Government and Politics
in Britain

To the memory of my father,
John Henry Kingdom

Government and Politics in Britain

John Kingdom

Polity Press

Copyright © John Kingdom 1991

First published 1991 by Polity Press
in association with Basil Blackwell
Reprinted 1991

Editorial office:
Polity Press, 65 Bridge Street,
Cambridge CB2 1UR, UK

Marketing and production:
Blackwell Publishers Ltd
108 Cowley Road, Oxford OX4 1JF, UK

Blackwell Publishers Inc.
3 Cambridge Center
Cambridge, MA 02142, USA

ISBN 0–7456–0592–3
ISBN 0–7456–0593–1 (pbk)

British Library Cataloguing in Publication Data
A CIP catalogue record for this book is available from the British
Library.

Library of Congress Cataloging in Publication Data
Kingdom, J. E., 1939–
  Government and politics in Britain / John Kingdom.
    p. cm.
  Includes bibliographical references and index.
  ISBN 0–7456–0592–3 (hardback) — ISBN 0–7456–0593–1
  (paperback)
  1. Great Britain — Politics and government. I. Title.
  JN231.K56 1991
  320.941–dc20   90–42900
                                                    CIP

Typeset in 11 on 12½ pt Sabon by
Wearside Tradespools, Fulwell, Sunderland
Printed in Great Britain by
Butler & Tanner Ltd, Frome

Contents

PART III   MOBILIZING THE *DEMOS*

Acknowledgements

I have received help from many people in the preparation of this book. Throughout the process of drafting and redrafting I have been grateful for the generous encouragement and advice of Professor Anthony Giddens of Cambridge University. In the latter stages David Held of the Open University made important suggestions. I owe enormous debts to John Dearlove of Sussex University and John Greenwood of Leicester Polytechnic, both of whom read an earlier draft in its entirety, giving encouragement and numerous practical suggestions which have materially enhanced the book in many respects. Throughout the process I have been helped and encouraged by Debbie Seymour and Tracy Traynor of Polity Press who have steered a complicated manuscript through the reefs and rapids of the production process. I also thank my colleague, Malcolm Stevens, who again read the entire script and discussed issues with me over an extended period. In addition, many other colleagues at Sheffield Polytechnic have kindly read particular chapters in areas of their expertise and generally offered encouragement and advice, including Jim Chandler, Phil Harris, Nigel Johnson, Dave Morris, Ralph Spence, Peter Vincent-Jones and Ann Wall. I owe special thanks to Professor Bob Haigh of Sheffield Polytechnic, without whose interest and help this book would simply not have been written. I am also grateful for careful work on the bibliography and glossary by Deborah Barham (aged 12). Most of all I thank my wife, Ann Barham. Not only has she been an exceptionally helpful copy-editor, she has used her consummate professional skill to prepare a first-class index which enhances the value of the book beyond measure. Needless to say, any errors, inconsistencies and idiosyncrasies are mine alone.

I am grateful to the following for their permission to reproduce material previously published elsewhere: Basil Blackwell and Polity Press for figure 14.6 from John Scott, 'The British upper class', in D. Coates, G. Johnston and R. Bush (eds), *A Socialist Anatomy of Britain*, 1985, p. 45; Owen Bowcott and the *Guardian* for the extract on p.249; The Campaign for Nuclear Disarmament, 22–24 Underwood Street, London N1 7JG, for figure 3.2; The Controller, Her Majesty's Stationery Office for tables 4.5 and 14.1 and figures 4.2, 5.3, 12.2, 12.3, 14.3, 15.6, 15.8, 16.8, 16.9 and 16.10; David Brindle and the *Guardian* for the extracts on pp. 154, 223 and 476; Economist Publications Ltd for the extracts from *The Economist* on pp. 405 and 472; Friends of the Earth Trust Ltd, 26–28 Underwood Street, London N17JQ for the picture on p. 4; the *Guardian* for figure 5.2; Martin Linton and the *Guardian* for the extract on p. 249; Macdonald & Co. for table 12.1 from *The Civil Servants* by P. Kellner and Lord Crowther-Hunt, 1980; Mary Evans Picture Library for the pictures on pp. 31, 57, 75, 114, 161, 164, 200, 270, 293, 310, 350, 384, 482, 489, 514, 527 and 550; Paul Nettleton and the *Guardian* for the extract on p. 344; Newspaper Publishing PLC for the extracts from the *Independent* on pp. 278, 377 and 510; Punch Publications Ltd for the cartoons from *Punch* on pp. 16, 137, 145, 149, 211, 219, 314, 340, 366, 444, 504, 520 and 562; Melanie Phillips and the *Guardian* for the extract on p. 123; Popperfoto for the pictures on pp. 61 and 262; Times Newspapers Ltd for the pictures on pp. 83, 93, 180, 228, 340, 388, 428 and 456; Martin Wainwright and the *Guardian* for the extract on p. 570. I should also like to thank the staff of the Mary Evans Picture Library, the Punch Cartoon Library and Dave Clark of *The Times* for their help in obtaining illustrations.

PART I

Introduction

No one is unaffected by politics. Speaking very broadly, it is about the way people organize their lives together in a community. The important collective decisions which shape the very quality of life – our wealth, our health, our education, our morality – are all essentially political in their nature. Studying and talking about politics is a necessary part of the good life which we seek. To be denied the right to do this is one of the first symptoms of the oppression of the human spirit. We can better enjoy the experience of talking and thinking about politics if we first ponder the essential nature of the subject and the terms and concepts associated with its study. This is the purpose of the first part of this book.

1

Studying Politics

In this chapter we introduce some of the terms and concepts central to the study of politics. It should however be remembered that their real meaning can only be truly seen in their *use* and should become clearer with continued study. Regard this chapter as a series of introductions such as you might receive upon arriving at a party. Like people, the terms and concepts of politics will reveal their full subtlety only with the familiarity of prolonged acquaintance. Initially the chapter examines the essential nature and the basic concepts of **politics** and **government**. This leads to the identification and definition of a range of key related concepts including **power**, **authority**, **legitimacy**, the **state**, and **society**. Finally we address the actual **study** of politics, concluding with comments on this book's approach to the subject and how it may be used.

Encountering politics

Human social life is not a tranquil experience. People seem able to argue and disagree over most things – education, nuclear weapons, US bases, the National Health Service, race, gender, Britain's place in Europe, the north–south divide, the future of Northern Ireland, and so on. Not only do people argue, they resort to violence. Today we see race riots, attacks on the police, attacks by the police, long and bitter strikes. We see blood and even death on our streets as women, blacks, the unemployed and the handicapped fight for their rights.

Even religious leaders will enter the fray, fighting for the rights of the underprivileged against the establishment and counselling the victims of the social battle. In the 1980s, the Church of England actually produced a report, *Faith in the City*, deploring the conditions of the poor in Britain's

Friends of the Earth on the steps of St Paul's
Source: Friends of the Earth

decaying and neglected inner cities. Throughout all, the unblinking eye of the mass media watches, reports, and incites.

There are limitless grounds for dissatisfaction with life in society; time and time again people find themselves denied the privileges and opportunities available to others. Some live in opulence, others in squalor. Some load their supermarket trolleys high, leaving empty cardboard boxes for others to sleep in. People hold beliefs for which they will fight and are even prepared to die. In 1913 Emily Wilding Davison fatally flung herself under the hooves of the King's horse in the Derby and other women threatened to starve themselves to death in Britain's prisons because they wanted the right to vote. Northern Irish prisons saw hunger strikes in 1981 and Bobby Sands's agonizing suicide by starvation on 5 May. People, and even the government, will also kill for their beliefs, as planted bombs and shoot-to-kill policies testify.

This widely disparate pattern of behaviour, involving matters great and small, serious and trivial, originating at home or abroad, involving ordinary people and the high and the mighty, which may be enacted within the great state institutions of Westminster, Whitehall and the Inns of Court, or in the streets and factories, share little in common except for one thing: they, along with thousands of other such examples, would be recognized as *events in politics*. It is clear that if we are to study this subject seriously it is necessary to make some order of a world of bewildering complexity; to try to distil the essence of the activity known as *politics*. This is by no means easy; scholars continue to dispute the definition of politics.

What is politics?

> I hope I will not destroy faith in the omniscience of professors entirely if I now confess that I do not really know what my subject is.
>
> F. F. Ridley, 'The importance of constitutions', *Parliamentary Affairs* (1966: 312)

Politics arises from certain basic facts of human existence: that people generally choose (indeed find it necessary for survival) to live together, and that they differ in multiple ways in their opinions as to how the community should be organized and the nature of the decisions it makes. The source of conflict may either be the simple fact that individuals are self-interested and greedy, never able to feel content with their lot, or that they hold differing views on big moral questions about how mankind should live. Such disputes are inevitable because the world's resources are finite (no one can have all he or she wants) and the range of opinion on moral questions is limitless.

However, when we come to address directly the fundamental question 'What is politics?' we find it impossible to give a simple answer. Politics can be seen variously as concerned with the art of *compromise*, the exercise of *authority*, the acquisition of *power*, and as a form of devious *deception*. It is not the case that any one of these categories of definition is correct and the others wrong, but rather that politics is a many-sided concept, only to be understood if viewed from various angles.

Politics as compromise: the 'art of the possible'

This well-known but enigmatic definition (authorship of which is attributed variously) retains its resilience because it encapsulates a particular view of politics as a process of compromising which has been attractive to western minds since the time of the famous Greek philosopher Aristotle (384–322 BC). Amongst modern thinkers it is most eloquently expressed by Bernard Crick:

> Politics is not just a necessary evil; it is a realistic good. Political activity is a type of moral activity; it is a free activity, and it is inventive, flexible, enjoyable, and human.
>
> (Crick 1964: 141)

However, if such a view of the meaning of politics were rigidly adhered to, there would be little material for political scientists to study in the real world of violence, murder, duplicity and self-interest. Yet this definition remains important for several reasons.

- It defines the pure essence of politics.
- It stands as an ethical ideal (what politics *ought* to be).
- It provides a measure against which real-world systems of politics may be judged.

The view of politics as compromising and conciliatory activity might suggest that it is opposed to the idea of sovereignty and rule by a central authority. This is wrong because differences cannot be reconciled without some overarching authority, even if this is no more than the idea of the *agreement* (or contract) reached between the parties. In the real world politics must entail the exercise of authority. This leads to a second definition.

Politics as authority

David Easton, an influential American political scientist, argued that politics was concerned with the **'authoritative allocation of values'** (1953: 129). The key word here is **authority**: the right of some person or institution (king or government) to make decisions affecting the community. A man with a gun, or a man with a large wallet, may be able to get his own way but he will not have authority if those obeying him do so with reluctance and a sense of grievance. Such rule is unstable; those subjected may be expected to revolt when they glimpse their chance. Authority is derived from legitimacy.

Legitimacy This is a central concept in the study of politics and is closely related to the idea of authority. When a government enjoys **legitimacy** people will obey its dictates because they believe it right to be ruled in this way. This is a key to the success of any political system, and explains why military dictatorships which may take over as a result of an armed *coup* are soon looking for some means of restoring civilian rule.

Forms of authority The great sociologist Max Weber (1864–1920) distinguished three kinds of authority: *rational legal* (bestowed by normative rules – constitutions, elections, and so on); *traditional* (conferred by history, habit and custom – like a hereditary monarchy); and *charismatic* (where the personal qualities of the leader are such as to inspire the confidence, and even adulation, of the masses).

Of course, to say that a government enjoys legitimacy does not necessarily imply that it is *good* government; legitimacy merely resides in popular consciousness. Hence political regimes will devote considerable time and energy, not to making policies for the people's education, welfare, and so on, but to the shaping of attitudes – the process of **legitimation**. We shall see that a great deal of British political life serves this end. For example, when the Queen was crowned by the Archbishop of Canterbury the British people witnessed a tradition whereby the monarchs of old sought to present their earthly power as a manifestation of the will of God.

While it is clear that the exercise of authority is a part of politics, it presents a rather legalistic, simplistic picture of the real world. Rulers cannot expect to possess legitimacy all the time; in a complex society there are always elements regarding the particular government of the day with distaste, if not loathing, and wishing to oppose and destroy it. Governments can aim to maintain themselves by deception of the masses and by force. Hence politics is a rather more murky arena than the authoritative-allocation-of-values definition would allow. This leads to an analysis of one of the most central concepts in politics – power.

Politics as power

The American political scientist Harold Lasswell gave the discipline a memorable catch-phrase in the title of his book *Politics: Who Gets What, When, How?* (1936). For Lasswell the essence of politics was **power**, and those who get most of what is going are the powerful. Power can be defined as the ability to achieve some desired effect, regardless of what opposition may exist. It is the ability to make people act in a manner in which they would otherwise not. Legitimacy is one form of power, but a glance at the world today quickly reveals that many regimes are based on cruder forms, particularly physical force and violence.

> I put for a general inclination of all mankind,* a perpetual and restless desire for power after power, that ceaseth only in death.
>
> Thomas Hobbes (1588–1679; English philosopher) *Leviathan* (1651: ch. 11)

Concentration on pure power rather than authority takes us beyond the trappings of government into shadowy corners behind the throne. Very often the authority of the government is nothing more than an empty legal (*de jure*) title; the real (*de facto*) power to get what is wanted, when it is wanted, lies elsewhere. Although some are content to study only the trappings of the state, it should be a central task of political analysis to track down the real source of power, to find the constitutional Mr Big, though the trail can often resemble the Yellow Brick Road to the elusive end of the rainbow.

We will discover later in this book that the most important approaches to the study of politics centre around hypotheses about where real power lies. Does it lie with the people, *some* of the people, the talented, the wealthy, the aristocracy, Parliament, the Cabinet, the Prime Minister, the civil service, the mass media, the professional classes, the managers of industry, the controllers of capital, and so on? Alternatively, does it lie outside the state territory altogether with multinational corporations, supranational groupings like NATO, or mighty superpowers like the US.

In British politics, power – like wealth – is unevenly distributed; some

---

* The terminology in this and other quotations is not intended to exclude women; it is merely an example of sexist language and is itself a manifestation of male power (see chapter 4).

people have much while others have little. It is partly based upon great wealth, often in the form of property. However, there may be other bases for power, such as race, gender, professional expertise (doctors, for example), the holding of high state office (like judges), or the occupation of key management positions in large, powerful organizations.

Power under capitalism No one can ignore the Marxist view of power within society, which sees it as linked with the fundamental question of the way a community produces the material things it needs to survive. In a **capitalist** economy such as Britain the vital tools, machines, factories, and so on are owned not by the community as such, but by a relatively small number of private individuals – the capitalists. This fact gives them immense power, to the extent that they can ensure that the government will operate in their interest. They can be said to constitute a *de facto* 'ruling class'.

The Italian Antonio Gramsci (1891–1937), an activist as well as a thinker (for a considerable time imprisoned by the fascist Mussolini), further developed the idea of hidden mechanisms of power through a particular view of the concept of **hegemony** (domination). As a neo-Marxist (one who adapts the basic principles of Marxism to better explain the world today) he believed that class domination is maintained through the capitalists' ability to monopolize the leading positions in society (in the press, the judiciary, the army, the civil service, the church, and so on). They are able to use their positions to create an **ideology** (a shared set of ideas claiming to give a universally applicable theory of man and society) portraying their dominance as part of the natural order of things, thereby legitimating their supremacy. Gramsci believed that it was this which forestalled the revolutions predicted by Marx (though he also believed it would be possible for the working class itself to develop a rival sense of hegemony and change the nature of society in its own interest).

Politics as deception

> Get thee glass eyes;
> And, like a scurvy politician, seem
> To see the things thou dost not.
> King Lear in Shakespeare's *King Lear*

A popular use of the term 'political' denotes devious, shifty activity aimed generally at securing personal self-interest, usually position or office. It is a kind of activity which can take place at the micro level (within political organizations), or the macro level (concerning the relationship between the rulers and the ruled).

> One has to be a bit of a lowbrow, a bit of a murderer, to be a politician, ready and willing to see people sacrificed, slaughtered for the sake of an idea.
>
> Henry Miller (1891–1980; American writer), *Writers at Work*

Deception in micro-politics It was probably in this sense that the word 'politics' was first used in English, as a term of disapproval applied to the activities of those engaged in faction, intrigue and opposition to established governments. People who are 'politicking' are usually understood to be plotting, advancing their own interests by nefarious means. The use of the term in this way often describes the behaviour of individuals in large organizations, where those engaged in politics (from planning to oust the chairman, to gaining an extra waste-paper basket) are unlikely to be contributing to the organization's collective goal. Clearly much activity of this kind takes place within government. Indeed the British Cabinet itself was originally a secretive group of ministers plotting quietly as a *cabal*.

This view of politics is often linked with the ideas of the Italian thinker Niccolo Machiavelli (1467–1527), and to be labelled 'Machiavellian' is usually taken as insulting. However, Machiavelli's essential point was that intrigue and plotting were justified by the greater purposes of government. In other words, he believed the old adage that the ends justify the means: 'when the act accuses, the end excuses'. This leads to deception at the level of macro-politics.

Deception in macro-politics This level of deception is by far the more important to the outcome of politics and was enunciated by Benjamin Disraeli (1804–81), the great nineteenth-century Prime Minister, in an oft-quoted aphorism that politics was 'the art of governing mankind through deceiving them'. Legitimation itself can be seen as a form of deception. The perceptive English political essayist Walter Bagehot (1826–77) placed particular stress on deception of the masses as a key to successful government (see pp. 260–3). Today one is presented with a great mist of this deceptive activity (including official secrecy) and the attempt to shine a searchlight through it is one of the principal duties of the political scientist.

> Politics is the art of preventing people from taking part in affairs which properly concern them.
>
> Paul Valéry (1871–1945; French writer), *Tel quel*

> Politics and the fate of mankind are shaped by men without ideals and without greatness. Men who have greatness within them don't go in for politics.
>
> Albert Camus (1913–60; French philosopher and writer),
> *Notebooks, 1935–42*

As we conclude this discussion on the nature of politics, it should be apparent that all our definitions are inextricably interwoven. There is no doubt that society harbours many conflicting interests which must be reconciled, often by the exercise of authority, and the process is clouded by evidence of great inequality of power and much devious behaviour.

What do political scientists study?

Individuals and groups disagree over ends and means in most walks of life and there are countless institutions which can resolve such conflict, including religious groups, trade unions, clubs, schools, universities, business firms, families, and so on. Does this mean that these are political institutions? Some academics do in fact study the politics of small communities, usually taking a psychological perspective, but behaviour of this kind is not political in the sense understood by the political scientist. How then do we delineate our subject matter? The particular focus of attention for the political scientist is the **state** – a very special, unique, and profoundly important social formation.

The state

A state is a community formed for the purpose of government. The Ancient Greeks talked of the **city-state** (sometimes termed the **polity**, from the Greek *polis*, meaning city or state) and today we speak of the **nation-state**. There is some philosophical dispute as to the nature of the concept of state, the German philosopher Hegel (1770–1831) giving it a particularly meta-physical significance as the highest expression of human existence; only through allegiance to, and service in, the state could individuals fully realize themselves. Generally the state is taken to be a community with the following characteristics (Lasswell and Kaplan, 1950: 181).

- A clearly defined territory.
- A legitimate government.
- Sovereignty within its territory.
- An existence recognized by other states in international law.
- A 'persona', in which it is able to make treaties and have obligations and rights which are independent of the individual members of the community or

government. In this personified sense it is common to read of the state doing this and that: prosecuting people (state prosecution), providing welfare (welfare state), being sinned against (crimes against the state), keeping secrets (state secrets), educating citizens (state education), and so on.

- Perpetual succession – rulers may change but the state continues to exist, with no alteration to its commitments and responsibilities.
- Universality – all those living within the jurisdiction of the state (there are some exceptions for diplomats) are subject to its rules. Unlike other associations (say, sports clubs or a church), members do not have the right to leave (unless they emigrate, though in this case they would soon come within the jurisdiction of some other state).
- The right to use force and coercion against members. Weber saw this as the most singular characteristic of the state, distinguishing it from all other organizations. If other agencies, say bouncers outside a disco, teachers, or even parents, use force to achieve their aims they may find themselves subject to the law, but the state can legally imprison people, harass them, and even kill them. From this it becomes starkly obvious that control of the state apparatus confers great and threatening power.

The state and society The notion of the state may be differentiated from that of **society** in that the former is constructed and based upon law, while the latter is an organic entity arising naturally from the free association of people (sometimes termed *civil society*). In the state, individual members stand as *citizens* with legally prescribed rights and obligations, but no such conditions attach to them as members of society, where they are constrained more by moral and ethical norms. The same distinction was made by the German sociologist Ferdinand Tonnies (1855–1936), who spoke of **Gesellschaft** (a community formed by some kind of artificial, man-made contract) and **Gemeinschaft** (a community arising naturally from bonds of affection or kinship). The distinction is profoundly important in political thought. Philosophers who view the state as a contract, without deeper ties, are those who reject conservatism and collectivism in favour of radicalism and individualism.

The national community is both the state *and* society simultaneously, a fact which is a source of friction. While all citizens of the state are legally equal, as members of society they can be decidedly unequal. When the legal equality of citizenship is markedly at variance with the real level of societal equality, there will be the potential for political tension.

Government

Few would deny that the idea of **government** lies at the heart of political science. Indeed no society has ever been found which did not have some form of government (Mair 1970). It can take various forms: it may be *constitutional* (limited by laws, see pp. 38–42), *absolutist* (unlimited by laws), *primitive* (a chieftain's rule over a tribe), or *pluralist* (consisting of several

> Government, even in its best state, is but a necessary evil; in its
> worst state, an intolerable one.
> Thomas Paine (1737–1809; English radical whose thoughts fuelled the
> American Revolution), *Common Sense*

institutions sharing the role). Following Aristotle, it is customary to group forms of government in terms of the number of rulers, thus distinguishing **monarchy** (rule by one person), **aristocracy** (rule by an enlightened few), and **democracy** (rule by all the people – the *demos*). However, each of these may be said to tend towards its corrupt variant, respectively termed **tyranny**, **oligarchy** and **mob-rule** (see figure 1.1).

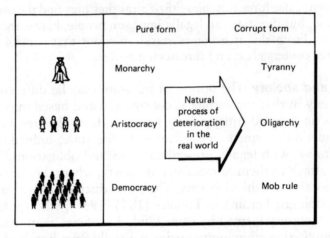

Figure 1.1   Forms of government

Government and self-interest   The fatal deterioration of the forms of government is usually attributed to the corrupting influences of power, which may lead those who hold it to act in their own self-interest rather than in the interest of the community. The historian Lord Acton (1834–1902) observed memorably:

> Power tends to corrupt, and absolute power corrupts absolutely. Great men are almost always bad men.

The selfish tendency of human beings is a hard truth which forms the starting point for much political thought. The key issue is reconciling the need for government with the common good. The Scottish philosopher David Hume (1711–76) believed that 'every man ought to be supposed a knave and to have no end other than private interest', arguing that it was crucial for a state to devise a form of government which would inhibit the corrupting tendencies.

A republican and free government would be an obvious absurdity, if the particular checks and controuls [*sic*], provided by the constitution, had really no influence, and made it not in the interest, even of bad men, to act for the public good.

(Hume 1882 edn: 6–7)

The Philosophical Radicals of the nineteenth century, who followed the utilitarian ideas of Jeremy Bentham (1748–1832), took the individual pursuit of self-interest as the key to understanding human behaviour. They sought to design institutions which would bring the interests of the rulers into coincidence with those of the people. This school of thought was very influential in shaping many of our modern institutions, including the legal system and the system of representative government from which has evolved the present form of British government – **liberal democracy** (see chapter 2).

Government and politics Government will necessarily entail politics. In primitive societies where institutions have taken only the most rudimentary form, political activity has still been found. In developed societies, politics is often seen as being about the formal working of the **machinery of government** – taking control of it, influencing its decisions, reforming it, changing those in office, and so on. However, it is important to remember that politics does not belong exclusively to the world of political institutions. It also takes place in the board-rooms of industry, the country houses, the trade unions, the streets, the schools, the hospitals, clubs and pubs where people gather and express their feelings, hopes and anxieties about public issues.

The state and the government

It is very important to recognize that the state and the government are conceptually distinct. In Britain, the Queen is the head of state, a position serving to underline the distinction. For practical purposes it is usual to regard the British government as the collection of around a hundred secretaries of state, ministers, junior ministers and their various assistants drawn from Parliament. In contrast, the state can be seen to comprise a much wider set of institutions over which the government has control (the civil service, the Bank of England, the local authorities, the health authorities, various quasi-autonomous bodies, the nationalized industries, the judiciary, the military and the police). Some theorists would go even further and include the mass media, the institutions of the capitalist economy, the schools, and even the trade unions (Middlemas 1979).

In theory the state is a passive machine which the government takes over like the driver of a car. This belief is a central plank in the theory of British liberal democracy. However, as will be shown throughout this book, the state machinery has a power and momentum of its own and can be very difficult for governments, particularly Labour governments, to control.

The political and the non-political

It will be apparent that if politics is about reconciling diverse interests it must have extremely wide manifestations; indeed there is no area of life which can be seen as intrinsically non-political. Some people find this thought peculiarly disturbing and it is common to hear calls to 'take education (or health, or the siting of power stations, and so on) out of politics'. If something is to be taken out of politics, where is it to go?

We have seen that politics is a process whereby differences and conflicts about community life at the level of the state are resolved through conciliation, the exercise of authority and power. However, politics is by no means the only way of resolving such differences and three particularly important alternatives are:

- the *economic market place*, allowing the forces of supply and demand to set prices and determine who gets what;
- *rational decision-making*, weighing up the pros and cons of a case by experts in order to arrive at the 'best' solution;
- the use of *violence*, where the unsatisfied, sadistic or greedy attempt to take what they want by physical force.

All these methods of resolving a community's disagreements are present in Britain today, though each has limitations.

The market In the eighteenth and nineteenth centuries classical economists believed that the **market** was a wondrous mechanism for bringing buyers and sellers together at a mutually acceptable price which resulted in the optimum allocation of resources within society.

However the market raises difficult ethical problems. In the first place it is undemocratic, favouring the economically strong against the weak because it does not *redistribute* resources; it gives only unto him or her that already hath (that is, can afford the price). Thus, rather than taking matters out of politics, it creates a new basis for dissatisfaction and conflict. Secondly, not all disagreements can be determined by the laws of supply and demand. Matters such as the level of sex and violence on television, the decision whether to send the task force to Argentina, the degree of religious toleration to be allowed within society, lie in a territory of value-judgement and morality of which the market is quite innocent. Indeed, because the capacity of human beings to disagree over value-judgements is potentially limitless, there are infinitely more areas of dispute to be settled by politics than by the market.

Rational decision-making The idea of making communal decisions on the basis of rational criteria seems highly attractive; it is the argument for the use of experts (town planners, architects and the like). Certainly, if we are ill we can think of nothing more sensible than a visit to the doctor. A faith in rationality was the basis of the thinking of the Philosophical Radicals in the early nineteenth century. They argued that decisions were rational to the extent that they would tend towards the maximization of the sum total of communal happiness, or utility (hence **utilitarianism**). Many continue to seek the holy grail of rationality. Organizational theorist Herbert Simon (1947) believed that state decision-makers should arm themselves with all the available information, calculate the outcomes of all possible courses of action, and choose the best as the policy for the community. This seems eminently reasonable, but in practice there are certain intractable problems besetting such processes.

- The principle is essentially elitist and paternalistic, based on the notion that certain people know what is best for the masses.
- There is a difficulty in deciding who the experts are to be; obviously election cannot be the answer.
- In reality, experts can never be sure that they have all the information necessary to make the 'right' decision.
- Experts, being human, may be tempted to place their own personal interests before those of the community.
- Experts invariably disagree with each other.

Rational decision-making also carries with it connotations of a threatening 'Big Brother' style of bureaucratic rule. Both fascist and totalitarian communist governments can be accused of trying to govern by putting experts in charge, while the call to replace politics with managerialism is ever-present in Britain.

Violence In the real world there can be little doubt that making and enacting collective decisions for communities is often accomplished by various forms of physical force and **violence**. Two world wars, the Nazi extermination of the Jews, the treatment of blacks in South Africa, the silencing of dissidents in Eastern Europe, and the brutal suppression of the students by the communist regime in China in 1989 can leave no one in any doubt of the harsh reality of human brutality. In the Suez crisis, in Northern Ireland, and in the Falklands war Britain has revealed itself completely willing to seek violent solutions to political problems. After the Falklands war, Mrs Thatcher employed the language of force on the home front, speaking of the 'enemy within'. This turned out to be Britain's miners, who were to find themselves embroiled in a physical confrontation with the state's blue-helmeted agencies of violence.

> War is nothing more than the continuation of politics by other means.
>
> Karl von Clausewitz (1780–1831; German military expert), *Vom Kriege*

Increasingly guerrilla warfare is chosen by groups wishing to gain their ends or make their voices heard as an alternative to participating in conventional political processes. Today anybody can be the subject of violence: thousands of civilians have been killed over Northern Ireland, hijacks and atrocities such as the Lockerbie air disaster can occur anywhere, and in 1989 the Ayatollah Khomeini set a chilling precedent with his 'death sentence' on author Salman Rushdie because his book *The Satanic Verses* gave religious offence. However, like the market and the rational decision-making model, violence does not seem very effective at resolving the problems it confronts. Often, when the fighting has ceased, the parties are obliged to sit around the conference table to seek a durable solution. The Northern Ireland and Arab–Israeli conflicts, for example, remain open wounds, no nearer a solution despite the high price paid in blood.

"Maurice has always been politically active."

Reproduced by permission of *Punch*

Is there really a world beyond politics?

In spite of the claims that the market, rational decision-making and violence take place in realms beyond politics, the evidence is that the real world of politics as studied by political scientists is an extremely muddy terrain and we find that these three spheres are themselves sucked into the political quagmire. It will become apparent throughout this book that when reformers believe they are taking an issue out of the sordid world of politics by handing it over to the market or the experts they delude themselves.

Similarly, the idea that violence is not part of politics is unrealistic.

Hence, in defining what is political we must be guided not by the nature of the subject matter but by the way people react to it. If we accept that politics is about reconciling diverse interests then it follows that, when people voice disagreement about anything it becomes political. The world which some believe to exist outside politics is a fantasy land, as inaccessible to mortals as that discovered by Alice when she went through the looking glass.

> Man is by nature a political animal.
> Aristotle (384–322 BC; Greek philo-
> sopher), *Politics*

Political Science

A master science?

> Every intellectual attitude is latently political.
> Thomas Mann (1875–1955; German writer),
> quoted in the *Observer* (11 Aug. 1974)

Throughout the history of western civilization, there runs a great tradition of **political thought**. Thinkers such as Socrates, Plato, Aristotle, Machiavelli, Rousseau, Hobbes, Locke, Bentham, J. S. Mill, Hegel, Marx and Russell have applied their minds to profound questions relating to politics. The subject is also the stuff of much great drama, literature and art. The study of politics was described by Aristotle as the 'Master Science' and it is not difficult to see what he meant. All we do in our lives, in society, the sciences and arts, will be influenced by politics; it is through politics that the totality of social existence is orchestrated.

A science of politics?

Political scientists do not wear white coats, peer through microscopes or carry test tubes. Is **political science** really a science? Can it produce the systematic, ordered, predictive propositions associated with a study such as physics? This is not a new question. The work of Aristotle, which involved him in a famous classification of the constitutions of the many Greek city-states, was just as systematic and 'scientific' as was his work in the natural sciences. However, the advent of Galileo and Newton in physics led to developments which seemed to transport the physical sciences into new realms of precision, uniformity and prediction.

> Politics is not a science . . . but an art.
> Otto von Bismarck (1815–98; Prusso-German statesman),
> speech, Reichstag (15 March 1884)

Yet some social scientists have tried to build a body of **political theory** – laws of society and politics which resemble those of the physical sciences. Karl Marx (1818–83) was one of these. We have already seen how he argued that the ultimate power in industrial society resides in those owning the capital used to produce the things needed to sustain life. However, this state of affairs is merely temporary, argued Marx, borrowing from the ideas of Hegel, under whom he studied. (Hegel believed in **determinism**, that events moved in some great predetermined pattern through three stages – *thesis*, *antithesis*, and finally, *synthesis*.) Marx predicted that the working class necessarily created by industrialization would overthrow its capitalist oppressors and establish a new Utopian society where people would not be allowed to own property and the state would cease to exist. Of course his predictions have never been confirmed anywhere and scholars have argued that his reasoning was flawed. The influential contemporary philosopher Karl Popper (1957) asserts that historical determinism of this kind, which he terms *historicism*, must always be illogical because, put simply, what people do will depend on their state of knowledge, and we cannot foretell the future state of knowledge (if we could it would not then be *future* knowledge). Revolutions have occurred (as they had before Marx) but without the features Marx predicted.

Under the influence of *logical-positivism* (a school of philosophy holding that only statements capable of being disproved can be meaningful), the post-war era saw renewed efforts by political scientists to steer the discipline towards rigorous theoretical propositions by the use of careful techniques and methods of empirical observation. In this effort to ape the objective observational methods of the 'hard' sciences they sought to ally the discipline more closely with anthropology and psychology. The movement was termed **behaviouralism**, meaning that the raw data was to be only that which was objectively observable as *behaviour*. One result of this was a preoccupation with things which could be observed, or more particularly, things which could be counted and thereby subjected to statistical analysis. The problem with this development was that many of the studies (attitude surveys, voting statistics, and so on) were rather boring and, more importantly, were essentially trite. They did not go to the really big questions of politics, such as: What is power? Where does it really lie? Why do states go to war? Why do people die of starvation?

Others, including Max Weber, were sceptical of the idea that people and organizations could be studied in this way. Human beings reason and interpret the world, and the proposition that they are best treated as unthinking molecules in a test tube is dubious, if not ludicrous. He argued that the study of human affairs should take account of reason, motives and emotions in order to afford a deeper level of understanding, which he termed *verstehen*.

Today few would deny Weber's argument and the narrow preoccupation with quantification is confined to a backwater of the discipline. Ironically, as the hard sciences push further into the unknown they encounter less rather than more precision in the phenomena they observe and are obliged to construct 'uncertainty principles' and 'chaos theories' resembling the uncertainties which have long confronted the social scientist. Yet behaviouralism has left a legacy in that the political scientist can no longer allow his or her mind to dwell for too long in the stratosphere of abstraction and metaphysics like medieval scholastics who disputed how many angels could balance on the point of a needle. Hence, the modern discipline of political science combines both a positivist orientation with a rich source of ideas and intuition. It is conceived in terms of a large number of interrelated subdisciplines taking particular focuses and methodologies.

- *Political theory* examines theories of political institutions, including the law, the state, systems of representation, forms of government, and so on.
- *Political philosophy* searches for highly generalized answers to major questions such as the meaning of freedom, justice, equality, rights, and so on. Ultimately **political philosophy** addresses the biggest question of all: What is the nature of the 'good life' and what must the state do to promote this?
- *Political economy* examines the state in the economic system. It is a form of economics which challenges the market orientation of much economic theory.
- *Political ideas* is the study of political thought throughout the ages. Most major philosophers have been concerned with political questions.
- *Political sociology* has the virtue of looking more towards the world of ordinary people for an understanding of politics. It is concerned with how political attitudes are formed and how they are influenced by those with power. This can involve psephology, the study of elections and voting behaviour.
- *Political institutions* is the study of the working of the state institutions. Traditionally it was preoccupied with a sterile account of rules and laws rather than behaviour, but no self-respecting political scientist would be guilty of such a narrow vision today. Within institutions there is much real political activity.
- *Policy studies* focus on the policy-making process of government and are centrally concerned with the analysis of power.
- *Comparative government* searches for general truths about politics derived from widespread examination of groups of countries. Conceptually straightforward, it can be immensely daunting in practical terms.
- *International relations* is the study of the ways in which states relate to each other in war and in peace.

Not only does political science embrace its own subdisciplines, it is multidisciplinary in that it draws, magpie-like, upon a wide range of disciplines throughout the social sciences (see p. 21).

About this Book

Peering behind the facade

The political scientist must be attentive to the real world and, before all else, must endeavour to describe it faithfully as it appears, seeking, like Machiavelli, to peel away the facade in search of a deeper reality for, as we observed above, much in politics is about deception. Textbooks in the orthodox liberal-democratic tradition betray a tendency to describe what they see as a beautiful stately home. Like overawed paying visitors, they are content to admire its ornate facade outside, and its fine draperies and furniture inside, but remain too timid to push aside the curator to get beyond the red ropes into the living quarters of the aristocratic family of today. A central concern of this book is to encourage the habit of enquiry, of looking beneath the surface or, where we are not permitted (and we are talking about one of the most secretive systems of government in the world), to remain conscious of the limitations of conventional pictures and to be intellectually open to those theories advanced about what *might* be there.

The implications of looking behind the facade

Much orthodox writing on British politics, while purporting to take an objective position, really subscribes to what can be shown logically to be a biased view.

- Objectivity is taken to mean describing without a commitment to any political ideology; thus the political system is detailed in much the same way as the internal combustion engine might be.
- The implication of this approach is that the state is an apolitical machine which does not favour any particular interest within society.

In fact the idea of the state as a neutral machine, easily controlled by anyone sitting in the driving seat, is highly contestable. **Marxism** holds the contrary view – that the state is controlled by the owners of capital. Hence, by declaring the state to be impartial and apolitical the orthodox texts are making a political (anti-left) statement. Rather than peeling away the facade they are actually assisting the process of concealment; indeed they themselves become part of the facade.

The interdisciplinary perspective

It follows from the above that our approach should embrace a wide range of disciplines. The social sciences study one single, complex reality, and the different disciplines are artificial territories staked out to facilitate detailed microscopic study of particular aspects. However, the disciplines can hinder understanding if they are allowed to dominate our view of the world, blinkering our eyes to other perspectives. The narrow disciplinary approach is nowhere more inappropriate than in the study of politics. If it is to deserve the title 'master science', it must look at all aspects of life; to fail to do so is to lay one more brick in the elegant constitutional facade.

Hence, while this book is rooted in the territory of political science, it is open to other perspectives. It is, for example, an inescapable fact that many of the forces acting upon the political system are *economic* in origin, whether they originate from the stock exchange or the plight of the homeless. To understand the British constitution we require a *legal* perspective, though this must be seasoned with an understanding of the balance of power within society, which breathes life into the constitution. The discipline of *sociology*, concerned with education, culture, class, racism and gender, which fuel much political activity, must also have a central place. Underlying all is the *historical* dimension. In almost all chapters we would be quite unable to comprehend the present state without understanding the patterns of earlier development. We do not take an historical perspective 'for history's sake', or by way of neat chronological introduction; we do so for reasons of intellectual necessity. The politics of today is only an ephemeral bloom on the tree of the past; history for us is not a set of 'stories of old', it is part of a chain of events linking contemporary problems and circumstances indissolubly with the past and leading into the future.

There is also an important *geographical* dimension to politics. Britain is part of a world economy populated by 'developed' and undeveloped countries and giant multinational corporations, many of which are richer than states. This international perspective does not end with the world economy, there is also a political order arising from the balance of military power, various political alliances, and a global ecological system innocent of national boundaries, serving to underscore the interdependence of states in the modern world.

The position of this book

This book rejects the notion that politics can be studied as if those involved are laboratory rats, or molecules in a test tube. It also rejects the idea that a political system is a sealed machine which can be explained without considering the economic, social and international environment. If the book consciously subscribes to an underlying value position it is a belief that it is in the nature of a polity to make its members *citizens*, rather than a random aggregation of individuals fending for themselves in a jungle. The distinction is that citizens have their status legally defined and all are entitled to equal *rights*, as well as being subject to the same *obligations*. Wherever the political system seems to work unfairly, giving one group an advantage over others, then it is important that this should be observed and explained rather than ignored or obscured.

Using this Book

The chapters of this book represent an exceptionally wide-ranging introduction to British politics. The expectation is that it will be studied over some time (one or two years) and the chapters generally reflect a sense of cumulative development so that, for example, chapter 4 is written on the assumption that chapters 1, 2 and 3 have been mastered. However, it is also the case that each has a clearly discernible focus and assumes no detailed prior knowledge of the topic. Hence the chapters can (under the direction of the teacher/tutor) be studied in a different order without major conceptual difficulty. Each chapter concludes with a summary of main points, a list of key terms and concepts, questions for discussion (which may be treated as essay topics to be completed under various conditions chosen by the teacher/tutor, or used for group discussion), and a guide to further reading.

The summaries and key terms and concepts

The summary of main points is intended to highlight the essential thrust of the discussion in the chapter, and provide a means of quick recapitulation and an aid to revision.

The lists of key terms and concepts are intended as a form of self-testing upon completion of each chapter. One should feel able to give concise definitions of all these before proceeding. Usually they are explained fully in the chapter and brief definitions are given in the Glossary at the end of the book.

The Glossary and Chronology

The Glossary can be used variously as an aid to revision, in essay writing, and to provide speedy clarification of a meaning during the course of reading. The definitions offered are necessarily brief and when greater clarification is required it should be sought in that part of the text where it is dealt with most fully (as indicated in the index). New terms appear in **bold** type when they are first mentioned.

The Chronology will enable you to see at a glance the sequence of the major events in British politics and their relationship to world events. It is often surprising to discover what happened when.

Further reading

The study of politics at an introductory level is essentially concerned with reading and thinking. We are not able to study our subject in a laboratory and we cannot manipulate the real world in order to conduct experiments. There is of course a real world of political activity, and it is profoundly dangerous to forget this fact, but the amount any individual can find out by direct observation is minuscule and, in the early stages of study, we must rely on accounts from various sources, including the mass media, historians, and academics from the range of disciplines discussed above.

The further reading suggested at the end of each chapter cannot pretend to be comprehensive and students should feel free to explore the literature of the disciplines according to their particular interests. The recommended sources are chosen for various reasons: sometimes the work is a classic, sometimes it is controversial, and sometimes unusual. Generally the suggestions are made because they are regarded as of an intrinsically high quality as well as being stimulating.

Where books for light relief are included this is not a joke. Much literature, light and serious, addresses the big questions of life and politics. It is important to remember that politics is not something outside normal social experience, unable to explain everyday problems; on the contrary, it lies at the very root of our social condition.

Discussion

However, mere width of reading does not constitute good study practice; it must be accompanied by thought and a search for understanding. It is better to study a limited number of sources thoroughly, so that they are understood, than to try to cover a wider range in order to commit things to memory 'parrot fashion'. The subject requires thought as much as factual knowledge, and we develop this through argument and discussion with others. This was the essence of the method employed by Plato in the Grove of Academos (hence 'academic') in Ancient Greece, and in spite of the breathtaking advances in modern information technology, it cannot be bettered. Talking seriously about politics is more than an academic enterprise, it is part of the process of being a citizen; it is itself an element of the good life (the prohibition of such talk is a sign of oppression). It can also lead to self-revelation: we can better understand the way we are by recognizing the forces which govern our environment. For example, many people (often working class, women, or members of ethnic minorities) blame themselves for various forms of 'failure' in their lives rather than entertain the possibility that they have been subject to greater political forces.

However, this possibility of gaining understanding of one's life can be dangerous; it is sometimes better for the powerful if those without power *do* blame themselves for their conditions. You will see throughout this book that there are various ways in which this is encouraged.

Assignments and questions for discussion

The assignments and questions included at the end of each chapter are integral to the study. The assignments ask you to use a wider range of skills than are required for essay writing. They are to encourage you to see in the media a further rich source for understanding the contemporary world. The 'essay-type' questions may be discussed in groups, made the subject of an address by one member to the others, or used as the basis of an essay. They are posed in order to address your mind to certain issues of fundamental importance in the chapter. Even so, the more you study the more you will realize that there are many variants upon them and teachers and tutors will provide a never-ending supply!

Topics for debate

These are intended to be controversial and should be used to stimulate sustained argument. The process of taking part in academic argument and debate can (under the stimulus of the adrenalin coursing through our veins as a result of anger, indignation, or frustration over the impertinence or stupidity of others) stimulate thought in a way that lone contemplation may not. Of course discussion and debate is empty and sterile if one does not read and think by way of preparation. If people attend your debates without having done this you are entitled to shred their egos with your knowledge and wit.

Key points

- A common definition of politics is the resolution by compromise and conciliation of the conflicts which must inevitably arise in any community.
- Politics necessarily entails the concept of authority, an accepted form of power exercised on behalf of the community by some institution such as a monarch, dictator or government.
- It is possible to speak of politics in the context of any organization (a firm, a school, a club, and so on), but for the most part the political scientist is interested in the politics of the nation-state.
- In the abstract, the state is a community, with a territory, within which it enjoys legal sovereignty. Practically speaking, the state is manifest in a range of institutions including Parliament, the courts, the civil service, the army, and so on. In Britain the monarch is formally the head of state.
- The government of the day, as an institution, may be in control of the state, but is conceptually distinct from it.
- The decisions made through politics (resolving disputes and competing claims within society) can be made by other means (the market, rational

decision-making and violence) but the idea that politics can be removed from life by those favouring any of these alternatives is an illusion. The nature of politics is such that it intrudes naturally; it is not something which we can decide to employ or not.

- The study of politics should be concerned with looking behind the great formal facade of the processes of government to understand where power lies; to understand who gets what, and why they get it.

Review your understanding of the following terms and concepts

art of the possible	monarchy
authority	aristocracy
authoritative allocation of values	democracy
legitimacy	*demos*
legitimation	tyranny
power	oligarchy
de jure	mob rule
de facto	liberal democracy
capitalism	machinery of government
hegemony	market
ideology	rational decision-making
state	utilitarianism
city-state	violence, political
polity	political thought
polis	political science
nation-state	political theory
society	determinism
Gesellschaft	behaviouralism
Gemeinschaft	political philosophy
government	Marxism

Questions for discussion

1 What is politics?
2 'Politics is "the art of the possible".' Discuss.
3 Distinguish between the concepts of 'state' and 'society'.
4 'Violence is the abrogation of politics.' Discuss.
5 'Education should be taken out of politics.' Why do people say this? How realistic is their suggestion?
6 To what extent can the study of politics be described as a science?

Topic for debate

This house believes with Camus that 'men who have greatness within them don't go in for politics'.
    or
This house believes that politics offers a means of apportioning the resources within a community which is ethically superior to the free market.

Further reading

Cornford, F. M. (ed. and translator) (1941) *The Republic of Plato.*
A highly accessible edition of the great masterwork which raises many of the questions and conundrums of the study of politics today. Also a model of the Socratic method of discussion. Written in the form of dialogues, it can be acted out by members of a group.

Crick, B. (1964) (2nd edn, 1982) *In Defence of Politics.*
A classic essay on the idea of politics as a peaceful and highly desirable process of conciliation.

Barry, B. (1970) *Sociologists, Economists and Democracy.*
A lucid examination of two schools of the study of politics lying outside the mainstream: sociologists, and a school of 'economists' who apply the ideas of rational man developed by the utilitarians (now called the public choice school).

Lasswell, H. (1936) (reprinted 1958) *Politics: Who Gets What, When, How?*
Classic statement of the power view of politics.

Mackenzie, W. J. M. (1969) *Politics and Social Science.*
A breathtaking 'Cook's Tour' of a wide range of approaches to the study of politics.

Miller, J. B. D. (1962) *The Nature of Politics.*
Stresses the ubiquity of politics, arguing that it will always be found in some form or other.

For light relief

Bertolt Brecht, *The Caucasian Chalk Circle.*
Much political activity revolves around questions of property. Who owns what? What is the moral authority for ownership? Brecht's play makes brilliant use of analogy to explore these great questions.

PART II

Politics in Context

A central theme of this book is that politics is not an activity taking place in a vacuum; it is a pattern inextricably interwoven into a social and economic fabric. In order to establish this from the outset, this part examines the context of British politics defined in terms of its **legal environment** (the constitution), the **international setting** (the world capitalist economy and the world political order) and the **social context** (the complex social organization and the attitudes which form the political culture). The substance of these three chapters remains a backcloth to the remainder of the book.

2

The Constitution: the Unwritten and the Unknowable

In this chapter we discuss the British constitution as a set of rules and prescriptions establishing the legal framework in which governments operate. This is not a simple matter; what is, and is not, part of the constitution is not always easy to discern, and the opinions of experts can vary. Moreover, the constitution does not stand above politics; its content, the way in which it changes, the criticisms people make of it, are all manifestations of political behaviour. The chapter falls into four main sections. This first is concerned with the **concept of a constitution**, examining the importance of its study to political scientists. This is followed by an identification of the **sources of the constitution** and a study of the way it evolves. The second and third sections focus on some of its key principles – the way it **limits the activities of government** and its capacity to **protect the rights of individuals**. The final section addresses the important debate over **constitutional reform**.

Seeking the Constitution

Defining the constitution

All kinds of organizations (from sports clubs and hamster societies to trade unions and political parties) have **constitutions**. They usually do two things: define the powers of those holding office and guarantee the rights of ordinary members. At the level of the state the principle remains the same. Hood Phillips describes a constitution as

the system of laws, customs and conventions which define the composition
and powers of organs of the state, and regulate the relations of the various
state organs to one another and to the private citizen.

(Hood Phillips 1987: 5)

However, another meaning of the term portrays the state constitution as a
description of everything which takes place on a regularized basis in the
process of government. This is a *behavioural* definition; it is found by
discovery rather than laid down by prescription, and was rather the way in
which the political essayist Walter Bagehot approached the study in his
famous work of 1867, *The English Constitution*. Even today books and
courses on politics are entitled 'British Constitution'.

For the most part, this chapter adopts the first definition – the constitution
as a set of rules prescribing the regularized behaviour which takes place in
the process of government. However, this focus does not mean that the
distinction between the prescriptive and descriptive aspects of political life is
ignored. Indeed, it is particularly important to observe the dissonance
between the two, for the belief that they coincide (that the prescriptive rules
describe actual behaviour) has given the study of constitutions a bad name. It
is quite clear that two games of cricket, although played according to the
same rules, will be quite different and, although for Englishmen politics
might lack the nuances of the revered game, its reality reflects a myriad of
factors of personality and environment upon which the constitution can only
remain silent. Life is breathed into a constitution by a host of political
Truemans and bureaucratic Bothams.

Why study the constitution?

The inevitable discrepancy between prescribed and actual behaviour can
render the study of formal constitutions a limited approach. This has led to
another tradition of writing on British politics (following the 'behavioural
revolution') which ignores the constitution altogether. However, this has as
many dangers as an excessive constitutionalism, for there are three good
reasons for studying the rules of the game.

It bestows authority Politics is pre-eminently about power. In prescribing a
framework the constitution bestows a particular form of power on certain
players – legitimate power, or authority. Thus, for example, the Prime
Minister can send people to war and generals can have them shot if they
refuse to fight, the police can arrest citizens, and judges can send them to
prison.

It represents a political prize More generally it should be recognized that
the constitution is itself *part of* the political process. Although it has usually
reflected change, rather than caused it, those engaged in the historic struggle
have seen the constitution as their ultimate goal. Thus, for example, after

Magna Charta, and the Charter of the Forests signed by King John

Published as the Act directs. June 11 1801 by J. Swatird, N° 112 Holborn Hill.

Source: Mary Evans Picture Library

humbling King John, the barons insisted that the new order be enshrined in the signing of the Magna Charta at Runnymede in 1215, the Glorious Revolution of 1688 led to the Act of Settlement in 1701, and the rising nineteenth-century bourgeoisie, the working class and the suffragettes made the constitution their political goal by calling for the extension of the franchise (the right to vote).

It shapes political consciousness Finally, even if the political analyst wishes to dismiss the constitution as a facade masking the reality of power, it remains important to study because of what people believe it to be. Thus, for example, even if people did not really possess effective freedom of speech (say because of problems of access to the media) it would remain important to political analysis that they *believed* themselves to have it; their consciousness would be part of the political culture (see chapter 4) determining their behaviour.

Britain's elusive constitution

For those with neat and tidy minds the British constitution exhibits the rather frustrating characteristic of not actually existing at all, or rather, not existing in the form of a nicely bound slim volume available from a bookshop. An American citizen can spend an edifying half-hour perusing the constitution on the bus or as a bedside companion. In contrast, the British constitution is notorious for its mysteriously **unwritten** manifestation. This is not strictly true because most of it certainly can be found in written form. However, the provisions are *uncodified*; the various elements have not been drawn together in a single document grandly entitled 'The Constitution'. This is just as well, for if all the material was bound together, the British counterpart of the American patriot would be faced, not with a light read, but something approaching the seven labours of Hercules.

The constitution takes this form because throughout history those in power have never wanted to make a dramatic renunciation of the past and start again. If Britain had experienced a popular revolution, then it is likely that the new rulers would have erased all trace of the *ancien régime*, as has happened, with variations, in many polities, including great ones such as France, Russia and the US (and indeed happened briefly in England under the Cromwellian regime).

Efficient and dignified elements

In looking at constitutions one must be alive to the fact that all may not be as it seems. In 1785 Paley noted how in 'the actual exercise of royal authority in England we see these formidable prerogatives dwindled into mere cere-monies', and in the nineteenth century Bentham and the great constitutional authority, Dicey, both charged the eighteenth-century constitutional chro-nicler, Blackstone, with being beguiled by what were no more than *fictions*. The passage of time has much to do with this, and Bagehot likened the constitution to an elderly gent giving to wearing the fashions of his youth, the outward finery belying the changes taking place beneath.

However Bagehot did not believe that the outmoded garb should be consigned to the dusty shelves of the constitutional curiosity shop in the way that the reforming radicals would have. He discerned a special significance in empty 'ceremonies', arguing that all well-established constitutions consisted of two elements: the **efficient** and the **dignified**. The former regulated the work of those getting on with the job of ruling, while the latter fulfilled a vital function in generating the authority they needed by supplying a glitter or 'theatre' to entertain the masses.

> The lower orders, the middle orders, are still, when tried by what is the standard of the educated . . . , narrow-minded, unintelligent, incurious.
>
> (Bagehot 1963: 63)

Bagehot believed that it was useless to expect working-class people to understand or even take any interest in the arcane mysteries of government, but they could be kept happy and deferential if they were given sufficient pageantry at which to gawp and wonder. Modern political scientists agree with Bagehot that in order to survive a political system must incorporate some mechanism for securing *legitimacy*.

The idea of dignified elements in a constitution means that we cannot ignore things which on the surface seem irrelevant to policy-making; they may be important in shaping mass attitudes. In addition we must be alert to the possibility that various state institutions may no longer play the part formally assigned to them; indeed we see throughout this book that imperceptible shifts from the efficient to the dignified pages of the constitution take place continuously.

Sources of the constitution

The constitution flows from five sources: royal prerogative, statutes, common law, convention and authoritative opinion (figure 2.1).

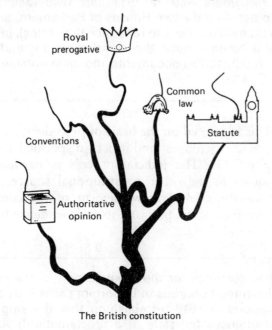

Royal prerogative

Common law

Conventions

Statute

Authoritative opinion

The British constitution

Figure 2.1 The British constitution flows from five sources

The royal prerogative This is a set of privileges enjoyed exclusively by monarchs since medieval times. *Personal* prerogatives are held by the monarch as a person and *political* prerogatives as head of state. The latter are the most important to the efficient constitution and include the rights to declare war or make peace, pardon criminals, dissolve Parliament, appoint ministers and assent to legislation. With the gradual erosion of the effective powers of the monarchy these, like the Crown Jewels, have been carefully preserved. They are now inherited by the Cabinet and the Prime Minister.

Statute These are no more than ordinary laws passed by Parliament. It is a rather unnerving fact that a law intended to change the constitution is not required to undergo any special procedures, as is usually the case under written constitutions. Thus the monumentally important extensions of the franchise were all made by politically motivated governments with little elevated thought of democratic or constitutional principle. Similarly, in 1986 the government was able to erase from the political map part of the local government system (the GLC and metropolitan counties) to do little more than settle a political score with left-wing councils.

> Statutes override all other constitutional sources. Some, such as the 1688 Bill of Rights (defining the relationship between Crown and Parliament) and the 1701 Act of Settlement (determining the succession) are extremely venerable. More recently, there have been the Parliament Acts of 1911 and 1949 (determining the relationship between the two Houses of Parliament) and the 1963 Peerage Act (enabling peers to renounce their titles). In addition to statutes, and having much the same character and force, are certain revered historical documents, the most notable of which is the Magna Charta.

Common law This is formed on the basis of precedent, from an accumulation of decisions made by judges (and juries) in specific legal cases throughout history (see p. 523). The judicial process is particularly useful for resolving ambiguities in the other constitutional sources. The two great virtues claimed for the common-law element of the constitution are its reflection of the wisdom of the past and its independence from the political process.

> Common law accounts for the greatest part of the constitution. Examples from the hundreds of important cases include the *Case of Proclamations* in 1610 (establishing that the king could not create new offences by issue of a proclamation); *Anderson* v. *Gorrie* in 1895 (the immunity of judges); and *Bradlaugh* v. *Gossett* in 1884 (the supremacy of Parliament over the courts in regulating its internal affairs).

Conventions These are regularly observed practices, having no legal basis and not enforceable in the courts. All states must evolve conventions to breathe life into their constitutions if they are to be flexible enough to survive. (The conventional elements of the constitution are the most easily changed.) However, in no other countries are conventions as important as in Britain, where they regulate the key processes of government. Democracy itself is based on conventions limiting the prerogative powers of the Crown and enabling them to be exercised by elected leaders. The Cabinet, the epicentre of government, is known only through convention.

In addition, there are many lesser conventions. For example, MPs never tell lies to the House, or to be more precise, no MP ever accuses another of having done so. In 1987, Labour MP Tam Dalyell broke with this, accusing Margaret Thatcher of lying over the Westland scandal. Consequently, he was 'named' by the Speaker; that is, barred from the chamber. There can be disagreement as to whether or not a convention actually exists. For example, some have argued that in cutting off relations with the TUC, Mrs Thatcher broke a newly minted convention of consultation with interest groups.

Although conventions may be regarded as the most obviously 'unwritten' part of the constitution, they are probably the most *written about*. This is necessary because there is more need for guidance in an area where the formal law is silent. This leads to the final source.

Authoritative opinion It is considered appropriate that learned works of great authority and wisdom be regarded as legitimate constitutional sources, though there may be difficulty in defining precisely what is meant by authority. Great age is taken as important because it may be presumed that ancient texts distilled the wisdom otherwise lost. Examples of such treasures include, among others, Fitzherbert's *Abridgement* of 1516, Hawkins's *Pleas of the Crown* (1716) and Foster's *Crown Cases* (1762). Of course not all authorities agree; indeed it is in their nature to be disputatious. The very belief that one can discover the constitution from the authorities of the past is itself open to question and was challenged by the Philosophical Radicals.

Change and development

All constitutions are political but Britain's is particularly so because its provisions can be changed as part of the normal process of politics. This is potentially threatening because, following the game metaphor, it is obvious that it would be quite impossible to play if the rules were not fixed. If we behave like William Webb Ellis of Rugby School, who during a particular game in 1823 is said to have picked up the football and run, we are no longer playing the same game.

Of course, a constitution cannot work if it is entirely inflexible and, even in the US, where its veneration rouses religious fervour (there have been only 26 formal amendments), small changes occur continually through judicial

> A written constitution need not be inflexible. Since 1809 Sweden's constitution has been amended over 200 times – like the workshop hammer, with several new heads and shafts, one wonders whether it is any longer the same thing.

decision and the establishment of conventions. However, written constitutions are usually given a propensity to resist change; they are **entrenched** through deliberately cumbersome processes of amendment. The unwritten nature of the British constitution might suggest that it is highly unstable and but a flimsy defence of citizens' rights. There is some truth in this, though it contains both conservative and flexible elements.

Amending the US constitution

In the US, amendments to the constitution must be first proposed and then ratified, both deliberately cumbersome procedures. Proposals may be made by two-thirds majorities in both houses of Congress voting separately, or by a national convention called by Congress at the request of two-thirds of the state legislatures. Ratification may be made by vote of three-quarters of the state legislatures or by state conventions in three-quarters of the states.

Art or Nature: are constitutions machines or organisms? There are two broad theoretical views on constitutional change: the mechanistic and the organic.

The **mechanistic** view sees constitutions as machines designed and created by men in order to give them the kind of government they desire. The English philosophers Thomas Hobbes (1588–1679) and John Locke (1632–1704) belong within this tradition, though it was Jeremy Bentham and the Philosophical Radicals who really addressed the issue of *rational* constitutional reform. The essence of their position was that, if a constitution was to serve the needs of a people at any particular time, they should be able to deduce from first principles the kind of constitution required. For this school of thought statute law is the obvious constitutional source.

In contrast, the **organic** view argues that a constitution grows and develops naturally like a living organism; for thinkers of this school it is a thing of untouchable beauty. Frequent references in literature liken the British constitution to a great tree. Blackstone's view of the constitution, with its veneration of the past, would belong in this category, and the cover of Sir Ivor Jennings's *The British Constitution* (1966) is actually adorned with a picture of a spreading oak.

While the mechanical contrivances of political inventors has died away ... the goodly tree of British freedom selecting from the kindly soil and assimilating its fit nutriment still increases its stately bulk ... Outliving the storms and vicissitudes of centuries, deeply rooted in the habits and affections of the people, it spreads far and wide its hospitable shade.

W. E. Hearn, *The Government of England* (1868)

> Poems are made by fools like me,
> But only God can make a tree.
> Alfred Joyce Kilmer (1888–1918), 'Trees'

The organic idea has a distinguished pedigree, extending from the Ancient Greeks. The German philosopher Hegel, and T. H. Green (1836–82) in England, also conceived the state in organic terms. It was one of the main proponents of this view, Edmund Burke (whose powerful writing in the eighteenth century was to provide a rationale and rallying cry for the Conservative Party under Peel), who suggested that the constitution should be treated with religious awe as a repository of the collective wisdom of the ages. He argued that it was

> a presumption in favour of any settled scheme of government against any untried project, that a nation has long existed and flourished under it.
>
> (Burke 1782: 146)

This distinction is related to the question of the moral justification for constitutions, leading into an important area of philosophical debate centring on a distinction drawn between positive law and natural law.

Positive law is laid down by some human agency, say a government or a monarch, or through the accumulation of customs. It is in essence entirely the product of human design. Prominent amongst the positivists was the Philosophical Radical John Austin (1790–1859), who saw law as nothing more than the commands of the sovereign. Bentham was himself influenced by Austin, though he believed that the utility principle (the greatest happiness of the greatest number) should replace the will of the sovereign as the basis for law-making. For some this approach (legal positivism) is unsatisfactory because it lacks a justification for the law.

Natural law is a system of law supposedly derived from something more fundamental than the dictates of any earthly sovereign. This idea can be traced back to the Ancient Greek philosophers, particularly the Stoics, whose ideas were adopted by the Romans when seeking a system of law which could extend over their empire independently of the customary laws of different lands. For some, natural law can be said to derive from an expression of the will of God [though various philosophers, including Grotius (1583–1645) and Immanuel Kant (1724–1804), argued that this is virtually a special kind of positive law with God as the sovereign]. Others argue that it is derived from the idea of certain 'natural rights'. However, this introduces the problem of what these rights actually are. For Locke they included security of life, limb and property, while the US constitution begins by speaking grandiloquently of certain 'inalienable rights'.

Development and change in the British constitution have shown both organic and mechanistic characteristics. Common law and conventions have evolved gradually, while statute law has facilitated some great leaps, such as the nineteenth-century extensions of the franchise. The two contrasting views are marked by more than a dispassionate search for the truth, they have been used to support political positions. For Burke's followers (the landowners), the organic and mystical view provided a basis to resist the forces threatening to erode their privileges, while for the rising industrial bourgeoisie, desiring to shape the constitution in their interests, the radical mechanistic view was irresistible.

Limiting Government

The essence of **constitutional government** is **limited government**. This is held to be necessary because there can never be any guarantee that the rulers will not exercise power in their own self-interest. Most political thinkers have shared the view that power corrupts.

This limitation can be secured by other institutions, the law, or popular control, and is sought in certain fundamental principles: the **separation of powers**, the **rule of law** and **parliamentary sovereignty**. The first was regarded by the French jurist Montesquieu, in his *L'Esprit des Lois* (1748), as the key to British democracy. The last two were seen by Dicey as the twin pillars of the constitution (1959: xvii), a view which continues to colour much constitutional writing today (Harden and Lewis 1986: 4).

The separation of powers

The idea of dispersing or separating power between various institutions so that they will curtail each other's actions is based on the theory that there are distinct functions of government, each of which can be entrusted to a different institution. Montesquieu followed the English philosopher Locke in arguing that the best safeguard of freedom was to ensure that those making the laws (the **legislature**) should not also be those with the power of executing them (the **executive**). Similarly, the independence of the judiciary (judges) meant that those making and executing the laws would themselves be bound by them. The founding fathers of the American constitution were deeply impressed by the doctrine and today the executive (the President), the legislature (Congress) and the judiciary are not only separate, but have extensive power to limit, and indeed interfere with, each other; the constitu-

> The accommodation of all powers ... in the same hands ... may justly be pronounced the very definition of tyranny.
> James Madison (1751–1836; one of the American founding fathers), in *The Federalist* (1788)

In February 1989 the Senate Armed Services Committee voted against the newly installed President Bush's nominee, John Tower, as Defence Secretary, a decision subsequently confirmed by the full Senate. Tower had been seen as a hard-drinking womanizer with too cosy a relationship with defence contractors.

tion works on the basis of 'checks and balances'. It is not unusual for the president to be thwarted in his policy ambitions by both Congress and the courts; indeed at times the system seems in danger of grinding to a complete standstill as vetoes are exercised like power-assisted brakes. Further separation is inherent in the US constitution through its federal structure, apportioning jurisdiction between the federal government and the states.

In fact Montesquieu was wrong in thinking that the British constitution embodied a separation of powers. Bagehot was to stress that the 'efficient secret' of the constitution is not a separation, but a *fusion* of powers (figure 2.2), through the medium of the Cabinet, which was head of both the executive and the legislature. Furthermore, the Lord Chancellor is head of the judiciary, a member of the Cabinet (in the happy position of receiving two salaries) and of the legislature, when he sits on the 'Woolsack' as the Speaker of the House of Lords. To increase the fusion, the House of Lords, as well as being part of the legislature, is the final Court of Appeal. The judiciary also makes laws through the doctrine of precedent (see p. 523). Moreover, the growth of a myriad of administrative tribunals means that the executive also acts widely in a judicial capacity, and through the practice of

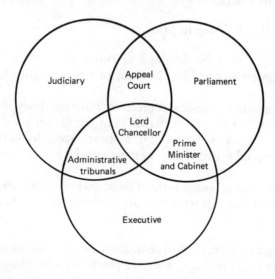

Figure 2.2 A fusion rather than a separation of powers

delegated legislation (see p. 287) is able to make laws without going through the normal legislative process.

The logical consequences of this fusion within the British constitution is that there is little scope for applying checks and balances. The government is virtually unimpeded by Parliament, which it completely dominates through party discipline (see pp. 283–7), and the courts have no authority to examine and veto legislation in the same way as the US Supreme Court. Furthermore, the doctrine of the sovereignty of Parliament (see p. 41) means that a judicial decision disliked by the government can be neutralized by a new statute.

The rule of law

This principle holds that the law is above the whims of any individual ruler. It can be traced back to the Ancient Greeks and lies at the heart of the idea of constitutional government. It has been brought to bear throughout history wherever people have sought to resist arbitrary rule or despotism; in the middle ages the notion that the monarch was subject to God and the law provided a fundamental rationale for challenging royal absolutism. However, to be meaningful the abstract principle must be specified in practical terms. Dicey (1959) saw its manifestation in the following three precepts.

- No person can be punished except for a distinct breach of the law.
- No person, whatever his rank, is above the ordinary law.
- The general provisions of the constitution are the result of judicial decisions made by an independent judiciary in deciding particular cases, rather than of declarations by rulers.

However, these break down in practice.

- Innocent people may be detained in order to *prevent* them committing crimes, or can be arrested on the basis of police suspicion that they might commit one.
- There are various categories subject to different laws. For example, the Trade Disputes Act (1906) conferred immunity from liabilities in tort upon trade unions; judges, MPs and diplomats are accorded extra privileges; the police have special powers, and members of the armed forces are subject to martial law.
- Much of the constitution is formed from statute rather than common law, and the government can pass any law it pleases in a truly despotic manner (see chapter 10).

Nevertheless, Dicey's formulation remains important to modern politics. It is really a statement of ideology, a prescription for liberalism (freedom from government intervention), which is inhospitable to the idea of socialism, Keynesianism (see pp. 390–2) and the welfare state, all of which require a positive rather than a negative (or minimal) state.

In Britain, the practical meaning of the rule of law has varied throughout history (Harden and Lewis 1986: 8) but today it largely holds that the government will operate within the law (this is not to say that it, or its agents, such as the secret services, do not sail close to the wind), but there is no requirement that the courts review the substance of any law passed, as happens in the US. This leads us to the most important criticism of any characterization of the rule of law in the British constitution: it is logically incompatible with the second of Dicey's great 'pillars' – the doctrine of the sovereignty of Parliament.

Parliamentary sovereignty

Popular sovereignty, the essence of democracy, was achieved in Dicey's views by means of the legal supremacy of Parliament. Though an obvious fiction today (see pp. 304–5), this doctrine enshrines the outcome of the prolonged constitutional struggle culminating in the Glorious Revolution of 1688, when the Bill of Rights set out the supremacy which Parliament had gained over the king through a succession of common-law decisions dating from the fourteenth century. However, not until the nineteenth century, following the great Reform Acts which changed the political system out of all recognition, was the principle formally enunciated by Dicey as the one fundamental (or entrenched) element in the British constitution. He described parliamentary sovereignty as

> the right to make or unmake any law whatever; and . . . that no person or body is recognised by the law of England as having a right to override or set aside the legislation of Parliament.

> (Dicey 1959: 39–40)

From this it follows that the courts have no power to review the constitutionality of legislation (thus inhibiting the separation of powers), and that no Parliament is bound by existing laws (thus denying the rule of law).

At the time Dicey wrote, the generally accepted doctrine of **sovereignty** was that put forward by John Austin, who argued that there must be in every state some body in which is vested ultimate unlimited power. This concept of sovereignty had no particular moral justification, the constitution being nothing more than the dictates of the ruler, but Dicey distinguished between two forms of sovereignty – *legal* and *political* – arguing that morally the latter was supreme. Thus the sovereignty of Parliament was derived, not from its inheritance of the absolute powers of the monarch, or from God, but from the people, through the principle of democratic representation. This is the key to the British liberal-democratic constitution. The people do not govern themselves, they elect representatives to Parliament, which governs the country through its committee – the Cabinet. Parliament is loyally served by the neutral machinery of the state, comprising institutions such as the judiciary, the civil service and the police force.

However, we shall discover later in this book that, in the real world of modern politics, Parliament as such is by no means supreme in law-making because it is controlled by political parties. Similarly, the neutrality of state institutions is a matter for considerable debate.

Protecting Individual Rights

In addition to regulating the working of the institutions of government, a constitution also guarantees **civil rights** – the freedoms of, and protections for, ordinary citizens. The two functions are not really distinct; the quantity and quality of personal freedom offered is linked with the nature and degree of the state's authority. Many written constitutions include positive guarantees of fundamental freedoms. In 1787, the framers of the US constitution neglected this and ten amendments were passed subsequently as the Bill of Rights. This guaranteed freedom of worship, speech, assembly, and to petition for redress of grievances; from deprivation of life, liberty or property by unlawful means; from cruel or unusual punishments; and security from unreasonable search of persons or houses and private papers and effects.

Glorious Revolution

The 1688 Bill of Rights marking the Glorious Revolution is not like that of France or the US. It is concerned with the rights of Parliament in relation to the monarch, rather than those of citizens in relation to the state, and confers various privileges upon MPs.

However, in Britain the laws protecting basic freedoms are nothing more than the ordinary laws of the land, and they are granted only *negatively*. That is, they are not actually conferred by the constitution; they are merely not withheld. Citizens can do anything which is not expressly prohibited by law; the freedoms are said to be *residual*. This means that there is nothing to prevent the government enacting harsh laws, which leads many critics to call for a US-style Bill of Rights for Britain (see p. 342). Of course, under certain circumstances people may be quite happy to relinquish freedom. Mill argued in his *Essay on Liberty*, in the nineteenth century, that freedom should be permitted only up to the point that one person's freedom impinged upon that of another, and much modern legislation (e.g. libel laws) limits freedom in order to protect others.

When we consider fundamental rights which have a direct bearing on politics we are particularly interested in freedom of the *person*, of *speech*, of *association* or *assembly* and of *property*. We examine these in the following sections.

Freedom of the person

The right to move about one's business has long been regarded as a central pillar of the temple of liberty. In the eighteenth-century case of *Leach* v. *Money and Other* (1765) it was held that a general warrant for the arrest of unnamed persons was illegal and void. In *Liversidge* v. *Anderson and Another* (1942) it was held that 'every imprisonment is *prima facie* unlawful, and that it is for a person directing imprisonment to justify his act'. If a person has been wrongfully imprisoned he or she has a range of remedies available in civil and common law, on grounds such as malicious prosecution, false imprisonment, assault and battery.

In addition there is the classic guarantee of individual liberty in Britain – the writ of habeas corpus – enabling anyone confined to demand to be brought before the court for a just trial. During its history the writ has served a variety of purposes, including removing apprentices from cruel masters, freeing slaves, and establishing that a husband has no right to detain his wife against her will.

However, the executive has the authority to limit freedom of the person by taking on unrestrained powers of arrest on the basis of great national emergency. The Emergency Powers (Defence) Act (1939) gives the Home Secretary the right to detain anyone whom he 'has reasonable cause to believe' may be of 'hostile origin or association', which means, in effect, that anyone may be so detained providing that ministers argue that they acted in good faith. Under emergencies, even habeas corpus can be suspended, as was the case, for example, in the fight against the Chartists (see pp. 163–4). The policy of internment in Northern Ireland, and the operation of the 'sus' law against young West Indians, have represented further serious infringements of freedom of the person.

Freedom of speech

It is clear that in a democracy the freedom to express political opinion is fundamental, and throughout the world the absence of such a right is held by liberals to be one of the most visible symptoms of oppression. Yet in Britain the freedom is restricted in various ways. Individuals are protected from verbal assault by others through the laws of slander and libel. There are also laws on obscenity, though the impossibility of deciding what exactly is obscene often produces ludicrous scenarios, such as the *Lady Chatterley's Lover* trial. The most serious restrictions on freedom of speech tend to come from the agencies of the state. In Britain the repressive apparatus, though often lying dormant, carries a formidable potential which is thrown into starkest relief in the reporting of politics by the media and the important question of government secrecy (see pp. 362–7).

Freedom of association

Politics is essentially about collective behaviour and the voluntary association of individuals. However, the constitution places a great many restrictions on the freedom to associate. There have been, for example, the crimes of conspiracy and public nuisance, and the common-law offences of riot, rout and unlawful assembly. These have now been codified in the Public Order Act (1986) and do not all exist in their original form. However, the police retain extensive powers to act in the event of a breach of the peace, or even the suspicion that such a breach might be likely to occur. Under normal circumstances the authorities claim to exercise their discretion in a liberal manner, but within this velvet glove of tolerance and forbearance is the clenched fist of state repression (see chapter 18): people can be bound over to keep the peace, road blocks can stop movement (as in the miners' strike of 1984–85) and powers to disperse crowds can curtail rights of assembly. In 1988, after a long battle in which the government sought to remove the rights of workers at the Government Communications Headquarters at Cheltenham to membership of a trade union, those refusing to relinquish such rights were sacked.

Freedom of property

This is the key freedom in a capitalist society, which is based on the private ownership of property. The Englishman's home is often said to be his castle, where he may defend himself from his enemies as well as seek repose. This is a view shared by the law, and in *Semayne's Case* (1603) it was declared that if thieves enter a man's house to commit robbery or murder, he, or his servants, are entitled to kill them in defence of life and property. In *Stroud* v. *Bradbury* (1952), the rights of 'free born Englishmen' to defend themselves against the intrusions of a council sanitary inspector with 'clothes prop and spade' were defended. However, when the forces of the state wish to enter private premises they find little practical impediment. It is not difficult for the police to obtain warrants, and in cases where they have made illegal entry the courts have taken a surprisingly lenient view where the object has been the suppression of left-wing or radical forces. In *Elias* v. *Pasmore* (1934), the illegal seizure by the police of documents belonging to the National Unemployed Worker's Movement was held as excusable on the grounds of state security.

Dubious rights

When considering individual rights it becomes apparent that in Britain these are so hedged with qualifications, ambiguities and what has been praised as the 'glorious uncertainty of the law' that it is difficult to know what one may actually do without impediment. In the ironic words of Hood Phillips:

> A citizen's person or property may not be interfered with – unless it may. A person is not liable for what he speaks or writes – unless he is. No liability attaches to one who takes part in a public meeting – unless it does.
>
> (Hood Phillips 1987: 39–40)

A Written Constitution?

In spite of the praises heaped on the mysterious virtues of the British constitution, its unwritten, or uncodified, manifestation is not universally acclaimed. Some argue that the twin guarantees of limited government and protection of individual rights would be far safer if codified in the form of a written constitution and placed beyond the meddling hand of the government of the day through entrenchment. This would have implications for parliamentary sovereignty, the rule of law and the operation of checks and balances, and would entail the enactment of a **Bill of Rights**.

A written constitution would mean the end of parliamentary supremacy, some laws would have to be so entrenched that they could no longer be changed by normal legislative means, and Parliaments would be bound by the constitutional amendments of their predecessors. Moreover, new laws would be subject to judicial review to ensure their harmony with the fundamental laws. In addition, the Cabinet would be subject to checks from both the Commons and the judiciary. It would even be possible to increase the power of the monarchy and Lords (probably with changed composition – see pp. 267–9) to provide further counterweights.

A Bill of Rights would formally enshrine the individual rights discussed above, which are at present little more than tenuous privileges with no guarantees. Britain could give itself such a bill quite easily by incorporating the provisions of the European Convention on Human Rights, ratified by the government in 1951 but not enacted into law. Thus, although British citizens cannot use the convention as a basis for taking a case to the domestic courts, they can use it to appeal to the European Court of Human Rights once they have exhausted the judicial avenues available to them at home. The court has found British governments in violation of human rights on a number of occasions (homosexual rights, immigration, telephone tapping, and the operation of the Prevention of Terrorism Act). In addition to protecting citizens in general against an oppressive state, the enactment of such a bill would be particularly important for trade unions (which are merely collections of ordinary citizens). In most western societies, the ability of organized labour to pursue its collective interest is afforded the status of a constitutional right, but in Britain the approach has been to confer certain 'privileges' or immunities. This carries the connotation that the unions are, in some dubious way, placed above the law (Griffith 1980: 12) and makes it easier for governments to remove such privileges, as happened in the 1980s.

The political debate: limited government or individual rights?

It must be remembered that constitutional reform is never out of the realm of the political, and choruses of constitutional disapproval are intoned from right and left. However, although employing similar rhetoric, the motives of each are quite different.

The call from the right: limited government The right is haunted by the spectre of 'big government', which is seen as directly opposed to the liberalism (minimal government) required by capitalism and established by the nineteenth-century constitution. All extensions to the role of the state are portrayed as the first steps along the dark road to totalitarianism and the right has found much cause for alarm. The social legislation of the late nineteenth century had set restrictions on the hours people could work, regulated conditions in factories and, in the case of children, prevented them from working at all, even insisting that they go to school. The 1909 Liberal government made further inroads with the introduction of national insurance and state pensions, and two world wars rolled forward the state frontiers into the era of the welfare state. Numerous quangos (see p. 444) mushroomed to extend state tentacles into scientific, industrial, educational and artistic life. In areas such as race relations and gender equality, *tutelary law* was introduced to deny the Englishman his right to express his racial and sexual superiority. Moreover, such relaxations in state control that did come about were not the sort the right welcomed: the permissive society of the 1960s reduced state regulation of personal morality, even permitting adults to read alarming works about upper-class ladies fornicating with gamekeepers.

During the 1960s and 1970s, as Labour looked increasingly like a natural party of government, the right became preoccupied with the idea of a written constitution. The cause was given great prominence by the distinguished Conservative lawyer Lord Hailsham (later Lord Chancellor) in 1976, when he delivered the BBC Dimbleby Lecture. He lamented that the British constitution had become an 'elective dictatorship' (see p. 211), posing considerable threat to ordinary citizens by its intemperate tendency to interfere with their lives. At the same time the thinkers of the 'New Right' were dusting up some archaic nineteenth-century economic theory, which required maximum freedom from the state in order to somersault through an economic time-warp into a pre-Keynesian world of unbridled capitalism (see chapter 13).

The advent of the Thatcher government in 1979 produced the opportunity to put ideas into practice and curb the dangerous threat of 'elective dictatorship'. However, establishment fears for the liberty of the man in the street suddenly evaporated, though in the event the new policies were more concerned with the liberty of the man in the *City*. The state was certainly rolled back, but the arm of the repressive state was extended to suppress any rising social unrest resulting from the policy.

The call from the left: protecting the individual The interest in liberties is by no means a prerogative of the right. The restoration of ancient medieval rights has been an historic rallying cry for radicals challenging the established order. Today left-wing concern for liberty is institutionalized in bodies such as the National Council for Civil Liberties (NCCL), a pressure group established in 1934 by left-wing intellectuals (Peele 1986: 146). Although fears associated with police suppression of public disorder were very apparent in the 1970s (e.g. the notorious Red Lion Square Disorders of 15 June 1974), the years of the Thatcher government were to see a resurgence of left-wing attention to individual rights.

Of particular concern were the excessive powers of the police to arrest, or harass people on scant evidence of crime; the militaristic use of the police in industrial disputes; the use of the Official Secrets Act to curtail freedom of speech; government secrecy, and electronic surveillance by the state over left-wing or working-class political activists. Thus the case from the left for a written constitution is not to limit the range of government but to entrench that part of the constitution which has guaranteed the individual rights of the citizen from the coercive power of the state.

Conclusion: Unwritten and Unknowable?

The fact that the constitution is unwritten means that it can never be said to be entirely known; it is always subject to interpretation and dispute. In defence, it could be argued that the constitution is already a written one which remains uncodified; yet to attempt to codify all the relevant material into a document of manageable size would rob it of its infinite subtlety. Moreover, the great virtue of flexibility would be sacrificed: no longer could changes take place imperceptibly to accommodate subtle social developments. Lawyers would become overpowerful, their fingers stained by the acrid alchemy of politics; indeed British judges, unaccustomed to meddling in such areas, would be like bishops trying to quell raucous altercations in a whorehouse. With the loss of parliamentary sovereignty would go the sovereignty of the people; non-elected organs of the state (Lords, monarchy, judiciary) would be able to thwart the wishes of an elected government. This would bring an unexpected problem for the left in that a socialist programme could be thwarted by upper-class judges. Moreover, throughout the world evidence suggests that written constitutions do not work with anything like the neatness implied by the legalists, and some countries with model bills of rights are guilty of serious abuses of freedom. Finally it can be argued that the entire exercise would be futile because the reality of the polity lies in the economic power structure of society, which would be unaffected by changes in constitutional architecture.

However, the vagueness of the unwritten constitution has meant that in reality the checks and balances adjudged necessary for limited and democratic government have in large measure stemmed from the willingness of members of the political elite to observe informal rules or conventions and practise self-restraint. This was a flimsy bulwark, and from the mid-1970s the two-party system began to disintegrate with the emergence of a third political force in the form of the Liberal and Social Democratic parties. After some fluctuations in fortunes, the effect of the change was to give the Conservatives a seemingly impregnable hold on office (see pp. 213–16), so that, under Margaret Thatcher, they began to ride roughshod over conventional niceties such as respect for opponents, consultation with affected interests, acceptance of local democracy, and so on (Wass 1986: xi).

In December 1988 citizens roused by this erosion of rights formed a Charter 88 movement calling for a written constitution conferring a Bill of Rights, the rule of law, open government, electoral reform, reform of the House of Lords, greater control over the executive, independence of the judiciary, legal remedies for abuse of power by the state and protection of local government. This movement was unique in that it brought together as bedfellows figures from both left, right and centre of the political spectrum.

Modern politics reminds us that the constitution is only part of the political landscape, the full extent of which we shall explore in the following chapters. This entails the study of certain institutions of which the constitution remains formally ignorant, and the identification of those parts of the constitution which may have passed from the efficient into the dignified realm. Underlying all is the distribution of power within society, which overrides all else and determines how the polity actually works. Yet the constitution remains central to political life, a crucial element in legitimation and an obscure object of desire for all actors, whether they be reformers or conservatives. Today it appears to be in a state of crisis, failing to limit government and preserve the individual freedoms expected in all other developed polities. The depth of the crisis will become apparent throughout the chapters of this book.

Key points

- The term constitution is used to denote either all that happens in the process of politics and government or the set of rules prescribing the powers and processes of government.
- In this latter sense (which has been the perspective of this chapter) a constitution may be said to do two things:
  (a) limit the powers of rulers;
  (b) safeguard the rights of citizens as individuals.
- It is difficult to discover the British constitution because it does not exist as a single document. It is thus described as unwritten, though in fact many documents are involved and much is written about it.
- The constitution is said to flow from five sources: the royal prerogative, statute, common law, convention and authoritative opinion.

CHARTER 88

W e have been brought up in Britain to believe that we are free: that our Parliament is the mother of democracy; that our liberty is the envy of the world; that our system of justice is always fair; that the guardians of our safety, the police and security services, are subject to democratic, legal control; that our civil service is impartial; that our cities and communities maintain a proud identity; that our press is brave and honest.

Today such beliefs are increasingly implausible. The gap between reality and the received ideas of Britain's "unwritten constitution" has widened to a degree that many find hard to endure. Yet this year we are invited to celebrate the third centenary of the "Glorious Revolution" of 1688, which established what was to become the United Kingdom's sovereign formula. In the name of freedom, our political, human and social rights are being curtailed while the powers of the executive have increased, are increasing and ought to be diminished.

A process is underway which endangers many of the freedoms we have had

The time has come to demand political, civil and human rights in the United Kingdom. The first step is to establish them in constitutional form, so that they are no longer subject to the arbitrary diktat of Westminster and Whitehall.

We call, therefore, for a new constitutional settlement which would:

Enshrine, by means of a Bill of Rights, such civil liberties as the right to peaceful assembly, to freedom of association, to freedom from discrimination, to freedom from detention without trial, to trial by jury, to privacy and to freedom of expression.

Subject executive powers and prerogatives, by whomsoever exercised, to the rule of law.

Establish freedom of information and open government.

Create a fair electoral system of proportional representation.

Reform the upper house to establish a democratic, non-hereditary second chamber.

Place the executive under the power of a democratically renewed parliament and all agencies of the state under the rule of law.

Ensure the independence of a reformed judiciary.

Provide legal remedies for all abuses of power by the state and the officials of central and local government.

Guarantee an equitable distribution of power between local, regional and national government.

Draw up a written constitution, anchored in the idea of universal citizenship, that incorporates these reforms.

- The importance of conventions is far greater in the British constitution than in that of any other country.
- A constitution does not stand above the process of politics in the way that the rules of, say, netball stand above the game. The process of politics involves interpreting the constitution and seeking to change it.
- Reformers from right, left and centre of the political spectrum call for a written constitution, for both political and rational reasons.

- In reality the British constitution can be seen as extremely fragile, requiring government willingness to impose self-restraint if it is to furnish the range of freedoms expected in a true democracy.
- For many commentators the 1980s saw the constitution in a state of crisis as the willingness of government to impose self-restraint was called into question.

Review your understanding of the following terms and concepts

constitution	positive law
unwritten constitution	natural law
dignified and efficient elements	constitutional government
royal prerogative	limited government
statue law	separation of powers
common law	rule of law
constitutional convention	parliamentary sovereignty
authoritative opinion	legislature
entrenched provision	executive
constitutional amendment	sovereignty
mechanistic view	civil rights
organic view	Bill of Rights

Assignment

Answer the following questions about the extract from *Charter 88* on p. 49.

		% mark
1	Do any of the demands in *Charter 88* imply a constitutional separation of powers? Explain your conclusion.	15
2	What does *Charter 88* say about provision for a system of administrative justice?	15
3	How might a Bill of Rights improve upon the existing provision made for the protection of civil liberties in Britain?	15
4	Why do you think the chartists call for a non-hereditary second chamber?	15
5	Why do you think the modern chartists want a written constitution?	40

Questions for discussion

1 Identify the sources of the British constitution and evaluate their relative importance.
2 Outline the advantages of a written constitution.
3 'The British constitution is itself more dignified than real.' Discuss.
4 Discuss the principal ways in which you think the introduction of a written constitution would change British politics.
5 Contrast the arguments from the left and the right in British politics for a written constitution.

6 'So-called individual or human rights are no more and no less than political claims made by individuals on those in authority.' Discuss.
7 How secure are the rights of individuals in Britain today?

Topic for debate

This house believes that the absence of a Bill of Rights leaves British citizens in a disconcerting position in relation to the state.

Further reading

Bagehot, W. (1963) *The English Constitution*.
First published in 1867, this is a classic and immensely readable account of the way government worked during the fleeting period of genuine parliamentary government (see chapter 9 of this book). Bagehot, with his journalistic skills, sought to describe what he believed actually happened, rather than what the laws said should happen. It was, however, immediately overtaken by events as Disraeli's 1867 Reform Act ended the period Bagehot described.

Chrimes, S. B. (1967) *English Constitutional History*.
The nature of the British constitution is such that it is always necessary for students to be aware of its historical progress. This slim volume is concise yet erudite on the subject.

Dicey, A. V. (1959) *Introduction to the Study of the Law and the Constitution*, 11th edn.
This classic account (first published in 1885) may be said to have taken over from where Bagehot left off in 1867, but has neither the flair nor political insight of the former. Dicey is the classic exponent of the theory of liberal democracy, though his heart is perhaps more with liberalism than democracy.

Hailsham, Lord (1978) *The Dilemma of Democracy*.
A prominent and rumbustious Conservative politician and lawyer (and Lord Chancellor), Lord Hailsham's views must be read with due caution. His dilemma of democracy is perhaps a problem felt more acutely when the electorate is misguided enough to elect a Labour government. Yet a thought-provoking and stimulating study.

Harden, I. and Lewis, N. (1986) *The Noble Lie*.
Adopting a US-style approach (critical legal studies) this explores the gulf between the orthodox approach to constitutional theory, which derives largely from Dicey even amongst those who wish to refute the nineteenth-century scholar, and the reality of the structure of political power today.

Holme, R. and Elliot, M. (eds) (1988) *1688–1988: Time for a New Constitution*.
A volume of essays to mark the tercentenary of the Glorious Revolution, this is generally critical of the constitution as a vehicle for politics in the 1980s. A number of distinguished contributors (mainly political scientists) argue variously for reforms to different parts of the constitution.

Scarman, Lord (1974) *English Law: the New Dimension*.
Arguments by a distinguished lawyer for constitutional reform.

For light relief

William Golding, *Lord of the Flies*.
Allegory exploring the tragedy that occurs when constitutional rule breaks down
and man's savagery takes over.

George Orwell, *Animal Farm*.
Fable satirizing Russian revolution and, by extension, all revolutions. New tyranny
replaces old.

3

The World Context:
This Sceptred Isle

The purpose of this chapter is to stress that British politics cannot be seen as a self-contained, independent process. The ship of state negotiates a stormy sea of world affairs and the idea promoted in much political rhetoric, and many traditional textbooks, that the government rationally charts its course with political compass and sextant is illusory. We examine Britain's place in the world order in economic and political terms. The chapter contains three main sections. The first seeks to identify and explain the factors leading to Britain's particularly intimate relationship with the **world economy**, and the associated concept of neocolonialism. The second section focuses on world politics and Britain's position in **supranational associations**. The final section examines one of the most compelling issues relating to Britain's place in the international order – its relative **post-war decline**.

The exogenous perspective Much orthodox writing on British politics assumes a high degree of control on the part of the rulers. If the economy does well it is to our credit, and if it fails we embark upon an orgy of self-recrimination. Explanations which look inwards are termed **endogenous** and they are essentially short-sighted. The tendency to seek endogenous explanations arises from various factors, including the arrogance that assumes that we are in control of our destiny, a 'Rule Britannia' conviction that Britain controls world events, the patriotic rhetoric of politicians, and intellectual laziness. Yet ironically, few countries have been more closely enmeshed in the economy and politics of the modern world, where events such as wars, economic crises and third-world poverty create an uncontroll-able turbulence. Any study which ignores this is clearly incomplete and, perhaps, worthless. When we direct our attention at such underlying *external* forces we are adopting an **exogenous perspective**.

Britain on the world stage

Many texts dwell with pride on the idea of Britain's unique insularity (physical and metaphorical) and the conviction, implicitly or explicitly, that its political system is superior. A much-vaunted factor is the country's geographical position, shielding it from physical and cultural invasion or other forms of contamination. As it was for Shakespeare's John of Gaunt, it has been

> [a] fortress built by Nature for herself
> Against infection and the hand of war.
> (*Richard II*, Act 2, Scene 1)

The last invasion took place in 1066, and the defeat of the Spanish Armada in 1588 encapsulated in a legendary way this advantage. Yet despite its protective insularity, more than in most countries Britain's world position has shaped the nature of the polity. Despite the proud emphasis on the unbroken thread of constitutional development from the distant past, the modern polity developed in a radical manner as Britain stepped dramatically onto the world stage during the great age of discovery and continued to play a leading role through the industrial revolution. Despite the '1066 and all that' of the history books, Britain was first an unknown land of barbarians, next a distant and unimportant Roman outpost, and then an insignificant medieval kingdom remaining largely cut off from mainstream European culture, trade, politics and dynastic ambitions.

The revolutionary developments placing Britain at the hub of the world were the result, not of any particular skill on the part of the ruling elite, but a confluence of several rivers of good fortune. This added to the protective geographical insularity and associated naval strength a high degree of unity given by small island status, a self-sufficient agricultural system, a reserve of vital raw materials, and an early industrial genius. Such factors produced the rise of industrial capitalism and the newly powerful capital-owning **bourgeois class** which created the modern British state.

Britain in the Capitalist World Economy

Although Britain belongs to a number of international institutions, nothing preoccupies the establishment, and influences political affairs, as much as the **world economy**. Indeed it is upon this that the undoubted greatness of the modern British elite has been based.

The capitalist world economy today: neocolonialism

Pre-capitalist world empires grew out of the desire of powerful states to establish hegemony over wider areas, usually the territory of their weaker neighbours, in an essentially exploitative relationship. However, these empires were relatively self-sufficient, perishing when they ceased to be so.

The coming of industrial capitalism saw a new form of empire with a stronger military and financial base. The forces of the state were used to help private capitalists exploit the labour and raw materials of the colonies, leading to a world economy based on sea trade routes. **Colonial rule** was established either through permanent settlements, with a new ruling class imposed on the old order, as in North America, Australia, Northern Ireland and South Africa, or through direct rule by means of an administrative system linked to the 'mother country', as in the case of India.

Yet the new empires were also unstable, costly to maintain and prone to revolts and pressure for independence. Those governed on the basis of settlement were particularly problematic, having greater **autonomy** (self-government) and military strength: America was able to break free as early as 1776. Although in the 1930s Germany, Italy and Japan sought unsuccessfully to establish new empires (precipitating the second world war in the process), and after 1945 a new empire was established in Eastern Europe based on socialist Russia, the twentieth century saw the gradual dismantling of the old European colonial empires.

However, contrary to the hopes of the subject races, this era of emancipation did not mark the end of their subjugation or exploitation. Advanced capitalism, through the medium of multinational conglomerate companies, has become so mighty that it can function without the cost of political control over large sectors of the globe. In this system of **neocolonialism** legally independent states are dominated through economic penetration. This world, of which Britain is very much a part, may be portrayed in terms of three readily recognizable **zones**: a core, a semiperiphery and a periphery (Wallerstein 1979).

- *The core zone* comprises certain of the successful (and less successful) European colonial powers of the previous century, together with three strong capitalist economies which did not form political empires: the US, Germany and Japan. From within these countries, where broadly based economies allow generally high material standards of living (though not without class differences and inequality), the world economy is directed.
- *The semi-peripheral zone* is formed by ex-colonial settlements (Latin America, the white Commonwealth and South Africa), where the development of a bourgeois ruling class through white settlement, some initial wealth, and political and military strength, has facilitated capital accumulation and economic development. The oil-rich countries of the third world have begun to enter this zone with ambitious development programmes.
- *The peripheral zone* of the capitalist world economy comprises the third world countries, with their poorly developed, narrowly based economies, low levels of consumption, and riven with disease, poverty and starvation.

Thus Britain today, no less than in the great age of Victorian prosperity, is a country enjoying material standards sustained by exploiting a large portion of the globe. The multinational conglomerates reach out voracious tentacles from their headquarters in the core states to the underdeveloped economies where wages are low and the potential workforce submissive. Economically dependent on the core states (as markets and the source of vital imports and loans), those at the periphery are rarely in any position to control the price of their exports and find it almost impossible to accumulate sufficient capital for self-sustaining growth. The appalling plight of the people in these states is increasingly brought into British consciousness by television, though this does little to alter the way world capitalism operates. British teenagers wear low-priced trainers made by workers whose entire weekly wage would not buy them a pair, and whose sight is gradually destroyed by long hours in close proximity to the chemicals used in their manufacture. By virtue of the high cost of research and technology in modern industrialization, even indigenous extractive industries are controlled from outside. The non-oil-producing periphery states find their position worsened by the willingness of the core states to make huge loans in order to stave off world recession. Thus they develop crippling debts, obliging them to aim for enormous trade surpluses.

Britain is a founder member of this capitalist world economy with a very special relationship to it which can only be understood by reference to its historical development, which we examine below.

The era of mercantilism

The great 'age of discovery' beginning in the fifteenth century opened up a New World, and a new world economy developing from the mid-sixteenth century, traversing the Atlantic, to be shared by Portugal, Spain, Holland, France and Britain. This sea-borne trading network was based on **imperialism**, with the emphasis on protecting the colonies themselves and trading with them. The period was characterized by greedy competitive struggle between the European powers for territory, raw materials and people. Britain was uniquely fitted to survive in this environment, possessing enough farmland to be self-sufficient, and completely safe from land attack. While other European states warred on land, Britain could develop a strategy of oceanic domination of a world trade in commodities and slaves. The British state accepted without question the role of assisting the commercial efforts of its merchants and settlers in the struggle to dominate the New World, and trade wars were fought for some 150 years. To protect trade, Navigation Acts were passed granting monopolies to British merchants. The colonies

---

The British Empire is one of the greatest enslavers of human beings in the world.

Paul Robeson (black American singer; victim of colour prejudice), quoted in *News Review* (3 Oct. 1946)

themselves were treated as state property and brought under the control of Parliament. Ultimately, with the gaining of India and Canada and the defeat of France in the Napoleonic wars, Britain emerged as the supreme world power, a role prized so highly that the subsequent determination to retain it accounts for much in British politics.

In these heady days the English ruling class bestrode the world with arrogance, aggression, and a conviction of racial superiority which reverberates to this day. In the colonies ancient cultures and families were torn apart; while merchants bartered for the slaves' bodies, missionaries traded in their souls. The essence of foreign policy was to maintain naval supremacy and prevent the rise of any rival power in Europe. The only cloud on the horizon was the successful rebellion in the American colonies in 1776 (where the settlers could endure British greed no longer) and the running sore of Ireland, where similar discontents were felt (see pp. 93–9).

British imperialism: Bombay police fire on rioters
Source: Mary Evans Picture Library

Although this world empire covered one-fifth of the globe it continued to be based on protection; Britain drew wealth from its colonies but remained self-sufficient at home. The mercantilist doctrine was to expand exports while limiting imports, thereby amassing wealth in the form of gold bullion. However, the events of the industrial revolution were to transform radically the nature of this world economy and Britain's relation to it.

The era of free trade

The **industrial revolution** beginning in the eighteenth century and continuing unabated even during the Napoleonic wars was a further good fortune for the English elite. Domination could be amplified through superior industrial productivity and the expanding capitalist enterprises were able to feed on raw materials from the colonies and disgorge manufactured goods to the world. With a considerable advantage over all competitors **free trade**, rather than mercantilism, became the rallying cry of the new bourgeoisie: Britain abandoned protection and threw open its doors to all-comers, urging others to do likewise. The principle of **comparative advantage**, enunciated by the economist Adam Smith (1723–90), required that each country specialize in the thing it did best. Of course Britain was incomparable best at manufacturing, and it was here that the greatest profits could be made. The country produced a third of the world's manufactured goods and half its iron, steel, coal and cotton goods.

The cost of this policy was to expose British agriculture (through the relaxing and ultimately the repeal of the corn laws in 1846) to destructive competition and an ensuing loss of national self-sufficiency, but the commitment to free trade remained unshaken. 'Nowhere did the transformation, the reduction of agriculture to a subordinate role, go further than it did in Britain' (Deane 1963: 188). This radical redirection in policy cannot be underestimated; it was perhaps the most decisive event in modern British history (Gamble 1985: 55). The bourgeoisie were fully prepared to risk the future of the whole of society in the interests of industrial capitalism and the creation of wealth on an unprecedented scale.

Britain, although powerful in terms of naval strength, colonial possessions and industrial might, became locked into the world economy in a state of dependency for food, raw materials and markets. Industry, finance and commerce flourished and state policy acquired an international outlook going beyond the confines of the empire. The state was brought under the control of the newly enriched bourgeoisie through far-reaching constitutional reforms and pledged itself to a world policing role in order to secure the vital trade routes. The pound (sterling), fixed to the gold standard, became the universal currency necessary to lubricate world trade (a reserve currency), and a world economic system emerged with a financial, trading and communications network centred on London. Britain had established an economic empire which extended beyond the bounds of its political one.

Yet this openness to the world economy was reckless, requiring a corresponding openness from others (including those not benefiting from it). Hence it contained the seeds of ultimate decline.

Signs of decline

After so exhilarating a start in the industrial race some initial relative decline was inevitable. The very markets which Britain opened up and supplied with manufactured goods could be penetrated by rivals. However, Britain's eclipse by Germany and the US was accomplished, not by following the teachings of Adam Smith but by denying them and erecting tariff barriers designed to protect their fledgling industries from Britain. Free trade was seen as nothing more than a self-serving pseudo-philosophy designed to justify and perpetuate the domination of the world by the British bourgeoisie.

> Englishmen know instinctively that what the world needs most is whatever is best for Great Britain.
>
> Ogden Nash (1902–71, US poet), *England Expects*

In response, a movement led by Joseph Chamberlain grew up in Britain seeking to reduce the vulnerability resulting from the openness of British markets. Tariff reform, a fundamental question addressing Britain's future as a world power, became a burning political issue at the beginning of the twentieth century. The reformers envisaged a new era in which an enlarged and protected empire, united as strongly as the UK itself, would take on the world from a position of impregnable self-sufficiency. A worldwide nation-state was envisaged, dominated, through settlement or by paternalistic administration, by English culture. However, in 1905 the election of a Liberal government committed to free trade effectively ended the debate.

In spite of the rise of its rivals, Britain continued to see itself as a **world policeman**, guarding the trade routes with its navy and maintaining a balance of power in Europe. The international monetary system continued to centre on sterling, London remaining the hub of world insurance and banking. British capitalists continued to invest vast sums abroad and draw incomes as *rentiers*. Yet the costs were high: the intense competition between the European powers culminating in two great world wars left Britain gravely enervated and obliged to look to the US for succour.

The United States and the special relationship

> Great Britain has lost an Empire and has not yet found a role.
>
> Dean Acheson (US Secretary of State), speech at Military Academy, West Point (5 Dec. 1962)

Both the US and Germany had threatened British dominance yet, in defeating one of these rivals in two horrific wars, Britain was obliged meekly to succumb to the hegemony of the other, the one which had actually rejected British rule in 1776. However, this was the strategy dictated by the logic of a free world economy, so vital to the interests of British capital. The US was seen as the state best able to take over the torch of free trade Britain had so long carried.

Despite its overwhelming importance in the post-war era, the 'special relationship' with the US is one of the least-discussed topics in textbooks on British politics. The relationship was indeed decidedly 'special' for the English elite, enabling Britain to enter into a double act with the US and continue to play the part of a world policeman (though very much Laurel to America's Hardy).

> **Give us the tools and we will finish the job.**
> Winston Churchill, as US Lend–Lease legislation
> going through Congress, broadcast (9 Feb. 1941)

The special relationship did not arise spontaneously; there was a festering legacy of American hostility towards the British establishment. Once the US economy had come of age it began to appreciate the advantages of free trade, and the British empire, particularly in the 1930s when it briefly became protectionist, was seen as a serious potential threat. Furthermore, Labour's 1945 election victory deeply disturbed the Americans, who questioned the wisdom of any aid which would finance socialism. The **Lend–Lease** agreement whereby the Americans had assisted the British war effort was abruptly halted, exposing the precarious state of the so-called victor. Britain was obliged to petition cap in hand for further loans for food, which were obtained only on harsh conditions and an agreement not to impede the access of American goods to the markets of the empire.

Hence it was necessary for Britain to court the Americans diligently and foreign policy revealed a desperate desire for the US to use its dominant position to create order in the world economy. The interests of British capitalism were seen to lie in two vitally important conditions: maintaining the international trading network and securing capitalist ideology against communism (through the concept of the cold war).

Reconstructing world capitalism: the Bretton Woods Agreement

As the US became convinced of the need to secure the capitalist world economy against communism its attitude towards Europe softened. Funds were supplied through the generous **Marshall Aid programme**, beginning in July 1948, to refurbish West European capitalism. The programme also served the purpose of providing markets and investments for the Americans.

In July 1944 a conference of 44 nations at **Bretton Woods** in the US established a base for healing the wounds inflicted upon the world economy. Aware of the dangers inherent in the nationalistic competition of the 1930s, the emphasis in the new order was to be on cooperation, cohesion and free

A 'special relationship' and its ambiguities
Source: Popperfoto

trade, based on a sound medium of exchange – the US dollar – to which other currencies would be tied (and through the dollar to gold) at fixed **exchange rates**. At the heart of the system was to be an International Monetary Fund (IMF), largely administered by the US, and a World Bank to make loans to weak countries in order to speed their recovery. Exchange rate changes would require IMF permission and countries securing loans would be obliged to accept conditions concerning domestic economic policy.

Naturally, this system was designed to favour the interests of multinational capital against those of the working class. Experience showed that typical conditions for IMF loans included tax reductions in order to stimulate private investment, and cuts in public spending on welfare policies. British Labour governments found it necessary to succumb meekly to these demands (Benn 1980: 49–50); the political risks of attempting to stand up to the IMF were exemplified by the downfall of Michael Manley's government in Jamaica. Although the legal and political sovereignty of member states was technically unimpaired, in effect they were seriously weakened, while the dominance of the US (and its multinational industrial allies) was rendered unchallengeable.

The long boom

The result of the Bretton Woods Agreement was an astonishing new era of plenty for the core states of the capitalist world, with an unprecedented growth of international trade, a **'long boom'** beginning in 1948 and continuing for some 25 years. This was **advanced capitalism**. 'Economic miracles' were wrought in West Germany, Japan and France, which themselves became able to challenge US supremacy. With high levels of employment, profitability and prosperity, it became common to speak of a post-capitalist society in which the slumps associated with old-style capitalism had been removed.

In Britain political adversity appeared to be replaced by consensus, liberal democracy (minimal government) by social democracy, with the two major parties benignly sharing assumptions about the genius of the mixed economy and the welfare state (see pp. 206–14). Apparently capitalism had been saved; all a state had to do was manage the level of demand to iron out slumps and the private sector could be relied upon to do the rest, ensuring prosperity for all (Keynesianism, see pp. 390–2). The boom was fired by a third 'technological revolution' involving the use of advanced techniques of automation and electronics which flowed from the US to raise productivity to new pinnacles. It was also a result of the stability induced by the world leadership which the US had taken over from Britain. However, it was not to be a boom without end, for it was sustained by features which could not be counted upon to last for ever.

World recession

In the mid-1970s the capitalist world edifice came tumbling down into crisis. World trade, which had grown at an annual rate of 8.5 per cent during 1963–72 fell to around 5 per cent, with industrial stagnation, high rates of inflation and unemployment standing side by side. The reasons for this are subject to debate but a number of factors were important.

In the first place, the growth of **monopoly capitalism** saw giant **multinationals** (unconstrained by territorial boundaries) which had restricted the opportunities for governments to influence their own economies and apply counter-cyclical policies. Moreover, the world economy was becoming so tightly integrated that slumps were no longer confined to particular states; once a recession set in, it was likely that all would crash together.

Secondly, technological advance cannot continue smoothly for ever. Mandel (1975: 21) argued that periods of innovation tend to last for around 25 years, to be followed by a further 25 years of slump when the scope for further growth is exhausted. After refurbishing their technology as part of the post-war reconstruction, the capitalist countries reached a point when they could go no further owing to the costs of replacement and update.

Decline in the US was a third contributory factor. The financial burden associated with its anti-communist militarism throughout the world began to take its toll, with the sordid entanglement in Vietnam being particularly devastating. West Germany and Japan, unencumbered by such commitments, had caught up and no longer needed large-scale importation; indeed they themselves began to penetrate the internal US market. In 1971 the US balance of trade slid into deficit for the first time in the century. In addition, US-based multinationals began to seek capital outlets in the more prosperous economies. Dollars no longer needed to buy American goods were stockpiled in West European banks (particularly in London) as Eurodollars, where they became a further source of credit to multinationals.

These developments were outside the control of national governments and accelerated at bewildering speed to fuel spiralling inflation in the increasingly stagnant capitalist economies, which were unable to meet wage rises with increased productivity (Pillay 1981: 59). The banks became unwilling to hold Eurodollars, finally forcing the devaluation of the dollar in 1971, which signalled the end of the financial stability of the Bretton Woods Agreement. Currencies could no longer be tied to the dollar by fixed rates. The collapse of the system enabled governments to sustain home demand by increasing the money supply in their domestic economies and allowing exchange rates to float downwards (see p. 392). Further fuel for inflation came from price rises instigated by the multinationals as a response to falling profits.

The oil crises Although sometimes cited as causing the collapse of the capitalist economies, the oil crises following the Yom Kippur war of 1973, which saw a quadrupling of oil prices by the Organisation of Petroleum

Exporting Countries (OPEC), did not in itself precipitate the end of the long boom, though it acutely amplified the fundamental problems. As the world economy began sluggishly to pull itself out of the mire (some countries were able to 'export' their unemployment by repatriating migrant workers), a second oil crisis was precipitated in 1979 by the Iranian revolution, which resulted in a halving of its oil production and a doubling of world prices. The effect of this was to set off resounding repercussions throughout the capitalist world, with reduced profits, balance of payments deficits (and associated deflationary measures), unstable money markets, alarming levels of third world debt, high inflation (13 per cent by 1980), mass unemployment, rising interest rates (which discouraged investment) and economic stagnation.

After the crisis

The oil crisis signalled the beginning of a new climate for the world economy, one particularly inclement for Britain. An intensified struggle for survival was apparent throughout the capitalist world as cooperation between states was replaced by competition, with increasing protection of home markets and thrusting attempts to penetrate those of others. Among the developed states, Germany, Japan and the US proved best fitted to survive, though the protectionist fight between them was to dominate the world economy. The markets of the weaker capitalist economies (particularly those of Britain) were increasingly penetrated with heavy imports of manufactured goods. In the peripheral zone, countries with oil sought to industrialize and improve their position, leaving the others to form a degrading *fourth world* of obscene levels of poverty and deprivation. Within the core, the US enjoyed the great advantage of its own oil sources, insulating it from the direct effects of higher fuel prices, while Britain fortuitously found the self-inflating lifejacket of North Sea oil. The OPEC states began to lose their advantage as the demand for oil dropped.

In 1978 the IMF Articles of Agreement were revised to mark the formal end of the Bretton Woods Agreement, abolishing an official price for gold and allowing members to choose their own exchange rate arrangements. The 1980s saw governments relinquishing their hold over domestic economies and throwing themselves on the mercies of the free market. Competition between the advanced capitalist countries prevented the re-emergence of a new internationally acceptable currency for world trade. Within the European Community agreement had been reached in 1973 to fix exchange rates between member currencies, and float together against the dollar – the 'snake in the tunnel'. The more flexible European Monetary System was introduced in 1979, though Britain typically remained aloof, awaiting the 'right moment' – the eve of the 1990 Conservative Party conference.

By the late 1980s the problems of floating exchange rates were becoming apparent, with high volatility and irrational movements caused by currency speculation, and a summit meeting in Tokyo in 1986 called for improved monetary coordination. In Britain the issue of whether or not to allow the pound to float was hotly debated, with Chancellor Lawson and the Treasury at loggerheads with Mrs Thatcher, who favoured floating, avowing 'You can't buck the market'. This tension was eventually to lead to Lawson's resignation in 1989.

The simultaneous occurrence of inflation and high unemployment suggested that Keynesian demand management (see p. 391) would no longer work once the boom conditions had passed. Increased public spending only led to inflation as large public sector wage rises were not matched by increased productivity. The increase in domestic demand made prices rise, undermining export potential, and sucking in imports (see table 3.1). Monetarism, the favoured policy of the IMF, reigned supreme, particularly in Britain (see pp. 393–9): welfare expenditure was reduced so that the taxes which threatened the capitalists' profits could be lowered.

Table 3.1 Britain's trade with the world (in £ million)

	1982	1983	1984	1985	1986	1987
Imports	56,624	65,581	78,760	84,905	85,568	94,016
Exports	55,314	60,590	70,373	78,263	72,834	79,852

Source: Data from *Monthly Digest of Statistics* (June 1988: table 15.4)

The multinationals had also been hit by the oil crisis and they increasingly exported capital out of the advanced economies into low-wage underdeveloped ones with passive workforces and often repressive and sexist regimes, such as South Korea and the Philippines. Although the system was a form of neocolonialism characterized by extensive exploitation, the trade share of these dependent economies rose, with some benefits (albeit below the level warranted by the labour invested) for the people.

In each country the legitimation of the governing elites depended upon their ability to improve the health of the national economy. For the governments in the more vulnerable countries life became politically difficult. Britain, with its traditionally open economy, was particularly at risk from the outflow of capital, which put profits before the patriotism sometimes expected of the working class in times of war or recession. In 1979 restrictions on such outflow were removed, resulting in a surge of investment, both directly in factories on foreign soil, and by purchasing foreign government bonds and company shares. Figure 3.1 shows the balance between investment in the UK from overseas and the UK outflow into other economies. The latter exceeds the former by a factor of three and has been a major headache for the home economy.

The crisis in the world economy was useful to the forces of the political right at home. A body of thought, gathered loosely together under the title of the New Right, sought a range of endogenous explanations for the ills in the British economy. These will be examined throughout this book, but broadly

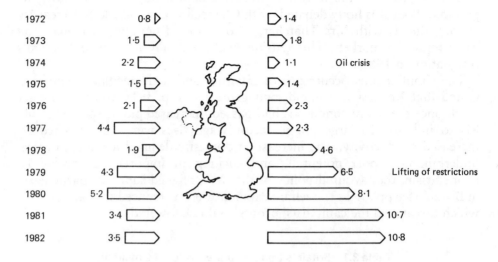

Figure 3.1   The balance between investment in the UK from overseas and the UK outflow into other economies

Source: Data from *Annual Abstract of Statistics*

the blame was placed upon Labour governments, the growth of social democracy (with welfare state feather-bedding and spendthrift bureaucrats), the consultative practices of government (giving too much power to labour and the trade unions and making the country 'ungovernable'), immigration (Enoch Powell's 'rivers of blood' visions), Keynesianism (leading to government debt), high taxation (removing the incentive of the high-earners to generate wealth), and extravagant local authorities (to be dubbed the 'loony left'). Generally the workers of Britain had become soft; they had, in Norman Tebbit's words, retreated into a 'post-war funk'. The fall of Edward Heath's government at the hands of the miners in 1974 symbolized the state of Britain for the right, which mobilized opinion through the media in favour of extreme right-wing solutions so that Margaret Thatcher's government was able to justify the economic medicine of monetarism (see p. 394). This was to launch a colossal attack on the concept of social democracy, the welfare state, local democracy, and so on.

This policy was mightily assisted by a number of exogenous variables, including the windfall of North Sea oil and the Falklands war, which restored confidence in Mrs Thatcher just at the right time. In addition, from 1983 the world economy began a period of renewed growth, with the US setting the pace. Inflation continued to fall and by 1986 oil prices were also falling, permitting more expansionist policies.

The Political World Setting

I am not an Athenian or a Greek, but a citizen of the world.
Socrates (470–399 BC; Greek philosopher), in Plutarch, *Of Banishment*

Although it is possible to speak of a world economy, there is nothing resembling a world polity. States have sought jealously to protect their autonomy and the idea of a world government, which could settle inter-state disputes without war, has been little more than a philosopher's pipe-dream. Yet ironically, while seeking zealously to retain the concept of national sovereignty, states have, as we have seen, been forced to relinquish true independence before the iron laws of world capitalism.

The role of the state in the modern world

The modern form of world capitalism discussed in the previous section contains enormous potential for political catastrophe. Billions of the world's population live at subsistence level or below, constituting valueless surplus labour and having little to lose from violent rebellion. Hence the mixtures of the modern political world are marked 'highly inflammable' and the role of the state must entail two contradictory functions: serving the gargantuan needs of multinational capitalism and at the same time seeking to legitimate the system (to prevent revolutions) by protecting citizens.

Thus, states can subsidize production costs, offer tax incentives, minimize risks, provide an infrastructure of communications and utilities, educate the working class, reduce labour costs through welfare policies, and so on. Yet, while states will go to almost any lengths to appease them, the multinationals show little loyalty in return. Shipping lines will fly 'flags of convenience' to avoid paying the taxes and meeting the working conditions required by their true countries of origin. Firms will cynically switch capital from one country to another as tax rates fluctuate, seek out tax havens, and when exploitable resources run dry will fly like the proverbial bat out of hell.

Because of the effects of the world economy it is not possible to identify a purely *political* dimension to the international context of British politics. However, certain features can be isolated for separate scrutiny, including the extraordinary phenomenon of the **cold war**, the permanent backdrop for post-war international politics, and a range of **international associations** which contain something of the germ of an international polity.

The cold war

The cold war between the capitalist and communist blocs was a divide based on psychology and ideology, arising from a consuming and paranoid fear of

FORTY YEARS OF NATO

Do we have to go on like this?

Figure 3.2 The futility of the cold war as depicted in a leaflet produced by the Campaign for Nuclear Disarmament (CND)

communism (an ideology based on equality and the common ownership of property) amongst the capitalist elite. The bizarre phenomenon claimed no casualties in the bloody manner of, say, the Somme, but its real effect in terms of human suffering among the poor nations of the world was incalculable. It has been particularly important to the British ruling class as a means of maintaining consistently anti-socialist attitudes among many ordinary people, and of ensuring that the US would assume the mantle of guardian of world capitalism. The prospect of defeating Germany in the second world war contained pause for thought on the part of the capitalist establishment, since it would leave Russia supreme in Europe. Indeed the prospect was rather more disturbing than the ultra-right German empire which the fighting was all about in the first place.

> If we see that Germany is winning the war we ought to help Russia, and if Russia is winning we ought to help Germany, and in that way let them kill as many as possible.
>
> Harry S. Truman (US President 1945–53), in *New York Sunday Times* (24 July 1941)

It was Winston Churchill, on a highly publicized tour of America (stunned by his unexpectedly overwhelming rejection by the British electorate after the war), who added to the cold war lexicon when, in a dramatic public speech in Fulton, Missouri, in March 1946, he declaimed: 'From Stettin in the Baltic to Trieste in the Adriatic an **Iron Curtain** has descended upon the Continent'. The actual term 'cold war' was coined by the Americans and given wide currency by the influential journalist Walter Lippmann.

The British view of the Soviet threat was finally accepted in the US, becoming an all-consuming passion of their foreign policy. The essence of the idea was that both blocs acted as if at war (manufacturing weapons, conducting acts of espionage and practising economic and political subversion) without actually coming to blows. For the capitalist bloc this had the advantage of keeping the population permanently hostile to all left-wing policies and politicians (talk of improving the condition of the working class could be portrayed as sedition and treachery). 'Reds under the beds' scares were fanned by the media and in the US the hysteria reached epic proportions in the medieval-style witch-hunts of McCarthyism, when famous figures were pilloried for left-wing sympathies and sometimes hounded from the country (compellingly captured in Arthur Miller's play *The Crucible*).

Arms manufacture became deeply entrenched in the cold war logic (Thompson 1980), constituting for the capitalist bloc a vastly profitable enterprise which could proceed apace without the inconvenience of physical damage to the economic infrastructure. Yet the arms race had deep implications for world politics, demanding a use of resources more extravagant than that of any real war, while billions in the third world continued to live (or die) in pain, indignity and squalor.

Our scientific power has outrun our spiritual power. We have guided missiles and misguided men.

Martin Luther King (US civil rights campaigner; assassinated 1968),
Strength to Love (1963)

The cold war was also manifest in the supposedly **non-aligned world**, with the US bolstering up a motley collection of oppressive anti-socialist regimes in accordance with an intellectually crude 'domino theory'. An anti-communist war was fought in Korea with active British support, the democratically elected socialist government of Chile was illegally and violently brought down by an American-backed insurrection, and the fatal embroglio in Vietnam dragged on to its conclusion of undignified withdrawal (mitigated only by a spate of *Rambo* movies in which American hawks could fantasize on how things might have been).

Britain generally supported the US in its adventurism. Although this commitment seemed to weaken under Wilson (when support for the Vietnam position was half-hearted), it saw a revival under Mrs Thatcher, whose foreign policy appeared to amount to supporting whatever the US felt inclined to do. This included resigned acceptance of the US invasion of the Commonwealth country of Grenada in 1983 and active support for the air attack on Libya in 1986. In November 1988, when the US refused a visa to allow Yasser Arafat of the Palestine Liberation Organisation to address the United Nations, Britain was the only country (apart from Israel) not to vote in opposition.

From the initial moves by Churchill, governments of all shades maintained full commitment to the spirit of the cold war. It was a Labour prime minister (Attlee) who agreed to an independent nuclear deterrent, a policy loyally pursued by both parties when in power, despite the presence of NATO and the US 'nuclear umbrella'. (With imagery appropriate enough for a 'cold' war, Bevan declared that, without the atom bomb, a Foreign Secretary would go 'naked' into the world conference chambers.)

The cold war enabled the Conservatives to maintain their historic claim to be the party of patriotism, making electoral support no less than a national duty. When Labour adopted an anti-nuclear stance, mass opinion had been so shaped as to render the policy suicidal.

Military alliances Although resting upon the psychology of fear rather than objectivity, the cold war justified various military alliances into which Britain enthusiastically entered. The major one followed a dramatic *coup* on 25 February 1948, when a new communist government took office in Czechoslovakia, after USSR interference in free elections. It led to an alliance which was soon superseded in 1949, after the Russian blockade of Berlin, with a wider one including the US – the North Atlantic Treaty Organization (NATO). The US was to be the biggest contributor to the NATO budget and, with its vast armoury, could provide a 'nuclear umbrella', its strategic dominance entailing a major loss of sovereignty by other members. The true limits of British independence in international relations were underlined by Mrs Thatcher's declaration that to refuse the US leave to launch its Libyan attack from British bases was 'unthinkable'.

> Militarism ... is one of the chief bulwarks of capitalism, and the day that militarism is undermined, capitalism will fail.
> Helen Keller (1880–1968; blind, deaf and dumb US writer and lecturer),
> *The Story of My Life* (1947)

Melting the ice Throughout the post-war period the degree of frost in the cold war had fluctuated, with attempts at *détente* (an ending of strained relations) followed by aggressive imperialism. However, although the cold war was good for arms manufacturers and posturing statesmen, it imposed absurd economic burdens on both the superpowers. The decline of the US, and Britain, compared with Germany and Japan, underlined this, and the damage was even greater in the USSR. In the 1980s, moves towards a more permanent thaw came with the accession of Mikhail Gorbachev. His programme of domestic and constitutional reform (*perestroika* and *glasnost*) set off reverberations throughout the eastern bloc and one by one hard-line totalitarian regimes in the Stalinist mould were popularly rejected. These developments met with approval in the capitalist bloc and the multinationals began to dream of penetrating new markets. Meetings between Gorbachev and President Reagan even led to reductions in the nuclear arsenals. In January 1990 Richard Pearl, former US Assistant Defense Secretary, told Congress it was 'simply no longer possible to imagine a cohesive Warsaw Pact, led by Soviet troops, forcing its way through the centre of Europe' (*Observer*, 20 Jan. 1990) and President Bush began to contemplate major defence cuts. Mrs Thatcher, however, to the dismay of the British Treasury, remained suspicious. In 1990 the defence budget as a proportion of national income was the highest in Western Europe at 5 per cent (compared with 4 per cent in France and 3 per cent in West Germany).

The United Nations Organization

In the cold-war atmosphere of military alliances, ideological incompatibilities and class tensions, forces for the creation of a world polity (to render war, not a glorious expression of national sovereignty, but a crime) appeared unlikely to make much headway. However, the idea that world peace could be so assured has long tantalized philosophers, and the United Nations Organization (UN) was intended as a step along this road.

The League of Nations The League of Nations, a precursor of the UN, was established in response to the insanity of the first world war through the Treaty of Versailles in 1919. Here was a forum where nations could seek diplomatic solutions to their differences, but the enterprise collapsed into the tragedy of the second world war.

Establishing the UN Thus when the UN was formally established in October 1945 it represented an attempt to pick up the pieces of the earlier abortive effort. In 1941 Britain and the US had signed an Atlantic Charter, and the following year 29 other countries signed an agreement (the Declaration of United Nations) to work together to defeat Germany, Japan and Italy. A further 21 nations joined and agreed to set up a permanent organization for world peace, the basic structure being determined after further negotiations at the Yalta conference in February 1945. From this time the UN has grown, partly under the stimulus of decolonization, so that by the 1980s there were 157 member states with their headquarters in New York. Its structure comprises the following agencies.

- *The Security Council.* The UN is headed by a Security Council consisting of five permanent founder members (Britain, France, the US, the USSR and

China) and ten others serving two-year terms. The permanent members hold a veto over council decisions, which has usually inhibited decisive action.

- *The General Assembly.* This is the main forum, bringing together all member states, which send delegations headed by their foreign ministers. Each has one vote regardless of size, giving a political prominence to weak countries not always welcomed by the strong. The assembly meets regularly and may be summoned for emergency meetings in crises (Suez, the Cuban Missile Crisis, and so on).
- *The UN Secretariat.* The assembly is serviced by a 4,000-strong Secretariat – a bureaucracy drawn from all states, headed by a Secretary General, whose role is to alert the assembly to threats to peace and conduct negotiations between disputants. In addition it can send its own peacekeeping forces to trouble-spots.
- *The International Court of Justice.* Disputes involving international law may be adjudicated by the International Court of Justice located at The Hague and presided over by judges (serving for limited terms) from member countries.
- *Specialized organizations.* The UN has also fulfilled a range of social and cultural functions through specialized agencies such as UNICEF (children), WHO (Health) and UNESCO (education).

Yet this is not world government; it neither passes laws nor imposes taxes, and member states retain full sovereignty. Its purpose is to facilitate dialogue and promote harmony, the value of its resolutions lying only in the extent to which they create a pressure of world opinion. Generally countries are loath to accept resolutions which restrict their autonomy. The UN was quite unable to prevent the Falklands war, and the British government steadfastly refused to follow the UN desire to open talks about the islands' future. Obviously, if powerful countries refuse to be bound by resolutions supported by third world countries, the principle that 'might is right' must continue to set the tone for international relations.

Retreating from empire: the British Commonwealth

> I have not become the King's First Minister in order to preside over the liquidation of the British Empire.
>
> Winston Churchill, speech at Lord Mayor's Banquet (10 Nov. 1942)

Disastrously weakened by the second world war, Britain still retained a ludicrous level of imperial commitments. Although the US was not happy with the concept of a British empire (a bar to potential markets), it tolerated it as a reward for the enormous military and financial commitments Britain had undertaken in the interests of world capitalism. Yet imperialism could not be sustained; not only did it impose unrealistic burdens on the 'mother country', it was detested by most of the colonies. Hence a process of retreat, very distressing to the old English colonial establishment, was painfully negotiated, to be virtually completed in 1967, when troops withdrew from east of Suez. The bitter pill of vanishing splendour was sugared by the evolution of the British Commonwealth, a means whereby the old order could delude itself that it still ruled the world. Initially this had consisted of the 'white' dominions of Canada, Australia, South Africa and New Zealand, but after 1945 these were to be joined by the 'new Commonwealth' formed from the colonial territories of Asia, Africa and the West Indies.

Today the British Commonwealth is a loose family of nations with no formal rules or constitution, united under the Crown rather than the British government. It is based neither upon treaty nor legal agreement; member states are sovereign, with the right to leave if they wish (as did Pakistan and the Republic of Ireland).

The Commonwealth's role in world politics is debatable, but since its membership encompasses a considerable diversity of cultures, political systems and economies, its potential as a force for international cooperation and understanding should perhaps not be dismissed too lightly (Ramphal 1988). However, the legacy of empire does little to provide a cultural heritage conducive to a harmonious partnership of equals. The collapse under the forces of indigenous culture of many Westminster-style constitutions, bequeathed to colonies upon their independence, demonstrated that the imposed rule had done little to inculcate English culture. Although the people are termed British subjects or Commonwealth citizens, since 1962 a series of Immigration Acts have eroded their rights to settle in Britain, stemming the immigration flow once the demand for cheap labour dried up. Furthermore, racism at home cannot be expected to win the confidence of Commonwealth leaders or their people. Thus it is hardly surprising if some members of Britain's black community detect in the amicable meetings at Buckingham Palace and Downing Street, where Commonwealth leaders, resplendent in their traditional costumes, pose for photographs with the Queen or Prime Minister, more than a whiff of 'Uncle Tomism'.

For its part, the UK disdains Commonwealth support when making important foreign policy decisions (like Suez or the Falklands). Nowhere has this been more clearly revealed than in the issue of sanctions against the white South African regime, which threatened to shatter the association completely during the 1980s. Even the Queen was reported alarmed by Mrs Thatcher's hard capitalist line, which treated the wishes of all other Commonwealth members with contempt.

It seems that the British Government sees black people as expendable.

Bishop Desmond Tutu (black South African civil rights campaigner), speech (1986)

Britain in Western Europe

> We are part of the community of Europe and we must do our duty as such.
>
> Lord Salisbury (1830–1903; Conservative leader), speech (11 April 1888)

In spite of the empire, the special relationship with the US, and a long history of European rivalry and warfare, it is in Western Europe that British cultural roots really lie, and there has been an inexorable pressure towards greater integration, particularly during the post-war era. In 1949 a Council of Europe was established to facilitate cooperation across a wide front, producing the *European Convention on Human Rights*, signed in 1951 but not incorporated into British law (see p. 45). In 1960 the European Free Trade Association was formed as a trading area including Britain, Austria, Denmark, Norway, Portugal, Sweden, Switzerland, Iceland and Finland.

> We must build a kind of United States of Europe.
>
> Winston Churchill, speech in Zurich (19 Sept. 1946)

The European Communities (EC)

By far the most important of the European institutions are the European Communities, often lamented in traditional textbooks for threatening a loss of British sovereignty. Membership is thus seen as a great constitutional watershed. It is stressed that while other associations to which Britain belongs are *intergovernmental*, having no superior institution to which member states must bow, the EC is **supragovernmental**: its institutions are distinct from, and *superior to*, those of member states. Yet while it is true that 42 weighty volumes of legislation promulgated by the European institutions were incorporated overnight into British law, the effective loss of sovereignty to the US in questions of defence and internal finance (through NATO and the IMF), and the working of the world economy dominated by the multinationals, are far heavier with political significance for Britain.

Initially Britain disdained membership, standing outside first the Coal and Steel Community established in 1951 (under the Treaty of Paris), and then the European Atomic Energy Community (Euratom) and the European Economic Community (EEC) – a *common market* for goods, both established by the Treaty of Rome in 1958. The world-power complex which inspired post-war British foreign policy decreed that the picture of the future should be painted on a wider canvas than Europe. While applauding the

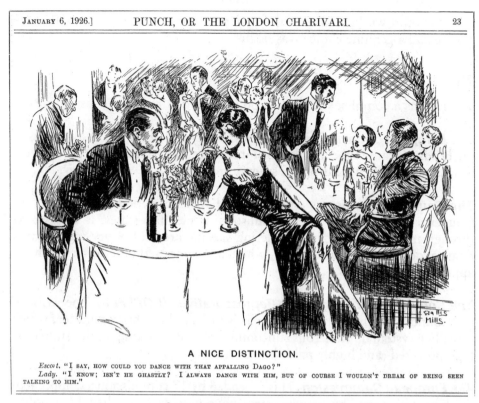

A NICE DISTINCTION.

Escort. "I SAY, HOW COULD YOU DANCE WITH THAT APPALLING DAGO?"
Lady. "I KNOW; ISN'T HE GHASTLY? I ALWAYS DANCE WITH HIM, BUT OF COURSE I WOULDN'T DREAM OF BEING SEEN TALKING TO HIM."

Source: Mary Evans Picture Library

willingness of Belgium, France, Italy, the Netherlands, Luxembourg and West Germany to bind themselves harmoniously together, Britain looked across the Atlantic for an alliance more worthy of its imperial grandeur. However, as events unfolded, Britain's relative economic decline during the long boom and the particular success of West Germany and France suggested that the decision had been misguided. The cold US response to the Suez crisis revealed that the 'special relationship' did not give Britain political omnipotence, and the unending quest for a world leadership role saw Britain turn back to Europe.

President Kennedy welcomed the move (Camps 1964: 336), but President de Gaulle of France smelt a rat, suspecting that Britain would be a Trojan Horse bringing US influence further into Europe, and in January 1963 he vetoed Britain's application. The process was restarted under Labour in 1967, and continued by the Europhile Edward Heath in 1970, reaching a successful conclusion in 1971. However, British feelings remained mixed and Labour voted against the principle of membership (though with 89 members either supporting the government or abstaining), as did 39 Conservatives. The Treaty of Accession was signed in 1972 and Britain formally entered the community on 1 January 1973. In 1975 the Labour government held a referendum on continued membership, but the full weight of the establishment was thrown behind the case for remaining in; any suggestion that the people had a genuine choice was bogus.

The structure of the EC

The EC has a complex structure of political and bureaucratic institutions.

The European Council This stands at the very top of the EC and consists of the heads of state of the member countries meeting around three times a year in what amounts to a European summit meeting.

The Council of Ministers The main policy-making body of the EC, the Council consists of the foreign ministers of member states. It also works through technical councils considering specific areas of policy (agriculture, finance, development, and so on), which are composed of ministers with the appropriate portfolios.

The Committee of Permanent Representatives (COREPER) The work of the Council and the technical councils is prepared by this committee, which is really a system of numerous subcommittees and working parties staffed by high-powered (and highly paid) bureaucrats.

The European Commission This is headed by 17 commissioners, appointed for four-year terms by member-state governments from their own politicians, one of whom they elect as president. Britain has established a tradition of appointing one Labour and one Conservative member.

The bureaucracy The European Commission is serviced by a large bureaucracy at Brussels of around 10,000, responsible for the implementation of Council decisions (usually working through the bureaucracies of member states). Like most civil services the Commission also initiates policy to be discussed by the Council, leading to charges that the EC is dominated by non-elected, faceless bureaucrats.

The European Parliament This is a unicameral (single-chamber) assembly with members (**MEPs**) popularly elected within their own states. (Before 1979 they were appointed by governments.) In all countries but Britain the electoral system is proportional representation (PR – see pp. 183–5). The original proposal for PR was amended by the British Parliament (presumably to prevent the people acquiring a taste for it), and the usual farcical distortions apply, the most grotesque occurring in the 1989 elections when the British Green Party secured 2,292,705 votes (15 per cent) yet gained not a single seat! However, PR *is* used in Northern Ireland for European elections. The province becomes a three-member constituency and the result is to give a seat to the Catholics which they would be denied under the

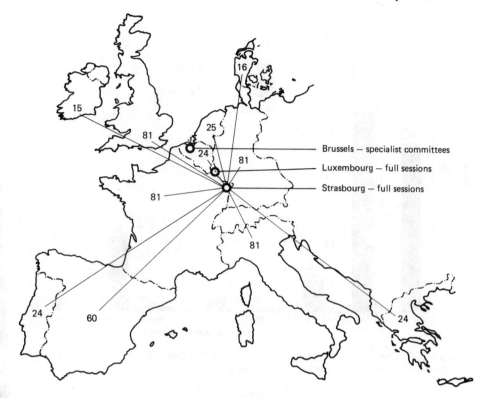

Figure 3.3 Members of the European Community and numbers of MEPs sent to the European Parliament

first-past-the-post method. The full picture for the 1989 election is given in figure 3.4.

The Parliament, which includes 81 UK members, meets at Strasbourg and Luxembourg and its many committees also sit at Brussels. In the semicircular chamber MEPs sit in blocs reflecting their national party affiliations (figure 3.5). The 1989 election saw gains by the left; in Britain Labour moved from having 32 seats to 45, while the Conservatives moved in exact reverse, from 45 to 32.

The European Parliament differs from most democratic assemblies in one significant respect: it is not a legislative chamber. However, although no more than a talking-shop, it has the power to reject the EC budget and dismiss the whole Commission and it became more assertive during the 1980s. Figure 3.6 demonstrates that it has also become more active.

The European Court of Justice The Court enforces and interprets EC law and its judgements are binding and enforceable by national courts. It also checks that domestic legislation does not conflict with community law, thereby infringing the British doctrine (myth?) of the supremacy of Parliament.

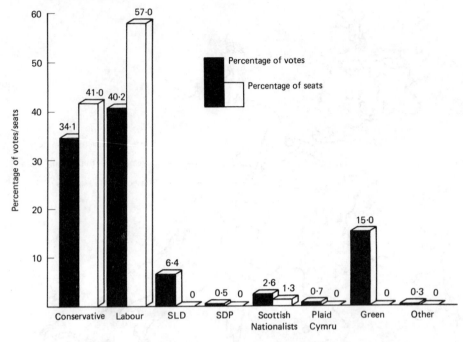

Figure 3.4   State of the British parties in votes and seats after the 1989 European Parliament election (excluding Northern Ireland)

The Economic and Social Committee This committee brings together representatives of trade unions and employers for joint discussions. Although having no formal powers, it is a nod in the direction of corporatism (see pp. 423–6), an approach more congenial to countries like France and Germany than Britain.

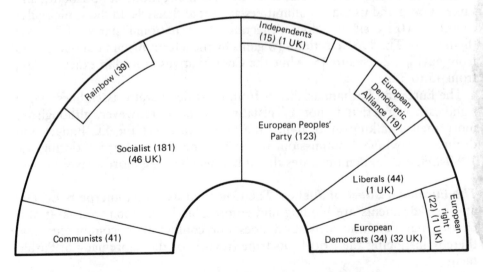

Figure 3.5   Likely political groupings in the European Parliament after the 1989 election

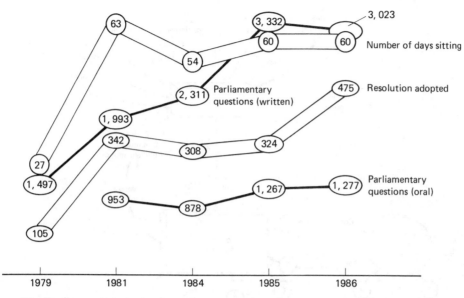

Figure 3.6 Increasing volume of work in the European Parliament since direct elections (1979)

Source: Data from *Social Trends* (1988: table 11.13)

The EC policy-making process

EC policy-making entails a lengthy process of deliberation and consultation (figure 3.7).

Britain's future in the EC

The success of the EC is a matter of considerable debate. The existence of NATO has prevented it from developing into a bloc standing between the USSR and the US, while progress towards political union has been at *l'escargot* pace. Within EC institutions, much debate is couched in nationalistic terms, member states competing for investment and employment. By remaining outside the community in the formative years Britain denied itself the opportunity to exert influence. From the very outset the six original members fought for national advantage in the Treaty of Rome itself; the Germans gained a free market for their manufactures and the French the Common Agricultural Policy (CAP) to protect their farmers (Blacksell 1981).

A number of aspects of British foreign policy, such as the continuing lure of America (strengthened under the Reagan–Thatcher axis), residual imperialist pretentions, and an unwillingness to accept monetary union, leads the partners to doubt the level of commitment. Much bitterness surrounded British contributions to the EC fund, which have exceeded the receipts gained, and Mrs Thatcher's style was applauded by her supporters as 'batting for Britain', rather than pursuing any ultramontane vision. In 1988 she replaced a commissioner who had been showing a dangerous tendency

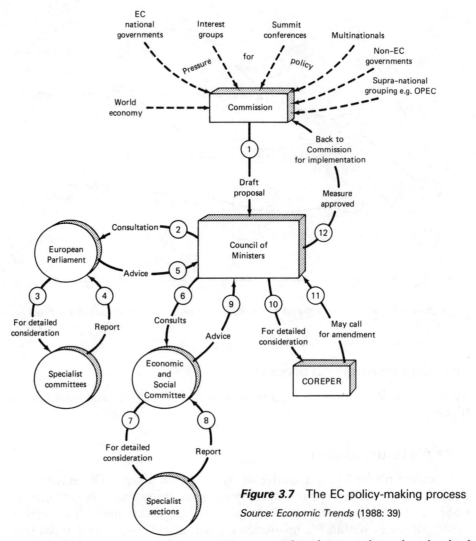

Figure 3.7   The EC policy-making process

Source: Economic Trends (1988: 39)

towards Europeanism with Leon Brittan, a Thatcherite whose loyalty had been so amply demonstrated when he appeared to lay down his political life for her in the murky Westland scandal. In July 1989 Sir Geoffrey Howe, the Foreign Secretary who had been appearing to play down the Prime Minister's anti-Europeanism, was unceremoniously sacked in a Cabinet reshuffle.

1992 and all that In 1986–7 a Single Europe Act was passed by the EC to lead the way to greater unity, with commitments to abolish trade barriers by 1992, create a more formal mechanism for cooperation in foreign policy, and strengthen social cohesion within the community. Although ratified by the British Parliament, in September 1988 Mrs Thatcher embarked upon a three-day tour of Europe in which she systematically enraged the partners by pouring douches of cold water on the notion of the social implications of a united Europe, most particularly in a notorious speech in Bruges.

> A centralised European government would be a nightmare. We have not rolled back the frontiers of the state at home only to see them reimposed at a European level.
>
> Margaret Thatcher, speech in Bruges (Sept. 1988)

In May 1989 the European Commission proposed a draft *Charter of Fundamental Social Rights*, a red flag to the New Right John Bull. The document listed a range of social concerns: conditions of work, rules for hiring and firing, minimum pay, worker participation, trade union rights, equality of opportunity, joint consultation, and so on. The Thatcher government wanted none of this. Indeed, in preparing its Employment Bill it announced that it would formally 'renounce' certain sections of the Council of Europe's 1961 *Social Charter*, to enable it to scrap restrictions on night work and hours of employment (*Independent*, 18 May 1989). The New Right in Britain saw in the EC a socialist threat, and the Thatcher vision of Europe was of convenient markets for capitalism, not for political union or help for the underprivileged. In her party's conference in 1988 she had assured delegates:

We haven't worked all these years to free Britain from the paralysis of socialism only to see it creep through the back door of . . . Brussels.

However, the British left has also opposed the EC, seeing its intention to create a free trade bloc with common tariff barriers against the rest of the world as very much at one with capitalism, representing a loss of power for the working class (see Benn 1979: 164). They argued that such a framework would prevent a Labour government from implementing an alternative economic strategy (requiring greater direct control over the home economy and curbs on the free flow of private capital). However, after its policy review the 1989 Labour Party line on Europe was much more favourable.

Conclusion: Decline and Fall

When Britain's position is considered in a world setting the picture is of economic and political decline since the late nineteenth century. The post-war chapter has been the most puzzling, and from the 1960s became a major preoccupation in political debate. Contingent upon relative economic decline has been a political decline which has been not relative but absolute; Britain was to see itself eclipsed by the US as the world leader in both military and political terms.

The search for an explanation has produced theories and prescriptions from both left and right, with blame attached variously to most political, social and economic institutions, though the full impact of historical British links with the world order are frequently ignored. Examination of these goes further than the idea of a passive state tossed on the tides of world affairs. Britain's particular attitude towards the world is itself a factor. The remarkable overseas expansion of the state, and its location at the very epicentre of the world economy, were to bequeath as legacies attitudes which would lead to decline – delusions of grandeur and an obsession with free trade.

Folie de grandeur

In the closing stages of the second world war Britain could not have fought on without the 'tools' provided by American dollars, a position of heavy dependence which was to persist into the era of peace. So keen was Britain to develop a close relationship with the US that it undertook massive political and military burdens in the post-war period, more crippling than in the days of empire (when it had been possible to tax the colonial territories). Britain was willing to rearm, to maintain forces in West Germany and other bases around the world, to develop the highest level of military expenditure in Europe, and to give active support to the US in the Korean war. As the icing on this cake a highly visible presence was maintained throughout the world in the form of ornate embassies and a glittering diplomatic service.

The economic consequence of this desire to cling to the days of greatness was that sterling continued to play an international role as a reserve currency. Although assisting the international movement of British capital, it placed crippling burdens on the domestic economy, forcing a continuing preoccupation with the balance of payments, to the exclusion of other economic objectives.

However, the post-war era also saw the gradual dismantling of the British Empire which, although it had never become the trading bloc envisaged by the tariff reformers, was a deeply symbolic process. Its replacement by the Commonwealth could be but cold comfort; it left the 'mother country' with some dignified vestiges of imperial splendour but bestowed no real political authority. Membership of NATO (and later the EC) further marked a newly subservient status. Yet illusions about the position persisted amongst the British ruling class and foreign policy continued to reflect a bygone age. Such illusions were rudely shattered when British world authority was put to the test in the Suez crisis. This was the culmination of events surrounding Britain's relinquishing of its Middle East power base.

The Suez crisis In 1954, amidst bitter dissension within the ruling class, Churchill reluctantly agreed to withdraw troops from the Canal Zone. This visible loss of power and prestige was deeply distressing to old-style patriots and a Suez Group formed amongst Conservative MPs, including the ever-zealous guardian of the 'English way of life', Enoch Powell, to express nostalgia for the great imperial past.

> We are not at war with Egypt. We are in an armed conflict.
>
> Anthony Eden (1897–1977; Conservative leader),
> Commons speech (4 Nov. 1956)

The fears seemed justified when, in March 1956, King Hussein of Jordan dismissed General Glubb, the creator of that great symbol of British domination, the Arab Legion. In July, Colonel Nasser of Egypt, generally suspected of anti-westernism and thought to be behind Glubb's dismissal, nationalized the Suez Canal Company. A diplomatic solution was ruled out when the USSR vetoed a UN resolution in the Security Council, and an ill-fated military action ensued with the arrogant and preposterous intention of toppling Nasser. This was taken in covert collusion with the French and the Israelis, and based on the bogus pretext of the need to separate the warring factions in the Arab–Israeli conflict. Israeli forces were encouraged to advance on the canal with pre-arranged British RAF cover. Once the true facts were known Eden's position as Prime Minister became untenable. The greatest humiliation was the chilly response from the US. Not only did the 'special' partner openly disapprove, it refused to intervene to halt a run on sterling until an undignified withdrawal of the Anglo-French forces was effected.

The last of the gunboats: the Suez Crisis
Source: Times Newspapers Ltd

Suez deeply embarrassed the British establishment and ruined the Prime Minister, Eden, who within six months had resigned on the grounds of ill health. Clearly there was within the establishment a large body of opinion regarding the adventure as an insanity, a fantastical journey through a constitutional time warp into the days when the ruling class believed in its divine ordination to rule the world.

The Falklands war In 1982 events in the South Atlantic allowed the decrepit lion again to yawn its arthritic jaws and chauvinistic Britons to shake the dust off their old Union Jacks. It is said that Eden was an unlucky politician and Mrs Thatcher the opposite; this was certainly borne out in their choice of wars. Gunboat diplomacy was made to work again, as one internally unpopular right-wing regime sought to bolster its sagging image by fighting another.

It was in early 1982 that Argentina invaded the Falklands (or Malvinas) Islands, one of the few tiny jewels remaining in the British imperial crown. As the British task force set sail towards the South Atlantic, the US Secretary of State shuttled to and fro between London and Buenos Aires in a desperate attempt to find a civilized solution, but he was no more successful than was the UN Secretary General in later efforts. The troops landed on East Falklands and, after three and a half weeks' fighting, secured an Argentinian surrender amidst orgasms of hysterical patriotism from the English press. The immediate cost of the exhilarating adventure was that 1,000 young men did not return home to their families alive, while the prize was that a rather inclement and hitherto little-known rock in the South Atlantic remained dubiously, and in the face of UN resolutions, forever England. In the aftermath, occasion was found for Britain to display its tendency towards crippling overseas commitment by constructing a permanent garrison, 'fortress Falklands', a costly symbol of great power status.

However, though an unmomentous cameo on the world stage, the events were of incalculable importance for the morale and hegemony of the British establishment. The Conservative government was able to avert the forecast electoral disaster in 1983, going on to further victory in 1987. The events gave a new strand to the fabric of Thatcherism, that of 'resolution', a word freely used during the war and capitalized on in victory. It was to justify forcing the working class to swallow all kinds of unpleasant medicinal compounds, as extravagant rhetoric promised more 'resolution' against the 'enemy within'.

Hence there is rather more to the *folie de grandeur* than meets the eye. Although imposing heavy costs on the home economy, the role has for long been of key importance for the pattern of hegemony at home, the English elite using its world power to justify its rule at home.

A free trade *idée fixe*

We have seen that British greatness was built and sustained by a policy of free trade, though the gains were for the controllers of capital, not the working class. As world conditions changed during the twentieth century, Britain's markets were penetrated and many home industries destroyed. Yet the global orientation of British capital means that today the number of British multinationals is second only to that of the US. For the domestic economy this has meant persistently low levels of investment (generally half that of rivals) and restricted productivity (Gamble 1985: 16). Fixed investment as a percentage of gross domestic product (a measure of production in the whole economy) in Britain for the period 1960–80 was only 18.3, compared with 24 per cent for West Germany and 32.5 per cent for Japan. The state's willingness to see capital pouring out to the low-wage, cruelly exploited economies of the third world was signalled in one of the first acts of the Conservative government of 1979: the complete removal of exchange controls.

Still a 'Sceptred Isle'?

British politics cannot be studied in isolation. Most of the issues examined later in this book are related (sometimes directly and sometimes indirectly) to Britain's historic and present relationship with the world. Never again be taken in by the 'Sceptred Isle' mythology of British insularity.

There are few areas of domestic policy where international pressures are without influence; despite the posturings of politicians, the idea of national sovereignty is largely a myth. Political and economic agreements, relationships and organizations create forces and set parameters in most areas of government policy. Because the bloc to which Britain belongs (indeed is a founder member) has been the capitalist one, the ideological and practical effects of the wider world tend to be anti-socialist. The post-war pressures from the international institutions have generally been for less welfare statism, less working-class power, more private enterprise, and more cold-war expenditure. Moreover, in addition to direct effects, Britain's world role has left enduring legacies to the British political culture in terms of racism, xenophobia, class deference, and so on, which are examined throughout this book.

Britain's global future The global factor in domestic British politics must become ever more dominant in the future. The political changes brought about by Gorbachev in Eastern Europe suggest new patterns of economic and political alliance. The likelihood of an enlarged world capitalist economy, the reunification of Germany, the possible enlargement of the EC and an uncertain future for NATO offer promises that are judged by commentators variously between exhilarating and deeply disturbing. A number of questions are posed. Will Eastern Europe move towards social democracy or the far right? Can defence expenditures be cut? What new world political and economic alliances will materialize? Will the US cede leadership of the world economy to Japan or a new Germany? Will the EC move towards greater socialism? Will it become more than a loose federation? The latter two prospects fill the British right with fear and promise strong political action at home. Whatever happens, the prospect for the states in the peripheral zone remains bleak as third world debt climbs unrelentingly.

In addition to political and economic factors, the modern world is enmeshed in patterns of interdependence resulting from the emergence or discovery of other global systems which bind countries together in a matrix of interdependence. Prominent amongst these is the impact of communications technology, which enables leaders and ordinary citizens of the world to speak with each other instantaneously and brings the horrors and excitements of world events into drawing rooms and mud huts through the medium of television. Television represents a tremendous force in world politics; it effectively led to the end of the Vietnam war, and the British government had to take strenuous action (to the admiration of astonished US leaders) to prevent the British people from witnessing the ugly side of the Falklands conflict. Moreover, the greater awareness of ecological systems, which are essentially global, compels leaders to recognize the limits of their moral right to pursue certain policies, particularly energy policies. Other factors to impinge upon domestic politics are world disease (chillingly demonstrated in the AIDS crisis), the uncontrolled growth of the world population, the horror of world terrorism (whereby mice-like states may roar at the superpowers, rendering them impotent dinosaurs). Underlying all remains the bleak threat of nuclear war and the grim possibility of proliferation under the insistent pressure of the world arms salesmen. This is a world which no country can escape, and which no explanation of domestic politics can ignore.

Key points

- British politics cannot be seen as an autonomous activity; the state is locked into a world economic and political system which influences much internal political activity.
- The modern world economy can be conceptualized in terms of three zones: a highly developed and wealthy core, an underdeveloped and impoverished periphery, and a middle section. The relationship between the wealthy and impoverished states is a form of neocolonialism, with domination and exploitation exercised through money rather than guns.
- The world system consists not only of states, but of multinational corporations which span the globe, are more wealthy than the states, and can blackmail and destroy regimes by the way they shift their capital from one country to another. They are generally controlled from the core states by the capitalist class.
- Britain, as the first country to industrialize, played a crucial role in developing the world economy, remaining a firm advocate of the concept of free trade, a policy generally in the interests of capital rather than labour.
- There is no such thing as a world political system; states do not subsume their interests to a supranational organization or power.

- However, although states will not relinquish their political autonomy, the real loss of autonomy to the world economic system, and to the system of military alliances consequent upon the cold war, has gone unacknowledged.
- Underlying Britain's relative decline in the world has been an obsession with retaining a world leadership role, developed during the days of the British Empire, which the economy could not support, and a fixation with free trade, which opened the world's markets to British capital but also exposed the home economy to damaging competition so that many industries were destroyed. In the post-war era much British investment has been in multinational companies which set up outside the country.

Review your understanding of the following terms and concepts

exogenous and endogenous explanations
bourgeoisie
world economy
colonialism
autonomy
neocolonialism
zones of the world economy
mercantilism
imperialism
industrial revolution
free trade
comparative advantage
world policeman role
'special relationship'
Lend–Lease

Marshall Aid programme
Bretton Woods Agreement
exchange rate
advanced capitalism
'long boom'
monopoly capitalism
multinational corporations
cold war
international associations
communism
'Iron Curtain'
non-aligned world
détente
supragovernmental organizations
MEP

Assignment

In your local library trace some newspaper articles about the elections to the European Parliament of Thursday 15 June 1989. Try to answer the following questions. Use quotations (referenced) to illustrate your answers.

		% mark
1	Outline and discuss Edward Heath's vision of the Europe of the future. Contrast it with the Thatcher vision.	25
2	Compile a chart showing the relative performance of the British political parties in the European elections of 1984 and 1989.	25
3	How do the papers explain the rise of the Greens in the 1989 election?	25
4	In what ways do you think the Euro-elections force the British parties to modify their policies?	25

Questions for discussion

Because this chapter is concerned with the link between the international environment and internal politics some of these questions may be easier to answer when further chapters have been studied.

1   Explain the meaning of the term 'neocolonialism' in the context of the modern world economy.
2   How far is it true today that Britain has a 'special relationship' with the US?
3   What were the implications of the mid-1970s oil crisis for internal British politics?
4   'Britain's relative post-war decline was largely attributable to its leaders' delusions of grandeur.' Discuss.
5   What have been the implications of the cold war for internal politics in post-war Britain?
6   'The unwillingness of the state to sacrifice national sovereignty means that the United Nations is doomed to fail.' Discuss.
7   'The Commonwealth is a mere shadow of the British Empire with no political or economic substance.' Discuss.

Topic for debate

This house believes that the idea of 'batting for Britain' in the EC undermines the basis of the Community.
      or
This house believes that the imperatives of Britain's military alliances mean that the idea of national autonomy in world politics is a complete illusion.

Further reading

Armstrong, P., Glyn, A. and Harrison, J. (1984) *Capitalism since World War II.*
A critical analysis by economists with a keen appreciation of the political dimension of the subject. Examines the long boom and its disintegration, concluding with an analysis of Thatcherism and the 'left alternative' to it.

Deane, P. (1963) *The First Industrial Revolution.*
Detailed account of the industrial revolution in Britain. Ultimately critical of the minimal role played by the government, which is blamed for the later eclipse by rivals.

Gamble, A. (1985) *Britain in Decline.*
Chronicles the relative decline of Britain and advances an explanatory thesis. Also considers the implications for internal British politics.

Gardener, R. N. (1956) *Sterling–Dollar Diplomacy.*
Anglo-American relations.

Harris, L. (1985) 'British capital: manufacturing, finance and multinational corporations', in D. Coates et al. (eds), *A Socialist Anatomy of Britain*, pp. 7–28.

Mandel, E. (1978) *Late Capitalism*.
A well-known Marxist interpretation of the long boom. Stresses the role of technology.

Thompson, E. P. (1980) 'The logic of exterminism', *New Left Review*, 121 (May–June), 3–32.

Wallerstein, I. (1979) *The Capitalist World Economy*.
Outlines the zones of the capitalist world economy.

For light relief

A. Sampson, *The Seven Sisters*.
Penetrating account of the oil crisis.

4

The Social Context: Our Disunited Kingdom

In this chapter we examine the social context in which British politics is enacted. A political system does not stand above society as an autonomous machine in the way suggested by conventional liberal-democratic accounts. It is part of society as our weather system is part of the ecology of the planet. It has long been proclaimed that British society is benignly cohesive, but we shall argue that this unity has been a veneer concealing the cracks beneath. The chapter includes five principal focuses. The first examines the **political culture**, noting how unity was secured through English conquest and subjugation of the people of Wales, Scotland and Ireland. The following four sections expose great divides arising from **geography**, **class**, **gender** and **race**.

Political Culture

What is political culture?

Political culture is a rather vague concept referring essentially to the set of attitudes citizens hold towards society and the political system. It is a recognition that the maintenance of a regime is dependent upon thoughts as well as actions. For this reason much political activity at all levels is symbolic, aiming to make people happy with the system – to *legitimate* it. It will become apparent throughout this book that the legitimating function has been performed very well in Britain.

Deference and hegemony The best political culture for a capitalist state is a **deferential** one, where the masses willingly accept the distribution of power and wealth and there is little popular desire for change or for participation in government. Indeed, the essence of deference is that ordinary folk believe the act of running the state should be left to those who 'know best'. The prevailing common sense dictates that the existing order is natural and beyond challenge. Deference was noted by Walter Bagehot in 1867, when he argued that the masses were too stupid to understand the reality of government, but were beguiled by a 'theatrical show' provided by the monarchy and other *dignified* elements of the constitution.

Although the virtues of deference are questionable (for Aristotle, not to be involved in politics degraded man to the level of the beast), texts in the orthodox liberal-democratic tradition greatly admire it. They portray the ordinary person's distaste for involvement as a sign of good sense rather than humility. This wondrous passivity was demonstrated in the depressions of the 1920s and 1930s, as well as in the unemployment of the 1980s, all of which were weathered with patience and stoicism.

The feeling that things must be accepted has been seen as a major characteristic of the British and helps to explain why so many working-class people have not voted for Labour, the party set up explicitly to represent their interests (see pp. 198–9). Antonio Gramsci argued that those wishing to dominate society encourage such a view in order to maintain their hegemony (see p. 8).

A crisis of deference?

A classic investigation of British political culture was carried out in the early 1960s by the American political scientists Almond and Verba (1963), who admiringly enthused that in Britain they had found a veritable jewel of a polity – nothing less than the ideal conditions for liberal democracy.

However, by the 1970s orthodox writers began to fear that the polity was turning sour. Surveys suggested that people were more willing to resort to forms of protest such as unofficial strikes and demonstrations (Marsh 1978). When a miners' strike precipitated the downfall of the Heath government, the liberal-democratic apologists were thrown into panic, prophesying an epic crisis for British democracy. They began a Cassandra-like lament that the country was becoming 'ungovernable' (King 1976). However, the obituary for deference was greatly exaggerated. In 1980 Almond and Verba 'revisited' the British political culture in a study which confirmed that, although there was cynicism, and even willingness to support unlawful violence against the state, this was confined to a small, unpopular minority (Kavanagh 1980). Labour leaders were actually disowning the actions of their own non-deferential left-wing elements with as much ferocity as the Conservative leaders. Throughout the 1980s the rulers managed the feat of persuading the masses that increased social suffering, cultural impoverishment and increasingly large differences in wealth were necessary for their own good. Deference was by no means in its coffin.

Yet the political culture is not as seamless and homogeneous as is thought.

In the remainder of this chapter we shall examine four great fissures which cut through the 'One Nation' envisioned by liberal-democratic apologists: spatial location, class, gender and race.

Uniting the Kingdom

From early times the unity of the British Isles was seen by the English as essential for their security. They needed to capitalize on the insular position provided by nature and remove both the possibility of challenge from within, or the establishment of bases for challenge from overseas. The Wars of the Roses followed by the Tudor dynasty saw the establishment of the central authority of the Crown, making the island better able to defend itself. In 1603 the Crowns of Scotland and England were united under the Stuarts with the accession of James VI of Scotland as James I of England. The 1707 Act of Union completed the process by uniting the two Parliaments, though the Scots retained independent legal, educational and religious insitutions. The *United Kingdom* itself was formally established in 1800 with the parliamentary union of Great Britain and Ireland under Westminster. Scotland and Wales, under English domination, subsequently followed a unified pattern of development into the agricultural and industrial revolutions and the age of empire.

> The so-called British Empire is in reality an *English* Empire, in which Ireland, Scotland and Wales formed the original colonies.
>
> F. A. Ridley, in *Socialist Leader* (Feb. 1948)

The Disunited Kingdom

Yet today new schisms disfigure the political map of the UK, with Scotland, Wales and northern England increasingly disenchanted with rule from the south-east. A major cause of the trend is the long-term decline in the economic base of the north, and associated social processes such as middle-class migration (Curtice and Steed 1988: 331). Those remaining nurse a sense of regional injustice, a perception of an imbalance in policy towards different areas. Not only have the deprived areas felt neglected, but the efforts of their local authorities to improve conditions have been frustrated by the government at Westminster.

Moreover, underlying this **north–south divide** is an historical sense of cultural subjugation felt by the Celtic fringes. Voting patterns in Scotland and Wales warrant Labour governments (as do those in northern England), yet they are ruled by a government chosen by the English. In effect they stand as colonies, with no lawful way of altering the policies affecting them. In November 1988 a tartan shot was fired across the English bows when

Twentieth-century slum, Glasgow 1957
Source: Times Newspapers Ltd

Scottish Nationalists robbed Labour of a gigantic 19,500 majority in the Glasgow Govan by-election, leaving the Conservatives with a humiliating 2,000 votes. In Wales incendiarists make symbolic attacks on English holiday homes. The **nationalist** call for independence on cultural grounds is likely to be augmented by the call for political rights. Increasingly the United Kingdom becomes a constitutional curate's egg – united only 'in parts'.

Ireland: a terrible beauty

Yet the political problem of a fringe population unwilling to accept the English yoke is by no means new. With its grim chronology of violence, Ireland mocks claims to unity. Today the problem of Northern Ireland seems an incomprehensible religious conflict, explained in terms of the 'hot-headedness' of the red-headed men, disdainfully contrasted with the secular rationality of the English, who have long avoided religious war. This is wrong; the problem is about racism, imperialism, cruelty, injustice, class domination and violent resistance – it is a political issue. Perhaps more than any other, the Irish problem has roots deeply embedded in a long and vicious history.

Though uncomfortably close to England, Ireland remained stubbornly separated by the Irish Sea, making English domination more difficult than in either Wales or Scotland. Conquest was finally completed by the Tudors, though the Irish, like the aborigines of the New World, lacked enthusiasm for subjugation on their own soil. In the English civil wars the brooding malcontents saw their chance to favour the Royalist cause, but in the aftermath they incurred terrible English wrath in the form of reconquest first by Cromwell, and later by William of Orange (in the famous Battle of the Boyne of 1690). They were relegated to the status of second-class citizens in their own country – barred from state office and the professions, and denied the right to own land. The territory of the south was confiscated by the English, who lived comfortably at home as absentee landlords while extracting crippling rents from dispossessed tenants. In the north, where resistance was fiercer, domination required a policy of settlement similar to that in the New World. A Scottish Presbyterian landowning settler class emerged around Belfast, ruling the natives and dependent upon English mainland support. Initially the settlers, like their counterparts in America, showed some resistance to the English navigation laws but were quelled in the battle of Vinegar Hill (1798). The following Act of Union of 1800 was adorned with manacles rather than wedding rings.

The industrial revolution altered the relationship. The Protestant-led north shared in English prosperity though, as workers, the conditions of Catholics were deliberately made worse than those of Protestants. The English excluded the south from the process of industrialization altogether, finding it more useful as a granary to feed workers on the mainland.

Thus you have a starving population, an absentee aristocracy, and an alien Church, and in addition the weakest executive in the world. That is the Irish Question.

Benjamin Disraeli (1804–81; Conservative leader), Commons speech (16 Feb. 1844)

The Home Rule Bills For the Irish, the concept of a United Kingdom was a farce, a fact realized in his later years by Gladstone, who determined with fervour to right the wrong (Bentley 1984: 245). His first Home Rule Bill of 1886 was defeated in the Commons, but he was able to introduce a second in 1893. This fell in the Conservative House of Lords, where the opposition reflected not only the self-interest of landowners, but the imperialists' convictions that colonizing Ireland could not be anything other than divinely ordained.

The events surrounding the third Home Rule Bill were dramatic, revealing class hatred at its most naked. Although the Liberals had become convinced home-rulers there were other matters to occupy them in the government of 1906–9, including their bitter battles with the suffragettes and with the House of Lords. They lost their overall parliamentary majority, becoming dependent upon the support of Irish MPs, and to win this Prime Minister Asquith pledged himself to another Home Rule Bill. The Conservatives, who regarded the Irish MPs as inferior in status and not worthy to vote on issues of constitutional import (Cross 1963: 123–4), believed them to be black-mailing the Liberals. Moreover, it became apparent that they considered themselves, and the class they represented, to be above the constitution. In 1906 Balfour had declared:

> The great Unionist party should still control, whether in power or whether in opposition, the destinies of this great Empire.
>
> (Blake 1985: 190)

In the frenzied opposition to the bill the Protestants of the north armed themselves as the Ulster Volunteers, under the fanatical leadership of Edward Carson, and Conservatives on the mainland contemplated a *coup d'état*. Conservative leader Bonar Law (himself of Ulster descent) declared chillingly to a crowd outside Blenheim Palace:

> There are things stronger than parliamentary majorities . . . I can imagine no length of resistance to which Ulster can go in which I should not be prepared to support them.
>
> (Cross 1963: 177)

No left-wing orator would dare utter such sentiments; the Conservative Party began to look like a guerrilla band (Bentley 1984: 365).

The Easter Rising However, this impending holocaust which promised revolutionary consequences for British politics was eclipsed in June 1914 with the assassination of the Archduke Franz Ferdinand of Austria-Hungary. The bill was passed but placed in cold storage for the duration of the first world war. Yet Irish activists, unable to trust the English, sought assistance from the Germans and, on Easter Sunday 1916, a republic was declared. This was put down harshly, the English toasting their triumph with the blood of martyrs through executions and imprisonments. Robert Casement, a British Consul in Germany who had enlisted enemy assistance, was hanged for high treason and his standing was undermined by diaries deliberately circulated to reveal him a homosexual.

I have passed with a nod of the head,
Or polite meaningless words.
All changed, changed utterly:
A terrible beauty is born.
W. B. Yeats (1865–1939; Irish poet), 'Easter 1916'

In the post-war general election Sinn Fein (the republican party) gained an overwhelming victory in Ireland and those elected refused to sit at Westminster, establishing an independent Irish Parliament, the Dail. They renewed the republic of Easter 1916 and appointed a president (Eamon de Valera) and government to run the country. At the same time an Irish Republican Army (IRA) was formed under Michael Collins, to which the British responded in 1920 with measures which Asquith said 'would disgrace the blackest annals of the lowest despotism in Europe' (Taylor 1965: 155). The infamous Black and Tans, men chosen for their penchant for violence, were recruited to assist the Royal Ulster Constabulary (RUC) in a reign of terror.

The 'solution' After much tortuous negotiation, Prime Minister Lloyd George and the Irish politicians signed a compromise treaty on 6 December 1921 giving birth to the Irish Free State (Eire). The 26 counties of the south received dominion status on the Canadian model, and the six of Ulster remained as a UK province with an elected bicameral (two-chamber) assembly (Stormont) and an executive exercising certain devolved powers. The fact that Ulster had far more autonomy than Wales or Scotland reflected hopes that it would decide in time to reunite under Dublin. The effect of the arrangement was to leave the Ulster Catholics as second-class citizens deprived of hope and opportunity. They were to live in ghettos in the poorest housing, do the most unpleasant jobs and receive the worst education. The constituency boundaries were gerrymandered (manipulated for electoral advantage) to ensure Protestant political dominance. For the south, the 'solution' had come not as a result of cool statesmanship but through violence and bloodshed, leaving a fermenting sense of grievance. This hardened over the years and 1949 saw Eire's departure from the Commonwealth.

Northern Ireland today: the killing streets Although the settlement contained the germs of further violence, up to the 1960s the Irish question ceased to be a scourge of British politicians. Like working people elsewhere in the UK, Catholics in Ulster appeared willing to accept their lot. However, economic decline was to fan the old embers of discontent; the heavy dependence on industries in irrevocable decline (shipbuilding and textiles) produced unemployment higher than in the rest of the UK, pressing most heavily on Catholics. Prime Minister Terrence O'Neil attempted to attract new industries and sought closer involvement with the south. At the same time, a new generation grew into political awareness, and young Catholics looked with hope for reforms in civil rights as part of a worldwide trend. These movements alarmed old-style unionists and a reaction set in under the inspiration of ranting demagogue the Reverend Ian Paisley. The B-Specials, an auxiliary unit of the RUC, attacked civil rights demonstrators, leading to a retaliatory rejuvenation of the IRA, which had effectively disarmed.

Since this time the politics of Northern Ireland has festered as a running sore on the British body politic. The divisions are not only reflected in battles between political parties, they are overlain with the machinery of violence and death; Protestants organize as the Ulster Volunteers and Catholics as the

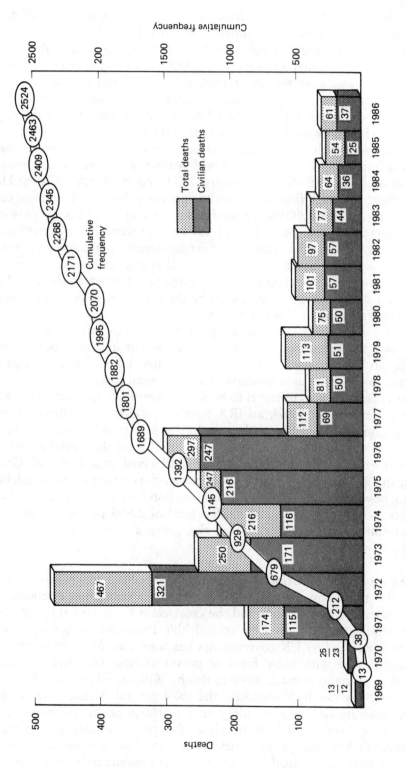

Figure 4.1 Violence in Northern Ireland: deaths associated with the civil disturbances

Source: Data from *Social Trends* (1988: table 12.25)

IRA. The police force – the RUC and the B-Specials – are Protestant dominated. The British government, drawn inexorably into the seething discontent, pressed for civil rights for Catholics and began to make attempts to revive the economy. However, in 1969, following a request from the Northern Ireland government, it took the fateful decision to send in the army, ostensibly to restore the peace. From initially welcoming the move, Catholics were to develop a feeling of menacing harassment and the pattern of violence began an unremitting escalation (figure 4.1).

Subsequent developments were to see the powers of state repression increase, hardening Catholic and world sympathy for the IRA. Internment without trial was introduced in August 1971 and in March 1972 the Heath government assumed *direct rule* over the province. Stormont was suspended and a Northern Ireland Office created under a Secretary of State, a poisonous chalice for any British politician. In 1974 the Prevention of Terrorism Act was rushed through Parliament (following devastating bombs in pubs in Guildford and Birmingham), outlawing the IRA and further extending police powers. Special (Diplock) courts were created in Ulster which dispensed with juries, and the treatment of prisoners by the state was to be condemned by the European Court of Human Rights.

Evidence that the RUC had adopted a 'shoot to kill' policy in 1982 occasioned the notorious Stalker affair, in which a British police officer heading an enquiry into the matter was impeded in his investigations, subjected to character assassination, and suspended from duty in May 1986, just days before he was to travel to Belfast to interview the chief of the RUC, Sir John Hermon. In 1984, an IRA bomb exploded in the Brighton hotel housing Conservative Party leaders, including Margaret Thatcher, attending their annual conference. In the escalation of violence the feared British SAS became involved, shooting eight IRA men and a civilian at Loughall, County Tyrone in 1987 and, on 6 March 1988, to an echo of excited public celebrity, gunning down three IRA alleged would-be bombers in Gibraltar (no bomb was ever found). By the end of 1988 a total of 2,695 people had died as a direct result of the conflict during the previous two decades (Lambert 1988b).

Seeking a political solution Northern Ireland politics sees religious groupings rather than conventional ideological parties contesting elections. The gerrymandered constituencies and the cross-class Protestant support meant that Stormont was captured by an indelible Protestant majority, and the solution advocated by UK governments has been seen in terms of breaking this stranglehold with some form of **power-sharing executive** (a kind of coalition). Efforts were made towards this by William Whitelaw in 1973, but were deeply resented by Protestants: the 1974 general election saw 11 of the 12 seats won by Unionists standing on a platform hostile to the policy. A general strike was called to paralyse the province and the executive collapsed. Further attempts by James Prior in 1982 were no more successful.

Another possible political solution is for the republic to be more involved in Ulster's affairs. In November 1985 an Anglo-Irish Agreement was signed by Margaret Thatcher and Irish Premier, Dr Garret Fitzgerald, establishing a forum in which the republic could comment on Northern Irish affairs. This provoked fierce criticism from a number of Conservative MPs and Treasury minister Ian Gow resigned in protest; he was to be assassinated by an IRA bomb in July 1990. Two Unionists resigned on the grounds that it was the thin end of a wedge designed to reunify Ireland as a republic. Enoch Powell has consistently argued that unification of Ireland is the covert goal of British governments.

In the meantime grim ceremonies continue to mark bitter anniversaries such as the Battle of the Boyne, the Siege of Londonderry, deaths of hunger strikers, 'Bloody Sunday', and so on. The provocative marches, demonstrations and military-style funerals incite violence. British governments continue to argue that it is the 'men of violence' who stand in the way of a peaceful rational settlement, yet it cannot be forgotten that it is English 'men of violence' exploiting the ill-fated island over centuries who have bequeathed this grim legacy.

Class in British Politics

> The history of all hitherto existing society is the history of class struggles.
>
> Karl Marx (1818–83; German-born philosopher and father of communism), *The Communist Manifesto* (1848)

Defining social class

Generally speaking, **social class** is a term used to categorize people on the basis of background, wealth, manners, accent, privilege, and so on. It is essentially about hierarchy and inequality, denoting social divisions similar to those indicated by words like 'caste', 'rank', 'degree' and 'status'. Class is adjudged to have been of greater political significance in Britain than anywhere else in the English-speaking world (Butler and Stokes 1969: 90). There are various ways of defining class, including the following.

Occupation Occupation is a key variable, being generally correlated with a

Table 4.1 The Registrar General's social classes

I	Professional
II	Intermediate
III	Skilled non-manual
IV	Skilled manual
V	Semi-skilled
VI	Unskilled

range of other factors – accent, social background, leisure activities, life-style, housing, and so on. The Registrar General's categories (table 4.1) used in official surveys are based on this type of classification. A widely-used alternative occupational definition is that devised by the advertising industry, aiming to place people in categories reflecting their consuming propensities.

Social Class: Institute of Practitioners in Advertising (IPA) definition

In order to persuade the right people to covet the right material things, the advertising industry classes people as follows:

Class A   Higher managerial, administrative or professional
Class B   Intermediate managerial, administrative, or professional
Class C1   Supervisory or clerical, and junior managerial, administrative or professional
Class C2   Skilled manual workers
Class D   Semi-skilled and unskilled manual workers
Class E   State pensioners or widows (no other earnings), casual or lowest grade workers, or long-term unemployed

---

Income This basis is not necessarily the same as occupation; there can be impoverished poets and vicars, and millionaire scrap metal merchants. Generally income shows wide variations between the few high and the many low earners. The early years of the post-war period saw some degree of reduction in income inequality, a trend enhanced by the tax system. Since the 1980s, however, this movement has reversed, the rewards of the top ten earners improving, under the stimulus of a theory that incentives to the cream would benefit everyone else, even those in 'Cardboard City'. Table 4.2 shows how the top 10 per cent consistently gains an astonishingly large slice of the cake.

Table 4.2 The 'top ten': percentage share of the top 10 per cent of earners in the post-war era

Year	Before tax	After tax
1949	33.2	27.1
1964	29.0	25.1
1973–4	26.8	23.6
1981–2	28.3	25.6
1984–5	29.4	26.5

Source: Data from Atkinson (1983: 63); *Social Trends* (1988: table 5.14)

Wealth In spite of large salaries earned by professionals, there remains in Britain today a basic dichotomy between a wealth-owning minority and the great mass who own relatively little (see table 4.3).

Table 4.3 Distribution of wealth in Britain (percentages)

Year	Top 1 per cent	Top 5 per cent	Top 10 per cent
1923[a]	61	82	89
1966[a]	31	56	69
1976[b]	24	45	60
1985[b]	20	40	54

[a] England and Wales only.
[b] UK as a whole.
Source: Data from Atkinson and Harrison (1978: 159); *Social Trends* (1988: table 5.21)

Self-assigned class In addition there is a subjective class structure, which is shown by inviting people to assign themselves to class categories. The tendency in the post-war era has been for people to see themselves as going up rather than down in the world. Thus table 4.4 shows that in a sample of 3,066, 59 per cent saw their parents as working class, but only 48 per cent put themselves in that category.

Table 4.4 Self-rated social class, Great Britain, 1986 (percentages)[a]

Social class	Self	Parents
Upper middle	1	2
Middle	24	17
Upper working	21	12
Working	48	59
Poor	3	8
Don't know/no response	3	2

[a] Sample size = 3,066.
Source: Data from British Social Attitudes Survey, 1986

Class in Marxist terms

Class is central to Marxist analysis. Here the division is more specific, being determined by the mode of production. Under capitalism it is essentially a *dichotomy* (division into two classes): a small upper class (or *bourgeoisie*) owning the capital needed in production, and the large working class (or *proletariat*) with only their labour to sell, for a wage. The basic relationship between the two is exploitative: indeed Marx saw the top class as able to control the state in its own interests – it was a 'ruling class'. He believed that a class struggle would inexorably drive the pattern of history towards revolution and ultimately to the emergence of a fairer society. However, as we see throughout this book, politics can prevent the overthrow of capitalism in various ways. In contrast, Weber saw class as based on a fundamental

---

Property is organised robbery.

George Bernard Shaw (1856–1950; Irish dramatist),
Preface to *Major Barbara* (1907)

distinction between creditors and debtors, believing that Marx's classes were merely a special case of this dichotomy.

> Misery and poverty are so absolutely degrading, and exercise such a paralysing effect ... that no class is ever really conscious of its own suffering. They have to be told of it by other people.
> Oscar Wilde (1854–1900; Irish author and dramatist), *The Soul of Man Under Socialism* (1891)

An anatomy of the classes

Although the terms are used loosely, most discussion on British society and politics speaks of a threefold division into *upper class, working class* and *middle class.*

The upper class   The British upper class has evolved over many hundreds of years through a process of fusion and fission which amalgamated the landowning aristocracy, the lesser gentry, the financiers and the bourgeoisie which emerged as a result of the industrial revolution (Scott 1985: 29–35). In 1923, before the Labour Party and the welfare state had made any inroads into the pattern of wealth distribution, this powerful alliance constituted the richest fifth of the population, owning 95 per cent of the nation's wealth. By 1972, with the welfare state at its peak, the richest fifth still claimed as much as 85 per cent, leaving 15 per cent to be shared amongst the rest (Urry 1985: 59–60). The holding is cumulative since it generates considerable unearned income.

In addition to the holders of great wealth there are the mega-earners: the Royal Commission on the Distribution of Income and Wealth (1976: 10) estimated that there were some 65,000 very highly paid employees in Britain in the 1970s – mostly managers, members of the established professions and higher civil servants. At the top of this mega-earnings league in 1990 stood Lord Hanson, narrowly beating rivals such as Tiny Rowland of Lonhro, with a bulging annual pay packet of £1.5 million. If he works a 40-hour week for 48 weeks a year, he gets around £13 a minute – an incentive indeed. (There are also certain freakishly high, and usually short-lived, salaries of entertainers and sports personalities, the popularity of whom could serve to legitimate the culture of inequality.)

Members of this class share much in common in terms of social background, life-style, education (normally public school and Oxbridge) and professional life. They also hold together by kinship (and old school) ties: an imaginary family might well have one son in the army, one in the civil service, and another in the established church, while the daughter might marry someone in the City. Indeed, arranged marriages ensure that family wealth will be augmented rather than dispersed, while their accountants and lawyers work assiduously to minimize the effects of death duties and other forms of tax.

Professional and social life reinforces commonality. Membership of London clubs, golf clubs and the Freemasons preserve a sense of exclusiveness, which is celebrated in ceremonies and great sporting events like the Lord's Test, Ascot, Wimbledon, Cowes, the Boat Race, the Grand National, and so on. At all these venues are secret places where ordinary folk may not go: the Long Room at Lord's, the Royal Box, the Royal Enclosure, and so on.

The presence of the upper class is venerated with archaic symbols: a reigning monarch, a fully fledged aristocracy, a House of Lords, and a host of ancient sinecures (offices with no duties attached to them) such as Lord Lieutenant of the County and High Sheriff, all of whom enjoy prestige, wealth and privilege, and claim noble birth. The exclusion process is strengthened by a preoccupation with dress, manners and accent (mocked in Bernard Shaw's play *Pygmalion*). These symbols of ancient privilege serve to maintain the legitimacy of the principle of tremendous inequality in wealth and opportunity which can be produced by modern capitalism. This explains why the British bourgeoisie sought, not to overthrow the bastions of privilege, but to ingratiate itself with the old elite through a process of social climbing.

An Englishman's way of speaking absolutely classifies him. The moment he talks he makes some other Englishmen despise him.

Professor Higgins, in Alan Jay Lerner's musical, *My Fair Lady* (1956)

In terms of ideology it is hardly surprising that the upper class exhibits a high degree of homogeneity, though there remains a broad division between the paternalistic strain inherited from Tory traditions – a belief that privilege carries duties – and the hard-nosed whiggish tradition of individualism and competition resuscitated as Thatcherism. In addition, much is made of notions of racial superiority (racism): members of the class saw themselves as shouldering the 'white man's burden' in the great days of empire and of being 'born to rule' (part of the rationale of the public school system). The class has shown a genius for survival, strengthening itself by selectively assimilating talented or successful members of the lower orders, sustaining itself like a vampire sucking the life-blood of its victims. This lack of rigid 'structuration' (Giddens 1979: ch. 6) helps to legitimate the system (in theory anyone can become a millionaire).

Not surprisingly, members of the upper class unfailingly vote for, and support in other ways, the Conservative Party, of which many are members, regarding its election to government as a major imperative which they will go to any lengths to secure.

The working class This essentially Marxist concept does not actually describe what people do. 'Work' can range from stock-brokerage to road sweeping and, although condemned to idleness, the large body of unemployed are generally regarded as belonging to the working class. The essential feature of this class is that its members lack wealth and, more importantly, do not own the capital upon which wealth accumulation is based. They are the 'working class' in that their *labour* is the only thing they have to sell.

Yet this great majority of the British people can only be designated as a class in the very loosest of senses and it lacks the homogeneity ascribed to it by Marx. There are multifarious distinctions within it in terms of race, colour, spatial distribution, income, gender, occupation and, most importantly, in the way they perceive the capitalist system in which they live.

A shrinking class? In Britain there has been a steady trend of upward mobility in the post-war era. Table 4.5 shows, for example, that in 1972, 16 per cent of the middle-class respondents had working-class backgrounds; by 1983 this had risen to 23.6 per cent. This upward mobility which swells the ranks of an intermediate stratum does not accord with the Marxist dichotomy.

The charm of Britain has always been the ease with which one can move into the middle class.

Margaret Thatcher, in the *Observer* (27 Oct. 1974)

The middle class Despite his essentially dichotomous view of class structure, Marx did recognize a no-man's land of 'middle and intermediate strata' between the two great social formations. However, he believed that the obligation to sell their labour, and hence their inability to accumulate capital, would mean that the intermediate class would ultimately become part of a massive proletariat. This has not happened in Britain (Mandel

Table 4.5   Movement between classes, 1972 and 1983 (percentages)

Father's class	Respondent's class		
	Middle	Lower middle	Working
1972			
Middle	57.7	23.2	19.1
Lower middle	31.2	31.9	37.0
Working	16.0	22.7	61.2
1983			
Middle	62.0	22.2	15.8
Lower middle	34.2	34.3	31.5
Working	23.6	23.8	52.6

Source: Social Trends (1987: table A.10)

1983: 201–2), a fact with very important implications for the legitimation process. It becomes possible to argue that the growth of a vast intermediate class represents a process of *embourgeoisement* (see p. 176) which has on the one hand eroded the old upper class, so that all that remains is an empty and harmless husk, and on the other, left an insignificant rump of ne'er-do-wells, an echo of the working class. Much media analysis discusses politics and society in these terms, with the intermediate class commonly divided into two, upper middle and lower middle, distinguished on the basis of occupation. The Thatcher era, with its attacks both on the welfare state and trade unions *and* on the old upper-class professions, was seen by many as the final seal on the creation of this middle-class-dominated society, which enthusiasts preferred to call a *classless* society.

This view is part of a *managerial revolution* thesis arguing that the traditional structure of the capitalist world has metamorphozed. Although sizeable firms which are run by their owners can still be found, the emergence of the giant national and international firms characteristic of advanced capitalism has broken the simple structure of the capitalist class, leading to an apparent fissure between ownership and actual control of industry. The former is more dispersed through share-ownership and the latter is in the hands of professional managers. It is these managers who now have the real power.

However, there are various objections to this thesis (see pp. 434–6). Many of those who are classed in official statistics as middle class are really performing routine, boring, low-paid, unrewarding jobs, indistinguishable from unskilled manual work. They constitute a camouflaged 'underclass' within the white-collar sector (Giddens 1979: 288).

Hence it can be argued that the managerial revolution thesis contains an element of mythology designed to legitimate or obscure the continued holding and control of great wealth by the few (Scott 1985: 38). Indeed, during a decade of Thatcherism 'old money' prospered as never before in the post-war era (*Sunday Times*, 8 April 1990). In terms of the relationship to wealth and capital, the new middle classes have far more in common with the working class. The essential vulnerability of the non-capital-owning members of the middle class was demonstrated throughout the 1980s as members of professions such as university lecturers and doctors were

---

Is he rich, or is he rich!

The Duke of Westminster ... not only owns a sizeable chunk of London ... and large slices of Cheshire, North Wales, the Scottish Highlands, Vancouver, Hawaii and Wagga Wagga, he has an income reported to be of around £10,800 an hour ... and inherited something between £500 and £1,000 million.

Sunday Times (20 Feb. 1983)

threatened by a government intent upon reducing the tax burden placed upon capitalism.

Thatcher's children

For some acolytes of the New Right, the era of Thatcherism was seen as the period when Britain became a classless society. At the end of the first decade of her regime there existed a large group within the population with no adult memories of full employment, trade union involvement in policy-making, plentiful funds for education, an inviolate National Health Service, the notion of rights to the welfare state, and so on. A MORI poll (May 1989) revealed that 'Thatcher's children' tended to be tougher than their middle-aged counterparts across a wide spectrum and keener to set up their own businesses. They also evaluated social problems differently.

Worries	% of 15–28-year-olds worried	% of over-28s worried
Aids	45	21
Risk of nuclear war	43	34
Drug addiction	34	41
Threat to environment	34	42
Increased government control over people's lives	28	33
Risk of terrorism	25	34
Poverty in Britain	25	31
Cruelty to animals	21	18
Third world poverty	13	14
Apartheid	10	6

Yet xenophobic characteristics, lack of concern for third world poverty or apartheid were shared throughout the population. Women were less enamoured of the Thatcher package than men.

A subclass? It is impossible to argue that British society is characterized by mass pauperization, exploitation, and the accumulation of surplus value (profit) into fewer and fewer hands, as prophesied by classical Marxism. Living conditions for the average person are clearly much better than in the 1840s. However, during the 1980s a new question was raised as the gap widened between a prosperous majority in secure, well-paid employment and a depressed minority forming a **subclass** of many millions of socially vulnerable people with very little chance of fending successfully for themselves. These include the unemployed, poor, homeless, elderly, handicapped, chronically sick, disabled, ethnic minorities, single-parent families, those with low educational attainments, and those who simply refuse for ethical

Table 4.6 Inequality in family income, UK (percentages)

Year	Bottom fifth	Next fifth	Middle fifth	Next fifth	Top fifth
1976	0.8	9.4	18.8	26.6	44.4
1981	0.6	8.1	18.0	26.9	46.4
1984	0.3	6.1	17.5	27.5	48.6

Source: Data from *Social Trends* (1987: table A.8)

reasons to enter the 'rat race' of competitive society. Table 4.6 shows that between 1976 and 1984 the trend in family income was towards greater inequality. In July 1989 a Salvation Army report revealed that there were 75,000 homeless people in London alone.

Ghost of Christmas Present

Children are begging on the streets this Christmas. Thousands more, destitute, will wake up on Christmas morning in bed-and-breakfast hotels where living conditions would be scorned by a Third World cockroach. In December 1988 these ... are facts of English urban life.

The *Independent* (24 Dec. 1988)

The establishment This is a rather vague though expressive term popularized by journalist Henry Fairlie writing in the *Spectator* in the 1950s (Thomas 1959). '**The establishment**' denotes a class defined largely as a cohesive body of individuals monopolizing power and authority, a closed group consisting of those in control of the leading institutions (the church, the monarchy and aristocracy, the mass media, the traditional professions, Parliament, the army, the civil service, the City, and of course the owners and managers of industry) (Sedgemore 1980: 11). It has much in common with the Marxist idea of a ruling class and is a term disliked by many of those alleged to be part of it.

We, as middle-class socialists, have got to have a profound humility ... we've got to know that we lead them because they can't do it without us ... and yet we must feel humble to working people.

Hugh Gaitskell (1906–63; Labour leader), conversation with Richard Crossman (Aug. 1959)

Domination by class

The effects of class in British politics are profound and will become apparent throughout the pages of this book. They are felt in voting behaviour, through pressure groups, in the media, in the realm of ideas and attitudes, in education, and in health. They may be traced in the operations of all the institutions of the state – Parliament, the civil service, local government, the police and the judiciary.

There can be no doubt that much domination within society is based upon class. Owners of capital dominate their managers, managers dominate their workers, professional people dominate their clients, and so on. Does class domination go further than this; can one class collectively dominate the whole of society in a politically significant way? In other words, is *class hegemony* possible? This important question is explored further in chapter 14.

From class to gender

You cannot trust the interests of one class entirely to another class, and you cannot trust the interests of one sex entirely to another sex.

David Lloyd George (1863–1945; Liberal statesman), speech (1911)

The Monstrous Regiment: Sexism in British Society

The First Blast of the Trumpet Against the Monstrous Regiment of Women.

Title of a pamphlet by John Knox (1505–72; charismatic Scottish preacher)

British culture is **sexist** and **patriarchal**: in all classes men tend to dominate women. This remains true although from 1979–90 Britain had a woman Prime Minister. Indeed, other patriarchal societies – India, Israel and Pakistan – have also had women leaders, but they remain lonely swallows showing very little promise of a feminist summer.

British patriarchy

A woman's social position is largely fixed by the men in her life, mainly her father and husband. Working-class culture is particularly male dominated, with the trade unions bastions of patriarchy. The domination is betrayed in

---

The *divine right* of husbands, may, it is to be hoped in this enlightened age, be contested without danger.

Mary Wollstonecraft (1759–97; early feminist writer), *A Vindication of the Rights of Woman* (1792)

---

the very language we speak, with the repetitious use of the male pronoun to denote both sexes (as in the quotations in chapter 1): not only are committees headed by chairmen, God is a man and so is Father Christmas. In the human race we are all *Homo sapiens*; there appear to be no *Femina sapiens*.

The modern pattern of domination by gender did not originate with the capitalism which dominates life today. In primitive cultures of tropical Africa women are forced to spend the day in hard physical labour while the men remain largely idle, Asian civilizations retain rigid sexist traditions, and in Muslim law the treatment of women is harsh indeed. As long ago as 300 BC, in an idyll by Theocritus, Praxinoa, a fine lady, rushes away from a show at the royal palace telling her friend: 'I must be getting back. It's Diocleidas's dinner time, and that man's all pepper; I wouldn't advise anyone to come near him when he's kept waiting for his food' (Seltman 1956: 134). However, male domination, and the concept of the family unit, have proved functional for capitalism by providing a means for the reproduction and maintenance of labour. Women rear children as future workers as well as caring for the capitalists' labour force quite free of charge. In addition, they are expected to perform a caring role in the domestic sphere by looking after the old, the sick and the handicapped.

Mother is the dead heart of the family, spending father's earnings on consumer goods to enhance the environment in which he eats, sleeps and watches the television.

Germaine Greer (Australian-born feminist writer),
The Female Eunuch (1970)

Women and work

The multi-faceted subjugation of women is nowhere better illustrated than in paid employment. The growth of capitalism made possible a sharp distinction between two forms of work: the *commodity production* of industry and *domestic production* at home. However, the latter is not usually considered real work at all (Rowbotham 1973: 68) and housewives socialized by the commodity production ethos tend to reply to enquiries with: 'Oh I don't

---

The oldest profession?

Even when women have full rights, they still remain factually down-trodden because all house work is left to them. In most cases house work is the most unproductive, the most barbarous and the most arduous work a woman can do.

V. I. Lenin (1870–1924; Russian revolutionary leader),
Collected Works (vol. XXX: 43)

have a job'. Figure 4.2 illustrates the extent to which housekeeping continues
to be a substantial activity among married women today, while remaining
largely outside the male experience.

For most women, paid employment must be fitted around the full-time
domestic production role, yet this has not significantly altered the basic
organization of work practices. The effect is to exclude women from many
sections of the labour market (Garnsey 1982: 440). An additional problem is
that of the single-parent family, of which there are around a million in
Britain. The term is largely a euphemism for families without a man, since
marital break-up, or unintended pregnancy, usually leave the children in the
care of the mother. The position can be particularly degrading as the great
need for an income, coupled with an inability to give a full-time commitment, often oblige women to accept menial, low-prestige occupations which
no one else wants. Immigrant women, sometimes from particularly sexist
societies, are even more vulnerable, often accepting sweat-shop conditions
and denied unionization. Even women in the professions can expect to be
dominated by their male colleagues and to be passed over for promotion,
while those returning to work after child-rearing will be obliged to occupy
positions far lower than their qualifications warrant.

The propensity to gravitate towards menial jobs means that, unlike men,
women tend to work in a limited number of occupations. Over half are in
three service sectors – distributive trades, secretarial and miscellaneous
services (e.g. catering, cleaning). They are also found predominantly in
caring work such as nursing and education (mainly primary) and social
services (Barret 1980: 156), thereby reinforcing the cultural definitions of

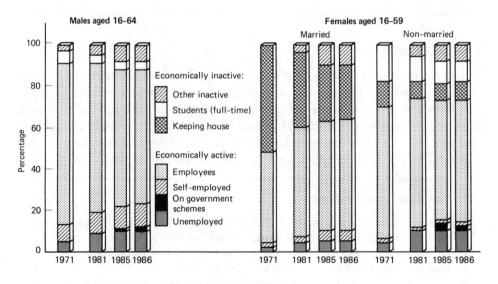

Figure 4.2 Population of working age by economic status

Source: Social Trends (1988: chart 4.2)

their identity as carers and servers rather than creators. Although constituting some 40 per cent of the labour force, women receive only 25 per cent of the total wages paid (Wainwright 1978: 168).

The women's realm: explaining subjugation

Subordination is often excused on the grounds that women are supreme in their own special world, the family, which is presented as part of the order of things, as natural as birth itself. Yet societies can exist without the family; it is a cultural creation. Moreover, women are not really supreme here: their subordinate position in the labour market makes them dependent upon the wage-earner returning like the mighty hunter each evening (Hartmann 1982: 459).

> The Queen is most anxious to enlist everyone who can speak or write to join in checking this mad, wicked folly of 'Woman's Rights', with all its attendant horrors, on which her poor feeble sex is bent.
>
> Queen Victoria, letter to Sir Theodore Martin (29 May 1870)

Most arguments for male domination have at their root some form of *biological determinism*, suggesting that women's social position is the natural result of innate physiological and psychological factors. They are designed for child-rearing rather than hunting, for caring rather than fighting. They are also said to be more compassionate, more emotional, but less rational and less creative than men. This argument is substantiated by the fact that in the arts and sciences, as well as in industry, commerce and politics, the great figures are overwhelmingly male. However, this imbalance can itself be seen as evidence of domination throughout history. In fact once breast-feeding has ceased there is no further biological reason why women should be the child-rearers. The division of labour is socially determined.

Another argument is that women are weaker. This presents a paradox in that they are left to do housework, which has been estimated variously as around a 99-hour week of physically demanding labour. Indeed, it was not the physical demands of labour that drove women from the workplace; in the early stages of industrialization they were welcomed by capitalists since their subordination made them highly suitable for passive submission to the imperatives of the factory. Indeed, the machines often reduced the need for physical strength. However, technology also reduced the demand for labour and male workers organized together as trade unions to drive women out, a trend supported by legislation from a male Parliament in the form of Factory Acts.

However, this is not to dismiss physical strength as a factor determining the relationship between the sexes. Historically speaking, it is not woman's lower capacity for physical work which led to her domination, but her lower capacity for violence. The gentlemanly Victorian adage 'Never strike a woman' has not amounted to much. Crimes of violence against women are commonplace, though it is an area which the police (a bastion of the male establishment) prefer to view with a blind eye, on the grounds of not interfering in domestic matters. Thus it can be argued that women have been subjugated throughout the ages because they are physically weaker than men. 'Women have been *forced* to do "women's work"' (Mitchell 1971: 103). It is a case of one of the oldest rules of politics, that 'might is right'.

> **Not all are serious – some are just husbands killing their wives.**
> Commander G. H. Hatherill of Scotland Yard on the subject of
> murders in London, quoted in the *Observer* (21 Feb. 1954)

Political implications

Male culture does not welcome women in politics. This is amply demonstrated in the suffragette battle for the franchise (see pp. 165–7). Generally women in British society are far less political in their behaviour than men. This is predictable: being confined to, and isolated within, the home they lack the opportunities to develop collective consciousness either as women or in class terms. Moreover, they have long been prey to sexist culture propagated by the media, including a very special *genre*, the woman's magazine, perpetuating the biological determinist picture of women as sex objects and the natural carers of men and children. As a result, many working-class women are themselves fierce advocates of the 'woman's role in the home' and can be strong opponents of the woman's movement which, by implication, devalues the lives they have led and the commitments they have made.

Yet by depoliticizing women the working class has done its cause considerable harm. Allowed to be prey to socialization by the media, they have remained deferential and given great support to the Conservative Party. The radical potential of women was recognized by the establishment, which resisted the extension of the franchise for so long and, even when conceding, restricted it to those who had reached the mature age of 30 (see p. 167).

A further result is that women's issues have tended to remain off the political agenda, they themselves have not become political activists, at work they are far less unionized than men, and they even tend not to support their husbands when on strike. They have been poorly represented on the TUC and, although trade union attitudes have become more sympathetic, there remains much deep-seated sexism. Parliament remains predominantly a male club (see chapter 10), seen at its most bizarre when pontificating on abortion, viewing the foetus as male property placed in the womb for safe keeping.

However, the women's movement is now a more serious part of politics and a number of concessions have been gained in the areas of equal opportunities and pay. Women have been involved in some major political affairs, including the 1976–7 strike by Asian women in the Grunwick photographic processing factory over unionization, and the Greenham Common encampment protesting against Cruise missiles. Yet a fundamental weakness is that, because women form such a vast constituency, the movement is fragmented by class divisions and consequent differences in goals. The problems of middle-class women (career frustration, wasted education) appear on the surface light years away from those of their working-class counterparts (low pay, menial jobs, domestic servility).

The male establishment retaliates with one of its traditional weapons – mockery and derision. In the same way that the accents of trade unionists are ridiculed, attempts to alter sexist language are laughed at quite openly in the media. In debate one finds a sniggering subtext suggesting that feminists are physically unattractive, or lesbians, and *Private Eye* carries a regular section entitled 'WIMMIN' in which readers are invited to submit examples of 'loony feminist nonsense'.

Government policies of the 1980s were particularly bad for women, with much rhetoric on the theme of the family as a caring unit. In this way women could be blamed for low educational standards, drug abuse among the young, juvenile delinquency, and so on. In social policy the intention was to shift the care of the old, chronically ill and handicapped from the state to working-class women with a policy termed 'Care in the Community' (Griffiths 1988). The freezing of child benefit payments was also specifically targeted at women.

Women have served all these centuries as looking-glasses possessing the magic and delicious power of reflecting the figure of man at twice its natural size.

Virginia Woolf (1882–1941; English writer), *A Room of One's Own* (1929)

This section has but touched on the deep sexist ramifications veining the political system. It will be apparent in every subsequent chapter that the world we are examining is one of sexist dominance. Here there are no female chief constables, field marshalls, lord chancellors, bishops or heads of nationalized industries. The vast majority of cabinet ministers, judges, higher civil servants, MPs, councillors, soldiers and police are male. Even the NHS is run by men, demonstrating their assumed right to control women's bodies as well as their minds. They scrape their cervixes, scan and remove their breasts, moralize over the contents of their wombs, and woe betide any female obstetrician attempting to respond to the desire for natural childbirth.

British Racism

The political culture of modern Britain cannot be understood without recognizing its deep-seated, indelible **racism**. Many white people are blind to the country's racial problem, believing it to be non-existent, exaggerated for political reasons, or unimportant, though few with a West Indian or Asian background could feel this way. For them race, and racism, lie at the very heart of their social and economic experience.

Source: Mary Evans Picture Library

What is racism?

The human species may be said to consist of several races distinguished by superficial physical characteristics (size, colour of hair and skin, etc.). These are only broad distinctions: many individuals do not fit the physical type which their racial origins demand and intermarriage further blurs the picture. Recognition of these differences is not racism. Racism is the practice of discrimination against people on the grounds of race. Some regimes (the fascists of Europe in the 1930s and the whites in South Africa) are openly based on the belief that racial differences justify inequality in the distribution of wealth and life-chances. The implication is that some races are superior to others. Apart from being ethically objectional, this is quite impossible to prove because of differences in cultural environments. It is about as logically defensible as the distinction Gulliver encountered in Lilliput based upon the method of eating a boiled egg, which resulted in bloody war for 'six and thirty moons' between the 'Big-Endians' and 'Little-Endians'!

The roots of British racism

> British thought and British society has never been cleansed of the Augean filth of imperialism.
>
> Salman Rushdie in *New Society* (9 Dec. 1982)

The British have long attributed their supremacy to God: He made them mighty, and they frequently enjoin Him to 'make us mightier yet'. Hence it is not surprising that Jews in particular have been despised; indeed the late-Victorian poet, W. N. Ewer, mocked:

> How odd,
> of God,
> to choose,
> the Jews.

From Shakespeare's *Merchant of Venice* to Dicken's Fagin they have been depicted as miserly and grasping. Similarly, the Irish (notwithstanding Wilde, Shaw, Joyce, Behan, et al.) have long been considered inferior to the English. Today, along with blacks, they are the butt of obscene and offensive jokes told by 'comedians' appearing on national television.

The great age of discovery revealed to all West European eyes a vast world of 'savages': inferior beings to be tamed; trained; deprived of their land, culture and property; and used as slaves. The seventeenth-century slave trade made the English curiously interested in race. Part of the justification for this abomination was a belief that Africans were so inferior in character and brain that to be enslaved by the white man was actually an improvement in their condition.

The development of the empire as an integral part of British capitalism has a particular significance for today's racist attitudes. The status of great imperial power encouraged superiority: the English gained control of the British Isles and defeated European rivals in the pillage of the New World where they had subjugated the indigenous populations. By the closing decades of the eighteenth century, once the Indian subcontinent had been retrieved from the French, the British Empire was the largest the world had ever experienced (see chapter 3). Truly they were a master race. Victorian scientists pictured mankind in terms of a great hierarchy, with the white Englishman invariably at the top and the negro just above the ape at the bottom.

> Take up the White Man's burden –
> And reap his old reward:
> The blame of those ye better,
> The hate of those ye guard.
>
> Rudyard Kipling (1865–1936;
> Indian-born British writer),
> 'The White Man's Burden'

Of course the superiority claimed by the English was attributed to its dominant class, not to the lower orders labouring in conditions scarcely better than those of slaves. However, the extension of the franchise obliged the establishment to win their approval and support, and this seemingly impossible enterprise was accomplished through the Disraelian concept of 'one nation'. In this great legitimating myth the empire became a unifying symbol serving to bestow something of the splendour of the upper class on even the most lowly Englishman; they were part of the race which ruled the world. Although the principal purpose of this ploy was to secure votes, it was to bequeath a lasting side-effect in an extraordinary sense of **xenophobia** (fear of foreigners) with peculiarly significant consequences for race relations at home.

The pattern of immigration

> All those who are not racially pure are mere chaff.
> Adolf Hitler (1889–1945), *Mein Kampf* (1925–6)

Contrary to the Victorian theory of racial superiority, the British 'race' is in no sense pure; it is a mongrel breed including Celts, Anglo-Saxons, Romans and Normans, which could find no class for itself at a *Homo sapiens* Crufts Show. After 1066 the country was host to further waves of immigration: the medieval period saw large numbers of Jewish settlers; at the end of the seventeenth century came the Huguenots escaping persecution in France; and in the eighteenth century famine in Ireland brought a further major influx. It was never in the British nature to welcome these additions. In 1601 Elizabeth I issued a proclamation to remove the country's few black people and in 1605 an Act was passed restricting the rights of aliens. However, time generally soothed irate feelings and the immigrants were well integrated, some to become very successful (indeed, amongst the most successful of all were William the Conqueror, William of Orange, the Hanoverians and Prince Albert!). Intermarriage frequently meant that the only sign of foreign origin was a strange name, and sometimes even these were changed.

A new wave of immigration began in the years immediately following the second world war, when labour shortages sucked in workers from India, Pakistan and the West Indies through recruitment drives by public bodies such as the NHS and London Transport. Although the first of these (mainly men) met with characteristic resistance, they were welcomed insofar as they could relieve the working class of the most menial and boring work. In addition, they were buoyed up by the expectation that things could only get better. However, such optimism was illusory. A second British-born generation remained as black as its parents and found itself subject to the same level of racism, remaining excluded from better jobs, confined to poor housing in inner-city areas, and with inferior education and health care.

The problems intensified as the long boom of western capitalism ran out of steam. Unemployment began an inexorable rise amongst the black population, which was particularly vulnerable as robots moved in to take over jobs characteristically undertaken in manufacturing and textiles. Adding insult to injury, they were seen as one of the *causes* of unemployment and discriminatory practices were increasingly applied so that unemployment rates for blacks rose to double those of whites (see table 4.7).

Table 4.7   Employment status of working-age men by ethnic group, 1984–1986 (percentages)

	White	West Indian and Guyanese	Indian, Pakistani and Bangladeshi	Other (African, Chinese, etc.)
In employment	79	63	64	60
Employees	66	55	49	49
Self-employed	11	–	15	10
On government scheme	1	–	–	–
Unemployed	10	21	17	12
Economically inactive	12	16	19	28

Source: Data from *Social Trends* (1988: table 4.6)

Manifestations of British racism

Modern British racism does not take the open and violent forms seen in Nazi Germany, the American deep south, or South Africa today, but it permeates every nook and cranny of social life. It is found in the membership of clubs and societies, sport, housing, newspapers, employment, education and in everyday language. The most openly racist whites have a rich lexicon of

> We shall have to start progressively removing their rights. If bloodshed and racial strife are the result, then all I can say is that that is an acceptable price to pay for clearing out the immigrants.
>
> Anthony Reed-Herbert of the National Front, quoted in *The Times* (24 June 1976)

derogatory terms ranging from 'our coloured cousins', 'nigger' and 'wog', to the more obscene. Such attitudes are found in all state institutions, with the police subject to particular criticism (see pp. 545–6). Though well-meaning liberals deplore racism, they themselves are products of an inescapably racist culture, falling easily into patronizing attitudes which can sap black morale.

When in the 1930s Hitler and Mussolini were taking power in Germany and Italy, Britain had its own fascist movement, led by Sir Oswald Mosley. Fascist parties have continued to exist, including the National Socialist Movement, the National Front and the British Movement. In addition to their traditional anti-semitism, the establishment of an all-white Britain remains a prime goal of such movements.

As racist patterns continue, the threat of further resistance, including violence, increases. One result has been for blacks to turn inwards, forming ethnic colonies or ghettos in the decaying centres of the old cities, where they live a self-contained existence, overtly abandoning the ambition to participate on equal terms in British society. It is the young with no experience of a home other than Britain who feel the greatest sense of alienation and despair and who are likely to vent their frustration in riot. By the late 1980s most major cities had experienced clashes between young blacks and the police (see chapter 18).

Institutional racism

Racism has been **institutionalized** through legislation passed by both major parties designed to restrict coloured immigration. In 1958 race riots in Notting Hill marked a grim watershed, leading the Conservative government to pass the first post-war Immigration Act in 1962. This restricted entry from the black Commonwealth to those able to show they were coming to a specific job, or able to offer a particular skill. Women were subject to strict physical examinations, including the degrading internal virginity test.

The hard reality of the Smethwick election result in 1964 (when an openly racist Conservative candidate using the slogan 'If you want a nigger for a neighbour, vote Labour' won a stunning victory) and increasing anti-black hysteria, led the Labour government to introduce even tougher restrictions in 1965, with deportation by the Home Secretary (without a court hearing) of any 'illegal' immigrant of less than five years' standing. A new style of rhetoric, speaking of the 'small crowded island', transformed what had been right-wing views into respectable orthodoxy. Home Secretary Roy Jenkins, hitherto a notable advocate of the humane society, stressed the 'social factor' limiting the number that could be absorbed. In 1968 (fearing more immigration precipitated by turbulent events in Kenya) the Commonwealth Immigrants Act (dubbed the 'Kenyan Asians Act') was rushed through Parliament in only two days.

In 1971 the Conservative government consolidated the position with an Act restricting entry to those with parents or grandparents born in Britain. This permitted Commonwealth citizens only the opportunity available to all foreigners of applying to the Home Secretary and having to prove four years of 'good behaviour'. They were reduced to the status of the exploited migrant workers in other West European capitalisms. The Act also extended state powers to deport, providing a basis for further official harassment of blacks. In 1981 the Thatcher government passed a British Nationality Act effectively closing the door to non-whites, while keeping another open for 6 million patrials and 200 million in the EC. In 1984 the immigration rules were changed by the Conservatives in response to anxiety within the party about alleged abuses of the arranged marriage system in Indian culture (Bhavnani and Bhavnani 1985: 152). In late 1989, after the dreadful massacre of Chinese students in Tiananmen Square, there were grave fears for the future of residents of Hong Kong, which was due to be handed over to China in 1997. However, the government steadfastly refused to give them British citizenship on the curious grounds of preventing the possibility of them *all* wanting to settle in Britain. However, provision was made for 50,000 of the colony's elite, dubbed 'essential workers', and their dependents to settle in Britain, paradoxically to encourage them to stay in Hong Kong.

Brothers in law: race relations legislation

Feeble attempts to cushion black morale have come in the form of race relations legislation in 1965, 1968 and 1976 designed to outlaw discrimination, and the establishment of the Commission for Racial Equality (CRE), formerly the Race Relations Board, to monitor race relations. For liberal critics, the CRE is merely a toothless watchdog, more concerned with legitimation than improving the life-experiences of blacks.

Racism and politics

The politics of Britain logically gives blacks and working-class whites more reason to unite than divide, yet racism in Britain 'appears at its strongest among unskilled working people' (Walvin 1984: 143). Even within the active left there is a strong vein of racism, particularly evident in the trade unions. The employment of immigrants has been seen as depressing wage levels and taking employment from indigenous workers. The TUC has pressed enthusiastically for action against illegal entrants and there is a lengthy catalogue of disputes involving racist behaviour by members and officials.

Although Labour has received more solid support from blacks than from working-class whites, its trade union roots have inhibited its response to them. The Scarman Report on the 1981 Brixton riots stressed that black people in the UK

> do not feel politically secure. Their sense of rejection is not eased by the low level of black representation in our elective political institutions.
>
> (Scarman 1981: 16)

Yet the party remains strongly opposed to black sections, thereby denying blacks the distinct political voice allowed to women. Another problem has been Labour's rejection of the New Urban Left movement (see pp. 503–5), for it is at the local government level that black political activism has been most evident.

Racism, class and politics

On the post-imperial stage racism has supported both capitalism and class domination. The first wave of post-war immigration was very good for capitalism: immigrants' willingness to undertake uncongenial, low-paid work made possible the survival of a number of traditional industries, such as textiles, in an increasingly competitive world economy. Unlike that of gender, the racial division does not cut across class. Black people belong largely to the working class, so racism weakens working-class solidarity, particularly at those very times when capitalism is at its most vulnerable – economic recession. The establishment therefore has good reason to welcome, and indeed encourage, working-class racism.

It is sometimes alleged that there is a gentleman's agreement among politicians not to use race for political advantage, liberal political scientists arguing that race is an insignificant factor in general election results. This is entirely bogus; racism helps sustain class domination. From the 'one-nation' appeal of Disraeli, Conservatives have laid great stress on patriotism as more honourable than class loyalty. Yet patriotism is not merely, in the words of Doctor Johnson, 'the last refuge of a scoundrel', it is also the first refuge of the racist.

It is an experience which people disbelieve when I tell them, but as I go about on public transport in Britain, the commonest thing is for a West Indian or an Asian to come up to me and say: 'Mr Powell, may I shake your hand? I have always admired you. You are absolutely right – carry on'.

Enoch Powell (maverick Conservative MP), quoted in the *Independent* (10 Sept. 1988)

The racist vote was most effectively garnered for the Conservatives by Enoch Powell, whose lurid speeches lamented the submergence of a halcyon English age under the great alien tidal wave. These sentiments set off resonances throughout society, drawing London dockers out in a strike of clamorous adulation and providing an ecology for the resurgence of a British fascist movement and of the National Front. A Gallup poll exposed the hard truth that 75 per cent of the population were broadly sympathetic to Powell's sentiments (Marwick 1982). Fascism had given racism a bad name but Powell helped to rehabilitate it, making it 'respectable amongst those

who saw the Tory party as the epitome of conformist respectability'
(Bhavnani and Bhavnani 1985: 150).

> As I look ahead I am filled with foreboding. Like the Roman, I seem
> to see 'the River Tiber foaming with much blood'.
>
> Enoch Powell on immigration, public speech in Birmingham (4 April 1968)

Powell fell foul of non-racist party leader Edward Heath and was
promptly ejected from the Shadow Cabinet, yet he helped to propel the
Conservatives into office in 1970. He was known to be greatly admired by
Margaret Thatcher, who herself had warned of the danger that 'this country
might be swamped by people with a different culture' (Sivanandan
1981: 145). Upon becoming Conservative leader she could be seen as 'a poor
man's Enoch Powell' (Johnson 1985: 114). Although convention, or cowardice, normally forbids politicians to speak as openly as Powell on the subject
of race, a government is able to signal its views with encoded messages about
'the British way of life' and the undesirability of sanctions against South
Africa.

Conclusion: Covering the Cracks

Hence it must be concluded that Britain's deferential, united civic culture is
rather more complex and tense than that venerated by liberal-democratic
apologists. The working of the polity cannot be explained in terms of a large
natural consensus. The geographical, class, gender and racial cracks in the
social fascia are only smoothed over with political polyfilla and concealed
beneath unwritten constitutional wallpaper. It is in exploring how this is
accomplished that one gains the key to the true spirit and genius of the
system. This exploration begins in the following chapter.

Key points

- Britain is often said to possess a cohesive political culture, to be 'One Nation'.
  The absence of proletarian revolution is taken as evidence of this.
- Another explanation for the absence of revolution may have lain in a long
  tradition of deference amongst the mass of the people towards the 'natural
  rulers' of society.
- Deference can be encouraged by the elite classes who are able to establish
  hegemony by fostering a political culture in which 'the way things are'
  becomes accepted as 'the way things always must be'.
- However, today the problems of Northern Ireland, class tension, the emergence of a new 'subclass', sexism and racism give pause for thought.

- Britain has a patriarchal political system in which women are not encouraged to take part.
- The British have not been traditionally hospitable to immigrants. This has become a particularly tense issue today because colour prevents the long-term assimilation of those with West Indian or Asian ancestry.
- Within and beneath the apparent calm of middle-class-dominated British society there remain several brooding bases for political schism.

Review your understanding of the following terms and concepts

political culture	subclass
deference	establishment
north–south divide	sexism
nationalism	patriarchy
power-sharing executive	racism
social class (upper, middle, working)	xenophobia
class in Marxist terms	institutional racism

Assignment

Study the extract from the *Guardian* and answer the following questions.

		% mark
1	What evidence of institutional racism did the CRE find in this case?	25
2	What explanation can you offer for the fact that both Labour and SLD parties appear to have practised institutional racism?	25
3	Given that local democracy is generally considered desirable, why should the SLD criticize its local branch for courting the racist vote?	25
4	What does this case tell us about the problems of race relations legislation and the power of the CRE?	25

Questions for discussion

1 How accurate is it to describe the United Kingdom as a cohesive political culture?
2 What are the factors which prevent the successful instigation of a power-sharing executive in Northern Ireland?
3 In what way do you think deference among the British working class contributes to the hegemonic consciousness of the upper middle class?
4 'The rise of the middle classes has rendered redundant the Marxist distinction between the owners of capital and the workers.' Discuss.
5 Identify some of the important manifestations of sexism in British politics.
6 'Racism is largely a social phenomenon. It does not have any significant effect on politics.' Discuss.
7 'You can change your class, but not your colour or gender. Herein lies a deep problem for British politics in the future.' Discuss.

A continuing tale of sham and shame

Melanie Phillips

WHAT a peculiarly unpleasant council Tower Hamlets appears to be. The recent disclosure that it is to press ahead with a new council house lettings policy despite legal advice that this will break the Race Relations Act is but the latest chapter in an apparently endless saga of racial discrimination by this local authority's housing department. It is a saga, moreover, in which the ruling SLD (who choose to style themselves Liberals) have sought to slough off responsibility for their actions on to their Labour predecessors. These Liberals maintain that their hands are clean, despite being severely criticised not only by the Commission for Racial Equality but by their own party, which has the grace to be ashamed of their activities.

Last year the CRE published a report detailing the results of its investigation into the overlapping issues of homelessness and discrimination in Tower Hamlets. The report painted a shaming picture of institutional racism permeating the council's housing policies over a number of years. In an area of startling deprivation, Bangladeshis, who amounted in 1981 to some 9 per cent of the total population, formed no less than 69 per cent of the borough's homeless people, compared with white people who amounted to only 18 per cent of the homelessness total. The CRE investigation found "enormous housing stress and mis-

ery" among the Bangladeshis, with gross overcrowding and slum conditions. It discovered racial discrimination among the council's emergency rehousing procedures, and that white families were twice as likely as Bangladeshis to be offered permanent accommodation within three months of an application to be rehoused. It also drew attention to the council's policy of refusing to consider Tower Hamlets families for rehousing if part of the family was still in Bangladesh.

The CRE investigation covered the years 1984 and 1985, when the council was ruled by the Labour party. However, its report was published last September, two years and four months after the SLD took control in May 1986. The report stated that, since the investigation, there had been "no significant changes" made to the council's housing policies that would eliminate the kind of discrimination identified in the report. As a result, in November 1987, it had served a non-discrimination notice under the Race Relations Act, putting the law behind its request to the council to stop discriminating against the Bangladeshis. Almost one year later, however, at the press conference launching the report, CRE officials expressed their disappointment that the council was still dragging its heels over complying with the legal notice. In fact, the council's housing policies had by now drawn the ire of the national Democrat leadership. Severely embarrassed by the council's policy of evicting Bangladeshi families on the grounds that they had been made "intentionally homeless" because they still had family in Bangladesh, the Democrat hier-

archy repeatedly told the Tower Hamlets Liberals that their policy was unacceptable.

The SLD For Racial Justice, find the whole thing pretty disgusting. They have said the Tower Hamlets Liberals have courted the racist vote by treating the Bangladeshis as second-class citizens, that councillors have consistently failed to address the needs of the Bangladeshi community and are only interested in keeping white families together; and that the party should dissociate itself from people they say are unfit to be its members.

Guardian, 31 March 1989

Topic for debate

This house believes that women have no place in politics.
>   or

This house believes that the working class should leave politics to those who know best what is good for the country as a whole.

Further reading

Almond, G. A. and Verba, S. (1963) *The Civic Culture* (reprinted 1989).
This remains a classic text in spite of criticism.

Almond, G. A. and Verba, S. (eds) (1980) *The Civic Culture Revisited*.
Quite different from the original study, this book of readings re-evaluates the civic culture in the light of events.

Bagehot, W. (1963) *The English Constitution*.
First published in 1867, before members of the establishment felt any need to regard the sensibilities of the working class, this 'classic' on the constitution reveals the extent of the disdain felt by the nineteenth-century elite for the masses.

Giddens, A. (1986) *Sociology*.
This brief but critical introduction illustrates how the discipline of sociology addresses many of the questions important to the study of politics. Argues that human beings are not the helpless puppets that deterministic theories imply; they make their own history, and there are many alternative forms of political system.

MacDonald, M. (1986) *Children of Wrath: Political Violence in Northern Ireland*.
Argues that the colonization of Ireland, with its native–settler division, created a problem which could not be resolved. Stresses the ironic fact that the colonizing power needed the disloyalty of the native in order to justify its hegemony.

Marwick, A. (1982) *British Society Since 1945*.
Although largely silent on the issues of Northern Ireland and gender, this is an accessible and wide-ranging introduction to British society, in terms of literature, science, philosophy and the arts.

Walvin, J. (1984) *Passage to Britain*.
Examines the pattern of immigration into Britain and the problems faced by blacks today.

Greer, G. (1970) *The Female Eunuch*.
An important and entertaining book which set the tone of much debate.

For light relief

Much literature, both from home and abroad, deals with themes which divide societies: class, race and gender.

Martin Amis, *London Fields*
Surreal vision of London life: four people bound together in a modern urban torment of class, wealth and squalor, destroying themselves and the world.

Jilly Cooper, *Class*.
A witty and amusing essay by a proud daughter of the upper middle class which sees the whole thing as a bit of a giggle. A very British attitude which serves to legitimate the suffering of others.

Henrik Ibsen, *The Doll's House*.
A powerful drama about women's oppression.

George Bernard Shaw, *Pygmalion*.
A witty but subversive comedy on upper-class manners and gender relationships by the Irish genius. Better to see the play performed than read it, of course. (Alternatively, see the musical version, *My Fair Lady* – but less subversive!)

Virginia Woolf, *A Room of One's Own*.
A classic essay from a feminist viewpoint.

PART III

Mobilizing the *Demos*

The Greek word *demos* means the people as a whole, and when they are masters of the government, then the polity can lay claim to the title democracy. Few polities today would not at least pay lip-service to the notion of democracy, but none fully realize its demanding ideals. Before there can be even a pretence of democracy there must be mechanisms whereby the *demos* will be mobilized to participate in the processes of politics. In this section we evaluate the principal means whereby this is accomplished in Britain. Above all we are interested in fundamental questions concerning the ability of the state institutions to permit genuine and unimpeded entrance of the masses through its portals. Can all enter with equal ease or are there signs saying 'Members Only', 'Keep Off the Grass', 'Men Only', or even 'Whites Only'?

It is clear that in this section we are moving to the very heart of British politics and we encounter some of the very big questions of social life, illuminating not only the nature of the polity we inhabit but the very quality of life. We first look at the way people form attitudes about politics. Do they believe they are able to participate in, or influence, government? These attitudes do not form spontaneously; they are socially constructed by experience and can be conditioned through the process we term '**mind politics**', a layer of political activity which people encounter before being allowed anywhere near the ballot box. Chapter 6 examines the most visible mechanism of participation, the **electoral system**. When everyone has the right to vote the *demos* would indeed appear mighty; or is it? We consider the grudging manner in which the powerful few in Britain extended the franchise to the mass, and did so in a way calculated to minimize damage to their own privileges. Chapters 7 and 8 examine the main products of the fully extended franchise, which extend participation beyond the voting booth: the modern **political parties**. When these are understood one has some important keys for unlocking the mysteries of the British political system.

PART III

Mobilizing the Demos

5

Mind Politics:
What We Think

In this chapter we turn to the processes which shape the attitudes people hold; that is, to the politics of the mind. **Mind politics** arises from the need for social stability. There are various ways of maintaining this, ranging from the brutal use of force and fear, through attempts by the state to ease the effects of inequality (say by means of a welfare state), to a more subtle psychological process which removes from the disadvantaged the desire to resist. While the British state has not been unwilling to employ force against citizens, it is ultimately necessary that the mass of the people accept their lot with some degree of contentment and passivity. In other words, the system must be *legitimated*; the distribution of power in society and the form of government must be accepted by the mass as being right and proper. We shall see throughout the chapters of this book that legitimation takes place variously, involving most government institutions. Here we are particularly concerned with institutions which directly impinge upon ideology and attitudes. The chapter has three broad sections. The first examines influences encountered by the young, including the family, the church, and school. However, mind politics is not confined to the young; we are subject to influences throughout life until the day we die, and thus we also examine the arts and the world of advertising. The second section concentrates on the **press**, a profoundly important source of politically biased mass persuasion. Finally we consider **broadcasting**, the most potent instrument of the mass media.

Political Socialization

Defining political socialization

The process whereby people acquire their attitudes towards politics is termed **political socialization**. A major flaw in typical studies of political socialization is a preoccupation with voting behaviour, seeking to explain the words of W. S. Gilbert:

> How Nature always does contrive
> That every boy and ever gal,
> That's born into this world alive,
> Is either a little Liberal,
> Or else a little Conservative!
>
> (*Iolanthe*, Act II)

There is much more to the socialization process than explaining the mysteries whereby boys and girls grow up to be Conservatives, Liberals, Labourites, or even Social Democrats or Communists. It is upon the socialization process that the stability of the whole system depends; it determines whether successive generations will vote at all, whether they will be apathetic abstainers, cynics or revolutionaries.

A central goal in legitimating a deferential and submissive political culture is to promote the notion of the neutral state. This is accomplished by the ostentatious veneration of basic constitutional principles such as the rule of law and the political impartiality of the state institutions. We shall see in later chapters that these institutions (the civil service, the police force, the judiciary, and so on) themselves play a part in the socialization process in many subtle ways.

However, in addition to the state's direct role in reproducing the all-important attitudes, there is a range of non-state institutions extending into civil society including the family, the church, the education system and the arts. Moreover, there are also institutions specially created to talk to (not to communicate with) the masses: the mass communications media. Each of these justifies a book in itself and can only be touched upon briefly here.

The family

> They fuck you up your mum and dad.
> They may not mean to but they do.
> They fill you with the faults they had
> And add some extra, just for you.
>
> Philip Larkin (1922–85; English poet),
> 'This be the Verse'

Today we think of the family as a small 'nuclear' unit consisting of two parents and their children. However, in pre-industrial Britain 'extended' families were the norm in which grandparents, cousins and so on would live in close proximity in rural communities. Industrialization, and its consequent urbanization, changed this pattern irrevocably by drawing people from their roots to the new, densely packed towns. Today the nuclear family is the first source of attitude formation we encounter. Despite the role played by mothers, this is an essentially patriarchal organization and sexist attitudes are reproduced in this way. Girls can be trained to do housework, while boys can be taught to be superior. Xenophobia and racism may also be learnt through the family, where views can be aired in private which might not be articulated outside.

> Far from being the basis of the good society, the family, with its narrow privacy and tawdry secrets, is the source of all our discontents.
>
> Edmund Leach (British social anthropologist),
> in the BBC *Reith Lectures* (1967)

The family is also a power structure in which parents will exercise authority, though they will characteristically do so on the basis of their love for the family and their desire to do the best for them. Hence we grow up understanding that authority is generally in our own interests. This can help explain why the Conservative Party lays great stress on the family: it can help to reinforce a social organization in which the position of a dominant class is accepted on the grounds that it acts in the interest, not of itself, but of the whole nation.

However, the family can also socialize people into non-capitalist values such as mutual care and equality, which is why it cannot in itself provide a sufficient basis for mind-shaping in a capitalist society.

Religion and the church

Today Britain is a secular society with little time for religion; faith in science has replaced faith in a God. However, the church has played an immeasurably important part in British politics throughout history. Until modern times most educated people were formally church officials, and leading office holders such as Thomas Becket, Cardinal Wolsey and Archbishop Cranmer were important political and administrative figures. The English Reformation saw the church become formally wedded to the state as the Church of England, with the monarch at its head. Today the bishops sit in the House of Lords and the crowning of the monarch takes place in Westminster Abbey.

During the industrial revolution the early capitalists drew guidance and divine inspiration from the puritan doctrines of nonconformity, with their stress on frugality and saving, which justified the great accumulation of wealth necessary to consolidate their position through ownership of increasing amounts of capital. Yet the bourgeoisie saw the Church of England as the religion of the upper middle class, and social advancement has often required a switch from nonconformity to the Anglican version of Christianity for the upwardly mobile (Mrs Thatcher herself crossed this divide).

From the eighteenth century, with the growth of the great urban masses, important social services were pioneered by the churches, including early ventures into mass education in the eighteenth and nineteenth centuries. These were made by nonconformist and Anglican organizations, competing for the minds of the population.

However, the version of Christianity offered to generations of British children has not stressed the love of one's neighbour. Capitalism is about selling dear, buying cheap, and becoming better off than one's neighbours; it could not operate if people did unto their neighbours as they would have them do unto them. Hence British Christianity has been concerned to explain the divine ordination of inequality in this world, with the promise of better conditions confined to the next. The sentiments of Christianity as purveyed to the masses by the establishment de-emphasized material things, making a particular virtue of the passive acceptance of one's lot. Thus it has been an anaesthetic to keep the poor content and brand as blasphemous attempts to seek material betterment through left-wing activities. Marx saw religion as a key part of the apparatus of subjection and exploitation.

> Religion is the sigh of the oppressed creature, the heart of a heartless world, just as it is the spirit of an unspiritual situation. It is the *opium* of the people.   (Marx 1969: 304)

Britain's non-Christian religions   The presence in Britain of large numbers with Hindu and Moslem backgrounds has presented new issues for the polity as religious and racial issues have become enmeshed. This is not essentially a new problem; Britain's Jewish population has long existed within the predominantly Christian culture. However, as the ethnic minority communities gained in self-confidence they began to make certain religious claims with political overtones, such as the right to Moslem schools within the state system, which were generally rejected by the government on the grounds that they would not lead to smooth integration. Moreover, the more fervent (sometimes fundamentalist) views of these communities led to clashes over matters of morality. The 'death sentence' passed by the Ayatollah Khomeni on author Salman Rushdie because of the blasphemous tone of his book, *The Satanic Verses*, found some support among Britain's ethnic minorities, who took to the streets in demonstrations and symbolic burnings of the book.

Turbulent priests?   Another development concerned the Anglican Church, for long regarded as the 'Conservative Party at prayer' and close to the heart of the establishment. However, the 1980s saw Anglican church leaders,

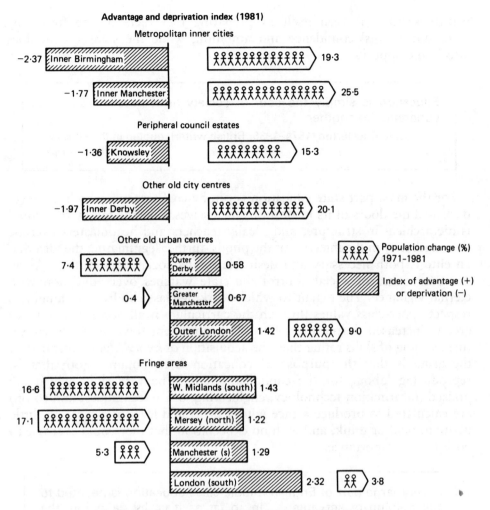

Figure 5.1 Inner-city polarization by type of area

Source: Data from Church of England report, *Faith in the City* (1985)

including David Jenkins, Bishop of Durham, and David Shepherd, charismatic ex-England cricketer and Bishop of Liverpool, attacking the government in a manner unheard of in the past. Policies were described as 'wicked' and in 1985 the Archbishop of Canterbury commissioned a report on Britain's urban problems, *Faith in the City*, which was a damning indictment of government policy in the older industrial cities (see figure 5.1).

The education system

The British school system is sharply divided into two sectors: the private system of public schools (with their umbilical link with the ancient universities) catering for the upper middle classes, and the state system for the masses. They have provided fundamentally different kinds of education: the private sector has seen itself as preparing the rulers of the future by increasing pupils' confidence and ambition, while the state system does largely the opposite.

> Education is simply the soul of society as it passes from one generation to another.
>
> G. K. Chesterton (1874–1936; British writer), quoted in the *Observer* (6 July 1924)

For the most part state education is run by civil servants who have never darkened the doors of its institutions themselves. Like the family the school is hierarchical in structure, and ideally teachers and headmasters exercise their authority in the interests of the pupils, further legitimating the idea that an elite is both necessary and desirable in any social organization. As an obvious source of social control the state watches over education with eternal vigilance. The extent to which working-class children are taught to respect upper-class values through the curriculum is all pervasive, and was greatly increased during the 1980s. The movement towards utilitarianism (the learning of skills rather than the acquisition of *knowledge*) is justified on the grounds that the purpose of education is to obtain a job; that is, reproducing labour for the capitalist system. The very skills which are praised (information technology, engineering, office techniques, and so on) are calculated to produce a race with a depressed level of aspiration, little desire to read or think, and with no expectation that they could ever rise to positions of importance.

> A very large part of English middle-class education is devoted to the training of servants ... In so far as it is, by definition, the training of upper servants, it includes, of course, the instilling of that kind of confidence which will enable the upper servants to supervise and direct the lower servants.
>
> Raymond Williams, *Culture and Society* (1958)

Generations of British children have come to understand their culture through what is alleged to be the history of their country. In reality it is the history of the elite: the subject has been taught mainly in terms of kings and their conquests. The heroes of school texts are figures like Richard the Lionheart and Henry VIII; of John Wilkes and Thomas Paine children have remained largely ignorant. Although he worked in England, and lies buried in Highgate Cemetery, a British child can confidently expect to negotiate the scholastic assault course without ever encountering the towering intellect of Karl Marx, whose presence has left its imprint on the pages of every academic discipline. The cruelties practised in the name of the British Empire have rarely featured, while the evil conditions brought about through the industrial revolution are reserved for the esoteric subdiscipline of economic history, and here the emphasis is on the great march of technology rather than its human implications. The history of women lies similarly unread, and indeed largely unwritten.

Increasingly ethnic minorities have challenged the relevance of the history of the British aristocracy as a basis for understanding their own cultural backgrounds and this has led to some modifications (though opposed by racist working-class parents). Yet the obliteration of the history of those from the black Commonwealth is really no stranger than the exclusion of working-class history. The difference is that the ethnic minorities have not yet had time to be socialized into the belief that the history of the high and mighty is, in some metaphysical way, the history of the whole nation.

The direct analysis of politics is discouraged in British schools and is not classed as a 'strong' subject by careers masters and mistresses, or university admissions officers. However, in marked contrast, the study of economics, taught by exploring wondrous motions of the free market, is recognized as a fitting basis for a rigorous approach to the social sciences. As Education Secretary, Sir Keith Joseph made strenuous efforts to prevent the development of politics teaching in schools. Even more abhorrent to the government of the 1980s was the unholy discipline of 'Peace Studies'. When cold war was invoked to legitimate the vast diversion of funds from social policy into financing the armaments industry, such a discipline could seriously undermine the state's continuing policy of anti-Russian propaganda, particularly when Mikhail Gorbachev, the charismatic Soviet leader, began to excite the minds of ordinary citizens in the west. In the 1980s the concept of a 'common core curriculum' was devised not merely to ensure that certain necessary subjects were being studied in state schools (they already were), but to resist developments away from 'patriotic' teaching.

The idea of the state paying for education as a *consumption* good (to be enjoyed in its own right as a gift of citizenship) for pupils rather than as state *investment* in industry is presented as unfair to taxpayers. Government rhetoric stresses that the beleaguered middle classes must expect 'something for their money'; that is, workers to service their cars, make their televisions or, from the higher reaches of the system, remove their gall stones. Of course many teachers are unhappy with an atmosphere which sees education in purely utilitarian terms. This accounts for the tense relationship between the teaching profession and government; teachers are poorly paid and generally belittled by politicians.

The arts

Literature and ideas present a particular problem for a capitalist society. Ever since Gutenberg set up the first printing press in Mainz in 1457, the power of literature has been at once cherished and feared by the mighty. Although offering a means of legitimating their position by directly shaping mass attitudes, it carries dangerous powers for inciting rebellion and exposing the privilege of the few to the eyes of the many. At first, even the idea of a Bible which everyone could read was seen as a calamity, and the distribution of radical newssheets during the years of industrialization was regarded as an insidious virus in the body politic.

It is in the thoughts and aspirations of Beethoven, Tolstoy, Dostoevsky, Milton, Shelley, and so on that the human spirit can learn to soar, but a workforce with a soaring spirit has had no place in the logic of capitalism. The growth of mass literacy has always contained a potential threat to the state, a fact which contributed to the retarding of education until the end of the nineteenth century, when it was accepted that industry could no longer function without an educated workforce. However, the 'uses of literacy' have been restricted to demeaning mass culture which has usurped the real world of art and ideas. People have been offered, and largely knowing no better have accepted, the culture of a 'candy floss world' and 'sex in shiny packets' (Hoggart 1958). In the pop music world of the young (which generates vast wealth for record companies), love and romance, or at least sex, conquers all. If true happiness comes with love there is little need to question the system that draws one from the sunshine into the mindless workplace for a pittance, or (as in the 1980s) makes one unemployed as a deliberate policy *pour encourager les autres*. The essence of pop culture is its elevation to the status of 'stars' (through the powerful apparatus of mass persuasion) those who think nothing, have nothing to say, and can be counted upon to make no social impact other than to induce mass mental torpor. Today, 'high culture' (classical literature, music, and so on), with its subversive message, is seen as the preserve of the upper, and upper-middle classes.

Advertising

Free-market capitalism is based upon the belief that if everyone buys and sells wisely, according to the way they perceive their self-interest, all will be well. The consumer is said to be sovereign. This is a quite bogus claim in practice because real people are denied enough information or wisdom to know what is in their own interest. Modern capitalism is not at all happy to leave people to decide for themselves what they want; it is concerned with telling them what they should want, and making them want what is most profitable to produce. For this reason the giant corporations which dominate the economic landscape devote huge proportions of their budgets, not to making products or rendering services, but to shaping people's minds (brainwashing). There is even a separate, entirely non-productive mega-industry devoted expressedly to getting into our heads and shaping our thoughts – advertising.

Naturally advertising, although usually promoting a particular product, generally subscribes to the ethos of free-market capitalism and usually favours the political right in politics. However, the political place of

"I like it. It's colourful, eye-catching and deceptive!"
Reproduced by permission of *Punch*

advertising in mind politics goes even deeper. We shall see in chapter 6 that it plays a direct part in politics, with the Conservative Party in particular investing enormous funds to sell itself to voters.

> Freedom of the press in Britain is freedom to print such of the proprietor's prejudices as the advertisers don't object to.
>
> Attributed to Hannen Swaffer (1879–1962; British journalist)

The Press

The concept of a free press

Part of the process of legitimation is a loud exhortation of the rights of the **free press** and independent broadcasting. These values were fought for in the eighteenth century against a secretive ruling class, when it was necessary to smuggle reports of proceedings out of Parliament. A free press is held to be one of the defining characteristics of the liberal state: a democracy must have freedom of speech for its journalists and free access to information for citizens. However, under capitalism this freedom must logically suggest a capitalist-controlled media because the newspaper industry is itself part of 'big business' (though not always a very profitable part in terms of immediate return – see Jenkins 1986).

The British are great readers (or at least great buyers) of newspapers, circulation figures being the highest in the western world (table 5.1). Because

Table 5.1   Reading of national newspapers, 1986

Newspaper	Readership (millions)	Percentage of adults reading each paper	
		Men	Women
Dailies			
Sun	11.4	28	23
Daily Mirror	8.9	23	17
Daily Mail	4.7	11	10
Daily Express	4.5	11	9
Star	4.3	12	8
Today	1.1	3	2
Daily Telegraph	2.9	7	6
Guardian	1.5	4	2
The Times	1.2	3	2
Financial Times	0.7	2	1
Any national morning paper	29.8	71	63
Sunday papers			
News of the World	12.8	30	28
Sunday Mirror	9.3	22	20
People	8.4	20	17
Sunday Express	6.2	15	13
Sunday Today	0.8	2	1
Mail on Sunday	5.0	12	10
Sunday Times	3.5	9	7
Observer	2.4	6	5
Sunday Telegraph	2.3	6	5
Any national paper	32.8	76	72

Source: Data from *Social Trends* (1988: table 10.6)

the country is small, the major British newspapers are national ones, producing considerable uniformity of view and centring on London. The eagerness for newsprint is not matched by enthusiasm for serious weeklies where a more detailed analysis might be found. Sales were buoyant in the 1960s, but most were finding it hard to survive by the 1980s: *New Society* and the *New Statesman* were forced to combine in 1988 in a fight for survival. However, although these might influence the opinions of the intelligentsia, including newspaper journalists themselves, they are not direct agents of mass socialization. Table 5.2 illustrates the mass readership preference for lightweight material, with magazines devoted to television the clear favourites.

Table 5.2   Reading of the most popular magazines, 1971 and 1986

Magazine	Readership (millions)		Percentage of adults reading each magazine (1986)	
	1971	*1986*	*Men*	*Women*
General				
TV Times	9.9	9.5	20	22
Radio Times	9.5	9.1	20	21
Reader's Digest	9.2	6.8	16	14
Smash Hits	–	2.3	5	5
Weekly News	4.5	2.0	4	5
Exchange & Mart	–	2.0	7	2
Women's				
Woman's Own	7.2	5.0	3	18
Woman	8.0	3.8	2	14
Woman's Weekly	4.7	3.3	2	12
Family Circle	4.4	3.0	2	11
Good Housekeeping	2.7	2.6	2	9
Woman's Realm	4.5	2.2	1	8

Source: Data from *Social Trends* (1988: table 10.7)

Partisanship

Britain is unusual amongst democratic countries in having an openly **partisan press**, most newspapers unashamedly supporting the Conservative Party – a fact with direct consequences for the political culture. In addition, there is a recognized division between the quality press for the upper classes, and the tabloids for the working class. Amongst the former *The Times, Daily Telegraph, Sunday Telegraph, Financial Times* and *Sunday Times* support the Conservatives, leaving only the *Guardian,* and the newly established *Independent,* supporting the centrist parties and the Labour right wing. Among the tabloids the *Daily Express, Sunday Express, Daily Star, Daily Mail, Mail on Sunday, Sun, Today,* and *News of the World* support the Conservatives, leaving the *Daily Mirror* and *Sunday Mirror* favouring (right-wing) Labour. In addition there is the Communist *Morning Star* (formerly the *Daily Worker*) taking a clear socialist position, but with a minuscule circulation. Thus, what is often described as the 'left-wing bleat' of press bias in favour of the Conservative Party is well founded; it is one of the few unambiguous 'facts' of British politics. During the 1983 general election Conservative newspapers accounted for 78 per cent of a total circulation of over 14.5 million (Butler and Butler 1986: 493). Table 5.1 demonstrated how the tabloids well outdistance the quality dailies in circulation, and amongst these the lion's share is split between the *Mirror* and the *Sun,* with sales of around 3 and 4 million respectively (note that actual readership exceeds this by a factor of around 3).

In addition to the nationals there are provincial morning and evening dailies but these are in decline, being confronted with right-wing 'free-sheets' containing mainly advertising from private firms and human interest stories, force-fed through the letterboxes of urban households.

The newspapers spread a continual message of Conservative Party competence, *The Times* attributing the 1987 general election result to 'the good sense of the majority of voters'. There is an extremely close association between newspaper readership and voting, dwarfing many of the other electoral variables, and perhaps as great as class and sectoral cleavage (see p. 178) (Dunleavy 1985). Not all readers are aware of the bias: the calculatedly yobbish down-market appeal of the *Sun* actually leads one-third of its readers to believe it to be a Labour paper (Newton 1986: 324)! Yet the extent to which newspaper bias affects voting should not be seen as the central issue. Between elections they exert an insidious influence on attitudes, fertilizing the social soil for the voracious roots of the tree of capitalism and its necessary inequalities.

Content: 'All the news that's fit to print' (motto of the *New York Times*)

News does not come in labelled packages; it must be selected from a great buzzing mass of reality, and there are various conventions determining what is to be printed. Because selling newspapers is business, profit-maximization means maximizing circulation. This results in a quest for the lowest common denominator, with the tabloids favouring sensationalism, trivialization and, in addition to news, much soft pornography (featuring working-class girls), giving them a highly sexist character. There is also a deep-seated racism in the sentiments expressed and language used, which breaks out into hysterical jingoism whenever foreign relations become in any way turbulent. In the Falklands war, in an orgy of bellicose press chauvinism, the Argentinians became the 'Argies', and the infamous *Sun* headline 'Gotcha!' invoked, in locker-room parlance, the image of a patriotic grip on the testicles of the Argentinian body politic. Much day-to-day reporting is preoccupied with the doings of the high and mighty in various walks of life. The activities of the royal family (and other members of the aristocracy) are lovingly detailed and the words of certain (acceptable) politicians accorded pride of place on any topic from which they choose to descant.

The reporting of political events concentrates on the immediate, with a marked absence of background analysis. Hence, for example, an IRA bomb is news, portrayed as entirely unrelated to the long-term suppression of the Catholics in Ulster. Yet the coverage of political news is as scanty as the clothing on the models pouting from the pictures.

Behind all reporting is a continuing subliminal pro-capitalist hum; marauding tycoons (including the owners of the papers) are portrayed as charismatic buccaneers rather than greedy bullies. The Labour Party and trade union leaders are regularly mocked, given demeaning nicknames, and featured in carefully selected photographs which make them appear funny, ridiculous, or demented. In contrast, Conservative politicians, and other establishment figures, tend to be accorded great gravitas. The *Mirror* may be distinguished to the extent that it favours the right wing of the Labour Party to the Conservatives, but it is equally harsh on the left.

> The Times has made many ministries. When, as of late, there has been a long continuence of divided Parliaments, of governments which were without 'brute voting power', and which depended upon intellectual strength, the most influential organ of English opinion has been of critical moment.
>
> Walter Bagehot (1826–77; political journalist), *The English Constitution*
> (1867: ch. 1)

Hence, we read as 'news' that which other people feel it fit to print, and the crucial exercise of journalistic discretion does not randomly favour all sections of society equally. To understand the reasons for this it is necessary to examine press ownership, journalists, and the extent to which the press is subject to regulation.

Ownership

The proud boast that the British press is not owned or controlled by the state must be countered with the observation that it lies squarely in establishment hands. Never widely dispersed, ownership narrowed down even further during the post-war era.

The celebrated *Times*, founded in 1785, was not intended to be read by the masses and, though inescapably an organ of the establishment (a 'parish magazine' for the upper classes, recording their births, marriages and obituaries), it claimed for much of its life to be a newspaper of national record (offering an objective, definitive account of events). The rise of the 'popular' papers followed the extension of adult literacy at the end of the nineteenth century with the creation of the *Daily Mail* (1896), *Daily Express* (1900), *Daily Mirror* (1903) and *Daily Sketch* (1908). These were the first mass-circulation papers and were to generate vast revenues from advertising, thereby keeping down the price. They were owned by private individuals who became formidable **'press barons'**, wielding awesome power. Their position was regularly recognized by elevation to the peerage: Alfred Harmsworth of the *Mirror*, *Mail* and *The Times* (regarded as the father of modern journalism), became Lord Northcliffe, his younger brother Harold, who took over the *Mail* on his death, became Lord Rothermere, and the Canadian Max Aitken of the *Express*, became Lord Beaverbrook. A second generation of press barons included Cecil Harmsworth King, nephew of Lord Northcliffe, who hugely expanded the family empire into the world of magazines and television. A rival empire was the Thompson organization headed by Lord Thompson of Fleet, a Canadian who had expanded his interests from Canada to Scotland, where he had become a millionaire through commercial television. He bought the *Sunday Times* in 1959, and *The Times* in 1966.

> I run the *Daily Express* purely for propaganda and for no other purpose.
>
> Lord Beaverbrook, to the Royal Commission on the Press (1948)

Modern concentrated ownership is in the classical advanced capitalist model, with complex multinational conglomerates combining diverse interests in electronic communications, broadcasting, cable TV and the leisure industry. This renders possible the sustaining of unprofitable newspapers by cross-subsidization for political reasons (Thompson 1982). The new-style media barons are typified in Robert Maxwell, the publisher who purchased the British Printing and Publishing Company (descended from the Harmsworth empire and including the *Daily Mirror*), and Rupert Murdoch of the mammoth News International which owns, amongst others, *The Times*, *Sunday Times*, *Financial Times*, *News of the World* and the notorious *Sun*. The *Observer* and *Today* were bought up by Tiny Rowlands's Lonrho, a mighty multinational with no previous interest in newspapers. (An exception to the rule is the *Independent*, founded in 1986 – a national newspaper owned by a consortium of its workers.) The concentration is even found in the so-called local press, once a basis for radical leadership, about 50 per cent of which has been progressively bought up by a few large companies (see figure 5.2).

> What the proprietorship of these papers is aiming at is power, and power without responsibility – the prerogative of the harlot throughout the ages.
>
> Stanley Baldwin (1867–1947; Conservative leader), attacking Lords Rothermere and Beaverbrook in an election speech (18 March 1931)

Owners have always exercised editorial control and both Maxwell and Murdoch continue the tradition. Upon buying the *Mirror* Maxwell declared: 'I have invested £90 million. There can only be one boss, and that is me' (Bower 1988). Murdoch conducted a continuing crusade in favour of the free-enterprise culture so close to the heart of 1980s Conservatism, even attempting to persuade his *Sun* readers that the notorious 1988 budget was in their interests with a headline 'Lots of Lovely Lolly'. When Lonrho engages in the controversial takeover battles which are its life-blood, the *Observer* is to be found, to the surprise of no one, lined up on the side of its paymaster, as in its fight over the ownership of Harrods.

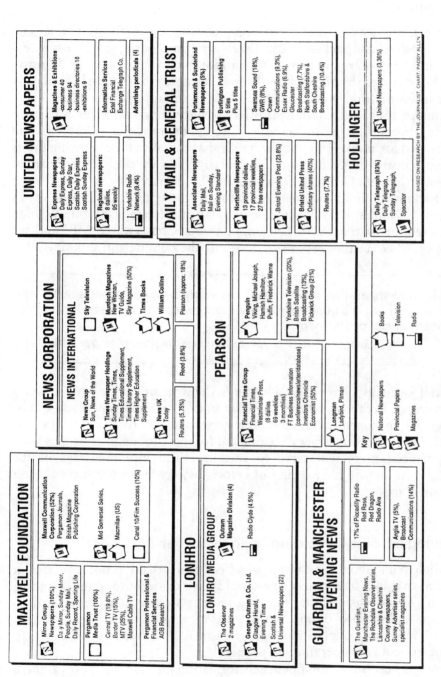

Figure 5.2   The empires of the media barons

Source: Guardian (12 June 1989, p. 21)

Journalists

Leading journalists, including editors, usually come from middle and upper-middle-class backgrounds. Establishment figures, particularly ex-government ministers, frequently turn to journalism as a sideline: Winston Churchill distinguished himself in the field, as does Roy Hattersley today. A career in journalism, with an inside track to the top, is one of the many glittering prizes the establishment offers bright young Oxbridge graduates. In their careers they get to know leading figures in the arts, business and politics, and are unlikely to bite the hands that can offer them enticing titbits of useful information. Editors in particularly live very close to the heart of the establishment. Geoffrey Dawson, for 29 years editor of *The Times*, moved comfortably in the country houses of the upper classes; one of his successors, William Rees-Mogg, was a pillar of the establishment; William Deedes, editor of the *Daily Telegraph*, was a Conservative MP; and his successor, Max Hastings, seems to personify the hunting and shooting set.

[Journalists are] nameless men and women whose scandalously low payment is a guarantee of their ignorance and their servility to the financial department.

George Bernard Shaw, *Commonsense About the War* (1914)

Even if journalists have radical leanings, the structure of the news industry will largely neuter them. Editors can alter stories, career advancement can be blocked by management and, in the final analysis, recalcitrants can be sacked. The process of career development for those of humbler origins from the provincial press will serve to socialize them into the ways of the establishment or will filter them out before they reach the precincts of Fleet Street or Wapping.

Behaving sensibly: avoiding lying in the sun

The whole point about the concept of a free press is that it is not *regulated*. It is argued that in a free society one should have the right to 'publish and be damned'. Those who feel they have a grievance are free to make recourse to the courts and the laws of libel. This, however, runs up against the problems of most 'freedoms' offered under capitalism: it is a freedom for the rich, offering but cold comfort to most people.

There has been some attempt at self-regulation through the Press Council, a body of laymen and editorial and managerial representatives from within the industry, set up on a voluntary basis in 1963 to protect their freedom, hear complaints, chastise malefactors for misreporting and so on. However, this is generally agreed to be a toothless watchdog, and has been made

JUSTICE and the PRESS

Reproduced by permission of *Punch*

something of a mockery by tabloid reporters plumbing depths of unprofessionalism (fabrication of 'news', malicious character assassination of public figures) that other newspapers could not reach. However, rivals have not been slow to follow the coach and horses driven by News International through the Press Council's gate and, to add insult to injury, individuals castigated by the Council, far from being damaged, have actually gained promotion in their careers.

The commercial activities of the press barons can be examined by the Monopolies and Mergers Commission (MMC). However, although there have been some token investigations into the voracious activities of the conglomerate juggernauts, these have failed to halt their march. The parlous state of the newspaper industry often means that a takeover is more in the nature of a philanthropic rescue than a predatory operation and an investigation is seen as a rather impertinent examination of the teeth of a gift horse. To prevent the takeover would kill the title altogether and reduce press plurality.

Of course, what freedom of the press means in a class society is the freedom of the wealthy to manipulate the ideas and attitudes of the masses, providing a leverage on the polity regardless of which party is in power. It is only in times of crisis that the state overtly demands that the press becomes its instrument. In two world wars dishonest reporting was deemed necessary to stiffen the resolve of the working-class population to sacrifice their lives, and the newspaper barons were flatteringly brought into government to ensure their cooperation.

Broadcasting

Although radio is by no means dead, television has become the organ of a truly mass culture in Britain. Its power over minds is Orwellian, a fact testified to in advertisers' willingness to contribute millions of pounds to the coffers of the commercial companies. It can sell anything from soap powder to soap opera and is recognized by politicians as a searing spotlight which can heighten their fretful hour on the political stage, or consume them like moths near a candle flame. Margaret Thatcher made mastery of the medium her first priority. In news reporting, the projection of visual images suggests a reality greater than that of the printed word, defying scepticism and compelling belief.

Consequently television is a major factor in British politics, completely transforming the nature of elections, giving an immediacy to political debate, creating a cult of personality politics hiding the true nature of issues from the masses, helping to transform the executive, reducing the role of Parliament, and projecting the monarchy into a new era of political theatre. It has become the principal means whereby people gain the information which forms their perception of the political world (Glasgow University Media Group 1976). Figure 5.3 shows that the working class have a greater propensity to view, though in all classes the habit is increasing.

Unlike the press, broadcasters are not permitted freedom of expression; there are mechanisms for control based on two regulatory bodies: the British

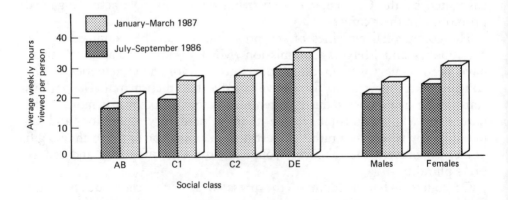

Figure 5.3 Television viewing by social class and gender

Source: Social Trends (1988: chart 10.4)

Broadcasting Corporation (BBC) and the Independent Broadcasting Authority (IBA). Members of these are selected by the government from the bosom of the establishment and require no particular expertise or knowledge of broadcasting, or indeed of anything else. They lie within the British tradition of amateurism where, in the old cliché, who you know is rather more important than what you know. Although their roles are different, each delegates matters of day-to-day operation to a Director General whom they appoint.

The BBC is seen as a particularly venerable public institution (affectionately known within establishment circles as 'Auntie'). It came into existence in 1927 as the successor to a private pioneer, the British Broadcasting Company. It has a Royal Charter to broadcast and is financed independently of the Treasury through licence fees paid by consumers. In its early years, under its legendary Director General, Sir John (later Lord) Reith, the BBC built up a reputation for elitism, pomposity, and sycophancy towards the institutions of the state, particularly the monarchy. (It became so much an arm of the establishment that it resembled a crusty government department, a veritable ministry of culture, where wireless news readers, though invisible to their audience, wore evening dress, the uniform of the upper class.) The development of television has lessened this, though vestiges remain, as in the reverent tones of commentators at great state or sporting occasions (if attended by royalty), such as the Lord Mayor's parade or Royal Ascot.

The BBC began television broadcasting from Alexandra Palace in 1936 and by 1966 was transmitting to virtually the whole of the country. It enjoyed a comfortable monopoly until a traumatic challenge came in the form of commercial television. If the BBC stood for the high Tory element within the ruling class, commercial television was to stand for its thrusting, free-marketeering spirit. In 1954, after prolonged political infighting among various factions within the upper class (Wilson 1961), the ITA (later to become the IBA) was created by the Conservative government. It had the responsibility of licensing and granting (renewable) franchises to private companies broadcasting on a regional basis and financed by advertising. The ITA's patronage was regal, and the franchise to operate commercial television was described by Lord Thompson (who became a millionaire by so doing) as a 'licence to print money'.

With the creation of commercial television a new kind of media baron appeared (typified in the gigantic personality of Sidney Bernstein of the Granada empire) from the world of capitalism and competition. They recognized that the companies could only attract the life-blood of advertising by building up mass audiences, which did little to raise cultural standards. The BBC, though free of this restraint, felt obliged to ape the populist strategy, so that *ratings wars* raged continually. Popular submissiveness was reinforced with soap operas, inane quiz shows, and other vulgar forms of entertainment. Although the regional structure of commercial television implies plurality, in fact the biggest companies belong to massive leisure and media conglomerates. Most major programmes made by the regional companies are intended for national transmission through a networking system and the main news programmes come from London.

Subsequent developments in broadcasting included breakfast TV, commercial and BBC regional sound broadcasting, and the establishment of a second commercial channel, Channel Four, a wholly owned subsidiary of the IBA. This managed to stay out of the ever-downwards spiral, even permitting the airing of some non-orthodox points of view, including features with a more than usually left-wing orientation and gay programmes. The future of television promises to be even more turbulent with the advent of more channels, the use of satellite dishes to receive foreign programmes, and cable TV, all to be largely controlled by the very same media kings who own the existing companies and the press.

The impartiality requirement

Both the BBC and the IBA are formally required in their charters to be **impartial** in their presentation of news. However, this means impartiality between the political parties and opposing interest groups, it does not mean any general impartiality between social classes. Indeed there is a consistent anti-working-class bias in news programmes which has been demonstrated by the Glasgow University Media Group in an extended systematic study since 1976. In industrial disputes the spokesmen for the upper classes (management or state) tend to receive deferential treatment and are allowed to define the terms of the debate. In contrast, union leaders are often interviewed in a hostile manner, in a setting likely to detract from their dignity (a jostling picket line, for example).

The apparent balance is really a contrived political debate where, in spite of seemingly heated exchanges, all points of view actually fit within a consensus acceptable to the establishment. Although it can be argued that this merely reflects a natural conservatism within British politics, it is equally likely that it contributes to it. In the structuring of political debate (deciding what can and cannot be said) the broadcasting media influence, not day-to-day decisions between left or right, but the scent in the cultural air we breathe. Views outside the narrow central orthodoxy are rendered 'loony' and even 'unpatriotic'.

Television journalists

Television journalists are generally drawn from the ranks of the press and consequently have the same characteristics and propensities. Indeed, the need to appear respectable before the camera puts a particular premium on an accent which can only be acquired at great expense outside the state school system. This tendency towards upper-class domination is strengthened by the high kudos associated with television careers amongst the young and it is a prized niche for Oxbridge graduates. It is interesting that the few black television journalists speak with particularly impeccable upper-class English accents.

Whenever it appears that the establishment cannot count on the kind of

Reproduced by permission of *Punch*

reportage desired, the underlying conviction that broadcasters should be subservient to the state is forced out into the open, making a mockery of the claims of independence with overt and covert political interference.

Political interference

There are certain formal means whereby governments may influence the media, including the D-Notice system, the lobby system, and the Official Secrets Act (see chapter 12). However, of far greater importance is informal pressure. The powerful do not need actively to control the broadcasters, they can rely on their sympathy. John Reith laid down the ground rules at the time of the General Strike (1926), recording in his diary that the government 'know that they can trust us not to be really impartial' (Stuart 1975: 96). He suppressed news which the government did not want broadcast, establishing that 'the vaunted independence of the BBC was secure so long as it was not exercised' (Taylor 1965: 246).

The BBC's unwillingness to displease was demonstrated in 1962 when the programme *That Was The Week That Was* introduced a level of popular satire hitherto unseen. Its style was little more than that of an Oxbridge undergraduate revue, part of the middle-class movement which generated *Beyond the Fringe* and the magazine *Private Eye*, and its stars and producer were from that same environment. However, gamekeepers made effective poachers, and the programme startled deferential working-class viewers reared on the unctuous tones of Richard Dimbleby. Amongst other things it stirred up the Profumo scandal, made the Macmillan government uncomfortable, and disturbed the establishment generally. As a result the Director General, Hugh Carlton Greene, lost his nerve and the programme was taken off at the end of the year on the blatant pretext of an impending general election, which did not actually materialize until 1964.

The BBC and its Director General are responsible for day-to-day management and are ultimately answerable to the Board of Governors, consisting of government appointees, with formidable powers to hire and fire. Generally, a cautious policy of appointment reduces the need for sacking, but should an incumbent decide, like Becket or Sir Thomas More, to turn from his official patron and serve a higher god, their martyrdom can be speedily effected. The 1980s saw the Thatcher government roused to fury, culminating on 29 January 1987 with the sacking of Director General Alasdair Milne. This move was foreshadowed in the menacing appointment of Thatcherite Marmaduke Hussey as Chairman of the Board of Governors for the purpose

---

We all know that Ingham [Thatcher's press secretary] spends his time manipulating the press.

Frank Dobson (shadow leader of the Commons), quoted in the
Independent (11 Jan. 1989)

of stamping out suspected leftist sympathies in the BBC, and it was he who delivered the *coup de grace* (Milne 1988).

Informal pressure became much more intense in the 1980s when, from the first, the Thatcher government felt that the media were failing to observe an appropriate degree of subservience, quickly diagnosing the problem of too many liberals in the establishment kitchen. During the Falklands war the government, mindful of the effect that reporting of the Vietnam war had had on the American public (exposing the falsity of government accounts and the horror of the enterprise, effectively ending the war), restricted the broadcasting of news of the British task force and would not permit the rapid transmission of television pictures to British audiences (Select Committee on Defence 1982: xiv).

In 1985, in a rather disreputable behind-the-scenes manoeuvre, pressure was placed on the Board of Governors by Home Secretary Leon Brittan, leading to the cancellation of a *Real Lives* programme which included an interview with a convicted IRA 'terrorist'. Even a fictional drama, *The Monocled Mutineer*, offended patriotic taste and was castigated by government. In 1986 Norman Tebbit weighed in with heavily intimidatory tactics against the BBC and their reporter Kate Adie for her temerity in reporting the launching of the US attack on Libya from Britain in non-jingoistic terms. His attack sought to call in question her professionalism and damage her career and sent a shudder down the spines of all journalists. Only the stout-hearted (without mortgages and children to maintain at private schools) would be inclined to risk such wrath, which was no doubt the real purpose of the broadside. In 1988 a radio series examining the security services, *My Country Right or Wrong*, was banned, only to be broadcast later when found to be harmless.

> What changed between January and March 1987 was not the facts or the quality of the programme but the scale to which the [BBC] governors' political and personal views intruded into the corporation's whole management.
>
> Duncan Campbell, referring to the banning of his controversial programme *Cabinet*, quoted in the *Independent* (30 April 1988)

As a further means of bringing the BBC to heel the government began to consider undermining its finances. There was talk of introducing advertising to remove the independence of the licence fee system, thus tying the BBC more closely to the structural constraints of capitalism. However, the report of the Peacock Commission on broadcasting was to disappoint the government by supporting the status quo. By the late 1980s government intimidation had made the BBC extremely nervous about causing offence. It had even decided to cancel a play criticizing the handling of the Falklands conflict (eventually transmitted some time later), beginning to concentrate on safer targets like battles within the Labour Party and the weakness of Neil Kinnock as its leader.

In 1988 a Broadcasting Standards Authority was established under the chairmanship of a pillar of the establishment, ex-editor of *The Times*, Sir William Rees-Mogg. The government insisted it would be concerned only with standards of decency and not interfere with the political content of current affairs programmes, though opponents feared that once established it would be but a small matter to extend its remit. The appointment of the right-wing Lord Chalfont as a Deputy Chairman of the IBA in 1989 was also seen by critics as overtly political and was said to indicate the lengths to which the establishment was prepared to go to bring about biased broadcasting (*Sunday Telegraph*, 19 Feb. 1989). However, as Richard Hoggart has pointed out, it cannot be assumed that there are no people in broadcasting for whom the goal of genuine neutrality is real (Glasgow University Media Group 1976: xii). Some courageous reporting shows that the independence of the broadcasting media is real, but can never be taken for granted.

Conclusion: Mind Politics

The philosopher David Hume said that 'beauty in things exists in the mind which contemplates them'. **Mind politics** seeks to make the British pattern of existing privileges seem beautiful in the mind of the mass; to lead people to believe that they are not exploited and that profound inequality in most aspects of their lives is a natural and good thing. Although all inegalitarian polities must achieve this if they are to survive, none has done so as smoothly as Britain. Our exploration of how this great psychological balancing act is accomplished has begun in this chapter but it has not ended; it must continue throughout the book for it is part of the genius of the British political system.

Key points

- In order for a polity to function there must be some broad consensus on its desirability; it must enjoy legitimacy. Thus there is a mental, as well as a behavioural, dimension to the study of politics. This mental climate is sometimes termed the political culture.
- People's attitudes towards politics are developed through a process of political socialization.
- There are various agents of political socialization. The important ones identified in this chapter include the family, the school, the church, the arts, advertising and the mass media.
- It is in the interests of those with wealth and power to lead others to share their own views of what this consensus should be; that is, to share their ideology.
- There are many ways in which the powerful can influence the process of political socialization (through control of education, the media, use of adver-

tising techniques, and so on). This can be seen as a manifestation of the hegemony of the dominant class.

- This hegemony is not absolute; ideologies contrary to the one favoured by the dominant establishment interests may circulate. In the 1980s the Church of England revised its traditional stance to become a centre for ideological dissent.
- Politics can thus be seen as a fight for the minds of people as well as for material things.

Review your understanding of the following terms and concepts

political socialization   press baron
free press   broadcasting impartiality
press partisanship   mind politics

Assignment

Study the extract from the *Guardian* on p. 154 and answer the following questions.

		% mark
1	Consider whether statements by church leaders are likely to have any impact on government policy.	10
2	Construct a reasoned defence against the bishop's attack on the 'simplistic idolatry of an all-embracing abstract entity called the market'.	30
3	'Church leaders should refrain from making overtly political statements.' Discuss.	40
4	What effect do you think a politically outspoken church has on the political culture?	20

Questions for discussion

1 Identify the main agents of political socialization in Britain and discuss their relative importance.
2 'Socialization in Britain has consisted essentially of removing the will of ordinary people to question existing norms.' Discuss.
3 'A political culture is more clearly manifest in people's behaviour than it is in what they say in response to questionnaires.' Discuss.
4 Is the concept of a free press compatible with the freedom of individuals and multinational corporations to own newspapers?
5 'Crusading journalists cannot expect to get very far in a system where newspapers are largely financed by capitalist advertising.' Discuss.
6 'The news is not news until its appears in *The Times*.' Examine the political implications of this statement.
7 'The independence of the BBC is secure so long as it is not exercised.' Discuss with reference to British politics in the 1980s.

Bishop hits at 'selfish' Thatcherism

David Brindle
Social Services Correspondent

THE Bishop of Durham, Dr David Jenkins, yesterday publicly attacked Mrs Thatcher's belief that social advance depends on senior churchmen setting a moral lead.

He also strongly criticised the Government's faith in the market and the sovereignty and resilience of the individual.

"Three terms of a Thatcherite government cannot wipe out, even if it tries to ignore, what has been learned and demonstrated about our human and social inter-dependence," he said.

"The budget has, I believe, declared that the Thatcherite answer to socialism is selfishness. We have to find a better way of living . . . for the sake of humaneness and for the sake of humanity."

Dr Jenkins was addressing a conference in Newcastle upon Tyne of the British Association of Social Workers. He said the role of social workers was under threat as society wrestled with the conflicting questions of caring for the individual and interfering in his life.

At the same time, there was deepening despair about care for the poor. "There is no pretence, I think now, of giving any sort of priority to caring through the political and social system.

"Caring must come from that private charity and private morality, which can in no way be influenced or contributed to by politicians or by the manipulations of economics, but must come from strong moral leads given by people like bishops and chief rabbis.

"Money is for those who can make it. And those who cannot make it must not be allowed to get in the way of its being made."

Later, Dr Jenkins confirmed he had been referring to the recently disclosed meeting at Chequers, at which Mrs Thatcher had invited him and 11 other bishops to discuss the Church's role in setting moral standards. He said he was glad the issue was now in the open.

In his address, he said the "simplistic idolatry of an all-embracing abstract entity called the market" had no chance of forging a sustainable society.

It was nonsense for some groups in society to pretend that free individual choice was available to those affected by ill-health, old age, mental or educational handicap or family affliction. "The Government has no concern for individuals as such — only for those individuals who can do well under the auspices of enterprise consumerism."

Guardian, 24 March 1988

Topic for debate

This house believes that the idea of the free press is nothing more than a useful myth.

    or

The British education system cannot provide 'education for leadership' unless it

also provides 'training for submission'.
       or
The British have the press they deserve.

Further reading

Cockerell, M., Hennessy, P. and Walker, P. (1984) *Sources Close to the Prime Minister: Inside the Hidden World of the News Manipulators.*
Written from an insider perspective, the title says it all.

Dennis, J., Lindberg, L. and McCrone, D. J. (1971) 'Support for nation and government amongst English schoolchildren', *British Journal of Political Science*, 1(1), 25–48.
Claimed, debatably, that English schoolchildren were less supportive of the political system than those in other countries.

Glasgow University Media Group (1976) *Bad News*, (1980) *More Bad News*, (1982) *Really Bad News*.
A relentless empirical examination of British styles of television news reporting, exposing a consistent bias in favour of the 'respectable' establishment interests.

Hollingsworth, M. (1986) *The Press and Discontent: a Question of Censorship.*
Details an alarming right-wing bias in the press.

Jenkins, S. (1986) *The Market for Glory: Fleet Street Ownership in the Twentieth Century.*
Asks why certain men have the desire to own newspapers, finding the answer not in profit, but in the quest for influence and glory.

Piven, F. and Cloward, R. (1972) *Regulating the Poor.*
Shows how in a capitalist society the welfare state can serve a socializing function.

Seaton, J. and Pimlot, B. (eds) (1987) *The Media in British Politics.*
A book of essays discussing most of the important issues in this area and calling for greater attention from political scientists.

For light relief

Barry Hines, *Kes.*
Goes into the mind of a working-class boy, and the narrow world it is permitted to perceive.

Evelyn Waugh, *Scoop.*
A satire on contemporary journalism.

Orson Welles, *Citizen Kane.*
A classic film exploring the motives of a newspaper baron.

Henrik Ibsen, *An Enemy of the People.*
Shows how mass opinion is turned against a man trying to put their collective good against the interests of capitalism.

6

The Electoral System:
Parsimonious Democracy

In this chapter we scrutinize the machinery supposed to make Britain a democracy, the means whereby ordinary citizens formally participate in politics. The chapter has five principal sections. The first addresses the underlying concept of **representative democracy** and outlines the mechanics of the electoral system. In the second section we examine a vital part of British political history, the **evolution of the electoral system** and the **extension of the franchise**. The next section turns to **voting behaviour**, asking why people vote, why some vote against their apparent economic interests, and why some vote in a stable manner while others are more volatile. We examine the British electorate as a whole and analyse the way it has changed, noting the impact, and relative importance, of race, gender and class. We then look at the behaviour of politicians during the **election campaign**, one of the most visible and symbolic events in modern politics. We conclude with an analysis of a great electoral divide cutting deep fissures into the political map and consider certain critical problems in the British electoral system, including the issue of **electoral reform**.

Representative Democracy

Democracy

Over three hundred years before the birth of Christ, Ancient Greece consisted of many small self-governing city-states. These adopted a variety of methods and institutional frameworks for conducting public affairs, and the thinkers of the time were presented with a unique laboratory for the empirical study of government. As we saw in chapter 1, many of these philosophers, particularly the Athenians, saw democracy – rule by the people – as the most desirable form of government, a belief which they bequeathed to modern civilization.

Democracy and representative government

In order to be entirely democratic a system of government should permit all citizens to take part in the making of public policy. There have been examples of such **direct democracy**: the Greek city-states made some provision for it and in early parish government in Britain all members of the community would meet in the church precincts to make decisions about their roads, bridges, matters of law and order, and so on. The government of the small communities formed by the New England settlers in America was also widely participative in character, while today the Swiss cantons (small units of local government) make provision for local citizens to be involved in decision-making. However, direct democracy is generally an impractical form of government.

The Greek city-states were very small and intimate, covering areas of around 30 square miles and usually with fewer than 20,000 citizens. Citizenship was restricted by means of slave status for many, while abortion, infanticide, and a liberal attitude towards homosexual relationships ensured population control. Yet even these polities were too large to govern themselves purely on the basis of direct democracy. A mass forum cannot conduct the kind of deliberation and analysis necessary for public decision-making and the function must be entrusted to a smaller group. If the democratic ideal is to be protected, the choice and accountability of these becomes of supreme importance. The Greek city-states attempted to do this variously with provisions for popular discussion, deliberation, voting, office-holding by rotation, and various forms of penalty for unsatisfactory officials. In Athens people would elect candidates to a large panel, from which the office-holders would be selected by drawing lots, giving each an equal chance. The Greeks believed that those like Macbeth, with 'high-vaulting ambition', who thrust themselves forward for high office, would be the most unsuitable.

In these early constitutional means of approximating the democratic ideal we see the origins of **representative government**. Although a state may be run by a small group of rulers, not unlike a monarchy or an aristocracy, they are not there by virtue of any personal right (birth, wealth, religious status, physical might, or even intelligence), but as *representatives* of everyone else. When they act, they do so in the name of the people, and the people retain the right to control and even remove them.

Representative government in Britain

Although Britain formally has a system of representative democracy based on elections, it falls a very long way short of the models devised by the Athenians. Indeed, for a long time it was believed by the ruling establishment that only a relatively small proportion of the population should be allowed to vote. Ordinary people were said to enjoy 'virtual representation', meaning that the aristocracy could be assumed to take the views of all classes into consideration when making decisions. However, the right to vote (the franchise) was gradually extended as a result of the willingness of radical leaders to fight for what they believed to be their rights. Those who regarded themselves as the ruling class became fearful of the possible consequences of mass rule and were obliged to think of new ways to limit democracy.

In the first place, they limited representation by ensuring that working-class people would find it very difficult to enter Parliament by keeping MPs unpaid, charging electoral deposits, refusing to adopt them as candidates, developing party machines to fight elections, and generally inhibiting the rise of a working-class party (see chapter 7). In addition, they developed a special, highly elitist theory of representation in which MPs were supposed to act according to their own discretion without any particular regard for the views of constituents. The idea had received its most authoritative enunciation by Edmund Burke (1729–97) in a famous address to his constituents in Bristol, when he stressed that what they were to expect from him was not servitude, but the exercise of his own 'judgement and conscience'. This view remains deeply ingrained in British political culture, part of the all-important machinery of deference in which the masses forgo their right to influence the high and mighty. An alternative view of representation is that of the **mandate**, whereby election to office obliges one to fulfil promises made to win votes (the **manifesto**). In the reality of political life today we find both views coexisting, with politicians choosing the one which best suits their argument.

The Tamworth Manifesto

A set of electoral promises was first made in 1834 by the Conservative leader Peel, on an historic occasion when he addressed the 586 electors of his Tamworth constituency. The 'Tamworth Manifesto', marked a new style of campaigning based on the notion of a mandate.

The electoral process today

The modern electoral process, pared down to its essentials, entails voters, constituencies and candidates.

1 *The voters.* Today Britain has a **universal franchise**. With certain exceptions (peers, aliens, bankrupts, imprisoned criminals, people of unsound mind, and those guilty of electoral malpractice) all citizens over the age of 18 are eligible to vote.

2 *The constituencies.* The basis for representation is spatial; MPs represent divisions of the country, termed **constituencies** (there are 650, including 17 in Northern Ireland), and a general election is in effect a number of simultaneous contests electing one member for each area. In theory, constituency populations should tend towards equality (at around 66,000). To reflect population change, the overall pattern is monitored by Boundary Commissions, independent bodies chaired by the Speaker of the House of Commons, which recommend changes every 10–15 years. These can have important political consequences. Recent readjustments in the inner cities to take account of declining populations have wounded Labour, and the party opposed the 1979 proposals, even taking the matter to court.

3 *The candidates.* Almost any resident British citizen over 21 (not 18) may stand; the excluded are those not eligible to vote, members of the police force and armed forces, certain civil servants, judges and ordained clergymen. Virtually all candidates clothe themselves in the garb of a party, which they gain through selection by the local party organization. Each candidate must formally appoint an agent, who ensures compliance with electoral law. In addition, the agent will probably be the campaign manager (organizing press conferences and so on). Agents are usually faithful party supporters, well versed in the arts of political intrigue.

The main electoral event in British politics is a general election, which follows a number of stages.

1 *Naming the day.* The election date is not fixed by law, a government's term of office is merely subject to a five-year maximum. This gives the Prime Minister the undemocratic advantage of effectively choosing the election date by dissolving Parliament at the most politically convenient time. Mrs Thatcher finely judged the 1983 battle to capitalize on the 'Oh what a lovely Falklands war' factor.

2 *The campaign.* In the run-up to the election, candidates and parties conduct publicity campaigns designed to woo voters. These take an increasingly sophisticated form (see pp. 179–81).

3 *Determining the result.* Voting in Britain, unlike that in many other countries, is the essence of simplicity, voters being merely required to mark an 'X' alongside the name of a candidate. The one with the largest number of votes – the **'first past the post'** is the winner. In this **simple plurality** system the absolute number of votes is immaterial; MPs are regularly returned with well below 50 per cent.

4 *Forming the government.* A general election ultimately results in the emergence of a government, formed from the party with an **absolute majority** (over half the seats) in the House of Commons. In a two-party system a simple majority will necessary be absolute, but with more parties complications set in; the emergence of a *hung Parliament* (with no party able to govern alone) becomes possible, and politicians have to retire to smoke-filled rooms to consider coalitions (or minority governments). In

Show of hands for a Liberal candidate, 1842
Source: Mary Evans Picture Library

1974 the narrowly defeated Prime Minister Edward Heath (with 297 seats) conducted a tentative and ultimately abortive flirtation with the Liberals (14 seats) before conceding defeat to Labour (301 seats). Conditions of uncertainty are not as foreign to British politics as is sometimes suggested – the period 1914–45 involved some form of coalition or minority government for all but nine years.

By-elections

Sometimes elections are called in particular constituencies owing to the death or retirement of a sitting member. These are termed by-elections, and are interesting for various reasons. They provide opinion polls upon which the popularity of a government and its policies may be assessed and allow minority parties to shine. They also stimulate political debate and are hyped up by the media, sometimes suffering mid-term blues. However, they provide a poor guide to long-term trends. Invariably the party in power will fare badly as a result of a 'protest vote' from those wishing to administer a 'kick in the pants' without actually unseating the government, and the minority parties sometimes dramatically elected are usually returned to the wilderness come the next general election.

However, the bare essentials of the process as outlined above do not reveal its problems and defects and give little sense of politics. In the rest of this chapter we shall consider these more interesting matters.

Economizing with Democracy: Evolution of the Electoral System

The evolution of Britain's electoral system is not a boring account of legalistic reform, nor a psephological nightmare of figures, swings and majorities, but a story of violence and political struggle in which the prize was hegemony over the state. Reforms were not based on rational thought, nor an enlightened desire for democracy on the part of the powerful; they were born of a slow and painful political labour.

The motive behind the electoral reform movement was a belief (perhaps misguided), prevalent since the seventeenth century amongst those wishing to secure social and political change, that entry into the House of Commons would advance their ambitions (Miliband 1984: 20–1). This meant that there was no fundamental challenge to rock the constitutional boat and British history was more tranquil than it might otherwise have been.

A democratic travesty

At the beginning of the nineteenth century the system was a democratic travesty. Of a total population of 16 million, a mere 400,000 were eligible to vote in parliamentary elections. Of the two chambers in Parliament, one (the House of Lords) was reserved for those of noble birth and the other (the House of Commons) was largely peopled on the basis of patronage and corruption. MPs came from two types of constituency: *counties* showed no consistency in size or population, but each returned two MPs, with the right to vote tied to landownership, while *boroughs* were towns which had at some time been granted royal charters entitling them to members of Parliament. In the latter the rights of franchise varied widely and, although in some there was almost universal male suffrage (right to vote), the scope for malpractice was considerable. In the so-called 'rotten boroughs', the population had shrunk since the days of medieval splendour so that a mere handful of citizens enjoyed an absurd right to an MP (Dunwich had fallen into the sea and Old Sarum had a population of zero). In 'pocket' boroughs, rich landowners were able to control elections through threats and bribery, while the new thriving and populous industrial towns, many with highly efficient local government institutions, remained starved of representation. Furthermore, voting was not secret, and candidature was restricted to the wealthy since MPs were obliged to be entirely self-financing. As a result, Parliament was held securely in the grip of a landed establishment.

Forces for change

In common with most other institutions, the electoral system was transformed to suit the purposes of the new bourgeoisie spawned by the industrial revolution. In the early stages of industrialization the aristocracy had shared some interests with the bourgeoisie as the railways scored the surface of their land and the mines burrowed beneath, and paid for the privilege of so doing. However, this congruence of fortune withered. For the emergent order the archaic practices of law, administration, and indeed government, were not the cherished legacies praised by Burke, but barriers to enterprise, trade and social advancement. The clash was typified in the 1815 corn law, which blatantly favoured landed interests over commerce. The bourgeoisie realized that the parliamentary compost required some more earthy additives before it could be sufficiently fertile for the bloom of private enterprise.

Justifying claims for a stronger voice in Parliament through the utilitarian philosophy propounded by Philosophic Radicals such as Jeremy Bentham and James Mill, they called for representative government through rational and fair elections. These noble sentiments were really intended to serve bourgeois class interests, but to promote reform they required allies, whom they found in the bottom half of the curious social sandwich in which they were squeezed. Here was a class which they themselves had, as Marx said, 'called into existence', whose potential for insurrection, made more ominous by the chilling excesses of the French revolution, threatened the social order. It offered a force which, if harnessed, could drive the piston of reform as well as the steam which drove their industry.

Working-class agitation Napoleon's defeat at Waterloo in 1815 had produced little relief from the misfortunes that war had heaped upon the poor. Economic slump, the return of soldiers, and Irish immigration produced unemployment, destitution and rising costs. In the resulting social unrest, the workers, with little idea what the solutions to their troubles might be, were willing to accept the leadership of middle-class radicals working for a reform which promised them a voice in Parliament.

Radical agitation operated on a number of fronts, involving the formation of Hampden Clubs (named after a great seventeenth-century parliamentarian), radical city newspapers, strikes, marches, mass meetings, and political discussion classes to prepare ordinary people for rule.

The Representation of the People Act 1832

Although working-class agitation was easily suppressed by state violence (as in the Peterloo Massacre in 1819), voters felt that the Whigs were better able to reduce the tension in the long term. In 1830 they were returned to government after almost 50 years of continuous Tory rule. The scene appeared set for a democratic revolution, but once in office they revealed no less a respect for property than the Tories. The difference lay only in their view that factories, machines, raw materials, and even the urban labour force, could represent property as well as rolling acres in the countryside. In the 1832 Reform Act many small boroughs lost their members and seats were redistributed to the more populous counties and new urban kingdoms where the bourgeoisie reigned. However, the size of the electorate was not greatly increased (from around 500,000 to only just over 700,000), corruption was not eliminated, and wealthy individuals could still exert undue control.

The working class gained nothing. The franchise was parsimoniously extended only to middle-class property-owners (valued at £10 a year), MPs remained unpaid, and potential candidates faced a prohibitive property qualification. Of course, the Whigs had never wanted popular democracy; they had dreamed only of a prudent middle-class control over Parliament from which they could command their empire of trade at home and around the world.

The Chartist movement

The radicals' disappointment led to bitterness, violence and renewed calls for electoral reform. In 1836 William Lovett formed the London Working

Men's Association which drew up a *Charter* incorporating the following demands:

1   universal manhood suffrage;
2   annual election of Parliaments (to render the purchase of votes prohibitively expensive and give the electorate frequent opportunities to call their representative to account);
3   abolition of the property qualification for candidates;
4   payment for MPs (to enable the poor to stand);
5   equal-sized constituencies (to make all votes of equal weight);
6   secret ballot (to prevent intimidation).

The working class were now more receptive and working men's clubs developed under the name of **Chartism**. However, in response to Parliament's rejection of their demands, those within the movement who favoured violence rather than reasoned argument took the initiative. The government's reaction revealed it to be as willing as its Tory predecessors to use draconian methods involving imprisonment, vigilantes (special constables and spies) and the army. By the late 1840s Chartism was a spent force, battered by the power of the very state in whose government it wished peacefully to participate.

Demonstration for reform, Hyde Park, 1866
Source: Mary Evans Picture Library

The Representation of the People Act 1867

However, in the 1860s, partly as a result of unease over the American civil war, popular attention again focused upon electoral reform as a means of containing unrest. In 1866 a Liberal reform bill was defeated by a combination of its own rebels and Conservatives. The government resigned, to be replaced by a Conservative minority government led by Disraeli who, to the surprise of many, promptly introduced the 1867 reform bill. This dropped the restrictive property qualifications and enfranchised all male urban householders. In 1868, with around two and a quarter million eligible voters, it was possible to speak of a *mass electorate*. This had far-reaching consequences: to attract mass support and keep out working-class parties politicians were forced to think beyond the limited role hitherto assumed by government and take serious interest in social conditions, education, and the rights of trade unions.

> The politician who once had to learn how to flatter kings has now to learn how to fascinate, amuse, coax, humbug, frighten or otherwise strike the fancy of the electorate.
>
> George Bernard Shaw, *Man and Superman* (1905)

The 1867 Act further underscored the moral supremacy of the Commons over the Lords. It also marked the end of the ascendancy of Parliament over the executive. The so-called 'Golden Age', which began in 1832, was closed by the rise of disciplined parliamentary party cadres (see p. 197) affording ministers a grip over the legislature that would have been envied even by the Tudors. From this time the voters, not the House of Commons, would choose governments.

The full impact of the reforms could not really be felt without certain other measures. The 1872 Ballot Act made voting secret: workers were no longer placed in the position of risking their livelihood by voting against their employers. The Corrupt and Illegal Practices Act (1883) reduced the opportunity of the wealthy to use their financial muscle in influencing voters, and the following year the electorate was almost doubled by the Franchise Act. This introduced virtual universal male suffrage by extending the 1867 provisions to the rural constituencies. The Redistribution of Seats Act (1885) had the profound effect of making the working class a majority of the electorate (McKenzie and Silver 1968: 9). However, MPs were still not paid as such and voters were obliged to select from two competing factions of the elite, rather than choose genuine working-class representatives.

Votes for women

Throughout the reform era, the phrase 'one man, one vote' meant exactly that; women continued to be regarded by middle and working class alike as political ciphers. Though less documented than the fight for male rights, the struggle was an epic one, and the size of the incremental increase threatened to be considerably larger than any introduced before. This fact was contemplated with grim consternation by the male establishment and had much to do with the intensity of their resistance.

> The most important thing women have to do is to stir up the zeal of women themselves.
>
> J. S. Mill (1806–73; English philosopher), letter to Alexander Bain
> (14 July 1869)

The achievement of universal male franchise was a particularly potent catalyst. The idea of a middle-class male monopoly might have irked some of their wives, but extending the right to all males, regardless of social status, education, or degree of political sophistication, was infinitely more intolerable. In 1897 Millicent Fawcett founded the National Union of Women's Suffrage Societies, but her approach was too timid for some and in 1903 Emmeline Pankhurst (1858–1929) and her two daughters established the Women's Social and Political Union, which was to become the most famous instrument of the **suffragettes**.

> Women had always fought for men, and for their children. Now they were ready to fight for their own human rights.
>
> Emmeline Pankhurst (1858–1928; suffragette leader),
> *My Own Story* (1914)

The movement began with an emphasis on education and propaganda, but the pipe-smoking, leather-armchaired establishment and Asquith's Liberal government were uncompromising and prepared to employ the same powers of state force that had resisted the working class. Suffragettes were subject to indignity and violence, including ridicule, physical attack, forcible ejection from meetings, imprisonment and hard labour. Hunger strikers were sadistically force-fed through the nose, an ordeal leaving some permanently injured. To avoid creating martyrs the government passed the notorious 'Cat and Mouse' Act in 1913, enabling it to release weakened hunger strikers only to reimprison them upon recovery. Yet they could not prevent Emily Wilding Davison's dramatic martyrdom when, in the same year, she hurled herself under the galloping hooves of the King's horse in the Derby.

War and the franchise Where Asquith would not help the women the Kaiser could. The arrival of an enemy at the gate produced domestic truce and the Pankhursts rallied their supporters behind the flag. On 15 July they staged their final demonstration, marching down Whitehall to demand not the vote, but the 'right to serve'.

The result was the 1918 Representation of the People Act, which A. J. P. Taylor describes, with apparently unintended humour, as the victory 'of the radical principle of "one man one vote"' (1965: 94). However, enfranchisement still stopped short of full equality: men could vote from the age of 21, but fear of a radical vote among young women, engendered by socialist revolutions in Europe, reserved their participation to the mature over-30s. (This anomaly was not remedied until the 1928 Equal Franchise Act, which was followed by the 1929 Labour victory, thus justifying establishment fears.) Despite this, the extension still added more new voters than all previous franchise acts together. It also gave women the right to stand for Parliament, and later that year Lady Astor, amidst much ceremony, 'made history' as the first woman to enter the House, though the auspicious occasion did not mark the opening of any floodgates.

War also led some to muse on the anomaly that, while young people of just over 18 were required to fight and die for the government, they were not entitled to vote for it. It was not until the 1960s, with improvements in education at all levels, many more adolescents going up to universities, and a prevailing cult of the young, that Harold Wilson, in sympathy with the spirit of the age (to the shock of the establishment, the Beatles received MBEs), lowered the voting age to 18 in the 1969 Reform Act. However, his reward was rebuff in the next general election.

• • •

The extension of the franchise had been gradual and grudging. The effect of the 1832 Act was to give the vote to a mere 20 per cent of the men in England and Wales. After 1867 this became 33 per cent, reaching 67 per cent in 1884. Full adult franchise was withheld until 1918. No major concession was secured without the threat of violence and disruption and, even when secured, the extensions never precipitated the earth-shattering social consequences hoped for by the reformers and feared by the establishment. The explanation for this lies partly in the way the vote has been used; that is, in the electoral behaviour of the population. It is to this that we now turn.

Voting Behaviour

People voting

The Philosophical Radicals argued that if everyone voted, governments would be forced to rule for the good of all. This seemingly commonsense view causes the white ruling class of South Africa to quake, led the nineteenth-century bourgeoisie to fear 'mobocracy', and explains their reticence in extending the franchise. Yet universal franchise has not resulted in anything resembling the popular rule that might have been envisaged. This conundrum is partly explained by the curiously restricted (Burkean) notion of representative government developed by the dominant elite. It may also be explained in the way people have used the vote; that is, in their *electoral behaviour*, the study of which is known as **psephology**.

> The returns from voting are usually so low that even small costs [time, energy, etc.] may cause voters to abstain.
>
> A. Downs, *An Economic Theory of Democracy* (1957: 274)

Why do people vote? Since any single voter, even in a marginal constituency, has a negligible impact, it can be argued that a rational being would not vote at all, but would be better occupied tending pigeons, watching television or reading Shakespeare. Some countries (such as Australia) attempt to combat the disinclination to vote by making it compulsory, but the right to **abstain,** to say 'a plague on both your houses', is itself a democratic freedom. Despite this, the turnout in British general elections, though not up to the standard of most European polities, remains high (figure 6.1).

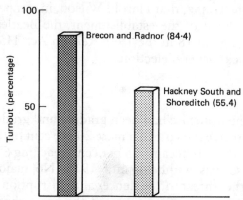

Figure 6.1   The highest and lowest turnouts in the 1987 general election

What do people vote for? Conflicting interpretations of what exactly one is supporting when placing an 'X' on the ballot paper reflect different views on the function of elections. Ostensibly voters are supporting a *candidate* but even charismatic figures attract very few personal votes. Most feel they actually vote for *parties*, a view reinforced by the theory of the mandate. Alternatively, many see a general election as a presidential-type contest in which they are choosing a future Prime Minister (see pp. 328–9).

Stability and volatility

Studies have shown that most people are stable voters, supporting the same party each time (Butler and Stokes 1969), while their more capricious fellows are described as **'floating voters'**. Figure 6.2 indicates an increase in net

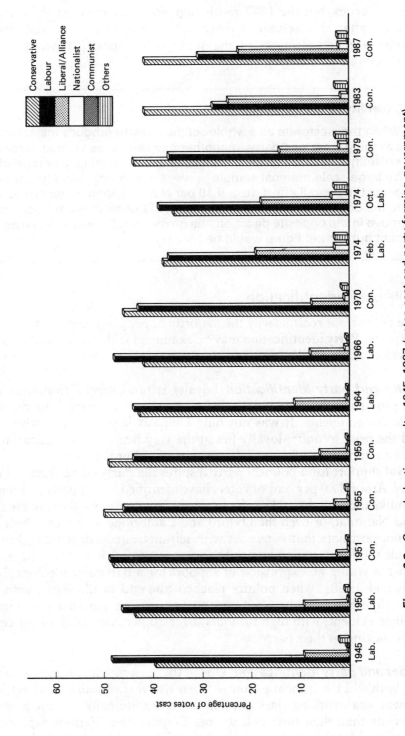

Figure 6.2 General election results, 1945–1987 (votes cast and party forming government)

Source: Data from Butler and Kavanagh (1988: table A1.1)

volatility during the 1970s and 1980s, with increasing voting for centrist and national parties, but the 1987 result suggested that the electoral earth was resettling after this seismic activity. The explanations for **stability** and **volatility** are key elements in the study of electoral behaviour and are considered in the following sections.

Volatility in the electorate

When the electorate as a whole seems likely to produce majorities swinging from one party to another it is said to be volatile. *Gross volatility* refers to the total amount of vote-switching, as revealed by large-scale national sample surveys, while *net volatility* represents the overall effect. (e.g. If 10 per cent of Labour voters switch to the Conservatives, while 10 per cent of Conservative supporters move in the opposite direction, the gross volatility would be 20 per cent but the net figure would be zero.)

Stable party identification

There are various reasons why the majority of people repeatedly vote for the same party. **Party identification** may be examined with respect to the concept of loyalty and to gender, race and class variables.

Loyalty and party identification Loyalty is fundamental to human existence, producing the cohesion needed by groups to withstand the rigours of hostile environments. It was not only Dumas's legendary trio who recognized the need to unite; loyalty lies at the very heart of politics, facilitating the formation of associations – basic units of political action.

Loyal support for a political party inspires the *Party Identification Voting Model*. Around 80 per cent of voters have identified with a party in a manner not unlike the way they take sides in other great contests – the Cup Final, the Grand National, or even the Oxford and Cambridge boat race. This model does not postulate that voters act with self-interested calculation; they vote without thinking, responding only to vague mental *images* of the parties. Neither is voting an expression of support for a particular ideology. In the 1950s and 1960s, when politics reached 'the end of ideology', with little policy differentiation between the parties, strong partisan identification remained evident, with high turnouts (over 80 per cent), and 90 per cent of voters sticking to their party.

Gender and party identification One of the reasons why the male establishment withheld the franchise from women was fear of radicalism. Yet in the post-war era working-class women have traditionally shown a greater propensity than their husbands to vote Conservative. Various explanations were offered for this. In the first place, women were less exposed to the forces

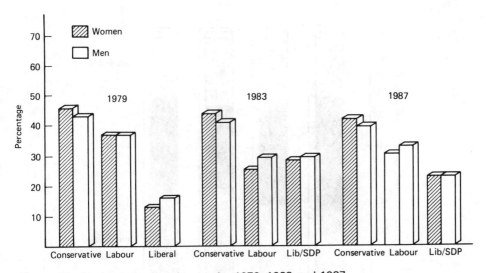

Figure 6.3 Voting behaviour by gender 1979, 1983 and 1987

Source: Data from Sarlvik and Crewe (1983: 92); Dunleavy and Husbands (1985); ITN/Harris Poll in the *Independent* (13 June 1987)

making for heightened class consciousness associated with employment in large industrial undertakings – camaraderie, unionization and collective leisure activities through clubs, pubs and sport. An alternative explanation was the greater longevity of women, who consequently had more chance to lose the radical fervour of youth (Hills 1981). Both these explanations would suggest that there is no real correlation between voting and gender, the causal factor lying in some other variable. Indeed, there are so many differences between the social experience of men and women in Britain that any suggestion that they vote differently because of some biological gender-based reason must be highly suspect. Moreover, the distinction between male and female voting behaviour has diminished. The 1979 general election was the first in which more men voted Conservative than Labour, and in the 1987 election the respective voting behaviour of the sexes was indistinguishable (see figure 6.3).

Age and party identification There is a belief that younger people are more likely to question established values and favour radical policies. This is why, when full manhood suffrage was conceded, the franchise was at first limited to those over 21. Figure 6.4 shows that voting in the 1987 general election tended to confirm this pattern, though the differentials give no cause for establishment alarm and do little to substantiate Shakespeare's claim.

> Crabbed age and youth cannot live together:
> Youth is full of pleasure, age is full of care
>
> Shakespeare, *The Passionate Pilgrim*, xii

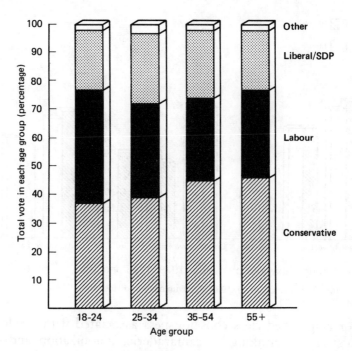

Figure 6.4   Voting by age, 1987

Source: Data from MORI in Butler and Kavanagh (1988: 275)

Race and party identification   Generally blacks have been less inclined to register to vote than whites (Todd and Butcher 1982: 13). Those of Asian descent are more likely to vote than their white constituency neighbours, while Afro-Caribbeans are less so. In both cases the strong preference has been for Labour (figure 6.5). However, there are grounds for predicting that non-manually-employed Asians, a growing sector, will gradually desert Labour (Studlar 1983). A poll conducted for the *Asian Times* and the *Caribbean Times* supported this prediction (see figure 6.5).

Social class and party identification   The most durable explanation for party identification has been that based on class. In four successive general elections in the 1960s and 1970s some 80 per cent of the middle class consistently voted Conservative, while about 70 per cent of the working class supported Labour (Gallup 1976). Yet class identification does not provide a complete explanation. There is a significant amount of cross-class voting.

Stable cross-class voting patterns

Cross-class voting occurs in the case of working-class Conservative and middle-class Labour voters.

Working-class Conservatives   This phenomenon is crucial to the pattern of

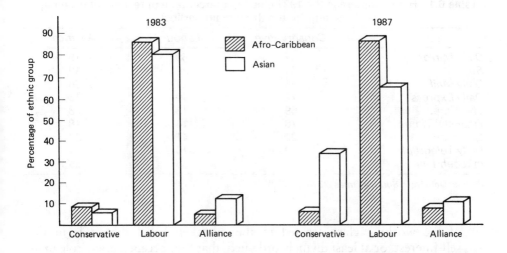

Figure 6.5 Voting intentions of ethnic minorities, 1983 and 1987

Source: Data from Anwar (1984: 11) and Butler and Kavanagh (1988: 278-9)

hegemony in British society, for without it the upper or upper-middle-class elite would be unable to maintain its supremacy. Though this obvious mathematical truth haunted the nineteenth-century establishment, they need not have lost any sleep, for around one-third of working-class voters were consistently to support a party with its origins in the aristocracy and deliberately favouring the preservation of traditional privileges and inequalities. The puzzle has excited various hypotheses.

- *Political deference.* In Britain's deferential political culture members of the working class may be said to vote for their 'betters', whom they believe, in some mystical sense, to be 'born to rule'. Thus Norton and Aughey perceive working-class Conservatives as individuals who 'prefer, despite not having ... privileges, what is known and predictable in the system, and who believe that this is how things should be' (1981: 175).
- *Social aspiration.* For many of the working class, the desire for self-betterment is seen in ruggedly individualist, rather than wetly collectivist terms. D. H. Lawrence speaks of his own working-class community in which 'it was a mother's business to see that her sons "got on"' (1950: 119). The individualism in Conservatism appeals to this sense of envious aspiration, and to 'be Conservative' in a working-class community can, in a snobbish way, represent social improvement in itself.
- *Neighbourhood.* Working-class voters in predominantly middle-class areas show a greater propensity than others to be Conservative. It may be, of course, that people choosing to move into such areas do so because they already hold such values.
- *False consciousness.* Marxists, notably Gramsci, have argued that members

Table 6.1   How voters read the 1987 election (percentage of readers of each paper voting for the three main parties)

	Conservative	Labour	Alliance
Daily Mirror	22	59	18
Sun	51	29	19
Daily Mail	55	11	34
Daily Express	72	10	18
The Times	59	13	28
Financial Times	78	14	8
Guardian	22	41	37
Daily Telegraph	69	10	21
Independent	31	33	35

Source: Data from *Sunday Times* (23 Aug. 1987)

of the working class are led to the mistaken belief that it is in their self-interest, or at least divinely ordained, that they accept a lowly role in life. This **false consciousness** is fostered through ruling-class control over the economy, the institutions of the state and the mass media (Gramsci 1971), which had forestalled the revolution predicted by classical Marxists. Table 6.1 reveals the close correlation between a newspaper's partisan complexion and its readers' voting patterns.

•   •   •

However, underlying this debate should be a realization that the British working class is not driven by left-wing attitudes, neither is it notably egalitarian by instinct. There is much genuine support for many of the policies and leanings of the Conservatives, including those on race and immigration, the Commonwealth and Britain's position in the world, nuclear disarmament, council house sales, the monarchy, the aristocracy, law and order, penal policy, capital punishment, education, higher education and academic research, the arts, trade union reform, social service 'scroungers', sexual morality, gays, and so on. The popularity of Enoch Powell between the 1960s and 1980s testifies to many of these sentiments, and the television character Alf Garnett, a grotesque caricature of the working-class Conservative, evoked ready recognition to become a loved national symbol.

Middle-class socialism Although attracting less attention, a not insignificant 20 per cent of the middle class support Labour. There are various possible explanations for this, including the following.

- *Intellectual socialism.* Middle-class intellectuals are almost by definition more likely than others to take a reasoned, rather than an entirely self-interested, view of politics. Much Labour support and leadership has been drawn from the intelligentsia, and the elitist Fabian movement was a significant force in the party from the outset. In 1987, the Conservatives fared markedly worse in those Conservative city constituencies (including Oxford and Cambridge) with high concentrations of professional middle classes, university dons and students (Curtice and Steed 1988: 332).

- *Residual class loyalty.* Not all upwardly mobiles pull up the ladder; some retain a sense of fidelity to the values of their parents. Hence, during the 1987 election campaign, when Labour looked unlikely to gain the services of an advertising agency owing to lack of funds and (more significantly) resistance from boards of directors, employees of Boase, Massimi, Pollitt (BMP) offered their services voluntarily, as did various prominent figures in the arts.
- *Public-sector employment.* Public-sector employees are predominantly middle class and, by the 1970s, had grown to around 30 per cent of the workforce. They have a career interest in the welfare-orientated policies of Labour and a natural antipathy to the Conservative mission to roll back the state. (One exception to this is the police force, a part of the public sector which Conservatives cherish.)
- *Mistrust of the 'New Right'.* The increasing dominance of the 'New Right' (see p. 214) since 1979 has alarmed old-school Disraelian Tories, including prominent figures who were quickly branded 'wets'. Although electoral defections tend to go to the Alliance, they are often tactical votes for Labour.

Volatile voting patterns

However, by no means all voters are stable. Non-stable voters are particularly important because, although constituting only a small proportion of the electorate, they precipitate the **electoral swings** which can sweep governments from office. A movement of only 3.6 per cent in 1964, for example, served to erase a seemingly impregnable Conservative majority.

Partisan dealignment Since the general election of 1945 the overall level of class-based voting for both major parties fell until over half the electorate was rejecting the class imperative (Crewe 1986: 620). This was confirmed using a sophisticated multidimensional definition of class as well as one based simply on occupation (Rose and McAllister 1986). Figure 6.6 shows **partisan dealignment** between 1945–58 and 1987, using the IPA classification (see p. 100). The collapse was particularly injurious to Labour. Between 1945 and 1970 its share of the vote had stood, like the Conservatives, at around 45 per cent, but it subsequently plummeted to reach a nadir of 27.6 per cent in 1983, recovering slightly in 1987 to 30.8 per cent.

Explaining partisan dealignment Several hypotheses have been advanced to explain partisan dealignment, including the rise of a third-party force, tactical voting, changes of social structure, geographical cleavage, new sectoral cleavages, and the emergence of a more discerning electorate.

(1) *The third force.* During the 1970s the bipartisan model of British politics was threatened as a rejuvenated Liberal Party offered electors a

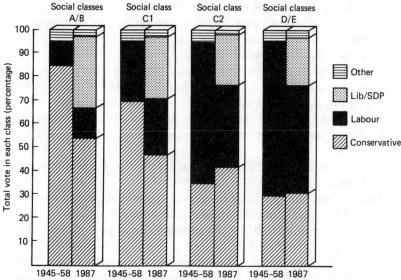

Figure 6.6   Partisan dealignment: class voting, 1945–1958 and 1987

Source: Data from Abrahams (1958) and ITN/Harris Poll in the *Independent* (13 June 1987) (for definitions of social class see p. 100)

third choice. Its share of the vote rose dramatically from 7.5 per cent in 1970 to 19.3 in 1974 (see figure 6.2). The SDP further muddied the partisan water when it entered the fray in March 1981. After forming the Alliance their support remained buoyant (25.4 per cent in 1983 and 22.6 per cent in 1987) though, owing to the electoral system, seats were not delivered in proportion. This volatile period also saw a rise in the nationalist vote, which in 1987 stood at 7.3 and 14 per cent in Wales and Scotland respectively.

(2) *Tactical voting.* The entry of a third horse in the electoral race opened the door to **tactical voting**. This amounts to supporting a party, or candidate, which is not the first choice in order to *prevent* the election of the least-liked party. There was some evidence of this in the general elections of the 1980s, a trend the centre parties sought to encourage.

(3) *Shrinking working class.* The tendency of the working class to acquire middle-class values and life-styles (**embourgeoisement**) has been accelerated by the information technology revolution and the ethos of aggressive individualism promoted by the Conservatives. Although working-class loyalty to Labour may have remained solid, long-term electoral movement away from the party may be explained by the class itself becoming smaller (Heath et al. 1987). From the early 1970s the percentage of manual workers in Britain has declined from around 47 to 34, while the proportion of people belonging to the salaried managerial class has risen from around 18 per cent to some 27 per cent.

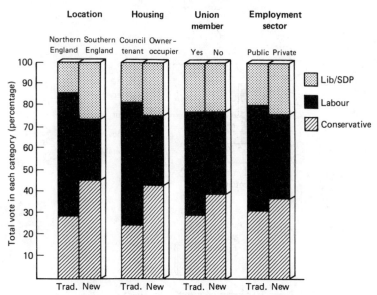

Figure 6.7 Voting patterns of the 'traditional' and the 'new' working class, 1987

Source: Data from I. Crewe in the *Guardian* (15 June 1987)

(4) *A new working class.* Crewe has identified what he has called a 'new working class' which may be contrasted along a number of dimensions with the 'traditional working class', swelling the ranks of the working-class Conservatives (see figure 6.7). Among the skilled working class Labour's share of the vote fell from 45 per cent in 1979 to around 34 per cent in 1987.

(5) *Geographical cleavage.* Since the 1970s a major new trend has altered the electoral geography: Britain has been described as 'a nation dividing'. It was once possible to speak of a national swing at election time which would sweep the country uniformly, enabling psephologists to predict the composition of Parliament from relatively few results. However, today Britain cannot be said to cast nationwide verdicts. It has become riven by a deep fissure between the north (voting predominantly Labour) and the south (Conservative). (There is a lesser Labour–Conservative divide between the west and the east.) This divide is not a new phenomenon, having been present in the 1930s, but it was largely erased in the 1945 Labour landslide (Johnston et al. 1988: 9).

Intimations of the reopening of the division were seen in the 1970s, when nationalist movements in Scotland and Wales urging a break with England gained momentum (see figure 6.2), and in the 1979 general election Scotland moved clearly to Labour against the national trend. In the contests of 1983 and 1987 the regional differentiation continued (Curtice and Steed 1988: 332). There are serious implications in the divide, the trends posing a severe threat to the government's legitimacy (see figure 6.8).

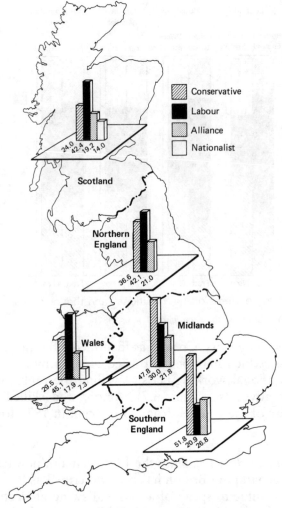

Figure 6.8 A national mandate? Regional support for the parties after the 1987 general election (percentage of votes cast)

Source: Data from Butler and Kavanagh (1988: table A1.2)

(6) *Public–private sectoral cleavage.* New **sectoral cleavages** have emerged in British society since 1945 (Dunleavy and Husbands 1985). There is a fundamental dichotomy between Labour voters, whose lives are predominantly locked into the public sector, and those operating largely within the private sector, who vote Conservative.

(7) *Consumer voting.* The **consumer voting model** characterizes voters as shoppers in a political market place, making choices to maximize their self-interest like consumers in the mythical economic market (Downs 1957; Himmelweit et al. 1985: 70; Rose and McAllister 1986). Thus voters choose policies which they believe to be to their advantage in the same way as they choose a powder that 'washes whiter', or a lager to

reach hitherto inaccessible parts. The model gained adherents in the era of partisan dealignment, for when blind loyalty weakens, issues and policies are more likely to be examined. The influences affecting these hypothe-sized customers in the political supermarket include factors such as policy promises, a party's campaign, issues of the day, and feelings on the competence of the party to govern.

However, the idea that voters behave in this way is based on unrealistic assumptions about individualism and rationality. The theory is developed by a right-wing school, the **public choice theorists**, who argue that democracy leads to wasteful expenditure because voters will naturally be greedy, and politicians try to outbid each other in the promises they make. However, in reality much electoral choice is not made on rational grounds. In the first place, there are the strong emotional attachments in the form of loyalty, and secondly, the views of electors may be manipu-lated through the process of mind politics.

Hence the model can offer only a partial explanation of voting behaviour. In 1988 it was still the view of leading psephologists that 'the voting decisions of some three-quarters of the electorate ... are largely decided before the dissolution of parliament' (Butler and Kavanagh 1988: 241).

Influencing Voters: Politicians and the Election Campaign

Packaging the parties

Despite its weaknesses, the consumer voting model is important in a way its proponents did not intend, for while it may not account for much of the behaviour of *voters*, it does explain that of the leading actors (politicians, pundits, parties, and the parasitic psephological media), all of whom operate as if it were true. Politicians like to think that the country is enraptured by their comings and goings, and make punishing efforts to inform, analyse and persuade. Such activities reach their climax in the grand celebration of the **election campaign** which, whether or not affecting voting behaviour, is one of the most compelling symbols of modern politics.

Traditionally a campaign involved an initial unveiling of the manifesto, followed by hustings and public meetings, door-to-door canvassing, flatter-ing constituents and kissing sticky babies, with candidates fighting individual constituency battles. Although these localized contests still take place in a ritualistic manner, the real campaigns are conducted by the central party organizations, with a degree of sophistication undreamed of a few decades ago. It is a battle of media men and large-scale advertising. Enormous sums are spent, particularly by the Conservatives, with their backing of mighty capitalist enterprises desperate to see them elected.

Once the campaigns are under way the politicians become passive products, to be packaged and sold. Their actions (speeches, interviews, photo opportunities, cuddled lambs, and so on) are planned in detail. What

Campaigning in the television age
Source: Times Newspapers Ltd

they say, how they dress, their hair-styles, where they go, whom they meet, which politicians or party they attack, which section of the electorate they target, by whom they will be interviewed on TV, is decided for them after careful analysis. Even the manifestos can be written by media men (the 1987 Conservative manifesto was drafted by John O'Sullivan of *The Times*). Backroom boys like Tim Bell and Gordon Reece (Thatcher media gurus) become as familiar to *aficionados* as the politicians themselves.

Campaigns are physically and psychologically gruelling. Politicians rise early, travel daily to and from London, attend frequent strategy meetings, write and rewrite speeches, give daily press conferences, sweat before TV cameras, and snatch only a few hours' sleep in each 24-hour cycle. They are constantly under the scrutinizing eyes of the media, eager for a gaff or an encounter with a banana skin. For Labour, the position is made worse by the general press hostility, though Conservatives have the strain of knowing that the mighty forces of capitalism are counting on them to deliver the political goods.

These hi-tech campaigns are increasingly dominated by TV (Harrison 1988: 139). Slick party political broadcasts make extensive use of skills developed in TV commercials. In 1987, a highly acclaimed production presenting Neil Kinnock was written by Colin Welland and directed by Hugh Hudson, director of the equally acclaimed film *Chariots of Fire*. Its showing was said to have lifted the Labour leader's popularity by 16 points in the polls (Harrison 1988: 154).

In all this the role of the public is reduced to total passivity. People cannot confront, and heckle, in the manner of the traditional hustings (a foot projected through the screen will do nothing to register opposition to the relentless talking head) and questioning can only take place vicariously through the medium of the professional interviewer (whose line may be governed by a desire to remain in employment after the election). The development of 'phone-ins', permitting the public to address politicians directly by telephone while others listen, does little to capture the robust spirit of true debate. Questions are carefully monitored beforehand and the programme controllers can reduce an awkward or abusive caller to mute impotence at the press of a button.

Monitoring the campaign

The analogy with selling in the market place is extended by the heavy use of market survey organizations (such as Mori, Marplan and Gallup), which are commissioned to conduct polls on voting intentions and related matters for the media and the parties. This is an increasing trend and with 73 national surveys, 18 surveys in marginal seats, and over 100 surveys in individual constituencies, the 1987 contest was 'the most exhaustively polled ... in British history' (Butler and Kavanagh 1988: 124). There are grave dangers in such saturation. It does more than inform; it influences and persuades. Any idea of genuine consumer choice is as bogus as it is in the commercial world. Polling also introduces the possibility of influencing the result through the 'bandwagon effect'. It is suspected that some people, believing with Oscar Wilde's Lady Bracknell that statistics 'are laid down for our guidance', may be swept along like sheep in an effort to be on the winning side. For this reason some countries ban polling during the campaign.

Whether the new approach to campaigning is desirable and effective is debatable. Familiarity with modern advertising tactics may arouse suspicion rather than persuade voters. Such techniques, with their short, easy-to-remember messages rather than detailed analysis, exorcize all subtlety from discussion, and the sheer quantity of coverage may induce boredom (a serious threat to democracy). Finally, the great expense and energy consumed in this intense heat is largely wasted. The Conservative campaign for the 1987 election was often in disarray, appearing lacklustre by comparison with Labour's chariot of fire, yet it was the Conservatives who found themselves drinking the champagne with a handsome parliamentary majority.

Conclusion: Distorting Democracy

The British electoral system: the case for

The present electoral system is said by its supporters to be quintessentially

British, having evolved to be uniquely fitted to the political culture. Any change in pursuit of some supposedly rational improvement would represent an artificial interference and lead to unanticipated difficulties. Its simplicity and ease of operation are also singled out for praise: it requires none of the complicated and time-consuming calculations found in more sophisticated systems of proportional representation. Furthermore, it is easily understood and voters are used to it. A consistently high turnout is thought to demonstrate public satisfaction.

The use of many small constituencies is said to permit close links between MPs and people, while the geographical basis for representation ensures that the interests of far-flung regions are articulated in Parliament. The system also produces stable majorities and an ethos of strong government, part of a political culture which relishes the smack of a stern matron. Single governments can count on a full term, enabling them to enact programmes without fear of a *coup*.

The case against

Yet the system has many critics. In the 1970s, an orchestrated reform campaign of academics and politicians gained considerable momentum but came to nought (Finer 1975), partly due to a lack of strong public feeling but, more importantly, because the defects have for long well served the two dominant parties. However, in the changed conditions of today it is necessary to re-evaluate the system. It may be accused of a number of failings.

   1 *Disenfranchisement.* In a single-member constituency only one set of opinions can ever be represented in Parliament and many votes are wasted. Even votes cast for successful candidates are superfluous where majorities are large, as was the case with many northern Labour votes in 1987. Such constituencies remain impervious to national swings and voters are therefore unable to influence the national political scene. This evil is compounded where local party oligarchs become the effective electorate through their right to select the candidate (the 'selectorate'). This corruption of the democratic process could be reduced by some form of **primary election,** passing the choice to the party membership (closed primary) or the public at large (open primary).

   2 *The third-party effect.* Third parties with widespread national support may not be in a position to win any constituencies. The Alliance parties were particularly vulnerable, attracting 7.4 million votes in 1987, only some 3 million fewer than Labour, yet securing only 22 seats compared with Labour's 229 (contrast figures 6.2 and 7.4). Conversely, minority parties with spatially concentrated support can achieve a parliamentary presence quite out of proportion to their *national* popularity. In 1987 the Scottish and Welsh nationalists were able to secure six seats with only half a million votes. (Even so, they gained under 1 per cent of

the seats with around 1.7 per cent of the votes.)

3 *Over-amplification of opinion change.* It has been estimated that a shift in support from one party to the other of only about 1 per cent will result in a change in Parliament of about 13 seats.

4 *Extremism.* The two-party system may force parties to adopt extreme positions, to the neglect of the middle ground.

5 *Discontinuity of policy.* The fact that government change entails a complete clean-out may threaten continuity of policy. This can partly explain the 'stop-go' policies which have impaired Britain's economic performance in comparison with Western Europe, where continuity is secured through centrally dominated coalition government.

6 *Limited choice.* The pressure towards bipartism means that, in spite of talk about consumer models, voters are offered only two very broad policy *tables d'hôtes* from which to choose.

7 *Minority governments.* Governments can lack moral legitimacy. Once there are more than two horses in the race it is quite possible for successful candidates to emerge even though rejected by well over 50 per cent of the electorate. Anomalies at constituency level are transposed to Parliament: in 1987 the Conservatives gained 42.3 per cent of the votes cast but 57.8 per cent of the seats. Since 1935 no party of government has polled over half the votes cast, even though almost all have enjoyed substantial *parliamentary* majorities. It is actually possible for the party with the parliamentary majority to poll fewer votes than the opposition, as was demonstrated in 1951 and February 1974.

Reforming the system: proportional representation

Yet far from being the only one possible, the British electoral system is in fact a rather rare curiosity in the modern world. Most polities seek an assembly reflecting the pattern of voting in the country on the principle of **proportional representation** (PR). If Britain had used PR in 1987, when the Conservative, Labour and Alliance parties polled 42.3, 30.8 and 22.6 per cent of the votes, they would have been awarded 275, 200 and 146 seats respectively (as

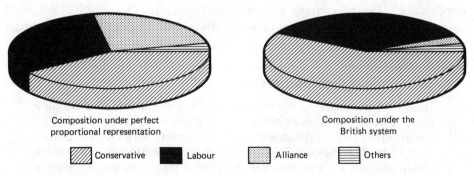

Composition under perfect
proportional representation

Composition under the
British system

Conservative   Labour   Alliance   Others

Figure 6.9 Distorting democracy: the composition of Parliament as it was in 1987 and as it might have been under perfect proportional representation

they were manifestly not), resulting in coalition government with a policy based on compromise, rather than dominance by an extreme ideology (see figure 6.9). There are various forms of PR, of which the following are well-known basic models.

The alternative vote system This is a well-known method of election, but does not produce genuine PR because it operates on the basis of single-member constituencies. However, it does ensure that members have an absolute majority by considering the alternative preferences of those voting for minority candidates (see figure 6.10).

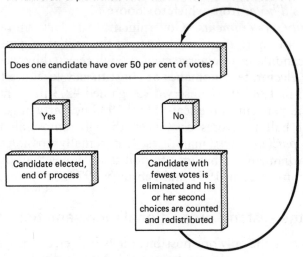

Ballot papers contain the names of candidates as in the British system. However, rather than make a single choice the voter places candidates in the rank order of preference. After this all first preferences are counted.

Does one candidate have over 50 per cent of votes?

Yes

No

Candidate elected, end of process

Candidate with fewest votes is eliminated and his or her second choices are counted and redistributed

Figure 6.10 The alternative vote system

The party list system Widely used in Western Europe, this system is based upon multi-member constituencies. Voters merely indicate the *party* of their choice, having previously studied each party's list of candidates (in order of importance). The percentage vote obtained by each party is calculated, and seats are awarded on a pro rata basis. Candidates are returned in the order shown on the list.

The multi-member constituency

This is fundamental to the concept of PR. If in a given constituency party X polls 60 per cent of the votes, party Y 30 and party Z 10, a minimum of ten candidates must be returned if strict proportionality is to be maintained. This implies that constituencies cannot be small; indeed a 'constituency' may be a large region, or even a whole country.

Single transferable vote (STV) STV systems bear certain resemblances to the alternative vote system, and are probably the best known. A version was used in Britain between 1918 and 1948, when multi-member university seats existed, and it was also recommended by the Kilbrandon Commission on the Constitution for the separate assemblies advocated for Wales and Scotland. Although it requires multi-member constituencies, these may be relatively small. The procedure is as follows.

1 Voters record on the ballot paper their order of preference for candidates.
2 An **electoral quota** (EQ) is calculated on the basis of the formula:

$$EQ = \frac{\text{Number of votes cast}}{\text{Number of seats available} + 1} + 1$$

3 First preferences are counted and those obtaining the EQ are elected. Surplus votes for successful candidates are then redistributed on the basis of second choices, so that further candidates reach the EQ. Thus no votes are wasted. (If all seats cannot be filled in this way, the last candidate is eliminated and those ballot papers are redistributed on the basis of second choices.)

Effects of PR in Britain The introduction of PR would in all probability change the nature of British politics fundamentally.

● Parliamentary representation of minority parties such as the Alliance and the Greens would increase at the expense of the old duopoly.
● Hung Parliaments and coalition government would become more likely.
● The centre parties, despite their minority status, would be placed in pivotal positions and could expect to remain part of successive coalitions.
● In the longer term the centre parties might lose their minority status, becoming more attractive once people felt that votes would no longer be wasted.
● Alternatively, electors might decide that they preferred a two-party system, and reduce their propensity to support minority forces.
● Voters would have an element of choice between the candidates of the party they support.

An agenda for change?

The two major parties have resisted reform in order to protect their self-interest, yet as the nation divides Labour's position is no longer clear cut. How might things change? In the event of a hung Parliament the minority parties might be able to secure promise of electoral reform as the price of supporting one or other of the giants. This was the vain hope of the Alliance in 1987, yet by this time their strong presence, consistently splitting the anti-Conservative vote, meant that the system was working against Labour as well.

A crisis of legitimacy?

In December 1988 the journal *New Statesman and Society* launched *Charter 88*, inviting citizens to add their names to a lengthy list of distinguished public figures, artistes and academics calling for a range of reforms to the British body politic in order to halt the insidious erosion of civil rights. Prominent among their demands was the call for proportional representation, seen as a bulwark of genuine democracy.

At the end of the twentieth century Britain finds itself with an electoral system which thwarts the popular verdict. The affluent south-east, with its many constituencies, high levels of working-class Conservatism and split anti-Conservative vote, seemed to guarantee impregnability and, after her 1987 victory, Mrs Thatcher talked confidently of another ten years as premier. Yet two serious problems remained for the Conservatives. In the first place, there was the loss of pride for those in the tradition of 'one-nation' Toryism. More importantly, there was the threatened crisis of legitimacy if the dispossessed and unheeded were to come (like the Catholics of Northern Ireland) to the conclusion that the system gives them no constitutional means of influencing government. This would remove one of the great stabilizing forces in British political history: faith in Parliament as a means of promoting political change.

Key points

- British democracy is based on the principle of representative government, in which a few people govern on behalf of the many.
- Representative government may have various interpretations, but in Britain it is taken to mean that the representative is permitted considerable autonomy from those represented.
- The evolution of the system has been slow and grudging. Extensions to the franchise were not given willingly by those in power; they have been bitterly fought for. The two least powerful sections of society – the working class and the female population – were long denied voting rights.
- The British electoral system uses the simple plurality, or 'first-past-the-post' method. This is a very crude system and very unusual today.
- Although bringing enormous disadvantages, the system has favoured the continued dominance of the two main parties; this explains its persistence.
- The study of voting behaviour has concentrated on seeking reasons why people vote one way or another. Gender and race have not been seen as really significant independent variables. Class has been regarded as the principal determinant.
- The class explanation has come under fire since the 1970s yet it remains the best predictor of voting behaviour.
- Throughout the 1980s, voters in Wales, the midlands, the north and Scotland rejected the Conservative Party, yet the government remained securely in office, thereby demonstrating, by something of a *reductio ad absurdum*, the

undemocratic nature of the British electoral system.
- The alternative to the British system is some form of proportional representation. However, this can only be introduced by a party (or coalition) in office. By the end of the 1980s the possibility of Labour and the centre parties combining for this purpose was being discussed, along with other calls for constitutional reform.

Review your understanding of the following terms and concepts

direct democracy	cross-class voting
representative government	false consciousness
mandate	electoral swing
manifesto	partisan dealignment
universal franchise	tactical voting
constituency	embourgoisement
first-past-the-post	sectoral cleavage
simple plurality election	consumer voting model
absolute majority	public choice theory
Chartism	election campaign
suffragette	primary election
psephology	proportional representation
abstention	multi-member constituency
floating voter	alternative vote system
electoral stability	party list
electoral volatility	single transferable vote
party identification	electoral quota

Assignment

Study table 6.2 and answer the following questions.

		% mark
1	Why are by-elections called?	5
2	Examine the differences in turnout between general elections and by-elections. What explanations would you offer for this difference?	20
3	Examine the pattern of third-party support in these elections. Try to explain this in terms of political developments taking place at the time.	25
4	Drawing on the data supplied, consider whether by-election results offer a good basis for predicting the results of general elections.	50

Questions for discussion

1 What reasons may be advanced to explain the fact that a substantial proportion of the working class have always voted Conservative?
2 'For all its defects, the British electoral system ensures strong government.' Discuss.

Table 6.2 Parliamentary by-elections, 1974–1987

	Oct. 1974–May 1979	Previous general election (Oct. 1974)	May 1979–June 1983	Previous general election (May 1979)	June 1983–June 1987	Previous general election (June 1983)
Number of by-elections	30	–	20	–	31	–
Turnout (percentage)	57.3	70.5	61.2	73.1	58.4	67.5
Votes recorded by party (percentages)						
Conservative	45.1	34.8	23.8	33.7	16.0	23.3
Labour	36.6	44.8	25.7	35.2	14.9	14.8
Liberal[a]	10.9	17.3	9.0	8.0	15.0	10.9
Social Democratic Party[a]	–	–	14.2	–	5.6	3.0
Plaid Cymru	–	–	0.5	0.4	0.3	0.3
Scottish National Party	2.7	–	1.7	1.4	–	–
Northern Ireland parties	–	2.6	23.3	20.1[b]	47.4	47.4
Other	4.7	0.5	1.9	1.1	0.8	0.2
Total votes recorded (=100%) (thousands)	1,058	1,288	715	852	1,235	1,410

[a] The Social Democratic Party was launched on 26 March 1981. An SDP candidate contested a parliamentary seat for the first time in the by-election held at Warrington on 16 July 1981. Since that date, the Liberal and Social Democratic Parties have contested 28 by-elections with only one of the parties putting up a candidate in each.
[b] Two of the by-elections were in the same constituency, Fermanagh and South Tyrone and as the votes recorded at both have been included the votes cast at the general election have been recorded twice.
Source: Social Trends (1988: table 11.11)

3 Why has the extension of the franchise to the working class in Britain been so grudging?
4 How important is the concept of the mandate in British politics?
5 What might be the effects of the introduction of primary elections into British politics?
6 How important is the concept of social class in explaining voting behaviour in Britain?
7 Evaluate the legitimacy of Conservative government of Wales and Scotland from Westminster in the light of recent general elections.

Topic for debate

This house believes that the time has come for the introduction of proportional representation in Britain.
   or
This house believes that it is more rational to abstain than to vote in British elections.

Further reading

Butler, D. and Kavanagh, D. (1988) *The British General Election of 1987.*
The latest in a long line of Nuffield election studies dating from 1945, in which the authors selflessly continue a tradition to 'seek immortality in the footnotes of others' – false modesty however, because the studies are complete in themselves, lively, accessible to students, and very conscious of the politics behind the numbers.

Butler, D. and Stokes, D. (1969) *Political Change in Britain.*
Something of a classic in the field, though much subsequent writing has questioned its explanations and predictions.

Dunleavy, P. and Husbands, C. (1985) *Democracy at the Crossroads: Voting and Party Competition in the 1980s.*
Presents the sectoral cleavage model.

Finer, S. E. (ed.) (1975) *Adversarial Politics and Electoral Reform.*
Essays attacking the electoral system and a strong case for proportional representation.

Heath, A., Jowell, R. and Curtice, J. (1985) *How Britain Votes.*
Stimulating challenge to the theory of dealignment. By redefining class the authors are able to argue that although working-class support for Labour is still secure, the class itself is shrinking.

Himmelweit, H., Humphreys, P. and Jaeger, M. (1985) *How Voters Decide.*
Read this to gain understanding of the consumer voting model. The authors try to show that attitudinal variables are more relevant than class in explaining voting.

Rose, R. and McAllister, I. (1986) *Voters Begin to Choose: from Closed Class to Open Elections.*
The authors use sophisticated techniques (automatic interaction detector or tree

analysis) to demonstrate that definitions of social class have steadily weakened as explanations of voting behaviour.

For light relief

Douglas Hurd, *The Truth Game.*
A stylish novel by a leading politician.

H. G. Nicholas (ed.), *To the Hustings.*
Entertaining short stories.

Dennis Potter, *Vote, Vote, Vote for Nigel Barton.*
A television drama giving a realistic picture of the role of the agent in an election.

R. Tressel, *The Ragged Trousered Philanthropists.*
A witty and ironical novel (first appeared in 1914) in which the working-class protagonists ruminate on life. They are seen as 'philanthropists' because it is their willingness to be poor which allows the rich to stay rich.

H. G. Wells, *Ann Veronica.*
Controversial when first published, this study of the relationship between men and women is set against a suffragette background.

Virginia Woolf, *Night and Day.*
A suffragette novel.

7

The Politics of Power: a Life History of the Party System

This chapter is the first of two on political parties. Here we introduce the basic concept of the modern political party and examine its evolution in Britain. The chapter comprises seven sections. This first examines the concept of the **mass party** and the place of ideology in party politics. The following sections identify a series of key periods, taking the concept of the evolving **party system**. This is because parties should not be seen in isolation; it is in their essential nature to be linked through competition and cooperation. The concluding section evaluates British two party politics.

Defining parties

Though unknown to the constitution, parties dominate the real world of politics. There is no corner which they do not touch; they are the organic symbols of the modern age of mass politics. Essentially a **political party** is an association of individuals with a common set of beliefs and political goals, sharing a desire to take control or become part of the government by constitutional means. For some commentators, the intention to gain office overrides all other considerations. Parties are portrayed as vote-maximizing machines, analogous to profit-maximizing firms of the economic market, with little ideological commitment and prepared to pursue any policy commanding support (Downs 1957: ch. 7). Such a characterization may assist analysis but is not a description of reality. Parties reflect ideologies and interests, which give each its particular character.

Parties and ideology Broadly speaking, an **ideology** is a systematic theory

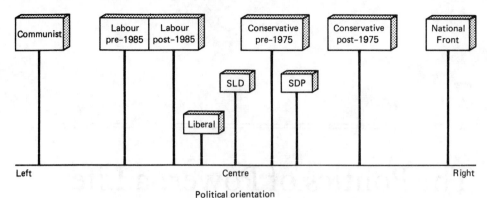

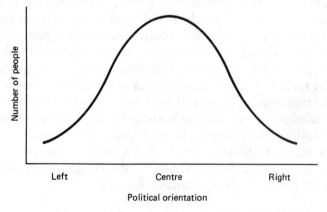

Figure 7.1 Notional positions of the parties along the left–right continuum in the post-war era

Note: SLD = Social and Liberal Democratic Party; SDP = Social Democratic Party

of human society from which a programme of political action can be derived. The most common basis for distinguishing parties ideologically is in terms of a left–right dichotomy. This tends to parallel that between **collectivism** (all members of society work together) and **individualism** (people only look after themselves). In terms of actual policies, those on the right subscribe to a characteristic package, tending to be *against* coloured immigration, the welfare state, state ownership, unilateral nuclear disarmament, and so on, and *for* capitalism, nuclear deterrence, hanging and a tough penal policy, selective education, the House of Lords and aristocracy, private education and health care. The right often lays a special claim to be for *freedom*, though this tends to mean freedom for the capitalist economic market. For the most part, the left-wing position is the reverse of all these attitudes.

However, a more realistic conceptualization of the left–right dichotomy is in terms of a continuum, with an infinite range of intermediate positions indicating tendencies rather than hard positions (see figure 7.1). It is generally believed that most members of the British public are nearer the centre than either extreme, as shown in figure 7.2. Even this concept is

Figure 7.2 Distribution of the population along a left—right continuum

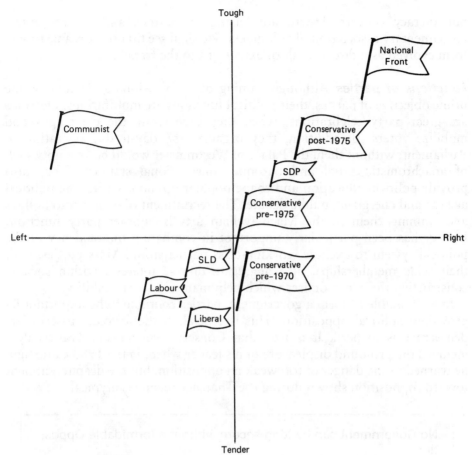

Figure 7.3 A notional two-dimensional distribution of the political parties in the post-war era

Note: SLD = Social and Liberal Democratic Party; SDP = Social Democratic Party

simplistic; in addition to substantive policy there are ideological questions related to means. It is possible to take a *tough* or *tender* attitude towards society, and preferences may not coincide with the left–right divide (Eysenck 1951). Fascists, with extreme right-wing ideologies, have taken tough attitudes, but so have communists. The addition of this dichotomy creates a two-dimensional matrix as shown in figure 7.3.

Parties and interests However, in the real world of British politics, parties do not merely embody abstract ideologies. In spite of their rhetoric they are enmeshed in a society fragmented with conflicting interests, and they generally subscribe to ideologies, not for ethical reasons, but in order to favour some sectional interests over others.

The modern mass party The major British national parties are not small, tightly knit bands, they are large associations consisting essentially of three elements: a **parliamentary cadre** of elected MPs (the parliamentary party), a bureaucracy concerned with administrative matters, and a large extra-parliamentary association of volunteers. We shall see that this organizational form evolved as a direct result of extensions to the franchise.

Functions of parties   Although gaining office by winning elections is the prime objective of parties, their political functions are multifarious. Elections are great party celebrations, when they orchestrate the campaigns and mobilize voters. In addition, they organize the day-to-day operation of Parliament; without them the Palace of Westminster would be an empty shell of anachronistic ritual and baroque constitutional statuary. They also provide political education and shape popular opinion, setting the political agenda and energizing public debate. The recruitment of people into politics and training them in the Machiavellian arts is another party function: Labour has been particularly important in combating the tendency of the political system to exclude working-class participation. Mass parties, with their wide memberships, also aggregate diverse interests within society, constructing the compromises which help maintain social stability.

Even if unable to form a government, parties continue to be important by providing political opposition. This is crucial: without voices to criticize, democracy is in peril. It is true that Conservative minister Francis Pym incurred the profound displeasure of his leader when, in the 1983 campaign, he warned of the danger of too weak an opposition, but the deep resentment towards opposition shown during the Thatcher regime is atypical.

> No Government can be long secure without a formidable Opposition.
>
> Benjamin Disraeli, *Coningsby* (1844: bk II, ch. 1)

The party system

Parties in a democracy cannot exist in isolation. During their evolution, the British parties have been inextricably entwined, the fortunes of one usually having implications for the others. Though remaining distinct they have cross-fertilized each other with philosophy, policy, strategy and organizational form. They have even made physical contact, to fight, or to hold together in the warm embrace of coalition, sometimes even exchanging vital fluids as factions have surged from one to impregnate the other. It is for this reason that we speak of a **party system**; any party can only be understood as part of a wider whole. It is usual to classify party systems in terms of *number*, but it is helpful to consider also their relative dominance, thus distinguishing four types.

- **Multi-party.** Any system with more than two parties. The assumption is that they have comparable degrees of power and governments are always coalitions.

- **Two-party.** Two parties share dominance, either being capable of securing an overall majority and forming an entire government. In the real world, minor parties always exist and a more realistic term is *two-party dominant*.
- **Single-party dominant.** There are several parties, but one stands like Gulliver among the Lilliputians, able to command either an overall majority and govern alone, or be the dominant partner in successive coalitions.
- **Single-party.** Such 'systems' are unlikely to arise naturally, but occur where the constitution permits only one party. They are found mainly under totalitarian regimes (like Nazi Germany or communist Russia), usually after the opposition has been wiped out.

The modern system is best understood through its evolution. We may identify a number of stages, beginning with the genesis of the modern mass party.

Genesis

From the settling dust of seventeenth-century constitutional struggles emerged two parliamentary groupings – the Tories, a landowning cadre avowing fidelity to the King, and the Whigs devoted to trade and the parliamentary cause. These dominated into the nineteenth century. As cadre parties they existed only at the parliamentary level and MPs were sustained in office by various forms of corrupt electoral practice. They had little ideology save the protection of self-interests.

These primitive organisms were forced under the radical sun, to crawl from the mud of eighteenth- and early nineteenth-century court and parliamentary intrigue onto the hard ground of democracy. The nineteenth-century extensions of the franchise cut the cadre system to ribbons and are the key to the emergence of the modern party.

The Conservatives: the era of Peel and Disraeli

By the 1820s, under the leadership of the Duke of Wellington, the Tory Party appeared to be dying, with little hope from any extension of the franchise. However, following the 1832 Reform Act, it experienced an unexpected revival under its resourceful leader Sir Robert Peel (1788–1850), who gave it a *raison d'être* beyond self-interest. He signalled the advent of manifesto politics in his famous election address, the Tamworth manifesto, when he identified the party with a long and respectable intellectual tradition of English thought. This he termed **conservatism**; insofar as the party was to have an ideology this was to be it. Derived from the ideas of the Whig, Edmund Burke (see pp. 36–7), it was a view of the nature of change and stability, rather than a social prescription, suggesting that there was more rationality behind a naturally evolving society and its institutions than could be discerned by reason. This should be venerated and conserved, rather than subject to the meddling attentions of radicals. The view implied respect for tradition, including the Crown, the aristocracy, the established church, private property, and law and order. Not surprisingly, it was exceedingly attractive to those whose interests lay in preserving the status quo; the landed gentry were happy to wear the title 'Conservative' as their badge. Thus can the modern Conservative Party be said to have risen, phoenix-like, from the ashes of the old Tory Party.

> The right honorable gentleman [Sir Robert Peel] caught the Whigs bathing and walked away with their clothes.
>
> Benjamin Disraeli, Commons speech (28 Feb. 1845)

However, a crisis occurred in 1846, when the party split over the repeal of the corn laws which ended tariff protection for agriculture, favouring commerce and industry at the expense of land. Two groups reflecting the divergence emerged within the party. The more radical one (containing many who had entered Parliament as a result of the 1832 Reform Act), favouring free trade, moved towards the Whigs, with whom they finally merged. Those remaining, the landed interests, once again seemed vulnerable and liable to extinction. Yet again the party was to find a political messiah to lead it out of the wilderness. Benjamin Disraeli (1804–81) was not only able to part the difficult waters of further extensions of the franchise, he created an image for the party which would carry it forward into the era of mass politics.

> I had to prepare the mind of the country [for reform] and ... to educate our party.
>
> Benjamin Disraeli, speech in Edinburgh (29 Oct. 1867)

Disraeli's inspiration was to perceive how the interests of privilege could be allied to those of the ordinary folk whose votes were needed. With a rallying cry of 'One Nation', he argued that the Conservatives were the natural guardians of *all* sections of society. The empire was evoked as the symbol to unite all Englishmen as members of a great white master race. The cost of forging this life-saving bond was a paternalistic commitment on the part of the landed interests to the welfare of the poor and some modest social reform. The strategy was so effective that it was a Conservative government in 1867 which felt confident enough to extend the franchise to manual workers. Working-class support was to remain the vital secret of the party's success. Disraeli had laid the foundations for the modern Conservative Party.

However, after Disraeli's death the party began to lose its way as the old-style Tory traditionalists reasserted their influence. It was saved by the tormented obsession of Gladstone, the Liberal leader, with the Irish question, which split his own party in 1886, propelling a group of unionist defectors, led by the leading radical Joseph Chamberlain, to the Conservative ranks. Subsequently the party acknowledged its commitment to Ireland's continued link with the mainland by adopting the title 'Conservative and Unionist Party'. The transfusion returned to the party some Whiggish blood, embracing the virtues of enterprise and commerce and enabling it to accommodate the rising bourgeoisie destined to dominate the social order. The Tory and Whig strands offered a formidable electoral potential and, although the emphasis has shifted from time to time, they have remained fundamental to the party's remarkable width of appeal.

The Liberals: the era of Gladstone

Although the Liberal Party existed in name until 1988, it was a major force for only around half a century. During its heyday it experienced some great periods of office, the results of many of its policies standing as its monument. Yet, like a figure in classical tragedy, the party (and its great leaders) seemed to contain from the first the seeds of self-destruction.

The modern party was formed by the marriage between the old Whigs and the free-trade faction which left the Tories in 1846. This not only helped to spawn the modern party, but provided one of its greatest figures, William Ewart Gladstone (1809–98), whose austere figure, the very antithesis of the polished Disraeli, dominated the party in the nineteenth century. The ideological rationale of **liberalism** lay in radicalism and reform; it opposed the Conservative view of slow organic change and was impatient with outmoded institutions of government and administration. It supported the interests of business and commerce, free trade, efficient (though minimal) government, economy, home rule for Ireland, nonconformity, parliamentarianism and limited social reform.

> You cannot fight against the future. Time is on our side.
> William Ewart Gladstone (1809–98; Liberal leader),
> speech on the Reform Bill (1866)

The emergence of mass parties

The two great Reform Acts hardened the fluid parliamentary alliances with a new sense of party discipline, greatly enhancing the leaders' authority, not only over the House, but over their own parties. Gladstone and Disraeli dominated both, forging the characteristic two-party system with its **adversarial** style of parliamentary thrust and parry. It was no longer possible to gain election on the basis of bribery and corruption and the two leaders recognized the need to spread their ideological messages to the mass of voters. They fostered organizations in the constituencies (registration societies) to ensure that all sympathizers were registered to vote. The local associations were also given the crucial responsibility of choosing candidates.

To oversee the local activists two London clubs – the Carlton for the Conservatives, and the Reform for the Liberals – became embryonic party headquarters. In addition, federations of local organizations (the National Union of Conservative and Constituency Associations and its reflection, the Liberal Federation) were established to forge a sense of national unity. The existence of a mass membership suggested problems of control: the Conservative Union seemed content to serve the leaders, but the Liberal Federation claimed a right to influence party policy. However, Gladstone would have little truck with such a notion. Despite this, both associations held annual conferences in which the toilers in the constituency fields could voice their opinions. Thus, by the end of the nineteenth century, the mould for the modern system had been cast. Parties were mass organizations, strongly led by elites, seeking to win office on the basis of a broadly ideological position and obliged to court the electorate with policy promises.

Challenge to the Established Order: the Rise of the Labour Party

One of the remarkable aspects of franchise reform was the failure of a working-class party to capitalize on the potential in the mass vote. It was a manifestation of the power and genius of the ruling classes that they managed to make the mass franchise mean a choice between two elites rather than real participation (see pp. 160–7). However, the conditions did not satisfy the active members of the working class, who sought to enter the parliamentary stage themselves.

Labour pre-history

The Labour Party was born in 1900, the result of a long and painful confinement. Though crushed by the establishment, the Chartists had argued from the 1830s that the way to improve working-class conditions lay in securing a parliamentary voice. In 1869 the trade unions created a Labour Representation League but, although succeeding in getting 2 of its 13 candidates returned in 1874, it showed little promise. In addition, some working-class candidates managed to enter Parliament under the Liberal banner, so that by 1885 there were 11 Trade Union Liberal MPs. However, among the various self-inflicted wounds suffered by the myopic Liberal Party was the persistent refusal of constituency associations to nominate working-class candidates. Keir Hardie, Ramsay MacDonald and Arthur Henderson were all spurned – had they not been there might never have been a Labour Party.

Moreover, despite the meagre improvements in their condition, the working class remained content to vote for either factions of the elite duopoly and, when an Independent Labour Party (ILP) was formed in 1893, it aroused pathetically little enthusiasm. However, within the working-class movement a more aggressively socialist New Unionism began to challenge old values. This impetus was strengthened in the late 1890s when both traditional and new unions suffered damaging defeats in large strikes, making the case for direct parliamentary representation more compelling.

During the 1880s and 1890s a new intellectual dynamic came from three political associations. At the extreme left was the London-based Marxist group, the Social Democratic Federation (SDF), led by H. M. Hyndman. Of different character was the intellectual Fabian Society, founded in 1884 by George Bernard Shaw and the indefatigable social researchers Sidney and Beatrice Webb. The society took its name from Quintus Fabius Maximus ('the Delayor'), a Roman general who achieved success by small, cautious moves and delaying tactics rather than reckless bravado – such was the avowed strategy of **Fabianism**. Most important was the ILP, founded to pursue a moderate kind of socialism and numbering amongst its members Philip Snowden, MacDonald and Hardie. However, these associations did not promise to achieve much on their own; in the 1880s there were only about two thousand active socialists in the whole country.

Emerging from the womb

In 1900, the Trades Union Congress (TUC) made the momentous decision to seek a direct parliamentary presence. The might of 65 trade unions, with their hundreds of thousands of members, was combined with the intellectual vigour of the three small organizations to establish a new political force: the Labour Representation Committee (LRC). Significantly, its strategy was in the moderate Fabian tradition, and it has always been possible to distinguish between true **socialism** and 'Labourism' within British politics, a fact which has proved bewildering to socialists. Indeed, the frustration was felt at a very early stage by the SDF, which hastily disengaged itself from the inhibiting embrace. Organizationally the party took much of the outward form of the existing parties (with an annual conference and a National Executive Committee at the centre of its extra-parliamentary organization). However, it had materialized in the opposite way, its mass organization predating its parliamentary cohort, a fact which was to have important implications for its internal power structure.

The reaction of the Conservative government was intensely hostile. It portrayed the movement as nothing less than a threat to the very constitution, requiring harsh confrontational tactics. A series of judicial decisions, culminating in the infamous Taff Vale Judgement of 1901 (holding that unions could be cripplingly sued for the tortious acts of their members), convinced more unions of the need to combine under the new banner and Ramsay MacDonald, as the LRC's secretary, worked to develop a national mass organization to rival those of the traditional parties.

> MacDonald owes his pre-eminence largely to the fact that he is the only artist, the only aristocrat by temperament and talent in a party of plebeians and plain men.
>
> Beatrice Webb (1858–1943; founder member of Fabian Society),
> *Diary* (May 1950)

Labour and the Liberals

Although a fundamental principle of the new party was to remain free of the established elites, an early pragmatic advantage was gained by a secret agreement between MacDonald and the Liberals. Each would withhold candidates from selected constituencies to unify the anti-Conservative vote. Through this strategem the new party signalled its entrance onto the parliamentary stage in 1906 with 29 MPs, who together took the title Parliamentary Labour Party (PLP). The election also saw the return of 24 Lib–Labs, so that for the first time there was in Parliament a formidable working-class phalanx. However, their prime object was to avoid radical

FEBRUARY 13, 1886.]   PUNCH, OR THE LONDON CHARIVARI.   75

ELEVATION.

Wife (of newly-elected Working-Man M.P. to her Visitors). "'OW D'E DO, MRS. FUZBUSH! PRAY TAKE A CHERE, M'UM. THOUGH I HAM A LADY NOW, IT WON'T MAKE NO DIFFERENCE IN MY MANNERS!"

Source: Mary Evans Picture Library

display and ingratiate themselves with the establishment by demonstrating *responsible* behaviour (Miliband 1961: 28). An early success was the Trades Disputes Act of 1906, reversing the Taff Vale Judgement. Yet at this stage Labour did not seem any threat to the Liberals, who went on to form a highly distinguished government, laying the foundations of the British welfare state.

However, these were turbulent times. The Liberal programme led to a dramatic confrontation with the House of Lords, resulting in the 1911 Parliament Act and near civil war over Ireland (only averted by the first world war). During these events Labour became more closely wedded to the Liberals, a development derided by its left wing. It was argued that to become a significant political force the party needed to forge for itself a distinct identity. The first world war provided an opportunity for this.

The People's Budget and the House of Lords

Lloyd George as Chancellor needed to raise £16 million in extra revenue to finance the government's planned social programme as well as build *Dreadnought* battleships for defence. He determined that the money should come principally from the rich, and saw the landlords, against whom he had been conducting a campaign, as the most suitable targets for new taxes. Not surprisingly, these measures shocked the landed interests and gravely alarmed the King, weakened by an arduous life of 'four gargantuan meals a day together with endless wine, brandy, whisky and cigars' (Cross 1963: 106), and the 1909 budget was rejected by the House of Lords, precipitating a constitutional crisis.

Asquith dissolved Parliament over the issue and in the ensuing electoral campaign Lloyd George launched a series of vituperative attacks on the landed interests as leeches on the common people. Yet the undying love of these common people for their King and aristocracy reasserted itself and, in 1910, the government went from its landslide position to a narrow majority. Asquith pushed ahead to a full-scale reform of the upper house and a second general election on the issue was held the same year. Again the Liberals secured a small majority, enabling them to introduce the Parliament Act (1911) formally limiting the legislative powers of the upper house (see chapter 9).

The Inter-war Era

The year 1914 marks the beginning of the Liberals' decline (Wilson 1966). It was the party's misfortune to be in office at the outbreak of war. As Prime Minister, Asquith became the leader of a coalition in 1915 but soon proved unequal to the task. 'His initiative, if he ever had any, was sapped by years of good living in high society' (Taylor 1965: 14) and, following a series of military defeats, he was ousted in 1916 by fellow Liberal Lloyd George, who formed a new coalition government with Conservatives, rather than Liberals, in the majority, thereby inflicting a grievous wound on his party.

For Labour, war provided a taste of office and a chance to demonstrate patriotic qualities. It had shed its pacifist garb and MacDonald (supported by the pacifist ILP) resigned the leadership to be replaced by Henderson. As the war progressed, Henderson's influence increased; he was even included in the War Cabinet, though dealings with international socialism led to his expulsion in 1917. This left him free for party affairs, preparing for a major role in post-war politics which Liberal disarray seemed to promise. With MacDonald and socialist intellectuals such as Sidney Webb, Henderson drew up a new constitution with a clearly socialist tone, including the famous *Clause Four*, with its commitment to the Marxist goal of public ownership. It also recognized the importance of widening the membership and provision was made for individuals to join constituency associations in their own right rather than as trade unionists. The 1918 conference formally approved a wide socialist programme drafted by Webb, entitled *Labour and the New Social Order*, which was to be the mainspring for policy for the next 30 years (Pelling 1968: 44).

The 'Coupon' election

The immediate aftermath of the war proved disastrous for the Liberals. Lloyd George rushed into an opportunistic general election to capitalize on victory by offering further coalition government in alliance with the Conservatives. Coalition candidates were endorsed with a letter signed jointly by Lloyd George and Bonar Law, dubbed the 'coupon' by Asquith, leader of the independent Liberals, in sarcastic evocation of the wartime jargon of rationing. Asquith lost his seat and only 28 of his supporters were returned, but Lloyd George had played into the hands of the Conservatives, delivering his own party into the consuming fires of a political netherworld.

Though not faring well against the anti-socialist pact, Labour had demonstrated its muscle by fielding 361 candidates, a considerable increase on its previous best of 78 in 1910, and the freak circumstances gave little indication of real political trends. The coalition proved unpopular and, after a string of by-election failures (mainly gains for Labour), Bonar Law agreed to destroy what he had helped create. At a momentous meeting at the Carlton Club in 1922, Conservative MPs agreed that it was time to say goodbye to Lloyd George, before he destroyed them as he had the Liberals. As a by-product, a new institution had been created within the Conservative Party, known to this day as the 1922 Committee.

The Liberal wound could not be healed with the break-up of the coalition and candidates fought the ensuing election as either 'Lloyd George' or 'Asquith' Liberals. Labour strength in Parliament rose to 142, outnumbering the combined force of both factions and claiming second-party status. Many of its more able members were returned to the parliamentary fold and the number of ILP-sponsored candidates reached 32, producing an influx of intellectuals and giving the party a wider appeal and more rhetorical virtuosity. Its new constitution and policies attracted able young Liberals despairing of the chasm in their own party.

Labour: a viable alternative government

As the party gained in parliamentary strength the heady possibility of taking over the reins of government became increasingly real. These ambitions were realized at the end of 1923 when Baldwin dissolved Parliament over tariff reform. Although the Liberals revived with 158 seats, Labour increased its presence to 191 (39 ILP). Because of the single-issue nature of the election the government, despite its 258 seats, had been decisively rejected and the Liberals felt justified in supporting Labour, which momentously ruled for ten months as a minority government. Not surprisingly, so tenuous a period of office produced little in the way of social reform and was attacked by socialist purists. This was a hard judgement on the leaders, who had been faced with a task which had hitherto been the preserve of those with wealth, position, and a solid tradition of parliamentary organization. Labour providing a government was, like the proverbial dog walking on its hind legs, remarkable for being done at all.

Labour versus the establishment However, the experience offered a grim illustration of the power of the establishment to thwart the working class. Horrified at the prospect of Labour rule, it went to unprincipled lengths to undermine the government with alarmist propaganda and deceit. Anglo-Russian relations was an area of particular sensitivity. When the Foreign Office was unable to reach agreement with Soviet emissaries a group of Labour MPs intervened. Opponents jumped on this as evidence of left-wing pressure and a massive anti-communist campaign ensued. The final straw came in the Campbell Case, when the Attorney General decided to drop sedition proceedings in a minor case against the editor of a small communist journal. This was fanned up as evidence of corruption of the judicial process and the Liberals grew nervous, withdrawing their support and forcing MacDonald to dissolve Parliament. The ensuing election campaign saw one of the shabbiest scandals of British politics – the Zinoviev letter (see p. 564). Chilling press warnings that a vote for Labour was a vote for a soviet system resulted in the establishment regaining its hold on the tiller.

Yet the value of parliamentary action to the working class was to be underlined when trade union recourse to direct industrial action proved abortive. In 1925, Chancellor of the Exchequer Winston Churchill put the country back on the gold standard, precipitating a crisis in which alarmed mine-owners called for drastic cuts in wages. Events culminated in the calamitous general strike of 1926, the abysmal failure of which led to a renewed commitment to the Labour Party. With 288 seats Labour emerged from the 1929 general election for the first time as the largest single party. This was a turning point in British politics. The Liberals had crossed the electoral Rubicon in that the inbuilt bias of the first-past-the-post system began, inexorably, to weigh against them. The future seemed to lie only in some form of union with Labour, and a second minority government was formed, though for the Liberals the embrace was to be that of the deadly praying mantis.

MacDonald's disgrace However, events were to shake Labour to its foundations. From the outset the government was severely hamstrung by the Liberals in the Commons and the Conservatives in the Lords. Problems were exacerbated by economic depression, the Cabinet split over the question of cutbacks in public expenditure (the most severe to be in unemployment benefit) as a condition of international loans, and on 23 August 1931 MacDonald resigned as Prime Minister. However, the following day he stunned his colleagues by accepting the King's invitation to form a Conservative-dominated *National Government*. Many saw this as despicable treachery and, together with a few followers, he was disowned. In the coalition MacDonald became a prisoner of his Cabinet. In leaving the gold standard, he agreed to the very thing which Labour had been warned off when in office, and none of the dire predictions followed. Without his party he was obliged to fight the next election on the basis of the coalition. 'National candidates' went to the country for a 'doctor's mandate' to heal its maladies and secured overwhelming endorsement (Labour faring disastrously with only 46 seats), the Conservatives gaining the lion's share of seats and dominating the coalition.

> There are no professions he [MacDonald] ever made, no pledges he ever gave to the country, and no humiliation to which he would not submit if they would allow him still to be called Prime Minister.
>
> Viscount Snowden, House of Lords speech (3 July 1934)

These events marked the end of an era for Labour, fortunes remaining at a low ebb until the prospect of a general election in 1935 saw some moderation in the anti-MacDonald hysteria. Clement Attlee became leader, the first to lack genuine working-class credentials, and the party, though not recovering its 1929 position, revived with 154 seats, while the Liberals drifted further into the wilderness.

The close of an era: the second world war The second world war had a significant effect on the party system and led to the further entrenchment of the Labour Party, which at first refused to join the coalition, but later agreed, subject to the condition that it would not be led by the discredited Chamberlain, whose policy of appeasing Hitler was exposed as folly. Thus it

The decline and fall of the Liberals

The disintegration of the Liberal Party remains one of the great cautionary tales of British politics. Within a single decade from 1914 it had descended from control of the House of Commons to a parliamentary presence of only 42 MPs and their leader rejected by the electorate. By 1929 it was represented by 20 MPs. There is no simple explanation and no single cause; rather there was a confluence of unfavourable circumstances, together with something of a death wish within the party. One historian likened the demise to that of a frail old gent, troubled by a variety of serious ailments (the rise of Labour and the suffragettes, the problems of Ireland), whose misfortunes were to be compounded while crossing the road by a violent meeting with a rampaging bus (the first world war); his state of health is easy to diagnose, but the actual cause of death is rather difficult to ascertain (Wilson 1966: 20–1). The story is something of a political whodunit and, in pondering any possible denouement, a number of suspects may be assembled along with the butler in the political drawing room:

- a congenital tendency to fragment;
- strong personalities whose ambitions or convictions overrode matters of purely party interest;
- the misfortune to be in power at the outbreak of the first world war;
- an inability to adapt its principles to the harsher climate of the twentieth century (Dangerfield 1936);
- the loss of leading personalities and potentially radical reformers like Chamberlain, Dilke, Churchill and Lloyd George;
- the rise of Labour and the Liberals' willingness to allow it to gather strength through the indulgence of electoral pacts (Wilson 1966: 19);
- an ending of the old social cleavage between landowners and capitalists who began to unite under the Conservative banner (Taylor 1965: 172);
- failure to recognize the importance of the Labour movement and embrace its leading figures under the party banner (several were rejected as parliamentary candidates);
- the defection of activists and supporters to the growing Labour Party in the inter-war years;
- the prolonged fight with the suffragettes, which showed insensitivity to the call for democracy;
- the British electoral system, which magnified small disparities in the votes cast into large differences in the number of seats.

could claim to have brought Winston Churchill to the premiership. It did well in the apportionment of offices, with Attlee and Greenwood both in Churchill's first war cabinet of five. When the Cabinet was enlarged in 1940,

Bevin was brought in, along with the extreme left-winger, Cripps. Attlee's position as party leader was strengthened as he became generally recognized as deputy prime minister, taking control of home affairs administration and gaining a reputation for efficiency and incisive decision-making. Internally the party became more stable than at any time since the 1920s, Bevin establishing a harmonious working relationship with Attlee. The political climate became uniquely favourable as, with the publication of the Beveridge Report, public opinion welcomed socialist ideas and the concept of the welfare state.

The Era of Consensus: Parties Without Ideologies

> **The masters now**
>
> We are the masters at the moment – and not only for the moment but for a very long time to come.
>
> Lord Shawcross (member of 1945 Labour government), Commons speech
> (2 April 1946)

After the war Churchill agreed to an early election and the party battle resumed. In 1945, the pattern of support gave every indication of a breathtaking revolution in British politics. A Labour landslide produced a majority over the Conservatives of 180, the first overall majority in its history. The swing in the marginal seats introduced a new kind of Labour MP drawn from the professions, helping to break Labour's cloth-cap image and giving a broader representative character. The government embarked upon an agenda intended to shake the foundations of British economic and social life, but within a regime of severe post-war austerity which was to colour perceptions of the party.

The aura of office increased the authority of the Labour leader within the party. Attlee was, for example, able to make the momentous decision to manufacture atom and hydrogen bombs without consulting colleagues. Yet in spite of the verdict of the people he was deeply concerned to win the respect of the capitalist establishment, even expelling from the party those whose views were too far to the left. His authority also stemmed from trade union loyalty, gained in large measure through his close relationship with Bevin.

For the establishment, events suggested unnervingly that the people, having come through the nightmare of war, had finally had enough of upper-class rule. There was much alarmist talk in stately drawing rooms, but the threat of calamity concentrated Conservative minds, enabling them again to demonstrate the protean qualities which have preserved them throughout the entire era of modern politics. Under party chairman Lord Woolton, the skilled architect of the Conservative recovery was R. A. Butler, who recognized that the ideological heartland had shifted to the left. He also saw that the umbilical link binding the unions to the Labour Party meant that they would be regularly consulted in a new age of interest group involvement in government. His strategy was not to oppose the drift, but to challenge Labour at its own game and steal its support in the country. Liberal democracy (minimal government) had given way to **social democracy**, in which the state assumed a positive role in social and economic life.

By the end of the hectic term the government was showing fatigue strains. Many stalwarts were well past their prime, some stricken with illness, some dead, and in the country people were weary of austerity. In the 1950 general election Labour narrowly clung to office but, lacking confidence to govern, Attlee, with a political death wish, went back to the country the following year. This time Labour polled the record number of votes ever cast for any British party, but the idiosyncrasies of the electoral system gave the Conservatives the majority, thereby easing the palpitating establishment (and American) hearts.

Butler had fashioned a bipartisan **consensus** which suited both sets of leaders in that it ruled out any hopes for a third contender by swamping the ideological central ground. This began a period of the peace spoken of by the Archbishop of York in Act IV of Shakespeare's *Henry IV* (Part 2), when

> both parties nobly are subdued;
> And neither party loser.

Yet the tranquil consensus view is misleading; there were powerful undercurrents. Labour was never entirely suited to erecting the manifesto tent in the middle of the ideological field and indulged in enervating, and electorally costly, infighting. A fundamentalist minority, led by Aneurin Bevan, vehemently opposed the leadership. The dissidents were mainly the newer members, highly articulate and able to propagate their views through their journal – *Tribune*. After tenacious resistance, in 1955 Attlee was finally persuaded to go, in favour of the sternly moderate Gaitskell (1906–63), but the new leader inherited a worsening discipline problem. The supportive trade union old guard was passing on and the largest union, the TGWU, had come under the leadership of the left-wing Frank Cousins.

The Suez crisis In the Conservative Party there was also a faction that did not fit easily with the consensus model, though in this case it was on the right. When Churchill finally relinquished the leadership, party and government seemed healthy and the succession passed to the smoothly aristocratic Anthony Eden. Yet despite an early general election success in 1955, domestic problems mounted, and by spring 1956 his popularity rating nose-dived from 70 to 40 per cent (Butler and Rose 1960: 36). He was certainly in no state to handle the momentous Suez Crisis of 1956 (see pp. 82–4), which traumatized the British establishment. A right-wing Suez Group advocating tough action was incensed by the ignominious withdrawal, while another faction of around 40 MPs expressed abhorrence at the dishonest pretext for the British invasion. Although there was strong jingoistic support for the action from the constituencies (Nicolson 1958: 133), Eden retired in humiliation, leaving the party in morbid contemplation of a possible two decades out of office.

Winds of change: the Macmillan era

> The Conservatives know there are books to read, pictures to look at, music to listen to – and grouse to shoot.
>
> Harold Macmillan (1894–1986; Conservative leader), quoted by Nigel Nicholson in Thames TV programme, *The Day Before Yesterday* (1970)

Eden's departure exposed the arcane and elitist process whereby the party chose (or more accurately, did not choose) its leader. Party elders Lords Salisbury and Kilmuir appear to have conducted soundings within the Cabinet and Harold Macmillan (1894–1986) was preferred over the diligent and admired Butler. Yet the choice was to prove inspired. With an Edwardian dilettantism concealing shrewd recognition of the consensus era, he was able not only to rebuild the weakened substructure of the party, but modernize its facade in line with the times. In addition, he restored self-confidence at home and repaired the damage to Anglo-American relations. Macmillan earned the cartoonists' nickname 'Supermac' yet, despite his success, some on the right wing mistrusted him. In 1960 the Monday Club was formed to commemorate 'Black Monday', when he made his celebrated speech about the need for change in racist South Africa.

> The wind of change is blowing through the continent. Whether we like it or not, this growth of national consciousness is a political fact.
>
> Harold Macmillan, speech in South African Parliament (3 Feb. 1960)

Labour in the wilderness The Suez crisis did not help Labour as much as was expected. Although shocking the intelligentsia, a mood of popular jingoism generally prevailed, which was shared by many Labour supporters (Pelling 1968: 118). In 1959, the party suffered a third successive defeat, the Conservative majority increasing to 100. This led to serious self-doubts for Labour. The party seemed to have squandered its post-war inheritance and younger members began to talk of revising policies. In 1956 Anthony Crosland had published *The Future of Socialism*, arguing, among other things, that in an age of affluence public ownership was an embarrassing

> By far the most radical man I've known in politics wasn't on the Labour side at all – Harold Macmillan. If it hadn't been for the war he'd have joined the Labour Party . . . Macmillan would have been Labour Prime Minister, and not me.
>
> Clement Attlee (1883–1967; Labour leader), quoted in James Margach,
> *The Abuse of Power* (1981)

anachronism (Crosland 1956). The revisionist theme was taken up by Gaitskell, who confronted the traditionalists head-on in a momentous 1960 party conference, where he suffered an heroic failure to remove Clause Four from the constitution. He also fought a battle to resist unilateral nuclear disarmament, which he finally won the following year, having gained the support of four of the largest unions.

> Do you think that we can become overnight the pacifists, unilateralists and fellow travellers that other people are? . . . There are some of us, Mr Chairman, who will fight, fight and fight again to save the party we love.
>
> Hugh Gaitskell, speech to Labour Party Annual Conference (5 Oct. 1960)

The Night of the Long Knives The Conservative Party also had difficulties with economic problems and falling popularity. On 13 July 1962 a desperate Macmillan reversed the action of *Julius Caesar*, turning on one-third of his Cabinet colleagues in the greatest blood-bath in modern political history: 'The Night of the Long Knives'.

Scandal: the Profumo affair Notwithstanding the general misfortunes, it was a more sordid affair which brought the leader's failing touch to a wider, tabloid-reading public. The Profumo scandal arose from an intriguing *ménage à trois* involving a government minister, a high-society prostitute (Christine Keeler), a Russian naval attaché, and a host of exotic bit players including Mandy Rice Davies (a prostitute), Stephen Ward (an alleged procurer of ladies for the gentry) and a mysterious man (believed to be a respected pillar of the establishment) featured only in photographs wearing a black mask (and little else). It is doubtful if the public were concerned with the security aspects of the affair; indeed it is doubtful if there *were* any security aspects. The massive newspaper coverage demonstrated that the main interest lay in the intoxicating contemplation of hanky-panky in high places.

The party's image was also not helped by the penchant of the early 1960s for cynicism and lightweight satire. Oxbridge undergraduates began poking fun at the establishment in the theatre (*Beyond the Fringe*), in the press (*Private Eye*), and on television (*That Was the Week that Was*). The last was so feared that it was taken off the air (see p. 150).

Constitutional change in the Conservative Party

Macmillan's retirement in 1963, on the grounds of ill-health, produced one of the most controversial events in the history of his party and led to a major change, the significance of which was not to become fully apparent until the 1980s. The patient Butler was again the natural heir, but the aristocratic Sir Alec Douglas-Home was conjured up by the establishment from entombment in the House of Lords by renouncing his title (as did Lord Hailsham) to take up the torch. It was felt that Macmillan, who influenced the succession from his sick-bed, had acted autocratically, and the method of appointment became a topic for serious debate.

> He is used to dealing with estate workers. I cannot see how anyone can say he is out of touch.
>
> Lady Caroline Douglas-Home, speaking of her father's suitability as Prime Minister, quoted in the *Daily Herald* (21 Oct. 1963)

Home continued a tradition in which the party's leaders came from its Tory rather than its Whig strain, but he seemed out of touch with the age. The 1964 election campaign saw him ravaged by the adroit new Labour leader, Harold Wilson, who mocked the aristocratic antecedents of his opponent. Labour secured a majority of four; with a different leader the Conservatives might have gained a fourth term. It was finally agreed that a ballot of the parliamentary party should become the basis for leadership selection and Home resigned to allow the new system to come into operation.

> As far as the 14th Earl is concerned, I suppose Mr Wilson, when you come to think of it, is the 14th Mr Wilson.
>
> Sir Alec Douglas-Home, BBC TV interview (21 Oct. 1963)

The Wilson era

Wilson had acceded to the Labour leadership in 1963 as a result of Gaitskell's unexpected death and brought the more conciliatory tone which helped win the narrow victory in 1964. His personal style was said to have been modelled on the charismatic and youthful President Kennedy. Although there were dissidents on questions of immigration, incomes policy and defence, they could only mutter in dark corners, while party conferences applauded their witty young leader.

By the beginning of 1964 Wilson felt confident enough to ask for a stronger mandate, gaining an overall majority of 96. The new Labour influx

TARGET PRACTICE

Reproduced by permission of *Punch*

was predominantly from the middle classes, giving the party a forceful professional image to back up Wilson's 'white heat of technology' rhetoric. Labour began to look like a 'natural' party of government and the seriousness of the threat to establishment hegemony was demonstrated by the intensity with which Wilson was attacked by the full might of the media.

> The Labour Party is like a stage coach. If you rattle along at great speed everybody inside is too exhilarated or too seasick to cause any trouble. But if you stop everybody gets out and argues about where to go next.
>
> Harold Wilson, quoted in Leslie Smith, *Harold Wilson: The Authentic Portrait* (1964)

Even so, there was surprise when the government was ejected in 1970 and a glittering decade, the 'swinging sixties', closed.

The Liberal Party During this consensus era the Liberal Party had been no more than a bit player on the stage; to some a buffoon, to others a figure of tragedy. In the bipartisan scenario it had no place, being neither regionally based, nor radical. The desperate condition was symbolized in the fate of its leader, Jeremy Thorpe, who in the 1970s became embroiled in the Norman Scott affair, a sordid scandal involving homosexuality, blackmail, threatened murder and even caninicide.

Liberal Party leaders since 1900

1900	H. Campbell-Bannerman		1945	C. Davies
1908	H. Asquith		1956	J. Grimond
1926	D. Lloyd George		1967	J. Thorpe
1931	H. Samuel		1976	D. Steel
1935	A. Sinclair		1988	Merger to form SLD; leader P. Ashdown

The Consensus Cracked: the 1970s

Heath: the coming of Selsdon Man

The Conservatives had embarked upon a new era under Edward Heath, the first leader to be elected and, significantly, the first to hail from the party's *petit bourgeois* strain. He had been chosen for his similarity to Wilson, the party applying Newton's Law of Motion to politics by attempting to counter Labour with an equal and opposite force, although the new style had failed to produce any immediate reversals. In 1966 the Conservatives had polled fewer votes than under Home, reducing their parliamentary presence by 50.

However, in the same way that the party revamped its policies and image after 1945, Heath had worked diligently in opposition to give it a managerial/technocratic image to match Labour's. A conference of businessmen and politicians at the Selsdon Park Hotel, Croydon, led to sightings of a new species of *Homo Conservatas* – 'Selsdon Man' – able to survive as well in the rugged terrain of private industry boardrooms as in the more temperate climes of Whitehall and Horse Guards' Parade. In 1970 Heath pulled off an unexpected *coup* (gaining an overall majority of 30 seats), surprising his own party as much as his opponents.

In government his rhetoric spoke of the need to free the forces of the market to induce greater efficiency in industry. As a long-standing Europhile, he led the nation into the Common Market (the European Economic Community) in 1973. However, increasing inflation and rising unemployment led to a return to the post-war remedies. The reversals, branded 'U-turns', were taken as evidence of weakness. To compound his agony Heath also experienced unrelenting opposition from the unions, Arthur Scargill of the National Union of Miners proving a particularly dark *bête noir*. In February 1974, Heath called an ill-timed general election to ask the electorate 'Who governs?' and, although a majority supported him, the idiosyncrasy of the electoral system again thwarted voters, Labour gaining the most seats, though not an absolute majority in Parliament.

The two-party system under pressure

Rather than resign immediately, Heath held talks with the Liberals in an effort to cling to office but, unable to reach an agreement for support in Parliament, he conceded defeat. The indeterminate situation forced Wilson to go once again to the country in October, but this did little to clarify the confusion, producing an overall majority of only three. The failure of either party to secure control introduced a dramatic new uncertainty factor into the battle, and there was talk of the old mould of two-party politics being shattered.

April 1976 saw the unexpected retirement of Wilson, bequeathing to James Callaghan rising inflation, bad union relations (partly created by Callaghan), and IMF-imposed monetarism (see pp. 393–4). All this was to culminate in a cold and gloomy 'winter of discontent' (1978–9) induced by public sector strikes, the media and some academics proclaiming a crisis of ungovernability.

The crisis deepened as by-election defeats rendered the government increasingly fragile until it could be sustained only with the life-support machine of a Lib–Lab pact. This development brought joy to Liberal hearts as they contemplated a new era in which a centre party might hold the balance of power. However, the government was defeated on 28 March 1979 on a vote of no confidence and the Conservatives returned rejuvenated. Again they had used their time in the reformatory of opposition gainfully, emerging ready to take British party politics into a new era, but not the one envisioned by the Liberals.

The coming of Thatcherism

> Any woman who understands the problems of running a home will be nearer to understanding the problems of running a country.
>
> Margaret Thatcher, quoted in the *Observer* (8 May 1979)

Heath's humiliation had placed him in bad odour and he was forced to submit to further ordeal by election. On 11 February 1975, to the amazement of many, a dark horse emerged on a second ballot as the leader.

Margaret Thatcher would have been unlikely to have had the support of the Lords, the party elders, the Shadow Cabinet or the constituencies, and was thus a clear beneficiary of the new electoral system (Blake 1985: 320).

The new leader was to seize radical initiatives on all policy fronts in a way never attempted before. The objective was no less than a frontal assault on the orthodoxy of post-war social democracy, corporatism and consensus. Thatcher's mentor was Sir Keith Joseph, who had himself experienced a political conversion to free-market philosophy. He had created the Centre for Policy Studies under **New Right** guru Alfred Sherman, and in this laboratory, outside the formal party machinery, a strange alchemy of neoliberalism was brewed which was to alter the course of British politics. A new broom was brought to bear on Central Office: Joseph became chairman of the Advisory Committee on Policy which, in the preparation for the 1979 general election, presided over 60 policy groups consisting of MPs and advisers (Riddell 1985: 31).

The election was critical. The new leader avowed that (being a woman) she would be permitted just one chance, and the spoils of victory promised riches beyond the dreams of avarice in the form of a gushing supply of North Sea oil available for generous policies ranging from tax hand-outs to increased welfare, according to political fancy. By the time of the campaign the party, its coffers now brimming with private-sector largesse, was in good shape for battle.

Enterprise man

I always dreamt of owning a Ferrari. I work very long hours, and I like to drive to and from work in a lovely luxurious car. I enjoy being stared at and seeing the car being admired.

Tim Bell, quoted in the *Observer* (22 April 1979)

Margaret Thatcher recognized the importance of the mass media in modern politics and, more than any leader before, was assiduous in her courtship of the cameras. Saatchi and Saatchi were engaged to harness the skills of Maddison Avenue. Tim Bell, who handled the account, revealed himself as the very apotheosis of New Right man. The relationship was to prove symbiotic. For the brothers Saatchi, company stock soared, and the general election result gave the Conservatives 339 seats, a majority over Labour of 60, and the country's first woman Prime Minister.

The Thatcher Era: Fractured Consensus or New Centre?

By the end of the 1980s it was possible to speak of a Thatcher era. Commentators varied in the extent to which they ascribed all developments to the domineering personality of the Conservative leader, but none could disagree that momentous changes had been wrought.

Thatcherism: the party begins to swing

Initially the new programme faltered. Not all the party shared the zealotry and the Cabinet contained a large element inherited from Heath which impeded radical progress. After the Crosby by-election in November 1981, in which Shirley Williams stole a Conservative seat for the Social Democrats, the deposed Heath mused on the possibility of future coalition governments in which he might be willing to serve. Unemployment rose and Mrs Thatcher's popularity sunk to an all-time low.

The Falklands factor Although things had already begun to improve, it was the astonishing good luck of the Falklands crisis which gave Mrs Thatcher the boost she needed. In an upsurge of popular bellicose chauvinism, the party was once again able to assume its mantle as the protector of Queen and empire, and the 1983 election was eagerly anticipated. Within her party Thatcher's ascendancy became virtually absolute; those who came to scoff very quickly began to pray. The years between 1983 and 1987 saw a flowering of the new ideology of Thatcherism (see p. 394) and the 1987 general election gave the Conservatives a third term with a majority of 102. However, the pattern of support became increasingly concentrated in the prosperous south-east, with the party showing less and less of its traditional 'one-nation' paternalism (see p. 177).

Within the party, the structure of class power had been radically changed as a result of Thatcher patronage. The Conservative majority brought into Parliament many new-style MPs with meritocratic backgrounds to replace the old-style knights of the shires. In April 1988, Major John Stokes, Conservative member for Halesowan and Stourbridge, enquired during Prime Minister's Questions whether 'there is still room in the party for the nobility, the gentry, and the middle class'.

Conservative Party leaders since 1900

1900	Marquis of Salisbury	1940	W. Churchill
1902	A. Balfour	1955	A. Eden
1911	A. Bonar Law	1956	H. Macmillan
1921	A. Chamberlain	1963	A. Douglas-Home
1922	A. Bonar Law	1965	E. Heath
1923	S. Baldwin	1975	M. Thatcher
1937	N. Chamberlain	1990	J. Major

Labour in the 1980s

As if on a see-saw, the fortunes of Labour sank lower as Conservative stock rose. As Mrs Thatcher had moved the Conservatives from the consensus umbrella towards the right, there were those in the Labour camp pushing in the opposite direction. Like the apostles of the New Right, the hard left abhorred the era of consensus; the Attlee, Gaitskell and Wilson years were depicted as a betrayal of fundamentalist principles. The doyen of the left, Tony Benn, practised public self-flagellation for his past involvement in government and, in 1981, narrowly failed to dislodge Healey in a provocative bid for the deputy leadership.

Although the trade unions had also shifted to the left, it was the constituency associations which became the most important centres for agitation. In 1973 the party had opened its doors to organizations of the left, a process which saw the emergence of Militant Tendency, with a vaguely defined extremist membership, as a party within a party, taking control of local branches and troubling sitting MPs. The principal demands of the left were:

- election of the leader by a franchise wider than the parliamentary party;
- compulsory reselection of all MPs between general elections;
- control of the manifesto to be vested exclusively with the National Executive Committee.

The first two proposals were accepted in 1980. For some, the pressures were too much: choosing flight rather than fight, in March 1981 they founded the Social Democratic Party. However, the reforms did not achieve the desired effect, for in 1983, following the resignation of Michael Foot, Neil Kinnock, who had moved from the left to the centre, became the first leader to be chosen under the new system (see pp. 237–8).

Expensive concessions to the left were unavoidable and Labour's 1983 manifesto offered unilateral nuclear disarmament, withdrawal from the EC, an end to council house sales, renationalization and increased taxation. It was described by Peter Shore from the party's right as 'the longest suicide note in history'. In the final stages of the campaign Labour support began to wilt before the new centrist alliance and only the quirks of the electoral system ensured survival. The party appeared to have reached a nadir. In 1987 Labour fought a much better campaign, yet again the result was failure when the Conservatives, with 42 per cent of the vote, gained a majority of 147 seats.

The new realism It became apparent to Labour leaders that the party had lost its moral claim of being tuned to the march of history and must think hard about its policies. A number of the Thatcher reforms had to be accepted. The new agenda had been recognized throughout Europe by socialist parties in or out of government, even in the USSR with the *perestroika* of Gorbachev, who established a surprising rapport with the British Prime Minister. A policy of reappraisal was started under rising star Brian Gould, with the intention of following the ideological lead of the Conservatives in much the same way that they had tracked Labour after 1945. For the hard left, this attempt to don Thatcher's clothes was a particularly perverse form of transvestism, but leadership and deputy leadership challenges in 1988 received an icy response. At the 1988 party conference Kinnock did not disguise the fact that Labour was not seeking undiluted socialism, stating:

> The kind of economy that we are faced with is going to be a market economy, and we have got to make it work better than the Tories make it work.

> (Bevins and Felton 1988)

Labour's revisionism began to bear fruit by 1989, the opinion polls consistently placing them above the Conservatives. The elections for the European Parliament brought joy to their hearts, giving 45 seats to the Conservatives' 32, and a succession of polls revealed them to be comfortably ahead on most counts.

Labour Party leaders			
1906	K. Hardie	1931	A. Henderson
1908	A. Henderson	1932	G. Lansbury
1910	G. Barnes	1935	C. Attlee
1911	R. MacDonald	1955	H. Gaitskell
1914	A. Henderson	1963	H. Wilson
1917	W. Adamson	1976	J. Callaghan
1921	J. Clynes	1980	M. Foot
1922	R. MacDonald	1983	N. Kinnock

The rise of the third force

One of the most dramatic developments of the system during the 1980s was the birth of the Social Democratic Party (SDP). It appeared at first to be very much a child of its time, though that time was to be short-lived.

The new grouping grew from a rib plucked from the breast of Labour, and its leading figures were all experienced parliamentarians, soon dubbed 'the Gang of Four'. William Rogers and David Owen were sitting MPs, while Shirley Williams and Roy Jenkins had served in previous Labour governments. The aim of this new designer party was to reclaim the centralist pastures and the rhetoric spoke of 'breaking the mould' of the old two-party model with its excessively adversarial style. They wished to re-introduce consensus government (supported by electoral reform) based on European-style coalitions.

By the end of 1981 they were able to claim 27 ex-Labour MPs, though only one Conservative, and in the country a mass organization of some 70,000 had mushroomed. The SDP signalled its presence with some notable by-election victories, two of which returned the remaining members of the Gang of Four – Shirley Williams for Crosby and Roy Jenkins for Glasgow, Hillhead.

From Alliance to merger The emergence of the new party gave renewed heart to the Liberals and in 1983 the two fought under a common Alliance banner to avoid splitting the protest vote. Ambitions were sufficiently high for them to contemplate office, and it was agreed that, under such happy circumstances, Jenkins would be Prime Minister. The result revealed that 26 per cent of voters had chosen the Alliance. Proportional representation would have entitled them to around 160 seats, but as it was they received a meagre 23. They fared no better in 1987, when 22.6 per cent of the votes bestowed a miserly 22 seats. After this, Liberal leader David Steel immediately set under way serious discussions on complete merger, which evoked much acrimony. Within the SDP the leader, David Owen, and a group of supporters ignored the majority vote, steadfastly refusing to abandon the notion of a separate identity. When formal merger as the Social and Liberal Democrats (SLD) took place in early 1988, he remained aloof to head the rump of the old SDP, although it proved to be in terminal decline.

Reproduced by permission of *Punch*

The fall of Thatcher

Events towards the end of 1990 were to shake the Conservative Party to its foundations. From a pinnacle of supremacy in 1987, with a popularity rating of some 48 per cent, Mrs Thatcher was to come crashing down. Dramatic resignations by Nigel Lawson, Chancellor of the Exchequer, and Geoffrey Howe, Leader of the House and Deputy Prime Minister, warned that all was not well in the Cabinet, the main source of dissatisfaction being the Thatcher view of Britain's future in Europe. Moreover, fierce hostility towards the poll tax had seen the Prime Minister's popularity plummet to around 29 per cent, the lowest since the pre-Falklands nadir in 1981. This time the party seemed unable to believe she could pull back to win a fourth term, and the result was the most brutal political knifing in modern political history.

In November Michael Heseltine launched a bid for the party leadership, forcing a humiliating second ballot (see p. 237) upon the Prime Minister. The men in grey suits, the party grandees, warned her to quit for fear the party would be irrevocably riven. Mrs Thatcher consulted her cabinet colleagues individually and the consensus was that she should go. Thus, astonishingly, the longest premiership since 1827, marked by three great electoral triumphs and a series of dramatic policy advances, was terminated, not by the electorate or even by the rank and file, but by the Conservative establishment. The events underlined the hard truth that the party has always combined absolute loyalty to the leader with utter ruthlessness when the failure comes (Bruce-Gardyne 1984: 22); electoral success must take precedence over all else. Yet a deep scar was left on the party.

Conclusion: Evaluating British Two-party Democracy

The British two-party model is held by apologists to have certain features peculiarly favourable to democracy, to be contrasted with the multi-party chaos rife throughout Western Europe. Much orthodox writing has extolled virtues such as the following:

- strong single-party government rather than unstable coalitions;
- a clear choice for electors;
- mandated government (the victorious party can be expected to execute all its promises);
- a clear mechanism for accountability (a whole government may be removed by the avenging hand of the electorate and no member of a discredited team can escape nemesis by creeping back in a newly-formed coalition);
- effective single-party opposition;
- moderate government with continuity of policy because parties seek the centre ground to maximize votes.

However, these virtuous features can all be subject to sceptical review. Indeed one can ask a fundamental question: does Britain really have a two-party system at all? We can examine this with respect to Parliament and to the country.

The party system in Parliament

The fact that two parties dominate Parliament does not mean that single-party government has invariably been the case. During the present century Britain has experienced some 21 years of government by a combination of parties, either in simple coalition, or as members of a National government. Moreover, there have been periods when a single party in office has lacked an absolute majority, being sustained only by an agreement with another party (see p. 326). In addition, the notion that two-partyism produces a regular alternation in office is unconvincing. Even in the post-war era, when the thesis has appeared most plausible, the Conservatives sustained the claim to be the natural party of government with the lion's share of office (see figure 7.4). If the 1987 government completes its full term, the party will have reigned for 30 years of a 47-year post-war period. Thus it is possible to argue that, in Parliament, Britain has something near a single-party-dominant system.

The party system in the country

This may be detected in two ways: in organizational structure, and in levels of electoral support. For much of the early part of the present century the Liberals coexisted with Labour in a three-party system. Since the 1970s, although the memberships of the new centre parties are relatively small, they are by no means inconsequential, having grown while those of the others have shrunk. They also contain some of the most enthusiastic workers; the Liberals in particular have made a virtue of local activism.

In terms of electoral support there is a greater diversity of parties in the country than in Parliament. This has been true ever since the emergence of Labour. Not until the immediate post-war decades did Labour and Conservative begin to carve up the popular vote, and the period was short-lived, ending with a groundswell of support for the nationalist parties of Wales and Scotland in the 1960s and 1970s, a resurgence for the Liberals, the birth of the SDP and the formation of the Alliance.

From the 1970s it was impossible to argue that Britain had a bipartisan electorate; in 1983 and 1987 the Alliance polled around a quarter of the total votes, not much less than Labour (28 and 30 per cent respectively) and over half the number polled by the apparently invincible Conservatives. In fact, the only way this invincibility could be broken under the electoral system would be for the electorate to focus on a single opposition party. This appeared to be happening in the dramatic result in the Mid-Staffordshire by-election of March 1990, where a collapse of the centre-party vote saw a 26 per cent Conservative lead over Labour converted into a 17 per cent Labour majority.

Verdict

Hence, the designation of the British polity as a two-party, or single-party-dominant, system can only be done in a highly qualified way. Such two-partyism as exists is in large measure a distorting result produced by the electoral system. There are other parties in the wings, and a change in the system would be their cue for a dramatic entrance. Soliloquies and dialogues

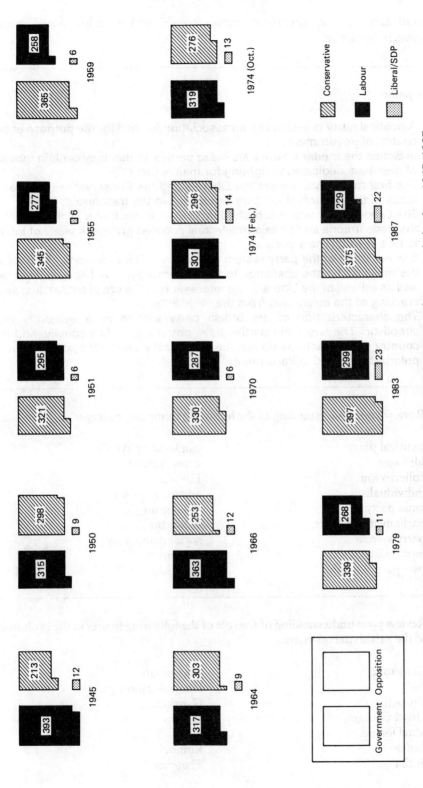

Figure 7.4 The party dispositions in the House of Commons after general elections, 1945–1987

would give way to turbulent crowd scenes and a rather more colourful *dramatis personae.*

Key points

- A political party is essentially an association formed for the purpose of taking control of government.
- In Britain the modern parties are *mass* parties, in that they contain thousands of members dedicated to fighting for their leaders.
- The first mass parties were the Liberals and the Conservatives, formed as a result of the nineteenth-century extensions to the franchise.
- The Labour Party was established in 1900 as a result of a joining together of the trade unions and certain intellectual socialist groups. It was not intended to be a revolutionary party.
- The evolution of the party system can be divided into periods: the genesis of the mass party; the challenge to the system posed by Labour's emergence and its eclipse of the Liberals; the inter-war era; the era of consensus; and the cracking of the consensus from the mid-1970s.
- The characterization of the British party system as a two-party one is simplistic. The two main parties have not shared office equally, and in the country voting patterns do not (because of the electoral system) mirror the polarization found in Parliament.

Review your understanding of the following terms and concepts

political party	single-party system
ideology	conservatism
collectivism	liberalism
individualism	adversary politics
mass party	Fabianism
parliamentary cadre	socialism
party system	social democracy
multi-party system	consensus
two-party system	New Right

Review your understanding of the role of the following figures in the evolution of the British party system

Gladstone	Macmillan
Peel	Douglas-Home
Disraeli	Gaitskell
Lloyd George	Wilson
MacDonald	Heath
Attlee	Kinnock
Butler	Thatcher

Assignment

Study the extract from the *Guardian* and answer the following questions.

Doctors launch pro-NHS party

David Brindle, Social Services Correspondent

DOCTORS opposed to the Government's health service reforms last night launched a single-issue political party with the aim of fighting more than 50 seats at the next general election.

The launch was staged in the Prime Minister's Finchley constituency in north London, one of the seats where the National Health Service Supporters' Party says it is certain to field a candidate.

It proposes to pick its targets mainly from the next 40 most marginal, plus ministerial constituencies and the seats of Tory MPs on the Commons standing committee considering the NHS Bill.

At a press conference earlier yesterday, the founders said the creation of the party was a last resort to try to stop what they considered the most damaging reforms

Dr David Watts, an Ayrshire GP and a former Liberal parliamentary and European candidate, said: "We see the Government hell-bent on rushing into the destruction of the NHS and we feel obliged to do something about it."

Dr Christopher Tiarks, a GP from Cardiff who stood in the Vale of Glamorgan byelection last year as an independent pro-NHS candidate, said: "After 10 years of confused and largely ineffective opposition ... the Government has been able to proceed unopposed to impose policies without proper debate and for which it has no popular mandate."

The strategy appears to be one of appealing mainly to dis-affected Tory voters. Dr Watts said many people felt strongly about the NHS but would not back Labour because of its other policies.

Guardian, 18 Jan. 1990

		% mark
1	Is the proposed Pro-NHS Party a political party in the true sense of the term? Explain your answer.	10
2	How astute do you regard the electoral strategy of the proposed party?	25
3	Would a system of PR improve or lessen this party's prospects?	25
4	What political effects could a party of this kind expect to achieve, short of actually winning seats?	40

Questions for discussion

1 Explain the concept of 'party system'. How would you characterize that of Britain?

2 What did Disraeli mean when he spoke of Peel stealing the clothes of the Whigs?

3 Identify the factors which led to Labour supplanting the Liberal Party as the main challenger to the Conservatives.

4　What were the reasons for the emergence of the mass party organizations in the nineteenth century?
5　What factors have given the Conservative Party its longevity?
6　Examine the effects of the two world wars on the evolution of the Labour Party.
7　Explain the reasons for the era of party consensus following the second world war.

Topic for debate

This house believes that Britain's so-called two-party system is artificially created by the electoral system.
　　or
This house believes that history shows that the British establishment will stop at nothing to keep Labour out of office.

Further reading

Blake, R. (1985) *The Conservative Party from Peel to Thatcher.*
A classic text updated to encompass the Thatcher phenomenon.

Drucker, H. (1979) *Multi-Party Britain.*
Questions the idea that British political culture is essentially bipartisan.

Ingle, S. (1987) *The British Party System.*
Lively and up to date. Particularly useful on the ideologies of the parties.

Pelling, H. (1968) *A Short History of the Labour Party.*
An economical account of the rise of the party with a commendably clear narrative.

Rose, R. (1980) *Do Parties Make a Difference?*
Examines the constraints which limit the freedom of action of parties in government, but written before the impact of Thatcherism was felt.

Sartori, G. (1976) *Parties and Party Systems: a Framework for Analysis.*
Analyses the nature of party systems, laying down criteria for defining a system as a two-party one.

Wilson, T. (1966) *The Downfall of the Liberal Party 1914–1935.*
A book with a thesis to explain the demise of the Liberals, but also very informative.

For light relief

George Dangerfield, *The Strange Death of Liberal England.*
Reveals the outward calm of Edwardian England as a facade concealing seething forces leading towards civil war.

Benjamin Disraeli, *Sybil, or the Two Nations.*
Celebrates the ideas of Disraeli's Toryism – a romance with a Chartist background.

8

Inside the Parties: Masses,
Leaders and Powers Behind
Thrones

Having examined the pattern of development of the party system in broad terms we turn inward to the organization and character of the parties themselves. The chapter falls into three sections. The first focuses on the anatomy of the **mass party organization**. The second examines the **internal party dynamics**: cohesion, power relationships, control mechanisms, and the basic relationship between mass membership and leaders. The concluding section analyses the location of the **parties within the structure of power** in society at large.

Anatomy of the Mass Party

In essence the British political parties can be said to comprise three elements: a parliamentary cadre of MPs, a central bureaucracy, and a large mass membership of voluntary workers in the country (see figure 8.1). In the case of the Conservatives and Liberals the parliamentary cadre predated the organizational network, while the Parliamentary Labour Party (PLP) was a limb of the mass movement. The emergence of the Social Democratic Party (SDP) in the 1980s was, like that of the older parties, a result of the initiative of the Westminster-based cadre. The explanation for the organizational similarities lies partly in the fact that all exist in the same environment and must fulfil certain necessary functions if they are to survive, and partly in the tendency they have to copy each other, a phenomenon sometimes termed contagion. We shall argue later that these similarities are largely superficial,

Figure 8.1 The mass party organization

masking important differences between the parties which are based on their relationship to the structure of power in society.

The constituency associations

The associations maintained in most constituencies have, throughout the century, been regarded as crucial for fighting national elections. Their role entails organizing local campaigns, distributing propaganda, holding meetings, liaising with the local media, canvassing, and so on. In addition, they raise funds, act as party recruitment agencies, and provide candidates. Each has an organizational structure with a chairperson and executive committee of some kind. Many (mainly Conservative) employ a full-time agent to add professional backbone. The selection of candidates is probably the most politically significant act undertaken by local associations, and this right to dispense patronage can be the reward for hours spent on wet doorsteps and in worthy meetings in draughty halls.

Ward associations The grass-roots structure may be further fragmented into ward committees, reflecting the community substructure within the constituency. These are very likely to be active in the politics of local government, and this is the most suitable level for the 'community politics' approach favoured by the Liberal Party.

Individual membership In principle anyone can join a political party. The constituency workers are volunteers devoting their spare time to political activity either as a hobby or an obsession; indeed, it is at this level that some of the fiercest zealotry is encountered, from the 'wild-eyed' hard left to the 'goose-stepping tendency'. Indeed, from the 1970s party memberships have fallen, tending to leave the zealots in command.

> There are a fair number of constituency parties in the commuter belt which are run by people who, frankly, might quite properly be labelled neo-fascists.
>
> Unnamed Conservative MP quoted in S. Ingle,
> *The British Party System* (1987: 83)

Membership is also a social activity, involving parties, whist-drives, concerts, and so on, the Young Conservatives' association being much admired as a dating agency and marriage bureau. Although willing to give them loyal support at the ballot box, few working-class people actually join the Conservative Party, which remains very much a middle-class preserve. At one time Conservative associations were controlled by local aristocrats, but they are now largely in the hands of small businessmen and professionals.

Affiliated associations In the Labour Party there is, in addition to individual membership, a form of indirect membership whereby associations such as socialist societies and trade unions affiliate with the party, giving it an extremely large mass membership on paper.

Intermediate-level associations Neighbouring constituency associations may combine at a level intermediate between the constituency and the centre, for purposes of coordination at area, regional or provincial levels. This was most significant in the SDP, where, because the party had to establish itself as a viable national force in the shortest possible time, the Area was the primary unit of association. Area members select candidates for the constituencies by postal ballot.

The federal organizations

The constituencies are united through federal associations. The first of these was the Liberal Registration Association, founded in 1861. In 1867 the Conservatives founded the National Union of Conservative and Unionist Associations headed by a president, a team of elected officers, and a central council consisting of representatives from all sections of the party. The Labour constituency associations form the Labour Party as such (the parliamentary cadre being the PLP).

The SDP began life by setting up a Council for Social Democracy while some of its members were still Labour MPs. The small body remained the representative of the mass organization and its supreme policy-making body.

It differed from its counterparts in the other parties in that it was headed by a powerful elected president who, with the leader, gave the party a Janus-like head.

Red flag and blue rinse: the annual conference

Each party holds an annual **conference** which, in an age of mass communications, is its most important shop window. Although bringing together all sections of the party, it is really a celebration of the mass membership. The event is a kind of jamboree in which all who have laboured in the fields on behalf of their leaders may draw near to pay homage. Conferences last for several days in the pleasant atmosphere of the seaside at the end of the season, but before the weather is too cold to enjoy a publicity-seeking dip. All takes place before the unblinking eyes of the television cameras, supplemented with a ball-by-ball commentary by the pundits.

Generally speaking the pattern involves a succession of debates on resolutions submitted by members, with speakers drawn from various sections of the party. Voting in the Labour conference has contained one striking feature in the form of the **block vote**, whereby delegates cast votes weighted in accordance with the size of their membership. The appropriate parliamentary leader (minister or shadow minister) will usually speak at the conclusion of the debate as a grand climax, and individual popularity is

The violence comes home: IRA bombing of the Grand Hotel, Brighton, during the Conservative Party conference, 1984
Source: Times Newspapers Ltd

gauged by the length and intensity of the applause. The audiences have their favourites: before he joined the ranks of fallen angels, Michael Heseltine, with his handsome profile and mane of golden hair, was accorded the adulation of a matinée idol. Generally, those attending conferences are zealots, and it is the more extreme views which gain the plaudits. Mrs Thatcher's legendary 'resolution' moved audiences to frenzied hero worship. On the other hand, a Conservative Home Secretary has the most difficult time since, whatever the measures proposed, and however tough the rhetoric, it will be unlikely to satisfy the bloodthirsty demands of the hanging-and-flogging school of penal reform.

Labour conferences often expose a sharp duality between the parliamentary leaders preaching the doctrine of moderation and trying on capitalist clothes, and the fundamentalist constituency prophets who see sackcloth and ashes as the only garb suitable for those who have repeatedly betrayed the faith. We shall see later (pp. 241–4) that Labour conferences are of more significance in party policy-making than Conservative; resolutions gaining the required support become part of the party's programme.

Conferences tend to spill out from the official centre, both socially and politically, into the surrounding environs. Parties of the non-political kind proliferate and there is a brisk business in fringe meetings where leading figures at the extremes of the party, who are 'managed' out of the main event, can expound their views in an atmosphere often more lively and stimulating than that found in the official forum. Increasingly the media show interest in the fringe; Michael Heseltine claimed that his views on regional imbalance given to the Tory Reform Group in 1988 received 'more serious coverage than for any speech I ever made at a Conservative conference' (Pienaar 1988). However, the organizers make strenuous efforts to ensure that the party boat is not rocked before the vigilant eyes of the media. Conservative leaders have demonstrated a clear superiority in the art of stage management, employing public relations experts to orchestrate their entrances and exits. In the Labour Party, speakers usually emerge who believe that, like justice, the washing of disgusting linen should be seen to be done, preferably on the launderette of television. However, Labour has become more skilled at protecting its image, debates on issues such as gay rights being carefully timed to take place when the cameras switch off for children's television. All the conferences conclude with a rousing speech from the party leader, the content and style of which are regarded as a key test of political virility, and the Labour Party places the final seal on its business with the fraternal rendition of 'The Red Flag'.

> No member of the [Conservative] conference wants to let down the party in front of the national (TV) audience. Everybody is on his best behaviour, naturally a great aid to the leadership.
>
> Ian Gilmour (Conservative MP), *The Body Politic* (1969: 80–1)

The executive bodies

The mass parties need **executives** to handle day-to-day business. The Conservatives have an Executive Committee consisting of around 150, including party officials, representatives of the constituencies and of business interests, MPs and Central Office. However, although not without importance, it is but a pale shadow of its Labour counterpart, the NEC.

The Labour National Executive Committee (NEC) is a key point of authority within the party. Acting on behalf of the conference, it exerts a greater dominance than any extra-parliamentary body in the other parties. With the exception of the leader, deputy leader and party secretary (who are automatically included), members are nominated and elected by the annual conference by the various sections of the party, as shown in figure 8.2. The trade unions have been in a position to control a majority of the NEC. The NEC elects its own chair and vice-chair.

Although the constitutional position of the NEC is to be the servant of the mass party, its practical role is better understood as one of leadership. It meets regularly and has a key position in policy formation, with various subcommittees producing statements on policy which are submitted as

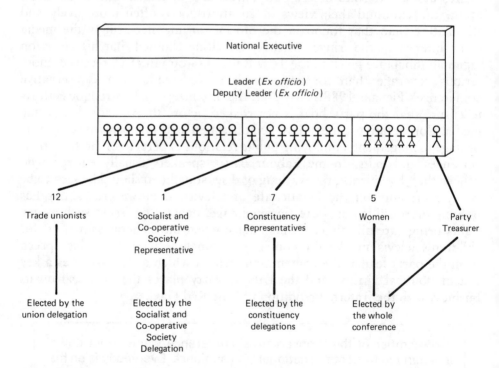

Figure 8.2 Composition of the Labour National Executive Committee

resolutions to be debated by the conference. Moreover the NEC, in conjunction with the parliamentary leadership, determines which elements of the programme will be included in the manifesto. It also has a party management and discipline function, supervising the mass organization at all levels and with the power to veto candidates selected by the constituencies.

The party bureaucracies

The **bureaucracies** are the professional skeleton for the flesh of the large voluntary army, manning party headquarters as career administrators not unlike civil servants. The Conservatives have their Central Office in Smith Square, while Labour has its Head Office. For long this was popularly known as 'Transport House' owing to its location in the headquarters of the Transport and General Workers' Unions, but in 1980 it moved, not without a certain symbolism, to rather less salubrious environs south of the Thames in Walworth Road.

The bureaucracies have a wide range of functions, including overseeing policy on candidates (such as number of female or working-class candidates) and maintaining a central list of select candidates. In day-to-day management and control they ensure that the voluntary arm will be effective while not challenging the authority of the leadership, coordinating local activities, providing a link between the leader and the mass membership, and giving advice and information to constituencies. They are also involved in public relations (liaison with the mass media and producing party literature), backstage management of the annual conference, organizing research into policy, and servicing backbencher's committees. Finally, they control party finances and raise funds.

Conservative Central Office (established in 1870) is largely a personal machine to serve the leader (Pinto-Duschinsky 1972). A significant development took place in 1906 and 1911, during opposition, when the key position of Chairman of the Party was created, to be held by an MP of cabinet rank responsible for running the Office. The appointment was to become one of the leader's most significant patronage gifts. In contrast, Labour Head Office was created by the National Executive Committee and is not formally responsible to the party leader. However, in practice its role has been little different from that of Central Office, though it suffers from the parlous state of the party's finances. The smaller parties maintain modest bureaucratic support, reflecting the lesser demands made by the small parliamentary cadres.

The parliamentary cadre

At the apex of the organizational pyramid sit the *parliamentary cadres* of MPs, including the leader, the front bench, and the backbench organizations. Though only the tips of the organizational icebergs they represent the most politically active sections and contain the leading figures. We will see in chapter 10 how, with their organization and party discipline, they provide the mainspring to drive Parliament (pp. 281–7). The extent to which the parliamentary cadres are independent of the rest of the party organization is one of the key questions of political analysis. Although elected by the people, they owe their chance to stand under the party label to the mass organization, so are in the confusing position of having to serve two masters. The issue of power within the parties is examined later in this chapter (pp. 241–4).

The life and soul of the parties: satellite groups

Within and around the parties is a constellation of smaller organizations or **ginger groups** consisting of various combinations of MPs and ordinary members. Although having separate identities, they owe their *raisons d'être* to the parent party, which they often feel an ideological compunction to influence. They can give a party much of its character, claiming variously to be its soul, its conscience, or its ideas bank, though they are often seen by the leaders as cancerous growths or diabolical incarnations requiring surgery or exorcism.

In 1883, the Primrose League was formed in an attempt to keep alive the 'one-nation' spirit of Disraeli-style Conservatism (Disraeli's favourite flower was the primrose). More recently the Bow Group was founded by Conservative intellectuals in 1951 as a counterpoise to Labour's Fabian Society. Its membership includes about 70 MPs and it professes a moderate policy view, disseminating its message through a journal, *Crossbow*.

When the right-wing Monday Club formed in 1960 to oppose Macmillan's position on South Africa it was mainly concerned with defence matters, but it went on to oppose any fellow MP considered too liberal. It has been accused of dealings with the National Front, but the coming of Thatcherism rather upstaged it, leaving it preaching mainly to the converted. The spirit of neoliberalism kindled by Heath in his early years as leader led to the establishment in 1973 of the Selsdon Group, and subsequently neoliberal views have been propagated by a rich vein of right-wing think-tanks welcomed by Mrs Thatcher, including the Centre for Policy Studies, the Adam Smith Institute, the Institute for Economic Affairs, and the Salisbury Group (publishing the extreme-right *Salisbury Review*). However, there were also anti-Thatcherite forces within the party. The Tory Reform Group, founded in 1975, professed a moderate brand of Conservatism, and after the 1983 general election over 100 Conservative MPs formed a group named Care to call for a more compassionate approach in social policy. In 1985 the deposed Francis Pym founded Centre Forward to oppose the government's extreme-right policies.

Away from the centre are the Young Conservatives and the Women's National Advisory Committee, both with highly organized national structures. Rather less well organized, and more bizarre in style, has been the Federation of Conservative Students, which was involved in ballot-rigging scandals and adopts an extreme rightist stance. In 1987 party chairman Norman Tebbit wound it up by withdrawing its grant from the party.

In the Labour Party there has been no shortage of ginger groups, the most well known of which is Tribune (propagating its views through the journal of that name), founded in 1964. Though often troublesome, it has been a highly respected body, including a number of prominent party figures. In 1950 Harold Wilson headed Keep Left, a band of MPs advocating more left-wing policies and in 1958 a group termed Victory of Socialism formed to oppose Gaitskell's revisionism. In the 1970s, with the rise of the left, two new groups were founded: the Campaign for Labour Party Democracy and the Labour Coordinating Committee, which sought successfully to gain control of the NEC and instigate reforms in the party constitution. Both these included activists outside Parliament, while in Parliament the Campaign Group was founded in 1982 as a more radical alternative to Tribune, with the aim of opposing what it saw as witch-hunts against left-wing fundamentalists. In addition, CND has always penetrated deeply into the Labour ranks.

On the Labour right is the Manifesto Group established in 1974, though the first two chairpersons went on to form the SDP. From the first the Fabian Society has exerted a profound influence on the party, providing some of its most illustrious figures as well as its intellectual dynamic, and exerting a continuing influence on policy. In addition there is the Cooperative Party, which acts as a partner to Labour by sponsoring around 20 of its MPs.

The Labour Party Young Socialists are organized on a national scale and tend to advocate extreme leftist policies, generally supporting Militant Tendency. The latter is an amorphous 'party within the party', believing in a mission to fight for socialism and opposing the Fabian tradition. It was criticized in an internal party report prepared by Lord Underhill in 1975 and, by the early 1980s, moderates felt that Militant tactics were seriously damaging the party. There was talk of witch-hunts and, in a largely symbolic gesture, Foot expelled the five members of the editorial board of its journal, *Militant*.

Like the party's young members, some of its women maintain an identity separate from the main body. In constituency associations they may form separate sections, which are coordinated through a National Labour Women's Conference, and women as such are represented on the NEC. Labour denies the right of a separate existence to its black members, who repeatedly call for special black sections. Indeed unconstitutional black sections have arisen in around 30 constituencies (*Sunday Times*, 9 March 1986), leading to the emergence of black candidates in the 1987 general election.

Of course, as we have seen, the most towering external presence for Labour is the trade union movement, which was largely responsible for its conception, delivery, and subsequent maturation. Less overt is the equally towering presence of the business organizations which nurture the Conservative Party, a matter we return to later in the chapter.

Inside the Parties: the Tweedledum–Tweedledee Myth

Figures 8.3 and 8.4 suggest that the anatomies of the major parties show a marked degree of similarity and textbooks have made much of this, painting a picture of party politics as a great battle between two equally matched Titans. However, this is part of the great legitimating myth of modern British liberal democracy. Looking more closely at the internal processes and power structure of each party we begin to discern significant differences, with major implications for their ability to win power and govern effectively. Important among these processes are internal cohesion, the selection of the leader, the exercise of patronage within the party, the selection of candidates, and policy-making style. Having examined these we shall seek the final answer to our question by looking for the powers behind the party thrones.

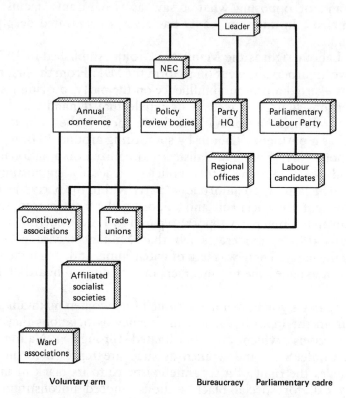

Voluntary arm   **Bureaucracy   Parliamentary cadre**

Figure 8.3 Organization of the Labour Party

Internal cohesion

In a multi-party system each party stands for a narrow interest or ideology, thereby ensuring a high degree of internal solidarity, but in a two-party model one of the *raisons d'être* of the party is the aggregation of many interests. Yet to attract votes it must present a united front, which produces

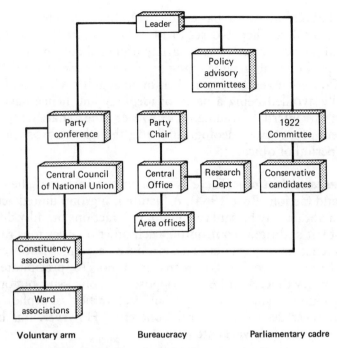

Leader

Policy advisory committees

Party conference

Party Chair

1922 Committee

Central Council of National Union

Central Office

Research Dept

Conservative candidates

Area offices

Constituency associations

Ward associations

Voluntary arm   **Bureaucracy**   **Parliamentary cadre**

Figure 8.4 Organization of the Conservative Party

an internal tension between the ideological forces of diversity, and political expediency. All British parties carry a deep-seated basis for schism; the Conservatives with their traditional Whig and Tory strains (now the wet–dry dichotomy), Labour bedevilled by a basic left–right divide, and the SLD composed of its Liberal and Social Democrat wings. The ways parties handle inner tensions constitute a key issue for analysis, and the evidence shows the Conservatives to be by far the most successful at achieving **internal cohesion**. In contrast, Labour has, throughout its history, been unable to find antibodies to counter the virulent factionalism coursing through its veins. A number of factors explain the difference.

Social composition Although the theory of a two-party system stresses the aggregative nature of the parties, and although the Conservative Party has always been able to put together a wide range of electoral support, its actual membership comes from a narrow and homogeneous social base within the upper-middle and aspiring lower-middle class. By contrast, Labour is more a microcosm of society, so that the class resentments fuelling political tension in the wider society are reproduced within its own ranks.

Office-holding A party which forms the government is constitutionally and politically induced towards coherence. The doctrine of collective responsibility, official secrecy, the need for Commons' support, the duty to represent the whole community, and so on, all conspire to unite. A long history of office has given the Conservative Party extensive exposure to these forces.

Ideology Labour avows a basic fidelity to socialist ideology, which can result in internal conflict. No set of ideas is completely unambiguous and socialism in particular can have a variety of meanings, implying contrasting strategies to different groups, ranging from Trotskyites to Fabians. By contrast, Conservatives, having as their main goal the winning of office, have traditionally avoided being a party of ideology and hence have harboured less basis for internal argument. However, the Thatcher era saw the development of a greater ideological divide, though this was countered by a continual period of office.

Tendencies and factions There is a distinction between the concepts of tendency and faction (Rose 1964). A **faction** is a group united across a wide spectrum. Labour may be said to contain two factions broadly differentiated in terms of left and right, confronting each other on questions ranging from nuclear defence to gay rights. This produces a fundamental cleavage. In contrast, Conservative disagreements tend not to precipitate the same formations every time. A and B may oppose C on one issue, but on another A and C may unite against B. Thus one sees rather amorphous and fluid **tendencies**, never destroying overall coherence. However, this became less evident during the divisive Thatcher years.

Internal power structure The Conservative Party, like its view of society, is essentially elitist, while Labour has a more democratic constitution. In the former, leaders exercise a unifying force, while in the latter they are obliged to fight, persuade and manoeuvre, with disruptive results.

Hegemonic consciousness Probably of greatest importance is the fact that, for various reasons, the Conservative Party considers itself (and is considered by others) the 'natural' party of government. Even when in opposition members remain united because they believe office is never far way. By contrast, some figures within the Labour Party see its role primarily in terms of protest.

The imperatives of capitalism In a capitalist state a key government role is unifying the competitive and potentially disruptive forces of private enterprise. As the party of private capital the Conservatives accept a key responsibility in this respect, forcing members to place a high premium on unity within the party ranks.

Choosing the leader

The way party leaders are chosen, and their security of tenure, is a central process in the internal life of the party, with important implications for discipline and policy-making.

Conservative Before 1965, the process whereby the Conservative leader emerged was shrouded in a mystique which would have been puzzling even to England's cricket selectors. The party elders, including the outgoing leader, would practise secret rites and make the decision on behalf of the mass membership. This was not necessarily either corrupt or even irrational; it permitted a sensitive attention to the qualities and nuances of the candidates and took account of the *intensity* of feeling in a manner denied by a simple one-person, one-vote election. However, it allowed the mass no chance to speak, which was why after the Douglas-Home debacle, a cumbersome three-ballot method of election by MPs was adopted in 1965. At the time little thought was given to the removal of the leader; the party felt no need for this, for its reputation for the prompt elimination of old warriors would be envied by the Mafia. With the exception of Bonar Law, every incumbent appointed during the century was either forcibly removed, or placed under heavy pressure to go. Thus, although the 1965 reforms made no provision for compulsory re-election, the unpopularity of Heath, and his carelessness in losing three general elections, led to a painful confrontation with the 1922 Committee, and he added to the distinction of being the first elected leader that of being the first to be 'un-elected'. Yet Margaret Thatcher, the triumphant though unexpected victor in 1975, was herself to experience the crueller side of the electoral coin. In November 1990, amidst deep unpopularity in the polls, the daggers were unsheathed and Michael Heseltine challenged from the back benches, forcing a second ballot by denying her the 15 per cent lead required for outright victory. At this point Margaret Thatcher withdrew from the contest in order to allow cabinet colleagues to enter without seeming disloyal. Hence the second ballot became a three-cornered fight between Michael Heseltine, Douglas Hurd (Foreign Secretary) and John Major (Chancellor of the Exchequer), who polled 131, 56 and 185 votes respectively. This left John Major only 2 short of the absolute majority needed to prevent a third ballot (between him and the nearest rival). However, Michael Heseltine withdrew, thereby preventing the final, and potentially disruptive, third round and John Major emerged as the new Conservative leader and Prime Minister. Heseltine was subsequequently rewarded with a seat in the new cabinet, though many thought the position of Secretary of State for the Environment, responsible for reforming the vexatious poll tax, an unenviable portfolio.

Because the Conservative Party sees itself, above all else, as the natural government, it will stand by leaders for as long as they can deliver the votes; like the manager of a league football team, the priority is victory. Thus, all deposed leaders are tainted in the party's memory with a fatal flaw: for Chamberlain it was Munich, for Eden Suez, for Macmillan the Profumo scandal, and for Douglas-Home and Heath it was ignominious defeat in the field. Accordingly, the pinnacle of unchallengeable supremacy attained by Thatcher by 1987 can be truly said to have been a result of her winning personality.

Labour From the beginning, the Labour leadership was elective, with voting the exclusive right of the PLP. In theory leaders were subject to annual re-election, with the possibility of challenge giving continuing intimations of mortality but, although Wilson unsuccessfully threw down the gauntlet before Gaitskell in 1960 and Tony Benn vainly challenged Kinnock in 1988, this has been largely a formality. In spite of constitutional limitations, evidence shows the tenure of Labour leaders to be more secure than that of their Conservative counterparts. Attlee was able to cling to office far longer than his younger colleagues wished; Gaitskell, although his reign was turbulent, died with his leadership boots firmly laced, and Harold Wilson was sufficiently secure after 14 years that his resignation came as a shock to colleagues and pundits alike. Even James Callaghan, after stormy battles with the left, was able to depart with dignity. The end of Michael Foot probably came closest to a Conservative-style hounding from office. He had proved an electoral liability, with the *Private Eye* nickname of Worzel Gummidge, a scruffy but well-meaning scarecrow featuring in a current television series.

Left-wing criticism in the 1980s blamed the method of election for the shortcomings of the leadership and, at a special conference at Wembley, it was agreed that the electoral college choosing the leader and deputy should be widened to consist of the trade unions (40 per cent), the constituency associations and the PLP (30 per cent each). (The left fought unsuccessfully for the whole of the Shadow Cabinet to be chosen in this way.) However, the outcome was not what the left had hoped for, the new electoral college choosing the right's 'dream ticket' of Neil Kinnock and Roy Hattersley. Paradoxically, the new system actually improved the leader's security in three ways: it gave authority over all sections of the party; the PLP lost any moral right to remove a leader by a vote of no-confidence; and the additional complications in the procedure could inhibit future challenges.

Liberal Until 1976 the Liberal Party had followed its traditional practice of allowing the parliamentary cohort, such as it was, to choose the leader. However, following Jeremy Thorpe's resignation over the Norman Scott scandal, it was decided to instigate a party-wide election. Generally, Liberal leaders appeared secure in office: Jo Grimond left with great dignity, continuing as a respected party elder; and although Thorpe's position became quite untenable, it is a tribute to the loyalty of his party that he remained for so long. David Steel, though subject to some rough treatment, remained secure until he voluntarily stood down in 1988 for the merger with the SDP.

SDP/SLD When the 'Gang of Four' established the SDP in 1981, each was a possible leadership contender. In 1982 the party made the choice through a postal ballot, Roy Jenkins defeating his only rival, David Owen. He did not last long, being edged out by Owen after the disappointing general election result of 1983. Owen was unopposed in the subsequent election, soon establishing himself as a dominant presence within the small party until they deserted him to merge with the Liberals. The Social and Liberal Democrats subsequently chose Paddy Ashdown as their first leader by postal ballot of all members.

●　●　●

The fact that Labour offers its leaders a more secure tenure does not necessarily allow the conclusion that they are the more powerful. Longevity does not necessarily indicate strength. It may be in the interests of party members to preserve a weak leader in the manner of the proverbial hanging gate, in order to enjoy greater freedom to rule from behind the throne. Caesar was slain, not because he was weak, but because he was powerful. The uncertainty of the tenure makes the party leadership a lonely position, many incumbents becoming brooding and paranoic, seeing enemies everywhere and fearing amongst their retinue those who, like the lean and hungry Cassius, lie awake at night and,

> ... be never at heart's ease
> Whiles they behold a greater than themselves.
> *(Julius Caesar*, Act I, Scene 2)

Patronage within the party

Leaders can counter the advantage others have to make or break them by using their own powers of party **patronage**. Those of Conservative leaders are almost unbounded: whether in office or opposition they appoint the front-bench team, the Party Chairman, and the significant officers of Central Office. An early Thatcher move was a thorough shake-up of the party bureaucracy, and her Cabinet was to become an echo chamber into which she could chant her convictions.

In contrast, the Labour leader is more tightly circumscribed. In opposition, the front-bench team is elected by the PLP, and must be taken into government. The powerful NEC is elected by the party, and appointments to the bureaucracy are made by the NEC itself.

Selection of candidates

To be a genuinely national force a party must field some 600 candidates, and their **selection** represents a widely based patronage exercise. Formally, the responsibility lies with the constituency associations, but for obvious reasons the national leaders have taken more than a little interest in the process.

The Conservative selection process In theory anyone can apply to be a Conservative candidate, and selection committees can be faced with the mammoth task of reducing an initial list of a hundred or so to a short-list of around six. Those in the select group become subject to various forms of scrutiny: they are vetted, interviewed, invited to deliver an address, their profession and life-style noted, and even their spouses may be vetted for acceptability on the speech platform and drawing-room. Throughout the process Central Office presence is felt. A Standing Committee on Candidates maintains a list of the potentially great and good, of which constituencies may avail themselves, and guidelines are issued on candidate policy. Yet local associations have traditionally resisted pressure from above. They have been unwilling to be more sympathetic towards working-class candidates and, in spite of the redoubtable member for Finchley, have tended steadfastly to shy away from women. Until the Maxwell-Fyfe reforms after the second world war it was possible for wealthy aspirants effectively to purchase the nomination by agreeing to finance their campaign and contribute to party funds, and a preference for breeding and education remains, with an overwhelming predilection for company directors. The typical Conservative candidate is resolutely middle class, white, married, and male.

The Labour selection process   The selection process in the Labour camp is significantly different from that of the Conservatives. The original list is considerably shorter because applications are restricted to those nominated by affiliated associations. In addition, the process is more markedly oligarchic and the decision reached by the general management committee is not placed before the wider membership for approval. Like Central Office, the NEC maintains a list of approved candidates which distinguishes between sponsored candidates (List A) and those nominated by non-sponsoring organizations (List B). **Sponsorship** means that the nominating association will meet a substantial proportion of the election expenses and make a contribution to funds. This can be a powerful inducement to an impecunious local association, and the advice of Oscar Wilde to the tempted is often followed; in the post-war era about half the Labour MPs could be described as politically kept men.

In spite of its undemocratic overtones, there are several arguments for sponsorship.

- It does not entail the use of *personal* wealth to gain office.
- It has been crucial to working-class participation in the polity so is good for democracy.
- It is in line with the original *raison d'être* of the party – to serve the interests of the labour movement through representation in Parliament.

However, sponsorship creates problems for Labour. Because the sponsors look to the safer seats when dispensing their largesse, the more radical candidates are left with the marginals. This has two debilitating effects: the PLP will present its least challenging face when in opposition, a time when it should be most virulent; and, being excluded from Parliament, the more radically minded can fall in on themselves in internecine warfare and leadership attacks.

The NEC generally exercises a greater influence than Central Office over selection, showing itself quite willing to impose its veto if candidates do not meet with approval, and sometimes taking firm steps to secure places for favourites. The constituency associations may of course resist centrally foisted candidates, as did the alarmed faithful of St Helens when offered the exotic Tom Driberg. Before the 1987 general election the NEC took a keen interest in candidates, particularly in the hard-left associations, and some were rejected. In the preparation for the Vauxhall by-election on 15 June 1989 a centrally favoured candidate, Kate Hoey, was imposed on the local association, despite their desire for a black candidate.

The requirement from 1983 that all Labour MPs undergo a mandatory process of reselection during each Parliament was intended to reduce the power of the leadership over MPs and came as a result of constituency pressure through a left-dominated NEC. A dramatic casualty of the new process was moderate, though maverick, Liverpool MP Frank Field, although the sitting member does at least have the advantage of being guaranteed a place on the short-list. In 1989 the party leadership mitigated the effect of the new system by securing a further change extending the choice of candidates to *all* local party members (on a voluntary basis).

• • •

A recurrent theme advanced by both activists and commentators is that the autonomous activities of selection committees will tend towards extreme candidates. Although in the early 1960s this thesis was shown to be dubious (Rose 1962), there can be no doubt that both major parties contain MPs with views which alarm their leaders.

Party policy-making: mass rule or iron law of oligarchy?

The ability to shape policy is probably the most significant index of power within a party. We may envisage two extreme models in examining this question: *top-down*, in which the mass obediently plays follow-my-leader; and *bottom-up*, where they expect the leaders to act as delegates in Parliament.

The emergence of the local associations in the nineteenth century created early fears that the unruly masses would gain control over the nation's leaders. Ostrogorski, in a famous study of parties at the turn of the century, issued dire warnings that the parliamentary parties had, like Frankenstein, created unlovely monsters which would soon destroy them and the process of representative democracy (Ostrogorski 1902). Others feared the reverse outcome – that the masses would be denied their democratic rights within the party. In the early 1900s the German/Italian sociologist Roberto Michels enunciated his well-known **iron law of oligarchy**, postulating that within any mass party ineluctible sociological and psychological processes would force the mass membership under the domination of a small elite (Michels 1962). His particular interest was the socialist parties emerging in Europe. He proceeded from a belief that they *ought* to be internally democratic, the iron law postulating a process of decay.

A number of factors determine the internal power relationship, including the party's evolution, its constitution, its experience of government, its attitudes towards office, and its leader's personality.

> Lenin's method leads to this: the party organisation at first substitutes itself for the party as a whole. Then the central committee substitutes itself for the party organisation, and finally a single dictator substitutes himself for the central committee.
>
> Leon Trotsky (1879–1940; Russian revolutionary), quoted in N. McInnes, *The Communist Parties of Western Europe* (1975: ch. 3)

The pattern of evolution Because the Conservative and Liberal parties originated as parliamentary groupings, the extra-parliamentary organizations were from the first seen as their handmaidens. Thus there was never any reason to address the question of who should make policy; it was clearly within the provenance of the leaders, themselves paid-up members of the ruling elite. This is why the attempts of Joseph Chamberlain and Randolph Churchill to impose some degree of democratic control over the policy within their respective parties came to nothing.

However, the conception, birth and growth of the Labour Party implied a quite different relationship. As an arm of the trade union mammoth, formed for the express purpose of representing its views and policies in Parliament, it was essentially subservient. Even the title 'leader' was initially avoided in favour of 'chairman', who was co-equal with the chair of the NEC.

Party constitutions Party constitutions are authoritative rules regulating internal affairs and formally *prescribing* the internal structure of power. Throughout the century Conservative literature has paid homage to the leader's supremacy in all important aspects of party life, while in the case of Labour, the constitution imposes an ostensibly democratic pattern of authority, with three centres of policy formation: the PLP, the NEC and the annual conference. From the outset it specified that policy, as contained in the *programme*, was to be determined by the mass through the annual conference on the basis of a two-thirds majority. In 1945, Harold Laski, chairman of the NEC, argued that if Attlee attended the three-power peace conference at Potsdam the party could not be bound by any agreement reached because the matters would not have been considered by the NEC (McKenzie 1967: 330) (an interpretation Attlee refused to accept).

For a considerable time the constitutional power of the conference was not a problem to the Labour leader because of the system of block voting: the six largest unions generally supported the leadership line. However, from the 1970s, the trade union leadership moved to the left, revealing the fundamental tensions in the party's constitution.

The Liberal Party constitution was decentralized in 1983, giving the rank and file a predominantly 'bottom-up' procedure (to be despised by Alliance partner David Owen as a form of anarchy). In 1986 a defence resolution of the executive was humiliatingly defeated by the conference, leaving leader David Steel in a position of some embarrassment. The SLD also established itself with a 'bottom-up' constitution.

The experience of government   When a party is in office its leader assumes the position of Prime Minister, inheriting the supreme policy-making powers of the Crown, and when ejected these clouds of glory may be trailed into opposition. This remains a natural advantage for Conservative leaders but, whenever they have experienced power, Labour leaders have also worn a halo of authority; both Attlee and Wilson enjoyed considerable personal ascendancy. However, such periods have been tantalisingly short-lived, punctuated by lengthy spells in the wilderness, when the steel discipline of office is softened in the heat of internal friction.

> What a genius the Labour Party has for cutting itself in half and letting the two parts writhe in public.
>
> Cassandra (William Neil Connor; 1910–67; Irish journalist) in the
> *Daily Mirror*

Attitudes towards office   Political parties exist to gain power, and policy is the key to this. The leaders are by definition concerned above all with electoral success and their policies can be expected to be framed accordingly. If the followers share the same hunger for office there will be little basis for disharmony. This model fits the Conservative conviction that they are the chosen ones and, as we saw in chapter 7, when on three occasions rudely displaced by Labour, the mass has loyally followed the inspiration of the leadership in a radical revision of policy. The Conservatives mass membership is in this sense a 'sleeping membership' (Gamble 1979: 40).

By contrast, Labour's ambivalence towards office weakens the leader and the idea of the left that it is better to lose the election than try to run the economy in a capitalist manner reduces the leader's moral claims over policy.

Personality of the leader   Asquith's view that the power of the Prime Minister is what the holder makes of it can be applied to the position of party leader. Labour's contentious policy revisionism in the 1950s and early 1960s in part reflected the combative character of Gaitskell, while the relative calm under Wilson can be largely attributed to his ability to smooth ruffled feathers and pour liberal quantities of oil on the party's sea of troubles. No leader in post-war politics has equalled Mrs Thatcher for dominance. Her reign as Prime Minister was preceded by similar dominance as party leader in opposition, the radical policy revision before 1979 coming about almost entirely as a result of her initiative.

Despite its ostensibly democratic constitution, the Social Democratic Party was presided over by the demonic presence of David Owen, and all policy bore his imprimatur. When unable to do this directly, as in the case of policy made by joint SDP–Liberal policy commissions, he worked to undermine the credibility of the bodies themselves, deriding the 1988 report on defence as 'fudge and mudge'.

Labour's policy review

Labour's third successive defeat in 1987 provided Neil Kinnock with strong grounds for stamping the leader's authority on the party. This he did, not by pressing his own policy views directly but by setting in motion a lengthy policy reappraisal, together with a 'Labour Listens' campaign designed to stress the need to shape policies to attract votes rather than reflect principles. The results of the review, with support for the idea of the market and the enterprise culture, and a weakening of the commitment to un-ilateralism, showed a clear victory for the moderate leadership.

Policy determination by the mass party, whether through conference resolutions or in some other way such as postal ballot, has been generally considered undemocratic because the views of followers have often been seen as more extreme than those of the leader and 'still further removed from the mass of those who actually provide the vote' (Butler 1960: 3). In the 1950s McKenzie argued that fears of policy-making by the mass party were unfounded: the imperatives of political life (electioneering, manifesto writing and governing) provided a Procrustean bed forcing the parties to become similar in organization, internal processes and leadership (McKenzie 1967: 635). In this model, each party in the post-war era was a confirmation of Michels's iron law of oligarchy.

The McKenzie view prevailed in the post-war consensus period, but it was always heroic in the case of Labour. Even if, in the long term, they got their own way, Labour leaders were obliged to shed considerable perspiration in the process. Does this mean that the internal democracy of the Labour Party represents a dangerous threat to representative democracy, while the centrally driven Conservative Party does not? In discussing this we are forced to go deeper into the operation of the parties to address a key question of British politics.

Conclusion: the Powers Behind the Throne

The British parties are not as self-contained as most discussions on the subject imply. The classic definition which stresses the distinctiveness of parties from pressure groups is highly misleading: Labour's marsupial link with the trade unions is more than matched by the Conservatives' relationship to the power of capital. Many Conservative MPs are themselves on the boards of the private companies in whose interests the party fights.

> We [the Conservative Party] need funds and I look to the City of London to give a lead in providing that support which as businessmen they should be prepared to give, in view of our efforts to make their business safe.
>
> Appeal made by Stanley Baldwin in 1926, quoted in R. McKenzie, *British Political Parties* (1967)

Although the constituencies work manfully in fund-raising, at critical points like general elections, the capitalist interests of Britain can be counted upon to reach for their wallets to achieve what is regarded as a key requirement of successful capitalism – a Conservative government. The Party Chairman has the task of rattling the begging bowl before industry, but this is about as difficult as fishing in a trout farm. Figures given by Conservative Central Office to the 1988 party conference, but not made generally available, disclosed that the party received £13.5 million in donations in the year ending March 1988 (*Independent*, 27 Dec. 1988). Moreover, various intermediaries exist for the specific purposes of propaganda and fund-raising.

(1) *The Economic League* was formed after the first world war by the ex-head of naval intelligence to raise funds for the party and propagate a 'Free enterprise' message. In addition, it compiles lists of 'subversives' and 'communists' to be blacked by employers, and has close links with the intelligence services in the fight against working-class movements.

(2) *British United Industries* was formed after the second world war, again for the purpose of fund-raising and propaganda.

(3) *Aims* (formerly Aims of Industry) is the best known of the fund-raisers. It was established in 1942 by a group of businessmen and has been active in every general election since. It originally produced propaganda undermining Labour's programme, and its celebrated Mr Cube campaign in 1949–50 featured a talking sugar lump who successfully saved Tate and Lyle from being dissolved in the thick working-class tea of post-war nationalization.

(4) *The Confederation of British Industry* (CBI) is, like the TUC, a *peak organization* (see p. 423) aggregating a wide range of business interests, providing money and exercising a continuing influence over Conservative policy.

The things they say

The CBI's character, and perhaps its main *raison d'être*, is geared to a dialogue with government ... But it must be emphasised that the CBI is politically neutral.

John Davies (Director General of the CBI), quoted in I. Gilmour,
The Body Politic (1969: 351)

---

(5) *The River Companies.* In December 1988 the *Independent* unearthed a murky trail explaining one of the strategies whereby the Conservative Party availed itself of funds from industry. In 1948 Lord Woolton, chairman of the party, wrote a letter to Winston Churchill, the leader, entitled *Party Finances*, stating: 'The treasurers and I have been much concerned by the fact that we have been told by our lawyers that, in the eyes of the law, a political party is not a body that is capable of receiving money by will or deed'.

Lord Woolton went on to explain that he had been advised by the best legal minds in the country to establish a body of trustees and 'a few companies' to receive bequests from wills, trusts and deeds of covenant. The result was the establishment of a secret network of companies named after English rivers, the memoranda of association of which prevented the shareholders from receiving any financial benefit. All profits were to go to the Conservative Party. However, some shareholders were recompensed in the form of honours, giving grounds for suspicion (*Independent*, 27 Dec. 1988). Demands for an enquiry into the 'river companies' were rejected in 1988 by Lord Young, the Conservative Secretary of State for Trade and Industry.

Not all capitalists use these intermediaries in bestowing their largesse: of the top 200 companies in Britain around a quarter inject main line into the veins of the party (Scott 1985: 52–3). Almost half the corporate donations come from banking, insurance, food, drink, and construction; the merchant banks are especially important, their directors often being active within the party organization.

Beyond the business pressure groups there are other interests lying close to the Conservative heart. 'Law and order' is always a central tenet, and the Police Federation, the 'trade union' of the force, openly declares its support with media statements and even advertisements in national newspapers urging voters to support 'law and order', a coded instruction to 'Vote Conservative' (see p. 555). In addition, the bulk of the press may be regarded as the effective public relations arm of the party and, under any theory of voting behaviour, its importance in maintaining a Conservative government is inestimable (Dunleavy 1985). The might of these shadowy interests behind the Conservative Party is incalculable: they can make and break politicians.

When Junior Health Minister Edwina Currie warned the public in December 1988 about the danger of salmonella in eggs, she roused the National Farmers' Union to fury and was forced to resign.

Though the penetration of the trade union movement into the Labour Party is profound, it pales by comparison with the capitalist establishment as a power behind the throne. Labour's funds must perforce come from the poorest section of society. The unions (since the Trade Union Act, 1913) collect a political levy from individual members and establish a fund to support political activity. It is not difficult to see why the 1984 Conservative legislation (designed to shatter its financial base by undermining the fund) represented a crisis for Labour. A similar restriction on business donations to the Conservatives would have produced outrage.

The fact that the two great estates of the modern realm – capital and labour – are so closely wedded to the major political parties leaves the minnows with little potential sustenance. However, both Liberals and Social Democrats were able to tap industrial sources and, following merger, one of the greatest benefactors, David Sainsbury of the supermarket leviathan, stayed loyal to David Owen, giving his rump SDP a continuing credibility.

When the parties are viewed within this wider framework, it becomes clear that their organizational similarities are of little real significance in understanding British politics. The parties reflect the power structure inherent in the politico-economic system. The idea propounded by scholars such as Schumpeter that they fight a battle as equally matched champions may be one of the more important legitimating myths of orthodox liberal political science.

Key points

- Modern political parties generally consist of three elements: a parliamentary cadre, a bureaucracy, and a mass membership organized throughout the country on a federal basis.
- The question of where the power lies within this tripartite structure is an important matter of political debate. Michels argued that an 'iron law of oligarchy' determined that all parties must ultimately fall under the domination of a small elite.
- It is often said that constituency activists are more extreme than the leaders. This was less obviously the case in the Conservative Party under Thatcher.
- The Conservative Party is less internally democratic than Labour, allowing greater authority to the leader in patronage, organization and policy-making.
- However, the 1980s saw Labour Party leaders making strenuous efforts to strengthen their grip over the mass membership on the grounds that moderation was required to win elections.
- For a variety of reasons, the Conservative Party shows greater internal cohesion than any of the other parties, which helps to make it such a formidable force in British politics.
- Contrary to the suggestion that parties are distinct from pressure groups, the

Labour and Conservative parties have umbilical links with the economic interests of labour and capital respectively.
- Hence, and unsurprisingly, the Conservative Party has enjoyed the lion's share of office-holding and can be regarded as the natural party of government in Britain.

Review your understanding of the following terms and concepts

constituency associations	party cohesion
ward associations	faction
affiliated associations	tendency
party conference	patronage
block vote	selection process
party executive	sponsorship
party bureaucracy	iron law of oligarchy
ginger group	party constitution

Assignment

Study the extract from the *Guardian* and answer the following questions.

		% mark
1	What does Neil Kinnock mean by 'alternative policies'? Why should he think that some members of his party might be afraid of them?	10
2	Compare the political task of Neil Kinnock with that of Hugh Gaitskell in the 1950s.	20
3	Does the need to 'embrace concepts such as the market economy and competitiveness and individualism' pose any threat to the ideology of the Labour Party?	30
4	Discuss the concept of individualism put forward by Neil Kinnock. Is it the same as that of the nineteenth-century Utilitarians?	40

Questions for discussion

1 Explain why the Conservative Party appears more cohesive than its rivals.
2 Is internal party democracy a necessary condition for effective democracy at the level of the state?
3 'The British electoral system will defeat any attempt to establish multi-party politics in Britain.' Examine this proposition in the light of the experience of the centre parties during the 1980s.
4 Compare and contrast the security of tenure of the Labour and Conservative party leaders.
5 'Too much power for the constituency associations in candidate selection will seriously damage the British system of party government.' Discuss.
6 Is it realistic to imagine that a party's policy programme can be made by means of a 'bottom-up' process?

Kinnock sets out 'price of victory'

Leader's speech

Martin Linton and Owen Bowcott

Mr Neil Kinnock brought the conference to its feet yesterday with a speech in which he asked his party not to be afraid of the alternative policies and the new thinking that will be the price of a Labour victory at the next election.

"Those who' say they don't want victory at such a price had better ask themselves what price they are prepared to pay for losing and who is going to pay that price," he said. . . .

He felt more certain than he had ever been that Labour supporters and potential supporters were looking to the party to press ahead with the policy review and develop the policies that would bring them to power.

There was no "slide to the right" in that and no "concession to Thatcherism." In any case the greatest concession to Thatcherism would be to let it win again.

But it did mean that the party would have to embrace concepts such as the market economy and competitiveness and individualism.

There was only one economy in Britain, a market economy, and "it will be the one we have to deal with when we are elected. And we have got to make it work better than the Tories make it work," he said.

He was amazed that any socialist could say that they did not like the idea of individualism. For him there was no test of progress other than the impact on the individual. It was the great inspiration of democratic socialism that it committed itself to collective means the whole purpose of which was the service, safety and care of the individual.

Guardian, 5 Oct. 1988

---

7 'The way British parties are financed undermines the democratic process.' Discuss.

Topic for debate

This house believes that the Conservative Party is the 'natural party of government' because it is the party of the country's 'natural rulers'.
    or
This house believes that the time has come for the Labour Party to break free from the trade union movement.

Further reading

Drucker, H. (1979) *Multi-Party Britain*.
See reading for chapter 7.

Ingle, S. (1987) *The British Party System.*
See reading for chapter 7.

Kavanagh, D. (ed.) (1982) *The Politics of the Labour Party.*
Useful book of readings. See especially the editor's article 'Still the worker's party? Changing social trends in elite recruitment and electoral support'.

Layton Henry, Z. (ed.) (1980) *Conservative Party Politics.*
Variable contributions from eminent scholars.

McKenzie, R. (1967) *British Political Parties.*
First published in 1955 and now much criticized (and rather turgid), but a major presentation of the thesis that the constraints of the political system have throughout history forced the parties to be very like each other.

Michels, R. (1962) *Political Parties.*
Classic statement of the 'iron law of oligarchy', first published 1920. Still a very readable book.

Muller, W. D. (1977) *The Kept Men.*
Examines the issue of trade union sponsorship of parliamentary candidates. Notes the modern trend towards younger, better-educated representatives.

Rose, R (1980) *Do Parties Make a Difference?*
See reading for chapter 7.

For light relief

Wilfred Fienburgh, *No Love for Johnnie.*
Love, romance and committee meetings in the Labour Party.

Chris Mullin, *A Very British Coup.*
Explores the problems for the Labour Party in dealing with the forces of the establishment.

PART IV

Government at the Centre

It is interesting to note that we do not arrive at the formal centre of British government until the middle of the book. This underlines the fact that the comings and goings of the high and the mighty in the state by no means represent the whole of the political story. In this section we address the most central and exhilarating concept in politics – power. We examine who holds it, who uses it, and who is able to influence the way it is exercised. Our search takes us through the most ornate institutions of government (the **monarchy** and **Parliament**), to the heart of the formal apparatus of state decision-making in the Westminster/Whitehall complex (the **Cabinet**, the **Prime Minister** and the higher **civil service**). Finally we delve even deeper into the mysteries of power in the state by seeking sources of political influence lying below the surface of ministerial pomp and splendour in the more shadowy recesses of political life.

We shall find in this section that, although all may not be as it seems, nothing is without significance; every cam and cog in the machinery of state power has a function, and the task of the political scientist is to try to discover what that is.

9

Pomp and Circumstance: the Living Dead of the Constitution

> In this chapter we examine the most ornate parts of the dignified constitution as they are found in Parliament: the **monarchy**, the **House of Lords** and the **House of Commons**. Here we see much constitutional flummery lovingly preserved from bygone ages, a celebration of the much-vaunted continuity of the British constitution. However, though appearing as lifeless as the waxworks at Madame Tussaud's, like the mystic ritual of the church and the courts, the ceremonial part of the constitution is by no means without significance. It induces respect and reverence for authority; it is the living dead of the constitution.

The physical setting

Parliament formally comprises the monarchy, the House of Lords and the House of Commons, with a very tangible presence as the picturesque Palace of Westminster situated grandly on the bank of the Thames at the end of Whitehall. It is one of the major landmarks of London, and during the holiday season a permanent queue of visitors (about a million each year) wait to be conducted on guided tours and purchase trinkets marked with the prestigious portcullis logo (which is also found on MPs' official notepaper). Within the palace the two great chambers, the Commons and the Lords, exude a cathedral-like aura calculated to intimidate all but the initiated, and around them a labyrinth of corridors, quadrangles and staircases lead to offices, committee rooms, smoking rooms, tea-rooms, and of course bars. MPs can be seen variously talking in intimate clusters, meeting groups of eager constituents, playing host to interest group representatives, or in secretive places of refreshment trying to avoid such encounters.

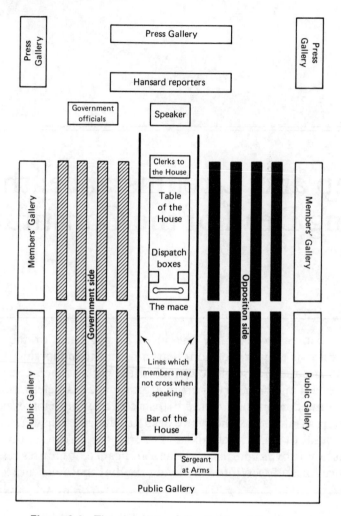

Figure 9.1   The chamber of the House of Commons

The chambers are surprisingly small and could not seat all members if they were to descend simultaneously. This is quite deliberate; the opportunity to rebuild was presented by the German Luftwaffe in 1941, but the decision was taken to retain the sense of intimacy conducive to debate. Figure 9.1 shows how the benches are arrayed in a hostile, confrontational manner and, in the Commons, commemorating a more colourful age, the front ranks are set a sword's length apart with the Mace, the symbol of authority, resting on the intervening table.

Parliamentary mumbo-jumbo

Westminster is a great home of **ceremony** and ritual. It is formally opened every year with a procession led by Black Rod, the officer responsible for maintaining order in the House of Lords, who carries an ebony cane for the purpose. He summons the Commoners to the Lords to hear the Queen's Speech, and all is conducted in Norman French. When he approaches the lower house the doors are slammed in his face (because in 1642, the last time the Commons allowed the monarch into their chamber, he arrested five members). Undeterred, he gives three solemn knocks, the doors are opened, and the MPs emerge in pairs, advancing like a *corps de ballet* towards the Lords, led by the Prime Minister and Leader of the Opposition.

The evolution of Parliament

The three elements of Parliament represent the great estates of the realm which have fought over the centuries for control of the state: the Crown, the aristocracy and the common people. Its origins lie in the assembly of Anglo-Saxon kings which met as the *Witangemot*. In Norman times kings governed with only their officials to assist them, although the country was divided into territorial units ruled by barons whom the kings would call together as the *Magnum Concilium* for discussion, advice, and to raise money. The barons began to demand more control over the royal authority and secured this through the Magna Charta signed at Runnymede in 1215. Herein lies the origin of the House of Lords.

The House of Commons was conceived in the kingly practice, from the thirteenth century, of calling additional meetings of the less-important local representatives, the commoners – knights from the shires and burgesses from the incorporated towns – as a further source of revenue. They would assemble humbly before the king, surrounded by his lords and nobles, who would tell them how much money he required and dispatch them to find it, leaving the aristocracy to discuss important matters of state.

However, the Commons, recognizing a source of power, demanded that the king listen to certain demands before payment. Expensive wars forced Edward III (1327–77) to summon frequent Parliaments, and the commoners took the opportunity to attach a list of desired reforms when approving the tax demands. As they held meetings of their own, away from the king and lords, the House of Commons began to materialize as a distinct entity. At the beginning of the fifteenth century Henry IV agreed that grants of money would only be initiated in the Commons, recognizing the lower house as part of Parliament.

The crucial power which the Commons held over the purse-strings saw the gradual erosion of the monarch's position. Coming soon after the profligate Henry VIII (1509–47), Elizabeth I (1558–1603) fully recognized this, and was careful to court Parliament with flattery and charm. However, the Stuarts lacked the Tudors' realism and Charles I sought to reassert royal authority and govern without parliamentary consent, by raising 'ship money' from all towns. John Hampden, a squire and member of Parliament, refused to pay this highly unpopular tax in a legendary and eloquent stand in the parliamentary cause. However, by this time the Commons had become powerful enough openly to oppose the King, and events led to the Civil War between the supporters of royal authority (Royalists or Cavaliers) and the parliamentarians (Roundheads), lasting from 1642 until 1652. It resulted in Charles losing not the Crown, but a head upon which to rest it. Britain entered upon a brief period as a republic with the Puritan Oliver Cromwell (1599–1658), though declining to be king, supreme as 'Lord Protector'.

The decision to restore the monarchy in 1660 saw Charles II return in glory from exile to be a *constitutional monarch* constrained by Parliament. In a grizzly ceremony that did not augur well for the future, Cromwell's corpse was disinterred and hung on the infamous gallows at Tyburn in January 1661, to mark the anniversary of Charles I's execution. The remaining Stuarts were too stupid and arrogant to accept the principle of constitutional monarchy, further skirmishes culminating in the Glorious Revolution of 1688, which placed William (of Orange) and Mary on the English throne with clearly restricted powers. Yet it was not until the 1701 Act of Settlement that the subordinate position of the monarchy *vis-à-vis* Parliament was satisfactorily established, made easier by the fact that the Hanoverian line (established in 1714 when the succession failed owing to Anne dying without an heir) produced kings with little interest in British affairs.

> I would rather hew wood than be a king under the condition of the king of England.
>
> Charles X of France (1757–1836)

The struggles also saw an increase in the power of the Commons over the Lords as a result of its control over the supply of funds. By convention going back beyond 1688 the upper house has acquiesced to the claim that money supply is in the sole gift of the Commons and could not be interfered with. Many lords had sided with the king and the upper house was abolished after the victory of the parliamentarians, only to be reinstated with Charles II's restoration. However, the Commons remained under the control of aristocratic and royal factions, both exercising a corrupt influence on elections and nomination. It was not until the great nineteenth-century Reform Acts that the lower house delivered the ultimate *coup de grâce*, through the supremacy derived from the moral authority of the popular vote.

Yet the message was not immediately clear to their lordships. In 1883 they rejected the second Irish Home Rule Bill and, when the reforming Liberal government replaced the Conservatives in 1905, 18 of its bills were rejected. Lloyd George's 1909 budget, in which he showed the temerity to tax the landed aristocracy, roused the lords to purple-faced indignation and a furious constitutional (or unconstitutional) battle ensued, in which a reluctant monarch was told he would have to rat on his aristocratic kinsfolk by threatening to create sufficient new government-supporting peers to quell their opposition. The result was the Parliament Act of 1911, which not only legalized the existing convention regarding financial legislation, but reduced the Lords' veto over other legislation to a power to delay for two years. In 1949 the Labour government, nearing the end of its life and fearful of the fate of its steel nationalization bill, shortened this to a year.

The Monarchy

The concept of constitutional monarchy

Britain has a **constitutional monarchy**, meaning that, although the Queen may be said to *reign*, she does not *rule*. Perhaps its last dying gasps as an agency of real government were heard under Victoria. First under the influence of her consort Albert (who took his authority very seriously), and later encouraged by the flattery of Disraeli, she made several efforts to exert the royal prerogative. It was the lot of the austere Gladstone, preaching the gospel of capitalism, to school the Queen in the art of constitutional rule and he can claim 'the main share of the credit for cutting the modern pattern of British democratic kingship' (Magnus 1963: 42–7).

Why study the monarchy?

A number of textbooks and commentaries on British politics and sociology omit the monarchy altogether. This may be intended to betoken a jettisoning of meaningless symbolism in order to concentrate on the hard world of reality, but it is a mistake, betraying a dangerously short-sighted and superficial vision focusing no further than Downing Street. The monarchy affects the nature of politics and policy by being a significant element in British political culture. The capitalist class needed it as a symbol to unite society while pursuing economic inequality.

The powers of the monarch

Today the monarch continues formally to hold the powers of old (the royal prerogatives), but they are generally exercised on the advice of the Prime Minister. They include appointing the government; patronage; legislation; emergency powers; and summoning, proroguing (dismissing), and dissolving Parliament.

Characteristics of the monarchy today

Though the succession has faltered from time to time, it is based on the hereditary principle, Queen Elizabeth II being the fortieth monarch since the Norman Conquest.

Today Buckingham Palace, the main royal residence, stands at the end of the Mall in some 40 acres of gardens. Together with Horse Guards' Parade, Westminster Abbey and the Palace of Westminster, all of which are within a cannon's shot of each other, it is part of a baroque Disneyland of the past, sleeping while it is gradually overgrown by a towering office-block jungle. Inside the palace, courtiers and flunkeys, with titles and sometimes costumes of a bygone age, perform the tasks of running the monarchy industry. Many of these, from the Queen's private secretary down, are themselves nobly born and treasure their families' links with the sovereign, passing the positions down through the generations. This modern monarchy is distinguished by the following characteristics.

Ceremony While Britain is not alone in having a constitutional monarchy (the Netherlands, Belgium, Spain, Sweden, Denmark and Norway all do the same), it is unique in the degree to which the pomp and ceremony of old has been unctuously preserved. (The Scandinavian monarchies have been slightly dubbed 'bicycling monarchies' by the British, because of their deliberate paring away of ostentation and display.) The British monarchy, although never able to match the French in its extravagant prime, can on great occasions in the royal life-cycle (births, weddings and funerals) reach a scale only matched in Hollywood epics.

Political impartiality Although informed on a weekly basis by the Prime Minister, the Queen remains insulated from the rough and tumble of politics. She (like all members of the aristocracy) does not vote, neither is she expected to express partisan opinions on the issues of the day. This is not to say that the mask does not sometimes slip. In May 1977 the Queen inserted some criticisms of the government's devolution proposals into a public speech. It was also widely reported in 1987 that she was disturbed by Mrs Thatcher's refusal to go along with other Commonwealth leaders on economic sanctions against South Africa. In 1988 Prince Charles criticized some of the implications of the government's social policy, earning a rebuke from Norman Tebbit, who alleged that the Prince's sympathy for the unemployed stemmed from his own absence of gainful activity (presumably a plea for a bicycling monarchy).

Popularity Before the second world war, shaken by the abdication crisis, the monarchy was in an uncertain condition. However, in the post-war era, with the coronation, weddings and many royal offspring, the public appetite for its dignified constitution grew to gargantuan dimensions. In addition to the sychophantic tabloid reporting, quality newspapers regularly carry the 'Court Circular', confident that readers will pour over the royal engagements with earnest concern.

Homeliness Like the Ewings of Dallas or the Archers of Ambridge, the Windsors of London present the public, not with a lone and aloof monarchical figure, but an extended family supported by a galaxy of bit players, from a topless Koo Stark to the Queen's press secretary. Indeed the Queen is faced with a similar rivalry problem to that of Snow White's mother, and by

December 1987 her personal popularity (measured as 'the member of the royal family you would most like to meet') had fallen from 34 per cent (in 1981) to 19 per cent, while the Princess of Wales had become almost the fairest of all, standing nearly equal to the Queen at 18 per cent.

> Life in Buckingham Palace isn't too bad, but too many formal dinners. Yuk!
>
> Diana, Princess of Wales, in letter to a former colleague, quoted in *Sunday Times Magazine* (26 July 1981)

Expense Finally it must be recognized that by any reckoning the monarchy does not come cheap. In 1761 George III agreed to surrender the income from the Crown Estate in exchange for a regular grant from Parliament, to be known as the Civil List. Although remaining constant for a considerable time, it was revised during the reign of Elizabeth II to keep pace with inflation (see table 9.1). In addition there are other expenses, including the upkeep of five palaces and the maintenance of the aircraft of the Queen's Flight. One of the most ostentatious sources of expenditure goes on the royal yacht *Britannia*, which in addition to normal annual running costs of some £2 million, requires a £5-million refit every three years. Yet royal wealth goes well beyond income received from the Civil List. The Queen possesses a considerable personal fortune, said to stand at more than £50 million in 1971, and enjoys an independent annual income of several hundred thousand pounds. Over the years this has been exempt from tax and death duties, giving the Queen a touch similar to that of King Midas, and enabling her to outdistance all aristocratic rivals, some of whom, even after the second world war, were actually richer than the king. Today, while they collect the tickets for the roller coaster and zoos in their estates, the wealth in the royal

Table 9.1 The Civil List, 1988 and 1989

Name	Amount (£)	
	1988	*1989*
The Queen	4,500,000	4,658,000
Queen Mother	390,300	404,000
Duke of Edinburgh	217,000	225,300
Duke of York	86,500	155,400
Prince Edward	20,000	20,000
Princess Royal	135,600	140,000
Princess Margaret	132,100	136,700
Princess Alice	53,500	55,400
Duke of Gloucester	106,300	110,000
Duke of Kent	143,500	148,500
Princess Alexandra	136,800	141,600
Refund by Queen	386,600	400,100
Total	5,535,700	5,795,200

coffers continues to swell. The Queen also owns an internationally renowned art collection, a stamp collection worth well over £1 million, the fabled royal jewellery, and two of the royal residences, Sandringham and Balmoral.

The real functions of the monarchy

If is it still true, as Bagehot argued, that the masses are beguiled and captivated by state pomp and display, then the monarchy remains an important feature of British political culture, offering the following features.

> The use of the Queen, in a dignified capacity, is incalculable. Without her in England, the present English government would fail and pass away.
>
> Walter Bagehot, *The English Constitution* (1867: ch. 2)

Intelligible government Bagehot believed that the monarchy gave intelligible government, arguing that 'the masses of Englishmen are not fit for an elective government; if they knew how near they were to it, they would be surprised and almost tremble' (1963: 97). For him the monarchy was a key element in the facade behind which the real process of government was conducted. It was a means of beguiling the simple minds of the masses (particularly women), who would not understand the real thing.

Symbol of national unity The monarchy is a symbol of national unity, a tangible object which may be venerated in collective displays of national narcissism, patriotism and xenophobia. Feelings of patriotism and racial superiority can be very dangerous and it may be seen as healthy if they are channelled off in support of a constitutional nonentity rather than used to swell the power and ego of a real ruler, as in say Nazi Germany.

Formal head of state Monarchy or not, any system of government will necessarily evolve a large element of dignified pomp and circumstance, such as opening Parliament, entertaining foreign leaders, opening hospitals and motorways, and launching ships. Without a sovereign the burden falls on elected leaders, thereby fattening their egos and removing them from the sharp end of real politics. In Britain the monarchy is able to share many of the formal activities of head of state, thereby relieving pressure on the Prime Minister.

Source of advice It is argued that the experience gained in office can make a monarch a valuable source of advice to politicians. In 1884 even Gladstone formally thanked Queen Victoria for her 'wise, gracious and steady exercise of influence' (Magnus 1963). However, it must be recognized that the life experience of the Queen (in spite of her known enthusiasm for television's

Coronation Street) can hardly be said to have brought her into contact with the aspirations and feelings of ordinary people; her circle of personal friends has remained securely within the aristocracy.

Vicarious splendour Finally, public policy under capitalism requires most people to live in relative poverty in order to make resources available to the elite. It is sometimes argued that the royal family can add colour to the lives of people with otherwise drab existences, and help maintain social stability.

The perils of monarchy

However, while supporters of the monarchy may point to positive virtues, and agnostics dismiss it as a harmless sideshow, more disturbing aspects may also be discerned.

> Kings are not born, they are made by artificial hallucination.
> George Bernard Shaw, *Man and Superman* (1905)

Vulgarization It is quite impossible to study the place of the monarchy in modern society without recognizing the way it is processed by the mass media. If Bagehot were to return from the dignified constitution in the sky he would have cause to rue the day he praised the virtues of an inert monarchy at which the masses could gape. Today they gape with decided vengeance, through the vulgarizing lens of the tabloid press, spurred by the money-making ethic of the media barons. These were to become obsessed with royalty, seeking to report with astonishingly poor taste and monotony their most intimate comings and goings, reducing them through the use of cloying, over-familiar diminutives ('Di' and 'Fergie', though *Private Eye* long insisted on referring to the Queen unregally as 'Brenda'). The obsession is at its greatest at times of royal procreation, with pregnancies followed with obstetrical fervour.

The 'Royals', without any particularly remarkable personal attributes or talents for good or ill, have been elevated to the status of show-biz celebrities and hounded all over the world by the *paparazzi*. In Britain, the royal-watchers, who lie for hours in long, damp grass to catch a glimpse of Prince Charles fishing, or lurk among the fruit stalls of Piccadilly for sightings of his wife emerging from Fortnum and Mason's, have been aptly named the

> Monarchy is the gold filling in the mouth of decay.
> John Osborne, quoted in Bernard Levin,
> *The Pendulum Years* (1976)

Our media monarchy
Source: Popperfoto

'rat-pack'. The pre-marital antics of Prince Andrew earned him the nickname 'Randy Andy', rendering the term 'dignified constitution' increasingly inappropriate.

Democracy as deception: bread and circuses Bagehot's idea that the monarchy provided the pageantry which ordinary people mistook for government was an open advocacy of deception. It arose from a widespread elite fear during the nineteenth century that the extensions of the franchise would result in chaos. Where J. S. Mill argued for more political education,

Bagehot preferred constitutional sleight of hand. Symbolic trappings of government provide a very effective way for a *de facto* power behind the throne to rule without full accountability. In the 1920s Spain was ruled by the dictator Primo de Rivera behind Alfonso XIII, and in the 1920s and 1930s King Victor Emmanuel presided over the dignified elements of the Italian constitution while Mussolini operated his fascist dictatorship.

The emperors of imperial Rome sought to divert popular attention from the problems of society with *panem et circenses* (bread and circuses). There is a sense in which the entertainment provided by the monarchy can serve a similar function today.

> If Her Majesty stood for Parliament – if the Tory Party had any sense and made her its leader instead of that grammar school twit Heath – us Tories, mate, would win every election we went in for.
>
> Alf Garnett in Johnny Speight, *Till Death us do Part* (TV series)

The impartiality myth Finally, the issue of political impartiality is open to question. Unlike the constitutional monarchies of Europe, Britain's does not stand alone; it is the tip of a formidable aristocratic iceberg based on inherited wealth and titles, the survival of which is one of the political wonders of the world. The existence of the monarchy legitimates social elitism and maldistribution of wealth, thus helping to keep the social soil fertile for capitalism. Disraeli's 'one-nation' brand of conservatism made the Crown one of its basic symbols. To be a patriotic member of society entailed support for the Crown, loyalty which could be expressed by voting Conservative. Looked at in this way, it becomes difficult to regard the monarchy as genuinely apolitical. The Conservative Party has always been the natural political home of the aristocracy, and the Queen and royal family do not need to vote, or otherwise express views, to indicate how deeply they are enstructured in the ruling establishment of Britain.

> Well, what are you socialists going to do about me?
>
> George V to Ramsay MacDonald, when he first presented himself at Buckingham Palace (1924)

Justifying monarchy

Yet if we are scathing of 'bread and circuses', government by deception, and the paternalism of Bagehot and his latter-day disciples, it does not necessarily follow that, in an age of secular politics, there is no place for the concept of constitutional monarchy. It is generally disastrous when rulers believe themselves to be almighty; the history of the world makes this amply clear.

> On the whole it is wise in human affairs and in the government of men, to separate pomp from power.
>
> Winston Churchill, speech in Ottawa (1952)

The parable of the Garden of Eden tells what happens to Adam when he believes himself to be all-powerful, and if Britain were a religious country, people and politicians could look to a God as a figure above earthly rulers. Thus, in a democracy, it is generally a good thing for politicians to be kept down to size. They are only ordinary people, supposed to represent the interests of their fellow men, and should be restrained from delusory self-aggrandizement through ceremony or pompous behaviour. This is why Mrs Thatcher's globe-trotting in the late 1980s was criticized by some as inappropriately imperious and as usurping the role of the real queen.

> The object of government in peace and in war is not the glory of rulers or races, but the happiness of the common man.
>
> Lord Beveridge (1879–1963; British economist), *Social Insurance* (1942)

The House of Lords

The monarchy is the tip of the iceberg; beneath it floats a silent edifice of ancient privilege, in the form of a fully fledged aristocratic class of titled lords and ladies, to be sighted on special occasions or in special places such as Ascot, Cowes, and most visibly of all, in the House of Lords. The general atmosphere of the upper house has long been seen as somnambulant; it has been likened to a mausoleum or adduced as evidence of life after death.

> If, like me, you are over 90, frail, on two sticks, half deaf and half blind, you stick out like a sore thumb in most places, but not in the House of Lords.
>
> Harold Macmillan (Lord Stockton), quoted in the *Observer* (19 May, 1985)

Composition

Today the House comprises some 790 **hereditary peers** and 370 **life peers**. In addition, there are 26 bishops and 19 Law Lords. It is one of the most curious of the curious anomalies in British public life, defying all logic of democratic and secular politics. Its composition was based on the principle of hereditary right enshrining the idea that certain people are 'born to rule', a distinction acquired by emerging from a particular womb at a particular time as a result of aristocratic impregnation. It is a question of breeding, something which the aristocracy know a great deal about from their herds and their racehorses. To this principle has been added, through the Life Peerages Act (1958), another which is equally undemocratic: life peers (who cannot hand down their titles) are chosen to sit in the House of Lords on the personal whim of the Prime Minister (and Leader of the Opposition). The theory behind this is that the upper chamber is revived with a transfusion of fresh (though rarely young) blood.

It might be thought that one small crumb of democratic comfort would come from the fact that members cannot stand for the House of Commons, thereby keeping would-be 'natural rulers' safely confined in what is generally regarded as a neutered chamber. However, this safeguard was removed, ironically by Tony Benn, one of Labour's most rigorous left-wingers. In 1960, after ten years as an elected member for Bristol South-east, he was thrown out of the Commons when compelled, upon the death of his father, to inherit the title Viscount Stansgate. He was refused re-entry even after winning the ensuing by-election in 1961 with an increased majority. His case, that election by common people should take precedence over 'feudal nonsense', was rejected by an election court which regarded a ruling of 1626 as a suitable guide for a decision in the 1960s (Benn 1980: 15). Yet continued debate and strong public feeling led finally to legislation permitting peers to renounce their titles; Lord Stansgate immediately became Tony Benn, and acts of renunciation were also made by Lords Hailsham and Douglas-Home in order to throw their hats into the ring in the contest to succeed Macmillan as Conservative leader.

Politics in the House of Lords

Though cryptically referred to in the Commons as 'another place', the House of Lords is linked to the lower house by a short corridor. The general atmosphere is leisurely: meetings take place from Mondays to Thursdays for about 30 weeks of the year and sittings are usually held at civilized hours between 2.30 and 7.00 pm. The chairman of debate is the Lord Chancellor, sitting on the traditional 'Woolsack' which symbolizes national prosperity through trade.

> This is a rotten argument, but it should be good enough for their lordships on a hot summer afternoon.
>
> Civil servant's note on a ministerial brief read out by mistake in a Lords debate; quoted in Lord Home, *The Way the Wind Blows* (1976)

Debates are rarely acrimonious and the Lord Chancellor does not pretend to be independent, often leaving the Woolsack to join the cut and thrust. The party machines do not dominate life in the Lords as they do in the Commons, around a fifth of members sitting as independents (**cross-benchers**), often having renounced their former allegiances. Of those owning party membership there were in early 1988 around 500 Conservatives, 145 Labour, 40 Liberals and 40 SDP.

> The House of Lords is not the watchdog of the constitution; it is Mr Balfour's poodle. It fetches and carries for him. It barks for him. It bites anyone that he sets it on to.
>
> David Lloyd George, House of Commons speech (21 Dec. 1908)

Of the regular party identifiers, Conservatives do not have an outrageous majority, but if the non-attenders were to descend upon the chamber from their country homes they would swamp the House. These are the 400 or so 'backwoodsmen' and, when the trumpet has sounded, they have forsaken the tranquillity of their estates to answer the call; as in 1968 to vote against a trade ban on Rhodesia, and in 1988 to ensure the safe passage of the unpopular poll tax legislation. Peers who had never voted before, and who did not even know their own leaders, were to be found wandering in bewilderment around the precincts of Westminster.

The functions of the House of Lords

> The House of Peers, throughout the war,
> Did nothing in particular,
> And did it very well.
>
> W. S. Gilbert (1836–1911), *Iolanthe*

The essence of the argument of those wishing to retain the upper house lies in the claim that it fulfils a number of important functions.

Legislation Most major bills begin their legislative journey in the Commons, but the Lords can propose amendments for consideration by the Commons and, if they wish to continue their opposition they have power to delay for one year. The fact that Commons debate is curtailed means that the Lords can be useful for tidying up legislation (see p. 289).

Criticism The Lords can guarantee a freedom of expression not found in the Commons, speaking out where elected mortals favour discretion. Unlike MPs, they are less dependent upon the party leader for patronage, and are beyond the age of vaulting ambition.

Informed comment The presence of certain life peers, appointed because of some particular expertise in non-political walks of life (the church, industry, or the academic world), can at times sustain a high level of debate on issues of the day, while the bishops inject a moral dimension conspicuously absent from the lower house.

Restraint The Lords can preserve Parliament's historic role of checking the actions of the executive. The lower level of party discipline means that there can be more sense of a separation of powers, and a full legislative veto remains in the case of any government seeking to pass a bill extending its life beyond five years. Furthermore, since 1979 something of a resurrection has been witnessed, with the upper house inflicting regular body blows on Conservative bills. The first notable defeat occurred in the first session (March 1980) over the imposition of charges for school transport, followed by a show of independence on a variety of issues, including council house sales, British nationality, telecommunication, the 'sus' law, postal ballots for trade unions, and housing and building control. On a number of occasions the threat of the delaying power meant the loss of the bill, and the government accepted unpalatable amendments. By June 1988, the Thatcher government had experienced over a hundred defeats (Gunn 1988).

Judicial decision-making One function which remains very much part of the living constitution is that of the final court of appeal in the judicial system. However, this is not performed by the Lords as such, but by the *Law Lords* (or lords temporal) headed by the Lord Chancellor, who in addition to his other roles is head of the judiciary (see chapter 17).

Political expediency There are various ways in which the House can be politically useful to a government. Prime Ministers can shift 'upstairs' ageing politicians who need putting out to grass. Moreover, those aspiring to high office in British government can circumvent the democratic rigours of the electoral process; a Prime Minister can make anyone a life peer and thence a cabinet minister, as did Margaret Thatcher when appointing David Young (thus Lord Young) to the politically sensitive position of Secretary of State for Employment.

Legitimation Finally, like the monarchy, the House of Lords helps legitimate the system of government through the popular respect accorded its noble and ecclesiastical members.

The future

There has long been widespread feeling that the House as presently constituted should not remain. Lloyd George regarded it with profound contempt, and the 1911 Parliament Act was intended only as a stop-gap, a prelude to thoroughgoing reform. In the modern era it is to Labour that people have looked for action, though they have done so in vain; the party barking in opposition but unwilling to bite when in office.

A 1968 white paper announced plans, not to abolish, but to introduce some half-hearted reforms in which the power of the chamber would be reduced and the composition altered to consist of around 230 salaried life peers, with a majority for the government of the day. Hereditary peers would be permitted to attend without voting rights. This was scarcely a great step in the direction of democracy; indeed it added immensely to prime ministerial patronage. The subsequent Parliament (No. 2) Bill introduced the following year was dashed on the rocks of an unholy alliance between the supporters of two unlikely bedfellows – Enoch Powell (who wanted things to stay as they were) and Michael Foot (who favoured bringing in the constitutional bulldozers).

In 1976 a private member's bill for complete abolition introduced by Dennis Skinner was narrowly defeated, and the following year the Labour conference expressed support for abolition. However, to the anger of the left wing, the 1979 party manifesto contained no such commitment.

Within the House itself a group of Labour peers produced a plan in 1977 which was more or less a repeat of Labour's 1968 white paper, and in 1978, a group of their Conservative siblings, anxious for their future after the Labour conference vote, suggested removing the hereditary element. In 1981, a Home Office minister, Timothy Raison, announced that the Conservative government was examining the question of reform, though preserving the principle of a second chamber. However, throughout the 1980s the House carried on to become a thorn in the Thatcher side, sailing dangerously close to the wind, causing her, according to a senior peer, to 'scream and kick her legs in the air' (Gunn 1988). Yet in May 1988 Lord Scarman, in his Radcliffe lectures to Warwick University, called for a strengthened upper house to resist the alarming trend towards the elective dictatorship of the Prime Minister (*Guardian*, 7 June 1988). The Labour Party's major policy review, completed in 1989, supported the principle of an elected second chamber.

More rigour or rigor mortis? One might ask why such an apparently unsightly blot on the democratic landscape has resisted constitutional clearance orders with such tenacity. The answer is that there are costs to any kind of change which those in power have been unwilling to meet. If the House were to be reformed to include more life peers it would be scarcely more democratic, and some would say less so. If it were to be democratically elected (like most other upper houses in the world), members would demand more powers (in the US, the upper chamber, the Senate, is the senior house) and competition would develop between the two Houses, introducing a new range of constitutional problems. Alternatively, a Guy Fawkes solution would throw a much greater burden on the Commons, necessitating radical reforms there. Hence, in spite of much huffing and puffing, no wolf has yet emerged with the lung power to blow the House down.

In the 1980s there emerged a surprising number of constitutional red cross officers keen to administer the kiss of life. They argued their case on the familiar Burkean grounds that the British constitution is a mysterious and wondrous thing: 'it is its very irrationality that in a strange, even perverse, way is its strength' (Baldwin 1985: 113). The conservationists have discerned in the twitches of the 1980s, not spasmodic death throes, but renewed constitutional vigour, and evidence that the effects of the Life Peerages Act were finally coming through.

However, there are deeper reasons why the preservation order remains operative. To the establishment the House has great symbolic value: it is one of the many remaining bastions of society which only the select may enter. It is thus a key symbolic element in British political culture, stressing the hierarchy and social exclusion which reminds the mass where they belong – on the outside.

The House of Commons

The House of Commons, the third element in the parliamentary triumvirate, is the only part which may be described as democratic, seating the 650 members chosen by popular election. It is also the chamber of the Prime Minister, the leading ministers and the opposition speakers. However, it is by no means free of flummery and ceremony; indeed, as a political force, the House can be seen as much a part of the dignified constitution as the Crown and the Lords.

In understanding parliamentary discourse there are various arcane terms which require translation. 'The usual channels' means consultation between party whips. In the chamber MPs refer to each other as honourable friends or honourable members for this or that constituency. Privy Councillors (ex-Cabinet members or leading members of the opposition parties such as Paddy Ashdown), although their formal authority is no greater than that of other MPs, enjoy certain privileges: 'right honourable', rather than merely 'honourable', they receive precedence in debate.

The Speaker

At the centre of life in the Commons is the Speaker, who chairs debate. The radio transmission of the Commons led to instant fame for Speaker George Thomas, the Welsh MP whose huskily intoned 'Order, order' became the signature tune of the broadcasts. Yet there is more to the role than this: adorned with wig, black robes and knee-breeches, the Speaker presides over a variety of solemn ceremonies often held in his official baroque house situated within the Palace of Westminster. Though considered an honour, the position was once unenviable, entailing risky dealings with the monarch on behalf of MPs, and a newly appointed Speaker makes a symbolic show of resistance, struggling against his colleagues as they try to force him to the chair.

I have neither eye to see, nor tongue to speak here, but as the House is pleased to direct me.

William Lenthall, in the House of Commons on 4 January 1642 in reply to Charles I asking if he had seen five MPs whom he wished to arrest. A classic statement of the Speaker's role.

The Speaker is chosen by MPs, usually from the ranks of well-respected but politically uncontroversial figures. The position of Thomas's successor was rendered unusually difficult when Mrs Thatcher, in an unprecedented move, tried to treat the office as one within her patronage, so that when Bernard Weatherill was elected by MPs in 1983 he was known to lack prime ministerial confidence and this weakened his authority (Heffer 1988).

The Speaker is attended by the Sergeant at Arms, who wears a sword and carries the Mace. He is responsible for maintaining law and order, will eject the unruly, including MPs banned by the Speaker, and can imprison enemies of the House in the clock tower of Big Ben. Each day the Speaker leads a

Yesterday as today: the arrival of the Speaker, 1884
Source: Mary Evans Picture Library

dignified procession into the House following the Sergeant, and during debate the Mace is placed on the table at the centre of the chamber. Members take this extremely seriously. Michael Heseltine etched his name in the history books when he brandished the formidable weapon in the face of the alarmed Labour enemy. However, by prostrating himself before the House the following day he gained forgiveness for his intemperate behaviour. However, when Labour MP Ron Brown did the same thing in April 1988 he refused to apologize and his party withdrew the whip for three months, the sternest punishment imposed by the party for 25 years.

In debate, the Speaker is supposed to call members fairly, and with due weight to their expertise, interest and status. Rulings are required on difficult points of procedure, on emergency debates, parliamentary privilege, and to determine whether bills are to be classed as *money bills* (thereby placed beyond the Lords' delaying power). The Speaker also keeps discipline. During the 1980s there were scenes which alarmed lovers of decorum, yet such turbulence is not new. Conservative opposition to Lloyd George's 'People's Budget' in 1909 reduced the House to uproar, giving the reaction of Labour backbenchers in 1988 to Chancellor Lawson's 'rich people's budget' the air of the proverbial vicarage tea party. Where MPs persist in bad behaviour the Speaker will 'name' them; that is, rebuke them by their real names rather than as 'Honourable Member for *X*', whereupon they are banned from the House for a prescribed period.

Parliamentary privilege

It is held that in order to operate effectively MPs must enjoy certain rights and immunities denied to ordinary people. These are termed **parliamentary privileges**, and to inhibit them in any way would constitute the serious offence of contempt of Parliament. Their purpose is to ensure free debate and they include immunity from court action for things said. Thus, for example, in 1987 Ken Livingstone was free to accuse Mrs Thatcher's party colleague and personal friend Airey Neave (killed by an IRA car bomb in the Commons car park) of nursing knowledge of treasonable activities practised by Britain's security officers in Northern Ireland (Pienaar 1987).

The timetable

The life of a *Parliament* is the period between two general elections which, except in exceptional circumstances, must not exceed five years. It is divided into *Parliamentary Sessions* of one year, commencing in the autumn. Each is further subdivided by *recesses* (holidays) over Christmas, Easter, Whitsun and summer. A timetable outlines the day's events and is the responsibility of a minister, the Leader of the House, who will liaise with the Opposition. From Monday to Thursday it is set out in the **Order Paper** in the following general pattern.

14.30   Prayers
14.35   Question Time (15.15 Tuesday and Thursday: Questions to the Prime Minister)
15.30   Miscellaneous matters such as the introduction of new members and ministerial statements
15.45   The major debate of the day
20.00   Debate on the Adjournment

Sometimes a debate will continue beyond the normal time for adjournment as an *all-night sitting* extending into the small hours, but on Fridays sittings adjourn at mid-afternoon, enabling members to return to their constituencies for the weekend.

The members

An MP's day There are no morning sittings (they were tried in 1967 but abandoned) and full-time MPs spend this time dealing with correspondence, attending committees, meeting constituents and receiving interest group representatives. However, the facilities for such activities are notoriously bad, MPs having to share offices and hold meetings in corridors and bars. In the afternoon they may attend debates in the main chamber, meet fellow MPs, feed information to gentlemen of the press, gossip and plot; Parliament being a hot-house of rumours, gossip, character asssassinations, secret agreements and broken confidences.

Private interests and public confidence Many MPs do not see the work of popular representative as a full-time job. Conservatives characteristically hold directorships of private companies, function in some professional capacity (such as barristers and lawyers), or are large-scale landowners. When James Prior was sacked from the Thatcher cabinet he soon re-emerged in public view as chairman of GEC, and when Cecil Parkinson departed in disgrace in 1983 he joined the boards of no fewer than nine companies. Some Labour MPs are also able to supplement their incomes by journalism and public relations work. It is argued in favour of these extra-curricular activities that they keep MPs in touch with the real world, though it is debatable how many ordinary people inhabit the board rooms of industry, the Inns of Court, or even the inns of Fleet Street or Wapping.

There are two levels of concern over the outside interests of MPs. First, there is the probability that they will lack time to attend to their parliamentary duties, and secondly, a fear that they may favour sectional interests. The Poulson affair, which involved prominent Conservative politician Reginald Maudling, led to the establishment of a Register of Members' Interests in 1975. This is an interesting tome, revealing a growing profession termed 'parliamentary consultant' – an opportunity for furthering British democracy in which members appear assiduous. So overt is the practice that the Speaker will choose MPs to speak, not on the basis of their constituencies, but because of the interests they are known to represent (Roth 1981: xxvi). It is not necessary for MPs to say how much they earn as 'consultants' or to state, except in the most formal terms, the companies employing them and the duties entailed. Moreover many companies adopt anodyne or deliberately misleading names. Occasionally a furore occurs as in March 1990, when Conservative MP John Browne was suspended in disgrace for not disclosing major business interests.

Characteristics of MPs It is misleading to do as many textbooks do, listing MPs characteristics *per se*, as if they are a single species. Labour and Conservative members differ significantly along most dimensions, and on some are poles apart.

> A Parliament elected by the universal suffrage of voters grouped according to geographical areas is about as truly representative as a bottle of Bovril is a true representative of an ox.
>
> Eleanor Rathbone, in the *Observer* (29 March 1931)

(1)   *Age.* The House of Commons tends to mirror the older population, with the 40–60 age group best served. The oldest member enjoys the title of 'Father of the House' and, with no compulsory retirement age, there is competition for the honour. Labour has tended to be an older party than the Conservatives, with some 20 per cent of its members over 60. The reason for the ripe age is the need to demonstrate ability (in business, the professions, academic life, trade union activity or local government) in some way in order to impress a selection committee. However, in 1970, the local Labour oligarchs of Merthyr Tydfil decided that at 83 their candidate, S. O. Davies, was beyond his best. He resisted their slight by fighting the election as an independent and winning handsomely, though his death shortly afterwards gave the constituency party what would in other circumstances have been the last laugh.

(2)   *Education.* MPs tend to be better educated than the average citizen. Over 50 per cent are graduates, and of these the majority in the post-war era went to Oxbridge. Although more Conservative than Labour members are in this category, the number of Labour graduates has risen since the second world war from 34 to 65 per cent (Mellors 1978: 50), though with an emphasis on the non-Oxbridge institutions. Traditionally the public schools have provided the pre-university education for the great majority of Conservative MPs (mainly Eton, Harrow and Winchester), though ex-public schoolboys have by no means been absent from the Labour ranks (see table 9.2).

However, under Mrs Thatcher the Conservative cohort began to change, with an influx of MPs from the meritocratic assault course (state grammar school and university) to the extent that they outnumbered those

Table 9.2   MPs' educational backgrounds (percentages)

Year	Conservative		Labour	
	Public school	University	Public school	University
1945	85	58	23	32
1959	72	60	18	39
1966	80	67	18	51
1979	77	73	17	57
1983	70	71	14	53

Source: Data from Butler and Butler (1986: 179)

from the traditional route (Burch and Moran 1984). State school alumni also became dominant in the Cabinet ranks.

(3)   *Class.* The class backgrounds of Conservative and Labour MPs place them further apart and are closely linked with the educational indicators. In terms of occupation, Conservative parliamentary parties have contained around 45 per cent classed as professional, 35 per cent businessmen, 20 per cent miscellaneous, and 1 per cent workers. In fact Conservatives are not merely businessmen, they are *big* businessmen. Of the 273 company directors elected to Parliament in the three decades following the second world war, no fewer than 245 were Conservatives. Thus they lie foursquare with the British capitalist establishment.

Labour has had a similar proportion of professionals, only around 10 per cent businessmen, 9 per cent miscellaneous, and 35 per cent working class. The party has changed since the second world war: by the mid-1970s the number of professionals had reached 50 per cent, though these were mainly teachers and academics – classic occupations for first-generation members of the middle class (Mellors 1978: 50).

(4)   *Race.* Racism in Britain has held back the representation of the large black communities in the cities; parties do not like to field black candidates for fear of losing votes. This is compounded by a disinclination of some groups, particularly those of Afro-Caribbean descent, to register or vote. The Conservative Party has a reputation for being tough on immigration and racial issues, but in 1976 it founded the Anglo-Asian and Anglo-West Indian Conservative Societies. The former was notably the more successful, with over 30 branches in England by the mid-1980s, members keen to move into the main body of the party, and strong promise of Asian candidates appearing in elections. In 1979 the party broke its all-white tradition and entered two black (Asian) candidates. However, the West Indians, politically preoccupied with problems of police racism, have found little in common with a party which has always made a strong police force one of its sacred cows.

The Labour Party has taken black activists into its ranks but has tried to walk a difficult path of balancing immigration control (to hold the working-class white racist vote) with a sympathetic policy on opportunities for resident blacks (to attract black votes). Since 1983 it has had to contend with a demand from some black leaders for separate sections. Although more black candidates have been nominated they frequently fight unwinnable seats. Yet the 1987 general election brought four black MPs into the House, all Labour.

(5) *Gender*. On balance Labour has fielded slightly more women candidates than the Conservatives, and has had more women MPs. However, the number has remained astonishingly low in spite of the towering presence of Mrs Thatcher herself. Since the ostensible purpose of Parliament is to represent society it is clearly absurd that only a minute proportion of MPs are women. A pressure group, the 300 Club, has that number as its goal for women MPs.

> I think ... that it is the best club in London.
>
> Mr Tremlow on the House of Commons in
> Charles Dickens's novel *Our Mutual Friend* (1864–5)

Parliament has the characteristics of a typical crusty Victorian establishment, with bars, smoking rooms, and large leather armchairs. One of the qualities of an MP is to be 'clubbable', to be able to tell a good joke, with the intimate whisper, sidelong glance, mischievous wink, and the raucous back-arching guffaw to accompany the denouement. This is not a world in which a woman can feel at ease.

> The House of Commons is not so much a gentleman's club as a boy's boarding school.
>
> Shirley Williams (SDP politician), on Granada TV (30 July 1985)

The 1987 general election was a record-breaking one for women in a variety of ways, producing the largest ever number of women candidates, the largest number of women MPs, and the first black woman MP (see table 9.3).

Table 9.3 Women in the 1987 general election

Party	Candidates fielded	Candidates elected
Conservative	46	17
Labour	92	21
Alliance	105	2
Other	84	1
Total	327	41

However, the shortage of women MPs is not essentially a fault of the House itself. Parliament is a social barometer reflecting the role and status of women in society, and here their function is not seen as robustly debating issues of the day, but being servile wives and mothers (Perrigo 1985: 126). Hence they tend not to seek nomination, if they do they are not favoured by selection committees (Mrs Thatcher was at first turned down on the grounds that as a mother of twins she could not possibly be an MP), and even when they are able to stand they have not proved electorally attractive.

(6)   *Amateurs or professionals – MPs' salaries.* This issue is a central factor in determining the kind of people who will become MPs. Before 1911 MPs were not paid, being expected to give their services freely, unsullied by pecuniary motivation. This reflected the fondness of the British establishment for amateurism and meant that, as on the cricket field, only the wealthy could participate. Until as recently as 1964 MPs were paid the equivalent of part-time salaries, working and lower-middle-class members being obliged to suffer considerable hardship, often unable to afford to eat in the parliamentary dining-rooms.

The issue is of deep political significance; there can be no effective representation of all classes within society if the majority of people are unable to meet the costs of being MPs. Even today the salary (together with certain expenses) equals that of only a relatively junior professional or executive in the private sector, with the Clerks of the House receiving more than the members. Many Conservative MPs resist the call for higher salaries. This constitutes a major threat to democracy, leading logically to government by the rich (Batty and George 1985: 171).

Conclusion: Dignified and Indignant

In this chapter we have seen three great estates of Parliament. The Crown, the Lords and the MPs are, in their different ways, all parts of the dignified constitution which time has passed by, leaving them empty husks, serving merely to legitimate the exercise of power by others. The reality of Parliament today can only be understood by reference to the organization of the parties within it. We turn to this in the following chapter.

Key points

- All polities and political institutions tend to contain ceremonial elements, though Britain is particularly rich in this respect. British political culture treats its ceremonial with profound respect, so that to deprecate it (say by opposing the monarchy) seems to contain almost a whiff of treason.

- Walter Bagehot, whose thoughts helped to shape British political culture, took an exceedingly elitist view of such ceremony, believing that its purpose was to keep ordinary people in the dark about the real process of government.
- The idea that the monarchy is above politics can be questioned: from the nineteenth century a rallying cry of Disraelian Conservatism has been the Crown. Furthermore, the Queen stands as the tip of an iceberg of wealth and privilege, the embodiment of anti-egalitarianism.
- However, the notion of monarchy can serve to remind people that the elected politicians are not to be venerated as almighty, a useful belief in a democracy.
- The House of Lords, with its composition audaciously based on breeding and prime ministerial favour, is the most undemocratic artifact of government in the developed world. The presence of the backwoodsmen means that the Conservative Party can always muster a majority for critical votes.
- Any idea that the House of Commons represents the people by being a microcosm of society is mythical. The working class, women and racial minorities are treated here as unfairly as they tend to be in many other walks of life.
- Much as it is enjoyed by people, the pomp and circumstance of the constitution has serious consequences for the nature of politics, tending on balance to legitimate the establishment by dignifying (indeed deifying) undemocratic inegalitarianism. It is part of the politics of the mind and has a deep effect on the political culture, generally inculcating an ethos of deference and/or passivity.

Review your understanding of the following terms and concepts

ceremonial
constitutional monarchy
peers (hereditary and life)

cross-bencher
parliamentary privilege
Order Paper

Assignment

Study the extract from the *Independent* on p. 278 and answer the following questions.

	% mark
1 'This decision reflects the great haste with which the government has prepared the Bill.' What possible function of the House of Lords does this statement bring to mind?	25
2 Why should the fact of 'Mrs Thatcher's personal interest in the measure' make the Lords' defeat 'unexpected'?	25
3 Examine the options available to the government at the time the article was written.	25
4 What does the lobbying of Parliament by the famous footballers from the 1950s tell us about the role of the House of Lords?	25

Lords defeat may hold up ID card Bill

THE GOVERNMENT were last night defeated in the House of Lords on their proposals for a football identity card scheme when peers voted by 124 to 121 to support an amendment for a phased introduction of ID card schemes, preceded by a trial period.

The defeat, which was unexpected given Mrs Thatcher's personal interest in the measure, is a severe embarrassment to the Government and casts doubt over the future of the Football Spectators Bill, which envisages a compulsory scheme imposed at the same time on all Football League clubs. According to the football lobby, the plan will now face a delay. There had been hopes to bring it in next season.

More than 30 Tory peers rebelled in support of a cross-party amendment empowering the administrator of the proposed Football Membership Scheme to institute a "phased and orderly introduction of the scheme" after a full assessment and report on the various options.

By JUDY JONES and CHARLES BURGESS

The amendment sets no deadline for the introduction of the ID scheme nationwide, which has been strongly contested by the football authorities and by both Labour and Conservative backbenchers.

Lord Hesketh, Under-Secretary for Environment, later persuaded Labour peers to abandon a vote on whether Welsh Football League clubs should be exempted from the scheme, after promising to consider their arguments.

Denis Howell, Labour's spokesman on sport, said: "This decision reflects the great haste with which the Government has prepared the Bill. These football membership proposals ought not to be inflicted on every football club in the land. Most clubs have no history of trouble at their grounds."

He added that most people would see the amendment as the most sensitive approach. "If the Government have any sense at all, they will adopt it," he said. "The Government will be well advised to take account of the strong feeling that have been expressed right across the political spectrum."

Irving Scholar, the Tottenham chairman, said: "This gives us hope that common sense will prevail and that the Government will see the error of its ways."

The Government are expected either to attempt to overturn the decision when the Bill is in the Commons, or to modify the terms of the Lords amendment.

Jack Dunnett, the Football League president and a former Labour MP, said: "The attendance was amazing. The fact that 34 Tories don't support the Bill showed that this really is an all-party issue."

Colin Moynihan, the Minister for Sport, said later: "We are going to consider the effects of the amendment very carefully. The Lords have expressed a clear view, and it is one we are going to take note of."

■ Five famous footballers from the 1950s, Jack Kelsey, Nat Lofthouse, Tom Finney, John Charles and Ivor Allchurch, yesterday lobbied Parliament to present a petition against the Bill signed by many of their contempories.

Independent, 21 Feb. 1989

Questions for discussion

1 Consider the possible composition of a reformed second chamber for the British Parliament. What methods of selection would you favour? What would be the role of your reformed chamber?
2 Consider the possible consequences for British politics if the monarchy were to be abolished?
3 'Without the attentions of the media the British monarchy would die.' Discuss.
4 Why do you think the process of government tends to be surrounded by ceremony and display? How would you account for the fact that Britain is so profoundly enriched (or encumbered) with such pomp?
5 'The most important reform needed by Parliament is the replacement of around 300 of its male MPs with women MPs.' Discuss.
6 'Parliament cannot be described as a representative assembly if its composition is not a microcosm of British society.' Discuss.
7 'The 1980s demonstrated that the House of Lords is a force to be reckoned with in modern British politics.' Discuss.

Topic for debate

This house believes that the abolition of the House of Lords is a prerequisite for making Britain a fairer society.
    or
This house believes that the presence of the monarchy enriches the quality of British social life.

Further reading

Bagehot, W. (1963) (first published 1867) *The English Constitution.*
Highly elitist and disdainful of the masses, but contains enduring truths about the relationship between the rulers and the ruled, and about the place of symbolism in government and domination.

Judge, D. (ed.) (1983) *The Politics of Parliamentary Reform.*
A varied collection on the reform debate in terms of both quality and intellectual perspectives. The opening chapter takes a neo-Marxist view, noting historically that the reforms which succeed do so because they are useful for legitimating the rule of the economically powerful.

Miliband, R. (1984) *Capitalist Democracy in Britain.*
Chapter 2 discusses the crucial importance of Parliament, not in government as such, but in legitimating government.

Mitchell, A. (1982) *Westminster Man.*
Academic, journalist and MP, Mitchell gives an insightful insider's view.

Norton, P. (1981) *The Commons in Perspective.*
A thorough introduction to the structures and procedures of the Commons.

Walkland, S. A. and Ryle, M. (eds) (1981) *The Commons Today*.
A collection of essays by eminent scholars covering many (though not all) important questions concerning the Commons.

For light relief

Julian Critchley, *Palace of Varieties*.
An entertaining insight into an MP's role.

Frances Edmonds, *Members Only*.
A sharp and witty analysis of the House of Commons as seen by a feminist who normally writes about another male preserve, the game of cricket.

P. Van Greenaway, *The Man Who Held the Queen to Ransom and Sent Parliament Packing*.

10

Parliament: Not to Reason Why

In this chapter we turn from the overtly ceremonial and structural aspects of Parliament to what appear to be its more active functions, our attention focusing mainly on the House of Commons. However, this does not mean that we have left behind the world of pomp and circumstance. In its day-to-day affairs the Commons continues to see much ceremonial, even in ostensibly businesslike matters. The chapter falls into seven sections. The first notes the importance of **political parties** in Parliament. This is followed by an analysis of certain central processes: **legislation, debate,** and **scrutiny of the executive.** The fifth section examines the all-important question of **reporting Parliament,** including an analysis of the role of the media. In the concluding section we try to look behind the formal picture to identify the **real role of Parliament** in the British political system.

The Parliamentary Parties

The idea that Parliament has a distinct identity of its own is really part of the dignified constitution; such life that it has is breathed into it by the political parties through their front-bench teams and their massed ranks of backbench troops (figure 10.1).

Today party leaders are invariably from the Commons; in earlier times they came from the Lords, but Salisbury, who retired in 1902, was the last of this breed. In 1906, after a landslide victory, the leading Liberals in the Commons – Asquith, Grey and Haldane – plotted (unsuccessfully) to dispatch their leader, Campbell-Bannerman, to the Lords, knowing that this would neuter him and allow Asquith in the Commons to become *de facto* Prime Minister (Cross 1963: 14–15). In 1963 Sir Alec Douglas-Home (as he

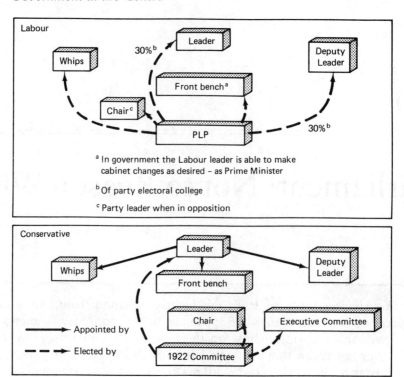

Figure 10.1 The parliamentary cadres

became) had to renounce his peerage in order to enter the Commons to become Conservative leader and Prime Minister.

Backbencher organizations

The backbenchers form themselves into separate organizations which meet regularly once or twice a week. The Conservative backbench association is known as the 1922 Committee in commemoration of the year in which members asserted themselves to end the post-war coalition (see p. 202). Before this they were easy prey to domination by their leaders. The chairman, who is elected annually, retains direct access to the leader and is always a commanding figure in the party. Proceedings are conducted informally with few rules; day-to-day affairs are organized by an executive committee of around 15, elected annually. When in government the party leader and ministers are not members, and the former attends only rarely, the event usually having the air of an occasion. Since 1965, Conservative backbenchers have assumed the key function of electing the party leader and the front bench has generally treated the 1922 Committee with respect.

The Labour Party formed its near-equivalent in 1923 as the Parliamentary Labour Party (PLP). In contrast to the 1922 Committee it is not exclusively a backbenchers' group; the leaders are also members. When in office it elects a chairman, but when in opposition the party leader assumes the position, though he does not select the front-bench team; this is elected annually. The party leader and deputy were themselves elected in this way until the reforms of 1980.

Owing to the vicissitudes of the electoral system the Alliance parties have been at their weakest on the parliamentary stage and their organization is more informal. At one time it was unkindly said that the Liberals could hold their meetings in a telephone kiosk, but after alliance with the Social Democrats they would certainly have needed an average-sized bus shelter.

In the upper house discipline is more relaxed. Although there is no equivalent of the 1922 Committee, there is a designated leader of Conservative peers and a chief whip, and the Labour leader and whips are free to attend the meetings of the PLP.

There remains an element of mystery about the workings of the backbench organizations. Although in the 1970s the PLP agreed to press reporting of its meetings, there is no constitutional requirement that they conduct their affairs before the public gaze. The rites of the 1922 Committee are practised behind closed doors and sinister stories have circulated, some of the earlier ones started, not surprisingly, by Lloyd George.

Policy-making

In both major parties the backbenchers form themselves into committees concentrating on particular policy areas, regions of the country and items of legislation. When the PLP is in opposition there is a feeling that votes taken should be regarded as resolutions binding the front-bench spokesman (the shadow ministers) in the House. This can threaten conflict, but is avoided by the Conservatives since shadow ministers chair the policy and regional groups. The potential influence of the committees is much weaker when a party is in government because the leaders become more remote.

Generally party leaders, not wishing to antagonize their troops, take soundings on the general mood through their parliamentary private secretaries and whips. It was Heath's reputation for aloofness which contributed to his downfall. The all-male club atmosphere of the House placed Mrs Thatcher at an unusual disadvantage, though she encouraged Cabinet colleagues to act as her agents in the informal socializing aspect of leadership.

The culture of obedience

The role of MPs today is largely one of humility, their lot being to follow the road of party obedience. Backbenchers have only a small chance of speaking in debate, and if they decide to devote themselves to earnest committee work their efforts may well go unnoticed. The first appointment an MP can expect will be as a parliamentary secretary or a junior minister (or shadow minister) to one of the less-important departments. There is little glamour in this, no invitations to appear on television or write articles, and they must cast envious eyes on the opportunities enjoyed by their seniors. If a backbencher does try to steal the limelight by writing a controversial article, or making a challenging speech, he runs the grave risk of incurring the displeasure of the party elders.

> The principle of Parliament is obedience to leaders. Change your leader if you will, take another if you will, but obey No. 1 while you serve No. 1, and obey No. 2 when you serve No. 2. The penalty of not doing so, is the penalty of impotence.
>
> Walter Bagehot, *The English Constitution* (1867)

Thus, backbench MPs (particularly those with professional backgrounds) may soon experience a sense of debilitating boredom. They spend their time in the tea-rooms and bars (of which there are seven and, because the Palace of Westminster is a royal palace, they are not governed by the licensing laws), sometimes appearing 'tired and emotional'. Those MPs who enter the House later in life and who may not expect to scale the political heights lack the incentives of the young to grovel before the party oligarchs, yet such members tend not to exhibit radical tendencies, being even more willing to show support on the basis of securing a quiet life.

The mavericks   There is a small category of MPs, who may be termed the mavericks, not fearing to speak their minds, scorning the party leaders and placemen, and grinning defiantly under the lash of the whips. Although risking their chances of office, they are more likely than their more docile colleagues to influence policy. Thus, for example, Enoch Powell caused both the Conservative and Labour parties to harden their lines on immigration policy. For the freedom to speak provocatively on this issue he effectively sacrificed his political career. Sometimes these rogue elephants spend their earlier years as orthodox careerists. Powell was Minister of Health in 1962, and Michael Heseltine, who was poised at the crossroads between orthodoxy and Mavericksville in the late 1980s, was, as Defence Minister, once a veritable pillar of the establishment. Tony Benn has moved progressively away from the Labour Party centre throughout his career. Others, such as Aneurin Bevan, began as wild men but accepted the warm embrace of orthodoxy in their more mellow years as the lure of office became stronger.

The mechanics of discipline   A key figure in the mechanics of **party discipline** is the **chief whip**, aided by assistants appointed from the ranks. In the Conservative Party the leader chooses the whips but in the PLP they are elected by MPs. In both cases, however, their loyalty is to the leadership, their function to ensure that members will always be in the House to vote as required (the title comes appropriately enough from the upper-class world of the hunt where the 'whipper in' is charged with the management of the hounds). The whips circulate weekly memorandums outlining the pattern of business, stressing the relative importance of the votes by underscoring the request to attend with one, two or three lines. Hence a 'three-line whip' indicates a matter of top priority with grave consequences for backsliding. There are various means whereby uncooperative MPs may be punished, ranging from a dressing-down in the chief whip's office, to a 'withdrawal of the whip' (a form of excommunication, to be restored only when the offender has purged his political soul). Labour has proved far more likely to use stern measures, even resorting to the expulsion of rebels. In 1954, on one celebrated occasion, the whip was withdrawn from Aneurin Bevan and seven of his supporters on the left.

Dead certainties

Lord Glenamora (Edward Short in his previous incarnation) reported macabrely (in the *Observer*, 26 Feb. 1989) how, as chief whip in the Wilson government, he had sick and unconscious members wheeled through the division lobby while hooked up to oxygen tubes.

From the 1970s MPs appeared less willing to accept discipline, resulting in a greater incidence of government defeats. During the Heath reign (1970–4) six such setbacks occurred, three on three-line whips, and some commentators saw this as heralding a new era of parliamentary independence. The thesis received dramatic confirmation when Labour took office in 1974 and suffered no fewer than 59 defeats. However, there were special circumstances, including minority government, followed by the most tenuous of majorities, concluding in the uneasy Lib–Lab pact.

The success of the Conservatives in broadening their social base in Parliament had costs in terms of discipline. The thrusting young meritocrats brought in on the Thatcher train were high achievers in education and business with less of the instinctive loyalty of their aristocratic forebears. During the 1980s there were many challenges (over matters as varied as rate-capping and charges for dental and optical tests) and some victories were gained (such as the 1982 amendment to the immigration rules). Dramatic revolts in April 1988 over poll tax and housing benefits also forced government concessions.

Bloody good news for democracy.

Speaker Bernard Weatherill, on the Shops Bill to bring in Sunday trading, put up by the government on a three-line whip and defeated; quoted in the *Independent* (24 Dec. 1987)

The constituency associations can be part of the machinery for discipline, recalcitrant MPs finding themselves ground between the upper and nether millstones. Thus, of the seven left-wing rebel MPs who voted against Eden in the Suez crisis, four failed to secure readoption as parliamentary candidates. When Francis Pym founded the anti-Thatcher group Centre Forward, his local association sought reassurance that he was not plotting a *coup*. Because of this local back-up, Conservative leaders only make recourse to the big stick of expulsion in exceptional circumstances. Thus, Sir Anthony Meyer, the Conservative MP with the temerity to stand against Mrs Thatcher for the party leadership in 1989, was deselected by his local party soon afterwards. In the 1960s, Wilson tried to evoke a similar kind of support, employing canine imagery to warn Labour rebels that although every dog might be permitted one bite, he should not forget that his 'licence' would need renewing. However, in the Labour Party local support for the leadership is by no means automatic; MPs from militant constituencies can be caught in a cross-fire, inducing a schizophrenic need to serve two masters. The 1980 reforms introducing compulsory reselection were promoted to strengthen the local associations by harnessing MPs as delegates who could be forced to defy the whips.

Disciplining the Lords The relatively weak position of the upper house renders party discipline a less important matter and *cross-voting* is considered acceptable. Although whips are appointed, they recognize that there are few sticks with which they can fright the souls of old warriors hardened with the scars of battles long ago. Equally, there are few carrots to dangle before the eyes of peers who already own much of the country, or are beyond the age of further ambition (at least in this world). However, the tough New Right line of the Thatcherites so alarmed the wetter of their lordships that 45 defeats were registered in the first time. The opposition they put up before the Local Government (interim Provisions) Bill (paving the way for the abolition of the GLC) earned the approval of Ken Livingstone, the condemned GLC leader, who experienced an eve-of-execution conversion to bicameralism.

> Three-line whips are very rare, and if I get 150 peers in to vote, using a really strong two-line whip, I am doing jolly well.
> Lord ('Bertie') Denham (Conservative chief whip in the Lords), in the *Independent* (27 April 1988)

Backbench opposition It can be argued that the real opposition to a government with an overall majority in Parliament is not the opposition as such but its own backbenchers; this is why governments take them seriously. On balance, the evidence is that the 1922 Committee, although having less formal authority, receives a more studious ear from its leaders than does the PLP. Even Mrs Thatcher followed the tradition.

The more secure the government's majority, the greater the likelihood that backbenchers will feel free to voice their dissent. They know they can beat their breasts and air their consciences without doing real damage. In 1964, when Labour had the barest of majorities, Wilson could enjoy loyal support, but after the 1966 general election the left began to exert pressure for changes, particularly in defence and commitments East of Suez. In the final analysis, however, members of the parliamentary parties are colleagues of the leaders, and discipline and cohesion are in their own interests.

Making Laws

Parliament is the British **legislature**; it is through the law-making function that its formal constitutional supremacy is manifest, being free to make any law it chooses and subject to no legal restraint from any other constitutional body. However, party discipline changes the meaning of this doctrine out of all recognition.

Types of bills

All Acts of Parliament begin life as bills, which broadly speaking, can be grouped into two kinds.

- **Private bills** are introduced by some body (a local authority or public corporation) wishing to gain some special power in the form of a *by-law*. In the nineteenth century these were very common as the local bourgeoisie (as councils or *ad hoc* authorities) sought new powers to develop the municipalities which supported the rise of capitalism.
- **Public bills** constitute the lion's share of all legislation, the resulting laws applying to all. It is by such means that most state policy is enacted. Public bills may also be introduced by private members.

Delegated legislation   In addition to bills passing through Parliament itself, much legislative power is delegated to civil servants, who frame detailed clauses through statutory orders and regulations. The purpose of this is ostensibly to free Parliament from what are often termed 'technical details'. This power is a serious threat to Parliament, and as long ago as 1929 the Lord Chief Justice Lord Hewart saw in it the dangerous 'pretensions and encroachments of Bureaucracy', in which he discerned a 'new despotism' (Hewart, 1929: v).

The legislative process

All bills must go through a lengthy **legislative process** (figure 10.2) which must be completed within a single session, otherwise they are 'lost' and cannot be resumed in the following session at the point they had reached. Under certain circumstances of political emergency a bill can be hurried

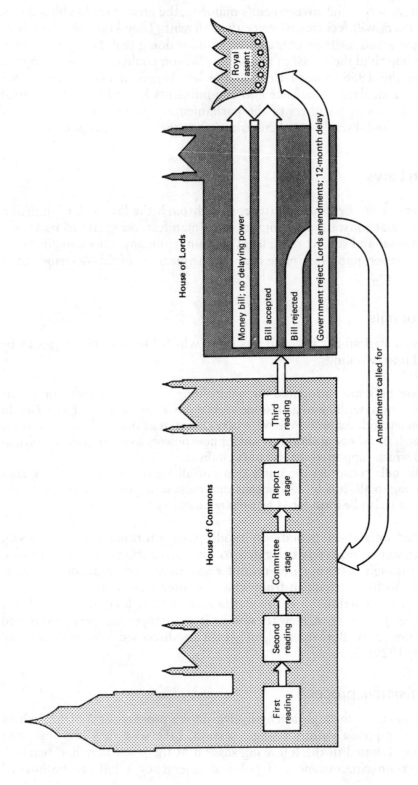

Figure 10.2 The legislative process

through with immense speed (in 1965 the Rhodesia Bill passed through the Commons in one day, as did the 1911 Official Secrets Act). Bills travel through both houses, passing through a number of stages.

1 *First reading.* This is a formality when the bill is introduced by its sponsor who, in the case of government bills, is a minister. It is then prepared in its final form by parliamentary draftsmen with the painstaking exactitude of constitutional lawyers.
2 *Second reading.* Here the broad principle of the proposed legislation is debated, but modifications are quite out of the question.
3 *Committee stage.* The bill is considered clause by clause, sometimes leading to small amendments. Apart from bills of major constitutional importance, meetings take place 'upstairs' in one of the **standing committees**. The term is a misnomer for, when any particular bill has been considered, the committee disbands; there is no continuity or opportunity for MPs to build up expertise in particular areas. Membership (around 15–50) reflects the party balance in the House, the government having the last say in all amendments.
4 *Report stage.* The full House has the opportunity to debate the clauses in detail and amendments may be made, though again voting follows party lines. In fact most amendments are actually introduced by the government as part of a tidying-up process. However, if the government's own supporters stand up the boat may begin to rock. In April 1988, for example, the Conservatives experienced their biggest backbench revolt since taking office in the report stage of the bill introducing the community charge ('poll tax'); their majority was slashed to a humiliating 25.
5 *Third reading.* This final Commons stage is nowadays largely a formality. There is no debate unless it is considered to be a matter of particular political importance, in which case six members must table a motion. No amendments are permissible.
6 *House of Lords.* From the Commons the bill proceeds to the Lords, where it follows a similar route. No real challenge to the authority of the Commons is expected, although during the 1980s there were some renewed attempts at self-assertion (see pp. 268–9). If amendments are made the bill is returned to the Commons for reconsideration and, if not accepted, the Lords, having made their point, are expected gracefully to comply. If they demur they have the power to delay for twelve months, which towards the end of a session can result in the loss of a bill.
7 *Royal assent.* In this final formality the Queen approves the bill, whereupon it becomes an **Act of Parliament**. Ever since Britain has been a constitutional monarchy this stage has been entirely ceremonial; the royal assent was last withheld in 1707.

Financial legislation

The House of Commons has a traditional role in controlling the supply of funds to the executive. It is this which helped to account for the growth in its power and today *money bills* are not subject to the Lords' delaying power.

However, the Commons' consideration of these proposals is largely symbolic (see pp. 386–90). It is far more likely that concessions will be made to powerful interest groups than to MPs acting in their own right.

Control of legislative debate

The essence of the legislative process is **debate** ('Parliament' derives from the French *parler*), yet British governments have become extremely adept at preventing such activity. The domination the majority party exerts over the legislative process goes further than ensuring support in the division lobby; it can actually restrict the amount of talking (and hence the amount of embarrassment, publicity, or inconvenience) during the passage of a bill. In 1902, standing orders were introduced enabling the government to decide what subjects could be raised, and for how long they would be discussed (dubbed 'Balfour's railway timetable').

Both front benches accept this curtailment, the opposition recognizing that they too may enjoy the advantages when in government, and negotiations between them are conducted by the whips through 'the usual channels'. Various devices which can be used to curtail debate include the following.

- *Committees*. Since the committee stage of bills is taken upstairs, the majority of MPs are excluded from the discussion about details.
- *Closure motions*. These permit the House to agree that the vote be put without further discussion, thereby ending the particular stage in the process.
- *The guillotine*. While tedious speakers are not actually decapitated, the debate itself is put under the blade. Discussion is cut off at a predetermined time, and the vote taken regardless. This frequently arouses opposition hostility and can be used to steamroller legislation and evade criticism.
- *The kangaroo*. Only a limited number of the proposed amendments are selected for discussion, 'hopping' over the others in the characteristic manner of the antipodean marsupial.

Early Day Motions

Citizens can often see reference to the fact that their MP has put down, or signed, an Early Day Motion, though they may never see any record of debate on the topic actually taking place. This perplexing situation arises from the fact that 'Early Day Motion' is today a colloquial term for a notice of a motion for debate given by an MP with no expectation that it will ever take place. It is merely a method whereby MPs can put on record their feelings on a particular subject, and perhaps canvass support, which they may do by inducing other members to endorse their motion by signing it.

Private members' legislation

It is here that Parliament comes nearest to a policy-initiating role, yet nothing better betokens the humility of the MP than the provision now made for members to introduce bills of their own.

In each annual session a mere ten Fridays are reserved for **private members' bills**, during which time members must attempt to negotiate all the hurdles. Demand outstrips the niggardly supply of opportunity and a crude process of rationing taking place, with a ballot each session in which the first 20 are selected. However, of these lucky ones, fewer than half will ever see their bills discussed, let alone complete the obstacle course to become an Act of Parliament. The reefs upon which private members' bills can founder are various.

Procedural problems Friday is a day when many return to their constituencies and there is a danger that the House will not be quorate. Malevolent rivals may 'talk' the bill out so that the debate does not close. Between 1976, when David Steel steered his abortion bill through Parliament, and 1988, when David Ashton introduced another bill on the same subject, there were no fewer than 15 private members' attempts to toughen up abortion law, all failing because of procedural devices.

Government attitude If a government wishes a bill to falter it can mobilize its majority to strangle it. Alternatively, if it welcomes the measure, government time can be made available. Such bills can be a convenient means of passing social legislation with which (for reasons of discretion or cowardice) government might not wish to be associated, such as, say, obscene publications, homosexual law reform, or abortion (Richards 1970).

Government takeover Sometimes a government will make known a number of topics upon which it would welcome legislation, so that any member successful in the ballot but bereft of ideas may inject the leader's inspiration into his or her veins. In addition, a government may induce a member to drop a bill in order to bring in a similar one of its own, as in the case of the Health Services Complaints Act (1965) and reform of the Official Secrets Act (1988). The results usually fall short of the original private member's bill.

●   ●   ●

Yet, despite the restrictions, some MPs use the opportunity to demonstrate parliamentary flair by steering through a successful bill, as did Roy Jenkins (obscene publication), David Steel (abortion law reform) and Margaret Thatcher (admissions to public meetings). Even if a bill meets an ignominious end, the MPs have had an opportunity to publicize their views, and may have done their careers some good by demonstrating their parliamentary virtuosity.

The value of the legislative process today

The legislative impotence of the House can be excused on the grounds that the process bestows the official seal of approval. Ordinary people can rest secure in their beds in the knowledge that the laws affecting their lives have satisfied their elected representatives, rather in the manner that a car might go through its MOT test. Yet if vehicles were examined in the way MPs examine legislation, the roads would be even more dangerous than they are. Scrutiny of this order produces only a false sense of security. The constitutional brakes may be failing and the wheels about to come off, yet Parliament is as rigorous as the man in the back-street garage with pockets full of greasy folding pictures of the Queen.

Although outwardly the process remains essentially that of the great nineteenth-century 'Golden Age' (see pp. 304–5), beneath the facade it has changed to become in large measure a dignified part of the constitution. However, like all such ceremonial its value lies in its ability to beguile and deceive. Although the legislative process may not have *policy-making* significance, it remains of considerable *political* significance as a means of legitimation.

Moreover, it would be mistaken to conclude that the Commons stages of the process are as devoid of substance as the royal assent. Parliament retains two key functions through the legislative process: *publicizing* and *criticizing* government policy. The progress of a bill is conducted in a glare of media attention which can stimulate public debate. Even though Parliament cannot change legislation it can, through the opposition party, expose the real meaning of bills, assess their impact, and identify the interests they serve. Although imperfect, and capable of being subverted, this critical function is not to be entirely dismissed as a contribution to democracy.

Debates in Parliament

A second major function is debate, Parliament's most characteristic activity. MPs such as Enoch Powell, Tony Benn and Michael Foot, who have been particularly identified with the parliamentary cause, have always stressed the profound importance of this function. (They were of course all virtuoso performers themselves.)

Opportunities for debate include the following.

- **The Queen's Speech.** Part of the ceremony of Parliament involves a speech delivered by the monarch in the House of Lords at the beginning of each session. This is a catalogue (written by the Prime Minister) of proposed legislation, which is debated over the following five days.
- **General government debates.** The government will normally devote around 15 days each session for debate on topics of its choice. In this way it can test

Gladstone defends his Home Rule Bill, 1893
Source: Mary Evans Picture Library

ideas, hear views on green or white papers, and outline its position.

- **Opposition Days.** Originally these were called Supply Days (of which there were 29), when the House would discuss the Estimates (see p. 387), the choice of topic determined by the opposition. These were really discussions on general policy and in 1982 were renamed. There are now 19 Opposition Days.

- **Estimates Days.** The Select Committee on Procedure recommended in 1981 that eight days should be set aside each session for debating the Estimates. In the event only three were allowed, with the topics chosen by a liaison committee.

- **Adjournment debates.** At the end of each day's sitting there follows a half-hour debate, traditionally to permit Parliament to consider grievances. The motion is chosen by a backbencher, often raising some matter of constituency interest, and is answered by a relevant minister. They are popular with MPs as one of their few chances to hold the floor, and the competition means that they must ballot for the opportunity. The final adjournment debate before a recess is a larger affair, with the motion decided by the party leaders.

- **Emergency adjournment debates.** At times of emergency a government may propose the adjournment of the business at the beginning of the day in order to concentrate on the crisis. Sometimes the House sits on a Saturday to debate an emergency such as the Suez crisis in 1956 and the Argentinian 'invasion' of the Falklands in 1982.

- **Emergency debates under Standing Order no. 9.** Here an MP can ask for an adjournment in order to debate a 'specific and important matter that should have urgent consideration'. The Speaker only agrees if convinced the urgency is genuine, and such debates are infrequent. Their value lies in allowing discussion of issues which the government might, for political reasons, wish to keep from the public eye.

- **Private members' motions.** In each session a number of Fridays are reserved for motions raised by private members. Although constituency matters may be raised, debates often centre on government policy.

Debatable virtues

The nature of parliamentary debate leaves much to be desired, and a number of criticisms are voiced.

Party domination The term 'debate' is rather a misnomer; there is little real cut and thrust and speakers tend to read from prepared briefs and rarely respond to points made. Final votes reflect, not the quality of wit or wisdom of the contributions, but party loyalty.

Backbench frustration At all times front-benchers are preferred as the official party spokesmen. In calling members to contribute the Speaker is supposed to look to those known to have particular expertise or interest in the matter, but most debates find MPs seething with rage at not having been called, and *ingenus* spend fruitless hours preparing speeches never delivered. Some are reduced to writing pleading letters to the Speaker (Wyatt 1973).

Superficiality The nature of debate can be criticized for emphasizing meretricious rhetorical skills. Members performing stylishly may triumph over less-articulate, but more sound, colleagues. When John Davies, the Director General of the Confederation of British Industry, was made a cabinet minister, his serious, non-histrionic style left members cold, drawing from party colleague Enoch Powell the mocking jeer: 'They've got a right 'un there' (Wyatt 1973). The parliamentary style is particularly ill suited to working-class politicians, who lack the background to fit them for the sophistry of Oxford-Union-style debate.

Weak in substance Yet despite the sophistry, debates tend to be of a low standard (not infrequently the Lords give a more informed treatment of a subject). Ministers rely blindly on a crutch of bureaucracy (providing statistics, arguments and information), while the opposition struggles to build its case on the basis of outside advice, intuition and invective. Though tea-rooms and bars abound to serve their bodily needs, backbenchers remain woefully ill-served for information.

● ● ●

Hence it must be concluded that debates in Parliament are generally party affairs in which Parliament, as the ordinary body of MPs, plays little role. In 1988 backbenchers claimed that Speaker Bernard Weatherill was over-conscious of the rights of Privy Councillors (Heffer 1988). Yet backbench MPs do not actually support each other very well; once the opening speeches have been made they drift from the chamber to places of refreshment, only to re-emerge for the front-bench winding up and to cast their all-important votes.

Scrutiny of the Executive

Though party domination renders the liberal-democratic notion that Parliament controls the executive illusory, it is said that the price of freedom is eternal vigilance, and the idea that Parliament should scrutinize the executive in order to discover and publicize its doings remains for many a key aspect of its role. In this section we examine the rights of individual MPs to probe through the device of the **parliamentary question**, and the attempts to restore some collective power of the Commons through an ancient instrument, the parliamentary select committee.

Questions in the House: a fretful hour

The first hour of the daily timetable directly after Prayers is **Question Time**. Here members of the government are questioned on areas within their responsibility, the occasion representing one of the few opportunities MPs have for acting on their own initiative. It is a relatively modern innovation, emerging during the nineteenth century as a means of protecting the power of Parliament against an enlarging executive (Chester 1981: 175).

Dealing with questions can be a testing experience for ministers. Although the answers are prepared by civil servants (work in the upper echelons of a department can come to a virtual standstill while this is being done), the hour receives keen media attention and those who cannot rise to the occasion may be earmarked as political liabilities; for junior ministers it can be make-or-break time.

Starred and unstarred questions Questions may, at the choice of the member, receive an oral answer (marked with an asterisk on the Order Paper) or a written one. With almost 50,000 questions tabled each session about three-quarters receive written answers. The distinction has considerable importance. Unstarred questions can be answered by civil servants and little media attention will be aroused unless the MP makes special efforts. In the case of **starred questions**, ministers are forced to become personally aware of the issue being raised, which gains publicity. Most importantly, the member will have the opportunity to challenge the minister through **supplementary questions**.

Supplementary questions When giving oral answers, ministers cannot get away with a mere recital of the civil servants' brief, they must also be prepared to deal with further follow-up questions. Skilful MPs will lure the minister to the dispatch box with an innocuous question, only to unsheath a rhetorical stiletto making probing and embarrassing thrusts. Supplementaries have steadily increased so that the number of questions answered each day has fallen from around 60 in the 1920s to around 20. This means that each day about 40 starred questions remain unanswered, though they will be printed in the following day's *Hansard* (the report of parliamentary proceedings) as if they had been. Successive Speakers have urged members to cut supplementaries, but such a move reduces MPs' power even further and has met with little success.

Prime Minister's questions The highlight of the Question Time circus occurs on Tuesdays and Thursdays, when questions are answered by the Prime Minister, and parliamentary broadcasts frequently place this at the top of the bill. In recent times, both Harold Wilson and Margaret Thatcher revelled in the opportunity to rally and enthuse supporters and ridicule opponents. There are more starred questions for the Prime Minister than colleagues, ranging over all issues of the day. Sometimes these can be deflected to the responsible minister, but to prevent this members have adopted the strategy of asking very specific personal questions, like enquiring into the Prime Minister's immediate plans and engagements, following this up with their real concern in the supplementary.

Problems with Question Time

The present system owes much to Balfour's reforms at the beginning of the twentieth century, which were intended to restrict rather than encourage the practice. Amongst other things, Balfour wanted to place Question Time at the end of public business rather than the beginning, when MPs were becoming weary and less combative and, although this was resisted, he managed to instigate the *written answer* and placed a fixed limit on the time available for oral questions. The procedure can be seen as something of a charade designed to foster the myth that MPs are important in their own right. A number of problems are associated with Question Time.

The rota The difficulty in raising oral questions is compounded by the rota system permitting particular ministers to be questioned on certain days only, causing a backlog. In an effort to improve their chances members began to give notice some six weeks in advance, resulting in many issues becoming 'stale', and in 1970 the period of advance notice was restricted to a fortnight.

Unstarred questions These are used increasingly (with a daily average of over a hundred) but represent a pale shadow of a parliamentary attack.

Time In spite of various suggestions for increasing the opportunity for oral questions (an extended question hour, a Friday session), Question Time remains a very inadequate 55 minutes. The reason given for the restriction is always on the theme of timetable overload, but it betrays the intent of party leaders to keep their troops passive and mute.

Evasion Ministers have great capacity to evade on the grounds that much public administration lies outside their formal control (local government, the nationalized industries, the NHS, and so on). In addition, they may refuse to answer questions on matters of security, including policing, on the grounds of 'public interest'.

Party domination Although much is made of the idea of MPs' freedom at Question Time, the parties insinuate their muscular tentacles. Governments can 'plant' questions, detailing tame backbenchers to elicit information placing them in a favourable light; alternatively, questions may be asked in order to crowd out those of the opposition. On the other hand, the opposition can wrest the initiative from their backbenchers by using the occasion for a concerted attack masterminded by leaders (Gould 1978: 87).

Scrutiny by committee

Much reforming impetus has focused on the revival of the parliamentary **select committee** as an instrument of scrutiny. In principle this is a body of

MPs drawn from all parties to fulfil some function on behalf of the whole House. They can enable it to regulate its affairs (the Procedure Committee), be involved in policy-making (in the nineteenth century they functioned rather like the royal commissions of today), or as a means of gathering information. One of the most successful has been the Public Accounts Committee (PAC), created in 1861 (see p. 390). In 1912 an Estimates Committee was created and in 1956 a successful Select Committee on Nationalized Industries. These provided a model and inspiration for a pattern of reform beginning in the 1960s.

The underlying case for greater use of **scrutiny committees** rested on the lack of information and expertise available to Parliament. Debates continually saw ordinary MPs, and even the opposition front bench, woefully out-gunned by the government. It was impossible to make intelligent and useful criticism without an adequate command of the technicalities of the matter under discussion.

The cause of reform was taken up in 1966 by Richard Crossman as Leader of the House. Committees were established on agriculture, science and technology, and education and science, and were invested with the power to 'send for persons, papers, and records', and to hold public hearings. However, for the government the experiment seemed like little more than an exercise in self-flagellation and it was allowed to languish. When the Conservatives returned to power in 1970 they looked more favourably at the idea and in 1971 the Estimates Committee was replaced by an Expenditure Committee working through six largely autonomous subcommittees, each specializing in a particular area (figure 10.3).

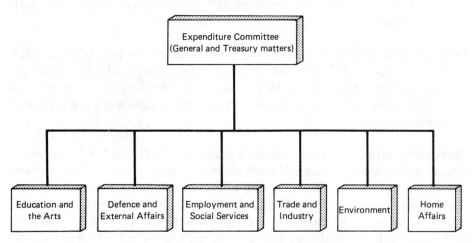

Figure 10.3   The expenditure committee system

A mandarin's charter   However, the new system continued to arouse official suspicion and hostility. Mandarins found developments singularly unnerving, and the Civil Service Department actually produced a kind of 'Hitchhiker's Guide to the Committee Galaxy' designed to keep civil servants out of trouble on hazardous voyages through the Palace of Westminster. This document was not intended for the eyes of MPs; indeed so secret was it that the Select Committee on Procedure had to use the force of the Lord Privy Seal in order to secure a copy. It outlined dark alleys of questioning down which civil servants should not allow themselves to be lured, including:

- advice given to ministers;
- matters of political controversy;
- confidential information supplied by firms or individuals;
- delicate information concerning foreign powers.

Furthermore, in no circumstances were MPs to be given extracts from cabinet papers, or be told anything about cabinet discussions. Information about the level at which any decision was made, and all documents on interdepartmental policy, were also to be clasped to the bureaucratic bosom. These guidelines constituted a mandarin's charter, a blueprint for government by bureaucracy.

The 1979 reforms The evident failure of the system called for a more radical restructuring, and a further report was produced by the Procedure Committee in 1978. This aroused no enthusiasm from the beleaguered Labour government, but a new Conservative government saw the reformist Norman St John Stevas as Leader of the House. Twelve new committees were created to cover the major spending departments:

Agriculture	Energy	Industry and trade
Defence	Environment	Social services
Education	Foreign affairs	Transport
Employment	Home affairs	Treasury and civil service

In addition, there were two covering Welsh and Scottish affairs respectively. Of the old committees, the only ones to remain were the PAC, and those on statutory instruments, European legislation, sound broadcasting, privilege, and the Ombudsman.

Although the committees' powers were not as great as envisaged in the Procedure Committee's report, they were superior to those of their forerunners. Members were able to choose the topic for investigation, they had greater powers to call for persons and papers, and were better staffed by the civil service. Working methods were left to the committees, but they were able to receive written and oral evidence from ministers, civil servants, local government officials and other interested parties, including pressure groups. They could also appoint outside advisers to prevent witnesses pulling the wool over their eyes. The committees were appointed for the complete duration of a Parliament and could not be disbanded by an irate government. Membership, controlled by a selection committee, reflected party strength in the House. They were kept small (around 11), with committee chairs shared between parties, though appointed by the whips. A liaison committee consisting of the chairpersons was created to oversee the general operation of the system.

Some were to produce stinging reports. The Treasury and Civil Service Committee, initially chaired by the prominent Conservative Edward Du Cann, was particularly scathing of economic policy in the 1980s. In 1988 the Home Office Committee criticized the way applications for British citizenship had been allowed to pile up and forced the appointment of more staff. Some commentators saw in the committees a new dawn for Parliament. However, the ultimate threat to restrict them was always present and surfaced dramatically in the enquiry into aspects of the Westland affair.

The Westland affair This issue concerned the leak by the Department of Trade of a letter from the Solicitor General criticizing Michael Heseltine, who was at odds with the Prime Minister over the way to save the Westland helicopter company. The Defence Committee decided to investigate: here was an opportunity for real scrutiny in an area where no question of national security could inhibit the enquiry.

In January 1986 the government refused point blank to permit key civil servants to testify, Mrs Thatcher claiming that this had 'major implications for the conduct of the government and for relations between ministers and their private offices' (*The Times*, 31 Jan. 1986). In place of the barred civil servants (Colette Bowe, John Mogg, Bernard Ingham and John Mitchell), the permanent secretary at the Department of Trade, Sir Brian Hayes, was sent in to play a straight bat that would have made Boycott look like Botham. When reminded of the committee's unqualified power to send for persons, papers and records, and to secure the attendance of whomsoever it wished, he unabashedly referred members to the memorandum of guidance to civil servants produced by Cabinet Secretary Sir Robert Armstrong, saying in effect that although a committee may get the horse to the water, the minister can still forbid him to open his mouth. Leon Brittan, whose behaviour in the affair was to lead to his ignominious resignation, refused to answer nine questions in succession, complaining that the observations of the committee were 'unworthy and unfair'.

Subsequently Sir (later Lord) Robert Armstrong, as head of the civil service, was asked by the Prime Minister to conduct his own enquiry, and after this he too went before the committee to stress once again that the civil servants would not appear. Thus Parliament was never to know the extent of Downing Street's involvement in what Armstrong admitted to be the 'discourtesy, impropriety, and unwisdom' of the leaked letter (Evans 1986b). When the committee's report appeared it was a damning indictment of those involved in the cover-up. Yet the sabotage did not end there; the Conservative majority on the committee delayed completion of the report by several months so that it was released just before the summer recess, thereby muzzling debate (Witherow 1986). Thus the government's ability to limit the damage arising from an event which some had predicted would unseat Mrs Thatcher in the manner of a British Watergate, was remarkable. No US executive could have got away with so much.

Committee scrutiny and the constitution

Many advocates of scrutiny committees cast envious eyes across the Atlantic, where congressional committees exert considerable sway in the political system and where the chairpersons are nationally recognized and important political figures. The US executive has good grounds to fear these commit-tees, as British television viewers witnessed in the Watergate and 'Irangate' hearings. However, no British system of legislative committees could ever operate with the same degree of authority. Congress is set within a constitutional separation of powers backed by a written constitution, whereas in Britain the Cabinet and Prime Minister are the dominant members of the House from which the committees are drawn. All the formidable powers of government to control Parliament can be used to limit its committees.

Moreover some (such as Enoch Powell and Michael Foot) argue that the whole development is misguided. Parliamentary debate is traditionally wide ranging, concerned with large generalities and points of broad principle. The concentration on details made possible by the micro-level scrutiny of the committees will result in losing sight of the ideological wood for the trees. The argument that MPs require more information in order to be better at their jobs may be fallacious.

Reporting Parliament

> Burke said that there were Three Estates in Parliament; but, in the Reporter's Gallery yonder, there sat *Fourth Estate* more important far than they all.
>
> Thomas Carlyle (1795–1881; Scottish author),
> *Heroes and Hero Worship* (1841)

If democracy is to work, people must be informed about the issues of the day. The mechanism for reporting Parliament is therefore crucially impor-tant. Although debate rarely leads to any direct change of policy, it can have a longer-term influence by shaping public opinion.

Problems of reporting Parliament

Although all debates and discussion are faithfully reproduced in **Hansard**, the official report of proceedings in the House (available for citizens to consult in public libraries), there are certain problems in the media reporting of Parliament.

- *Selectivity.* It is impossible to cover everything said in this palace of a million words, particularly if one includes the vast amount of committee work. Journalists must be selective, and try to choose the element of a speech or debate which will encapsulate its essential message.
- *Simplification and trivialization.* This further symptom of selectivity is particularly true in the tabloids, where single-syllable words are *de rigueur*. In the quality papers there is a tradition of amusing reporting in the 'Parliamentary Sketch' column, often highlighting the antics of some of the more bizarre and exotic parliamentary creatures.
- *Political bias.* The right-wing bias of the press (see pp. 139–40) means that the editorial selection will generally favour the Conservative Party. 'Rowdy-ism' of the extreme left can always expect to be reported in lurid detail.
- *Diminishing Parliament.* The media can reduce the importance and status of the House by encouraging speeches and statements from leading figures outside its precincts. This frees politicians from restraint by colleagues and can catch opponents unprepared. Even Enoch Powell, a fervent parliamentarian, frequently courted the media by pre-releasing the text of speeches and making major utterances outside Westminster under the eyes of the cameras.
- *Tame reporting.* Much of the reporting from Parliament merely relays the information disseminated by ministers through the lobby system, the press becoming little more than a government megaphone (see p. 366).

Live from the Commons: televising Parliament

No technological innovation has had a greater impact on the political life of the nation than the unblinking box flickering ubiquitously in the corner of the room. Campaigning is mainly a television art, and between elections politicians feature regularly in news stories, as pundits and chat-show guests and hosts, on phone-ins, and on 'question time'-type programmes. On Christmas Day viewers are even taken into their homes to share their festivities and hear them singing carols with their families. Although politicians are television stars, the cameras for long remained out of the House. On 16 March 1976 the Commons agreed in principle to the sound broadcasting of proceedings, regular transmissions beginning in April 1978. However, this was not to be the thin end of the television wedge.

The debate Those against televising Parliament argued that it would tend to highlight the 'worst' aspects of debate, encouraging members to play to the gallery and forget the serious matters before them. The unruly behaviour of Labour backbenchers in the late 1980s was seized upon as reason for keeping such scenes under wraps for fear of alarming the public. It was also argued that the problems of selectivity and trivialization would be magnified by the editing process which would, like sports coverage, concentrate on 'highlights' (Segal 1970: 303). Yet on the surface it would seem proper that the people, having been courted for their votes, should be allowed to witness the results of their choices. Political debate today takes place on television; if the cameras did not enter the House it would still take place in the studios between academics, journalists, and a chosen few media politicians or ex-politicians. But these are not the representatives of ordinary people, and when they speak they do so only for themselves. These are not public debates; they are private debates upon public matters.

Towards a nervous experiment In 1963, the distinguished broadcaster and scourge of evasive and wily politicians, Robin Day, argued a strong case for televising Parliament (Day 1963). The debate rumbled on and an important watershed was reached in 1986 when the Lords agreed to submit to the cameras. In 1988, despite vigorous opposition from Margaret Thatcher and Norman Tebbit, it was agreed with a majority of 54 that a ten-month experiment should take place in the Commons, and a select committee was given the task of deciding on the form the broadcasts would take. However, the committee's report brought dismay, with its determination to do everything possible to emasculate producers and exorcize all hint of the drama of real-world politics. The committee wanted Parliament presented in the unctuous tones of the old-fashioned BBC approach used for occasions like royal weddings, with cameras turning a blind eye to any raucous behaviour.

A spokesman for the Independent Broadcasting Authority argued that the cameras 'should have the same scope and freedom as a journalist sitting in the Press Gallery or a member of the public in the Strangers' Gallery (*Independent*, 8 May 1989). However, the desire of the committee was clearly to make the result as boring as possible to viewers, thereby limiting popular involvement as recommended by the nineteenth-century elitists. The historic first live broadcast of Commons debate took place on Tuesday 21 November 1989 with the debate on the Queen's Speech. Although officially an experiment, it was difficult to imagine that the cameras would ever leave.

> The resistance to cameras in the elected assembly has been stronger in Britain than other liberal democracies. By 1988, when the British Parliament finally agreed to an experiment, Australia, Austria, Belgium, Canada, France, Greece, Italy, Japan, Holland, West Germany and the US had all accepted the principle (see *Sunday Times*, 14 Feb. 1988).

Explaining resistance MPs' reticence is hardly surprising in the context of a political culture which arguably accepts the most closed and secretive system of government outside pre-*glasnost* Russia. Democracy, unlike justice, has been deemed better for not actually being seen to be done. Television offers Parliament one of the most potent ways to heighten its visibility, gain a popular voice for its members, and increase its power. This is the very last thing the executive wants. The public gallery is kept deliberately small and is usually full of sightseeing tourists rather than vigilant citizens. This is very convenient for those who emasculate the people's representatives. With a public gallery of some 50 million, things may change.

> A case of 'gently gently catchee monkey' and we, Mr Speaker, would be the monkey.
>
> Norman Tebbit (Conservative front-bencher),
> Commons debate on televising Parliament (9 Feb. 1988)

Conclusion: From Golden Age to Golden Sunset

An incessant theme of post-war political debate has been the reform of Parliament, the underlying critique centring on its inability to bridle, or even effectively scrutinize, the executive. Although formally regarded as the sovereign body within the constitution, it is like the aged parent of a hulking son grown to enormous proportions, who mocks any attempt to exert discipline.

The Golden Age of Parliament

It is sometimes argued that Parliament has never been strong *vis-à-vis* the executive and it is not in the nature of the British constitution that it should be. However, there was a 'Golden Age' of Parliament effectively extending from the first great Reform Act of 1832 to that of 1867, when MPs really mattered. This was before the parties began to dominate so completely, when governments were genuinely dependent upon the collective goodwill of the House, vulnerable to being turned out of office without a general election (as happened in 1852, 1855, 1858 and 1866), when ministers could be individually censured and forced to resign. MPs controlled the organization of the House and could shape policy through debates. Information could be demanded from the government, and where it was not available they could establish select committees to conduct authoritative investigations and even draft legislation.

During this period the legislative process began with a formal request for leave to introduce the bill, in which a justification for the proposed measure was required before it could be printed and presented for its first reading. Following this, the second and third readings, and the intervening committee stage, were genuinely critical scrutinies of general principles and particulars, in which MPs took their own time and demanded many amendments. In addition, Gladstone introduced financial reforms whereby public expenditure was subject to real financial control centring on the Estimates, the Budget, and the public accounting process (see p. 390).

It is clear from the discussion in this chapter that, in spite of the preservation of ceremonies and names of long ago, the House of Commons today bears little resemblance to that portrayed in the liberal-democratic model of representative government. Bagehot saw in the Commons (unlike the Lords and the monarchy) much activity of real government through its *fusion* (through the Cabinet) with the executive, which he termed the great 'efficient secret' of the constitution. Yet it was that fusion, together with party discipline in the context of a two-party system, which was to render the sovereignty of Parliament a palpable fiction. In the US, where there is separation rather than fusion of powers, the leaders of Congress are not members of the executive, neither do they depend upon executive patronage for advancement; thus they exert a formidable check upon the president.

Inhibitions to reform

All attempts to make the House of Commons more powerful *vis-à-vis* the government must founder on the rocks of the fusion of powers and party discipline; the very disease renders the House unable to administer the medicine to its lips. Only the executive has the power to bring about changes, but why should it connive in any reform designed to reduce its omnipotence?

Furthermore, not all MPs want to see Parliament more powerful. Old-style Conservative knights of the shires and businessmen entertain little ambition for office, seeing a seat in the House as a title to boost their egos and private earning capacities. They are happy enough to trust their party leaders to govern the country in their interests, while the local associations selecting candidates do not want their representatives to rock the establishment boat. There has long been a similar body of inert loyalists within the Labour Party, who see a seat in Parliament as a reward for faithful service to the movement; an old folks home where they may peacefully spend the eventide of their careers. Furthermore, the new breed of young, ambitious MPs of both parties see their future not as chairpersons of select committees, but as front-benchers, so they too will play the game. Moreover, a willingness to tolerate executive domination is entirely compatible with a political culture which sets great store by strong government. Voters would be considerably disturbed to find their representatives continually frustrating the actions of a mandated government.

The key to understanding Parliament lies in the parties. MPs are members of their parties first, and of the House second. The unity of Parliament is like that of a gigantic pantomime horse, in which two ill-matched thespians wrestle with each other about who should be the head end. In everyday political life there is no interest of Parliament itself, only the interests of the parties within it.

Denouement: the real function exposed

We have seen that the House of Commons can be said to fulfil a number of functions, including representation, legislation, debate and scrutiny, all of which contribute to the broader function of controlling the executive. However, it has been shown that in all these the power of the assembly is mythical; the government remains very securely in the Westminster driving seat. What then is the point of Parliament in the British political system?

Perhaps the answer to the question lies in Bagehot's interpretation of the value of the House of Lords and the monarchy: that they served to beguile and deceive the masses in order that the real process of government could proceed unimpaired by popular participation. Today this interpretation can be extended to the Commons: we can say that the House is an apparent (but bogus) focus of political life and government. For this reason politicians of all parties, representatives of powerful interest groups, the media, and civil servants, all pay unctuous tribute to the House; the paternalistic politeness of the peer to the flower-girl.

It is of course crucially necessary for the economically and politically powerful that the House of Commons *should* have this apparent centrality in British political life, because it stands alone in the constitution as the embodiment of the notions of democracy and participation. Without it there would be little to justify the exercise of state power. More than any other institution it can foster a popular belief that ordinary folk choose their rulers, call them to account, and shape the laws which determine how people shall live, and how the economy which underpins social life shall operate. In other words, it is one of the most powerful legitimating devices in the political system.

Key points

- The life of Parliament is largely controlled by the two main political parties. Parliament has no real identity as such (as the collective voice of the people).
- Party discipline, the absence of a separation of powers, and the tendency of

---

Review your understanding of the following terms and concepts

party discipline	Opposition Days
party whips	adjournment debates
legislature	emergency debates
bills, private and public	parliamentary questions
delegated legislation	Question Time
legislative process	starred questions
standing committees	supplementary questions
Act of Parliament	select committee
parliamentary debate	scrutiny committee
private member's bill	*Hansard*
Queen's Speech	'Golden Age' of Parliament

the electoral system to produce governments with unchallengeable majorities mean that the sovereignty of Parliament is in effect the sovereignty of the government.

● The principal functions of Parliament may be said to be legislation, debate, and scrutiny of the executive. In all these the government exerts an overwhelming dominance. This is true despite the efforts of reformers.

● Thus, in spite of the seemingly businesslike behaviour of politicians, and the earnest reporting in the media, the House of Commons serves largely to conceal the reality of power and government in Britain.

Assignment

Using your library, trace some newspaper accounts of the proceedings in Parliament for Tuesday and Wednesday, 13 and 14 March 1990, when a bill to restructure the NHS was considered. In addition, ask to see a copy of *Hansard*. Attempt the following questions.

		% mark
1	What was the method used by the government to curtail debate on the bill?	10
2	Why do you think the government wished to curtail debate?	10
3	Explain the tactical error made by Labour.	15
4	Why was business 'adjourned in grave disorder'. Who decides when such disorder occurs?	15
5	Choose one newspaper account and compare this with the account given in *Hansard*.	50

Questions for discussion

1 Explain the way in which the Labour and Conservative backbenchers organize themselves in Parliament. Can they exert any control over front-benchers?

2 What factors account for the high level of party discipline in the House of Commons?

3 'The legislative process was designed for the mid-nineteenth-century Parliament and is nothing more than an anachronism today.' Discuss.

4 What is the value of the parliamentary question today?

5 Evaluate the opportunity for private members' legislation in Parliament.

6 To what extent can select committees revive the ability of MPs to influence government?

7 Consider the possible implications of the introduction of television cameras into the House of Commons.

Topic for debate

This house believes that electoral reform is a prerequisite of any fundamental reform of Parliament.

     or

This house believes that the House of Commons is no more than a part of the dignified constitution.

Further reading

The reading suggestions below should be seen as supplementary to those indicated for chapter 9, many of which remain relevant to the discussion in this chapter.

Batty, K. and George, B. (1985) 'Finance and facilities for MPs', in Norton, P. (ed.), *Parliament in the 1980s.*
Generally an indictment of the facilities available for British MPs, and a gloomy prognosis for the future of Parliament unless things improve.

Chester, N. (1981) 'Questions in the House', in S. A. Walkland and M. Ryle (eds), *The Commons Today.*
Examines MPs' use of Question Time since its inception. Believes that changes must come in order to deal with the increased pressure.

Day, R. (1963) *The Case for Televising Parliament.*
The case put by one of Britain's great political television journalists.

Englefield, D. (ed.) (1984) *Commons Select Committees: Catalysts for Progress?*
Fairly optimistic analysis of the select committee system in its first Parliament.

Mackintosh, J. P. (1978) *People and Parliament.*
Political scientist and MP, Mackintosh saw Parliament as the centre of the political universe.

Marsh, D. and Read, M. (1988) *Private Members' Bills.*
Careful analysis of a subject not often studied with rigour. Stresses the need for government support if a private member's bill is to get anywhere.

Richards, P. G. (1970) *Parliament and Conscience.*
Illustrates the backbencher's role in legislating in sensitive areas of morality.

Richards, P. G. (1981) 'Private members' legislation', in S. A. Walkland and M. Ryle (eds), *The Commons Today.*
Argues plausibly that MPs should have the right to sit into the night in order to overcome the absence of parliamentary time for private members' legislation.

For light relief

Hilaire Belloc, *Mr Clutterbuck's Election.*
Satire on political life early in the century.

Howard Spring, *Fame is the Spur.*
A Labour politician's rise to power.

J. T. Storey, *Dishonourable Member.*

11

The Executive: of Cabinets and Queens

In this chapter attention turns from the elected assembly to the relatively small group of MPs who head the **executive** arm of government. Britain is said to have cabinet government: the executive is collective rather than singular, the principle of rule by the *one* having been repudiated in the long series of constitutional struggles against the monarchy. The chapter is in two broad sections. The first begins with an examination of the nature of **cabinet government** and its evolution. This is followed by a study of the anatomy of the modern Cabinet, identifying a range of associated political debates. In the second section we seek a deeper insight into the essential nature of the British executive by examining the distribution of power within the Cabinet. This leads in to the central debate on the role and power of the modern **Prime Minister**. Is it, or is it not, presidential in character? This debate tells us more about the living constitution than any other.

Defining the executive

The centre of political authority in any state lies in the **executive arm of government**. Decisions made here will determine how we live, how we are educated, our health, our employment, and even, where war is concerned, how we shall die. Formally the head of the British executive comprises the Prime Minister and around 20 other senior ministers – the Cabinet. This works through regular meetings (about once a week under Mrs Thatcher) in the Cabinet Room at the Prime Minister's residence, 10 Downing Street, a familiar TV backdrop for the comings and goings of the important and self-important.

The Cabinet Room in Downing Street, 1870
Source: Mary Evans Picture Library

An Anatomy of Cabinet Government

What is cabinet government?

Cabinet government entails the sharing of authority and decision-making based upon discussion and compromise between differing points of view. This is a self-moderating form of government which protects against tyranny and is quite different from the dictatorial, presidential or monarchical systems found in many countries of the world and throughout history. However, it is only convention which ensures that cabinet government will take place, and these particular conventions, though supremely important, are among the most fragile in the constitution. For this reason students of British politics are compelled to regard the nature of the executive as one of the most crucial areas of debate.

The debate: philosopher king or tyrant? The Greek philosopher Plato (427–347 BC) believed that a pure monarchy, with rule by a divine 'philosopher king', would be the most perfect form of government. However, this could only be realized in an ideal world; in reality it would deteriorate into the *worst* form – tyranny (see chapter 2). Regimes which have terrorized populations have characteristically been driven by single rulers – tyrants, dictators and demagogues whose very names have become synonyms for oppression. Constitutions are designed to prevent the rise of such people:

this is what the English sought to do in 1215 and 1688 and the Americans in 1787, and after Stalin the Russians vowed they would never again permit one person so much power.

Yet we will shortly see that the British executive knows no constitutional constraints, so a belief that we have cabinet government is important as a safeguard and as a basis for the legitimacy of the state. It is for this reason that one of the most crucial debates in modern British politics concerns the reality of cabinet government. There are grave fears that this may be but a myth, with the real power of the executive lying elsewhere.

Evolution of the Cabinet

It is dangerous to assume that the history of the Cabinet can be traced as a continuous line linking a distant past indissolubly to the present. The modern Cabinet owes much to political forces generated by the industrial revolution and the rise of capitalism and is linked with the nineteenth-century reform of Parliament and the party system. It is certainly true, however, that monarchs have, throughout history, tended to surround themselves with small bands of loyal advisers and confidants, and these are important in understanding the nature of the modern executive and the balance of power within it.

The Privy Council By the sixteenth century the practice of monarchical consultation had become institutionalized in the form of a **Privy Council**, a body which had itself evolved from a council of royal advisers in Norman times (the *Curia Regis*). The following century saw the Civil War and the establishment of a republic with government by means of *executive committees*. The system proved unworkable, leading to the Restoration in 1660. However, Charles II sought ways to re-establish what he believed to be his divine right to rule without parliamentary impediment. He found the Privy Council difficult to control and resorted to a smaller group, a committee of the council, or 'cabinet', though it was so described as a form of denigration – a synonym for 'cabal', a secretive, devious, inner group.

The modern Cabinet remains constitutionally a committee of the Privy Council; members are formally appointed as Privy Councillors, retaining the title for life (and referred to in Commons' debate as 'right honourable', rather than simply 'honourable'). Consigned to the dignified part of the constitution, the full Council nowadays meets only rarely, to mark great state occasions such as the sovereign's marriage or death.

The Glorious Revolution In 1681 Charles II dissolved Parliament, establishing an 'Oxford Parliament' as an alternative. The ensuing struggle led to the 'Glorious Revolution' of 1688, resulting in the flight of James II (who had acceded in 1685), and his ultimate replacement by William (of Orange) and Mary in a more clearly constitutional (limited) monarchy (see chapter 9). Matters of state were transacted in the full Privy Council rather than in the 'Cabinet' and, to prevent influence of the House through royal patronage, ministers were excluded from Parliament.

However, this principle was soon abandoned because Parliament wanted ministers in its midst for questioning. Had it been retained, Britain would have developed a separation of powers and a significantly different constitution. As it was, membership of Parliament, rather than being forbidden, became an essential requirement of office. Hence the way was cleared for a *fusion* of powers, to be seen by the percipient nineteenth-century commentator Walter Bagehot as the key (or 'efficient secret') of the constitution.

The Act of Settlement Later anxiety about the succession, resulting from the death of Queen Anne's son, was allayed in the Act of Settlement (1701), establishing the Hanoverian succession. It has been said that between the years 1714 and 1760, George I and George II, as Germans, showed little interest in British politics, thereby allowing the Cabinet to play an increasingly dominant role. This may contain an element of truth, but there were also more fundamental forces at work. Ministers had in fact met in the absence of the monarch during the reign of Anne (1702–14). When in 1784 George III (1760–1820) attempted to reassert a degree of royal authority he was castigated as unconstitutional; the model of the modern Cabinet had emerged. The constitutional problems besetting the previous century appeared to be resolved. The monarch reigned as head of state but the real power lay with the Cabinet, which had effectively hijacked the powers of the Crown (the royal prerogative). It did not, however, possess all the essentials of the modern Cabinet.

- Its responsibility was to the Crown rather than to Parliament, so that it was possible to govern without a majority.
- The parliamentary groupings (Whigs and Tories) were only loose coalitions – it was possible for a Cabinet to contain representatives of both and enjoy cross-party support in the House.
- Cabinet members were responsible only for their own ministries and quite prepared to speak against each other's policies.
- The resignation of the First Lord of the Treasury (the Prime Minister) did not mean that other ministers also had to depart.
- A significant number of MPs owed allegiance to neither 'party' and could be courted through patronage and bribery.

The industrial revolution The rise of the industrial bourgeoisie in the nineteenth century challenged the *ancien régime*; the new men entered Parliament through the extended franchise and dominated it through party discipline. The effect was to make the Cabinet even more powerful.

- Cabinets became more tightly knit with members drawn from one party only.
- Members accepted collective responsibility for policy.

- So long as their MPs remained loyal, governments enjoyed a degree of supremacy unknown since the Tudors.

Here was the modern Cabinet. Today it is a relatively autonomous body drawing authority from various constitutional and political sources, including its lineage to the Privy Council, its inheritance of the prerogative powers of the Crown, and its domination of the constitutionally sovereign Parliament.

The doctrine of collective responsibility

> Now, is it to lower the price of corn, or isn't it? It is not much matter what we say, but mind, we must all say *the same*.
>
> Remark attributed to Lord Melbourne (1779–1848; Whig Prime Minister), quoted in Walter Bagehot, *The English Constitution* (1867: ch. 1)

The constitutional basis of cabinet government is sometimes said to lie in the doctrine of **collective responsibility**. This implies a form of collective decision-making. It is interpreted variously by participants and commentators, but is generally said to entail the following features.

- All members play a part in formulating policy.
- All members support each other in public (even if privately disagreeing).
- Any member unable to lend public support to the collective policy should resign.
- As a corollary, cabinet debate is regarded as confidential (though those who resign earn themselves the right to give their account of events).

The doctrine probably originated in the eighteenth century when ministers sought to strengthen their hand *vis-à-vis* the monarch by sticking together. We encounter frequent reference to the doctrine today, its prescriptive force lying in the idea that collective decision-making will produce the moderation and balance which the constitution is unable to guarantee. However, we shall see throughout this chapter that in day-to-day politics the convention is honoured more in the breach than the commission.

Collective responsibility or political expediency? An important reason for the doctrine's persistence is political expediency (which is why we even find talk of a similar doctrine among the Shadow Cabinet). A united front has proved a valuable asset to a political party. Moreover, although referring to *cabinet* responsibility, it is extended in practice to all members of the government, amounting to around one-third of the parliamentary party. (In 1983 Nicholas Budgen, a mere assistant whip, resigned over the provisions of the Northern Ireland Bill.) The doctrine is thus little more than a basis for party discipline.

"*Our minutes are going to make pretty boring reading in 30 years' time with no one ever dissenting.*"

Reproduced by permission of *Punch*

The Cabinet and the government

Today journalists often write as if the terms 'Cabinet' and 'government' are synonymous. In the eighteenth century this was largely the case, but today the Cabinet is numerically only a small part of a complex governmental structure comprising over a hundred politicians, who form a hierarchy ranging from cabinet ministers to junior parliamentary secretaries assisting ministers (figure 11.1).

Cabinet structure

Within the hierarchy senior members have relatively wide areas of responsibility, as indicated by titles such as Home Secretary, Chancellor of the Exchequer, Foreign Secretary, Secretary of State for this or that, while junior ministers' portfolios cover only part of the work of a department. In addition, a Cabinet contains *ministers without portfolio* assuming responsibilities for areas of public concern. Ministers are not expected to have any special expertise in the areas of their portfolios; indeed regular cabinet reshuffles positively discourage this. They are *generalists* rather than *specialists*.

Figure 11.1   The Cabinet stands at the centre of a web of government

In addition there are:

Ministers in Cabinet	Ministers not in Cabinet
• Lord President	• Minister for the Arts
• Lord Chancellor	• Paymaster General
• Chancellor of the Duchy of Lancaster	• Attorney General
• Minister Without Portfolio	• Solicitor General
	• Lord Advocate
	• Solicitor General (Scotland)
Plus a miscellany of junior positions	

> We still thought in terms of appointing a statutory woman. 'Who should she be?' asked Ted [Heath]. 'Margaret Thatcher,' was my immediate reply.
>
> James Prior (Conservative Cabinet member), *A Balance of Power* (1986)

Composition Cabinets have been drawn largely from the social elite, a large proportion having aristocratic backgrounds and only a very small number coming from the working class (figure 11.2). However, in both major parties there has been, throughout the twentieth century, a steady increase in the lower-middle-class, *petit bourgeois* element, reaching a high point in the Thatcher Cabinets of the late 1980s. In terms of educational background, ministers have been by no means typical of those they govern, a high proportion having attended public school (particularly Eton) and Oxbridge (Guttsman 1963). Like Parliament, the Cabinet is largely a male preserve, women (Thatcher excepted) having only a token presence.

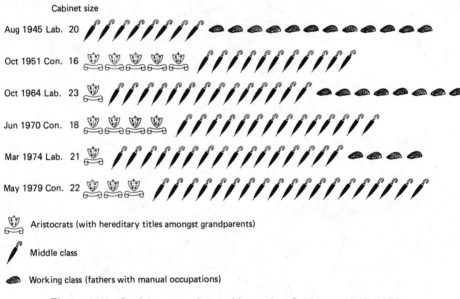

Cabinet size

Aug 1945 Lab. 20

Oct 1951 Con. 16

Oct 1964 Lab. 23

Jun 1970 Con. 18

Mar 1974 Lab. 21

May 1979 Con. 22

Aristocrats (with hereditary titles amongst grandparents)

Middle class

Working class (fathers with manual occupations)

Figure 11.2 Social composition of incoming Cabinets, 1945–1979

Source: Data from Butler and Butler (1986: 83)

Size The size of the Cabinet is not merely a technical matter, it has important implications for its constitutional role. Eighteenth-century Cabinets contained around 5–9 members, which grew to 12–15 in the following century and by Asquith's time had reached 23, whereupon the figure remained fairly constant (see figure 11.3). Although this might not seem very large for the task, it is so by international standards. The mighty US president, for example, surrounds himself with only around ten colleagues. Generally critics believe Cabinets to be too large for effective

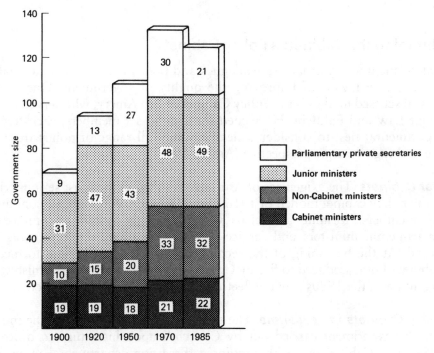

Figure 11.3   Size and structure of peacetime governments

Source: Adapted from Butler and Butler (1986: 82)

collective government, but there are various pressures tending to increase size which are hard to resist.

- *Growth in the public sector.* Since the nineteenth century, government has taken on many more areas of responsibility. After four years in office Wilson defended his Cabinet of 23 on the grounds that it was 'inconceivable that important sectors of our national life should be excluded' (Walker 1972: 35).
- *Bureaucratic pressure.* Representation in Cabinet remains politically important to departmental civil servants as they compete with each other for resources.
- *Interest group pressure.* Outside Westminster, groups see in cabinet composition indications of a government's intentions towards them. Doctors, farmers, teachers, trade unionists, and so on, will look for visible confirmation that they are regarded as important.

The British Cabinet has been criticized as fat and flabby, with a number of defects. It can be slow and cumbersome in decision-making; vulnerable to factionalism (Thatcher Cabinets being characterized in terms of 'wets' and 'drys'); liable to leak – 'The more you have,' said Harold Wilson, 'the more people can be got at' (Hennessy 1986: 149); unable to maintain collective responsibility; and lacking a strategic perspective, with ministers developing departmental tunnel vision.

Slimming the Cabinet: a Policy Cabinet

Critics, including journalists, academics and politicians, advocate a smaller Cabinet as a means of improving the quality of government. One of the most-discussed models is the **Policy Cabinet** of Leo Amery, who served under Bonar Law and Baldwin. He argued for around six members, each free of departmental ties, to consider collectively the full range of policy from an overarching, strategic perspective (Amery 1947).

War Cabinets The exigencies of war have resulted in the most serious trials of the policy cabinet model. In 1916 Lloyd George's **War Cabinet** contained five members, forming a nucleus within a larger system encompassing departmental ministers and service chiefs, who attended meetings as required. At the beginning of the second world war Chamberlain formed a Cabinet of nine, reduced to five by Churchill in 1940. Even the skirmish with Argentina in the 1980s saw the fleeting emergence of a War Cabinet.

Policy Cabinets in peacetime The nearest peacetime version of the model was the experiment carried out by Churchill upon his return to office in 1951. In a Cabinet of 16 he appointed three non-departmental ministers, described as 'Overlords'. This is generally regarded as a failure, with a return to 'normal methods' after only two years (Daalder 1964: 110–18).

The inner cabinet While outward forms remain the same, the Cabinet is subject to informal evolutionary processes beneath the surface. One such has been the rise of the **inner cabinet**, very much a political creation, even more unknown to the formal constitution than the Cabinet itself. The term is applied to a group of about five ministers closest to the Prime Minister, meeting independently. This can be seen as a threat to genuine cabinet government, carrying connotations of devious secrecy not unlike those evoked in the eighteenth century by the term 'cabal'. Yet in the inner cabinet the British system of government may be said to have evolved a Policy Cabinet informally.

However, the principle of the Policy Cabinet rests on a rather questionable proposition – that strategic policy-making can be separated from day-to-day matters. Douglas Wass, ex-joint head of the civil service, stated in his Reith Lectures: 'In my experience of administration I have found it almost impossible to think constructively about general policy issues if I have not been involved in particular practical cases' (1984: 29).

Cabinet committees

It is impossible to give an account of the working of cabinet government in Britain today without reference to the dense committee network in which it is enmeshed (figure 11.4). The growth of **cabinet committees** is one of the most significant constitutional developments of the century, yet it long remained cloaked in secrecy, with accounts pieced together from memoirs, leaks, the press, and occasional parliamentary statements. In 1972 Patrick Gordon Walker gave some clear indications in his book *The Cabinet*, Mrs Thatcher acknowledged them in the House in 1983, and the following year *The Times* published a detailed list, including names of chairpersons. In principle, committees are created to assist the Cabinet, which remains the 'parent' body. There are two broad categories: *ad hoc* and standing.

Keeping the people informed

He agreed that no Prime Minister has ever explained why the numbers and membership of Cabinet Committees were kept secret. Why were they? I asked.

There was a long pause. 'Erm,' said the former Secretary to the Cabinet. 'Well. Erm. Are we on the record or off the record?'

'On the record.'

'Then I think I'd rather not go into that.'

Lord Hunt (ex-Cabinet Secretary), interviewed by Michael Davie,
in the *Observer* (11 Oct. 1987)

Ad hoc *committees* These consider specific problems and thus have only ephemeral lives. The first was created in 1855 to handle the Crimean War, to be followed by others concerned with aspects of foreign policy. Towards the end of the nineteenth century, with a massive tide of legislation, others emerged to formulate policy and draft bills, and there are numerous recent examples. In 1984 an *ad hoc* committee addressed the abolition of the Greater London Council and the metropolitan counties, while Mrs Thatcher controlled strategy towards the 1985–6 miners' strike in this way.

Standing committees These date from a later period, the first being the highly successful Committee of Imperial Defence (CID) in 1903, which marked a watershed in cabinet government. The standing committees are concerned with particular areas of policy (education, defence, the economy, social services, and so on – see figure 11.4) and have continuing existence. To add to the confusion they are known mysteriously by code names, initials and acronyms (E for Economic and MISC for Miscellaneous).

Composition and functions The committees characteristically include a core of cabinet ministers with a central interest, some junior ministers, and civil servants attending as the secretariat or in their own right.

Official committees Paralleling the cabinet committees there is a system of official committees which meet in advance in order to prepare the ground. There is a danger here that decisions may really be made before the

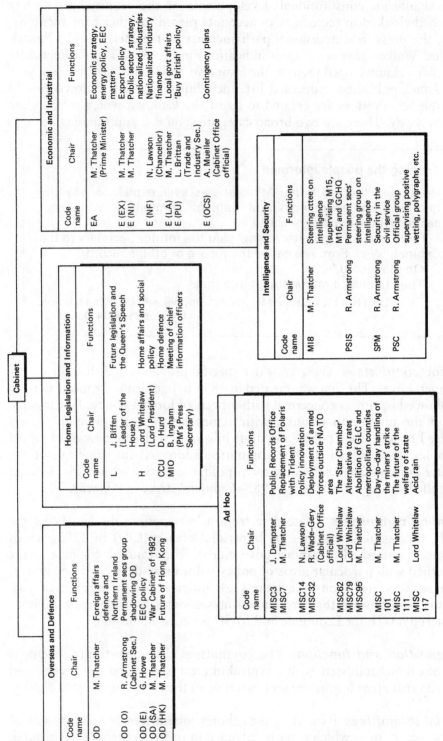

Figure 11.4 Some major cabinet committees of the 1980s

Source: Adapted from *The Times* (30 April 1984) and Hennessy (1986: 27-30)

politicians actually meet, with ministers being given briefs which foreclose their options.

> As I sat there first at the EDC (Economic Development Committee) and then at home affairs, I reflected on the way that cabinet committees as well as the cabinet itself are becoming part of the dignified element of the English constitution.
>
> Richard Crossman (Labour minister), *Diaries of a Cabinet Minister*
> (19 July 1965)

Government by committee? Although it is widely accepted that committees play an essential role in modern government, there is an underlying fear that they undermine cabinet government. As committees they should be subservient to the parent body, yet some have exceedingly high status, often being chaired by the Prime Minister or another senior minister and taking decisions with little reference to the Cabinet. Mrs Thatcher herself chaired standing committees on the economy, export policy, public sector strategy and oversight of the nationalized industries, and foreign affairs and defence. She also chaired *ad hoc* committees on the replacement of the Polaris defence system and on the future of the Falklands. This threat to cabinet government has long been present. The planning of the great 1944 Education Act was entirely the product of a committee led by R. A. Butler. In 1967 Wilson formally enhanced the status of cabinet committees by decreeing that matters should only be reconsidered by the Cabinet with the agreement of the committee chairmen.

> Most of my work when I was Minister of Education was done outside the Cabinet, and hardly referred to the Cabinet at all.
> Lord Butler, interviewed by Norman Hunt (later Lord Crowther-Hunt) in
> the *Listener* (16 Sept. 1965)

The Cabinet Secretariat

The Cabinet cannot be studied only in terms of politicians. Civil servants exert a dominant presence at the very heart of the executive in the form of the highly powerful **Cabinet Secretariat**. This is part of the Cabinet Office, a department of some 600 organized into a number of sections including the Central Statistical Office, which collects and analyses information for government, and an Historical Section compiling official histories. With the exception of its head, the **Cabinet Secretary**, the hundred or so civil servants comprising the secretariat are employed on the basis of secondment from other departments and there is much competition for these prestigious positions within the super-elite of the service.

Its ostensible functions are similar to those of any other committee secretariat: circulating information to the Cabinet and its committees, preparing and distributing papers and agendas for meetings, advising on procedure, and taking minutes. However, these functions give the secretariat far greater political significance than a formal description of its role would allow (see figure 11.5).

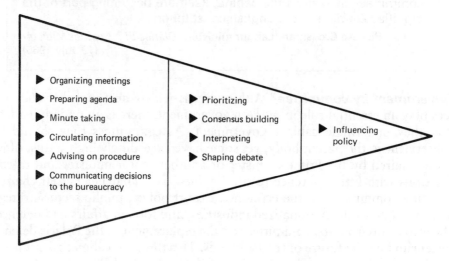

Figure 11.5   Administrative functions have political implications

Evolution At the beginning of the century it was traditional for the Cabinet to work informally, with no agendas, no minutes, and no officials present. The only records were ministers' notes and personal letters sent by the Prime Minister to the king, giving an account of discussions and conclusions. Sometimes ministers were unclear about the discussions and their civil servants would be obliged to consult each other to deduce what had been decided. This seeming madness had method: meetings were regarded as highly secret and the involvement of outsiders a violation of the constitution. However, the exigencies of the first world war were to undermine many constitutional niceties, including those surrounding the Cabinet. When Lloyd George took over he commandeered the much admired secretariat of the CID, including its head, Maurice Hankey, to service the War Cabinet; it was housed in huts in the garden of 10 Downing Street and known as the 'garden suburb'.

After the war the constitutionality of the innovation was reappraised; traditionalists wished to restore the old practices and opponents saw the secretariat tainted with Lloyd George's overbearing style. The Treasury saw it as rivalling its own position as the supreme coordinating instrument in Whitehall. However, the 1918 Haldane Report on the machinery of government recommended its retention.

Hankey was the main architect of the modern Cabinet Secretariat in both war and peace, and deserves an honoured place in bureaucratic history. He demonstrated the inestimable value of the new machinery, remaining at its head to serve five very different Prime Ministers (Lloyd George, Bonar Law, Baldwin, Ramsay MacDonald and Chamberlain) in a variety of circumstances including war, reconstruction, coalition, and both Labour and Conservative administrations. Today the Cabinet Secretary is frequently described as the most powerful civil servant in the country. Since 1983 he has been formally designated Head of the Civil Service.

The minutes how they run The nature of the cabinet minutes is a significant factor in understanding the importance of the secretariat. Initially Hankey kept near-verbatim accounts, attributing opinions and attitudes to individuals. However, this was criticized as unconstitutional and became modified to include only a general view of the debate, making it possible to use the minutes (or 'conclusions') as the directions for civil service action.

Now that the Cabinet's gone to its dinner,
The Secretary stays and gets thinner and thinner,
Racking his brains to record and report,
What he thinks what they think they ought to have thought.

Anon., quoted in S. S. Wilson, *The Cabinet Office to 1945* (1975)

This practice places the secretariat in a pivotal position, with disturbing possibilities. In a break during a meeting Richard Crossman examined the notes of Cabinet Secretary Sir Burke Trend and was shocked to see that the report of the Prime Minister's position was 'not the substance of what he had said, and if it had been the substance he would have divided the Cabinet' (Crossman 1975: 103–4). Michael Heseltine complained that the Prime Minister prevented discussion on certain matters and 'insisted that the Cabinet Secretary should record my protest in the Cabinet minutes', yet when circulated 'no record of my protest' was to be found (Heseltine 1986: 2).

The Shadow Cabinet

Even less known to the constitution than the Cabinet is the **Shadow Cabinet**, the front bench of the parliamentary opposition. Although featuring prominently in political debate, it is usually ignored in studies of cabinet government. The Shadow Cabinet constitutes a ready-made governmental cast waiting in the wings of the political stage; members are shadow ministers with shadow portfolios and the leader is the shadow Prime Minister. Today the practice goes even further to include a whole 'shadow government' ranged on the opposition benches. It is a particular feature of a two-party system, where the alternative government can be clearly known before the general election.

Evolution In the eighteenth century there was evidence of out-of-office parliamentary factions organized into groups and cabals to oppose those in office (Turner 1969). If a government seemed likely to fall, members would begin to circulate lists of possible ministerial teams – foetal governments lying curled in the womb. The relatively frequent fall of governments meant that there were always ex-ministers in Parliament able to provide well-informed criticism; thus the 'ex-Cabinet' is the natural forebear of the Shadow Cabinet. If a general election was to mean that a government would be removed *en bloc*, it followed that a new one must be ready to emerge overnight (Punnett 1975: 144).

The Shadow Cabinet today Of course the difference between the shadow and the substance is that the former has no executive responsibility. However, in many respects members conduct themselves in the same manner, holding meetings to discuss strategy and policy, appointing specialist committees, and practising collective responsibility and secrecy (which can be breached with leaks); there are even shadow inner cabinets.

Shadow Cabinets are valuable to democracy as a source of coherent critical comment on policies, and generally stimulate and elevate public debate. Americans do not see an alternative President until the election period, and do not see the Cabinet until after the result. With a Shadow Cabinet the alternative government is clearly displayed on the shelves of the Westminster supermarket in cellophane wrapping. The role of the Shadow Cabinet is officially recognized in the fact that the Leader of the Opposition and the chief whips receive state salaries (see table 11.1). Yet the value of the Shadow Cabinet is vitiated by the lack of information available to it; ex-mandarin Sir Douglas Wass (1984) has argued that it should be served by a special civil service department.

Table 11.1   Salaries of the Prime Minister and Leader of the Opposition

	Prime Minister	Leader of the Opposition
1937	£10,000	£2,000
1965	£14,000	£4,500
1985	£42,950	£28,601

Source: Data from Butler and Butler (1986: 67)

The Central Policy Review Staff 1970–1983: RIP

An interesting attempt to revitalize cabinet government was made in 1970 by Prime Minister Edward Heath in the establishment of a Central Policy Review Staff (CPRS). It was baptized with this stuffy title by Cabinet Secretary Burke Trend who, notwithstanding his own name, found 'Think-Tank', the US-style term preferred by Heath, rather too slick for the British civil service. However, the media preferred Heath's choice, giving it the wider currency dreaded by the mandarin. The CPRS was to be a small unit in the Cabinet Office, its role to:

- provide ministers with wide-ranging information to prevent departmental 'tunnel vision';
- offer additional advice on policy alternatives;
- promote interdepartmental cooperation;
- help to determine relative priorities within the government programme;
- provide continuing performance review in the light of overall strategy.

Heath briefed the infant CPRS on the lawn of 10 Downing Street, recalling how he had seen 'Cabinets which all the time seemed to be dealing with the day-to-day problems' with 'never a real opportunity to deal with strategy' (Heath 1972: 5).

The first CPRS head was Lord Rothschild, an academic and scientist personally chosen by Heath. Once appointed he played a major part in recruiting others, many of whom had personal connections in the Conservative establishment. The multidisciplinary composition drew representatives from the grove of Academe, industry and the civil service, and the impression was of a smart set of young intellectuals from society's privileged enclaves. Rothschild, 62 when appointed, described them with affectionate tolerance as 'a bunch of 15 anarchists' (Fox 1975: 285).

The career of the CPRS However, after the honeymoon years, the career of the CPRS took an erratic rake's progress, its function varying according to the government in office. When Wilson succeeded Heath in 1974 he did not, as some had predicted, abolish it, but purged its overtly political element and directed its attention away from immediate policy towards the longer term.

Mrs Thatcher, remembering with distaste the U-turns of Heath and his association with CPRS (Fry 1986: 98), was to prove the *pons asinorum* of the think-tank. Its role in financial matters was restricted: it was removed from PESC (see p. 392) and directed to consider the political implications of expenditure cuts. So enthusiastic was its response to its new-found role that reports alarmed even hardened monetarists, and judicious leaking led to considerable embarrassment. A report on the future of the NHS under private insurance forced the Prime Minister to her fervent conference declaration in 1982 that the service was 'safe with us'. She did not promise the same to the think-tank, however, and after her re-election the axe fell. Its demise was little mourned in Whitehall; it had been resented by bureaucrats, seen as essentially lightweight, and often ignored by ministers. Yet Wass (1984) regards something like the CPRS as essential if cabinet government is to be preserved.

Cabinet government: dead or sleeping?

The idea that Britain is governed by a tightly knit team is grossly simplistic.

The Cabinet today is but one body in a labyrinthine network of cabinet committees, department and interdepartmental committees, ministerial advisers, pressure groups, inner cabinets, the Cabinet Office, and a corps of mighty bureaucratic mandarins. In addition, members are fully occupied with departmental duties, with little time to devote to collective decision-making by discussion and reasoning across a broad front in the manner implied by the term 'cabinet government'. At the epicentre of all lies the ill-defined inner cabinet, presided over by the Prime Minister.

We have not yet fully covered the question of Britain's cabinet government. To do this we must delve deeper into the machine and address the key debate over the position of the Prime Minister.

The Prime Minister: Popular Monarchy

Who is the Prime Minister?

A key point to remember is that no one elects the Prime Minister as such; he or she is normally the leader of the party controlling the House of Commons. However, such control has been present less than is usually realized. Although Britain has had only three fully fledged coalition governments in the twentieth century, all in times of national emergency, governments with a single-party majority had, by 1988, held office for a total of only 44 years (see Butler 1978: 112–13). Under a coalition or party pact the Prime Minister is most likely to be the leader of the largest party, although the minority partners might enjoy power to influence the choice. Thus in 1987

Table 11.2   Age and experience of Prime Ministers since 1895

Name (and party)	Date of first coming to office	Age	Years in Commons before becoming PM
Salisbury (Conservative)	1895	55	15 (+19 in Lords)
Balfour (Conservative)	1902	53	28
Campbell-Bannerman (Liberal)	1905	69	37
Asquith (Liberal)	1908	55	22
Lloyd George (Coalition)	1916	53	26
Bonar Law (Conservative)	1922	63	22
Baldwin (Conservative)	1923	56	15
MacDonald (Labour)	1924	58	14
Chamberlain (Conservative)	1937	68	19
Churchill (Coalition)	1940	65	38
Attlee (Labour)	1945	62	23
Eden (Conservative)	1955	57	32
Macmillan (Conservative)	1957	62	29
Home (Conservative)	1963	60	15 (+13 in Lords)
Wilson (Labour)	1964	48	19
Heath (Conservative)	1970	53	20
Callaghan (Labour)	1976	64	31
Thatcher (Conservative)	1979	54	20
Major (Conservative)	1990	47	11

David Steel, of the Alliance, made it clear that serving in a Thatcher-led coalition would be 'inconceivable'.

The circumstances of political life mean that Prime Ministers will usually be of mature years, with substantial political experience (see table 11.2). In 1964, however, Labour's 13 years in the wilderness meant that Wilson had only been Secretary for Overseas Trade and President of the Board of Trade and Mrs Thatcher's experience was similarly slight, having served for only four years as Secretary of State of Education and Science. Lack of experience can be compensated for by youth: Mrs Thatcher took the reins at the relatively young age of 54, although at 48 and 47 respectively Wilson and Major were veritable infant prodigies, well below the average of 60. On the other hand, when Callaghan took over in 1976, at 64, he had reached the age where most people stop working and turn their attention to growing vegetables.

Evolution of the office

It was the Hanoverian succession which, through lack of kingly interest in things British, allowed Sir Robert Walpole (1676–1745), the First Lord of the Treasury, to fill the power vacuum in the Cabinet left by the monarch. He is usually credited with having been the first Prime Minister. However, the term was used as a form of abuse, to deplore his dominance over his colleagues. This had resulted as much from the power of personality as from his position and, after his fall in 1742, immediate successors were denied the same authority. However, by 1803, the time of William Pitt the Younger, the position of Prime Minister could be said to have been firmly established as a constitutional convention.

Yet to accept that one person would be the leader of the Cabinet was not to say that he or she should be supreme. The purpose of the struggles of the seventeenth and eighteenth centuries had been to end monarchy, not replace one king with another. Early Prime Ministers were regarded as *primus inter pares* (first among equals), with a responsibility to lead the Cabinet and represent it to the monarch, but not to dominate. Hence, when Bagehot highlighted the significance of the Cabinet within the constitution in the nineteenth century, he did not stress the role of the Prime Minister. However, subsequent developments saw a shift in the balance of power, so that in 1963 Richard Crossman argued in the introduction to a reprint of Bagehot's great work that

> the post-war epoch has seen the final transformation of Cabinet Government into Prime Ministerial Government.
>
> (Crossman 1963: 51)

The Prime Minister as President

The question of whether the Prime Minister has presidential powers lies at the heart of political debate today. It is helpful to address the issue by considering the nature of **presidential government**. In the real world systems take many forms. Some Presidents share power with a Prime Minister, as in France; others, as in West Germany, are mainly symbolic figures, rather like the British monarch. However, exponents of the 'presidential prime-ministerial' thesis think in terms of a powerful model such as that found in the US, where incumbents stand in a particular relationship with the other political structures.

- *The people*. Presidents are directly elected by the people, granting a populist legitimacy greater than that of any other institution. Moreover, they remain in direct contact through the media, regularly addressing the nation over the heads of other institutions.
- *The Cabinet*. The Cabinet is not elected but is personally chosen by the President on the basis of loyalty and commitment.
- *The legislature*. Presidents are not members of the legislature and their position is independent of it.
- *The party*. Presidents are not the leaders of their parties. If they were to disagree with them they would not lose office.
- *The bureaucracy*. The upper echelons of the bureaucracy are appointed by the President, again on the basis of commitment.
- *A personal department*. Presidents are served by a formidable White House staff, providing powerful intellectual and political support.

Yet despite their personal ascendancy, Presidents face certain *restrictions*. The separation of powers allows the judiciary to examine the constitutionality of executive actions, and the legislature can block presidential legislation and veto certain appointments.

The position of Prime Ministers appears to be quite unlike that of the President: there is no direct election by the people, the choice of Cabinet is restricted, they are not independent of the legislature, they are dependent upon their parties, the bureaucracy cannot be politically appointed, and there is nothing rivalling the White House staff to give personal support. However, our examination cannot end with the formal constitutional position; on the contrary, this is where it begins. We shall analyse this key question in terms of these points.

The Prime Minister and the people: the populist appeal

The direct line to the people characteristic of a US-style presidency is achieved through election and continuing personal contact through the media. More than any other institution of state, the President is the embodiment of the popular will. Formally British prime ministers do not have this direct relationship (see figure 11.6), being elected only as ordinary MPs. However, various forms of political practice provide an increasingly populist link.

General elections   It can be argued that a general election is little more than

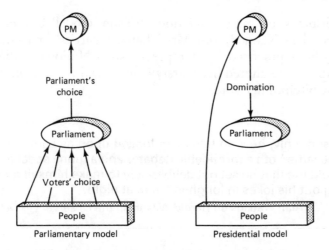

Figure 11.6   Choosing the Prime Minister

a presidential contest, people voting mainly on the basis of their feelings towards the party leaders. The style of modern British election campaigns contributes mightily to the presidential trend. Before the 1987 election Mrs Thatcher proclaimed: 'I can handle a big majority'.

The media Throughout the world, the media have transformed politics, making demagogy infinitely more feasible than ever before; at the touch of a button Presidents can address nations. The Prime Minister's press department monitors the flow of information to the people, feeding journalists with a 'carefully filtered version of what transpired' after each Cabinet meeting (Hennessy 1986: 5).

Public opinion polls Opinion polling arises from the application of market research techniques to politics; its general tendency to centre on questions of personal standing singles out leaders from party colleagues. Although the polls can confer authority, they can also be treacherous: it was her poor showing which led to the unprecedented and fatal challenge to Margaret Thatcher in November 1990.

Image-making Further presidentialization comes from the concern shown for the public image, or charisma, of leaders; as an ex-film star Reagan represented the apotheosis of this trend. A measure of this is shown at annual party conferences, where the leaders are unashamedly lionized, with stage-

> The acting abilities of Mr Wilson and Mr Macmillan were such that either could have earned a substantial living and devoted following on the stage of the theatre.
>
> Bernard Levin, *The Pendulum Years* (1976)

managed displays of mass adulation. Wilson modelled himself on the youthful President Kennedy but Mrs Thatcher carried image-making well beyond anything practised by her predecessors: following the advice of publicity experts she altered her hairstyle, her facial expression, her clothes, and even the pitch of her voice.

Quite suddenly, he who had been looked upon as something of a bore became both a formidable debator and a funny speaker . . . He once told me that he set out deliberately to make himself amusing, writing out his jokes in longhand, late at night.

Alan Watkins on Harold Wilson, in the *Observer* (19 Oct. 1986)

Political culture Finally, it can be said that, in all probability, the electorate at large actually likes to view politics in terms of a titanic struggle between leaders, for in the deferential British political culture there is a preference for strong, individualistic leadership. History is replete with examples of great individuals – from kings and generals to explorers and social reformers, yet despite the dutiful and worthy service of many eminent men and women, there are no 'great' committees or working parties to stir the imagination like Cromwell and Gladstone. Even the Knights of the Round Table and the Merry Men of Sherwood Forest had leaders who were by no means *primus inter pares*.

The Prime Minister and Cabinet

This relationship lies at the heart of the debate and contains a number of facets. Unlike presidential appointees, cabinet members are career politicians who will usually confess, like Macbeth, to vaulting ambition. Within the Cabinet sits the heir apparent and plots against the Prime Minister are regular features of political *reportage*.

Creating the Cabinet In forming a Cabinet a President makes wide-ranging choices from social, commercial, industrial and academic walks of life, ensuring that the team consists of trusted allies. Though a Prime Minister chooses a Cabinet, this is done within a limited framework of constitutional, administrative and political constraints. Within the Prime Minister's party there will be a core of senior members with strong followings who cannot be

---

Prime Minister, you will not bother yourself about the New Hebrides.

Reported reply from Foreign Secretary Lord Carrington when asked for details by Mrs Thatcher, quoted in the *Guardian* (1 March 1989)

---

omitted, moderate Labour leaders invariably being obliged to endure some unwelcome company from the far left. However, these constraints are not really inhibiting. Although there are some (the old, disenchanted or highly privileged) who scorn the Prime Minister's patronage (Lord Carrington, for example, Mrs Thatcher's wealthy Foreign Secretary, could afford an outspoken line), all ambitious MPs must tread warily.

The restriction of choice to Parliament affords Prime Ministers ample opportunity to get to know colleagues before appointing them. Any ideas that they are afraid to sack popular figures was exploded by Mrs Thatcher: by the late 1980s the Conservative backbenches rattled with the dry bones of political has-beens. Unlike Macmillan, Thatcher used more insidious 'salami tactics', slicing away colleagues one or two at a time, thereby avoiding the mass slaughter which weakened Macmillan.

Cabinet meetings Although colleagues are often statesmen of stature, demanding that their views be duly weighed, the conduct of the meetings (and committee meetings) remains securely under the prime ministerial thumb through the *chair*. This bestows control of the *agenda*, the power to decide what colleagues shall talk about. Wilson was able to prevent debate on devaluation, and Mrs Thatcher avoided consideration of economic strategy and the decision to purchase the Trident missile system from the US. Furthermore, as chairperson the Prime Minister decides who shall speak, when, and at what length, so potentially dissident voices can be limited or studiously ignored. Even seating can be manipulated to advantage: Heath placed the *ingenue* Margaret Thatcher at an inconvenient position around the table, from which she found it difficult to make interjections, and Lord Home tells how Macmillan took measures to avoid having the 'steely and accusing eye' of Enoch Powell facing him across the table (1976: 192). Finally, Prime Ministers can define precisely what was concluded at meetings through their prerogative to sum up and shape the content of the all-important cabinet minutes.

The inner cabinet The right to create inner cabinets enables Prime Ministers to encircle themselves with cronies. Thus the large number of 'wets' in the first Thatcher Cabinet was soon countered by an inner cabinet containing economic mentor Sir Keith Joseph, as well as Norman Tebbit and Sir John Nott.

Cabinet committees Cabinet committees could weaken a Prime Minister's position by enlarging the number involved in policy-making and increasing their supply of information. Yet in reality the Prime Minister orchestrates the system – appointing members, designating chairs, and chairing those critical to major initiatives. In 1979 Mrs Thatcher took control of the 'E' committees on the economy, which she packed with sympathizers. The main Thatcher strategy was to reduce the power of the *standing committees* by creating more *ad hoc* ones which she could dominate (Henke 1989).

Collective responsibility Presidents are not troubled by this doctrine, but it is fundamental to cabinet government, giving constitutional endorsement of a team approach. Where ministers feel they are inadequately consulted they have constitutional grounds for complaint. Yet today the doctrine decrees little more than that all support the Prime Minister's official line or resign.

> If the basis of trust between Prime Minister and her Defence Secretary no longer exists, there is no place for me with honour in such a Cabinet.
>
> Michael Heseltine, after his resignation over the Westland affair, quoted in *The Times* (10 Jan. 1986)

However, Margaret Thatcher was to discover the limits to this advantage. By 1990 the backbenches creaked with the weight of ex-cabinet members, many of whom muttered darkly of muzzled debate. Most dramatic was the departure of Sir Geoffrey Howe, whose resignation speech was to set in train the momentous process which led to her dramatic fall in November 1990. He lamented the futility of

> trying to stretch the meaning of words beyond what was credible, of trying to pretend there was a common policy ... That conflict of loyalty has become all too great.
>
> (*Independent*, 14 Nov. 1990)

The Prime Minister and Parliament

Is Parliament able to limit the power of the Prime Minister in the way that Congress limits that of the US President? Control of the executive is one of its most important constitutional roles, yet unlike Presidents, Prime Ministers have a number of effective means of dominating. They are members of that assembly and lead the majority party.

The timetable The parliamentary timetable is extremely congested and the organization of time for debate and legislation is of vital importance. This is the responsibility of the Leader of the House, who has a duty to fellow members to provide adequate opportunity for debate. Yet the Leader is actually appointed by the Prime Minister (until 1915 the Prime Minister *was* the Leader) and the two work hand in glove.

Debates Prime Ministers can be adroit parliamentary performers and the House provides an ample stage for the exhibition of their skills. Yet this unrivalled opportunity can provide rope for a noose; only the fit survive. Sir

Alec Douglas-Home was not one of these, his lacklustre performances leading to his downfall. Yet the odds remain heavily stacked in the Prime Minister's favour, with extensive civil service back-up for information. Both Wilson and Thatcher established great ascendancy over the House through the opportunities offered.

The power of dissolution Another threat is to dissolve Parliament, to act like Samson at Gaza and bring down the temple, putting all out of a job. There is reason to doubt the reality of this; an election precipitated by such a crisis would suggest unfitness to rule. However, it would be exceedingly unwelcome to most MPs and the fact that the threat is rarely made does not make it unusable. Indeed, it was made by Wilson after a near mutiny by George Brown and others over the supply of British arms to South Africa.

Timing the general election Presidents serve fixed terms of office, an important feature of democracy. However, the right to dissolve Parliament means that Prime Ministers can, in effect, fix the date of the general election. Of course mistakes may be made. Heath's decision to go for February 1974, in the midst of his battle with the miners, was seen as weakness, and he ruefully acknowledged to a group of ministers: 'I let you down by having an election at all' (Fay and Young 1976: 24). Yet Mrs Thatcher, whose popularity had plummeted to an all-time low, was able to set the 1983 general election a year earlier than was necessary in order to capitalize on the 'Falklands factor'.

The Prime Minister and the party

Having been elected by the people, a President's security of tenure is, politically speaking, absolute. Only upon some gross misdemeanour (such as Watergate) will the process of impeachment roll into action. By contrast, Prime Ministers sit precariously on top of the wall of party leadership. They occupy their positions only as long as the party is prepared to accept them. Yet for long the final act of the Humpty Dumpty scenario had seemed inconceivable owing to party loyalty and political expediency. Leaders were removed only when in opposition. However, the inconceivable happened when Margaret Thatcher was forced to resign by the party establishment in November 1990. Conservative Prime Ministers might ruefully note that this curb would be far less threatening to a Labour Prime Minister owing to the wider spread of the leadership electoral college (see p. 238).

Although a serious curb, it is a political rather than a constitutional instrument. Margaret Thatcher was dethroned because her party regarded her as an electoral liability, not because of her dominance, which, during an 11-year reign, had become legendary and was actually much admired by many within the party.

The Prime Minister and the bureaucracy

When American Presidents take office they sweep like new brooms through-out every nook and cranny of the White House. While their wives have traditionally changed furniture and wallpaper, they have changed the people, some three or four thousand of them. This is the **spoils system**, giving awesome power to reward, bribe and command. In contrast, when Prime Ministers take office they are faced with a granite mountain face of public bureaucracy, constitutionally as permanent and immovable as the Sphinx. Or are they? The idea that the public service is beyond the reach of political manoeuvring is but one more myth of British public life.

Choosing the people: the power of patronage Though not as dramatic and sudden as the presidential shake-out, Prime Ministers are able to control key positions and distribute considerable prestige and power. These powers were originally inherited from the monarch, and since Walpole's day Prime Ministers have used them to enhance their standing (see figure 11.7). Positions within the Prime Minister's gift include:

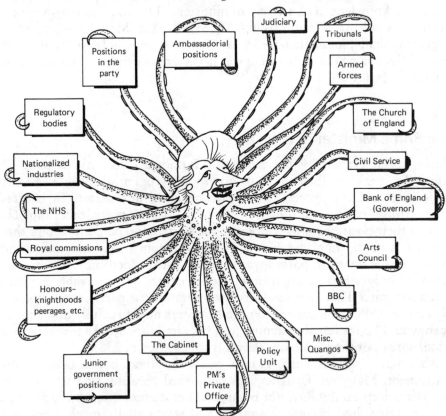

Figure 11.7   In an age of patronage to make Walpole blush, the tentacles of prime ministerial patronage reach deeply into the state machinery

- honours (peerages and knighthoods);
- state offices (armed forces, church and judiciary);
- government posts (from senior ministers to parliamentary private secretaries);
- key ministerial advisory posts;
- top jobs outside Whitehall (in water authorities, the NHS, nationalized industries, tribunals, royal commissions and committees of enquiry, the BBC, a diversity of quangos, and so on);
- party offices;
- top positions in the civil service and Bank of England (under the Thatcher regime).

Moreover, unlike a President, the Prime Minister is not accountable to any institution for these appointments, thus gaining untrammelled leverage.

> It was a political decision, a response to what was felt to be the wish of 'No. 10', and broke 30-odd years of useful precedent.
>
> Richard Hoggart on his 'manipulated departure' from the Arts Council (vice chair), in the *Observer* (29 Dec. 1985)

Shaping the machine In addition to the ability to make important state appointments, the Prime Minister shapes the very structure of government, thereby determining what it is capable, or not capable, of doing. Wilson, for example, created a Department of Economic Affairs (DEA) and the Civil Service Department (CSD) to usurp Treasury power. Departments have been amalgamated and split up, the administrative skyline being transformed overnight by demolition with high explosives: the CSD and CPRS both perished under Mrs Thatcher. In the early 1980s the government's battle with left-wing local authorities was resolved by wiping a whole tier of local government off the map (see p. 488).

A prime-ministerial department?

Unlike the US President, with a large White House staff, and a number of polities based on the British model (including Canada, Australia and New Zealand), Prime Ministers do not have departments of their own. They appear to stand alone against a Cabinet of ministers armed with information and advice provided by their bureaucratic forces. However, this is a misleading picture; today's Prime Ministers are by no means unsupported, having the backing of various agencies.

The Cabinet Secretariat A particularly close relationship can be built between the Prime Minister and the Cabinet Secretary. Although Sir (now Lord) Burke Trend, who served from 1963 to 1973, stated that he was 'not the Prime Minister's exclusive servant' (Hennessy 1985), the relationship has been likened to that between a minister and permanent secretary (Walker

1972: 54). From the beginning Lloyd George relied heavily on Maurice Hankey and Wilson worked closely with Trend, who accompanied him, for example, to Washington, to play Kissinger to Wilson's Nixon in the Oval Office (Wilson 1974: 947).

Mrs Thatcher established an exceptionally close working relationship with Sir Robert Armstrong, whom she referred to as 'my oracle' (Hennessy 1986). Indeed critics thought that the loyalty displayed here went beyond that appropriate to a neutral public servant. In its report, the select committee conducting the Westland enquiry argued that the Cabinet Secretary should not be the close confidant of Mrs Thatcher and head of the civil service at the same time.

Personal offices In addition, Prime Ministers have developed personal offices containing staffs of around a hundred. In the mid-1980s the Thatcher personal office comprised four sections.

- *Private Office.* Housekeeping functions in managing day-to-day affairs.
- *Press Office.* Managing the media presentation. This became a central point of politics under Bernard Ingham, Thatcher's press secretary, with some stormy controversies.
- *Political Office.* Responsibility for party and constituency matters.
- *Policy Unit.* Introduced by Wilson in 1974, and the most politically significant, since it is concerned with policy-making. Mrs Thatcher may be said to have needed such a unit more than her predecessors. She brought in a succession of eminent specialists, such as Sir Anthony Parsons, ex-British Ambassador to the UN. The composition changed continuously and the leaders, including Sir John Hoskyns, Ferdinand Mount, John Redwood and Brian Griffiths, became well-known public figures. So crucial to Mrs Thatcher was economic adviser Sir Alan Walters, that she refused to sack him when Nigel Lawson, Chancellor of the Exchequer and second-most important figure in the government, gave her a 'him or me' ultimatum in 1989.

Mrs Thatcher further demonstrated a penchant for advice and ideological support by maintaining contact with a number of right-wing intellectual groups, including the Centre for Policy Studies, the Institute of Economic Affairs, and the Adam Smith Institute.

> I resigned on a matter of fundamental principle, because it seemed to me that the Prime Minister [Wilson] was not only introducing a 'presidential' system into the running of the government . . . far too often outsiders in his entourage seemed to be almost the only effective 'Cabinet'.
>
> Lord George Brown, *In My Way* (1972)

What's in a name? A de facto prime-ministerial department? Some of those centrally involved in a policy advisory capacity have expressed dissatisfaction with the level of influence which can be achieved with the existing machinery. Sir John Hoskyns, in particular, felt disillusionment as his most radical ideas came to nought (Hoskyns 1985), and Berrill claims that the advice given to the Prime Minister is patchy and lacking in depth (Weller 1983: 61). Both have argued for a fully fledged prime-ministerial department. Hoskyns was particularly impatient with the democratic process of interest group involvement in policy-making (Riddell 1985: 270). However, there is a case against such a department.

> It would set the prime minister apart from the cabinet, frustrate cabinet cohesion, and symbolise the shift from cabinet to prime ministerial government.
>
> (Jones 1983: 84)

Some opponents of the idea appear content that existing arrangements stop short of this.

> In spite of ... developments I believe the Cabinet remains the supreme governing body and I believe it is right that it should be.
>
> (Wass 1984: 33)

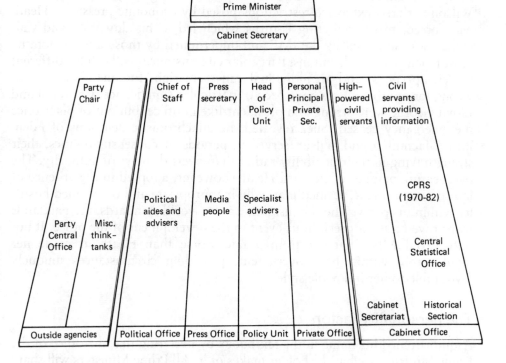

Figure 11.8 A Prime Minister's department?

Yet such a view may be sanguine. The ability of Prime Ministers to establish think-tanks and policy units at the drop of a hat or a handbag suggests that they need never be short of support when faced with cabinet dissidents. This could explain why, in spite of increased speculation in the early 1980s, a formal Prime Minister's Department has not been established. The existing informal arrangements (figure 11.8) serve to legitimate a *de facto* department, while formalization would invite accusations of constitutional tampering and presidential self-aggrandizement.

Conclusion: Britain's Popular Monarchy?

The Prime Minister has a number of weapons in the quest for dominance and power within the British executive, but most are double edged. They are potential powers, their reality depending upon two factors: the *prevailing contingencies* and the *personality* or character of the incumbent.

Contingencies of office

The circumstances surrounding their tenure are largely a matter of luck, but all Prime Ministers encounter squalls as well as fair weather. Attlee was obliged to reign during the years of post-war austerity, while Macmillan was lucky enough to inherit the years of plenty brought by the long boom. Wilson suffered extensive restrictions posed by economic pressures, Heath was forced into humiliating U-turns which led to his downfall, and Callaghan was squeezed by the IMF and undermined by those upon whom he most relied – the trade unions. Particular circumstances will call for different leadership styles, and an individual can seem right for one situation but wrong for another. Wars have been of particular significance: Churchill and Lloyd George were strong and president-like in office, but out of place once the emergency ceased; Suez revealed the anachronistic delusions of Eden. Both Macmillan and Wilson served in periods of consensus politics, their strength lying in their flexibility rather than overt displays of authority. The overbearing manner of Edward Heath, however, adopted in the absence of international threat, seemed markedly inappropriate and occasioned hostility within his party. Though insignificant by world standards, the Falklands war proved a most precipitous event in the development of the office. It not only saved Mrs Thatcher from a fate worse than Heath, it made her invulnerable within her government, providing circumstances uniquely favourable to her inflexible style.

The personality factor

Asquith etched his name in the textbooks by declaring that the office of the Prime Minister is what the holder makes of it. All Prime Ministers will share a propensity to exploit the powers available to them; as individuals who have risen to pre-eminence, they are likely to possess qualities of determination, political skill, ambition and a desire to dominate. However, like other people, each is unique, with a particular style, and the informal nature of the office permits a considerable variation in interpretation. This fact helps to explain why the debate on the power of the Prime Minister remains unresolved and of unquenchable interest to journalists and academics.

Prime Ministers had, for the most part, interpreted their role cautiously, content to preserve the constitutional status quo. Macmillan is credited with having been surprisingly radical, but Labour leaders were repeatedly accused of failing to harness the reins of power in the interests of the classes they purported to represent. However, this style of leadership was to change under Mrs Thatcher, the most domineering of post-war British Prime Ministers. Even before she came to office, the effect she might have was anticipated:

> No political leader that I have ever known has been less dependent upon the advantages and trappings that attend high office for the impact she made; and none more dependent on the force of her own character and mind.
>
> (Cosgrave 1978: xx)

Interviewed in the *Observer* (25 Feb. 1979), she baldly stated her rejection of the principle of cabinet government: 'As prime minister I could not waste time having any internal arguments'.

Reproduced by permission of *Punch*

> It is urgent because the Government, and Mrs Thatcher in particu-
> lar, are getting more and more dogmatic; they don't listen to
> anyone.
>
> Dr David Jenkins (Bishop of Durham), speaking of his personal campaign
> to protest against the 'wicked' aspects of Thatcherism, in the *Guardian*
> (27 Dec. 1988)

The Falklands war seemed to bring home to Margaret Thatcher in a blinding flash the real extent of her power; fields of potential constitutional energy were shocked into life. The weapons in the ancient monarchical armoury were brought into the open. The state relentlessly reasserted its authority under a philosophy so personalized that it bore the name 'Thatcherism'. In this era personalized politics in Britain came of age. For students of politics, one of the most important things about the New Right project is not whether or not it was a success, but that it was possible to try it with such ease. The programme uncovered important clues as to the true nature of the British constitution, revealing beneath the Dicean facade of popular supremacy an essentially monarchical character, with moderating influences residing only in unwritten conventions observed by those playing the game.

The surge of **populism** brought by Thatcher to this essentially monarchical culture produced a kind of **'populist monarchism'**, with the Prime Minister becoming, not merely presidential, but regal, overshadowing the Queen as the personification of the state. In a symbolic slip of the tongue, she proclaimed on television: 'We have become a grandmother', and unblushingly characterized her encounters with President Reagan as meetings of 'two heads of state'.

Elective monarchy?

Although the advent of a Conservative government in 1979 dissipated establishment fears of 'elective dictatorship', the 1980s saw Britain increasingly coming under a form of rule redolent of its ancient monarchical lineage. This was a consequence of the testing of ambiguities, myths and conventions which had long misted any clear vision of the British constitution and upon which the apologist textbooks have preferred to turn a benevolently blind eye.

The powers of the Cabinet are derived from the hijacking of the supremacy of Parliament (the key to all legitimate authority in the Dicean view of the constitution) through party control over the House of Commons. Hence the Cabinet can be said to possess greater power than monarchs of old, who were constrained by Parliament. Yet within the Cabinet sits the Prime Minister, who effectively inherits the royal prerogative, giving power

The Prime Minister as head of state
Source: Times Newspapers Ltd

(particularly through patronage) over all other colleagues. This is a truly despotic position.

What the 1980s showed was that the much-vaunted freedom from an overweening executive was not guaranteed by the constitution but depended upon governments observing conventions to remain within certain accepted limits. Thus Labour governments had always believed in their duties towards their capitalist neighbour, while Conservatives, dominated by the party's old tory strain, nursed a chastening sense of bourgeois guilt, accepting the ideas of the managed market, the mixed economy and the welfare state. Together they held any possible ravages of capitalism at bay to a greater extent than classical Marxists might be prepared to admit. Yet the despotic power lying dormant within the constitution remained, and a government blind to the political road signs and speed limits could career on a frightening course.

> The greater the power, the more dangerous the abuse.
> Edmund Burke (1729–97), House of Commons speech (7 Feb. 1771)

The Thatcher leadership took the constitution at its face value and citizens were presented with the alarming possibility that they had dwelt in a fools' paradise; that there was little to protect basic civil rights, Parliament, local democracy, the mixed economy, academic freedom, the welfare state and NHS, the trade unions, even the opposition parties, from radical executive action. Cabinet government, the main constitutional curb on an overweening executive, seemed to mean little. A child reared during the Thatcher years would be unable to understand why William Pitt (the Elder) was compelled to resign as Prime Minister in 1761 because the majority of his Cabinet refused to support his policy towards Spain.

> Unlimited power is apt to corrupt the minds of those who possess it.
>
> William Pitt the Elder (1708–78), House of Lord speech (9 Jan. 1770)

In 1988 the tercentenary of the Glorious Revolution was celebrated in a most muted manner (the privatization of the steel industry receiving far more publicity). The British and the newly monarchical government, in marked contrast to the French celebration of 1789 the following year, appeared to see little to applaud in the notion of freedom from tyranny. In December, *Charter 88* voiced fears for the effects of unbridled government, declaring:

> Our concern is with the law. No country can be considered free in which the government is above the law. No democracy can be considered safe whose freedoms are not encoded in a basic constitution.

Did the unceremonious fall of Thatcher demonstrate the power of the constitution? Some thought so. Hugo Young declared, 'finally the system, which says that this is cabinet and not prime ministerial government, reacted. There was a point beyond which it declined to be flouted' (*Independent*, 23 Nov. 1990).

Yet, although a number of eminent resignees from Thatcher Cabinets loudly lamented her style, she enjoyed an astonishing 11 years of supremacy, humiliating colleagues, replacing eminent figures with court favourites, emasculating local government, introducing the poll tax, insulting European leaders, undermining working-class associations, slamming the door on consultation, and so on. She strode the political landscape like a colossus with provocative braggadocio and disdain for views contrary to her own. Moreover, the ambition in the project was of audacious enormity, nothing less than the demolition of the British post-war social democractic state itself. Yet the constitution had no answers to this rapacity. There were no curbs, and when the fall came it was precipitated by a nervous party cadre suspecting that its leader had passed her electoral sell-by date.

By the end of the 1980s, after a decade of Thatcher rule, the monarchical character of the British constitution was laid bare. A President on the US model would actually have enjoyed substantially less power over the nation than did Mrs Thatcher. Yet contrary to popular feeling, the Thatcher dominance cannot be explained solely in terms of personality. As head of the Conservative Party she was the great hope of British capitalism. The idea that a non-capitalist-supported Prime Minister could use the potential in the office in the same way must remain extremely dubious. The establishment would soon sing again its 'elected dictatorship' refrain.

Key points

- Formally speaking, Britain has cabinet, as opposed to monarchical or presidential, government. This means government by a team, with decisions based on discussion, compromise and moderation.
- This system is recognized constitutionally in the convention of collective responsibility.
- Important issues associated with the analysis of cabinet government in Britain relate to its structure, its size, and the idea of the Policy Cabinet.
- The formal powers of the executive are inherited from the monarch.
- Cabinet government in Britain cannot be appraised without considering the office of the Prime Minister, who is constrained by the convention that he or she is only *primus inter pares* (first among equals) in the Cabinet.
- The Prime Minister is able to control the composition of the Cabinet and the nature of discussion, and to determine in retrospect what was actually decided by summing up.
- Control over the machinery of government allows a Prime Minister to have all the administrative back-up and advice that a personal department would offer.
- In important respects the Prime Minister is potentially more powerful than a typical President in a democracy because there is neither separation of powers nor a written constitution to restrain the executive.
- The Thatcher regime was a quite unique phenomenon in British politics, virtually ending the debate on the real extent of the powers of the office. It remains to be seen whether future incumbents will accept the old conventions of restraint.

Review your understanding of the following terms and concepts

executive arm of government

cabinet government

Privy Council

collective responsibility

Policy Cabinet

War Cabinet

inner cabinet

cabinet committees

Cabinet Secretariat

Cabinet Secretary

Shadow Cabinet

presidential government

spoils system

patronage

populism

'populist monarchism'

Assignment

Study the extract from the *Guardian* and answer the following questions.

PM set out to undermine Chancellor, says Smith

Economic debate

Paul Nettleton

LABOUR returned to the attack again yesterday on the circumstances surrounding the resignation last week of the Chancellor of the Exchequer, Mr Nigel Lawson.

Mr John Smith, the shadow Chancellor, opening a Labour-initiated debate on the economy in the Commons, said "no Chancellor can carry out his arduous duties without full support of the Prime Minister, a support which in the case of Mr Lawson was withheld because of a preference in favour of a part-time, unelected adviser."

The two crucial issues, Mr Smith said, were membership of the Exchange Rate Mechanism of the European Monetary System, and domestic policy in relation to exchange rate management.

Mr Smith said Mr Lawson had learnt from the failure of unfettered market forces during the early years of his chancellorship and moved towards participation in international efforts to manage exchange rates. That, he said, was why Sir Alan Walters had been invited back to Britain. "The lady did not turn."

It was precisely because Mrs Thatcher saw Mr Lawson as "unassailable" that she set out to undermine him, he argued. "Only the truly innocent believe that Sir Alan was just another adviser, one of these people who advise while ministers decide. He was more than that, he was a crucial ally of the Prime Minister.

"It was in the knowledge of his fierce opposition to joining the ERM ... that he was recalled to serve in No. 10. It did not take long for Sir Alan to become the alternative chancellor and we know the sad eventual outcome of all that."

Guardian, 1 Nov. 1989

	% mark
1 Would you describe Nigel Lawson's resignation as being in accordance with the doctrine of collective responsibility? Explain your reasoning.	20
2 Do the events of this resignation demonstrate the strength or the weakness of the Prime Minister's patronage powers?	20
3 Consider the accusation that Sir Alan Walters was more a 'crucial ally' than an impartial provider of advice. How far is this dichotomy of possible roles a general problem where ministerial advisers are appointed?	30
4 Contrast the Lawson resignation with that of Heseltine. Do they have any features in common?	30

Questions for discussion

1 Outline the essential features of cabinet government.
2 Critically evaluate the role of the Cabinet Secretariat in British government.
3 Discuss the function of the Shadow Cabinet in British politics.
4 How important is personality to the authority of the Prime Minister?
5 By what means is the British Prime Minister able to establish a direct link with the public? How significant is such a link?
6 In what ways would the establishment of a prime-ministerial department alter the process of government in Britain?
7 'The real question is not whether or not the powers of the British Prime Minister are presidential, but how far they are monarchical?' Discuss.

Topic for debate

This house believes that Margaret Thatcher was only able to be so dominant because her policies were ultimately good for private capital.
  or
This house believes that without cabinet government the British constitution offers no reliable safeguard against tyranny.

Further reading

Benn, A. (1979) *Arguments for Socialism.*
A stimulating essay expressing extreme distaste for presidential-style premiership.

Crossman, R. H. S. (1975–7) *Diaries of a Cabinet Minister.*
A uniquely frank record of cabinet government by a minister who never cast off his academic gown in an ambition to emulate Bagehot as the chronicler of his times.

Hennessy, P. (1986) *Cabinet.*
A lively account by a master journalist with an intimate knowledge of the geography of the corridors of power.

Hoskyns, Sir J. (1985) *An Agenda for Change.*
Written by an ex-head of Mrs Thatcher's Policy Unit, this essay contains a strong plea for more expert advice for the Prime Minister.

Mackintosh, J. P. (1977) *The British Cabinet.*
Something of a classic, with a good historical basis.

Wass, Sir D. (1984) *Government and the Governed.*
The text of the Reith Lectures delivered in 1984 by this ex-head of the civil service. Makes a case for a revised version of the CPRS rather than a prime-ministerial department, and expresses deep unease over the presidential trend of British government.

Young, H. (1989) *One of Us.*
Arguably the best book on Thatcher in government, with a clever punning title capturing her populist appeal and her determination to surround herself with like-minded people.

For light relief

W. Clark, *Number Ten.*

M. Edelman, *The Prime Minister's Daughter.*

12

The Village of Whitehall: of Ministers and Mandarins

In this chapter we look at a key agency of the state – the central government bureaucracy, known as the civil service. Constitutionally this is part of the executive arm of government, charged with responsibility for implementing government policies. We first examine the **evolution** of the modern civil service and the forces which shaped it. We also try to discover the kind of people civil servants are: the way they are **recruited** and their **educational and class background**. Next, we identify one of the most potent sources of government power – **official secrecy**. We also address the question of civil service **political power**, asking whether the bureaucrats really are the 'obedient servants' of Her Majesty's Government. In conclusion we assess the traumatic, though paradoxical, impact of the Thatcher years.

The constitutional position

The British civil service is the central government **bureaucracy**, its function in the great liberal-democratic scheme of things to administer faithfully the policies of the elected representatives of the people. Belief in this serves a vital legitimating function; when people vote for a government they must do so on the assumption that it will be able to take control of the levers of national power once in office. Writers in the apologist tradition have no difficulty in believing this to be the case. They seem determined to depict the bureaucrats as seventeenth-century painters portrayed the nobility of their day, in romantically idealized poses without warts or wrinkles. Taking no sides, and favouring no class against another, civil servants are pictured as being above the sordid world of politics. The service is seen as the very embodiment of the liberal-democratic ideal of the *neutral state*.

This tradition of approval in writing on the subject is partly explained by the fact that many specialists in the study of the civil service are themselves ex-members. Sir John Hoskyns, an outsider brought in by Mrs Thatcher to shake up this comfortable self-confident world, observed:

> No one is qualified to criticise ... unless he has first hand experience of working in it. But if he has worked in it, then there is a convention that he should never speak about it thereafter except in terms of respectful admiration.

> (Hoskyns 1984)

In this chapter, however, we shall try to substitute a microscope for rose-tinted lenses. We set the scene for our analysis by first identifying our specimens and the environment in which they civilly serve.

The civil servants

Not all state employees are **civil servants**. They may broadly be defined as servants of the Crown (in other words, central government) working in a civil (non-military) capacity and not the holders of political or judicial office.

Said unkindly in caricature to be rarely civil and never servile, members are popularly thought of as grey, anonymous, passionless beings who sometimes exercise discretionary power over one's life. They, and the study of them, are often characterized as rather boring, which may well be precisely what the establishment likes the masses to think; people do not look too closely at boring subjects. However, in spite of evident efforts by writers on public administration to avoid over-exciting their readers, the civil service is certainly not boring; its major preoccupation has been nothing less than running the country and influencing the policies which shape our lives. When one is seeking to explain the balance of power in society, and to understand why resources are allocated as they are, the role of the civil service must be central to the analysis.

Civil servants may be broadly dichotomized as industrial and non-industrial. Thus, although the civil servant of popular imagination wears a suit and carries a rolled umbrella, many are obliged to roll up their shirt sleeves, others work stripped to the waist in government dockyards, and the exotic Quentin Crisp entitled his autobiography *The Naked Civil Servant* because, when posing for students in state art colleges, he wore nothing at all. The non-industrial civil service consists of three main elements: the *Administrative Group*; a category of *specialist groups* employing scientists, technologists, doctors, lawyers, and so on; and a set of particular departmental classes employing *specialists* in particular areas such as taxation.

The service as a whole, from the mass of workers at its base to its tiny elite pinnacle, can be seen as a social microcosm. However, 99 per cent of these do not concern us; our focus is on the 1 per cent at the top of the Administrative Group, those whose daily lives bring them into intimate

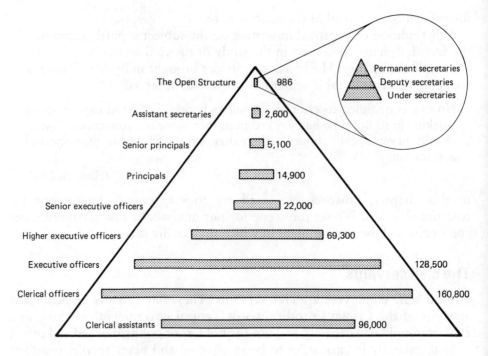

Figure 12.1   The civil service hierarchy: staff in post by grade in the non-industrial civil service, April 1988

Source: Treasury (1988b)

contact with the highest and most mighty in the confident and pompous world of the British establishment, who comprise the **mandarin** class, named after the officials in imperialist China (from *mander*, to command). These form a caste system (see figure 12.1): at the very apex is the permanent secretary, below him (rarely her) is the deputy secretary, and then the under secretary.

> Mandarin is not in fact a Chinese word; it was used to describe the Chinese officials (*Khiouping*) by the Portuguese colonists at Maca'o. Mandarins were appointed on the basis of imperial birth, long service, illustrious deeds, knowledge, ability, zeal, nobility and aristocratic birth. There were nine ranks of seniority distinguished by the buttons on their caps.

Though powerful, the mandarins are not elected and they cannot be removed by any democratic mechanism. A principal characteristic is their permanence: political storms may rage, and politicians be swept into the foaming seas of controversy and scandal, but the bureaucrats cling like pin-striped limpets to the solid grey rocks of Whitehall. Speaking of this elite corps, E. N. Gladden notes with awe:

On its record of public service it stands unchallenged, setting an example that the lesser breeds of official strive, almost hopelessly, to emulate.

(Gladden 1967: 199)

The structure of the civil service

Following nineteenth-century reforms, the civil service grew steadily until the 1980s, when it began to contract as a result of government policy. In 1900 there were only around 50,000 civil servants, but growth was promoted by two world wars, the emergence of the welfare state, and government acceptance of the responsibility for economic management. Figure 12.2 shows the largest departments at the end of the 1980s.

It is the great historic departments lying at the centre of government, including the Treasury, the Foreign and Commonwealth Office and the Home Office, which stand in Whitehall, the dignified corridor watched over by Nelson from the top of his column in Trafalgar Square and leading to the Palace of Westminster. With long histories predating the nineteenth-century reforms, their origins lie in the royal household. The newer departments, such as the Department of Social Security (DSS), the Department of Education and Science (DES) and the Department of Employment, reflect the changing role of government and lie in rather less grand areas of the

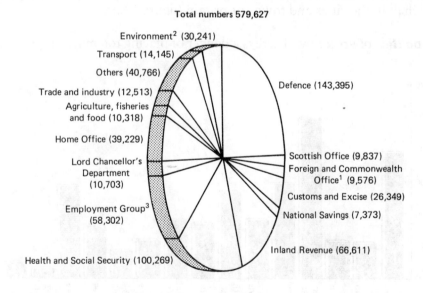

Total numbers 579,627

Environment[2] (30,241)
Transport (14,145)
Others (40,766)
Trade and industry (12,513)
Agriculture, fisheries and food (10,318)
Home Office (39,229)
Lord Chancellor's Department (10,703)
Employment Group[3] (58,302)
Health and Social Security (100,269)

Defence (143,395)

Scottish Office (9,837)
Foreign and Commonwealth Office[1] (9,576)
Customs and Excise (26,349)
National Savings (7,373)
Inland Revenue (66,611)

1. *Including Overseas Development Adminstration (1,540)*
2. *Including Property Services Agency (21,902) Crown Suppliers (1,773)*
3. *Including Department of Employment (42,102), Training Commission (12,165)*
   Health and Safety Commission/Executive (3,410) and Advisory Conciliation and Arbitration Service (625)

Figure 12.2 The largest government departments, April 1988

Source: Treasury (1988b: 3)

The ornate facade of Whitehall: the New Home and Colonial Office, 1875
Source: Mary Evans Picture Library

metropolis. In addition, there is a great network of *field agencies* beyond Whitehall in the cities and towns of Britain (figure 12.3).

The politics of structure   There is a danger of placing too much emphasis on

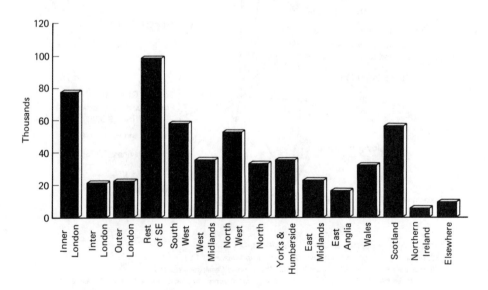

Figure 12.3   The national distribution of civil servants

Source: Treasury (1988b: 5)

structure and boring students with detailed textual analysis of turgid white papers written by obfuscating bureaucrats. However, structure is not some technical matter lying outside politics. Since it is not determined by constitutional rules, it may be changed overnight at the Prime Minister's whim – an important source of power.

During the 1960s and 1970s the fashion for departmental fusion created new giant departments for Defence, Health and Social Security (DHSS – see figure 12.4), Foreign and Commonwealth Affairs, Trade and Industry (DTI) and Environment (DoE). This has political implications, enabling governments to remove controversies from the public eye by resolving them in the corners of Whitehall rather than in Cabinet or Parliament. It also created political empires for prominent politicians, such as Richard Crossman at the DHSS, giving them a better chance of standing up for their services against the Treasury. However, by the mid-1970s, the climate began to change and the giant's limbs began to drop off. Energy, for example, left the DTI and Transport was re-established outside the DoE. In addition, Mrs Thatcher's desire to slim down the public sector led to certain functions being hived off to special semi-autonomous agencies (see p. 374). The splitting of the DHSS in 1989 also served the political goal of making health less integrated into the welfare state, more vulnerable to accounting methods of evaluation and, in the longer term, to partial privatization.

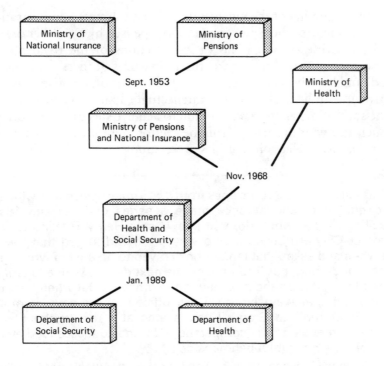

Figure 12.4 Departmental fusion and fission: the rise and fall of a giant

The Culture of Whitehall

The genesis of the modern civil service

Like many other institutions of modern British politics the civil service is not static and cannot be understood without reference to its past. Orthodox accounts stress the nineteenth-century reforms, which are said to have laid the foundations by replacing a corrupt system controlled by the old artistocratic order with one based on meritocratic principles. Less readily acknowledged is the fact that these reforms made this most powerful state institution the property of the bourgeoisie.

Early origins of the service can be discerned in the courts of the Anglo-Saxon kings, where administration emerged as a distinct activity, requiring the employment of full-time clerks who would accompany the king as he moved about the realm (Stenton 1941: 349). Essentially, they were the officers of the royal household and their functions persisted, despite a turbulent constitutional history which witnessed the struggle between monarchy and nobles, the conjuncture of church and state, the rise of the Tudors, the battle between the Stuarts and Parliament, the Glorious Revolution and the establishment of the constitutional monarchy. Gradually the old offices, such as the Chamber and the Wardrobe, gave way to newer ones, and the royal household itself became departmentalized to reflect various specialisms.

Up to the beginning of the nineteenth century, the state administration was not seen as a single service; patronage was dispensed by a number of separate political authorities heading the various sections of the royal household. Many positions were little more than sinecures (offices with no duties attached) and appointments were filled on the basis of nepotism (favouritism to relatives), with little attention to intellectual capacity. Civil servants were often the sons of the aristocracy too dull to achieve success in any other walk of life such as law or the army. Trollope's autobiography recounts the lack of rigour in his own selection. Salaries were supplemented by bribes: Samuel

---

I was asked to copy some lines from *The Times* newspaper with an old quill pen, and at once made a series of blots and false spellings. 'That won't do, you know,' said Henry Freeling to his brother Clayton. Clayton, who was my friend, urged that I was nervous and asked that I might be allowed to do a bit of writing at home and bring it as a sample on the next day ... With a faltering heart I took this on the next day to the office ... But when I got to 'The Grand', as we used to call our office in those days, from its site, St Martin's le Grand, I was seated at a desk without any further reference to my competency. No one condescended even to look at my beautiful penmanship.

Anthony Trollope (1815–82; English novelist), *Autobiography* (1883)

Going out of Whitehall, I met Capt. Grove who did give me a letter directed to myself from himself; I discerned money to be in it and took it, knowing, as I found it to be, the proceed of the place I have got him . . . But I did not open it till I came home to my office; and there broke it open, not looking into it till all the money was out, that I may say I saw no money in the paper if ever I should be Questioned about it. There was a piece of gold and 4/- in silver. So home to dinner with my father and wife.

Samuel Pepys (1633–1703; diarist and naval administrator), *Diary* (1 April 1663)

Pepys, who served in the Admiralty in the mid-seventeenth century, records the giving and receiving of gifts in the line of official duty.

The rise of the industrial bourgeoisie In the eighteenth century there were many who lamented the failings of the service and a campaign for reform led by Burke and Fox attacked sinecures and other malpractices. However, it was the impact of the industrial revolution and the rise of the new bourgeoisie which spawned the modern service. A critical element shaping bourgeois thinking was the experience of empire, and the model for the new central administration was found in the Indian Civil Service (ICS), the instrument of British sovereignty in India. This had evolved from the East India Company, under the inspiration of the poet and historian Lord Macaulay (1800–59), to become a complex machine for the exercise of British colonial rule. The ICS was manned by the brightest sons of the bourgeoisie, who would take the passage to India, there to reign in splendour as the epitome of the over-dressed, over-confident Englishman (depicted by writers such as E. M. Forster). It is clear from the fading sepia photographs that the adventure was luxuriantly pleasurable and exceedingly good for the ego.

The young bureaucratic conquistadores prepared themselves to rule a race about which they knew nothing, in a climate for which they were singularly ill suited, by means of the newly revived public school system with its umbilicus to the universities of Oxford and Cambridge. Their studies were largely confined to the classics which, under the stimulus of men like Thomas Arnold of Rugby, had undergone a renaissance as the most effective way of transforming the sons of rough-talking northern businessmen into scholars

What we must look for here is, first, religious and moral principles; secondly, gentlemanly conduct; thirdly, intellectual ability.

Dr Thomas Arnold (1795–1842; headmaster), address to his scholars at Rugby School

and (more importantly) gentlemen. These schools sought to place a stamp of conformity on their alumni through the study of the classics, obsessional team games, and a hierarchical sado-masochistic prefect system which simultaneously stressed a natural right to rule and passive obedience.

Macaulay had emphasized the importance of examinations in selecting candidates, though he did not believe that these need be in relevant disciplines, preferring to use the classics, the intellectual diet of the universities, as the best judge of all-round intelligence. As *generalists*, with no particular skills, they confidently sailed away to command a vast subcontinent peopled by those regarded as their social, racial and intellectual inferiors. The ICS seemed to the bourgeoisie to offer the very best possible model upon which to reform the central administration in order to control the inferior orders at home.

The Northcote–Trevelyan Report (1854)   This important official report, the vehicle for reform, was the result of an enquiry set up by Gladstone. Its driving spirit was Sir Charles Trevelyan who, as a zealous member of the ICS and son-in-law of Lord Macaulay, had observed its felicities at first hand. The report recommended that the separate departments of state be amalgamated to form a single *home civil service*. The work was characterized in hierarchical terms, ranging from mechanical, clerical drudgery, through a range of executive tasks, to the heady intoxication of intellectual cogitation and policy-making. Recruitment was to reflect these distinctions in appropriately Platonic terms: men of iron would labour at the lower levels, while the upper echelons were to be reserved for the men of gold forged on the public school–Oxbridge anvil.

A crucial feature of the reform was that 'merit' should replace aristocratic patronage and nepotism in recruitment. In this praiseworthy ideal lay the key to the bourgeois capture of the service. The examinations were to be geared to the Oxbridge syllabus, and neither the aristocrats nor the working classes could match the sons of the bourgeoisie in passing examinations in the classics. By this device the public schools were to assume the mission of manufacturing a ruling elite.

The report was warmly welcomed by Gladstone, who did not conceal his motives: the bourgeois class would have 'command over all the higher part of the civil service, which up to this time they have never enjoyed' (Morley 1903: 649). The old guard were not blind to the writing appearing on their decaying walls. Queen Victoria enquired in some alarm where 'the application of the principle of public competition is to stop' (Magnus 1963: 118).

The twentieth century   The fact that the civil service took the shape it did is by no means remarkable: it was fashioned in the age of high mid-Victorian confidence to serve a new dominant class. What *is* remarkable is that, as the twentieth century changed the world, with national debt, enervating wars, social democracy, high technology, widespread higher education, and spiralling economic decline, the model persisted.

The twentieth century was to substitute the positive interventionist state for the largely negative regulative state, the background upon which the Northcote–Trevelyan reforms had been painted. Increasingly critics saw the bureaucrats as ill suited to the government's new role, yet the old system was tenaciously defended. This is not surprising; it was exceedingly functional for maintaining an establishment grip on the central institutions of state.

To assess the extent to which the nineteenth-century pattern has been preserved we shall examine two interrelated features of the modern civil service which are woven into the warp and weft of the culture of Whitehall: *social composition* and the *nature of the mandarins' expertise*.

Representative bureaucracy: the social make-up of the modern service

In the post-war era the mandarins have been asked to run a complex welfare state and to manage the economy in pursuit of social goals such as full employment. Given their great potential influence over policy one is entitled to ask whether they can be expected to understand the problems of ordinary people. Do they know what it is like to sit at nights with a loved one in pain on an NHS waiting list? Have their lives brought them into contact with the unemployed, the discriminated against, the dispossessed, the poor, those harassed by the forces of law and order, or the homeless? Does the selection process aim for representative bureaucracy?

The Whitehall atmosphere has traditionally been likened to that of an Oxbridge college, with much attention to status, ritual displays of courtesy, esoteric speech codes involving the liberal use of Latin phrases and much cricketing jargon learned at Fenner's, and a general air of superiority. The upper echelons of the service cannot be said to represent the population they serve in terms of gender, race or social class.

Gender The civil service has a poor record as an employer of women. The great Victorian era which saw its birth was marked, amongst other things, by overwhelming male hegemony, shown in crusty all-male London clubs, limited education for girls, a male House of Commons, and the belief that women were not sufficiently intelligent or stable to vote. Although their opportunities in the service have improved (they are no longer forced to retire if they marry), women remain grossly under-represented at the upper levels. Their main virtue is seen to lie in the performance of mindless jobs, and it is at the levels of clerical officer that their presence is most prominent (figure 12.5). Although the Crossman diaries made Permanent Secretary Dame Evelyn Sharp famous, women remain extremely rare at this level: in 1988 there were none at all. Indeed, today women hold only one in twenty posts in the higher grades, and one in ten at the level of principal. In addition, 26,000 women were employed on a part-time basis, the most notoriously insecure of all forms of employment (Hughes 1988).

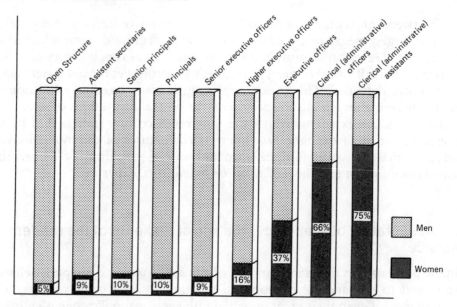

Figure 12.5   Proportion of men and women in the non-industrial civil service, April 1988

Source: Data from Treasury (1988b: 11)

Race The prospects for blacks in the upper reaches remain remote. Their presence is more evident in the lower levels, although even here they represent a minuscule proportion.

Social class Nowhere has the Northcote–Trevelyan legacy been more evident than in the social make-up of the service. The overriding impression is of social superiority; in Whitehall one is close to the heart of the British establishment in an atmosphere of power and privilege. The corridors linking the offices are those very corridors of power of political legend, and

---

Diary of Jim Hacker: Oct. 27th

'How many Permanent Secretaries', I asked Sir Humphrey, 'are there at the moment?'

'Forty-one I believe.'

A precise answer.

'Forty-one,' I agreed pleasantly. 'And how many are women?'

Suddenly Sir Humphrey's memory seemed to fail him. 'Well broadly speaking, not having the exact figures to hand, I'm not exactly sure.'

'Well, approximately?' I encouraged him to reply.

'Well,' he said cautiously, '*approximately* none.'

J. Lynn and A. Jay, *The Complete Yes Minister* (based on the TV series)

(1981: 355)

from the walls hang portraits of the men who have shaped the destiny of the nation, enshrined for ever in their pomp and dignity. The mandarins have traditionally come from the same social stratum as those at the heads of industry, commerce, the City, the army, the church, and professions such as law and medicine. They attended the same public schools and universities, belong to the same London clubs, and meet at the country house parties exotically caricatured by Anthony Trollope. Consequently they feel and think in the same way as those who wish to preserve a capitalist status quo.

Mandarins in the hereafter: life after death This is an aspect of Whitehall culture virtually ignored by textbooks, yet it is vital to any understanding of the importance of social background. Unlike many members of the working class, mandarins do not fear retirement; indeed some greet their professional demise with the relish of Christian heroes in Foxe's *Book of Martyrs*, so certain are they of paradise to come.

At the end of their careers they receive rather more than a pocket watch; titles are dispensed twice a year in the New Year and Queen's birthday honours lists. In other walks of life it is necessary to climb Everest, discover penicillin, or win an Olympic gold medal to qualify, but mandarins receive them automatically as part of the job. These awards reflect status reached rather than any particular contribution made, and the most prestigious, such as the Cabinet Secretary, usually receive peerages.

The rewards do not end with ennoblement. Though gone, the mandarins are not forgotten, their names are entered upon the revered list of the great and the good from which are chosen the members and chairs of quangos and government enquiries into this or that matter of public concern. Former Cabinet Secretary Lord Trend was recalled briefly to conduct a top-level enquiry into allegations that the former head of MI5 had been a Russian master spy. The ex-mandarins' great value lies in the conformity assiduously cultivated throughout their sheltered lives. They can be relied upon not to rock the boat in their solutions and conclusions.

There is also an alarming tendency, once the winter of retirement threatens, for ex-mandarins to migrate like starlings to the warm climes of the private sector, where they look for further reward in the strongholds of the capitalist economy they have served (in merchant firms, banks and industry) (Balogh 1968: 21). As the role of the civil service has increased throughout the century, so this seam of lucrative transfers has become richer.

In the 1980s, with the ethos of profit-seeking elevated to the status of beatitude, public service could increasingly be seen as a prelude to private gain (Doig 1984). A mandarin nearing the end of his career will feel considerable anguish if he has not ensured that when the Whitehall door closes one in the private sector is ready to open. Sir Leslie Rowan left the Treasury to head Vickers, Sir Edward Playfair went from Defence to International Computers and, amidst much controversy, the ex-head of the civil service, Sir William Armstrong, became chairman of Midland Bank.

However, the real concern here is not that these favoured beings are able to continue to draw upon their capital of privilege while others draw their meagre pensions, but that many civil servants in key positions with an eye on their retirement 'will wish to do well and will therefore be . . . inclined to take a general view of things not awkward to large private interests' (Balogh 1968: 23). It is not difficult to see why those with an unrivalled knowledge of the workings of the Whitehall machine, and of the people remaining in the pivotal positions, should be prized by large companies, including multinationals, which gain a direct line to the policy-making centre.

The expertise of the mandarins: gentlemen versus players?

The social bias in the upper echelons of the service is defended with the argument that the criterion for selection is not class but brains, that the apparent class domination is merely a consequence of the fact that those with the best brains issue from the loins of intelligent fathers who have had the wisdom to accumulate the wealth to afford the right school and university for their offspring. This is the flip side of the argument that those who attend inner-city slum schools perform badly because they, and their forebears, are of fundamentally low intelligence. It is all part of the idea that Britain contains two types of people – the masses and their natural superiors.

While doctors attend medical schools, lawyers study law, chemists chemistry, and so on, Britain's mandarins have remained untouched by the disciplines (sociology, economics, political science, civil engineering, defence, education, and even public administration) which would seen relevant to their work. This stands in sharp contrast to the practice in many other developed countries, where a more serious view is taken of training top civil servants.

The practice is defended by the argument that high-level work requires **generalist** rather than **specialist** abilities, a preference redolent of the nineteenth-century reforms. Yet in truth the reformers had little choice if they wanted to ensure that 'open competition' meant closed competition, reserving the places for the sons of the bourgeoisie: it was classics which the public schools taught, so it had to be classics in which the examinations were set. If they had been in engineering, perhaps the barbarians from the urban technical colleges might have entered the establishment gates. This approach was appropriate enough during the nineteenth century, since the state's minimalist 'night-watchman' role was to leave private capitalists with as much freedom as possible. However, the post-war era meant radical changes, requiring the mandarins to come out of the shadows of the *laissez-faire* economy and operate across a wide economic and social front. Critics bemoaned the fact that, throughout the post-war era, Britain was slipping behind its main competitors as inept mandarins, wrestling with problems they did not understand, applied irrelevant remedies. The cultivated air of effortless superiority was regarded as a sham concealing a shallow dilettantism.

The retention of the generalists' hegemony was legitimized on the grounds that only they could understand what was in the (equally generalist) minister's mind; that is, the best people to lead the blind would be the blind. Justification was also found in a kind of administrative ideology held to be peculiarly British which condescendingly declared that 'experts must be on tap rather than on top'.

However, with twentieth-century developments in education the system of class dominance could not be expected to continue unchallenged. The growth of the grammar schools and the rise of the provincial universities promised a proletarian invasion up the stairway of **meritocracy**. Yet it is an astonishing fact that the traditional dominance has been maintained, even in the face of strong and sustained calls for reform. This was accomplished by controlling recruitment, which remained in the hands of the mandarins themselves.

Skimming the milk: selecting mandarins

The selection of mandarins remains a highly controversial feature in modern British politics; it is the key to understanding the culture of Whitehall today. The principle established after the Northcote–Trevelyan Report was that potential mandarins would enter directly into what was to become a closed upper elite – the Administrative Class. This at once removed the inconvenience of working up through the ranks and precluded the possibility that any intelligent members of the lower ranks (the executive and clerical classes) would rise beyond their station. Subsequent reforms did not alter this principle; today would-be mandarins enter a special trainee grade which guarantees an inside track to the top. Numerous studies conducted throughout the twentieth century have illustrated how this process of selection has continued to operate as Gladstone intended: to discriminate in favour of the upper middle classes.

Although the pattern slightly wobbled in the 1960s as a result of university expansion, Oxbridge recruitment was back around its historic levels by the 1980s (Ponting 1986: 70). Table 12.1 demonstrates, not only the overwhelming preference for Oxbridge graduates, but a tendency for them to gravitate disproportionately towards the most prestigious departments – the Treasury, the Foreign and Commonwealth Office and the Home Office.

Vetting An additional safeguard against the barbarian at the gate is the process of vetting recruits. Although officially a means of excluding both communists and fascists, interest focuses rather more on those with leanings towards the former than the latter. 'Neither the vetting procedures nor the ideological climate in the upper reaches of the civil service required a man or woman to abjure strongly held conservative views; but there was a problem for anyone with more than mildly reform-oriented leaning' (Miliband 1984: 103).

Socialization The class bias is reinforced by working-class graduates'

Table 12.1   Oxbridge and non-Oxbridge top civil servants

Department	Principal and above			Deputy secretary and above		
	Oxbridge graduates	Non-Oxbridge graduates	Oxbridge as % of all graduates	Oxbridge graduates	Non-Oxbridge graduates	Oxbridge as % of all graduates
Foreign and Commonwealth	630	170	79	42	7	86
Treasury	110	51	68	10	3	77
Cabinet Office	55	46	54	7	3	70
Education	42	50	46	6	2	75
Civil Service Department	70	89	44	3	2	60
Overseas Development	98	141	41	2	0	100
Energy	49	100	33	3	2	60
Environment/Transport	299	668	30	14	2	87
Home Office	97	230	30	5	2	71
Trade/Industry	293	897	25	16	2	84
Northern Ireland	20	66	23	1	1	50
Defence	349	1,254	22	13	9	59
Employment	154	598	20	5	3	62
Health and Social Security	127	538	19	10	3	83
Agriculture	109	499	18	5	2	71
Wales	21	112	16	1	1	50
Scotland	48	375	11	3	5	37
Total	2,582	6,056	30	146	51	74

Source: Kellner and Crowther Hunt (1980)

disinclination to apply, owing to low expectations of success and the natural deference in British culture. This allows the mandarins to shed crocodile tears and speak piously of trying to 'drum up' interest among the lower classes. Although some entrants to the mandarin class are not from the elite inside track, this tends to have little effect on the general ethos. For the working class, aspiration to the upper echelons is a means of social advancement rather than an expression of radical consciousness. Moreover, rewards are dispensed by those in authority, who perpetuate the species by promoting in their own likeness in a Darwinian process of natural selection.

'Yes Permanent Secretary'

There are those who are always on the side of authority and quite exceptionally adept at formulating the answer that will be most acceptable to those at the top. It is no secret that they get on better than those who are outspoken and speak their minds.

E. N. Gladden (retired civil servant), *Civil Services of the United Kingdom* (1967: 199)

The Fulton Report: a substitute for action

The arrival of the Labour Party in office in 1964 led many to anticipate an attack on both the social exclusiveness of the civil service and its amateurism. Wilson was known to harbour strong feelings on the subject and had even expounded his views to a sympathetic political scientist, Norman Hunt, on radio. A committee was soon established under Lord Fulton with Hunt, as the Prime Minister's nominee, a key member.

Having put the service under a critical microscope, the 1968 Fulton Report castigated the 'cult of the amateur', declaring it obsolete at all levels. Great excitement was generated, the government announcing its intention to implement over a hundred recommendations, and the popular press spoke of 'Mugging the Mandarins'. However, one recommendation was politely declined – that entrants should be expected to possess *relevant* degrees. This seemingly small reservation had the effect of completely sabotaging the enterprise and ensured that no other reforms (such as setting up a civil service college and a special Civil Service Department responsible for recruitment and training) could ever make sense. Although Wilson's lips were seen to be moving, the voice heard in the Commons was unmistakably that of the mandarins, who subsequently made great show of implementing the proposals (even regularly publishing turgid accounts of *Actions on Fulton*). Norman Hunt was later to confess that in trying to see the reforms through he was but a dupe 'engaged in an unequal struggle with arch mandarin, Sir William Armstrong' (Kellner and Crowther-Hunt 1980: 63).

Ten years later, Parliament's Expenditure Committee (under chairman Michael English) found little evidence that the generalists had relaxed their stranglehold. After a further decade Clive Ponting was able to list a ludicrous catalogue of amateurism: in 1983 four of the senior officials responsible for controlling the entire defence budget of a mind-boggling £18 billion 'were all classicists who had read Greats at Oxford' (Ponting 1986: 85).

Thus it must be concluded that the culture of Whitehall is one dominated by the ideals of white, male members of the upper middle classes. The ethos is one of social exclusivity, rather like the London clubs (to which most mandarins belong), and all is reinforced by another feature of immense importance in British politics: secrecy.

Secrets of Success

> I know that's a secret, for it's whispered everywhere.
> William Congreve (1670–1729; Restoration dramatist),
> *Love for Love* (1695)

To outsiders, Whitehall may appear awe inspiring and intimidating, the place where great issues of state are decided with smooth efficiency by the Rolls Royce minds of the intellectual elite. However, two American scholars debunked such an image when, after an intimate examination, they reported it to be more like a gossipy 'village' than a rational machine. The inhabitants of Whitehall-on-Thames have, like other villagers, their own private world of shared experiences and are 'united by coherent patterns of praxis' (Heclo and Wildavsky 1972: 2). This image of village life is particularly apposite with respect to the sharing of information with outsiders: the locals like to keep themselves very much to themselves. However, the mandarins are supposed to serve the world outside their cosy environment, and the fact that they are miserly with information is a threat to democracy. The issue of **official secrecy** is thus central to understanding the way British government operates.

Information and power

Secrecy is endemic throughout British society and is a necessary feature of domination. Since information is power, a dominant elite is more secure to the extent that it can maintain a degree of ignorance among the masses. In true capitalist spirit, official information is seen as the private property of the high and mighty, who are as likely to distribute it to the rabble as they are to part with their land, wealth and capital. Secrecy, rather than flagellation, is the real *vice anglaise*, and the civil service, as keeper of the keys to the state informational vaults, has been able to make our system of government one of the most closed in the world.

The information withheld is of a particular kind – *truth*. This was made clear by Cabinet Secretary Robert Armstrong when he left the Australian courts agape by boasting of his bureaucratic ability to be 'economical with the truth'. There is no shortage of other kinds of information, designed to mislead, confuse and obscure. The civil service is a giant information processing factory, producing each week thousands of memos; lengthy answers to parliamentary questions; white and green papers; and masses of data on the state of society, the economy, the international situation, and so on. The creaking shelves of 'Government Publications' in any university library present precipitous mountain faces which only the most intrepid or foolhardy attempt to scale. However, all this can be seen as part of the process of legitimation: the turgid material disgorged from the Whitehall intestinal tract is there to daunt researchers and mask the true level of secrecy.

Political public information

Government spending on advertising was planned to increase by twice the rate of inflation from £109 million in 1988–9 to over £120 million in 1989–90. (This compares with £21 million in 1983–4.) The increase led civil servants to complain that they were being encouraged to 'expound half-truths, produce dodgy material and leak in the Government's interest' (see the *Sunday Telegraph*, 2 April 1989).

The key to British secrecy is often said to lie in the *Official Secrets Acts*. This is doubtful; its real basis lies in the hearts of those in power and the culture they seek to perpetuate. The Acts are but symptoms of the informational constipation which seizes up the bowels of government. However, we cannot ignore them because they represent an extremely convenient instrument for the truth misers.

The Official Secrets Acts

Britain is extremely good at passing Official Secrets Acts, having enacted them in 1889, 1911, 1920, 1939 and 1989. The most restrictive element in this corpus was for long the infamous section 2 of the 1911 Act. This made it a criminal offence for *any* Crown servant to disclose without authorization *any* information learned from his job. It was also an offence to receive such information, and to claim that the disclosure was in the **public interest** was no defence. Ironically, the 'public interest' is the most common basis upon which government itself claims the right to withhold information. Moreover, in the Ponting case the judge ruled that the public interest was no more than the interest of the government of the day: thus if it was not in the government's political interest for facts about the sinking of the *Belgrano* (in the Falklands war) to be known, then *ipso facto* it was not in the public interest for them to be known. For many, political rather than national interest seemed the motivation for prosecution, and the jury surprised everyone by aquitting Ponting.

It is an official secret if it's in an official file.

Sir Martin Furnival Jones (one-time head of MI5),
quoted in C. Aubrey, *Who's Watching You* (1981: 19)

It is easy to see why section 2 was described as a 'catch-all' provision or a blunderbuss: a civil servant could be imprisoned for disclosing the colour of the Whitehall toilet paper, or the number of biscuits consumed by a permanent secretary. The only way to remain safe would be to take the vows of a Trappist monk. Section 2 was originally intended as a subtle form of press censorship and was rushed through its parliamentary stages in under an hour by bewildered MPs fearing war with Germany. In 1971 it was reviewed by an official committee which declared it to be 'a mess' (Franks 1972: para. 88), arguing that no one was sure what it actually meant, or what actions involved a real risk of prosecution. This contravenes the notion of the rule of law that it should be known with reasonable certainty what behaviour might lead to punishment (Michael 1982: 37). However, for those who wish to keep things under wraps this 'mess' can be extremely useful: it gives them *carte blanche* to act as they please. If they wish to disclose they can regard themselves as having *authorized* release, but if more humble beings wish to do so, they can be penalized. Thus Sarah Tisdall, a Foreign Office clerk, was sentenced to six months' imprisonment in March 1984 for leaking information to the *Guardian* on the arrival of US Cruise missiles in Britain. As in the Ponting case, the prosecution appeared merely an expedient to avoid political embarrassment.

A right to know If we look to other countries we find a quite different view of the questions of government information, an emphasis not on the state's right to secrecy but on the people's democratic right to know. The first amendment of the US constitution declares that 'Congress shall make no law abridging the freedom of . . . speech or of the press', and the Supreme Court has generally interpreted this provision with a liberality alarming to the British establishment (Michael 1982: 127).

After the first world war, the UN General Assembly passed a resolution stating boldly that freedom of information was 'a fundamental human right'. Today Denmark, Sweden, Norway, France, Holland, Australia, Canada, Finland, New Zealand and the US have all passed laws guaranteeing citizens access to official information (Thomas 1987: 137). The essence of such legislation is that those who wish to withhold information should have to prove their case.

British moves towards legislation of this kind have been painfully sluggard. Governments have fought shy in spite of bold-sounding manifestos ai private members' bills introduced in 1978, 1981 and 1984. Labour came power in 1974 promising to reform the Official Secrets Acts and introdu freedom of information legislation. However, such ideas had little chance under the stewardship of Home Secretary Merlyn Rees, a man who disdainfully believed that such matters were 'of little day-to-day consequence to the MP, or to his constituents' (Rees 1987: 32).

As an alternative to a **Freedom of Information Act** came a feeble compromise in 1977 known as the *Croham Directive* – a 'modest' attempt to encourage departments 'to publish as much as possible of the factual and analytical material used as the background to major policy studies'. With sweet irony it was itself a 'confidential' document and had to be leaked (Ponting 1986: 205). One of its main effects was an increase in the scale of official smoke-screening, generating masses of uninteresting, useless information. Furthermore, in an age when other governments were bringing out freedom of information acts, the British government actually tried to do the opposite, introducing in 1979 the Protection of Official Information Bill to toughen official secrecy! This audacious measure was withdrawn as a result of the furore it aroused.

'Reforming' section 2 In January 1988 the government unprecedentedly placed a three-line whip (resisted by nearly 100 MPs) to kill a private member's bill introduced by Conservative MP Richard Shepherd. Reform was promised, but the white paper which duly appeared the following June (HMSO 1988) was highly disappointing. Critics (including Shepherd himself) alleged that the proposed reforms were more repressive than ever. No past or present employee of the security services, or of GCHQ, could ever disclose anything about their work. There was to be no defence on the grounds of public interest or that the information was already in the public domain. It was clear that individuals who had disclosed official wrongdoing in the past (like Clive Ponting, Cathy Massiter and John Stalker) would have been blocked under the new provisions.

The Official Secrets Bill appeared in November 1988 and, although the discredited section 2 was finally laid to rest, the position had not really been relaxed at all. Those charged under the old section (such as Sarah Tisdall) could still be prosecuted, as could journalists receiving official information.

Classified information

Section 2 has not been the only instrument of suppression. Franks reported 61 other statutes criminalizing the disclosure of information, though none punishing unnecessary secrecy.

It might be expected that MPs, as popular representatives, would enjoy certain rights to information, but this is very far from the case: mandarins are at their most wily when thwarting MPs, using various devices to evade both parliamentary questions and scrutiny committees (see pp. 297–301).

Technically Parliament could compel disclosure through its power to punish for contempt, but this power is rendered defunct by party discipline.

Official secrecy and the media

Official secrecy is a matter of central concern to the media, the *raison d'être* of which is disseminating information. However, the media are largely instruments of the establishment and bureaucrats can use this avenue to propagate the official line. A tidal wave of paper pouring from Whitehall is washed up on the beaches of Fleet Street and Broadcasting House each day; many journalists live by the source, faithfully trotting out the platitudes in the press releases, often using the very same sentences and phrases. So house-trained are they that officials have organized them into a formal club, the *Lobby*, complete with rules and regulations (Tunstall 1970). They meet in the Members' Lobby of the House of Commons where ministers throw titbits of information under a cowardly cloak of anonymity. Those stepping out of line and attributing words to particular people will have their exclusive membership cards removed. Anthony Howard likened them to sad prostitutes, waiting patiently to act as instruments for the gratification of ministers (Hennessy et al. 1984: 40). Of course not all journalists are lobby hacks and Whitehall poodles. Some, like Paul Foot and Duncan Campbell, crusade valiantly in the cause of the non-official version, although once officials begin to be alarmed a number of muzzles can be used. The beauty of the official secrets legislation is that it is an offence to *receive* information as well as to dispense it.

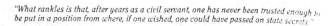

"What rankles is that, after years as a civil servant, one has never been trusted enough to be put in a position from where, if one wished, one could have passed on state secrets."

Reproduced by permission of *Punch*

The D-notice system This offers means of overt government control over reporting matters pertaining to (D)efence. It was introduced in 1906 as an alternative to formal press censorship and, although sometimes described as self-censorship or 'responsible journalism', it serves the interests of the establishment. The notices are issued by the Defence Press and Broadcasting Committee, composed of representatives of the media and senior civil servants and served by a full-time Whitehall secretary who is constantly available for advice. As a non-statutory body it relies on the media bosses playing the game in a sportsmanlike manner. Yet the system is abused in order to hide political embarrassment, and some of the braver souls of Fleet Street have refused to be silenced, resenting the suggestion that they themselves are unable to exercise responsible judgement.

A la recherche du temps perdu: ministerial memoirs

The publication of memoirs of political figures rarely poses any threat to security, yet the attempts to suppress them are often reminiscent of a Savoy opera. This is not surprising when it is realized that one of the most important reasons for secrecy is to avoid embarrassment in high places. During the Crossman Diaries case a further secret was revealed when we discovered the existence of unwritten 'guidelines' produced by the civil service. This gentlemen's agreement declared that memoirs should not disclose arguments in cabinet meetings, discussions on civil service appointments, discussions between ministers, and advice given to ministers by civil servants. In other words, they were merely to add to the boring, anodyne corpus of treatises supporting the cherished myths of the authorized version. Part of this code involved the inspection of proposed memoirs by the Cabinet Secretary.

Of course *Spycatcher* represents the apogee of memoirs cases, the Conservative government literally pursuing its prey to the antipodes. Here it was possible to argue that national security was involved because Peter Wright, the author, had worked for MI5. While the book was being freely circulated throughout the capitals of Eastern and Western Europe, as well as the Americas, the po-faced servants of the establishment were still trying, like obsessive school prefects, to conceal it from the eyes of their own people.

What I wanted to do was to show Wilson that we'd got him and that we wanted him to resign.

Peter Wright (former member of MI5), referring to a secret MI5 file on Harold Wilson, TV interview reported in the *Guardian* (14 Oct. 1988)

Power in Whitehall: Disobedient Servants?

The liberal democratic constitution portrays politicians as the masters in Whitehall, but in reality the relationship between ministers and mandarins is far from simple. The idea of a subservient bureaucracy is logically necessary to liberal democracy. If the civil servants are not the neutral instruments of the elected representatives, the whole system of cabinet government, Parliament and elections becomes a sham. Around the turn of the century the German sociologist Max Weber, a liberal troubled by the decline of liberal culture, noted in some despair the tendency towards rule by public bureaucracy in developed states:

> It is obvious that technically the large modern state is absolutely dependent upon a bureaucratic basis. The larger the state ... the more unconditionally this is the case.
>
> (Weber 1978: 971)

He warned of the horror of unimaginative, unelected officialdom trussing the body politic in red-taped bondage, and one of the central problems he addressed was curbing such power in the interests of liberal democracy. He constructed a theoretical *ideal-type* model of a bureaucracy recruited on the basis of merit, its members bound by clear impersonal rules, rigidly defined roles, and a disciplined hierarchy channelling power to the elected rulers at the top. Apologists for the British system see in the civil service many of these features, and Weber himself was one of its admirers.

The view of the civil service as *apolitical* and *neutral*, able to serve governments of left or right with equal fidelity, rests on the belief that there is a clear distinction between the functions of **policy-making** and **policy implementation**, and on the doctrine of individual **ministerial responsibility**. We shall examine these and then move on to consider in detail the nature of the relationship between ministers and mandarins.

Look Sir Humphrey. Whatever we ask the Minister, he says it is an administrative question for you. And whatever we ask you, you say is a policy question for the Minister.

House of Commons select committee questioning Permanent Secretary Sir Humphrey Appleby in J. Lynn and A. Jay, *The Complete Yes Minister* (based on the TV series) (1981: 336)

The politics–administration dichotomy

The belief that politics and administration can be separated underlies much writing on the public bureaucracy. The view was authoritatively enunciated in 1887 by Woodrow Wilson, who was concerned about corruption in

American public life. He argued that administration should be placed on a rational basis, divorced from the sordid world of political skullduggery. Yet the distinction is quite untenable in practical terms: no public servant implements a policy in a neutral, instrumental way, and all policy directives must be interpreted in the light of particular circumstances. In this respect the mandarins are, like judges and the police (see chapters 17 and 18), expected to exercise discretion in a politically significant manner.

Individual ministerial responsibility

Lying at the very heart of liberal democratic theory, this doctrine articulates the relationship between minister and department. Because ministers are elected, it is they alone who are *responsible* to the outside world (through Parliament) for departmental actions. Various corollaries follow from this: civil servants are not themselves supposed to speak concerning their work; they must remain anonymous; and when praise or blame is apportioned, it must fall on the minister who should, in cases of serious error, resign like an officer and gentleman. The Crichel Down affair (see p. 530) caused widespread disquiet over the doctrine.

Despite its detailed exposition in textbooks, the convention is largely illusory, honoured more in the breach than the commission. Mandarins are increasingly to be found addressing the media, their roles are overtly politicized, their names are becoming known to the public (Cabinet Secretary Sir Robert Armstrong found his a household word through his trials and tribulations in the *Spycatcher* affair), and they are likely to find themselves publicly blamed, as in the Vehicle and General case in 1971 and the Courtline crash in 1975. In the latter case, an official enquiry produced a hierarchy of bureaucratic shame, indicting humble officials and entirely absolving ministers, while in the Westland fiasco, civil servant Collette Bowe became famous as an instrument in the devious political strategy. In 1972, the governor of Holloway Prison (a public servant) was publicly rebuked by the Home Secretary for an 'error of judgement' in taking Myra Hindley, one of the 'moors murderers', for an early morning walk.

Moreover, ministers are now loath to attone for departmental sin by accepting the loaded pistol. In the Maze Prison breakout case, Northern Ireland Secretary James Prior sweated it out, producing the extraordinary result of the resignation of the prison governor instead. Although Leon Brittan resigned (belatedly) after the Westland affair, it was widely felt that Mrs Thatcher's office was at the epicentre of the affair, but she remained characteristically resolute in the face of calls for resignation. In contrast, Lord Carrington took the honourable way out after his servants at the Foreign Office failed to take due cognizance of developments leading to the Falklands war.

Yet despite evidence that the convention is largely mythical, the rhetoric of politicians and commentators pays it continuing tribute. Why is this? The answer lies in its political utility. It can be used variously to shield mandarins from criticism, resist civil service reform, evade parliamentary scrutiny, and as the basis for official secrecy. For politicians, the question of resignation is determined by political expediency not constitutional imperative; thus Carrington and Brittan were expendable, Thatcher as party leader, figurehead and inspiration, was not.

Mandarins and ministers: 'Yes Minister'

The nature of **bureaucratic power** is manifest in mandarins' day-to-day relationships with ministers. Does the evidence support the liberal-democratic view that they are the obedient servants of their political masters? According to some it does. On the basis of the experience of the post-war Labour government, Attlee is widely quoted as an apologist:

> I always found them perfectly loyal . . . That's the civil service tradition, a great tradition. They carry out the policy of any given government.
>
> (Williams 1969: 79)

This is a typical ex-politician's statement and it echoes through to the present day. In evidence to the Expenditure Committee Edward Heath avowed that in his experience the civil servants were definitely all 'under ministerial control' (Expenditure Committee 1977: para. 1877), while Harold Wilson declared that any minister unable to master his civil servants 'ought to go' (para. 1924). On gaining office, Richard Crossman confided to his diary with satisfaction:

> Now at last I was a Minister in charge of an important Department and I could take decisions [and] lay down the law.
>
> (Crossman 1976: 293)

The orthodoxy is also supported by academic researchers and journalists, Heady concluding that the mandarins preferred strong ministers who gave them a firm lead (1975: 131–5).

Mandarins and ministers: 'No Minister'?

Yet there is much reason to doubt the passive civil servant thesis. At a personal level the mandarins have numerous advantages over ministers.

- They are highly educated, long experienced, street (or corridor) wise to the ways of Whitehall.
- They have access to information and are able to control its flow to the ministerial desk.
- They have well-established connections with powerful interests impinging on the work of the department.
- They possess detailed historical knowledge of departmental policy.

- They are considerably more numerous than ministers and can work together informally and in committees (of which there are hundreds) within and across departmental boundaries.
- They enjoy great security of tenure, comfortable salaries (figure 12.6), and come from the confident upper classes, with a conviction of natural superiority.

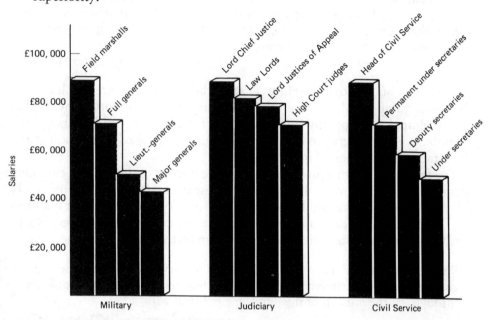

Figure 12.6 Civil service salaries compared with the military and the judiciary, 1989

Source: Based on data from *The Economist* (25 Feb. 1989)

Moreover, for ministers the support of civil servants is an absolute necessity: they answer parliamentary questions, write speeches, arrange meetings, draft endless memos and reports, and generally organize his or her life. The width of a departmental ambit means that no minister (or ministerial team) can possibly be aware of everything going on, even if blessed with the wisdom of Solomon, the strength of Hercules, and the tenacity of Robert Bruce.

It is not surprising, therefore, that an alternative body of evidence on the subject can be found. This comes not from textbooks, government publications, or officially sanctioned memoirs of the smug and cautious, but from exposés of those bold enough to publish against the wishes of the establishment. Among the most notable were the Crossman *Diaries*. From an initial state of euphoria Crossman was to feel that he had, as if in a horror movie, sought refuge in the very room where the vampire was hiding, and the accounts of his enervating battles with his formidable permanent secretary, Dame Evelyn Sharp, should not be read by those of a nervous disposition. Barbara Castle's diaries give an equally frank account of the realities of office.

To these may be added confessions of civil servants who have come out of the bureaucratic closet. Brian Sedgemore, first a senior civil servant and then an MP working as parliamentary private secretary to Tony Benn, was uniquely qualified to provide insight into the private world of public policy. From him we learn of the

> arrogant and subtle way in which they dealt with ministers when it mattered, . . . developing departmental policies which weak ministers could call their own, using delaying tactics, skilfully suborning powers of patronage that belonged to ministers.
>
> (Sedgemore 1980: 26)

For Kellner and Crowther-Hunt (1980) the mandarins are no less than 'Britain's ruling class'. Through these sources we enter a world making that of Sir Humphrey Appleby and Jim Hacker seem tame, and bearing little resemblance to the seraglio of caliphs and eunuchs evoked by textbooks and the establishment-minded inside dopesters.

The final proof of this pudding must be the flavour of the policies emerging from the Whitehall oven. During the post-war era these have consistently followed a centrist line and Labour governments, regardless of their manifestos, have pursued economic and social strategies generally acceptable to establishment interests. An Expenditure Committee report confirmed that:

> Some departments have firmly held policy views . . . When they are changed, the department will often try and reinstate its own policies through . . . the erosion of the minister's political will.
>
> (Expenditure Committee 1977: para. 137)

The potential influence of civil servants must be seen as a profoundly important conclusion, because ordinary people do not vote for civil servants and cannot remove them from office.

Managing the mandarins: the service in the 1980s

While it is clear that the elitist background of the higher civil service ensures that an arm of the establishment remains securely in government whichever party is in power, it does not follow that all bureaucrats are right wing, or that only Labour governments will be frustrated by bureaucratic obstructionism. The newer departments, associated with the welfare state and Keynesianism (see p. 349), have a vested interest in its maintenance. A body of right-wing thought (public choice theory) depicts bureaucrats as incorrigible wasters of public money, intent on enlarging their empires and 'oversupplying' their services (Niskanen 1973). Hence, the question of combating bureaucracy exercised the Thatcher government of the 1980s, and various attempts were made to limit its power, including the introduction of private-sector-style management, the removal of certain functions from the civil service in the process of 'hiving off', the politicization of the mandarins, and the use of ministerial advisers.

Management: private lessons? A major theme in civil service reform has been concerned with management, or its absence. The debate is by no means an apolitical consideration of efficiency techniques; it is about the structure of power. Put simply, governments have tried to induce mandarins to spend more time running their departments, and less on the policy-making functions. For the traditional mandarins, **managerialism** has been a life-or-death issue.

Calls for reform came long before the Thatcher era, including the 1961 Plowden Report and the 1968 Fulton Report. The creation of the Civil Service Department and the Civil Service College in the 1960s was intended to foster a new private-sector-style management ethos. In 1970, Edward Heath promoted the 'Selsdon Man' ideal of efficiency by introducing a team of businessmen into Whitehall. However, none of these reforms had any significant impact; they were skilfully neutralized by the mandarins, who preferred the intrigue of managing their ministers to the tedium of managing their departments.

However, Thatcherism, with its deification of the private sector, particularly as manifested in the world of big grocery, was to send tremors to the very foundations of Whitehall. This was a necessary part of New Right strategy since the new regime, intent on parting from the post-war consensus, needed more than any before it to break the back of Whitehall's legendary capacity to resist. Margaret Thatcher, as a radical ideologue, wanted a civil service which would obey, not argue and debate, and she threatened civil servants in a multiplicity of ways. As an early move, Sir Derek Rayner of Marks and Spencer's became in 1979 her special adviser on efficiency. He had already served as one of Heath's disillusioned businessmen and knew much of the wily ways of the mandarins. A system of 'scrutinies' was introduced with specially selected teams of young civil servants probing the practices of their elders.

> I made my first million by the time I was 30. What have you lot ever done?
>
> Allegedly Michael Heseltine's opening remarks to his mandarins upon arrival as Secretary of State for Defence, quoted by Katherine Whitehorn, in the *Observer* (16 March 1986)

In the changing climate, management systems – known variously by strange names and acronyms, such as MINIs, FMI and Joubert systems – began to proliferate, all intended to transform civil servants from administrators and policy advisers into managers and 'doers'. The environment of Whitehall became inhospitable to bureaucratic life-forms; at jolly parties at number 10, permanent secretaries learned to hold their views, like their vols-au-vent, close to their chests and leave as early as possible.

Hiving off Between 1979 and 1988 the size of the service was slimmed from over 700,000 to around 600,000. The ideological obsession with reducing the size of the public sector had further manifestations in a report in February 1988 from a committee of enquiry under Sir Robin Ibbs, head of Mrs Thatcher's Efficiency Unit, recommending **hiving off** parts of the civil service to become semi-autonomous agencies outside the framework of ministerial responsibility. The kind of agencies envisaged included the employment services section of the Department of Employment (responsible for job centres), the Meteorological Office, the Stationery Office, the Passport Department, the Driver and Vehicle Licencing Directorate, and the royal parks (see p. 446). Ironically, similar recommendations had already been made in 1968 by the somewhat left-wing Fulton Committee.

Advising ministers Repeated attempts by politicians to instigate alternative advice systems are eloquent testimony to their need, but the steps of Whitehall were long littered with the sun-baked bones of personal **ministerial advisers** who had come up against a bureaucratic wall of impeccably polite intransigence.

Only during the two world wars had advisers made any impression, suggesting that when the pressure is on the civil service is unable to cope with crisis. However, the 'outsiders' were quickly dispatched afterwards. One of the most notable of the post-war breed was Thomas Balogh (later Lord), brought in by Wilson in 1964 to advise on the economy. His experience proved exceedingly frustrating as the civil service systematically froze him out through a series of 'Yes Minister' ploys such as withholding documents and holding meetings behind his back. Heath's team of businessmen encountered a similar series of tight bureaucratic lips and cold pin-striped shoulders. The 1974 Labour government permitted cabinet ministers two advisers each, and Wilson also set up a special policy unit at number 10 headed by Bernard Donoughue from the LSE.

Although the Fulton and the English Committees had seen some value in the use of advisers, it was during the Thatcher era that the development was taken furthest. Advisers appointed during the 1980s became in some cases as well known to the public as politicians, with the hard-line monetarist, Professor Alan Waters, a familiar media figure. In the 1980s, a state of fear induced by the black cloud of anti-bureaucratic feeling emanating from Downing Street ensured that mandarins could no longer treat with disdain those close to the ministers.

Politicizing the service In order to secure a civil service which would obey, not argue, Mrs Thatcher took unprecedented interest in senior appointments. With her 'one of us' approach to personnel management, she was able to evaporate ideological dampness from the upper echelons. In this she was assisted by Cabinet Secretary Sir Robert Armstrong, who after the disbanding of the CSD and the early retirement of Sir (now Lord) Ian Bancroft, assumed the additional role of head of the civil service. A number of important positions became vacant during the early years, and other incumbents were encouraged to go. Sir Douglas Wass, the head of the Treasury, was, like Sir Gordon Richardson, Governor of the Bank of England, soon out of favour and was replaced upon his retirement in 1983 by Peter Middleton, a Treasury official who had caught the Prime Minister's eye.

Prudent survivors recognized that 'if you can't beat 'em', there remained only one sensible thing to do. Monetarists and managerialists began to emerge from the closets and oak panelling of Whitehall. By mid-1980s Lord Bancroft was able to note how the Whitehall 'grovel count' had risen (*Guardian*, 12 Nov. 1985). By the end of the decade over two-thirds of the mandarin class had been appointed under the Thatcher regime and all ministers were following their leader in taking a close interest in departmental appointments. A further means of taming the mandarins was the appointment to top positions of people from outside, as in the US spoils system. Sir John Hoskyns argued that industry and commerce should fill no less than two or three hundred such posts.

Conclusion: Whither the Mandarins?

The civil service plays a central role in politics and its greatest defence against the attentions of reformers has been its alleged political neutrality, in which prominent Labour politicians place their faith. However this neutrality has seemed real only because the political system has never thrown up a government with policies requiring a dramatic break with the central orthodoxy. Throughout the post-war consensus the neutrality thesis remained, as Laski had observed of the pre-war period, untested 'by the need to support a policy which . . . might well challenge the traditional values for which it has stood' (1938: 317). Laski believed that if such challenge were to occur, a point of crisis would be reached, though he thought, contrary to events, that this would involve a government of the left.

The movements towards a greater *politicization* of the service represent an insidious process of change, inevitably inviting comparison with Europe and the US. The use of advisers is redolent of the French *ministerial cabinet* system, while political appointments resemble the US spoils system or the West German *polititsche Beamten*. In the short term it could produce some new problems for politicians. What, for example, would a Labour leader do if confronted, not merely with an upper-class corps of disdainful mandarins, but a set of hard-nosed monetarists? Would these have to be retired off in favour of committed socialists? In the longer term it is clear that Thatcherist *ad hoc* developments could lead to momentous constitutional changes.

Key points

- The civil service is part of the executive, headed by the elected government through a system of ministerial posts.
- The key period in the formation of the modern civil service was the mid-nineteenth century, when the bourgeoisie used their new political and economic power to gain control of the state apparatus through a pattern of reforms which replaced nepotism and corruption with meritocracy.
- The modern civil service is said in the theory of liberal democracy to be permanent, politically neutral and anonymous. All these features can be critically questioned today.
- The mandarin class of civil servants are not mere ministerial puppets. They have traditionally enjoyed a significant role in shaping government policy, and can even be said to dominate their putative political masters.
- A key feature in understanding the role of the civil service in the political system has to be the pattern of recruitment. Studies have repeatedly demonstrated that the bias in favour of the public school and Oxbridge candidates deliberately sought in the nineteenth-century reforms has been maintained up to the present.
- Whitehall has a village-like atmosphere characterized by obsessional secrecy.
- In spite of their backgrounds and continuing social contact, civil servants are not necessarily right wing. They have a considerable personal stake in the welfare state, which is the most important factor in accounting for the expansion of the service.

Review your understanding of the following terms and concepts

bureaucracy	policy-making
civil servant	policy implementation
mandarin	ministerial responsibility
specialist and generalist	politics–administration dichotomy
meritocracy	bureaucratic power
official secrecy	managerialism
public interest	hiving off
Freedom of Information Act	ministerial adviser
D-notice system	

Assignment

Study the extract from the *Independent* and answer the following questions.

% mark

1 Why does the writer suggest that 'real-life Sir Humphreys' are drifting further from the stereotype? 5

2 Would you agree that the top civil service positions represent 'the highest echelon of the British establishment'? 5

Risen from a golden chair

Real-life Sir Humphreys — the permanent secretaries who head government departments and rule over Whitehall — are drifting further from the stereotype of the *Yes, Minister* television series every year that Margaret Thatcher stays in power. They are getting younger (in an élite stratum where anyone under 50 is positively youthful). They are less anonymous (in a world where a passport-sized photograph in a broadsheet newspaper was once regarded as excessive publicity). They are, most importantly, becoming more actively engaged in reforming the very system that they serve. Who are they? How are they picked and groomed? And who are the next candidates for elevation to the highest echelon of the British establishment?

Promotion is rare in the stratosphere of civil service ambition, for the simple reason that civil servants retire when they are 60, almost never earlier or later. As increasingly younger candidates are appointed to the top jobs, Whitehall watchers are beginning to wonder when the logs will jam. The appointment of Sir Robin Butler, as the Cabinet Secretary, Head of the Home Civil Service, and successor to Lord (Robert) Armstrong, effectively seals up the top job until 1998. He leapfrogged his seniors to take over at 50, becoming one of the youngest among his colleagues elsewhere in Whitehall, all of whom knew from that moment that their prospects of winning the seat next to the Cabinet table had vanished.

But some things continue unchanged. The vast bulk of the permanent secretaryhood is still male: there is only one woman — Dame Anne Mueller, second permanent secretary at the Treasury — and at 58 she probably has too short a remaining career to reach the very top.

One or two, like Terry Heiser, 56, at the Department of the Environment, have risen from state schools and the clerical ranks. Mr Heiser, though by no means a Thatcherite in personal politics, was singled out by the Prime Minister as a prime example of the "doer" qualities she energetically seeks in civil servants. Others, like Peter Levene (46, permanent secretary in charge of defence procurement at the MoD) or Sir Terry Burns (44, second permanent secretary and economic adviser at the Treasury), have entered as mid-life Whitehall outsiders from the world of private business or academia. Infusing outsiders into the closed Whitehall world has been the other main strand in Mrs Thatcher's reform ambitions.

But most are still Oxbridge-educated. Of the 32, 13 were at Oxford and eight at Cambridge; three were at the London School of Economics. Four of those from Oxford, numbering among the highest ranks, took the time-honoured route of studying classics: Sir Robin himself; Sir Michael Quinlan, 58, at the MoD; Peter Gregson, 52, at the Department of Energy; and Brian Unwin, also 52, running Customs and Excise.

Independent, 30 Aug. 1988

3 What tradition appears to guarantee that Sir Robin Butler can expect to remain Cabinet Secretary until 1998? Is this degree of permanence a good thing? 20

4 Why do you think there is only one woman among the top permanent secretaries? 20

5 How significant do you regard the presence of Peter Levine and Sir Terry Burns amongst the mandarins? Does their inclusion promise any sea-change in the character of the British civil service? 20

6 Does the extract justify the opening claim that the civil service is   30
   changing?

Questions for discussion

1 How useful is it to characterize the world of Whitehall as a village?
2 What factors lead to the view that civil servants will tend to dominate
   ministers in their professional relationship?
3 'Individual ministerial responsibility is a convention honoured more in the
   breach than in the commission.' Discuss.
4 How did the Northcote–Trevelyan reforms reflect the power structure of
   nineteenth-century British society?
5 Examine the political and administrative implications of hiving off certain civil
   service functions to semi-autonomous agencies.
6 What might be the long-term effects of the introduction of a 'spoils system'
   for appointing top civil servants in Britain?
7 Examine how the Thatcher government of the 1980s changed the role and
   structure of the higher civil service.

Topic for debate

This house believes that the real danger posed by the British civil service is not
bureaucratic rule, but bureaucratic capture by the economic elite.
   or
This house believes that the model of the British civil service is no longer able to
meet the needs of the modern state.

Further reading

Aubrey, C. (1981) *Who's Watching You.*
A disturbing account of the oppressive working of the Official Secrets Acts by one of
the defendants in the notorious ABC trial.

Castle, B. (1980) *The Castle Diaries 1974–6.*
Diaries and memoirs are often the best source of information on the secretive world
of Whitehall. Barbara Castle was one of the most energetic politicians of her era and
her account is lively and perceptive.

Crossman, R. H. S. (1975–7) *Diaries of a Cabinet Minister.*
Richard Crossman was not only a cabinet minister, he was an academic with very
strong views on government in general and on the minister–civil servant relationship
in particular.

Drewry, G. and Butcher, T. (1988) *The Civil Service Today.*
A highly readable and authoritative account.

Fulton, Lord (1968) *The Civil Service, Vol. 1: Report of the Committee.*
A detailed critique of the civil service since the reforms of the nineteenth century.

Contains the text of the Northcote–Trevelyan Report.

Fry, G. K. (1985) *The Changing Civil Service*.
A lively modern approach to the civil service, giving a scholarly summary of basic information, and with a critical edge.

Gray, A. and Jenkins, W. I. (1985) *Administrative Politics in British Government*.
Although by British authors, this book, in the style of Heclo and Wildavsky (see p. 407), is a rather livelier account of life in Whitehall than is common.

Greenwood, J. and Wilson, D. (1989) *Public Administration in Britain Today*.
The clearest and most readable account of the machinery of the British state available today. Essential reading.

Hennessy, P. (1990) *Whitehall*.
An immensely entertaining *tour de force*; not to be missed. The world of Whitehall is illuminated as never before.

Kellner, P. and Crowther-Hunt, Lord (1980) *The Civil Servants*.
Lord Crowther-Hunt was, in his former incarnation, Norman Hunt, the driving spirit of the Fulton Committee. This study casts a jaundiced eye on the official response to the report.

Kingdom, J. E. (ed.) (1989) *The Civil Service in Liberal Democracies*.
An introduction to the civil service in Britain and a number of other countries.

Mallalieu, J. P. W. (1941) *Passed to You Please*.
A short early polemic against overweening officialdom, with a penetrating introduction by Harold Laski.

Michael, J. (1982) *The Politics of Secrecy*.
Written by an American living in Britain, this notes with alarm the 'routine secrecy' of British government, which acts more like a private firm than a democratically responsible body.

For light relief

E. M. Forster, *A Passage to India*.
A study of the manners of the English in the Indian Civil Service.

J. Lynn and A. Jay (1981) *The Complete Yes Minister*.
Edited version of the television series. Perhaps not as astonishing as the real thing in the form of the Crossman *Diaries*, but shorter.

C. P. Snow, *Corridors of Power*.
While others find passion in love and sex, Snow finds it in the ambitions and intrigues of the men in pin-striped trousers. The title added a phrase to the English language.

Anthony Trollope, *The Pallisers*.
Enter the world of the nineteenth-century political establishment, with its intrigue, romance and arrogant power.

13

Getting and Spending: the Politics of Public Expenditure and the Economy

It is quite impossible to understand politics without appreciating the financial dimension. The chapter has three main sections. First we examine how the state determines its expenditure levels and raises money. This entails a study of the **nature of public expenditure** and its purposes in modern government. We then turn to the means whereby the level of public finance is fixed, how the money is raised, and the public accounting process. Next we note how public expenditure policy is concerned with more than simply financing the state; it has been used as an instrument of **economic management**, and we must therefore examine the nature and evolution of the **capitalist economy**. The final section assesses the extent to which the British approach to public expenditure can in itself been seen as a factor contributing to the post-war pattern of **economic decline**.

The nature of public expenditure

Put at its most simple, **public expenditure** is the money used by the agencies of the state in its multifarious operations from the waging of war to the emptying of the nation's dustbins. Its absolute level is beyond intuitive grasp – planned expenditure for 1988–9 was a mind-boggling £183,000 million. The lion's share of this is raised through taxation, supplemented with borrowing and through trading enterprises. Thus the state draws money from society, passes it from one agency to another, and returns it to society in the form of services and grants in a complex network of financial flows (see figure 13.1).

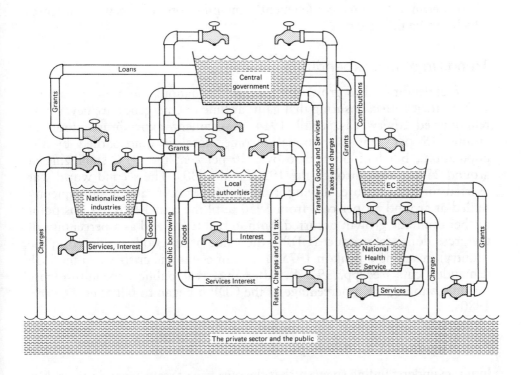

Figure 13.1 The flow of public expenditure

However, a rather more profound view of public expenditure conceives its true nature in more philosophical terms. Thus it may be seen as an expression of our propensity to live collectively in a community – one of the most important features explaining our survival on earth. A community is cemented by public expenditure. It ensures national security through defence, preserves and transmits our cultural heritage through education and the arts, and facilitates what many see as the mark of a civilized society – a welfare state in which the community collectively accepts responsibility for the care of all its members through taxation.

Public expenditure lies at the heart of politics in an ideological sense in that some people seek to deny the collective nature of our psyche. These are the **individualists**. They do not agree that the rich should be taxed to support the weak, and find their ideological home along the right of the political spectrum. Whether they would fare well alone in the jungle (or even outside the world of the Freemasons) is a moot point; Aristotle believed that we are by nature political animals, and it is certainly true that few people choose the

---

No man is an Island, entire in itself; every man is a piece of a Continent, a part of the main.

John Donne (1573–1631; English poet), *Devotions* (1624)

life of hermits, 'solitary confinement' remaining one of the worst tortures which can be inflicted.

Trends in public expenditure

Public expenditure has grown inexorably throughout the present century, with a ratchet effect ensuring that gains at time of emergency are never fully relinquished afterwards. Until 1914 government expenditure stood at around 15 per cent of national income (total income earned by the population), but had climbed to over 50 per cent by 1918, stabilizing at around 25 per cent through the 1920s and 1930s. The second world war exerted further pressure, driving it up to 75 per cent, and it subsequently settled at around 35 per cent from 1950 until the mid-1960s. At this point further dramatic growth occurred, both in real terms and as a percentage of the gross domestic product (GDP – the value of all goods produced in the country), reaching a peak in 1975, a time of economic crisis when the IMF demanded cuts (see pp. 393–4). After this, real public expenditure rose steadily, although as a percentage of the GDP it began to fall after the early 1980s.

The purposes of public expenditure

Intuitive understanding suggests that the purpose of state expenditure is, like that of a household, to finance its activities. Figures 13.2 and 13.5 show how it is used in two ways: providing services and making grants to others (**transfer payments**) in order to increase their purchasing power (pensions, student grants, and so on). Another purpose is less self-evident and has no analogue with family budgeting. The colossal scale of state finance means that it must disturb the balance in the rest of the private capitalist economy. For this reason, government is able to use its taxation and spending powers deliberately to influence the economy in what is termed **fiscal policy**. When post-war governments have made their getting and spending decisions, economic objectives have been as much in their mind as the services the money is intended to fund. The following sections will consider these two purposes in more detail.

Paying for the State

The services provided by the state must be paid for and figure 13.2 indicates the various broad areas of public expenditure and the relative cost of each. You will have noticed in figure 13.1 a number of taps interrupting the financial flows, and a key question of politics considers who has the power to open and close these. This is by no means a new question; it has been at the heart of British constitutional history and remains at the epicentre of modern political debate.

Controlling public expenditure: developing the machinery

We saw in chapter 9 how public expenditure lay at the heart of much constitutional development (pp. 255–7) and was the mainspring for exerting increased parliamentary control over the executive. The sovereign's crown was indeed hollow without a supply of funds, and as Parliament became the effective payer of the piper it sought to call the royal tune. By the time of Elizabeth I it had acquired a control over taxation which was to be consolidated in the Glorious Revolution of 1688. Since this time Parliament has remained nominally in control of public finance, although as we are about to discover, this is in practice largely a fiction.

Further important reforms came in the 1780s under the stimulus of Edmund Burke. Of particular significance was the creation of the **Consolidated Fund** in 1787, gathering together a rather muddled collection of public accounts into a single one into which all state revenue would flow, and from which all expenditure by the various departments would be drawn. This is in effect the government's bank account and is lodged with the Bank of England. The reform was intended to simplify public accounting and thereby improve parliamentary control. Although taking place through technical, boring-sounding processes, the control of state expenditure and fund-raising is about who gets what, when and how; it lies at the heart of political life. The system of public finance was mainly a nineteenth-century invention designed to serve a *laissez-faire* capitalist economy, fashioned by the industrial bourgeoisie as part of its greater creation – the liberal-democratic state. The way in which public expenditure is controlled can only be understood in terms of the nature of the British economy itself.

Britain's capitalist economy

In a capitalist economy such as Britain's, the means of providing the basic conditions needed by all citizens to sustain their very lives (land, raw materials, factories, machines, and so on) are for the most part owned by a relatively small proportion of the population in their private capacities, rather than by the public at large. These owners are termed the **capitalists**. Although it may be argued that since the second world war we have had a **mixed economy**, with certain key industries owned and managed by the state (the public sector), this mix has always been designed to maintain the dominance of the private sector (Miliband 1984: 95).

Capitalism has proved itself a particularly effective mode of production, with an incomparable ability to apply technology and expand voraciously to find new materials and markets. Although releasing a dynamic entrepreneurial spirit within mankind, and enhancing the material living standards of countless millions, the achievement is not without its costs, which have important consequences for the political system.

> [The capitalist bourgeoisie] has accomplished wonders far surpassing Egyptian pyramids, Roman aqueducts, and Gothic cathedrals ... It draws all nations into civilisation ... has created enormous cities ... rescued a considerable part of the population from the idiocy of rural life ... and ... has created more massive and more colossal productive forces than have all previous generations together.
>
> Karl Marx, *The Communist Manifesto* (1848)

The development of capitalism The capitalist mode of production first emerged in agriculture by replacing feudalism. Peasants were deprived of their historic rights to use land to produce crops for themselves in the notorious eighteenth-century enclosure movement, when landowners forced them to work over larger areas, using new machinery, for a wage. The industrial revolution saw the rise of industrial capitalism with large-scale mass production in the factories, which spawned the unholy urban centres.

" Oh, Mabel, is it not dreadful ?   What a miserable place to bring up such a lovely dog !"

Source: Mary Evans Picture Library

The capitalist order even brought with it a new philosophy – *utilitarianism* – an individualistic credo articulated by the philosopher Jeremy Bentham, who was himself a rather eccentric egotist. This rejected the idea of shared social obligations amongst members of society, elevating the rational pursuit of individual self-interest as the main objective in life. It argued that if everyone pursued their own personal interests the whole society would actually be better off; that is, the sum total of utility (or happiness) would be maximized.

Man is not a solitary animal, and so long as social life survives, self-realization cannot be the supreme principle of ethics.

Betrand Russell (1872–1970; philosopher), *History of Western Philosophy* (3rd edn, 1961)

Although individualism became the dominant principle of capitalism, it should be noted that not everyone subscribed to it. The Victorian era was also one of paternalistic philanthropy. Robert Owen (1771–1858), for example, sought to establish a form of cooperative socialism at his cotton mills at New Lanark, demonstrating that good wages and communal life were not incompatible with profitability.

The Protestant work ethic and the ethos of parsimony Another important part of capitalism is the concept of **accumulation**. When the early capitalists acquired wealth, they did not use it in the grand manner of merchants and landowners of old to make their lives comfortable or even voluptuous, but tended towards frugality and self-denial in order to amass greater wealth, like Dickens's Ebenezer Scrooge. In this way they could invest in yet more capital and amass further wealth quite beyond what they could ever need for personal survival. The cumulative effect was to consolidate the position of the capital owners and their families, forming a class which became increasingly dominant and exclusive.

The public be dammed. I am working for my shareholders.

William Henry Vanderbilt (1821–85; US millionaire railway owner), refusing to answer a reporter asking questions on behalf of the public

---

The importance of this aspect of capitalism was stressed by the sociologist Max Weber, who attributed it in large measure to religion – to Protestantism, or more particularly to the Calvinistic puritanism within Protestantism. The effect of this **Protestant work ethic** was, in Weber's view, to explain the ascendancy of capitalism in Western Europe by adding religious zeal to the lure of profit. This parsimonious ethic was to inform the approach to public expenditure. The prime goal was to become that of Victorian prudence – a *balanced budget* as advocated by Mr Micawber.

> Annual income twenty pounds, annual expenditure nineteen nineteen six, result happiness. Annual income twenty pounds, annual expenditure twenty pounds ought and six, result misery.
>
> Mr Micawber in Charles Dickens's novel *David Copperfield* (1849–50)

The Gladstonian era of public finance

Against this background, the key figure in a series of rigorous reforms was Gladstone, who determined that government finance should be as tightly controlled by the bourgeois paymasters as were their own prudently managed businesses. Public expenditure was viewed in the same terms as that of a family (or a firm). Money was spent, money was earned, and the main objective of control was to ensure that expenditure was as low as possible, and that it did not exceed receipts. The aim was to evolve a system which would damage the capitalists' profits as little as possible, taking just enough to keep open the trade routes and contain the potentially unruly masses at home.

The system was conceived in terms of an annual cycle which would balance expenditure and tax. Nominally based on Parliament, at its very heart was Her Majesty's Treasury, the centrepiece of Whitehall, and the Bank of England.

The Treasury Of all the Whitehall departments the Treasury stands nearest to Westminster both geographically (on the corner of Great George Street and Parliament Street) and in spirit (with the Prime Minister holding the formal title First Lord of the Treasury). It is one of the great centres of power, controlling almost every sinew of the body politic. Its political head (the Chancellor of the Exchequer) is the second most powerful figure in the Cabinet and its bureaucratic head a permanent secretary who, with the Cabinet Secretary, reigns supreme in Whitehall. The Treasury is organized hierarchically: moving down from the apex it is functionally differentiated, with various specialist *supply sections* each concentrating on the spending of a particular government department.

The Bank of England This is the government's bank, holding its account and with a prime responsibility to implement financial policy. In this it is by no means a passive instrument. On the domestic front it acts as the government's agent, managing the note issue, the national debt, government borrowing and government loans. In international matters it is similarly close to government, dealing in foreign currencies so as to maintain the value of the pound, buying and selling gold, and engaging in international discussion on financial and trade policy. In addition, it stands at the centre of the financial community. It is the bank of banks, holding the cash reserves of the clearing banks, providing them with facilities which an ordinary customer might expect from his or her own bank, and acting as a channel of communication between them and the Treasury. It also deals in the open market where, through its control over the issue of Treasury Bills and new issues of government bonds, it is by far the largest operator, regularly engaging in mammoth buying and selling operations which influence the whole economy.

The Gladstonian cycle

> It is the mark of a chicken-hearted Chancellor when he shrinks from upholding economy in detail . . . He is not worth his salt if he is not ready to save what are meant by candle-ends and cheese-parings in the cause of the country.
>
> W. E. Gladstone, quoted in F. W. Hirst, *Gladstone as Financier and Economist* (1931)

Through Gladstone's reforms Parliament was (nominally) given the kind of control over the economy which a Victorian husband would want over his family, overseeing three basic housekeeping functions:

1 granting of prior approval to planned expenditure (the estimates process);
2 considering the ways and means of raising the sum required (the budgetary process);
3 checking that all past expenditure had been conducted in a proper manner (the accounting process).

In reality, the reforms placed the *Treasury* at the centre by making it the agent of Parliament.

Prior approval: who gets what, when, how in Whitehall Beneath the atmosphere of restraint and courtesy in the village of Whitehall there is, as in Agatha Christie's village of St Mary Mead, an undercurrent of mistrust, competition and sublimated violence. 'Who gets what' in the interdepartmental battle for resources is the most important feature of the Whitehall wars. Prior approval is granted by means of the **estimates process**, entailing the allocation of funds to the spending departments, 'the most pervasive and informative operation of government' (Heclo and Wildavsky 1974: xii). The annual process begins around November with each department submitting to the Treasury estimates of expenditure plans for the coming financial year. This initiates a protracted process of bilateral negotiations between each department and the Treasury, having more in common with a north African *souk* than a rational decision-making process; yet the outcome is nothing less than the policy of Her Majesty's Government. The bilateral nature of the encounter is very significant, enabling the Treasury to increase its power through a 'divide-and-rule' strategy. By around March, when some degree of agreement has emerged, all departmental estimates are published by the Treasury and presented to Parliament by the Chancellor's second in command, the Chief Secretary to the Treasury. Approval is a formality. From the 1960s, this process has been complemented by the less parsimonious PESC system (see p. 392).

The budgetary process: who pays, when, how much? The second operation in the control cycle entails raising the money – the **budgetary process** – through a variety of forms of taxation (see figure 13.2). This is another annual process. Constitutionally the government's right to tax must be renewed by Parliament each year, which is why the Chancellor presents his annual budget. In Gladstone's view, the purpose of the budget was to raise enough money to finance the policies agreed to through the estimates process; no more and no less.

The budget is prepared over the course of the financial year in the bowels of the Treasury by special high-powered committees working in the deepest secrecy. In March, the proposals are embodied in the Finance Bill and the Chancellor, with the aid of his private secretary and various experts, begins to draft his Budget Speech – the focal point of Budget Day.

Parliament gives automatic approval to the proposals without debate and

A quiet pre-budget stroll for the Chancellor, March 1989
Source: Times Newspapers Ltd

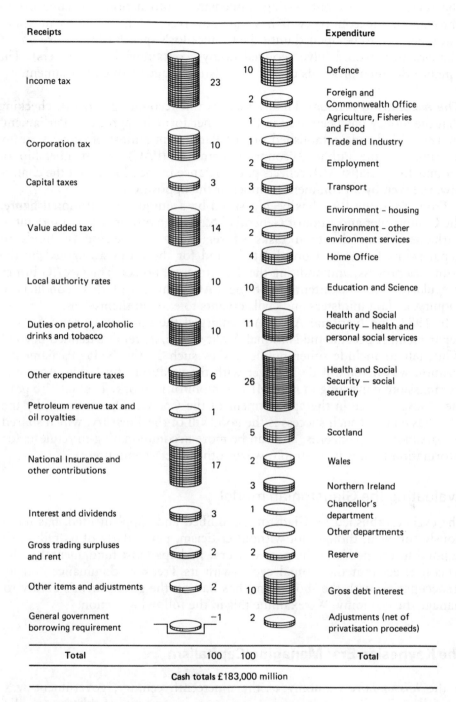

Receipts				Expenditure
Income tax	23	10		Defence
		2		Foreign and Commonwealth Office
		1		Agriculture, Fisheries and Food
Corporation tax	10	1		Trade and Industry
		2		Employment
Capital taxes	3	3		Transport
		2		Environment – housing
Value added tax	14	2		Environment – other environment services
		4		Home Office
Local authority rates	10	10		Education and Science
Duties on petrol, alcoholic drinks and tobacco	10	11		Health and Social Security — health and personal social services
Other expenditure taxes	6	26		Health and Social Security — social security
Petroleum revenue tax and oil royalties	1	5		Scotland
National Insurance and other contributions	17	2		Wales
		3		Northern Ireland
Interest and dividends	3	1		Chancellor's department
		1		Other departments
Gross trading surpluses and rent	2	2		Reserve
Other items and adjustments	2	10		Gross debt interest
General government borrowing requirement	−1	2		Adjustments (net of privatisation proceeds)
Total	**100**	**100**		**Total**

Cash totals £183,000 million

Figure 13.2 Planned receipts and expenditure of general government, 1988–1989 (pence in every pound)

Source: HMSO (1989: 369)

the revenue departments swing immediately into action. Revenue offices throughout the country will have already received instructions in sealed packages, not to be opened until the Chancellor's speech (if there are no tax changes they would have received decoys containing blank papers). The Finance Bill then proceeds upon a ritualistic voyage through Parliament.

The accounting process Finally there is the accounting process, checking that the money has been used in the manner formally agreed by Parliament. In 1861 Gladstone established one of Parliament's most effective scrutiny instruments, the Public Accounts Committee (PAC). Its membership of around 15 specialist MPs reflects party balance in the House, but the chair is always taken by a prominent member of the opposition.

From 1866 the PAC has been assisted by a unique constitutional figure, the Comptroller and Auditor General (C&AG), an officer who is a servant of Parliament with the twin tasks of regulating the release of funds to departments from the Consolidated Fund for the purposes agreed by the estimates process, and auditing the departmental books. The C&AG brings irregularities to the attention of the PAC, which will then conduct an enquiry, calling ministers and civil servants to explain themselves.

In 1983, the National Audit Act enlarged the purview of the C&AG's department. It became the National Audit Office, its remit extended beyond Whitehall to include other public bodies such as the NHS. Parliament's position was made a little stronger with the creation of a Public Accounts Commission, consisting of nine MPs, to monitor its work. The Act also gave the House a voice in the appointment of the C&AG. One reason why the PAC has enjoyed such success is the goodwill of the Treasury, which shared its parsimonious concerns, and can be more accommodating to requests for information than is its custom towards other select committees.

Evaluating the Gladstonian model

The cycle established by Gladstone, modified and supplemented, has tenaciously survived, though not without criticism, particularly of its failure to respond to the needs of the post-war era. Perhaps most fundamental is the general effect that the annual cycle (with its Treasury dominance and its preoccupation with the short term) has had on the government's ability to manage the economy. We examine this in the following section.

The Keynesian Era: Managing Capitalism

In the *laissez-faire* economy of the nineteenth century, government was generally viewed with suspicion as an infringement of liberty; public expenditure was a necessary evil to be constrained at all times. Despite an embryonic welfare state, the cheeseparing approach served well into the twentieth century; indeed the inter-war years are sometimes called a golden age of Treasury control. Economic depression resulting from a failure of capitalism enabled it to practise a firm monetarist policy (controlling inflation by limiting the quantity of money in the economy) and keep down public expenditure, in the belief that industry and world trade could only develop if there was confidence that the currency would hold its value.

Yet the economic depression persisted, threatening the legitimacy of the state. The classical economists had argued that unemployment would precipitate a fall in wages, which would automatically eliminate unemployment because profits would rise and more people would be taken on by employers. Yet although wages fell, unemployment persisted. With the spectre of the Russian revolution before them, the General Strike of 1926 appeared as a black cloud on the capitalists' horizon. Marx's prophesies of inevitable crisis culminating in the collapse of capitalism gained ominous plausibility as the economy began to look increasingly fragile.

Rescuing capitalism: the coming of Keynes

However, an alternative diagnosis and prescription was offered by John Maynard Keynes (1883–1946), who appeared like a knight in armour as the saviour of capitalism. In his *General Theory*, published in 1936, he argued that, contrary to the Gladstonian view, (macroeconomic) budgeting for the state was not the same as the (microeconomic) budgeting of firms or households. Constantly aiming for a balanced budget was simply an inappropriate goal and potentially harmful to the economy (and hence for the level of unemployment).

Keynes's diagnosis Keynes refuted the classical economists' view that the market would necessarily allocate resources in the optimum manner for society. Left to itself, the economy could reach a point of equilibrium (where aggregate demand equalled aggregate supply) below its full capacity and, in this state of recession, one of the under-used resources would be labour. He argued that cuts in wages, far from restoring full employment, would further depress the economy and produce the very opposite effect: less would be bought, less would need to be produced, and more unemployment would fuel an ever-downward spiral of depression. The slumps of the inter-war years seemed ample verification of this theory.

Keynes's prescription If the market, and hence capitalism, was to be saved, the state could not keep out of the economy as prescribed by classical liberal orthodoxy. It should take on the job of managing the market in order to ensure that it would operate at the level of full employment. More precisely, it should use its public expenditure function as a means of **demand management**. In times of slump the state should stimulate the economy by increasing the level of aggregate demand, using its gigantic purchasing power to buy materials, provide education, build roads, and so on. The effect of this would be to stimulate demand throughout the economy (more roads require the production of more materials). Of course, if the government merely financed its greater expenditure by increasing taxation there might not be any increase in aggregate demand because expenditure by citizens would fall. However, it could be financed by borrowing from its citizens, creating a *budget deficit*. Alternatively, in times of prosperity the government could adopt the opposite tack and run a budget *surplus*, thereby dampening down demand by reducing expenditure while raising taxes, which would serve also to eliminate the debts incurred earlier (the national debt). This strategy had the momentous implication that the idea of the *balanced budget* would no longer be sacrosanct.

The experience of the war years seemed to confirm Keynes's theories; massive government expenditure on arms virtually erased the unemployment which had plagued the 1930s. The war also saw an enormous increase in direct government intervention in various walks of life, and politicians' promises in areas such as health care, social security and education in order to keep people keen to fight and die, meant that Britain was destined to enter a quite new era of public expenditure after the war. The new orthodoxy was that government could, and should, accept a much greater responsibility for the well-being of citizens. This threatened the traditional role of the Treasury, which was to lose its grip on the nation's purse-strings.

The years of plenty: the Treasury loses its grip

Hence the decades of the long boom of western capitalism saw public expenditure being used for the quite new purpose of managing the national economy: stabilizing the trade cycle and maintaining full employment. Forceful spending ministers were able to push through expensive program-mes with no necessary implications in terms of tax increases. Moreover, in the expanded welfare state, people did not appear to mind paying taxes as much as the followers of the Gladstonian precepts had believed. It seemed that the boom would last for ever; the capitalist economy could be permanently protected from its own propensity to crisis by government management. Although Britain was still a capitalist country, the market was no longer an inner sanctum from which the state was excluded.

The principle of government intervention was advanced beyond fiscal policy in 1961 with the establishment of the National Economic Develop-ment Council (NEDC – known as Neddy). Set up by the Conservative government, this was a timid entry into the area of indicative planning (requesting and directing rather than commanding) and corporatism (see pp. 423–6), practised with success by some European rivals. In this new world of high public expenditure and **economic planning**, the nineteenth-century liberal ideas embedded in the Treasury philosophy were rendered anachro-nistic.

The need for a new approach: the coming of PESC In this new era voices were soon raised against the Treasury. After a critical parliamentary report on Treasury control a committee of enquiry was established under Lord Plowden (a Treasury man himself). Its report, *The Control of Public Expenditure* (Plowden 1961), recommended that expenditure decisions be taken on grounds more rational than those offered in the estimates process, with its narrow, single-year perspective. Decisions should be taken against a wider background of public expenditure as a whole, so that the value of competing policies could be weighed against each other, and considered over a longer time-scale in the knowledge of the anticipated level of resources. The result was the establishment of a **Public Expenditure Survey Committee (PESC)** to augment the estimates process.

PESC was composed of senior officials from various departments (including the Treasury), with the task of making annual five-year projections of future expenditure needs in the light of forecasts of economic growth. Its remit was to extend beyond the confines of Whitehall to encompass the full range of public expenditure, including the nationalized industries and local government. Before long, the process became an established part of public finance, producing a white paper around February, to assist Parliament in evluating the Estimates.

In 1964, the Wilson government created a special department concerned with economic planning: the Department of Economic Affairs (DEA). It was to incorporate representatives of labour and capital into the policy-making process by working through Neddy. More intervention in the market came in 1965, with a new quango, the National Board for Prices and Incomes (PIB), created to vet proposed increases. In 1966 a further quango, the Industrial Reorganization Corporation (IRC), was established with capital of £200 million to promote industrial development through state share purchase in companies with a strategic place in the economy.

The restoration of the Treasury However, the wheel was to go full circle. In the 1970s the 'hidden hand' of Adam Smith (the classical economist who had believed that left to itself the market would apportion goods in the best possible way) began to push up his creaking tombstone from beneath the Keynesian moss. The long boom of western capitalism was at its end. Inflation reached an alarming 24.7 per cent in 1975, yet unemployment, defying the Phillips Curve (which postulated an inverse relationship between the two) was also rising.

Britain reached a point of crisis where the state appeared unable to service its existing debts and was obliged to turn humiliatingly to the International Monetary Fund (IMF) for large-scale loan support. The concerted call from the IMF, the City, the financial markets, the Governor of the Bank of England and the media pundits was for a return to the monetarist principles of the Victorians (Keegan 1984: 88), and the cry came echoing back from the valleys of King Charles Street, where the Treasury stood like a rock emerging shining from beneath the retreating Keynesian tide.

Chancellor Denis Healey was forced to exert further controls over the money supply, cut public spending, trim public sector borrowing, and raise interest rates (which reached a record 15.5 per cent). Central and local government expenditure was subject to cash limits, and similar controls were imposed on the nationalized industries. In 1976 James Callaghan measured up the corpse of Keynesianism for the Treasury undertakers in his fateful declaration to the Labour Party conference: 'We cannot now, if we ever could, spend our way out of a recession'. The Labour government was already moving with some momentum towards monetarism before Thatcherism became a word in the economic lexicon.

Public expenditure under Thatcher: the end of Keynes

When Mrs Thatcher took up residence in Downing Street, Treasury control in the true Victorian sense experienced its real rebirth. While Labour had reluctantly relinquished its economic controlling mechanisms, the New Right Thatcher government dropped them like hot potatoes, making monetarist nostrums a key plank in its 1979 election platform.

The prescription was generally for less welfare spending in order to restore profitability, an end to consultation with trade unions in policy-making to ease the problem of government 'overload', the abandonment of Keynesianism to release the forces of the market, and privatization of the nationalized industries. Generally the state, and hence the area of life under democratic control, was to be 'rolled back'; the market rather than politics was to determine who got what in British society. Collectivism was to be replaced with individualism. The *individuals* in question appeared generally to be white, middle class and male. They would fight their way to the top not with welfare state feather-bedding, but with the even softer pillows of property ownership, mortgage tax relief, falling levels of taxation, private education, private health care, and the motherly embrace of legislation and a legal system designed to outlaw all activity likely to endanger property rights and the working of the market.

On the public expenditure front, balancing the books became once more the purpose of the budget. Public expenditure was again to be regarded as an evil, and the idea that the government had a duty to manage the economy in order to reach those parts of society which the market could not, was declared grave heterodoxy. In the Treasury, Keynesians were hunted like medieval witches, prudent young bureaucrats quickly deciding that they had really been closet monetarists all the time (Ponting 1986: 102).

Applying monetarism

The policy was different from that prescribed by **monetarist** guru Milton Friedman. He argued that the level of public expenditure and taxation did not have an important effect on the economy; a government need do no more than control the rate of increase in the **money supply**. However, the Thatcherite desire to make (and justify) tax cuts, attack welfare state 'scroungers', and so on, led to a form of monetarism which included in its strategy a particular obsession with reducing public expenditure; it could be described as 'fiscal monetarism'. As a result, the initial strategy had two broad thrusts: first, control of the rate of increase in money supply through a Medium-Term Financial Strategy (orthodox Friedmanism) and, secondly, reducing expenditure by public bodies, with a particular focus on eliminating the **public sector borrowing requirement (PSBR)** (the budget deficit – money borrowed from the private sector).

The Medium-Term Financial Strategy (MTFS) This entailed the setting of annual targets for the rate of monetary growth over four-year periods, to be published at the time of the Budget (see table 13.1). These were to be built into the PESC process, transmuting it into an instrument for cuts rather than for the rational planning of public expenditure. The original character of PESC was further eroded as its time scale became shorter and competitive bargaining replaced the corporate approach envisaged in the Plowden Report. Thus, by the late 1980s it was the custom for the Treasury to hold separate meetings with each department, unashamedly termed 'bilaterals'. Where the Treasury failed to reach agreement with the department the matter was passed up to the 'Star Chamber', a mighty cabinet committee presided over by the Prime Minister (Treasury 1989: 9).

Table 13.1 First targets for the rate of monetary growth

Financial year	Target (% growth)
1980–1	7–11
1981–2	6–10
1982–3	5–9
1983–4	4–8

Reducing public borrowing The government was passionately opposed to the Keynesian proposition that a budget deficit was not in itself evil, adhering to the Gladstonian belief that the state was best run like a household. Mrs Thatcher preferred to follow Polonius's advice in *Hamlet* that 'borrowing dulls the edge of husbandry'. The Thatcherite objection to the PSBR was that an excess of public expenditure over public income could be seen as an increase in the money supply. In addition, it was argued that the money borrowed by government is not available to be borrowed by the private sector, which would use it for productive investment to expand the economy (and therefore would not be inflationary because more would be produced), while the government would use it for funding such things as the welfare state and public sector salaries. The strategy of reducing the PSBR became more attractive with the failure to keep money supply within the targets (see below). By the financial year 1987–8 it had been transformed into a PSDR, a public sector debt repayment.

The failure of monetarism Yet Thatcherite monetarism did not work as had been promised. The targets were regularly exceeded and the average

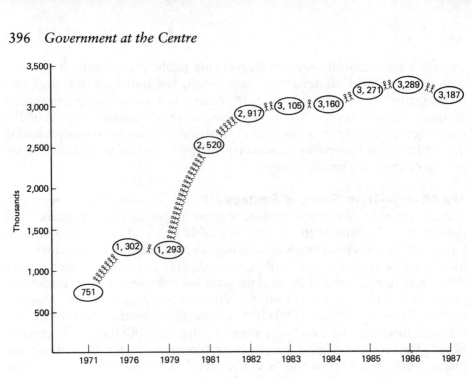

Figure 13.3   Unemployment in the UK, 1971–1987

Source: Data from *Social Trends* (1988: table 4.19)

growth of M3 sterling (a measure of money supply) was actually higher in the period 1979–85 than it had been at any time under the previous Labour government. In its calculations, the government replaced M3 with M0 (a *narrower* definition consisting of notes and coins in circulation, money in the tills of banks, and operational balances with the Bank of England), which most economists dismissed as entirely unrealistic in age of 'plastic' and computerized money. At the same time, there was a huge loss of industrial output and a horrendous price to be paid in terms of unemployment (figure 13.3).

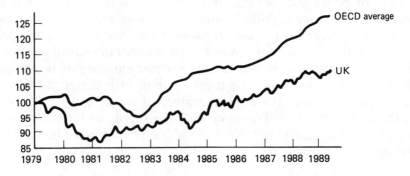

Figure 13.4   Index of growth in output since 1979

Source: Data from Cowe (1989)

Until 1984, investment and output were actually below 1979 levels, and even afterwards the climb was sluggish and well below the OECD average (figure 13.4). The balance of trade moved adversely and the growth in the economy actually went into reverse in the years 1980 and 1981, when the great industrial 'shake-out' occurred, remained erratic, and was never significantly better than that of rival economies (*Guardian*, 29 May 1987). The effect of tax reductions for the wealthy saw the balance of payments (the relative value of imports and exports, including 'invisible' trade such as services, as well as manufactured goods) plunge into deficit from mid-1987

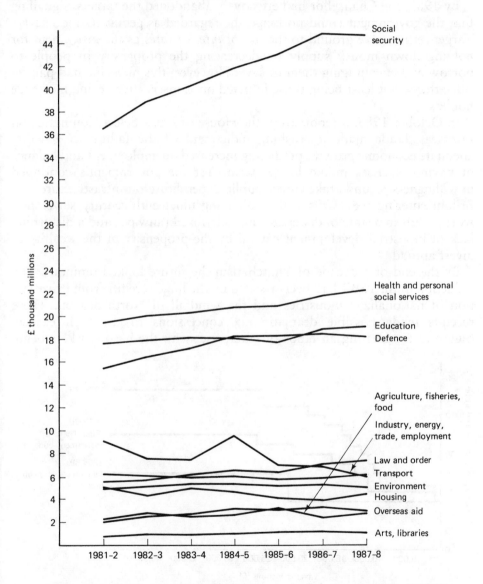

Figure 13.5 Public expenditure in real terms, by function, 1981/82–1987/88

Source: Data from *Social Trends* (1988: table 6.23)

as goods were sucked in from rival economies. By 1989, Britain was running the largest trade deficit ever in its history.

Moreover, the declared intent to cut public expenditure could not be achieved; it rose each year throughout the 1980s. Paradoxically, cutting public expenditure on economic infrastructure and services was counter-balanced by increased health, social services and social security spending necessitated by the effects of unemployment and poverty. Income support for the unemployed rose faster than any other category, reaching £44,478 million in the year 1987–8 (see figure 13.5).

By 1985, the Chancellor had effectively abandoned the targets, signalling that the government could no longer be regarded as genuinely monetarist. Target-setting gave ground to the use of *interest rates* as the instrument for holding down money supply by decreasing the propensity of people to borrow and encouraging them to save. However, this medicine had painful side-effects, not least being those inflicted on Conservative-voting mortgage holders.

In October 1985, a report from the House of Lords Select Committee on Overseas Trade made a crushing indictment of the failure to generate adequate economic growth, predicting increased unemployment and balance of payments crises in the longer term. Yet the government's continued unwillingness to undertake direct public expenditure on infrastructure saw Britain entering the 1990s with a decaying nineteenth-century sewer net-work, roads in a state of disrepair, unmodernized railways, and a disturbing lack of industrial development caused by the propensity of the wealthy to invest abroad.

By the end of a decade of Thatcherism the future looked ominous. The reduction in the PSBR had been assisted by the huge receipts from privatiza-tion of nationalized industries and the windfall of North Sea oil. These receipts made possible dramatic tax concessions to the high earners (figure 13.6), creating an ethos of enterprise, with the hard workers being

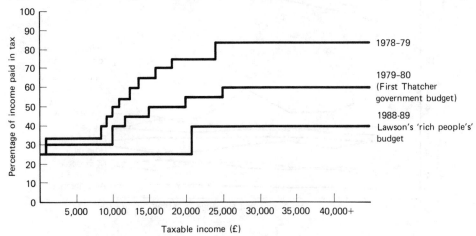

Figure 13.6   The changing income tax profile during the 1980s

rewarded and the poor with only themselves to blame.

One much-vaunted success of the government was the reduction of **inflation**. However, this was an ironic achievement because the classic claim of the monetarists had been that the reduced money supply would achieve this result. In fact inflation fell while the money supply was *increasing*, suggesting that the effect, though desired by the policy-makers, was largely the accidental result of exogenous factors. However, even this achievement began to look less secure by the end of the 1980s, the annual rate of the Retail Price Index (RPI) climbing to 7.5 per cent by the end of 1988 and reaching 8.3 per cent by June 1989, well above the OECD average. It remained a moot point whether the failure of monetarism was caused by the government's unwillingness to apply the nostrums according to the word of Friedman, or whether monetarism itself was an outmoded thesis which could make sense only in the context of the simple capitalist economies of the nineteenth century.

During 1989 a body of opinion developed that Britain's economic problems could only be solved by joining the European Monetary System, a move favoured by the Chancellor, Nigel Lawson. This was opposed by Mrs Thatcher and her economic adviser Sir Alan Walters. The unneighbourly tension between numbers 10 and 11 Downing Street reached fever pitch, culminating in the dramatic resignation of Lawson, to be matched by that of Walters.

Conclusion: Public Expenditure and Economic Decline

Explaining decline

The British economy has experienced relative decline *vis-à-vis* other countries of the developed capitalist world in the post-war era, and various hypotheses are advanced to explain this (see pp. 64–6).

In this concluding section we shall examine how far the patterns and traditions of the control of public expenditure in Britain have in themselves contributed to the economic problems. Broadly speaking, it will be argued that the Victorian traditions were so strong that they inhibited the state's ability to manage the market in the way implied by Keynesian analysis. We shall identify three culprits in this failure:

- the institutional setting of public expenditure policy-making;
- the competitive pattern of public expenditure decision-making in Whitehall;
- a failure to incorporate the vital economic interests into the public expenditure policy-making process.

The institutional setting

The two key institutions associated with public finance – the Treasury and the Bank of England – are both august establishments imbued with the liberal values of the nineteenth-century constitution. To them, the government regulating the economy is like the Pope conducting a service in the Golden Temple at Amritsar.

The Treasury Despite its overweening importance, the Treasury is a small, intimate department, its ambience adding to its strength by creating a tightly knit community in which everybody knows everyone else. Here an aroma of politics pervades the air in each committee meeting and in each information exchange in the fabled corridors of power. Long-standing personal relationships constitute the key channels of communication; trust between colleagues is built up and cemented over long acquaintance and counterpoised with a mistrust and suspicion of outsiders. Everything is conducted beneath a cloak of secrecy. Within this village atmosphere, orthodoxies emerge as unchallengeable wisdom, contributing to a 'Treasury view' – a set of attitudes towards policy and the proper medicine for this or that malady – which will tend to dominate all decision-making in Whitehall and Westminster.

Who are those with such dominance? They are called the Treasury men, a very special breed. Although their work sounds technical, they are dilettantes *par excellence*, hand-picked from the very cream of the civil service applicants, with no specialized knowledge of economics, accounting, or any of the policy areas in which public money is spent. Even within the Treasury the average time spent in any particular policy area is but a fleeting two years, so that they 'are clearly exposed to little danger of losing their amateur status' (Heclo and Wildavsky 1974: 65). Apologists will argue that the reason the Treasury men can move so lightly between policy areas is their renowned Rolls Royce minds; they are the exotic orchids of the Whitehall hothouse, cultivated in the fertile soil of Oxbridge.

> The good Treasury man is an able amateur ... He relies on ability to argue, to find internal contradictions, to pick out flaws in arguments whose substance he has not fully mastered and whose subtleties he can only be dimly aware of.
> H. Heclo and A. Wildavsky, *The Private Government of Public Money*
> (1973: 60)

The Bank of England The Treasury's influence is complemented by another formidable institution which, although not part of the civil service, lies at the heart of the governing establishment – the Bank of England. Nationalized in 1946, it remains formally autonomous from government, standing in the City of London like a veritable palace, served by pink-coated flunkeys. This is appropriate, for in the day-to-day political life of the country it plays a regal role.

Yet despite its overwhelming importance to the nation, the Bank is not a servant of the government; on the contrary, it can be the master, effectively shaping policy through the advice it gives. It can even be seen as a pressure group, using its close relationship with the Treasury on behalf of the banking sector of the economy against industrial capital and pressing its preference for high interest rates (Marsh and Locksley 1987: 223). In addition, the legendary secrecy of the British state is here amplified by the claims of necessary confidentiality, keeping out any prying eyes from Parliament, the media, and even the government. Generally, what is known about the Bank is what it wants known, information which is purveyed through its own, carefully edited, publications.

Given this enormous power, one must ask who is in control, and whether they are likely to be responsive to the needs of society. The Bank is formally under a Court, consisting of the Governor of the Bank of England, a deputy governor, and 16 directors, 12 of whom are supposed, in a quasi-democratic manner, to represent various interests throughout society. However, they come overwhelmingly from the male establishment galaxy, with public school–Oxbridge backgrounds and top jobs in multinational giants and the world of high finance. One token trade union representative sits like the timid dormouse at the Mad Hatter's tea party. The Governor is a key figure, even more grand than the head of the Treasury, moving in the world of the most powerful in society, fêted by millionaire capitalists, delivering speeches declaiming his views and theories, conferring with government, and in times of crisis exerting a domineering presence. Despite the dignity surrounding the office, and its estrangement from the ballot box, the position is a profoundly political one.

In 1964, the Wilson government learned very soon of this power. In its first year of office, being naturally enough unpopular with the financial sector, it suffered in the face of malicious speculation against the pound (selling sterling in the belief – or hope – that the market value of the pound was about to fall, and thereby threatening to *cause* it to do so), and Lord Cromer demanded that the government, notwithstanding its manifesto commitments, make all-round expenditure cuts. Harold Wilson records:

> In January 1965 ... I told him that Government expenditure was committed far ahead; schools which were being built, roads ... were part-way to completion ... Was it his view, I asked him, that we should cut them off half-finished ... The question was difficult for him, but he answered, 'Yes'.
>
> (Wilson 1974: 62)

The political salience of the position was recognized by Mrs Thatcher, who inherited as Governor Sir Gordon Richardson, appointed during the Heath regime. She determined not to reappoint him and, after a trawl in the waters of high finance, a replacement was found in Robin Leigh-Pemberton, chairman of National Westminster Bank. This was an overtly political appointment of an 'outsider' to the incestuous Treasury–Bank world, resulting in considerable furore (Keegan 1984: 197–8).

Victorian institutions in a Keynesian landscape The dominance of the Treasury and Bank has meant that nineteenth-century values have lingered like the smell of stale tobacco smoke in the redecorated constitution of the post-war era. Both could be but poor instruments for Keynesianism, placing a 'dead hand' on public expenditure in general, with little thought for industry, the level of employment, the wider economy, the longer-term goals of government, or the welfare state. Whatever the economic problem – falling pound, rising pound, balance of payments crisis, inflation or unemployment – the response was invariably a deflationary package. The result was a series of what were termed 'stop–go' policies. When the economy expanded, imports were sucked in, the trade deficit widened and the Bank of England would step in to buy sterling with its own foreign currency in order to maintain its value as an international reserve currency (see p. 82). As the foreign currency reserves fell, governments felt the need to deflate the economy (a 'stop' period) in order to reduce imports. Despite Treasury determination to defend sterling, devaluation came in 1967. However, deflation produced unemployment, calling for the stimulation of the economy (a 'go' period), and the cycle would begin again. Throughout the long-boom era, foreign exchange crises forced stop–go cycles in 1957, 1960, 1964, 1966 and 1973. Of course, an inescapable conclusion is that the Bank and the Treasury are unlikely to prove instruments of socialism or social democracy and Labour governments found in them a source of considerable resistance to their policies.

The pound in your pocket

From now on the pound is worth 14 per cent or so less in terms of other currencies. It does not mean, of course, that the pound here in Britain, in your pocket or purse or in your bank, has been devalued.

Harold Wilson's speech after devaluation of the pound (20 Nov. 1967)

Competitive decision-making in Whitehall

Linked with the dominance of the Treasury and Bank is the method of reaching spending decisions in Whitehall. Although Britain in the post-war era formally accepted the Keynesian package, the basic pattern of expenditure policy-making remained unchallenged. Thus the Treasury missed its historic opportunity to become a coordinating instrument in the economy. In spite of the PESC experiment, decisions on what each department would spend continued to be made through the old system of competitive infighting, with the Treasury persistently reducing expenditure regardless of the merits of the policy.

The failure reflected an inability to see the state in collectivist terms, as something over and above sectional interests; it was a manifestation of the

Victorian legacy of individualism. In this respect, the British system of government has compared unfavourably with the French, where the *Commissariat General du Plan* accepted the remit to coordinate departments in line with an overall policy towards the economy.

Failure to incorporate the economic institutions into policy-making

This same ethos prevented the successful constitutional implantation of institutions designed to bring together for the purposes of planning and policy-making the sectional interests within society – the representatives of finance, industry and labour. Neddy and the 'little Neddies' were never really integrated into the machinery (remaining arm's-length quangos). The dominance of the Treasury and Bank was to go so far as to kill off the Cinderella DEA, a pretender to the crown worn by these ugly daughters of the penny-pinching Gladstone. The IRC and the National Enterprise Board, lacking both sufficient powers and funds, were similarly unsuccessful in the late 1960s and 1970s respectively (see p. 463). Another area where labour failed to become incorporated into government policy-making was over incomes policy; indeed it was the unions' frustration with this which cost Labour the 1979 general election. The unwillingness to work in harmony was graphically illustrated by Heath's attempt to establish an Industrial Relations Court to coerce the unions (see pp. 528–9).

This non-corporatist bias saw its apotheosis in the Thatcher government. Here the declared policy was quite the opposite: to deliberately exclude economic interests from policy-making, using the police force and courts to drive labour into a position of submission with a battery of restrictive new laws (see pp. 427–8).

Keynesianism and the British state: a revolution denied?

In view of the way the British state has controlled public expenditure it is possible to argue that the New Right's general critique of the effects of Keynesianism can be seen as ill founded because the approach was never given a fair chance. 'The British state is so imbued with the liberal philosophy ... that sustained, coherent, and disinterested arbitration and sponsorship of the economy is extremely difficult, if not impossible' (Hutton 1986: 196). The result is that the British state has always remained subservient to the market order, with a persistent legend of minimal government etched into its institutional masonry – never open enough to engage in dialogue with industry, never coordinated enough to plan, and never autonomous enough to manage.

Key points

- In simple terms, public expenditure is money spent by the state in providing services. The scale of public finance is enormous (almost £200,000 million in 1988–9) and most of it is raised by taxation.
- Almost all government policies involve expenditure and the whole of the public sector is held together by a financial network. It is impossible to discuss political questions without recognizing the financial dimension.
- Public expenditure is controlled by Her Majesty's Treasury, which presides over a set of processes designed in the nineteenth century by the capitalist bourgeoisie.
- However, public expenditure is also an expression of our propensity to live collectively in a community. The principle of state-provided services, paid for by taxation, is fundamentally different from their provision by the capitalist system through the market.
- Because of its great magnitude, public expenditure cannot but influence the rest of the economy. This fact has offered post-war governments a chance deliberately to use their spending and taxation powers to moderate the working of the capitalist economic system (Keynesianism).
- However, by the mid-1970s, with the end of the long boom of western capitalism, the New Right emerged to criticize the Keynesian approach, arguing that employment had been maintained at too high a level (making the trade unions too powerful) and that government activity in the economy had crowded out the private sector.
- The New Right alternative to Keynesianism was monetarism, a return to Victorian principles.
- In terms of its declared intentions, the Thatcher government generally failed: money supply grew, firms went bankrupt, and unemployment and interest rates soared.
- Looking back over the Keynesian era, it can be argued that the nature of the British state, with its Victorian institutions, was such that true government

---

Review your understanding of the following terms and concepts

public expenditure	*laissez-faire*
individualism	Keynesianism
transfer payments	demand management
fiscal policy	economic planning
Consolidated Fund	PESC
capitalism	monetarism
mixed economy	money supply
accumulation	public sector borrowing
Protestant work ethic	requirement (PSBR)
estimates process	inflation
budgetary process	

management of the economy was never really practised. The ethos of low public spending, the minimal state, and the non-involvement of capitalists and unions in economic policy-making prevented the central control found in more successful competitors such as Germany and France.

Assignment

Study the extract from *The Economist* and answer the following questions. (N.B. In this article billion is used to mean 1,000 million.)

Britain's public spending

Shed a tear for the Treasury—and for the taxpayer

After this year's white paper, it may be harder to hold down public expenditure

HOW does a government hold down public expenditure when it is running a £14 billion budget surplus and planning, in the coming financial year, to run another that is even bigger? When Mr Nigel Lawson presented the results of last year's public-spending round back in November he boasted that spending was continuing to fall as a share of national income. But in real terms the planning total for 1989-90 represents a rise of 3.7% on the previous year. After four years in which the real level of public spending has been flat, it will rise by 7.6% between 1989-90 and 1991-92, the year in which the next general election will probably be held. Holding down the total will grow harder, too, as the government's various reforms start to take effect.

The white paper published on January 30th gives a detailed breakdown of spending. Its list of winners and losers is a good guide to the broad thrust of government policy and of demography. The Department of Employment has left the great days in the mid-1980s, when Lord Young invented a scheme a month to get people off the unemployment register. Its expenditure is falling. So is that at Lord Young's present home,

the Department of Trade and Industry. It has been shorn of almost all its loss-making nationalised industries. Its secretary of state now seems admirably keener to demolish an empire than to build one. Defence spending is flat; thanks to sterling's strength against the dollar, the costs of the Trident weapon system are far less than five years ago people thought they would be. The big gainers are the Home Office (more prisons) and health (more very old people).

These are the departments that have convinced the Treasury that they need extra cash. They prompt another question. If the budget surplus continues, can the Treasury keep its grip? Give people more choice (in education and now in health) and they will choose the best; raise their expectations with radical reform, and they will expect more public spending. Allow schools and hospitals more control over their budgets and pay, and their bills are more likely to creep up than down. Give the government's new executive agencies greater financial autonomy (as the Treasury now seems willing to do), and it may be harder to hold down their spending.

Economist, 4 Feb. 1989

		% mark
1	What is the Whitehall process which has led to the white paper referred to in the article?	10
2	Explain the meaning of the term 'budget surplus'. Briefly discuss its possible effect on the quantity of money in the economy.	10

3   Distinguish between actual and real public expenditure.   10
4   'It lists the winners and losers . . .'. What does this statement imply about   20
    the nature of public expenditure planning in Britain?
5   Explain why the writer of the article believes that the Treasury may be   50
    unable to 'keep its grip'.

Questions for discussion

1   'Public expenditure is a reflection of our propensity to live communally.'
    Discuss.
2   Outline the Gladstonian cycle of financial control. What were its principal
    objectives?
3   How can government use its powers of spending and taxation to manage a
    capitalist economy?
4   What was the purpose behind the establishment of the PESC process? To
    what extent were the original intentions fulfilled?
5   Explain how the monetarist approach to the government role in the economy
    differs from that advocated by Keynes.
6   What is meant by the 'dead hand of the Treasury'? Discuss its effect on the
    post-war economy.
7   'The role of fiscal policy is to bring the public accounts into balance and keep
    them there, and thus underpin the process of re-establishing sound money'
    (Chancellor Nigel Lawson, Budget Speech, Tuesday 15 March 1989). Discuss.

Topic for debate

This house believes that the 'failure' of Keynesianism is a result of institutional
factors in the British state rather than inherent defects in the approach.
    or
This house believes that monetarism as applied in Britain during the 1980s
restored Britain to superpower status.

Further reading

Armstrong, P., Glyn, A. and Harrison, J. (1984) *Capitalism Since World War II*.
Traces the years of the long boom of world capitalism. Argues for a 'socialist path'
to break the stalemate between classes which leads to stagnation.

Budd, A. (1978) *The Politics of Economic Planning*.
Examines the failures of the various attempts by British governments to plan the
economy.

Diamond, Lord (1975) *Public Expenditure in Practice*.
Written by a Labour Chief Secretary to the Treasury, this combines an insider view
of the nitty gritty of public expenditure with a philosophical perspective.

Friedman, M. and R. (1985) *The Tyranny of the Status Quo*.

Collaboration between the influential monetarist guru and his wife laments the failure of the Thatcher regime to control money supply in the manner prescribed.

Gamble, A. (1985) *Britain in Decline.*
Traces various explanations for decline, stressing the importance of world influences.

Heclo, H. and Wildavsky, A. (1974) *The Private Government of Public Money.*
A unique book, which shows those involved in the public expenditure process as real people.

Hodgson, G. (1984) *The Democratic Economy.*
Examines in a lively way the relationships between democracy, freedom, the economy, and economic policy-making.

Hutton, W. (1986) *The Revolution that Never Was.*
Argues that the British liberal-democratic legacy inhibited the state from effectively applying Keynes's principles.

Keegan, W. (1984) *Mrs Thatcher's Economic Experiment.*
Written by an economic journalist, this account contains the flavour of the real-world politics lying behind all expenditure policy.

For light relief

Hilaire Belloc, *Pongo and the Bull.*
The power of money and the moneyed classes.

H. G. Wells, *Tono-Bungay.*
Biting social comment on an entrepreneurial society with nothing of value to sell.

Tom Wolfe, *Bonfire of the Vanities.*
Brilliant satire on the world of capitalist high finance and its penetrating social implications.

14

The Politics of Influence

In this chapter we move beyond both the formal institutions of government and the overtly political structures to uncover the more shadowy forces in politics – the powers behind the throne. Where 'real power' lies is the greatest conundrum of the study of politics and one can never be sure if it has been answered. We find repeatedly that the apparent puppet masters are themselves dangling on yet further strings stretching away out of our sight in an infinite regression. In studying the politics of influence we are seeking to understand not who holds the formal power but who is able to get most of what they want from the system. This is the study of pressure groups and of the balance of power within society. The chapter falls into three main sections. The first introduces the concept of **group politics**. The next identifies major theoretical approaches to this study, analysing the theories of **pluralism** and **corporatism**. We also consider the neoliberal view that the group approach distorts the political process. The third section goes beyond the group approach to examine the **elitist** and **Marxist models** of power in society.

The Group Approach

In 1978, a number of protesters hurled from the public gallery of the House of Commons foul-smelling bags containing a substance later described as of 'agricultural origin' onto the heads of cowering members. In February 1988, to the alarm of the seated aristocracy, a hoard of Amazon women abseiled into the House of Lords, and others appeared uninvited on a BBC news broadcast. In 1978, members of the National Union of Public Employees produced for Britain an unforgettable 'winter of discontent', when household rubbish, sewage, and even human corpses were left to form grisly mountains. Trade unions strike, mount pickets, fight with the police, have their funds sequestrated by the courts, and the name Arthur Scargill is better known in the households of Britain than almost all MPs and many ministers, although its owner holds no office known to the constitution. Almost daily the news media report on the activities of protest marchers, demonstrators, delegations to Westminster and Whitehall and hurlers of eggs at the high and mighty. Although the constitution makes no provision for activities such as these, they are events in politics. They are concerned with influencing the authoritative allocation of resources. It is clear that the study of politics by no means ends with constitutions, elections, parties and institutions.

Once a party has been elected to office, the formal constitutional means whereby policy is influenced by citizens ends. MPs return joyfully to Westminster, the ballot boxes are stacked away in town hall vaults and returning officers and vote counters go back to some honest form of employment. To be sure, a government may take cognizance of public opinion during its reign, but such consideration places the population in a position of prostrate passivity and can hardly be dignified as democratic involvement. The operation of liberal democracy does not allow people to make policy, it merely permits them to choose between elites. However, the involvement of people in shaping policy is not confined to elections, it continues throughout the life of a government at the informal level of the political system through the activities of pressure groups.

The scholar most responsible for foregrounding groups in political analysis is the American Arthur Bentley, an economist who realized the futility of studying economic policy only in terms of institutions and office-holders. For Bentley, the process of government was essentially about the activities of organized groups, and in his major work, published in 1908, he averred compellingly that 'when the groups are stated, everything is stated' (1967: 208). Since Bentley, US political scientists have made much of the analysis of groups.

Definitions

It is not advisable to give a simple definition of pressure groups because they appear in many guises. It is more helpful to discuss certain *definitional issues*, such as the following.

Interest groups and pressure groups Although essentially different, these two terms are often used synonymously. However, an **interest group** is an association of individuals with a shared interest or concern, while a **pressure group** is one actively attempting to *influence* government with respect to that concern. Thus not all interest groups are pressure groups, but all pressure groups will be interest groups. The reason for the synonymous use of the terms is instructive, and lies in the fact that 'pressure group' carries certain sinister connotations of factions seeking to subvert the *general will* as expressed through the democratic process. Indeed, it was probably coined by US journalists as a term of abuse. Hence some modern writers (particularly those in the pluralist tradition – see below) tend to favour the more innocent-sounding 'interest group' for reasons of legitimation.

Pressure groups and political parties Many definitions stress a fundamental distinction between pressure groups and political parties which can be expressed in the following way.

- Unlike parties, pressure groups do not seek actually to enter government via the electoral system, they wish only to influence policy.
- Pressure groups have only a limited range of policy interests, while parties are concerned with the entire government remit. This is sometimes expressed in terms of different *functions*: groups are said to *articulate* interests and parties to *aggregate* them.
- Parties tend to be clearly located along the political spectrum, but pressure groups will seek to establish links at all points and try to gain access to a government of any political complexion.

Although a useful aid to thought, this distinction breaks down under scrutiny. The differences should be seen in terms of tendencies rather than clear orientations. We saw in chapter 8 that the Labour and Conservative parties are wedded to the interests of labour and capital respectively.

Types of pressure groups

An important dichotomy distinguishes groups on the basis of who they are fighting for – some high ideal or their own economic interest. Although scholars vary in their nomenclature, this distinction is fundamental.

Promotional groups These are groups whose policy goal is some value other than the particular interest of members; they are sometimes called *cause groups*. Thus, for example, the Royal Society for the Prevention of Cruelty to Children, the Society for the Protection of the Unborn Child and, say, the Antivivisection Society, fight for those unable to speak for themselves. Others pursue ideological or moral goals which will affect the whole of society. The National Council for Civil Liberties is concerned with the rights of all citizens and the Campaign for Nuclear Disarmament fights against nuclear weapons for the whole of mankind. Generally speaking, membership of promotional groups is open to anyone interested in the cause and they tend to attract zealots. Thus members of Mary Whitehouse's National Viewers and Listeners' Association expose themselves to corruption in the public interest, spending long unselfish vigils before their television screens for sightings of sexual hanky-panky in their mission to purify the airwaves.

A subdivision of this category is *self-help* groups such as Alcoholics

Anonymous, the Spastics Society, or the Prisoners' Wives and Families Society, where the goals are in the interests of members, although of course there are implications for society at large. Some groups are, by their very nature, strictly sectional: the Campaign for Homosexual Equality naturally tends to attract homosexuals as members, while the diversity of groups comprising the women's movement consists mainly of women. Table 14.1 indicates the range and size of promotional groups in Britain.

Table 14.1 Membership of selected promotional groups in the UK, 1986

Name	Membership (thousands)
Abbeyfield Society	12
Age Concern	124
British Red Cross	88
Civic Trust	241
Confederation of Indian Organizations	52
Conservation Society	4
Disablement Income Group	5
Friends of the Earth	28
Mothers' Union	188
National Association of League of Hospital Friends	470
National Federation of Gateway Clubs	60
National Federation of Women's Institutes	347
National Women's Register	23
NSPCC	255
National Trust	1,417
National Trust for Scotland	145
National Union of Townswomen's Guilds	150
Physically Handicapped and Able Bodied	18
Ramblers' Association	53
Rotary International	63
Royal British Legion	858
Royal Society for Mentally Handicapped Children and Adults	55
Royal Society for Nature Conservation	179
RSPCA	23
Royal Society for the Protection of Birds	506
St John Ambulance Brigade	60
Toc H	7
World Wildlife Fund	106

Source: Social Trends (1988: table 11.4)

Sectional groups The pursual of individual self-interest is the motive for much economic and political activity, and this category is the more numerous. Sometimes called *economic groups*, membership is generally restricted to those protected. The trade unions are a notable sub-category, their importance having been heightened by the enormous growth of the industrial public sector, making the government a large-scale employer. On the employers' side, there are business associations reflecting various sectors, and even multinational firms. Both unions and employers' associations coalesce into larger **peak organizations** – the Trades Union Congress (TUC) and the Confederation of British Industry (CBI) – to press their collective demands.

A further sub-category consists of *professional associations* such as the British Medical Association (BMA) and the Law Society, which claim to have rather more elevated goals than the mere economic well-being of their members (the health of society, the concept of justice), though they are certainly not inattentive to mammon.

The promotional–economic interest distinction can be blurred in practice. As we have seen, some promotional groups are formed on a self-help basis, while sectional groups often see it as in their own interests to pursue wider goals for society.

The individual in the group world

The logic of the group approach to political analysis is not only to downgrade the role of institutions, but also that of individuals. This makes sense insofar as one individual's vote is likely to have far less impact on public policy than the activity of a group. However, it obscures the fact that groups are led by individuals and can often serve as the power base of some dynamic activist, a *political entrepreneur* (Salisbury 1969). Dominance of this kind is of course predictable through Michels's iron law of oligarchy (see p. 241). In a study of the British 'poverty lobby' it was shown that out of 39 promotional groups concerned with income maintenance policy (such as Help the Aged, Gingerbread and Shelter), around half were driven by the dynamic of a political entrepreneur.

Similarly, in the area of economic interest groups the leaders are often charismatic players on the political stage. Throughout the post-war era, giants of the CBI and the TUC, as well as a variety of industrial and trade union superstars, have featured in the national news as visibly as cabinet ministers. Indeed, one of the principal objections to pressure group involvement in politics is that the leaders ignore the views of members, exercising not *collective*, but *individual* power. Thus, group politics does not eliminate the politics of individuals, it actually fuels it by augmenting their political weight.

The policy bazaar: the resources of pressure groups

A singular characteristic of post-war politics before the 1980s was government willingness to accept group involvement in policy-making. This reflected the consensus politics of the era and its explanation lies partly in the fact that the groups can have powerful bargaining counters in terms of expertise, cooperation and communication.

Expertise Many groups are, by definition, expert in particular fields – farming, medicine, the preservation of wildlife, and so on. The state bureaucracy is generally deficient in specialism at various levels; it cannot be expected to know everything, and where new problems arise it is likely that voluntary organizations will acquire expertise and information before government. Thus, for example, as AIDS began its fateful march through the population, the Terrence Higgins Foundation clearly understood the problem better than the mandarins.

Veto power There are areas where policy implementation would be impossible without cooperation. The 1971 Industrial Relations Act, for example, failed owing to trade union unwillingness to play ball. Coal cannot be mined without miners, education must have teachers, and only farmers can implement agricultural policy. To secure compliance concessions must be made, and a group's leverage increases in proportion to its monopoly of expertise. The BMA was in an immensely powerful position at the time the NHS was created, with threats of non-cooperation constantly rumbling. Of course circumstances can change. The National Union of Mineworkers (NUM) appeared mighty when its strike dislodged the Heath government in 1974, but by the 1980s its power had seeped away, owing to the break-up of its monopoly through the formation (with government encouragement) of an alternative union and the development of other fuel sources.

Communications Governments continually need to address sections of the population and a group organization can function as a conduit, giving an easy channel for targeting. Of course influence can be a two-way process: by permitting a group to enter the decision-making forums, a government obtains an opportunity to 'sell' its policies in the hope that representatives will go forth and spread the word among members.

Talking to government

To communicate with governments groups require some channel of access, which may be through the public at large, the political parties, Parliament, the executive, or the civil service.

The public It is in a group's interest to ensure a favourable climate of public opinion and there are numerous ways to achieve this. It may gain media attention through news stories; buy advertising space; organize marches, rallies and demonstrations; make mail-shots, and have its leaders appear as pundits on television and radio.

The press is critically important in public relations, but owing to its right-wing bias, groups of the left are unlikely to receive sympathetic reporting. In addition, in an era of mass communications, successfully influencing public opinion can be a function of wealth. Economically powerful interests may enlist the services of the advertising agencies – the professional persuaders – who reach parts of the subconscious other voices cannot reach. Less well-endowed groups are usually obliged to adopt more robust tactics, such as marches and demonstrations.

It is frequently said that appeals to the public at large, although eye-catching, are the least effective way of exerting influence. It may be a case of 'not waving but drowning'; groups resorting to public display often do so because either they do not understand the system, or they are denied access to other channels by a hostile government.

However, the view that 'most noise equals least success' may be something of a myth propagated to keep people passive. Desecrating a cricket pitch may not get a man out of prison, but if fundamental shifts in policy are to be achieved, the public consciousness may require a degree of electric shock treatment. Promotional groups make considerable efforts to attract attention; the director of the Child Poverty Action Group declared that 'coverage in the media is our main strategy' (Whiteley and Winyard 1984: 35).

Parliament Groups may attempt to make an impact on Parliament as a whole through some form of mass demonstration outside the Palace of Westminster, while individual MPs may be lobbied by delegations, besieged in their constituencies, and deluged with persuasive mail. They may be sympathetic to particular groups for various reasons. Deaf MP Jack Ashley campaigned with great fervour on behalf of the handicapped, with whom he had natural empathy. Sometimes the former profession of an MP leaves a residual loyalty to erstwhile colleagues, while groups based in a particular constituency can make a strong claim on the sitting member.

Groups try to cultivate long-term relationships with MPs, even inviting them to take up honorary positions in their associations. The relationship can be symbiotic, with some useful pay-offs for MPs, including lucrative retainers as 'parliamentary consultants'. Moreover, a reputation for specialist knowledge can be a basis for catching the Speaker's eye in debate and building a reputation.

Inside Parliament the general showpiece debates on issues chosen by the front benches afford few opportunities for influence by ordinary MPs. However, the committee stage is particularly useful (see pp. 287–9); amendments can be proposed and, even if defeated, valuable publicity is gained. Private members' bills provide a unique, though limited and expensive, opportunity for groups with friendly MPs actually to shape legislation. The upper house is not exempt from attention; its function of 'tidying up' bills affords a chance for one last-ditch stand.

It is sometimes argued that promotional groups are more interested in Parliament than are the economic giants, but this is far from the truth if one remembers the basic relationships with parties. Indeed, it is possible to view Parliament as a *functional* chamber where the members sit as representatives, not for geographical areas, but for industrial interests. Thus an MP might be more accurately described as the 'Right Honourable Member for ICI', or even 'Lord Channel Tunnel'. The danger of too cosy a relationship developing between groups and MPs led to the establishment of the register of members' interests (see p. 272).

Political parties   The orthodoxy that groups will seek friends in all political parties is questionable. In addition to the siamese pairings of labour and capital with the two major parties, the ideology of many promotional groups gives a partisan leaning. CND, for example, is wedded to Labour, and welfare groups like Age Concern or Shelter could find little cause for harmony with the Conservatives of the 1980s. The law-and-order lobby, however, traditionally expects a better crack of the whip from the Conservatives.

The executive   Direct lines to ministers at the heart of the decision-making centre might seem the most promising of all communication channels. The more powerful groups can demand meetings with ministers if they are so moved. Even under the Thatcher government, when ministers' consultation styles came to resemble that of Greta Garbo, the presidents of the royal colleges of surgeons, physicians, and obstetricians and gynaecologists demanded a summit meeting as the NHS careered towards crisis in early 1988. Again, when the 1988 local government bill sought in the notorious Clause 28 to ban the 'promotion' of homosexuality by local authorities, the artistic community trembled for freedom of expression and distinguished actor Ian McKellen sought a meeting with the arts minister. However, such close encounters often have no more than symbolic value; they are ritualistic exchanges, collapsing into bathos, and unlikely to result in any change in policy. Participants frequently report disappointment, ministers appearing uninterested, and under the control of suspicious, supercilious mandarins.

The civil service   Demonstrations can catch the headlines and meetings with ministers carry kudos, but it is the dealings which the groups have with the mandarins of Whitehall which have proved the most potent sources of influence. In these têtes-à-têtes the groups are at their most insidious. As a small village, Whitehall is full of intrigue, and those group representatives welcomed to tea may rest assured that the curtains will remain drawn; the genteel residents will not betray their secrets even to Commons select committees (see pp. 362–6). It is here that the technical resources of the groups (information, cooperation, expertise) are most valued, and where the symbiosis is most apparent. Consultation can shape the content of official publications, including **green papers**, which put ideas on the political agenda, and **white papers**, which declare government policy. Indeed, it may even be possible to keep issues from the public eye altogether. The group–mandarin duet sings even more *sotto voce* in the making of statutory instruments, where details of actual legislation are drafted in the privacy of the Whitehall offices.

Insiders and outsiders

It has been said that 'the more points on which pressure can be brought to bear, the greater will be the group's influence' (Smith 1976: 57). However, it is apparent that this view is wide of the mark. The most effective groups can be those needing the fewest channels of communication. Indeed, the sophistication commanded by the wealthiest groups is alarming: a new profession of **lobbyist** has emerged in which the skills and skulduggery of big business are brought to bear on public servants and the people's representatives. The fact that some groups can do better than others leads to an important distinction between them: some are **insiders** and others **outsiders**.

> Recently I had to do a job on the road issue and the civil servant I wanted to talk to wouldn't meet me. So I arranged for our MP to draft something like twenty written questions, questions which I knew he would have to do the work of answering. He soon got the message. You might call that blackmail. I call it a triumph for democracy.
>
> Douglas Smith (a lobbyist of Martin Dignum Associates), quoted in the *Guardian* (31 Oct. 1978)

Inequality of access, though a rather neglected area of direct study, is one of the most important features of group politics in the real world. Major British studies, such as those of the BMA (Eckstein 1960), the CBI (Grant and Marsh 1977) and the National Farmers Union (NFU) (Self and Storing 1962) (as well as the majority of smaller case studies and various symposia on the subject), have all concentrated on groups which are, in their different ways, largely successful, respectable and legitimate. The representatives of the select band of insider groups are themselves civil servant clones, having attended the same schools (public) and universities (Oxbridge). The relationship can be relaxed and informal, extending beyond tea in the corridors of power, to G&T in the clubs and restaurants of London, and even to weekends in country houses where the high can meet the mighty. Public service can be followed by private gain when, upon retirement and duly knighted, the ex-mandarins are able to take up lucrative appointments with those with whom they have previously been doing business (Doig 1984).

Factors determining status In practice the dichotomy between insiders and outsiders is not clear cut; rather there is a multiplicity of changing positions located along a notional insider–outsider spectrum. A confluence of factors will determine whether a group receives the Whitehall come-hither, including popular standing, stage of development, ideology, social compatibility, and leverage in the economy.

- *Public esteem.* The BMA has always gained mightily from the natural veneration which society accords to healers. On the other hand, groups espousing unpopular causes such as, say, the unification of Ireland or nuclear disarmament, can be safely snubbed by a government ever conscious that it will be judged by the company it keeps.

- *Stage of development.* New groups tend to start as outsiders. This may lead to various forms of 'non-responsible' behaviour, reinforcing outsider status. However, insider status may well be the ultimate goal, in return for which a code of good behaviour will be accepted.
- *Ideology.* Where the ideology of group and government clash, it is likely that neither will wish to be seen holding hands with the other. By choosing to remain outside the pale the group avoids any moral burdens of self-restraint and may kick more violently against the pillars of the establishment.
- *Social compatibility.* On the other hand, where the groups represent sections of society from which the decision-makers come, they will share norms, values and interests. They will not only speak the same language, they will do so with the same accent!
- *Economic leverage.* Certain interests (private industrial sectors and the City) enjoy a pivotal and unique position in that they shape the economic and political environment; governments of all complexions must therefore cater for their needs. Indeed Labour governments have been so concerned to reassure on this front that they have often subordinated their social programmes to favour private industry and the City.

These factors may either reinforce or come into conflict with each other. In addition, governments of left or right will evaluate them differently: the TUC went from a back-slapping 'beer-and-sandwiches' relationship with the Wilson government to a frosty cold shoulder from Thatcher. The suppression of dissidents is one of the hallmarks of totalitarianism, and when governments try to silence them, deride them, ban them, act as if they do not exist or seek to undermine their leaders, they can be said to gravely threaten democracy. The study of outsider groups is as important as that of the insiders. There are probably more of them than is normally realized, and their discovery will pose new debates about the efficacy of group-based representative democracy.

Explaining Group Politics

There are different theoretical perspectives on the politics of influence and the questions raised take the debate into the very heart of the power structure within the polity. In the rest of this chapter we shall examine the most important theoretical approaches to the politics of influence.

Pluralism

Much orthodox British study in the liberal-democratic tradition subscribes to a generally **pluralist** view of politics. The operation of groups is believed to remedy some shortcomings in representative government, including the following.

- A single vote cast about once every five years is so small an act that it can hardly be said to constitute participation.
- The principle of one vote per person fails to recognize the variation in the intensity with which views are held.
- People are denied influence over government between elections.
- Manifesto promises can be broken with impunity by mid-term.
- The voices of minorities are generally unheeded.

The modern variant of the theory is largely a US import deriving from Bentley. However, he saw group activity as a necessary and inescapable feature of *any* political system, and did not say that groups were unique to, or necessary for, liberal democracy. Yet subsequent political scientists developed the theory in this way. The freedom to form groups and make demands was seen as a hallmark of liberalism and the theory became a political version of the *laissez-faire* economic market place, fitting snugly within the framework of a capitalist economy. It was not merely a *description* of the way things were, but an ideology prescribing how they *ought* to be. Robert Dahl wrote extensively on the theory in the US, coining the term **polyarchy** to denote its benign nature. He regarded this as no less than a completely new theory of popular sovereignty (Dahl 1956), in which groups helped to exert the checks and balances so central to the American constitution.

In Britain, the interest in pluralism which had been present since the rise of the trade unions (exercising thinkers like Cole, Tawney, Russell, Laski and the Webbs) was reinforced by American commentators on the British scene, such as Samuel Beer (1965), and entered into the mainstream liberal-democratic orthodoxy.

The tenets of pluralism   This benign system, complementing representative democracy, may be portrayed in the following way.

- Groups provide a means of representation more effective than that afforded through institutions. The right to join such groups is a manifestation of the basic fundamental rights which liberal democracy holds dear.
- Public policy is the outcome, or resultant, of a number of group forces acting against each other. This may be compared with the mathematical vector diagram in which the *resultant* reflects the combined effect of all other forces (see figure 14.1). Thus the system tends towards a state of equilibrium, with all forces having some effect on the outcome.
- The point where the forces act is the government, which may be regarded as having no motivation of its own. It may be likened to a football referee, who does not kick the ball, has no desire to score, and cares not who wins. As recently as 1979, a study of British politics described the 'political style' as 'the balancing of group pressures' (Richardson and Jordan 1979: vii).
- No single group will dominate because, as in Newton's law of motion, for every force there is an equal and opposite which will act as a counterbalance.
- Competition will not threaten the integrity of society because each indi-

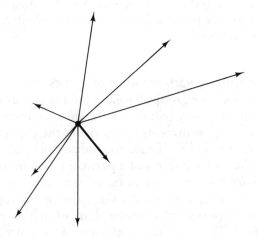

Figure 14.1 A vector diagram. The lines represent the magnitudes and directions of forces acting at a point. They produce a resultant which is the sum of their directions and magnitudes; thus every force is taken equally into account. This is analogous to a pure theory of pluralism.

vidual tends to belong to several groups; a loss on one front will be balanced by gains elsewhere.

- The larger the group the more influence it will have, thereby maintaining the democratic principle of majoritarianism, while not silencing the voice of minorities.
- People with intense feelings on an issue will tend to exert more pressure than the apathetic, thereby countering the unfairness of the mathematical equality in the one-person-one-vote principle.
- Those with a common interest, but not organized, will be accommodated because the policy-makers and other groups will regard them as *latent groups* ready to spring into action if threatened.
- Policies, as the product of bargaining and compromise, will tend to be moderate, fair to all, and conducive to social stability.

This of course is an abstract model, which the real world is supposed to resemble. Thus, while the idea that government is a complete nonentity is unrealistic (specifically rejected by Beer in the heyday of the theory in the mid-1950s – 1956: 23), a weak role for government is necessary to the theory, which is mainly concerned to legitimate the involvement of groups in policy-making. Lively (1978: 191) suggests two broad theories of the role of government in pluralism, neither of which sees it as a nonentity: the *arbiter* theory (government with enough power to ensure that the groups play by the rules) and the *arena* theory (government merely as one of the participants in the game). Although some revisionists have tried to argue that the theory is value free, intrinsically neither good nor bad, there can be no doubt that many scholars have believed it to be ultimately democratic.

With all its defects, it does nevertheless provide a high probability that any active and legitimate group will make itself heard effectively at some stage in the process of decision.

(Dahl 1956: 150)

The policy community variant Some pluralists give a more realistic version of the arena in which the groups bargain and fight, characterizing the various areas of government policy (education, finance, defence, and so on) as policy communities or **subgovernments** 'comprising the expert, the interested, and engaged' (Cater 1965: 17). Thus, to understand policy-making one must look at each policy area in terms of a particular community of ministers, civil servants, pressure groups, academics, consumers, and so on. Although in some respects these may be rivals, they also work together against other subgovernments in pursuit of a greater share of public resources (Richardson and Jordan 1979). This more complex view of the pluralist arena is shown in figure 14.2.

Evaluating the pluralist model

Few would quarrel with pluralism for stressing the role of groups in politics; they are indeed ubiquitous. However, one may question their uniqueness to liberal democracy; totalitarian regimes also have groups, including dissident movements. More importantly, it is doubtful whether their effect must automatically be benign and equitable.

To supporters of capitalist liberal democracy, pluralism is a welcome theory; it saves it from the charge that the electoral system, and other political institutions, are merely dignified elements serving only to legitimate class rule. Yet empirically it can be seen that group activity does not result in the elegant equity predicted; on the contrary, it is loaded against the underprivileged. In the first place, the pressure groups with the largest memberships are not necessarily the winners in the competitive battle; several other factors contribute to success. In particular, small, tightly knit associations (the City, the BMA) often have a degree of influence entirely out of proportion to their democratic weight. Moreover, the upper class (with superior education and so on) are generally better placed to operate pluralism, and the insider–outsider distinction demonstrates that there is no true equality of access.

> When I was at the [Health Education Council] ... the Ministry of Agriculture was in there like a ton of bricks acting virtually as a lobby for the National Farmers Union.
>
> Dr David Playfair (former Director General of the HEC), quoted in the *Independent* (17 Dec. 1988)

Groups are also defective as an alternative means of representation. Leaders are sometimes unelected, or elected on very low turnouts, and often

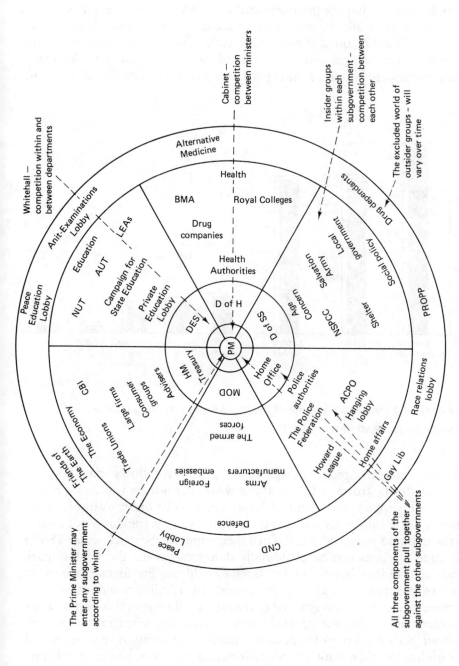

Figure 14.2 The pressure group world in terms of policy communities or subgovernments (simplified view)

have views at variance with members. Apart from trade unions, very few associations have procedures for consulting members. Among promotional groups, some are better able to attract public sympathy than others. Unpopular causes (like ex-prisoners and drug addicts) have great problems in raising funds, while others (such as animal welfare and children) (see figure 14.3) function on a big-business scale. Finally, the suggestion that government is a neutral referee is absurd: we have seen that the major political parties are bound to the economic interests with chains of silver and gold.

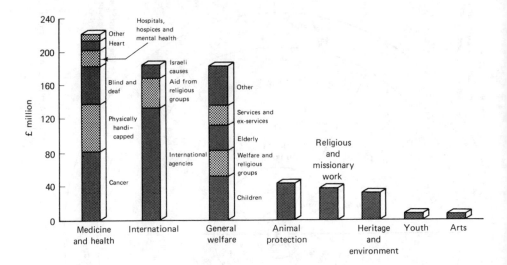

Figure 14.3   Voluntary income of the top 200 grant-seeking charities, 1986

Source: Social Trends (1988: chart 11.3)

Like the Ancient Greek Thrasymachus, pluralism allows that 'might is right', that strong groups will defeat the weak. Pensioners will be no match for the virile yuppies who demand lower taxation in order to inspire their exertions. Yet it can be argued that the purpose of government is not to give in to the rich and powerful but to curb their rapacity (Scattschneider 1960); weak game wardens can be profoundly dangerous when the wildlife park contains marauding beasts. In his farewell address President Eisenhower warned of the menacing growth in America of a 'military-industrial complex' threatening the sovereignty of government. Of course, this idea of weak government fits within the general liberal-democratic suspicion of government itself. As a kind of political *laissez-faire* (or anarchy) it removes moral responsibility from the state for inequalities and injustices: you cannot blame the referee if you lose the game. This can serve the privileged by inducing ordinary people to blame themselves rather than the system for their lack of success.

Because of factors such as these, the tendency of free-market pluralist politics is to produce a conservative, static society in which the privileged maintain their advantages and reformers are unable to make headway. Lindblom (1959) used the term **incrementalism** to characterize the way in which pluralism resulted in only small policy changes. Thus the Labour Party, on assuming office, has never been able to bring about anything resembling a socialist revolution.

Clearly the pure theory of pluralism does not explain the reality of the politics of influence in Britain. However, we can usefully turn to a variant of the theory – corporatism.

Corporatism

The **corporatist** thesis has long European antecedents, becoming interesting to British scholars during the 1970s as the limitations of pluralism were exposed. It is a form of politics in which government works in very close and deliberate collusion with the major interests in society. Clearly it has some family resemblance to pluralism, but as in many families the relationship is antagonistic rather than fraternal. A basic ethical problem arises with corporatism owing to its identification with the fascism of the 1930s. Phillipe Schmitter (1974) distinguished two forms – *state corporatism* and *societal corporatism*, arguing that the latter arose naturally within a society and unlike the former was *not* dominated by oppressive government.

The tenets of corporatism Societal corporatism is the variant to be found in modern liberal democracies and has the following characteristics.

- Politics is again seen in terms of groups, but unlike the pluralist scenario, they are not competitive, they work together.
- Government is not a passive referee, it plays a part in deciding who shall be consulted and has clear views on policy.
- The groups do not have to fight for access to government, they are welcomed in; they may even be created by government to represent interests it wishes to work with.
- Only a limited number of groups are included in the consultative network. These tend to be the representatives of capital and labour, and the result is **tripartism**, a *pas de trois* for government, the trade unions and employers.
- Those included tend to monopolize the right to represent their particular area of interest. Sometimes groups join together, forming peak organizations through which much consultation takes place.
- Special state institutions facilitate consultation and these can bypass those of the formal constitution.
- The relationship is reciprocal: not only do groups influence policy, government can influence groups, forcing them to modify their demands, gaining their cooperation in promoting and implementing policy, and disciplining their members to ensure its success.

Signs of corporatism in Britain In the early decades of the twentieth century Britain encouraged institutional growth among bodies representing labour and capital as a means of securing legitimacy for the state. There was even an attempt to set up a National Industrial Conference in 1919 and subsequently efforts were made formally to create a 'Parliament of Industry' (Middlemass 1979: 372). The age of post-war consensus saw renewed corporatist tendencies. The trade unions achieved some degree of hierarchical ordering under the TUC, as did employers under the CBI, and government showed a clear preference for consultation. A number of tripartite institutions appeared, particularly the National Economic Development Council, set up in 1961. In the mid-1970s, the Manpower Services Commission, the Health and Safety Commission, and the Advisory, Conciliation and Arbitration Service were established on a tripartite basis. In addition, there were hundreds of advisory and consultative councils concerned with particular industrial sectors and policy areas.

The corporate tendencies were not always restricted to the capital–labour duet. In other specific policy areas certain groups enjoyed particularly easy access to government, while others were excluded. Thus the BMA, the NFU and the National Union of Teachers enjoyed privileged access, while the ancillary medical professions, the environment lobby and smaller teaching unions shivered in the cold. Various policies had a corporatist flavour, particularly over prices and incomes, and the 1975–8 'social contract' gave labour and capital a voice in many domestic policies in exchange for cooperation.

However, whether this was real corporatism was always debatable, and by the mid-1980s the age appeared to be past. At an early stage Schmitter, who had once believed in the historical necessity of corporatism (even arguing that the western world was in for a full century of it), was quick to note the dramatic revolt in Britain among Conservative and capitalist interests after the mid-1970s (Lehmbruch and Schmitter 1982).

The pattern began to decay in the face of economic crisis. Heath's relationship with the unions marked an end to the beer-and-sandwich days of Wilson, and his confrontation with the miners was a red-letter day for British corporatism. The collapse of the Callaghan 'social contract' was a further illustration of the trend, and the 1979 Conservative government soon made it clear that it was not interested in beer and sandwiches with the trade unions, or even wine and pâté with the CBI.

The seeds of decline Corporatism was essentially a product of the consensus era. The *ménage à trois* of tripartism contained the seeds of its own destruction, its nature proving most fragile when it could have been most valuable – in economic crisis. Its vulnerability lay in certain intrinsic features.

- Trade unions were always liable to opt out once the benefits of full employment were no longer available to compensate for the concessions made to capital.

- Employers likewise become disenchanted as the rules and constraints to which they have agreed begin to erode profits.
- Militant forces within the trade unions are congenitally opposed to incorporation into capitalism.
- Large firms and unions will, on the grounds of self-interest, prefer to deal with government directly, rather than under a wider sectoral grouping.
- Governments with radical programmes will have little desire for the corporatist embrace, which tends towards the status quo.

Corporatism and pluralism It can be claimed that the corporatist interpretation explains nothing not already explainable in terms of pluralism. The terms 'pluralistic corporatism' and 'corporate pluralism' are coined to justify such claims, arguing that there are two pluralist traditions: the first emphasizing open competition between groups under a neutral state (the orthodox version), and the other a closed secretive one. However, such a view of pluralism robs it of its ability to say anything in particular: if it accounts for secretive, undemocratic government as well as liberal-democratic government it is saying little more than that 'groups exist'. The essential difference between corporatism and pluralism is that one stresses a central leadership role for government and the other its passivity as an essential feature of the liberal state. This is too fundamental a distinction to erase with pluralist sophistry.

Evaluating the corporatist model

Corporatism's link with fascism gave it an unpleasant odour; the resurrected version is sometimes termed **neocorporatism** in purification. For some, a neocorporatist style of government is a 'good thing', the answer to the wasteful competition generated by pluralism. Many of those actually involved in politics fall into this apologist category. It can appear as a great cure-all for national problems, engendering a classless camaraderie allegedly seen in times of war (indeed, the two world wars were great corporatist periods for Britain).

However, for others the corporatism of the post-war era was an undemocratic instrument of class rule. The world of participation became like an exclusive golf club, fine for the members but not so good for those beyond the fairways. Furthermore, trade union involvement in this exclusive world might be seen as little more than the opportunity to act as forelock-fingering caddies, labouring under the heavy burden of the capitalists' golf bags, and never invited into the bar. Even before its decline, it is doubtful whether corporatism was ever highly developed in Britain (see p. 403). Some crucially important interests, particularly the City, and many groups associated with welfare, remained outside the corporate processes and institutions, and even those included never entirely eschewed competitive pluralistic behaviour.

Although Britain has seen some corporate patterns of policy-making in

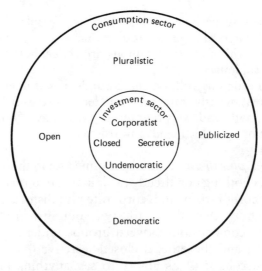

Figure 14.4   The dual state perspective

some areas, it has never looked like a *corporate state* (Cox 1988). One scholar saw it as 'a weakly developed system of corporatist interaction ... coexisting with a still healthy and important pluralist system of representation' (Grant 1984: 130). Thus the important question becomes: 'Which issues are decided in the corporatist style and which is the pluralist one?'. Cawson and Saunders developed the **dual state thesis** (figure 14.4) to explain this, arguing that issues affecting production tend to be settled in a corporatist style affording much power to capitalist interests, while those concerning the consumption sector (welfare and moral issues) are made pluralistically (Cawson 1986: ch. 7). Middlemas has spoken of a 'corporate bias' pervading political activity at many levels, suggesting a *desire* on the part of government to insulate itself from pluralist competition in order to best meet the needs of favoured interests at the expense of others. This bias has served to suppress class conflict, particularly during economic depression and war (Middlemass 1979: 371–85).

This makes the idea that pluralism can be 'healthy' while containing corporatist elements debatable. Indeed it can be seen as a disease to which pluralism is inevitably prone, a tumour threatening the life of the polity.

Politics without groups: New Right theory and public choice

New Right thinking has questioned the group interpretation of politics in both descriptive and prescriptive terms, doubting whether groups are as natural as Bentley asserted, or as desirable as pluralists have claimed.

By applying the methods of classical economic theory to political analysis, the *public choice theorists* attempt to explain political decisions (public choices) in terms of individual actors pursuing their own self-interests. Essentially an individualistic doctrine, it tends to negate any sort of group theory of politics, arguing that people are just too selfish to work together in pursuit of common goals. Olson (1968) suggests that a rational individual will not naturally become active in a group, or indeed a class, merely because it is fighting for a collective interest which he or she shares. The individual can do just as well by sitting back and letting others do the work. In the school choir it is easy enough to open the mouth soundlessly and enjoy the free meal after the concert. This is the age-old problem of the 'free-loader'.

Thus the idea that people tend to form groups (or even political parties) to protect their common interest is fallacious; the groups which do form would have formed anyway, existing first and foremost for some other reason. This, for Olson, is the explanation of the success of the capitalist interests in shaping policy. 'The multitude of workers, consumers, white collar workers, farmers, and so on are organized only in special circumstances, but business interests are organized as a general rule' (Olson 1968: 143). Groups which wish to influence government must develop a strategy for recruiting and retaining members. To do this they must offer **selective incentives** as inducements to join, use coercion such as a closed-shop arrangement, or resort to violence and intimidation. However, being artificial, these can never be entirely successful.

This theory is based on an economist's view of the world and has all the defects of that discipline. Political scientists study a real world of passion and emotion, not the abstract one of pure rationality inhabited by 'economic man'. Hence the theory is largely at variance with what we see. It may be quite true that one more person joining, say, Greenpeace, will not alter the course of history, but it will give that individual some deep psychic satisfaction, as an affirmation of identity and conviction. In the same way, many people join trade unions because they believe in the movement, wish for camaraderie, or want to make an ideological statement. As for the explanation of the success of capital in terms of superior organization, this is dangerously simplistic, ignoring the underlying imperatives of capitalism.

Group politics and the New Right   Olson further argues that the power of groups to veto government policy holds back economic growth. Only a trauma such as a revolution or war can break this choking stranglehold and free the economy (Olson 1982). This view is reinforced by other right-wing commentators. Samuel Beer believed Britain to have reached a state of paralysis or **'pluralist stagnation'** by the late 1970s as a result of governments' willingness to listen to group leaders who did not necessarily speak for the members and who were unwilling to accept restraint. The more groups involved in the process, the worse the problem becomes (Beer 1982: 31). This thesis has appealed to the New Right, with its deep antipathy towards union involvement in government.

The referee attacking the players   The New Right saw pluralism as admitting the barbarians at the gate into the hallowed chambers of the state and believed that the time had come to put a stop to consultative shilly-shallying. It was a case of 'cometh the hour cometh the woman'. The war cry was that the 'government should govern', and led to bitter confrontation with the steelworkers in 1980, the railwaymen in 1982 and, most dramatically of all, with the miners in 1984–5. A series of Acts of Parliament weakened the unions further: they lost legal immunities crucial for collective action, the weapon of secondary picketing was removed, the closed-shop laws were relaxed, and secret ballots to enable the apathetic mass to speak the voice of moderation and deference were made mandatory.

Insiders on the outside
Source: Times Newspapers Ltd

The new legislation brought the courts into the arena. Pluralist bargaining was replaced with force of law, and some unions found their funds sequestrated (appropriated by the government) on a crippling scale. This was backed up by government determination to enforce their policies by greatly strengthening the police force, which was seen in a new light of viciousness in the miners' strike and the Wapping newspaper dispute. By March 1988, the Manpower Services Commission's policy for industrial training (a flagship of corporatism) was being made by government on a 'take-it-or-leave-it' basis. Within the labour movement, the willingness of some unions to conclude single-union agreements and embrace new unemployment-creating technologies undermined the TUC as a peak organization. The government encouraged a fragmented trade union movement rather than one unified under peak organizations as required in the corporatist model. The breakaway miners' union was applauded and the TUC expulsion of the electricians' union in September 1988 led the government to end the TUC's automatic right to

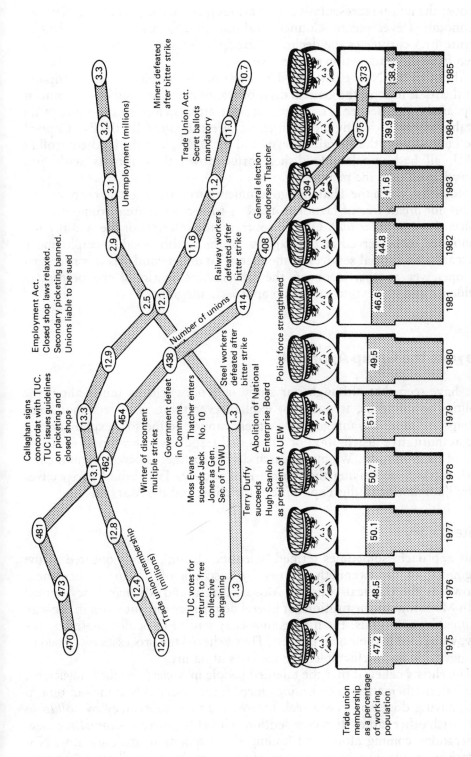

Figure 14.5 The death of corporatism   *Source:* Data from *Social Trends* (1988: tables 4.19 and 11.8)

choose the union representatives on various quangos, including the National Economic Development Council and the Health and Safety Executive. Figure 14.5 chronicles the decline of group politics under the New Right as seen from the trade union perspective.

Although the New Right and Thatcherism reserved its greatest antipathy for the trade unions, the general disapproval of pluralism and/or corporatism appeared to go deeper. Traditional insider groups close to the heart of the establishment, including the Institute of Directors, the CBI, the Bar Council, the Law Society, the Royal Colleges and the BMA, and the land-controlling NFU, all had unpalatable dishes thrust down their throats with little consultation over the menu.

However, when the Thatcher government turned its back on corporatism, it did not break free of factional interests to become a great trumpet of the voice of the *popular will*. On the contrary, the interests of the wealthy few continued to be served at the expense of the health, wealth, employment, education and social services of the many. To understand this it is necessary to open yet another door on the labyrinthine world of the politics of influence and go beyond the group approach altogether.

Beyond the Group Approach

We have seen that although our study of groups tells us much about the politics of influence, it does not explain everything. The fact that some groups are more advantaged than others cannot be the sole explanation of the authoritative distribution of values and resources in Britain, it is merely one of its *symptoms*. We must search deeper for the explanation, and enter dark recesses underlying the *structure* of society. Two broad perspectives offer illumination in this exploration: the **elitist** and the **Marxist**.

Elite theory

This approach, sometimes termed 'scientific elitism', was pioneered at the beginning of the twentieth century by a school of Italian thinkers now known as the classical elitists – Mosca, Pareto and Michels. They agreed with Marx that the institutions of liberal democracy did not work in the way claimed by apologists: the masses in society tended to be dominated by the few, who ruled in their own interest. They believed the processes discerned to be inevitable and ineluctable, like the laws of nature.

The elitists believed that the talented people in society (be they musicians, dentists, mathematicians or businessmen) would inevitably come out on top and, having done so, would seek to preserve their supremacy by *collusion* with each other rather than competition. This elite power is *cumulative*, new generations coming along and finding silver spoons in their mouths. Not surprisingly, the elite gains control of the state, by controlling the parties, securing the elective offices and monopolizing key official positions. It becomes a ruling class.

Elitist theory was rejuvenated in the 1950s by those sceptical of pluralism. In a famous study Floyd Hunter (1953) argued that a small, coherent corps of wealthy people dominated both the social and political life of the United States, while C. Wright Mills argued that the pluralist belief in countervailing forces was more 'ideological hope than factual description' (1959: 126 n.).

Elitism as an ideology There can be little doubt that Britain's political culture is elitist. This is both symbolized and reinforced in the unique, and elaborate, honours system. Titles continue to be inherited by those in the upper classes, with lesser ones reserved for the most successful members of the upper middle class, such as civil servants and businessmen. Peerages increase the power of the elite by giving seats in Parliament to those who come far nearer the royal box at Wimbledon than the ballot box.

Yet the idea that the elite class within society is able to cohere and collude to take over the state is palpably implausible. There is much rivalry, bitterness and hatred within the upper classes; indeed capitalism is based on this, under the name of *individualism*. Moreover, it is patently clear that those people at the top of the social heap are by no means the most talented or the best able to govern. The quest to understand how the balance of power and privilege in society is maintained is not yet over.

Marxist perspectives

For Marx, the key driving force in politics was a struggle, not between groups, but between classes. Liberal-democratic and pluralist theories assert that the state is independent of any particular class or interest in civil society; it is *neutral*. The Marxist perspective views this neutrality as bogus, asserting that under capitalism the state always operates in the interests of those with economic power – the capitalist class. There are, however, many schools of Marxist thought with conflicting views on how this domination is effected. At one extreme, the state may be said to be controlled through the conspiratorial activities of the upper class; this would be an **instrumental** perspective. At the other extreme, it may be held that the state is compelled to act in favour of the business interests by virtue of the logic of capitalism – a **structural** perspective.

The instrumental perspective The view of the state as an instrument of the ruling class is a feature of classical Marxist analysis, and Marx's description of the government as a committee for managing the common affairs of the bourgeoisie is regularly cited. A prominent exponent of this view is Ralph Miliband, who argues that

> there is a high degree of homogeneity among the members of the dominant class, much of it based on a marked similarity of social background,

education, and 'life styles' ... They constantly cross each other's paths in an incessant round of meetings, lunches, dinners, functions, and cere-monies, and as members of boards, commissions, councils, committees and institutions of the most varied kind.

(Miliband 1984: 7)

The view that the state becomes a limb of the dominant class can be supported in many ways. There are, for example, the recruitment patterns to the state institutions – the civil service, armed forces, judiciary, and so on – studied in the chapters of this book, which show the establishment directing its sons (and some of its daughters) into key positions. The manner in which, during the nineteenth century, the rising bourgeoisie reformed the state machine lends much credence to the instrumental view. Today the penetra-tion of the Conservative Party by business and finance, and the power of the establishment repeatedly to deliver a Conservative government, testify to the power of capitalism to dominate the state. This grip can be enhanced by control over the mass media, which cultivate an atmosphere of public opinion favourable to the hegemony of the dominant capitalist class.

Egg on the face of power

On 24 December 1988 the *Independent* revealed that the boards of the large food and poultry feed manufacturers, producing most of the eggs sold in British supermarkets, included a number of ex-Cabinet ministers and top civil servants (Sir Peter Carey, perma-nent secretary at the DTI, 1976–83; John Biffen, former leader of the Commons and a senior Conservative MP; and Lord Hunt, former Cabinet Secretary). Another big feed supplier had donated nearly £10,000 to Conservative funds in the 1987 election year. Little wonder that the government agreed to compensate egg producers for lost sales during the salmonella scare.

Control of the state can be enhanced by coherence within the dominant class. Pluralists argue that groups compete with each other, and economists argue that business firms do the same, so that, in both cases, the alleged effect is a mutual limitation of power. However, there is evidence of more coherence, if not collusion, than the competitive theories imply, and the multinational conglomerates of advanced capitalism make a mockery of competition. At the head of Britain's largest companies are the all-powerful directors, who each tend to sit on the boards of several companies: in 1976, eleven men held 56 of the 250 top directorships in Britain, as well as many others in smaller companies (Scott 1985: 44). In addition, although their interests can sometimes diverge (Marsh and Locksley 1983: 21–52), there are fundamental links between the City (which has been particularly influential in government policy-making) and industry. 'In terms of both ownership and control, banks, traders, and producers have come closer together the last 60 years' (Scott 1984: 45). Class solidarity is further promoted by intermarriage and various methods of excluding outsiders, ranging from freemasonry to inimitable upper-class accents.

The structural perspective However, although it may capture a deep truth about the *essence* of the state under capitalism, the committee metaphor should not be taken literally. The idea that any class consciously makes the state an entirely compliant instrument implies an unrealistic degree of collusion and conspiracy.

From the outset it can be argued that the very existence of state institutions (Parliament, the executive, bureaucracies, and so on) implies some degree of autonomy because these develop self-interests of their own. This is part of the explanation for the continued growth of social democracy, producing a large bureaucracy with an interest in expansion and self-preservation. Many civil servants and local government officers working in the welfare state have a firm ideological commitment to it and vote regularly for the Labour Party (see p. 178). In addition, politicians are highly ambitious and keen to remain in office. If the demands of capitalists were to threaten or inhibit their ability to do this (by making them support politically suicidal positions), they could be expected to resist.

Some writers even believe that the capitalist state can actually be highly insensitive to the needs of capital. Crouch argues that 'two of the most remarkable facts about liberal democratic societies are, first, the extent to which their ruling class mistrust the state and try to limit its activities, and second, the relative responsiveness of the polity ... to working class demands' (1979: 27). The structuralist explanation for the way the state serves the interests of capital is that it is essentially *autonomous*, but compelled by the structure of capitalism to perform certain necessary functions without which it cannot survive. The state must aim to stimulate economic growth, protect profits and facilitate private capital accumulation. The prosperity of the state depends on the prosperity of capitalism. In other words, the state is obliged to support the interests of those who gain the most from capitalism. Those occupying important positions in the institutions of the state are driven by the imperatives of capitalism as the actor playing Hamlet is driven by the imperatives of Shakespeare's script. This can help to explain why Labour governments have not made any serious impact on the distribution of wealth and privilege. The view is associated with the Marxist scholar Nicos Poulantzas (1973), who has conducted a long-running debate with Miliband.

Indeed, it can be argued that the nature of these necessary functions is such that, far from appearing as an instrument of the bourgeoisie, the state actually needs, and must be able to show, a degree of real autonomy in order to:

- provide services (social, economic, legal, and so on) which it is unprofitable for capitalists to provide for themselves;
- promote homogeneity within the dominant class, reconciling the fundamental conflict between finance capital, monopoly capital and non-monopoly capital (see Poulantzas 1973);
- provide political stability by acting as a mediator to absorb potentially disruptive demands by the underprivileged and ethical pressure groups;
- legitimate the capitalist system, by providing an ideology espousing the good of all.

The instrumental model is a **voluntaristic** one, allowing individuals choice in how they behave, while the structural one is **deterministic**, seeing the actors as puppets or role-players. The French philosopher Althusser (1969) believed that Marx was essentially a structuralist, although one can find both perspectives in his writing. Moreover, in real-world states we find a combination of the two: people have some choice but they are constrained by the system's structure. If politics is seen as a game of football, the capitalists are playing downhill and with the wind behind them. However, there is a referee with some autonomy (the state) and they are obliged to exercise some degree of skill to get the ball into the opponent's net.

Questioning the Marxist perspectives

There are of course arguments against the Marxist interpretation.

The managerial revolution thesis   It has been argued in one version of elite theory that a managerial revolution has taken place in industry. The old-style capitalists have been displaced by a diverse and non-organized body of anonymous shareholders, allowing control of capital to pass to a new managerial class of meritocrats, of lower social origins and without the same close identification with the state. Thus modern society may be seen as less elitist and more egalitarian in the opportunities offered to ordinary people (Burnham 1942).

For modern Marxists this is a fallacious thesis. They deny that power has passed to neutral meritocrats, asserting that it remains with the old upper class, though the latter has undergone an internal transformation. In the first place, the new ladder of meritocracy is also open to the sons and daughters of the upper class, and it is they who will have the best chance of climbing up. Moreover, the position of the meritocrats remains entirely dependent on their position in the bureaucracy; they can easily land upon the head of a snake and slither down to square one. Again, the meritocrats operate largely at the level of middle management, where their concern is with operational matters, leaving the traditional elite members, whose power remains based on ownership of property (and shares), in the boardrooms and in strategic control. Astonishingly, it was found that between 1850 and 1975 the proportion of chairmen of major companies with upper-class backgrounds remained stable at around 66 per cent (Giddens 1989: 219). In addition, the old upper class is sufficiently absorbent to permit the inclusion of outstanding aspirants from the lower strata who, with artificially cultivated upper-class mores, become neutered as potential agents of social change. Finally, although businesses are no longer in the hands of the old-style capitalists, there remains a small class holding large personal shareholdings, so that control of capital still remains in the hands of the few (Scott 1985).

Moreover, the power of the managers is dwarfed by that of the finance capitalists, moving in the world, not of commodities and production, but of banks and ledgers. These come from various walks of establishment life, including politics, the civil service and industry, and most hold titles. They also hold numerous directorships, thus coordinating the business system. Figure 14.6 illustrates how a mere nine individuals carried a network of 39

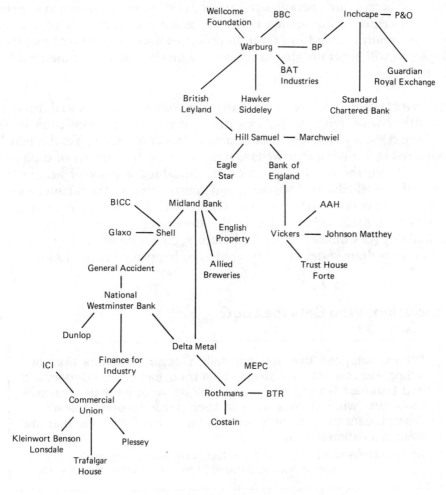

Figure 14.6 Top company links, 1976

Source: Scott (1985: figure 2.5)

companies in 1976. The strength of the controllers of capital is enhanced beyond measure through the presence of multinational companies, which can threaten to desert any country whose government does not cater for their needs.

The bureaucratic power model The idea that the upper class dominates government can be refuted by the suggestion that the civil service is a rational organization functioning in the public interest on the basis of high expertise. Max Weber noted the increasing role played in developed societies by public administrators who, with a monopoly of knowledge, and long experience, represented a potential threat to the hegemony of the elected rulers (see pp. 368–72). The public choice theorists of the New Right feared the bureaucrats as self-seeking individualists constantly exerting pressure for the expansion of their empire (Niskanen 1973). There is much in this; some Marxists accept bureaucratic self-interest as one of the reasons why the state enjoys a degree of autonomy. However, as we saw in chapter 12, the civil service recruitment and socialization processes have long ensured that those employed will generally sing in harmony with the interests of the establishment.

Welfare statism It may be argued that the post-war rise of social democracy, with a wide range of policies designed to ease the conditions of the working class, is hardly evidence of upper-class domination. Yet this may be countered by claiming that **welfare statism** serves the interests of capitalism by socializing the costs of production, furnishing a body of healthy and reasonably well-educated workers, and contributing to the maintenance of social harmony through legitimation (Gough 1979). If the economy runs out of steam, a *fiscal crisis* arises as the tax-borne cost of welfare erodes profitability (O'Connor 1973). If this occurs, the capitalist interests will soon rein in the welfare state. This appeared to be happening in the 1980s.

Conclusion: Who Gets the Loot?

> Do you suppose that you and half a dozen amateurs like you, sitting in a row in that foolish gabble shop, can govern Undershaft and Lazarus? No my friend: you will do what pays us. You will make war when it suits us, and keep peace when it doesn't ... When I want to keep my dividends up you will discover that my want is a national need.
>
> Andrew Undershaft, the wealthy industrialist, addressing his MP son-in-law in George Bernard Shaw's play *Major Barbara* (1907)

Explanations of group political behaviour range from the most benign version of pluralism to the most invidious form of elitist factionalism. All theories tend to devalue the role of government, and in this respect represent an important corrective to the constitutionalist descriptions of politics (favoured by the media), which see formal institutions as the beginning and end of political life.

One way to discover where the power really lies is to use the technique of Hercule Poirot and see who gets the loot. During the Thatcher era, the corporatist institutions became overgrown with trees and creepers, the path to Whitehall obscured with grass and moss, and the telephone to the TUC gathered a thick coating of dust. On the surface, a similar stance was also displayed towards the capitalist and professional interests, but the 1988 Lawson budget placed the loot most handsomely in the wallets and handbags of the wealthy at the expense of the rest. Marxist and elitist interpretations were made more compelling as the political system was stripped of its legitimating pluralist patina.

Thus influence is not to be explained primarily in terms of the activities of the groups, with success or failure contingent upon their skills and resources. The pattern of class power shapes the whole environment in which politics takes place, and this largely, though not entirely, predetermines the outcomes. The odds are always weighted in favour of capitalist interests. The struggles of pressure groups representing the poor and underprivileged must always resemble that of Sisyphus, whose torment in hell is to forever push a heavy stone to the top of a hill, from which it will invariably roll down again.

Key points

- The politics of influence takes place behind the formal scenery of the constitution; it is largely the domain of pressure groups whose goal is not office, but influence over government policy.
- There are two broad kinds of pressure groups: promotional groups seeking to advance some broad principle to benefit the whole of society, and sectional groups whose principal aim is to gain concessions for their own members.
- Pressure groups have a number of resources (expertise, veto power, the ability to communicate with their members and with the public) which enhance their standing with government.
- Pressure groups have various points of access to the political system, including public opinion, Parliament, political parties, the executive, and the bureaucracy. The last is often the most effective, not least because the relationship can be conducted in secret.
- Not all groups enjoy equal access to government; some are 'insiders', others 'outsiders'.
- Two principal theories explaining group politics are pluralism and corporatism, although there are a number of variants of these.
- Some theories about the politics of influence do not accept the primacy of the role of groups postulated by the pluralists. New Right theorists do not agree that groups are the natural unit of political activity, seeing group involvement as an unnatural phenomenon distorting the allocation of resources within society. Elitists and Marxists look for deeper sources of power within the polity.

- On the basis of asking the question 'who gets what?' the politics of influence appears to work largely in the interests of those who own and control capital.

Review your understanding of the following terms and concepts

interest group	corporatism
pressure group	tripartism
interest aggregation	neocorporatism
promotional group	dual state thesis
sectional group	selective incentives
peak organization	pluralist stagnation
green paper	elitism
white paper	Marxism
lobbyist	instrumental explanation
insider group	structural explanation
outsider group	voluntarism
pluralism	determinism
polyarchy	bureaucratic power
subgovernment	welfare statism
incrementalism	

Assignment

Conduct a research project on the resignation in December 1988 of junior minister Edwina Currie, with a view to assessing the power of the National Farmers' Union. Use your library to locate relevant newspaper articles; a key date for comment on the issues was 24 December (see especially the *Independent* for that day).

		% mark
1	Give a brief account of the events leading to Mrs Currie's resignation.	15
2	Identify some of the large food-producing interests in Britain today.	15
3	Would you agree that demographic changes within the Conservative Party mean that it is less responsive to the farming and landed interests? Explain your reasoning.	20
4	What evidence is there to support the view that Mrs Currie was forced to resign by the egg-producing interests?	25
5	Who said that 'the Thatcher years have been seen as anti-corporatist years'? What did he mean? Would you agree with the conclusion?	25

Questions for discussion

1 'In the analysis of politics, pressure groups are the really important units of analysis; more so than individuals or political institutions.' Discuss.
2 Discuss the problems facing the CND as a pressure group.
3 'Pressure groups are spontaneous formations and their activities are a natural extension of the liberal-democratic state.' Discuss.

4 'Interest groups which resort to loud public campaigns are revealing their impotence rather than their strength.' Discuss.
5 Could Britain have been described as a corporatist state at any time during the post-war era?
6 'Rational people do not join pressure groups.' Discuss.
7 'In all societies power will tend to be held by a small elite.' Discuss in the British context.

Topic for debate

This house believes that it was openness to pressure group involvement in government decision-making that led Britain to a state of near collapse in the post-war era.
  or
This house believes that the idea that all citizens enjoy equal opportunity to influence public policy through group activity is a myth.

Further reading

Almond, G. A. and Powell, G. B. (1966) *Comparative Politics*.
Classical US-style pluralism applied comparatively.

Beer, S. H. (1982) *Britain Against Itself*.
Bewails the power of the trade unions.

Bentley, A. F. (1967) *The Process of Government*.
The classic text which first appeared in 1908. Very readable and it is good to find out exactly what Bentley did and did not say.

Bottomore, T. (1964) *Elites in Society*.
Good introduction to elite theory.

Cawson, A. (1986) *Corporatism and Political Theory*.
Good account by a specialist in corporatism.

Coates, D., Johnston, G. and Bush, R. (eds) (1985) *A Socialist Anatomy of Britain*.
Set of powerful readings with masses of evidence to support the thesis that Britain has an all-powerful upper class with much influence over government. See especially the essay by Scott.

Dahl, R. A. (1956) *A Preface to Democratic Theory*.
Pluralism at its most optimistic by a doyen of the genre.

Finer, S. E. (1968) *Anonymous Empire*.
The first wide-ranging study of British pressure groups.

Grant, W. and Marsh, D. (1977) *The CBI*.
For some reason the CBI had remained beyond the scrutiny of political scientists until this examination.

Lehmbruch, G. and Schmitter, P. (eds) (1982) *Patterns of Corporatist Policy-Making*.
Comparative insight with some seminal contributions.

Middlemas, K. (1979) *Politics in Industrial Society*.
Presents the theory of 'corporate bias'.

Miliband, R. (1984) *Capitalist Democracy in Britain*.
Well-argued Marxist perspective.

Olson, M. (1982) *The Rise and Decline of Nations*.
The politics of influence from a public choice theorist.

Scattschneider, E. E. (1960) *The Semi-Sovereign People*.
Critique of the heavenly choir (of pressure groups) which sings with an upper-class accent.

For light relief

Bertolt Brecht, *The Good Woman of Setzuan*.
Brilliant satire on capitalism, taking a structural perspective. Thus the 'good person' is made bad when she tries to run a shop under capitalism.

R. B. Dominic, *Epitaph for a Lobbyist*.

George Bernard Shaw, *Major Barbara*.
Explores with humour and insight government–industry relations, exposing the greed and hypocrisy motivating the political world.

Frederick Raphael, *The Glittering Prizes*.
A nostalgic view of the privileged world where success comes as a matter of right to the scions of the establishment.

PART V

The Outer Reaches of the State: Worlds Beyond Whitehall

The media construction of British politics is characteristically centralist in orientation; this is understandable because constitutionally Britain is a unitary state under a supreme Parliament. However, when attention turns from the hot fires of policy-making to the cooler parts of the political room, where policy proposals are transformed into reality through the more prosaic processes of public administration, the media lens is revealed as distorted. There are a number of reasons why the juggernaut machinery necessary to operate the full range of public functions lies largely beyond the precincts of Westminster and Whitehall.

- *The evolutionary pattern.* Many of the important functions of the state grew up at the periphery rather than the centre.
- *The policy–administration dichotomy.* There is a long tradition of thought which sees the making of policy and its implementation as separate activities.
- *Commercialism.* Where the state enters into the world of industry it has been held that administration cannot be entrusted to naive civil servants.
- *Artistic and technical judgement.* The dispensation of state money to the arts (Arts Council) and the application of technical principles to decision-making (NHS) involve judgements beyond the scope of bowler-hatted bureaucrats or popularity-seeking politicians.
- *Personal morality.* Similarly, there are certain areas of personal morality felt to be beyond political judgement (e.g. race relations).
- *Freedom from political interference.* A fundamental plank of liberal democracy is that there are some state functions which must be politically neutral (e.g. broadcasting, police and judiciary).

- *National security.* Certain matters are kept beyond the eyes and ears of not only Parliament, but even of ministers. In Britain the security services are allowed to operate with few restrictions, sometimes at the fringes of legality.
- *Efficiency.* Where services are needed by a local community it is more rational to provide them through bodies familiar with local conditions.
- *Local democracy.* It becomes necessary, if the idea of democracy is to be real, to establish local machinery for participation and decision-making.

The most singular characteristic of this great world beyond London is some degree of autonomy from the centre. However, in moving from centre stage we are by no means leaving the world of politics, nor even the world of central government, for the tentacles of Westminster and Whitehall are long. We shall argue that arm's-length administration is often part of the strategy of the powerful to 'technocratize' important matters out of politics and hence out of the public domain.

15

Quasi-autonomy, Quasi-democracy: Arm's-length Administration

We begin our exploration of the non-Whitehall territory with a large group of diverse agencies, a rag-bag defying clear classification and, under the acronym '**quango**', sounding more like something Alice might have encountered than part of the machinery of government. Scholars and practitioners define quangos variously, some referring to them as Quasi-Autonomous National Government Organizations, while others replace 'national' with 'non', though this makes little sense. Better is the alternative QGAs (Quasi-Governmental Agencies), but this is little used and lacks the ring of 'quango'. They are set up by the national government, often on a statutory basis, but once in existence they are permitted a degree of freedom from democratic control and accountability. The chapter comprises four main sections. The first looks at the category as a whole, identifying some important subgroups. In the second section we examine a very special group within the overall category, the **health authorities**, looking rather like unelected local authority health committees. These are examples *par excellence* of bodies designed to allow experts, rather than democratic representatives, to take control. Next we consider the **nationalized industries**, which were for the most part given the special constitutional status of public corporations. In large measure the difficulties and contradictions encountered here represent in heightened form those of quangos in general. The fourth section analyses the programme of **privatization** which gathered momentum throughout the 1980s, identifying the new problems which this 'solution' to the old problems throws up with the creation of a new generation of **regulatory bodies**.

Introducing the Quango

Assessments of the number and nature of quangos differ, but generally they are government-created bodies operating beyond the control of Parliament in various areas of industrial, social, scientific, cultural, economic and artistic life. They are run by boards appointed by ministers from the list of the 'great and the good', consisting of the nation's trusted worthies – generally white, middle class and male. Usually funded from the national exchequer, quangos may be broadly classified as judicial, advisory, executive, consultative, commercial and regulatory.

"The committee on women's rights will now come to order.

Reproduced by permission of *Punch*

Judicial These are mainly tribunals, of which there are many hundreds; they are examined in chapter 17.

Advisory Such agencies represent a peculiarly British institution, their creation often being seen as a ploy by governments to avoid any real action. Their function is to examine specific problems and make recommendations. **Advisory bodies** lie thick on the ground – in 1979, the Pliatzky Report identified over 1,500 (1980: 1–2) – and may be classified as temporary and permanent. The former include the large, prestigious royal commissions addressing major issues such as the reform of local government or the police, their deliberations often taking several years and sometimes heralding momentous changes. The second category is the larger and includes some major bodies, such as the Central Advisory Council on Education which produced, *inter alia*, the important Plowden and Newsom reports, but many which remain largely unknown, such as the White Fish Authority, working diligently in some cobwebbed backroom of the state. They are known variously as advisory councils, consultative councils, working parties, boards, commissions, standing conferences, and so on.

Consultative These are forums reflecting the corporate tendencies in the British state (see pp. 423–6) and designed to bring together ministers, civil servants and representatives of pressure groups. The National Economic Development Council is a prime example of a **consultative body**, though there are hundreds of others. They were particularly important during the consensus era of British politics before government spurned consultation.

Executive These actually administer some function: disseminating information, like tourist authorities or the Health Education Council, or distributing public funds, such as the University Funding Council, the research councils and the Arts Council. Pliatzky identified almost 500 **executive bodies**. This group also includes certain semi-autonomous departmental agencies employing civil servants but responsible for sharply defined blocks of work, such as the Defence Procurement Executive within the Ministry of Defence. There are also Crown Bodies charged with the management of institutions such as the royal palaces, the British Museum, the National Gallery and Kew Gardens. The Ibbs Report of February 1988 recommended an increase in this category (see figure 15.1) by hiving off various civil service functions (see p. 374).

The largest hiving-off operation was announced by the government in May 1989. Eighty thousand civil servants responsible for the social security system were to form several semi-autonomous agencies to run the £50 billion benefit system on contract to the government. For the New Right the political implications of the policy were clear: the semi-autonomous agencies would be sitting ducks for subsequent privatization.

Quasi-local government There are a number of services administered on a decentralized territorial basis but not entrusted to elected local authorities. The abolition of the GLC and metropolitan counties led to some increase in these. Another major example was the water authorities, but the largest group within the category are the health authorities.

Commercial A very special element of the public sector has been concerned to operate in the commercial world like a private capitalist undertaking. This has comprised the nationalized industries in the form of public corporations, which we examine in detail later in this chapter.

Regulatory Regulation has long been a role of the state in order to protect citizens from exploitation, pollution and ill health, and is frequently entrusted to a quango. Today **regulatory agencies** are common in many

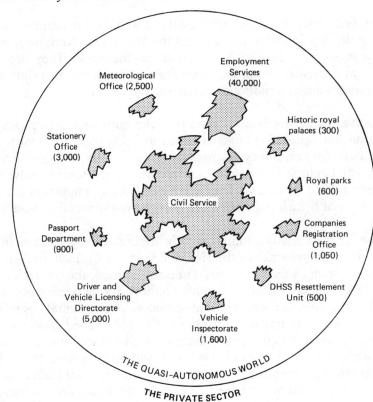

Figure 15.1 Chipping away the civil service: candidates for hiving off in 1988 (with staff sizes)

areas, such as standards of hygiene, working conditions, building standards, safety at work, the use of pesticides, quality of food, and so on. Increasingly regulation is viewed as an alternative to public ownership, particularly where the objective is to curb the use of monopoly power (see pp. 470–73). In addition, certain aspects of social life are now subject to regulation in order, for example, to outlaw discrimination on racial and sexual grounds.

Sick of Democracy: the National Health Service

The National Health Service is one of the most stark examples of the practice of placing important public services beyond the arm of democratic control. Health is our most valued possession. Although much political activity, and political analysis, sees the main goals in the battle for 'who gets what' in material terms of wealth and property, health is really of far greater importance to our quality of life. Because of this it has been held that health care in British society should be apportioned on the basis of need rather than wealth, and a National Health Service (NHS) was created in 1948 on the collectivist principle that rich and poor should have equal access to treatment. However, one effect of this was to place health care firmly in the realm of the political and in the health policy-making process there are the usual combatants (a wealthy minority, the politicians, the bureaucracy, the pressure groups, the masses, and so on). In addition, there is one other very singular feature: the technical experts have a much greater role than in any other policy arena. These are the doctors, who as a profession have enjoyed a remarkable degree of power, stemming not from their possession of capital, nor from the ballot box, but from the fact that they claim literally to hold the power of life or death. Their influence has accounted for a great deal in British health policy and is the reason why the NHS is run as a quango, away from the eyes and ears of democracy. How did this come about?

The wartime consensus

The second world war provided an important impetus towards the creation of the NHS with the establishment of a nationally based emergency medical service to treat casualties. The voluntary societies and local authorities which had been providing hospitals could hardly baulk at the takeover in time of great national need, and the pill was sweetened by central government willingness to shoulder the financial burden. During the war a broadly based consensus developed, embracing the coalition parties, the medical interest groups and local government: some kind of state health service was required to take the British people into the new age.

This was a natural consequence of war, when national solidarity was at a premium to ensure that large numbers of working-class men would agree to fight and die to preserve a political and economic system which had previously seemed impervious to their demands and insensitive to their sufferings. Austere food rationing did not prevent a liberal supply of the carrots required to maintain morale: the war-weary public was confidently assured that, if shoulders were put to wheels, it would be difficult to see the bread for the thick coating of state-provided jam to be dispensed in the future. Thus the impressive coalition consensus in no small measure reflected establishment concern for its post-war survival and fears of working-class radicalization.

This thinking was displayed in the famous Beveridge Report, *Social Insurance and Allied Services* (1942), often venerated as the blueprint for the British welfare state. It spoke of a new concept of freedom: instead of the essentially *negative* and *laissez-faire freedoms* to pursue trade and maximize profit, citizens were to be guaranteed *positive freedoms* from the 'evil giants' of want, ignorance, idleness, disease and squalor. An extended social welfare system was envisaged which could include a comprehensive national health service, available to all, and free at the point of delivery. In 1944 a white paper was published demonstrating this consensus over the goals and structure of a new health service.

Goals The accepted goals were comprehensiveness, accessibility, and democratic responsiveness.

Structure The service was to be a local government function with a Health Minister in a coordinating role. General practitioners (GPs), who were resistant to the idea of being state employees, were to be made something of an exception. They were only partially integrated into the system, with a Central Medical Board (replacing the old local insurance committees) to pay doctors on a capitation (number of patients) basis and ensure an even spatial distribution of their services.

The consensus cracked

However, the passing of the mood of wartime emergency saw a peeling of the paper which had masked the cracks in the walls of British society. Although officially the goals of the new service remained the same, the caring concept was refocused to embrace the health and welfare of the medical profession itself. The structure which actually emerged was a clear regression from the model tantalizingly dangled before the eyes of the public in 1944.

- It was not to be a single integrated service: a tripartite structure introduced an administrative division between hospitals, GPs, and the rest.
- It was not to be democratic, being largely located outside the local government system. Although the country was dissected territorially, the local controlling bodies were to be appointed by the minister, not elected by the local people. Regional hospital boards and hospital management committees were responsible for the hospitals, while executive committees controlled the GP services. Only certain community health functions (clinics, school medical service, and so on) were to remain with local government.
- It was not egalitarian (within the body of the NHS the tumour of private enterprise was to remain, feeding off the blood of the service, for the benefit of the wealthy).

The structure was a triumph for the medical profession, which was largely in control at all levels. However, the real significance of the NHS at this stage was probably its symbolism; it was a key instrument of legitimation for the establishment. The service was free at the point of use and collectivist in nature (funded from general taxation rather than personal insurance). It also showed some of the principles of a caring society that many Britons had been convinced they were fighting and sacrificing their lives for, and it was to become the most popular part of the welfare state.

In 1974, the quest to seal off the NHS from local democracy was completed when local government reform saw all its personal health functions given to a reorganized NHS and hospital management committees became **health authorities**. The deprivation of local democracy was compensated for by the creation of unelected community health councils (CHCs) to act as consumer watchdogs. In 1982 the structure was simplified, with 192 district health authorities (DHAs) becoming the key administrative units (figure 15.2).

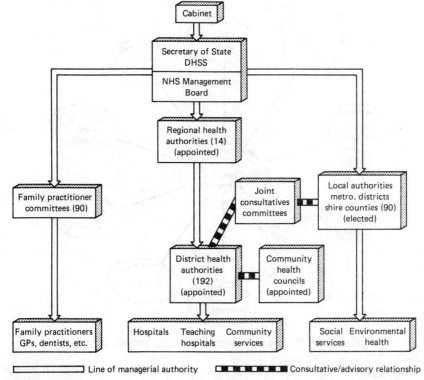

Figure 15.2 The administrative structure of the National Health Service, 1982

Quasi-local government: the concept of the health authority

Today the basic unit for running the NHS is the *District Health Authority*. This curious animal has much of the appearance of a committee of a local council, apart from the significant fact that on their journey to their positions members do not pass by way of the local ballot box. It stands at the centre of a local political force field (figure 15.3), its members appointed by the minister from within the community. This has been held to be a sufficient degree of democracy for the important matter of health care. DHAs assemble once a month, the meetings being generally held in public but, although the local press may send a word-weary hack, the general level of public interest is about equal to that shown towards the mating pattern of the North American warthog. This of course is a predictable (and intended) result of non-elective public activity; citizens have little cause to know about this shadowy freemasonry. The sheltered environment is a benign ecological system where the creeper of technocracy strangles the tree of democracy.

There are around 2,000 members sitting in the committee rooms of the health authorities of England and Wales and Aneurin Bevan (Minister of Health at the inception of the NHS) had argued that they were not to represent any special interests within the service. Until the late 1980s they included three broad categories: local government nominees, laypersons and members of the medical profession.

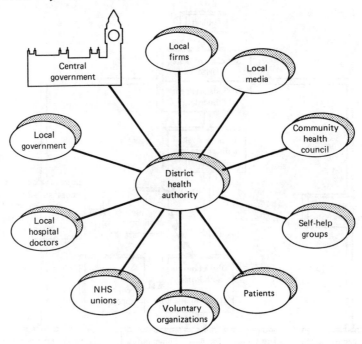

Figure 15.3   The local arena for health service politics

The chairperson This is the pivotal position, and the only one with a salary. The appointment represents a key patronage power of the Secretary of State and, during the 1980s, Conservative ministers increasingly made overtly political appointments, often placing local businessmen at the helm.

> They [the chairpersons] neither speak as elected representatives nor do they have the expertise of their own officials. And their attitude to the secretary of state and the department is necessarily pretty subservient – they want to keep their jobs.
> Barbara Castle (Labour Minister of Health), *The Castle Diaries 1974–6* (1980)

Laypersons These are surrogates for elected representatives, coming from relevant local interest groups and voluntary associations. In theory they should reflect the community in terms of factors like class, gender and race (there must be a trade union member, for example), but membership remains largely a middle-class preserve. Although lying ultimately in the hands of the Secretary of State, the choice is usually made at regional level under the eye of the chairperson and in the darkest secrecy (Steel 1984: 37).

The laypersons are by definition not experts, a state of primordial innocence the government appears keen to preserve. Like Adam, they are not encouraged to taste the dangerous fruits from the tree of knowledge, receiving only a few bland documents and regulations by way of introduction, and given virtually no training. They stand as hapless Davids against the Goliaths of medicine.

The professionals The presence on the DHA of members of the medical profession has meant that, in effect, they have been in the happy position of being their own employers, the state guaranteeing to pick up the bill for the policies they make. This stands in contrast to local government, where employees are legally barred from standing for election. The practice is legitimated on the grounds of the need for medical expertise. The assumption, perhaps based upon the Hippocratic oath (whereby doctors swear to put their patients first), was that doctors would not act to advance their own interests. Whether Hippocrates has ever revolved in his tomb is a matter for archaeological scholarship rather than political science, but the latter discipline has cast considerable doubt on the wisdom of Bevan's trust.

> Physicians of the utmost fame,
> Were called at once; but when they came,
> They answered, as they took their fees,
> 'There is no cure for this disease'.
> Hilaire Belloc (1870–1953; prolific and versatile writer),
> *Cautionary Tales* (1907)

Local authority nominees The presence of this category was the nearest the DHA got to democracy. Although not elected to their NHS positions, they had at least passed before the electorate at some point. During the 1980s, there was a move towards the party politicization of the DHAs, some Labour authorities sending members as cohesive political cohorts. This was balanced by the Conservative central government with overtly political appointments of chairpersons and other lay members. However, in January 1989 the government announced in a white paper its intention to purge the authorities of local authority representatives, replacing them with local business leaders – representatives not of the community but of private capital.

Power in the NHS: Doctor knows best

The healers in most societies, be they witch doctors or organ transplanters, are solemnly venerated; they offer the inestimable gifts of hope and even life itself. As society becomes increasingly secular, hospitals replace cathedrals and doctors inherit the sceptre and mace of the bishops. While the offer of new lungs for old is hardly a promise of eternal life, it is a step in the right direction, and doctors' calls for more expenditure are sure to arouse popular sympathy. Thus, in the three decades following the creation of the NHS, a close-knit *health policy subgovernment* emerged in which the doctors' professional organizations lay close to the heart of power (figure 15.4).

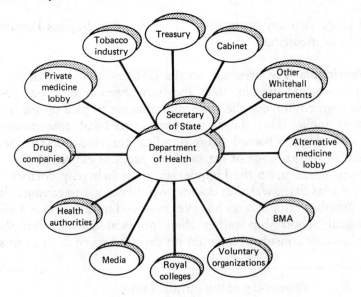

Figure 15.4 The central arena for health service politics

Governments responded to doctors' demands, ignoring those advocating greater concentration on preventative measures, in the belief that Canute had more chance of success than a British government trying to resist the popular tides of medical approval.

This example serves to demonstrate that power in society is not only based on the ownership of capital. One of the major results of the medical

---

The unhealth industry

Cigarettes provide government with one of their biggest and most reliable sources of revenue: they create tens of thousands of jobs in hard economic times; they present a healthy surplus on the balance of payments; they help the development in Third World countries where tobacco is grown.

P. Taylor, *The Smoke Ring* (1984: xix)

---

profession's close involvement with the policy-makers has been to gain widespread acceptance for its own special view of what a health service should be, reversing the old wives' tale to say that 'cure is better than prevention'. This medical definition of health sees the service as a means of curing and healing. It is physician based and largely excludes the **public health**, preventative functions of health care, which aim to eradicate environmental conditions damaging to health.

However, despite its seemingly independent power base, the medical establishment is (like the legal establishment) linked through family and social ties with the capital-owning stratum of society. Moreover, the **medical model of health** is one fitting snugly within a free-market economy where industries do not like to meet the expense of limiting pollution and even manufacture products (such as cigarettes) known to damage health.

> As to the cause of our illness
> One glance at our rags would
> Tell you more. It is the same cause that wears out
> Our bodies and our clothes.
>
> Bertolt Brecht (1898–1956; German dramatist and poet),
> 'A Worker's Speech to a Doctor'

Who gets healthy, how, when? Despite the seeming insulation of the NHS from the processes of democracy, it is clear that politics intrudes. Decision-making is concerned with the political allocation of health resources. In this there are winners and losers and, as in other areas of life, members of the higher social classes get a consistently better deal (figure 15.5).

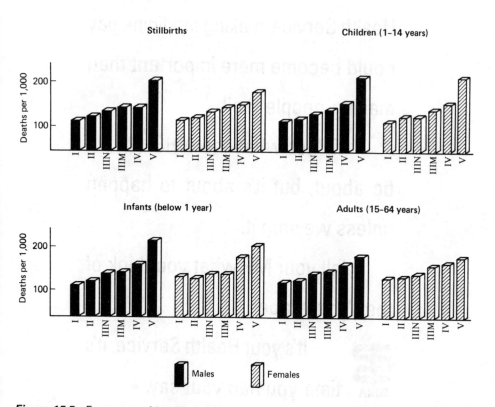

Figure 15.5 Four ages of health: relative mortality by social class (Registrar General's classification) and gender

Source: Data from Black (1980: 32)

Health politics in the 1980s: the quango model turning sour

Although doctors were singing a theme which harmonized well with the larger symphony of capitalism in Britain, the harmony was to turn to discord and the sweetness of the quango model turn sour.

Health politics in the 1980s provided a useful case study of power within British society. While Marxists would argue that the power of the medical profession is largely derived from its position as a segment of the dominant class, the corporatist view would see it more in terms of a particular power derived intrinsically from its own resources (monopoly of expertise, professional organization, and so on). It would be difficult to argue that the Conservative government of the 1980s, representing the interests of capital, was at one with the medical profession. Indeed, by the late 1980s the BMA, far from being the cosy insider close to the heart of the establishment, was beginning to take on the appearance of an outsider group, demonstrating, abusing ministers, and appealing to the public with advertisements.

In Mr. Clarke's sharp new Health Service, making medicine pay could become more important than making people well.

It's not what the NHS should be about, but it's about to happen unless we stop it.

Tell your MP what you think of the White Paper.

BMA It's your Health Service, it's time you had your say.

The BMA's advertisement in national newspapers, May 1989

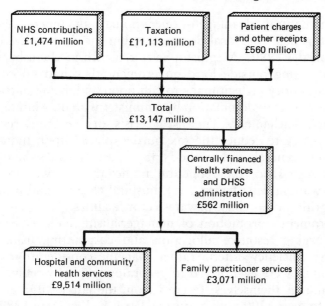

Figure 15.6 NHS funding and expenditure in England 1983–1984

Source: HMSO (1985)

The financing of the NHS, as built into the quasi-autonomous model, goes a long way towards explaining its problems in defending itself in the 1980s. Since its inception it had contained an implicit Faustian bargain between central government and the profession (Klein 1983: 82). In exchange for the everlasting life of clinical autonomy, unconstrained by elected representatives at the periphery, the doctors sacrificed their financial souls to the Whitehall devil by forgoing the autonomy promised by local taxation. Central funding, which is a mammoth operation (see figure 15.6), gives

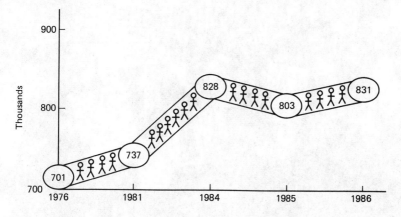

Figure 15.7 UK hospital waiting lists, 1976–1986

Source: Data from *Social Trends* (1988: table 7.23)

Whitehall the natural advantage of one who pays the piper. The immediate casualty of this deal was local democracy, but the doctors lived to rue the pact when, in the 1980s, Mephistopheles returned to claim his due. When under threat, being outside local government they had no core of local democratic authority or legitimacy to call upon and, being outside the civil service, were subject to domination by a minister with only limited accountability through Parliament. The fiscal crisis of the state resulted in a determined policy to reduce the tax burden placed upon industry by the welfare state in general, and by the NHS in particular. As the overall NHS budget was restrained, the reduction in health care was manifested in lengthening waiting lists (figure 15.7), hospital closures and instructions to health authorities to purchase private-sector facilities.

The government's promotion of managerialism challenged the doctors' hegemony, urging resource allocation and cost-cutting using 'rational', private-sector efficiency criteria rather than the consideration of patients' *needs*. Hospitals were even urged to generate income by selling services or the very buildings themselves, receipts from the latter surging from under £50 million to over £200 million during 1984–8 (*Key Data* 1989). Reforms proposed in the white paper of January 1989 revealed the government's clear determination to smash professional power. In addition to its controversial proposals to curb the doctors in various ways, subsequent working papers promised greater authority for administrators (including a say in decisions as

Doctors and nurses demonstrating against proposed NHS reforms
Source: Times Newspapers Ltd

to which consultants should receive merit awards), tight limitations on prescribing, and new, tougher disciplinary procedures. Moreover, the cherished role of the profession in policy-making was to be curtailed: at the top of the Department of Health there was to be a policy board consisting of civil servants, and industrial and business leaders, but excluding the government's own chief medical officer and chief nurse.

The weaknesses exposed here are to be found in all forms of quango: though outside the normal democratic channels of control and accountability, they are ultimately as much under the control of the central government (usually the paymaster) as it wishes to make them.

Prognosis: private grief

In addition to the managerialism and the cuts discussed above, the political health agenda also included a reversal of the essentially collectivist character of the service by taking it out of the fiscal system altogether. This was to take the debate back to pre-1945 days; there was much talk of private medicine, with the NHS as little more than a safety net for the poor.

Yet there is little doubt that the privatization of British health care was already happening during the 1980s. The number of private beds outside NHS hospitals increased by 54 per cent, while the number of private hospitals rose by 35 per cent. Even more important has been the change in the pattern of ownership, with giant US companies moving in to cash in on the Thatcher revolution. The greatest beneficiaries of the developments are members of social classes I and II, a quarter of whom have private medical insurance. Between 1979 and 1988 the number of people taking out private medical insurance more than doubled (Higgins 1988: 8–9); by the late 1980s nearly 10 per cent of the population were covered (*Social Trends* 1988: 128).

Nationalizing Industry

The post-war political landscape of Britain was characterized by large-scale state ownership of industry to the extent that the economy was described not as capitalist but as 'mixed'. The motives for state ownership were also mixed, and by no means all anti-capitalist.

The pattern of nationalization

Nationalization has occurred in two waves. The first, following the second world war, brought into state ownership coal, electricity, gas, rail, road haulage, air transport, steel and the Bank of England. The second took place from the mid-1960s under both Labour and Conservative governments, largely through state purchase of shares in a wide range of undertakings.

The motivations for state ownership

Broadly speaking, the reasons for state ownership of industry may be categorized as ideological principle, political expediency, or some combination of the two (Hanson 1963: 22), varying from one industry to another. The debate over the desirability of nationalization is fundamental, with tendrils penetrating into the structure of power within the state. The left has always been more favourably disposed for a number of reasons.

- *Marxist doctrine*. Nationalization can be seen as an attack on capitalism, and is included in the Labour Party's constitution in its famous Clause IV.
- *Imperfections of the free market*. Keynes showed that in the real world the free market does not produce the optimum allocation of resources. Nationalization is one means of regulating the market.
- *Balance of power within society*. The large-scale owners of capital are able to exert great influence over society. Thus public ownership can be seen as a means of restoring strength to democratic government.
- *Protection of workers*. Industrial relations in certain of the industries taken into state ownership in the immediate post-war period (coal and rail) were particularly bad, providing an important stimulus for nationalization.
- *Control of key industries*. Certain industries were adjudged too important to be left in the control of sectional interests. This became starkly evident in the second world war and special ministries were created to coordinate work in key areas. The same applies to the development of atomic energy and the exploration of the North Sea for mineral fuels.

Although the principle of state ownership of industry was deeply alarming to capitalist class interests, the nature of the post-war era was such that they could happily support it. The owners of outdated plant and machinery were relieved of the responsibility for modernization, and also given extremely generous compensation. Most industry remained in private hands so that Britain developed, not a socialist economy designed to tame the forces of capitalism, but a mixed economy, designed to make it work better in unfavourable circumstances. Private industry in general was able to benefit from a state-provided infrastructure encompassing power and transport facilities, and there were no serious disagreements between the political parties (L. Harris 1985: 26). Table 15.1 shows the extent of the mix in the economy on the eve of the collapse of the post-war consensus.

Moreover, the technical characteristics of certain industries rendered competition extremely wasteful (two railway lines for the same journey would clearly be absurd); they were **natural monopolies**. However, this gave them great exploitative powers in the economy at large and capitalists were well pleased to see them under state control.

The question of management was a key area of debate, and an orthodoxy emerged that this could hardly be entrusted to Whitehall mandarins with little knowledge of industry and trussed in red tape. It was argued that the

Table 15.1 Nationalized industries' share in the UK economy, 1975: the big nine
(percentage of total)

	Output	Employment	Investment
Post Office and Telecommunications	2.8	1.8	4.5
Electricity Board	1.5	0.7	2.9
British Airways	0.3	0.2	0.4
Coal Board	1.5	1.2	0.9
British Rail	1.2	1.0	1.0
National Bus Company	0.2	0.3	0.1
National Freight Corporation	0.2	0.2	–
British Gas	0.8	0.4	1.7
British Steel	0.8	0.9	2.0
Total	9.2	6.7	13.6

Source: Data from McIntosh (1976)

industries should be able to function with commercial freedom while retaining both public accountability and a responsiveness to overall economic policy. This called for a new kind of agency, which was to come in the form of the public corporation.

The concept of the public corporation

In 1908 a Port of London Authority had been set up to manage London docks and the Labour government of 1929–31 had created a London Transport Passenger Board; both had considerable autonomy. A prominent figure in drafting the legislation for the latter was the Minister of Transport, Herbert Morrison, who became a fervent advocate of the concept of the **public corporation**. He outlined his view in *Socialism and Transport* (1933), teaching his government colleagues to love this strange new constitutional animal.

The public corporation was to be a quango entirely owned by the state. It was governed by special statute rather than ordinary company law, with a constitution which could only be modified by legislation. Employees were not civil servants and their conditions of work would vary from one corporation to another. Most importantly, although each industry was to be linked into the system of central government through a *sponsoring department*, it was not subject to the full rigour of ministerial control or parliamentary accountability. In other words, it was deliberately quasi-democratic.

The model entailed a management structure broadly similar to that of any large industrial undertaking. However, the board of directors appointed by the minister was to be responsible, not to shareholders, but to the population at large through the minister. Essential actors in this set-up were the minister of the sponsoring department, the chairperson of the board, Parliament, and the consumer councils.

The minister Although the minister's powers were prescribed by statute, this gives little indication of the true role, which can be understood only by distinguishing between *formal* and *informal powers*. Formally the minister was excluded from the actual *management* of the industry, being confined to the appointment of the board and certain major decisions concerning the national interest. Yet these powers provided only the backcloth to ministerial activity; the real level of power was to be measured in the minister's informal ability to make things happen without seeming to, by issuing 'lunchtable directives'.

Celestial orbits

Barbara Castle (1980: 295–6) gives an insight in her diary of the politics of quango patronage. In 1967 she, as the sponsoring minister, wanted to get rid of the chairman of British Rail, Sir Stanley Raymond. Feeling that it would be politically dangerous to sack him outright she decided 'I would have to blackmail him into resigning'. Prime Minister Wilson chipped in by offering to give him a peerage 'If it will help'. The removal of the chairman was finally effected by making him head of another quango, the Freight Integration Council. Thus do the great and the good move about their celestial orbits.

The boards   The size of the boards varied between about 10 and 20, with a balance between full- and part-time members. Generally the former were chosen from within the industry, ostensibly for their technical and managerial expertise, while the latter were supposed to reflect various outside interests (local government, other industries, workers), though to a great extent they reflected the interests of private capital and the great and good of the establishment. For example, the four part-time members of the British Gas Board (just before privatization) shared senior positions in Pressac Holdings, Broadgate Holdings, Marks and Spencer, Metal Box, Barclays Bank, the Bank of England, the BOC Group, and Cadbury Schweppes. The overall result was a tight interlocking of the industries with the private sector at board level, with no suggestion whatsoever of socialistic workers' control.

The chairmen   The industries provided a major area for the exercise of ministerial patronage. With no statutory requirements that particular interests or skills should be represented, they were free to select whomsoever they wished. The chairmen generally became visible political figures, with much higher profiles than any civil servant and many politicians. Under the stimulus of Alf (later Lord) Robens of the Coal Board, a Nationalized Industries Chairman's Group was formed as a pressure group to articulate their collective views and demands. Always male, they came from the upper reaches of private industry, with skills in banking and finance, and were important in developing the links with private capitalism. At one time the chairman of British Airways, Frank (later Lord) McFadzean, was simultaneously joint head of Shell, actually operating from the imperious Shell building on the banks of the Thames, and in 1980 he went on to head Rolls Royce.

Parliament A principal purpose in the invention of the modern public corporation was to evade the eyes of Parliament. MPs could only debate the annual reports and accounts of each industry, the relevant legislation, and ministerial proposals (say to raise an industry's borrowing powers). However, the true level of restriction lay in the fact that the House was only able to question a minister on his *formal* responsibilities. The result was to limit Parliament, but not ministers, whose *informal* operation enabled them to exert influence while evading responsibility. Parliament was never happy with the restriction and the post-war period saw a pattern of continuing experiment and testing in order to extend its role. In 1955 a Select Committee on the Nationalized Industries (SCNI) was created to enable MPs to specialize, but this became a casualty of the 1979 reforms to the select committee system (see p. 299).

Consumer councils The public corporation model tended to preserve the independent, private-sector character of the industry, which did not augur well for consumer sovereignty in the face of a natural monopoly. This hard truth was implicitly recognized in the creation for most of the nationalized industries of consumer councils responsible for receiving complaints and influencing policy in line with consumer interests. However, these were ineffective to the point of farce. They were little known by the public, understaffed, and lacked the expertise and information to challenge the managers (McIntosh 1976: appendix p. 86). Eventually they became slightly more effective, the Post Office Users Council scoring some successes over telephone charges.

Problems with the nationalized industries

Textbook accounts of the career of the nationalized industries suggest that they were prevented from working effectively because of political interference. In other words, they were not permitted to act like private capitalist companies, seeking profit at every turn.

Combining commercial freedom with public accountability was an attempt to secure that most illusory of human desires – 'the best of both worlds'. The general power given to ministers to intervene in the 'national interest' meant that chairmen were frustrated in their commercial designs, but at the same time the industries could not effectively function in the national interest because of perennial criticisms of their economic performance. This fundamental contradiction was to bedevil the public corporations throughout their lives. Various factors led governments to interfere in the running of the industries, including:

- the initial desire to promote rapid post-war economic reconstruction;
- a desire to use the great economic leverage of the industries as an instrument of economic management;
- a Labour government tendency to emphasize the social interest role at the expense of commercial performance;
- a tendency to manipulate the industries for political advantage.

The result was a blurring of the roles of boards and ministers which was never satisfactorily resolved, although successive attempts were made to distinguish between policy (the domain of the minister) and day-to-day management (the domain of the boards). These were doomed to failure because of the impossibility of drawing such a distinction in practice.

The SCNI produced a wide-ranging and critical report on the whole question of ministerial control, advocating greater clarity in the respective roles of ministers and boards. Governments addressed themselves to the political problems of managing the public corporations in two important white papers in 1961 and 1967, but neither resolved the basic problems. The political imperatives were always at cross purposes with the commercial ones, and the capitalistic orientations of the board members left them unable to comprehend the essential ethical goals of public ownership.

The McIntosh Report: a corporatist solution   In the mid-1970s the government asked the National Economic Development Office (NEDO) to conduct a wide-ranging enquiry, resulting in the McIntosh Report (1976). This called for radical reform, arguing that all previous thinking had been simplistic and based upon a false analogy with the private sector. The nationalized industries operate in an area of high political sensitivity and should never have been expected to behave like private firms. However, its recommendation for a more corporatist-style approach, bringing all interested parties together in a policy council, was rejected in the 1978 white paper, which was largely a recipe for the status quo.

Early Thatcherism   The 1979 general election introduced a government committed more firmly than any of its precedessors to the view that the public corporations should function like private-sector concerns. Precise medium-term financial targets were set and tight restrictions were placed on grants and borrowing by extending to the nationalized industries the government cash limits system (here termed 'external financing limits') in order to reduce the public sector borrowing requirement and control inflation in line with Thatcher-style monetarism (see p. 394). Ministers took a Pontius Pilot interest in a number of disputes over wages and job losses.

The power of patronage was used to replace old Labour appointees with those whose style and ideology were more in keeping with the government's views. Lord Ezra (NCB) and Sir Peter Parker (British Rail) were removed and Ian MacGregor was brought (at enormous expense, including compensation to his employers) from the pinnacle of the capitalist world, first to head

British Steel and then the NCB. In each case he waged war with the unions as bitterly as the most doughty of Victorian capitalists. Sir (later Lord) John King took charge of British Airways, the Post Office and the Electricity Council were placed under safe ex-civil servants, and the tough Sir Michael Edwardes received considerable government support as chairman of British Leyland.

State shareholdings

This alternative form of nationalization is achieved by the state purchasing shares in companies and was to become the main instrument after the initial phase of post-war nationalization. The principle was by no means new; government acquired an interest in the Suez Canal in 1875, and shares in British Petroleum (BP) were bought to ensure naval oil supplies during the first world war.

These arrangements were even more congenial to private capitalists than the public corporation, allowing maximum managerial independence. The state has a position no different in principle from that of any other shareholder, and the company is led by its board. The case of BP was an exception in that, although the government allowed its shareholding to fall to less than 50 per cent, it continued to appoint two directors who maintained a right of veto over general policy. Cable and Wireless was another unusual case in that the government was the only shareholder, its relationship being more like that with a public corporation – appointing the board and scrutinizing the accounts.

Share acquisition: the crest and the break of the wave To some extent it was controversy surrounding the public corporations which led the Labour government to seek other ways of intervening, but the more important motive was to rescue capitalist disasters rather than control the industry. In 1966, an Industrial Reorganization Corporation (IRC) was established by the Wilson government with a capital of £200 million to promote industrial development through share purchase. Much effort went into supporting lame ducks and a trend towards mergers was encouraged. In 1970, the new Conservative government promised to end such support; the IRC was abolished and its holdings in profitable enterprises were sold. However, the problems of the economy embarrassingly forced the government to reverse its policy and the 1972 Industry Act facilitated further assistance to key industries. Firms supported included British Leyland, Cammell Laird and Rolls Royce, all of which were considered vital to the national economy.

The prolonged industrial slump caused by the end of the long boom and the oil crises in the mid-1970s left many capitalist undertakings reeling. In 1974 Labour returned to office, establishing an even more comprehensive policy of state aid than before. A National Enterprise Board (NEB) was set up in 1975 as a more powerful successor to the IRC. Shares were acquired in over 20 companies, including British Leyland, Rolls Royce, Chrysler,

Ferranti, Bear Brand, Fodens and Burma Oil.

However, the Thatcher 1979 government showed a marked distaste for this policy and abruptly reversed the trend. Lame ducks were given specific time limits to restore their plumage and the NEB was wound down. It was directed to sell off its investments and the responsibility for Rolls Royce and British Leyland was transferred to the Department of Industry.

State share purchase: the problems This policy was always controversial and subject to attack from both extremes of the political spectrum. The left saw it as propping up a capitalist system at a time when the weaknesses were finally being exposed, while the right viewed developments as a sinister pattern of creeping statism which distorted the market. The firms themselves found it difficult to pursue profits when the government was seeking social (employment) as well as commercial objectives. Finally, the fact that substantial funds passed from the public to the private sector raised constitutional questions of responsibility, since Parliament had little ability to scrutinize firms which remain private companies (D. Mitchell 1982).

Towards Privatization: the Full Circle

In 1981 the Central Policy Review Staff conducted an enquiry which proposed a system not unlike that of McIntosh's NEDO report. However, this made little impact for a more radical solution had begun to brew in the cauldrons of the New Right think-tanks – **privatization**.

The concept of privatization

Essentially privatization is the placing of functions which the state has been fulfilling in the hand of private organizations. Its advocates claimed the following advantages:

- restoring consumer sovereignty through competition;
- increasing efficiency through the profit motive and shareholder pressure;
- reducing public expenditure;
- reducing the public sector borrowing requirement;
- promoting worker ownership through shareholding;
- ending political interference in management;
- giving the public a sense of *real* ownership rather than the *illusion* of ownership through the impersonal concept of nationalization.

Generally these arguments came from the right, and the policy had several political advantages for the Conservatives. By increasing the size of the private sector, and introducing more opportunities for profit accumulation, it served its principal clientele, the owners of capital. Furthermore, the short-term cash gains from the sales generated colossal government income (rising from £377 million in 1979–80 to over £5,000 million in 1987–8), which could be used to fund tax reductions, so that those buying the lion's share were twice blessed. In addition, the policy offered a populist power base for the Conservatives by claiming to transform society into a *shareholding democracy* (figure 15.8) in the way that it had become a property-owning one.

The pattern of privatization

The steel industry had been denationalized by the Conservatives in 1951, but subsequently reclaimed for the state by Labour. In 1970 the Heath government had sounded much rhetoric about reducing the state, but the dissolution of the IRC and the sell-off of Thomas Cook and some pubs in Carlisle was no more than the thin gruel of symbolism. Even the Labour government made nods in the privatization direction when, during the 1976 sterling crisis, it sold part of the stake in BP, as a means of averting some of the public expenditure cuts demanded by the IMF. However, it was the 1979 Conservative government which launched the serious assault on the public sector. When it came to office state ownership was at a peak, producing 10.5 per cent of the gross domestic product, employing some 1.75 million people, with an annual turnover of £55 billion and annual investment of around £7.5 billion.

At first the approach was cautious. Although expressing a general desire to create a dynamic free-enterprise economy, the 1979 election manifesto placed very little stress on denationalization. However, the frustrations felt by the government and sponsoring ministers in dealing with the nationalized industries led to the bolder approach which developed the momentum to rewrite irrevocably the British political agenda. The programme was to generate a growth industry in itself. Merchant bankers, stockbrokers and lawyers grew even fatter and even richer as they vied with each other for the

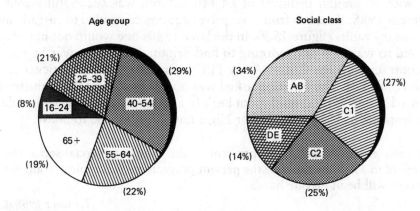

Figure 15.8   A share-owning democracy? Share-ownership of privatized companies and the Trustee Savings Bank, 1987

Source: Social Trends (1988: table 5.22)

lucrative opportunities to advise government, conduct sales and underwrite the share issues.

The early movement began slowly in 1979 with the government reducing its holding in BP, followed in 1981 by the disposing of its holding in Cable and Wireless as well as a majority stake in British Aerospace. The following year saw the sale of the National Freight Corporation (in the face of union opposition) in a management-led buy-out. As the movement gained momentum a major watershed was reached with the sale of 50 per cent of the equity of British Telecom. At a cost of £4 billion, this was the first large-scale public monopoly to be shifted into the private sector and Herculean efforts were made to ensure its success, with much expensive political advertising. This paid off in a clamorous demand from small investors resulting in a policy of strict rationing. Jaguar Cars, Enterprise Oil, Sealink Ferries and the British Gas onshore oil wells followed.

The sale of British Gas in 1986 represented an even bigger operation than Telecom. It was orchestrated by a massive advertising campaign, with TV commercials, mailshots and newspaper double spreads, taking as its theme the patronizing image of 'Sid', to stress the populist virtues of privatization. After this went British Airways, Rolls Royce and the British Airports Authority. Companies within British Shipbuilders were sold individually to different buyers, the Royal Ordnance factories were bought by British Aerospace, and the National Bus Company was disposed of as 70 companies, mainly by management buy-outs. By 1987, nearly 20 per cent of the adult population owned shares (*Social Trends* 1988: 97). The only cloud on the horizon was the intense opposition to the privatization of the water industry, which led to its postponement until after the 1987 general election, ostensibly for 'technical reasons'. (The bill eventually went through Parliament in 1989 amidst much controversy, costing Environment Minister Nicholas Ridley his job in the July 1989 cabinet reshuffle.)

Even after the 1987 stock market crash, spirits soon revived and British Steel, with an annual turnover of £4,116 million, was successfully sold in November 1988. Receipts from past privatizations continued to cascade into the Treasury vaults (figure 15.9). In the later 1980s one would not have been surprised to wake up one morning to find Britain conducting war by means of a contract with the British Army PLC, or receive a parking ticket from British Police Ltd. The question asked was not 'Why should this industry be privatized?', but 'Why should it not be?'. In a speech to the right-wing Adam Smith Institute in 1988, Chancellor Nigel Lawson was able to boast:

> We have privatised nearly 40 per cent of the state commercial sector we inherited in 1979. By the time the present programme is complete, some 60 per cent will be in private hands.
>
> (Treasury 1988a)

Likely candidates for the privatization trawl went well beyond the industrial to the very fabric of the state (figure 15.10).

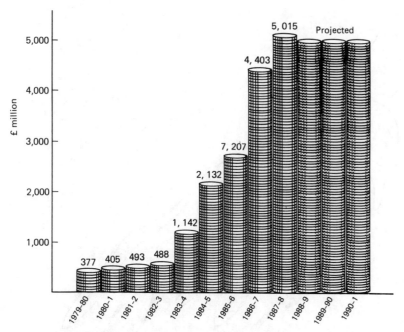

Figure 15.9 *Un embarras de richesse:* money raised through privatization, 1979–1991
Source: Data from Atkins (1988)

> Selling the family silver.
>
> Harold Macmillan (Lord Stockton) on privatization policy, House of Lords
> speech (1986)

For enthusiasts these years were euphoric, with soaring profits (table 15.2) for the privatized concerns (some with debts written off). However, the popularity of the programme was waning. A MORI poll published in May

Table 15.2   Examples of profit performance of privatized companies, 1981–1986

Company	Year privatized	Pre-tax profit/loss to financial year ending					
		1981	1982	1983	1984	1985	1986
Cable and Wireless	1981	64.1	89.2	156.7	190.1	245.2	295.0
Amersham International	1982	4.1	8.5	11.2	13.7	17.1	17.5
National Freight Consortium	1982	4.3	10.1	11.8	16.9	27.2	37.0
Jaguar	1984	−31.7	9.6	50.0	91.5	121.3	120.8
British Telecom	1985	570.0	936.0	1,031.0	990.0	1,480.0	1,810.0
British Gas	1986	−	430.0	803.0	909.0	712.0	782.0

Source: Data from *Financial Times* (25 March 1987)

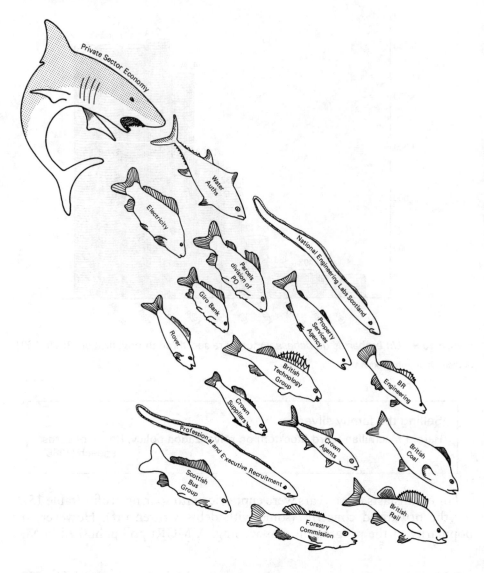

Figure 15.10   The privatization trawl into the 1990s

1989 showed that almost all the prospective privatizations evoked more hostility than support.

Beyond privatization

It is probably one of the most remarkable features of British politics in the 1980s that privatization was accomplished on such an astonishing scale with so little opposition. The case against it was never strongly put because the shift of the political agenda saw Labour, under the cloak of 'new realism', merely searching for alternative means of pursuing the same policy. However, the policy is one designed to serve the elite, giving to a few that which belonged to the many. Early in the programme Samuel Brittan (1983) had argued that the most ethically acceptable way to promote privatization would be to distribute shares free to the public, who already owned them.

Privatization robs the state of the chance to be a model employer and increases the power of private capital *vis-à-vis* the state. It also places consumers – the public and other industries – at the mercy of large, powerful natural monopolies. The control of these mammoths now that they have escaped from the game reserve of state control promises to become one of the most important political issues of the 1990s, giving birth to a new generation of arm's-length agencies. It is to these that we now turn.

Regulating the Natural Monopolies

The moral justification of *laissez-faire* is that the operation of the market will result in the optimum use of resources, thereby maximizing the sum total of satisfaction within society. Keynes and others demonstrated this to be a dubious proposition in the real world but, even in theory, it comes tumbling down once a monopoly emerges in an industry. Here there can be no competition and consumers and other firms suffer exploitation. One of the most important reasons why certain industries were originally taken into state ownership was that they were natural monopolies. Thus, paradoxically, the very area where the government was most keen to privatize, in keeping with its free-market philosophy, was the one where theorists have always agreed that the market will fail.

Hence, when the natural monopolies are privatized the government is obliged, for reasons of legitimation, to find ways of ensuring their sensitivity to the national interest. Significantly, this question has remained well away from the front pages of the political agenda, yet it is potentially the most significant political aspect of privatization, with far-reaching social consequences. In the following sections we consider two principal ways of curbing natural monopolies which can be used in harness or separately: fragmentation into smaller units (to introduce artificially some element of competition), or the creation of special regulatory machinery.

Creating competition: fragmenting the industries

In some areas competition has been introduced with ease. For example, the Department of Transport's road construction designs department was hived off to 15 private consultancy firms. In addition, a potentially formidable competitor for British Telecom's business services emerged in the form of Mercury, a consortium formed by the privatized Cable and Wireless, BP and Barclays Merchant Bank.

However, in many cases the idea of artificially created competition is rather fanciful. One regional gas company might be comparable with another, but they could never be expected to compete within the same territory for consumers. The same applies to water, rail and electricity, although it is claimed that the separate companies can compete in other arenas, such as the capital market and the stock exchange. It is also argued that consumers in high-charging areas will bring some sort of pressure for reductions when they compare their lot with those elsewhere.

Yet breaking the natural monopolies up into smaller companies is an unattractive option to government because it is likely to receive a lower price for the industry. This is why British Aerospace, where fragmentation would have been feasible and would have led to genuine competition, was offered as a job lot.

The controllers of the industries themselves show little appetite for such a solution (Brittan 1983). Sir Dennis Rooke, the most formidable of the leaders of the nationalized industries, fought a long and bitter battle to keep British Gas as a single company. Yet after privatization there were soon loud squeals from firms that it was overcharging industrial users. Similarly British Telecom, also kept as a single company, came under fire for lazy monopolistic behaviour, manifested in low standards of service and failure to maintain its (necessarily unprofitable) call-box network.

After these criticisms it became clear that the Conservatives would use a different model in the privatization of the electricity and water industries. In 1988 it was announced that the former was to be sold as two separate companies, one concerned with generation, the other with transmission. Similarly, the water industry was sold off as ten separate regional companies. In the longer term, the likelihood was that rail and coal would also follow this model. However, the fact remains that artificial fragmentation can never produce the degree of competition demanded in the perfect market model. Natural monopolies must always retain their privileged, potentially dangerous, position and require some further more direct form of regulation.

Regulation

Regulation is a relatively common feature in the US, where public utilities have long been run as private companies. Designed to prevent exploitation of consumers, unfair competition, or misuse of vital resources, it can be accomplished through the existing machinery, the concept of the golden share, or the creation of special new quangos.

Existing machinery At the time of privatization there were already various ways for the state to regulate private capitalism.

- *Regulatory quangos.* A number of watchdog bodies (consumer councils, ombudsmen, the Office of Fair Trading and the Monopolies and Mergers Commission) could be used to police the new leviathans. However, with their wider-ranging remits, they could not be expected to develop the necessary level of detailed understanding.

- *Fiscal means.* The taxation system can be used to provide incentives for firms to act in a certain manner and extract penalties for misbehaviour. The objection to this is the heavy reliance placed upon the concerns themselves for information, and the problems and costs of analysing it.
- *Special laws.* Although privatized companies are legally indistinguishable from private ones, it is possible to prescribe a special framework within which they operate. However, critics see this as diminishing independence and blunting commercial instincts.
- *Special articles of incorporation.* It is possible to require the amendment of certain articles of company law. For example, this may outlaw takeover in its early life, prevent ownership passing overseas and block material disposal of assets without ministerial consent. In two cases – Cable and Wireless and British Aerospace – such arrangements were made after privatization.

The golden share When an industry is privatized it is possible for government to retain for itself one share, which although worth only £1, is extremely special, giving the government itself the power to outvote all other shareholders on particular issues, such as undesirable takeover bids and asset sales. This device was used from the early days of the privatization programme, with **golden shares** held in Cable and Wireless, Amersham International, Britoil, Enterprise Oil, Jaguar and British Telecom. The concept is not really in the general free-market spirit of the Conservative privatization crusade and, although little is said on the possibility, a Labour government might use the principle to restore state control over the privatized sector without the inconvenience of renationalization.

New ad hoc regulatory agencies John Moore, as Financial Secretary to the Treasury, declared in a speech in 1985 that in order for the privatization programme to move into the heartlands of the public sector 'novel techniques' should be developed (1985: para. 23), entailing the creation of *ad hoc* regulatory agencies. The first of these to be established as a result of the privatization programme was the Office of Telecommunications (OFTEL) to watch over British Telecom (BT). Its duties were to lay down conditions ensuring that BT would observe social responsibilities (providing a universal service including uneconomic rural areas, maintaining emergency services and maintaining the call-box network) and hold price increases for domestic rentals and local calls below a fixed figure.

The early auguries did not suggest a firm regime; the government's avowed intention was to keep the regulation of BT as light as possible (de Jonquieres 1983). OFTEL began work with a modest staff of only 50 and it was evident that it would have to rely heavily on BT itself for information, carrying the risk that it would be vulnerable to **agency capture**, becoming not the watchdog of the state, but a tame guard-dog for the industry.

In the gas privatization both Peter Walker, the minister, and Sir Dennis Rooke, the chairman, showed a fervent desire to keep regulation to a minimum. Rooke declaimed: 'Regulation should be as light as possible and cover the smallest area' (Hargreaves and Lawson 1985). When the licence for British Gas was published in December 1985 it gave a decidedly hands-off role for OFGAS. Apart from abuse of monopoly powers and serious miscalculation, the setting of prices was left entirely to the company, constrained only by a price formula in the domestic market (to be revised every five years):

$$RPI - X + Y$$

where RPI = retail price index
  X = an arbitrary figure designed to squeeze efficiency from the company
  Y = an allowance for increasing costs as North Sea supplies become tighter

In the industrial sector there was to be no regulation; the great monster was permitted to roam freely through the jungle of the market, striking deals where and how it wished.

WANTED

Dynamic, thrusting individual to regulate 17 recently privatised companies. Ability to perform miracles (and understand RPI-X+Y) useful. Sense of humour essential. Staff of 150-200, annual budget £10m. Salary negotiable. Apply:

Saxton Bampfylde International, London SW1.

THE ECONOMIST FEBRUARY 25 1989

A third regulatory body, OFELEC, was planned. However, the emerging evidence suggested that this was taking an even more feeble appearance, a castrated poodle with rubber teeth rather than a watchdog. Privatization of the water industry posed particularly difficult problems of regulation, since the search for profit might threaten to compromise the health of the nation. Secretary of State for the Environment, Nicholas Ridley, established an Office for Water Services, headed by a director general, and a National Rivers Authority, with a remit to monitor pollution, yet even here government seemed determined to pursue a light-touch policy.

> The Government has never made any secret of the fact that it would consider relaxing the law if authorities are having temporary problems ... The water authorities cannot meet the [anti-pollution] standard overnight.
>
> DoE spokesman, quoted in the *Daily Telegraph* (12 Nov. 1988)

Prospects for regulation

The future for the regulation of natural monopolies in Britain promises to be controversial. Conservative governments show little appetite for it. When speaking in Parliament on the subject of the tobacco industry, Mrs Thatcher had stressed that 'we should be very slow indeed in thinking of imposing statutory regulation' (Goodin 1986). The whole purpose of privatization is to prise the fingers of the state, one by one, off the ball. One Conservative minister commented: 'Regulation? We want as little of it as possible' (Wilkinson 1985). In late 1989, when the US giants General Motors and Ford were bidding for Jaguar, Nicholas Ridley, as Industry Secretary, threw in the government's golden share (which allowed him to veto takeovers) gratis, greatly surprising the bidders. Control may have to come from extra-state forces. It is likely that pressure groups will become more important in protecting consumers, but of course this will mean that the interests of the articulate middle classes will be better served than those of the working class.

Privatization mania will not remove certain fundamental problems from the political agenda. People elect governments in the belief that they will pursue the national interest, and the threat posed by natural monopolies cannot be legislated out of existence. The view in the US is that for regulation to be effective it must be tough and aggressive; the 'light touch' favoured by the Conservative government promised many problems as Britain moved into the 1990s.

Conclusion: Government at Arm's Length

It is clear that a system of government which sets great store by secrecy and the evasion of accountability will always find much that is attractive in the concept of a shadowy world of quasi-democracy. It is entirely commensurate with the minimalist state preferred by capitalism. However, grave problems are raised.

Quangos in politics: an endangered species?

The idea that quangos can take matters out of politics is fundamentally fallacious (Chester 1979: 54). Anything will be political if people's views about it differ and they are allowed sufficient information to form judgements. In fact quangos are associated with all kinds of acutely sensitive political areas: unemployment, race relations, atomic energy, inner-city riots, police violence, local government reform, education, the NHS, grants to universities, the arts, broadcasting, and so on.

Quasi-democracy is criticized from left and right. The left view with misgivings the undemocratic features of a system of administration which deliberately places responsibility for the making and implementation of policy in the hands of unelected people who remain at **arm's length** from Parliament. For the right, the growth of the quasi-democratic sector is feared as an insidious encroachment by the tentacles of the state.

The Conservative Party has traditionally adopted an aggressively anti-quango stance, and upon coming to power in 1979 Mrs Thatcher announced open season on them. In the government's early years, before privatization captured its imagination, some zealous quango-culling claimed around 500 victims (a rather cosmetic figure because the numbers were reduced by some merging). However, the government was soon to discover that the quango, like the fox, could have its uses. It was to facilitate the policies of abolishing the metropolitan counties and the GLC, hiving off the functions of the civil service, and the massive programme of privatization.

Whither the quango? Hence the quango is not an endangered species in the constitutional wildlife park. It offers the rulers some extremely useful services, enabling politicians to wash their hands of embarrassing matters, disclaim responsibility for unpopular policies, evade parliamentary scrutiny and take certain matters off the political agenda. They also furnish a rich vein of patronage, placing thousands of positions within the gift of ministers.

We find that the famous and the pompous move to and from quangos from the other peaks of social, academic and economic life, names tending to reappear on this or that council, working party and advisory body with a degree of monotony. Virtually all can be counted upon to favour an establishment line, and if they develop a maverick streak, criticizing government policy, they can be removed as easily as they were appointed. Even the Director General of the BBC is not immune, as Alasdair Milne found to his cost. Hence there remains in British public life today more than a little whiff of early-nineteenth-century corruption and nepotism (Hood 1979: 40).

Key points

- Quangos are instruments of state policy-making and administration deliberately placed at arm's length from the institutions of democracy.
- The case for quangos is based on the proposition that there are certain areas in state administration which are 'technical' rather than political – a dubious proposition.

- The creation of the NHS as a quasi-autonomous system insulated from local democracy was an institutional recognition of the medical definition of health and the political weight of the doctors.
- Nationalization of industry in Britain took place in two waves: the first, following the second world war, facilitated by outright purchase of the industries, and the second from the mid-1960s, when the real motive was to support lame-duck industries rather than command the heights of the economy.
- The public corporations have, during the post-war era, represented a major arena for British politics. The essence of the problem stems from the attempt to combine the goal of state control of industry in the public interest with the demands of private capitalism.
- Throughout the post-war period there have been attempts to resolve the contradictions, but in the 1980s the Thatcher government decided to erase the problem altogether by privatization.
- However, this solution promised to bequeath a new set of problems caused by private-sector natural monopolies and a new generation of regulatory quangos to monitor them.

Review your understanding of the following terms and concepts

quango	nationalization
advisory body	natural monopoly
consultative body	public corporation
executive body	state shareholdings
regulatory agency	privatization
health authority	golden share
public health	agency capture
medical model of health	arm's-length philosophy

Assignment

Study the extract from the *Guardian* on p. 476 and answer the following questions.

		% mark
1	Explain in principle the idea of the 'internal market' for the NHS. Why are the doctors against it?	20
2	Contrast the relationship between government and the BMA in 1989 to that which existed in the 1950s, 1960s and 1970s.	20
3	What does the fact that the BMA is launching a '£600,000 press campaign' tell you about its power as a pressure group?	20
4	'The NHS: underfunded, undermined, under threat.' Given the nature of medical treatment, could the NHS ever be other than underfunded. Hence is the allegation fair?	20
5	What pressure groups might disagree with the BMA's position in this issue?	20

Doctors resume battle for NHS

**David Brindle, Social
Services Correspondent**

HOSTILITIES between the Government and the doctors reopened last night over adverts in today's newspapers placed by the British Medical Association at the start of a £600,000 press campaign against the planned health service shake-up.

Mr Kenneth Clarke, the Health Secretary, said the four adverts all contained untrue statements and the BMA was "deliberately seeking to frighten their patients to further the interests of their members".

The day before, Mr Clarke had appeared notably conciliatory, saying arguments over the proposals were now splitting hairs because his plans were "very experimental".

Dr John Marks, the chairman of the BMA's ruling council, said the minister's comments had not warranted calling off the advertising campaign.

The BMA adverts urge readers to lobby their MPs about the reforms. Each ends with the slogan: "The NHS. Underfunded, undermined, under threat." One attacks the plans for an internal health market, whereby patients may travel to hospitals run by different health authorities for treatment. It features a dejected-looking woman in a hospital bed, beneath the heading: "When you're 50 miles from home, every ward is an isolation ward."

A second, on the Government's goal of injecting competition into the health service, carries a picture of the Health Secretary gesticulating in full rhetorical flight and asserts: "In Mr Clarke's sharp new health service, making medicine pay could become more important than making people well."

A third, headed: "A complete list of the medical bodies who support the Government's plans for the NHS," features five blank columns.

The fourth is likely to cause most controversy. It shows rows of tinned processed peas, branded "Clarke's," on chairs in a family doctor's waiting room, with the heading: "If the Government's plans for the NHS go through, how will the patient feel?"

Guardian, 19 May 1989

Questions for discussion

1 Compare and contrast the case against the use of quangos by the left and the right respectively.

2 Which model of policy formation provides the most satisfactory explanation of the making of health policy in Britain: pluralism or corporatism?

3 Why was there a high degree of consensus during the second world war concerning the need for, and nature of, a national health service?

4 Identify the arguments for nationalizing much of British industry following the second world war.

5 Outline the basic structure of the public corporation. What were the objectives it was supposed to attain?

6 'Regulation of the natural monopolies will encounter essentially the same problems as did the public corporations, which will centre upon the intrinsic contradiction between capitalism and the public interest.' Discuss.

7 Evaluate the role of advisory bodies in British government and politics.

Topic for debate

This house believes that the process of privatization amounts to the foolhardy selling of the family silver.
    or
This house believes that if the privatized industries are permitted to pursue their rational self-interest the national interest will take care of itself.

Further reading

Cawson, A. (1982) *Corporatism and Welfare.*
The welfare state is made the central focus for the corporatist perspective.

Holland, P. (1981) *The Governance of Quangos.*
Holland has long written about quangos and their threat as an insidious extension of the state. Here the thesis is fitted into a wider New Right view of British politics.

Klein, R. (1983) *The Politics of the National Health Service.*
A lively book in which the NHS is seen as a microcosm of the political system, its lessons having a relevance extending beyond the confines of the service itself.

Manser, W. A. P. (1982) 'Nationalization or privatization: the case for each', *Banker*, 132 (December).
Gives a good framework of analysis of the privatization issue.

McIntosh, R. (chairman) (1976) *A Study of the UK Nationalised Industries.*
Gives a good account of the development of the nationalized industries, showing a keen awareness of their social role.

McKeown, T. (1979) *The Role of Medicine: Dream or Mirage?*
Argues that the medical model of health prevents society from making the most effective use of its health expenditure.

Navarro, V. (1974) *Medicine under Capitalism.*
A well-developed Marxist perspective. Sees the power of the doctors as a manifestation of the power of the capitalist bourgeoisie rather than an expression of their professional vantage point in the decision-making process.

Pryke, R. (1981) *The Nationalised Industries: Policies and Performance Since 1968.*
A critical study of the nationalized industries and the concept of the public corporation, on the eve of the privatization bonanza.

Wilson, J. Q. (ed.) (1980) *The Politics of Regulation.*
A book of readings by US political scientists and economists examining a set of problems which has hitherto not been of particular concern to British students.

For light relief

George Bernard Shaw, *The Doctor's Dilemma.*
Written 40 years before the creation of the NHS, this play exposes the frightening power of the medical profession. Read also the witty and perceptive introduction.

16

The Local State

Local government provides one of the most important theatres of politics in Britain today. The media construction of political life tends to see in Westminster, Whitehall and the Cabinet the holy trinity but, in so doing, they place the political thermometer too near the radiator of London. Throughout history it is in local rather than central government that ordinary people have encountered the reality of the state. The chapter comprises five sections. The first examines the **nature of local government** and the second looks briefly at its **evolution**. In the third section we consider **local politics**, identifying the principal actors in the drama. This leads to the crucial question of **finance**. Throughout, we will be conscious of the overpowering presence of central government and we conclude by evaluating models of the controversial **central–local relationship**.

The Nature of Local Government

What is local government?

Local government is the self-government of a subnational territorial unit of the state. It is found in virtually all developed states as a complement to central government and is generally seen as a sign of a healthy democracy. Because the local authorities have some degree of autonomy from the centre, the power of the state can be said to be fragmented; there is an element of balancing power, a mark of pluralism. Hence, the elimination of local government is generally taken as a sympton of totalitarianism. Indeed local government in Germany was one of the first casualties of Hitler's rise to power. It is this claim to autonomy from the central state that makes local authorities different from any other public agency.

Modern **local authorities** have the following characteristics:

- democratic control by locally elected representatives who form the council – a kind of local Parliament;
- power to levy taxes;
- clearly delineated territorial boundaries;
- large permanent bureaucracies – local civil services;
- multi-functional portfolios, giving responsibility for an exceptionally wide range of services;
- a legal identity or *persona* as a **body corporate** with a name (say Barnsley Corporation) in which all activities are carried out.

However, although democratically elected and able to levy taxes, local authorities are by no means entirely free. They are subject to the legal doctrine of **ultra vires** (beyond the power) which means that, however well intentioned, a local authority cannot exceed those powers given to it by Parliament. Thus an act which may be legal for an individual (say giving children free ice cream) will not be legal for a council.

What does local government do?

Local democracy is meaningless if not linked with the provision of services. Parish government today is of little more importance than the maypole dances performed on village greens. Yet if they had significant functions, parish councils would be, as in France, important features of communal life. Few studies stress the political importance of what local government does, but today this complacency is being shattered. Throughout the 1980s the debate has been politically charged.

Classifying functions   Local authorities are *multi-functional*, to be distinguished from *ad hoc* single-purpose bodies. They provide most of the state services required by ordinary people from 'the womb to the tomb'. These may be broadly classified as follows:

- *protective* – fire, police, consumer protection;
- *environmental* – roads, transport, planning, refuse collection and recycling;
- *personal* – education, careers, social services, housing;
- *recreational* – parks, sports facilities, theatres, art galleries, libraries;
- *commercial* – markets, restaurants, transport;
- *promotional* – employment creation, tourism, economic regeneration.

Allocating functions within the state   Is there any real rationale explaining why local government performs certain functions and central government the others? There are few theories to underpin such a discussion. While it is self-evident that some are best administered within the community, not all state functions delivered locally are entrusted to local government. For example, the NHS is run by *ad hoc* non-elected local bodies, the supply of electricity and gas was placed in the hands of public corporations, and the payment of income support is made by the civil service itself through local offices.

A basic premise of any rational explanation must be that there are certain services, say education, where the special qualities of local government (openness to local participation, sensitivity to the popular will) are of particular importance. However, other rational arguments might conflict with the conclusions reached. For example, from a socialist perspective, it would be unfair if the schools in one area were better than those in another. This calls for central administration to ensure equality of opportunity.

Saunders (1984: 25–8), in his 'dual state' thesis, associates the two levels of government with two key functions of the capitalist state: **investment functions** and **collective consumption functions**. Central government is concerned with providing investment which will enable the economy to work, while local government provides those services consumed by people in order to live and bring up their families (housing, education, social services, and so on). Broadly speaking, we can say that the functions of local government have been determined by the needs of capitalism. Hence the great Victorian cities emerged to house the labour force needed to feed the voracious appetites of the new factories. Public health, law and order, education, and so on all served the same master. They were desperately needed but too expensive (and unprofitable) for the capitalists to provide for themselves.

Defining local politics

Local politics means something quite different from local government. It is the process of settling differences and reaching compromises over public decisions relating to a local community. It may entail the activities of pressure groups and parties, the media, and various expressions of local opinion acting upon the institutions of local government.

It is often said that each area is a political system in microcosm – a **local state**. However, there is more to local politics than this. The concept of the local state may be helpful in particular kinds of analysis but its dangers are considerable; it is very much part of the apologist tradition. If local authorities are miniature states, they must have the *power* characteristic of all states to effect an authoritative allocation of resources and values within their territories. In fact local authorities have only a very low level of political autonomy (Castells 1977: 247); every breath they take is polluted with a Dickensian fog drifting from London. It will become clear throughout this chapter that virtually no aspect of local politics can be explained without reference to the presence of central government.

Evolution

The spirit of local government

Local government has a history extending from the earliest times, and from the first there has been a tension between the centre and the locality. Evolution saw a twin-track development, with two traditions – centralist and localist – which continue to colour modern debate.

- **The centralist tradition** arose from the ruling needs of royal authority. The key territorial unit was the **county** (originally small kingdoms). Kings would impose local agents, sheriffs and latterly Justices of the Peace (JPs) to collect taxes, recruit for the army, keep order and dispense justice.
- **The localist tradition** developed in an organic, evolutionary way by communities seeking to provide collective services such as roads and poor relief for themselves in the **parishes** and **boroughs**. Also part of the localist tradition were guilds, which developed from the twelfth century as associations of craftsmen and merchants seeking self-protection. Their interests lay in orderly, well-conducted, town life, and they lent a strong dynamic to civic administration to the extent that guild halls often became in effect town halls.

By the mid-eighteenth century local government was a patchwork counterpane. The centralist and localist traditions had coalesced to form a two-tiered pattern, with counties covering the whole of the country, containing parishes of various sizes and status, operating under the eye of the JPs and local landed interests, and boroughs (often controlled by the guilds) with royal charters granting them independence from the county jurisdiction.

The industrial revolution

However, the industrial revolution shattered this pattern. It was the cause of massive urbanization, drawing people from the countryside and spawning huge teeming communities around the factories, the like of which had never been seen before. The traumatic events precipitated the modern local government system.

The new centres did not necessarily grow up in those boroughs where municipal institutions were well established under the guilds. Often sleepy rural hamlets were transformed, within decades, into clattering urban machines, with a range of social and economic problems unknown to the *ancien régime* of squirarchy and JP, and quite beyond their ability to manage. Housing was hastily erected with little thought for comfort or sewage, while unemployment and abject poverty left many with little alternative to lives of crime – the dark alleys were fertile ground for footpads and prostitutes. On top of all was the urban ecology, better suited to the bacteria from the gutters and unholy privy middens than to people; disease

Nineteenth-century London slums
Source: Mary Evans Picture Library

of epidemic proportions was as much part of life as the dense smoke belching from the factories. The gross inequalities generated by the new order and the harrowing spectre of the French revolution and its aftermath haunted the bourgeoisie, leaving them in a state of perpetual fear of the Frankenstein's monster they had created – a vast new social force, the working class.

The initial response to the trauma of industrialization was necessarily localist. The infrastructure for local economic growth was inadequate and the capitalists realized that the success of their enterprises depended on efficient urbanization. They required a strong passive workforce, good roads, railways, freedom from disease, public transport, street lighting, and firm law and order. Hence the bourgeoisie claimed the municipalities, creating a granite landscape of confident town halls, the cathedrals of the age, and municipal pomp and splendour (Briggs 1963). This was accomplished by two broad means: establishing a range of *ad hoc* bodies, and *reforming* existing municipal institutions.

Ad hoc *bodies* These were essentially boards of leading citizens unable to wait for the creation of new municipal institutions and were established to provide some particular service (gaining the necessary statutory right through private Acts of Parliament). The movement gained great momentum, producing a complex network of special-purpose boards responsible variously for the poor law, burial, jails, asylums, sanitation, water supply, roads, street lighting, hospitals, civic improvement, education, and so on.

Reform of existing municipal institutions

Reform of existing municipal institutions This had a more lasting effect. Following the 1832 Reform Bill, which increased the power of the bourgeoisie through the Liberal Party, a number of important official enquiries were conducted into the state of municipal institutions. That into the operation of the poor law deplored the softness in the Speenhamland system which effectively provided money from the rates for paupers to supplement income. Bentham railed against this as a 'bounty to indolence and vice' and the 1834 Poor Law Amendment Act introduced savage reforms to end 'out-relief'. The poor were forced into workhouses of deliberately inhuman standards on the principle that conditions were to be 'less eligible' than those of the poorest worker. An inquiry into the state of the municipal institutions was deeply critical of the local administration by the old landed classes and resulted in the Municipal Corporations Act (1835). This aimed to spread the practices developed in the large industrial cities (prudent accounting, elections, efficient services, and so on) throughout the country.

> The truth, Sir, is that we have a chaos as regards authorities, a chaos as regards rates, and a worse chaos than all as regards areas.
> G. J. Goschen, House of Commons speech introducing bills to reform local government (3 April 1871)

Later the Local Government Act (1888) laid the foundations of the modern local government system. The practices which had been adopted by the municipalities after 1835 were extended to the counties. The original intention had been to establish a unified system to cover the whole of the country based upon counties, with a second (subordinate) tier responsible for certain defined functions. However, the efficient (mainly Liberal) municipal corporations resented losing their autonomy to the (mainly Conservative) counties and lobbied strongly to amend the bill, with the result that all boroughs with populations over 50,000 were permitted to remain independent as **county boroughs**. The Act met the unique metropolitan needs of the huge London conurbation with an entirely new administrative county, under a London County Council (LCC), with a second tier of 28 metropolitan boroughs (established in 1899) and three county boroughs (figures 16.1 and 16.2). The curious sytem was a recognition of the facts of social and economic life. It was, as Redlich and Hirst stated in a classic work of 1903, 'a

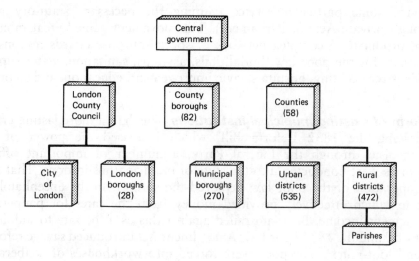

Figure 16.1 The local government structure in England and Wales at the end of the nineteenth century (actual numbers varied slightly)

system ... condemned by logic ... [but] approved by experience' (1970: 115).

The 'Golden Age' of local government The new pattern became established as modern local government. The responsibilities of the *ad hoc* bodies and voluntary societies were gradually taken over (not without some stout resistance and much political infighting). In addition, the authorities bought out the various public utility companies (water, public transport, electricity and gas). The late nineteenth century is sometimes seen as the high point of English local government, when the energy of capitalism was directed into municipal endeavour in the same way that it flowed into the national institutions. The economic leaders of society were also the political leaders, and the baroque town halls testify to the importance placed by the Victorian capitalists upon their municipalities and, indeed, upon themselves.

Into the twentieth century: reappraising the pattern

Although the nineteenth-century boundary pattern reflected the way of life induced by industrialization, there was no effective mechanism to ensure that the system would be flexible enough to accommodate subsequent demographic development. It became set in aspic, looking increasingly like a vintage car on the M1.

As the twentieth century progressed, railways, trunk roads, aeroplanes, telecommunications, radio and television made the country effectively smaller by enlarging the domain in which people lived their lives. The traditional heavy industries which urbanization had served went into decline and the urban–rural dichotomy was rendered outmoded as towns increasingly interacted with their hinterlands.

> The County Councils are likely to prove stronger and more exacting than local sanitary authorities have been, though here it must be recollected that manufacturers who find it convenient to pour their refuse into the nearest rivers will be very apt to seek a place on the County Councils.
>
> Leading article on the prospects for the new county councils, *The Times*
> (23 Oct. 1888)

Reforming the Great Wen The problems of London were the most acute; the LCC area and surrounding counties had experienced an enormous population growth, creating great housing demand and considerable traffic congestion. In 1957 the Conservative government set up a royal commission under Sir Edwin Herbert to drive through a wall of intransigence erected by the local authorities and the Labour Party (fearing loss of the control it had established over the LCC). This recommended a drastic redrawing of the 1888 boundaries, massively expanding the area from 75,000 to 510,000 acres, raising the population from just over three million to well over eight million, and engulfing parts of Kent, Surrey and Essex, and the whole of

Figure 16.2 The Greater London reforms

Middlesex. The newly staked territory would be divided into boroughs, with functions shared between two tiers. The government pushed the reform through and the old order gave way in 1963 (figure 16.2). The new Greater London Council (GLC) was responsible for those functions requiring coordination over a wide area (housing, major roads and traffic management). Before long it gained responsibility for public transport by taking over the London Passenger Transport Executive.

The 1974 reform In 1964 Labour came to office and Richard Crossman became Minister of Housing and Local Government. He soon foresaw problems for certain of his parliamentary colleagues in the piecemeal reforms suggested by the Boundary Commission (see p. 159), since constituency boundaries are tied to those of the local authorities. He saw a solution to the problem in comprehensive local government reform, and set up the Royal Commission on Local Government in England and Wales, chaired by mandarin Lord Redcliffe-Maud.

This reported in 1969, criticizing the complex maze of over a thousand authorities and recommending its replacement with an amazingly simple system of 58 unitary authorities (figure 16.3). There were to be three exceptions in the large conurbations around Liverpool, Manchester and Birmingham, where a two-tier system on the GLC model would operate. A forceful note of dissent from one of the members, journalist Derek Senior, argued for a two-tier model of 35 **city regions** (which stressed the essential unity of town and country in modern economic and social life), subdivided into a second tier of 135 districts.

The Redcliffe-Maud model was to end the division between town and country, submerging the autonomous county boroughs along with all other towns. The plan was indeed radical, promising far-reaching implications with its suggestion of Benthamite central orderliness rather than local democracy. However, the 1970 general election gave an unexpected victory to the Conservatives, who sniffed out a number of particularly malodorous

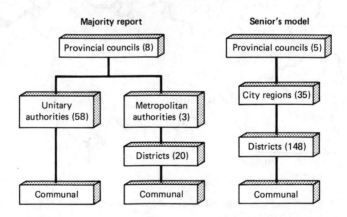

Figure 16.3   The Redcliffe-Maud recommended structure

political rats in the scheme. In particular, a **single-tier** principle, integrating rural areas with the densely populated urban strongholds, might easily find the new areas swamped by the Labour-supporting masses. In a new white paper, the government recommended preserving the **two-tier** principle.

The plan subsequently entered the statute book as the Local Government Act (1972), and in 1974 the 58 counties of England and Wales were recast in the form of 47 **shire counties** and six **metropolitan counties** covering the major conurbations of Greater Manchester, Merseyside, Tyne and Wear, West Yorkshire, South Yorkshire and the West Midlands, with populations ranging from 1 million to 2.7 million. These were based on the GLC model (figure 16.4). In the shire counties the main responsibilities (education and social services) rested with the upper-tier authorities, while in the metropolitan counties they lay with the districts.

In Scotland, the Wheatley Commission had played Tweedledum to Redcliffe-Maud's Tweedledee in the diagnosis of the problems, but the

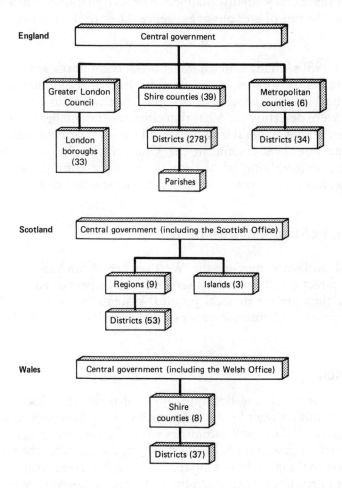

Figure 16.4 The local government structure after the 1974 reform

prescription was for a city-regional model. The resulting reform created a top tier of nine regions and 53 districts, plus three autonomous island councils.

For those favouring radical nostrums these reforms were seen as a missed opportunity of monumental proportions. They were said to be too timid and too conservative, the new counties were too remote, and the structure was anti-urban in that many ancient county boroughs, relegated to district status, lost much prestige and power. Despite the rhetoric of Redcliffe-Maud, which spoke of increasing the role of local government, the reforms actually removed the vital functions of water supply, sewage and personal health. The package was seen mainly as a political move by the Conservatives.

Abolishing the mets The next revision to the map was even more overtly political. The metropolitan counties and the GLC were seen during the 1980s as hotbeds of socialist insurrection and central government's patience with local democracy finally snapped. The extreme decision was taken to 'streamline' the reprobates out of existence (Dept of the Environment 1983).

● ● ●

During the 1980s, changes in capitalist production (large-scale undertakings being replaced by smaller, more flexible units – sometimes termed post-Fordism) had led to a process of *counterurbanization* in which people and industries were deserting the Victorian cities for the smaller towns. The local government map was again lagging behind the reality of industrial and social life. By the late 1980s some in the Conservative Party, including local councillors, were talking of abolishing the shire counties altogether and restoring authority to the non-metropolitan towns and cities.

The Local Political Environment

Each local authority mirrors the Westminster–Whitehall model in being under the direction of politicians served by large permanent bureaucracies. Moreover, they are set in local political systems involving local elections, political parties and interest groups. We examine these in the following section.

The council

Councils are formally the lynchpins of local politics; as local Parliaments they sit in chambers built by the nineteenth-century bourgeoisie scarcely less august than the Palace of Westminster itself. Council meetings usually take place once a month although, like Parliament, the idea that the full assembly is a decision-making body is a myth. Today most urban council chambers split along party lines, with disciplined Westminster-style voting and local

THE FIRST COUNCIL OF THE ROYAL BOROUGH OF KENSINGTON—ELECTED NOVEMBER, 1900

Source: Mary Evans Picture Library

'cabinets', reducing the majority of councillors to backbencher status.

Choosing councillors: local elections Local elections are of great constitutional significance. Dicey attributed the moral justification for the supremacy of Parliament to the popular election of MPs and a similar authority may be said to rest with councils. However, local electoral behaviour is yet another example of the insidious centralism within British politics (Newton 1976: 16). Since the national parties are usually represented locally, people vote on the performance, not of their council but of central government. For this reason national politicians and the media watch with interest, using local elections to gauge public feeling. Because national governments tend to be at their lowest ebb of popularity in mid-term, it is usual for local elections to show a swing in favour of the opposition party (table 16.1).

One of the most widely discussed features of local elections is the relatively low turnout (below 40 per cent). Those favouring centralism invariably take this as evidence that people do not want local democracy. However, in many areas one party enjoys so entrenched a position that, in the absence of proportional representation, there can be but little chance of change and hence little motivation to vote. In urban areas Labour enjoys greatest support, while Conservatives have green wellies securely planted in the mud of the shires. Hence polling is higher where the results are less certain (Fletcher 1969).

Motivations for council membership: why bother? The question of councillors' motivations is frequently addressed in conventional textbooks,

Table 16.1 Number of councils controlled by each political party after district and county council elections, England and Wales, 1978–1987

	Conservative	Labour	Liberal/SDP	Other[a]	Total
Counties					
Metropolitan (incl. GLC)					
1981	0	7	0	0	7
Others					
1981	19	14	1	13	47
1985	10	9	1	27	47
Districts					
Metropolitan					
1978	17	16	0	3	36
1979	10	18	0	8	36
1980	6	27	0	3	36
1982	8	23	0	5	36
1983	7	25	0	4	36
1984	5	25	0	6	36
1986	1	27	0	8	36
1987	1	26	1	8	36
Other					
1978	168	39	0	126	333
1979	161	62	1	109	333
1980	150	70	3	110	333
1982	143	71	3	116	333
1983	150	70	3	110	333
1984	145	69	2	117	333
1986	119	69	5	132	333
1987	128	69	8	128	333
London boroughs					
1978	17	14	0	1	32
1982	16	11	0	5	32
1986	11	15	2	4	32

[a] No clear majority party.
Source: Data from *Social Trends* (1988: table 11.2)

and even in official reports (though less commonly asked of MPs). The subtext of this enquiry suggests that working-class entry into local politics is, like the dog walking upright, a rather unnatural occurrence requiring some explanation. Thus we find that the reasons for becoming a councillor are usually generalized in rather unflattering terms such as prestige, self-improvement, seeking a better social life and, the most heinous crime of all, the pursuit of some ideology (that is, socialism). The Maud Committee on management in local government (1967) argued that 'councillors in interesting and progressive jobs' (middle-class Conservatives) 'see council work as a kind of supplement to their lives'; others 'in ... routine and undemanding jobs' (working class) 'may seek it as a compensation'. The criticism is generally part of an elitist ethos which seeks to exclude the masses from politics.

The calibre of councillors This debate is linked to the previous one and is also widely rehearsed, lying at the heart of the sustained establishment attack under which local government is obliged to live. The belief that the calibre of councillors has fallen since the nineteenth century unites middle-class politicians, academics and Whitehall mandarins. It has two basic strands – *class* and *centralism*.

The class case bemoans the retreat of the old landed and industrial elites from local affairs. Academic case studies (such as Birch 1959) argued that the managerial revolution in British capitalism (see pp. 104–5) meant that local industry ceased to be controlled by locals with an interest in municipal affairs. Hence the economic leadership of communities became separated from political leadership, to the detriment of quality. However, this does not explain why the superior classes were no longer interested in local government. A probable answer is that they lost interest as firms outgrew their locality and directed their attention upon central government; municipal leadership ceased to be crucial to profitability. As a result, the Labour Party made its early gains on the local front. Hence the lament over the calibre of councillors is in part an attack on increased working-class participation. For the establishment, democracy is supposed to mean a spectator choice between elites, not participation in the game.

Labour representatives usually make excellent councillors, because they are much more severely criticised than their middle-class colleagues. It is possible for a middle-class councillor to sit on a municipality for twenty years in a condition of half-drunken stupor without exposure and defeat at the polls; but Labour councillors receive no such indulgence.

George Bernard Shaw, *The Commonsense of Municipal Trading* (1908)

The new breed   The 1974 local government reform signalled a significant change in the composition of many urban councils. The feeling that socialist objectives might be pursued through local government began to develop within parts of the Labour Party and a new breed of councillor emerged – younger, more articulate, more self-confident and better educated. They began to challenge some of the traditional expectations of councillors, making a major contribution to politics during the 1980s as a vital part of a New Urban Left movement (see p. 503). Some of the new-style councillors (Bernie Grant, Ken Livingstone and David Blunkett) became national figures, well known through news and current affairs programmes and chat shows, even winning admission to the BBC pantheon, *Desert Island Discs*.

Political parties

Although modern local government is dominated by political parties, they have been neglected by political scientists. Dilys Hill (1974) argued that

'English local government operates in an atmosphere of relatively low public interest and party conflict is normally muted'. The Maud Report (1967) went so far as to conduct a survey on whether or not councillors belonged to parties, but did not consider it necessary to ask *which* party, leaving the data antiseptically apolitical. The Bains Report was extremely reticent on party politics, but where it did speak it implied that the effect was to undermine the 'efficiency and morale' of the officers (1972: 37).

Opponents of local party politics often hark back to some mythical age when independents supposedly ran the councils. In fact parties – that is, groups seeking collectively to take office – have long existed in local government. Even before the nineteenth-century reforms, electoral battles would take place to secure control of the various *ad hoc* bodies, as well as of the boroughs themselves. However, it was Labour which introduced modern, highly organized party operations into local politics. This development was deeply feared; the old Liberal and Conservative adversaries formed anti-Labour alliances, behaving like Tweedledum and Tweedledee when confronted by a

> monstrous crow as big as a beer barrel,
> which frightened both our heroes so,
> they quite forgot their quarrel.

Local national parties Today the term **'local political party'** is something of a misnomer. Although some are genuinely local, parties are usually offshoots of national organizations. This has three compelling centralizing implications for local government.

- There is close ideological identification between national and local parties, local election battles reflecting national politics.
- Local politicians often look to the national party for inspiration and guidance.
- National leaders expect to exert dominance over local parties, seeking to limit their autonomy for national party ends.

In addition, the respective ideological and policy positions of the local parties tend to be made in the image of those at national level. Thus, Jones confirmed that in Wolverhampton, Conservative councillors disliked rates, while Labour welcomed them as a means of taking from the rich to give to the poor (1969: 321). Dearlove, in a classic study of Kensington and Chelsea, was able to confirm the intuitive prediction that Conservative councillors favoured self-help, rather than collectivist solutions to social problems (1973: ch. 10). In the 1980s, a tough breed of New Right councillors (such as those of Bradford) seemed intent on outdoing their central counterparts in 'dryness'.

The impact of local parties The impact made by parties on local politics can be examined at two levels. Within the community they can act as

political catalysts, mobilizing local electorates, educating the public, stimulating interest in local issues, improving accountability through elections,
providing an avenue for political recruitment and training, aggregating and
articulating interests and offering citizens a means to participate.

Within the town hall the parties can gain complete control over the
machine in much the same manner as at Westminster. Indeed, to understand
town hall politics today one must speak the language of party control. Such
domination, particularly in the urban areas, has increased considerably since
the 1974 reorganization (RIPA 1980; Widdicombe 1986b) and is effected in
a number of ways.

- *The party group*. This is the local government equivalent of a parliamentary
  party. Groups can meet behind closed doors to plan a concerted strategy.
- *Committees*. These can be so composed to reflect the majority in the council
  chamber so that all policy can carry the stamp of the majority party.
- *Chairs*. The committee chairpersons have traditionally been very important
  figures in local government, often achieving celebrity status. The majority
  party can ensure its monopoly of these positions.
- *Local Cabinets*. Senior councillors from the majority party can form a Policy
  and Resources Committee, rather like a Westminster-style Cabinet.
- *Council leaders*. Similarly, if the political will is present, the leader of the
  majority party can become the effective council leader, a kind of local Prime
  Minister.

Modern politics is largely about organized action and parties are key
political units. Much recent local party development reflects the political
reality of urban life and those who oppose it may well be reflecting their own
political orientations. Parties generally threaten the establishment desire for
a passive population – hence the paranoia over increased party activity in the
1980s (see pp. 503–5).

Local interest groups

Owing to the propensity to treat local government as an apolitical branch of
public administration, local interest groups have received even less attention
than parties. However, this changed from the 1960s, as a result of an
increased behaviouralist emphasis in political science and also an apparent
rise in the number of local groups concerned with social policy (education,
housing and social services). Of course, the fact that local groups may be
shown to exist is not proof of a significant degree of pluralism in the
decision-making process. Newton identified over 4,000 organizations in
Birmingham, but only a small proportion could be described as politically
active (1976: 38).

In several respects local interest groups largely resemble those at national
level. Thus their channels of access will be (in order of effectiveness) to
officers, leading councillors, backbench councillors, and local public opin-

ion. Similarly, there were insider and outsider groups, and different scholars found variously evidence of pluralism, corporatism and elitism.

Insider groups These tend to represent respectable interests and have something to offer the authority in terms of resources and expertise. The category includes chambers of commerce, large firms, professional bodies, and sometimes trade unions. Saunders (1980) details the way in which the councillors of the London borough of Croydon worked hand in glove with private business interests to facilitate the commercial development of the town centre, confirming Dearlove's findings in Kensington and Chelsea (1973). Here we find a form of **local corporatism** of the 'gin-and-tonic' kind. It has not invariably been the case, however, that councils are captivated exclusively by capitalist interests. In Sheffield, for example, the local trade unions, through the Trades and Labour Council, enjoyed a close relationship with councillors (Hampton 1970). However, councils cannot ignore the structural imperatives of locally based capitalism.

Outsider groups Such groups include squatters, ethnic minorities, one-parent-family associations, civil rights movements, and so on, and are characteristically left out in the cold when the municipal banquets are held. Dunleavy (1981) noted how humble citizens' groups were excluded in favour of establishment interests in the area of local housing policy. However, one cannot generalize from the experience of right-wing councils. Some will take a radically different view of the kinds of groups they wish to embrace and will not slam the door on groups representing the injured and insulted. Indeed, great efforts were made by left-wing councils to work with the underprivileged during the 1980s.

Local pluralism in chains The extent to which local groups play a part in policy-making is related to local government independence from the centre. Robert Dahl, doyen of American pluralists, conducted a study of local government in New Haven (a city notoriously vulnerable to siege by Yale academics) which was to become celebrated amongst a relieved liberal establishment for demonstrating that the oligarchy of two centuries earlier had been replaced by **local pluralism** (Dahl 1961). Yet Dunleavy observed that the very nature of the approach was defective in that it excluded the influence of state and national actors (1980: 31).

If modern local government is subservient to central government, one might expect the economically powerful to turn their attentions elsewhere, an expectation supported by Cockburn's study of Lambeth. Here powerful local interests did not need to bother themselves with local government. 'Deals that matter most to them, over taxation and employment policy, grants and control, are deals done at Westminster and Whitehall' (Cockburn 1977: 45).

The politics of local bureaucracy

Local government depends on large **local bureaucracies**, staffed by permanent salaried officials, creating a politician–bureaucratic interface replicating many of the issues inherent in the minister–civil servant relationship. At the apex of the hierarchy are the senior officers who interact at the political level with the elected representatives in the process of policy-making: they are the municipal mandarins.

'Yes Councillor': municipal mandarins The respective resources of the actors in the town hall drama are similar to those on the Whitehall stage: the councillor is essentially a layperson, while the officer is a professional bureaucrat, able to play all the tricks of a poor man's Sir Humphrey Appleby. However, in the case of local government it goes further. For a number of reasons, the threat of overmighty bureaucracy is actually greater than at Whitehall.

Ministers are fat-salaried, full-time politicians, while most councillors are unpaid, part-time amateurs, unable to become as *au fait* with the workings of the machine or the technicalities of policy as the officers. This problem is compounded by the fact that, contrary to civil service practice, the top administrative jobs in local government are not the preserve of *generalists*; traditionally chief officers are exclusively professionally qualified *specialists*. Their authority is enhanced by their professional associations, giving them a dual loyalty and lending weight to their elbows in disputes with councillors (Dunleavy 1980: 117).

> The view of the expert can become too narrow. Professional enthusiasm can carry the expert beyond the bounds of good judgement, and 'Bumbledon' can be a real danger ... The control of the expert by the amateur representing his fellow citizens is the key to the whole of our system of government.
> *Report of the Royal Commission on Local Government in Greater London,*
> *1957–60*, Cmnd 1164 (1960)

There is often an underlying class dimension. Leading bureaucrats are generally from the middle classes and much of their work entails informal consultation with representatives of local elites, where they 'believe that they are behaving quite properly and [do] ... not see that they are consulting a minority opinion' (Hill 1974: 87). Some local bureaucrats deeply resent working-class councillors, whom they see as managers *manqué*, with delusions of grandeur (see Henney 1984: 321–41).

Local bureaucrats can be very useful to Whitehall as Trojan horses. Regular interaction between central and local bureaucrats, bypassing the elected representatives, results in an informal network whereby local mandarins are able to pick up the phone and contact their central counterparts on first-name terms. Labour councillors have even discovered 'moles' within their organizations, keeping Whitehall fully informed about their plans and strategies. In addition, a constant flow of demands and regulations, in the form of official circulars, emanates from Whitehall, setting standards and telling officials how to proceed under particular circumstances. These are by no means confined to matters of administrative minutiae; one of the most famous (Circular 10/65) sought to revolutionize the education system by abolishing grammar schools.

Management and managerialism

Because it gains power if bureaucrats are in a strong position *vis-à-vis* the politicians, central government has tried to increase the status of officers through the concept of **managerialism**. The issue of **corporate management** has been a particularly salient area of debate in the post-war era. The traditional style of management in local government (figure 16.5) entailed separate departments, each headed by a chief officer and responsible to a council committee. Critics alleged this to be cumbersome and lacking a sense of central control and direction. Moreover, the committee system gave too much power to councillors, particularly the chairpersons.

Early moves came from municipalities with particularly strong, ambitious figures at the top (Cockburn 1977: 19–24). Newcastle, under the dynamic leadership of T. Dan Smith, was quick to subjugate its councillors to the managerialists. In 1965, the retirement of the town clerk enabled the corporation to appoint Frank Harris, an executive from the Ford motor company, as an administrative supremo – a veritable **city manager**. Harris

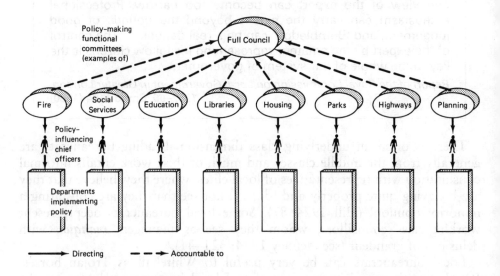

Figure 16.5 The traditional local authority pattern of control and management

set about the committees with the vigour of a Canadian lumberman, reducing them to six. He also established a 'board of directors' consisting of a few of the seniormost councillors. So impressive were developments in the eyes of the centre that a Committee of Enquiry into the Management of Local Government was set up in the mid-1960s under Sir John Maud. Its extensive research into the quality of local councillors supported the declining-calibre thesis, and the Newcastle experiment was endorsed with the recommendation that city managers, in the image of Harris, be encouraged to go forth and multiply. The report asserted that

> the local administration of public services is essential, that the organs of administration should be democratically elected bodies is not.
>
> (Maud 1967: vol. I, p. 68).

The promise of major reorganization in 1974 placed the existing management structure in a highly malleable state and local officials, with the connivance of the minister, decided to strike while the iron was hot with another committee of inquiry, from which councillors were entirely excluded. The Bains Report (1972) reiterated the message of Maud. The main

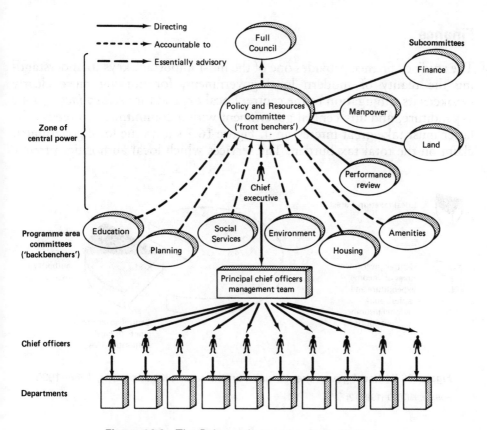

Figure 16.6   The Bains-style management structure

power was to be vested in a *management team* of chief officers, a *Policy and Resources Committee* of senior councillors, and a supreme highly-paid *chief executive* (figure 16.6). Bains gave the game away by advocating maximum 'delegation to the lowest possible levels'; in other words, as much decision-making by officers, and as little democracy as possible. The report was a hymn to bureaucracy, warning councillors that 'the skilled professional officer is not just a servant who is paid to do as he is told' (Bains 1972: 8).

It is not difficult to conclude that the hidden agenda of the management reform movement was to weaken local democracy and transform local authorities into field agencies of the centre. However, in one of the great ironies of the period, it became possible for highly politicized councils to don the clothes of the corporate managers and use the centralized structures to increase their own hold over the authority in order to pursue radical localist initiatives.

However, before we can fully understand the politics of local government and the role of the central government within this, we must address the key question of finance. Although they may be democratically elected, council-lors are powerless if their hands do not hold the municipal purse-strings. We turn to this in the following section.

Finance

The study of finance provides one of the most important keys to understanding the reality of modern local government, for nothing more clearly betokens its subjugation to the centre. Local expenditure is *ipso facto* public expenditure, and any central government with a commitment to reduce the latter must take great interest in it. Figure 16.7 shows the local government claim on the total tax burden. The services which local authorities provide

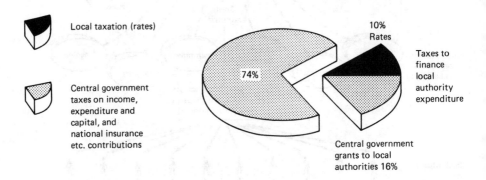

Figure 16.7   Local government's claim on the total UK tax burden, 1984–1985
Source: HMSO (1986: 2)

tend to be expensive because they are labour intensive, with no easy technological routes to savings, and throughout the 1980s the Conservative government pursued local government like a Victorian father cursed with a profligate son.

Local authorities have four methods of raising funds: fees and charges, local taxation, grants from central government, and borrowing.

Fees and charges

A local authority provides many services where charging is possible. In the nineteenth century, they were able to raise large amounts from services such as water, electricity, gas, roads and public transport, but the subsequent rise of the Labour Party contributed to a movement away from charging when, in its early years, it saw local government as a vehicle for socialism. Today the most important areas of local authority charging are in housing rents and, to a lesser extent, public transport.

The hand of the centre At first sight it might appear that central government has little influence over, or indeed interest in, the charges levied locally. However, if a service is offered below cost a subsidy is required from some other source of income – ultimately taxpayers. The Thatcher government took a profound interest in all local government services where profits could be made. A policy of **deregulation** was introduced to remove local government's monopoly status in the provision of certain services, compelling authorities to act like private companies. Public transport fares and housing rents were raised and the 1989 Local Government and Housing Act gave the centre the right to designate further services where charges should be levied.

Local taxation

In both political and constitutional terms local taxation has been by far the most significant element of local government income, not because of its level but because it has served to guarantee autonomy. The principal basis for local taxation was the **rates** – a property tax with liability based on the occupation of domestic and industrial property (broadly speaking, the greater its desirability, the higher the tax). The system came increasingly under criticism, accused of being:

- regressive (taking a greater proportion of income from the poor than the wealthy);
- outdated (first introduced in 1601 to finance the poor law);
- a disincentive to property improvement;
- lacking buoyancy (not rising automatically with inflation);
- insufficient in yield.

In addition, commerce and industry complained that the system was unfair to them; although contributing around 50 per cent of income they were not allowed a corporate vote in local elections. Moreover, it seemed fiendishly designed to penalize the propertied middle classes: over 50 per cent of the adult population were able to escape payment.

The hand of the centre The system had traditionally lain in neutral waters in the central–local battle. In 1980, Tom King, the Conservative Minister for Local Government, said, in response to criticism of grant cuts: 'If we'd started to determine ... rate levies ... then I'd accept that that would be a major threat to local democracy' (Douglas and Lord 1986: 31). However, in 1984 the government, desperate to reduce public spending and under pressure from its ratepaying supporters, broke the rules of engagement and introduced a system of selective rate limitation, soon to become known as **rate-capping**. This was generally targeted at Labour councils, which comprised 16 of the 18 authorities affected in the first year.

After the 1987 election victory the Conservatives were so emboldened as to go even further, replacing the rates with a **community charge**. Profoundly regressive, it was quickly dubbed a **poll tax**, because the principle was to levy an equal charge on each adult, regardless of property or income. Its purpose was to make councils unpopular with the working class as well as the middle classes. However, the bill introducing it aroused enormous hostility, negotiating the Commons with heavy whipping and surmounting the Lords only with a government summons to its hundreds of backwoodsmen. The last time a poll tax had been tried it had led to the Peasants Revolt of 1381, but in 1990 it was the middle classes which were revolting, with stormy, and sometimes violent, scenes outside council chambers as the new charges were fixed.

The non-domestic rate was greatly disliked by firms for its effects on profitability and was also reformed at the same time. Instead of paying a local rate fixed by a (perhaps socialist) council, industry was to pay a uniform nationally determined business rate which would be centrally pooled and redistributed to authorities on a per capita basis.

Central government grants

Central government commands the heights of the taxation system with an unparalleled fund-raising capability through income and sales taxes, as well as other forms of duty. Local government has been obliged to rely upon some of this revenue being passed back in the form of grants. There are in principle two types of grant which together constitute the Aggregate Exchequer Grant (AEG).

- **Specific grants** are made for a particular service (housing, education, police, etc.), usually on the basis of the centre contributing a given percentage of expenditure incurred. They made up about 20 per cent of the total exchequer grant, amounting to some £2.8 billion, in 1984–5.

- **General (or block) grants** contribute to the finances of local authorities by supplementing their rate income and may be used with local discretion. Central grants facilitate a redistribution of the nation's wealth through the national taxation system in favour of the poorer areas. The extent of this process of **equalization** is shown in figure 16.8.

Figure 16.8 Equalization between English regions through central grants, 1984–1985

Source: HMSO (1986: 31)

Baking the cake and slicing it up The calculation of the general grant involves two basic operations: determining the overall size of the cake and deciding how to share it out between the different authorities. In the first task the Secretary of State is assisted by an advisory body, the Consultative Committee on Local Government Finance, which brings together ministers, civil servants and local government. However, the final decision is a political one taken by the Treasury and Cabinet through the estimates and PESC processes. The second operation is not a matter of simple division; like a just parent with different-sized children, central government was supposed to ensure that the slice on each authority's plate would reflect its strength (the *resources* element of the grant) and the tasks it had to perform (the *needs* element). A third element to grant relief to domestic ratepayers was added in 1966 (when it was renamed the Rate Support Grant – RSG). However, in 1980 the wise parent was replaced by the nineteenth-century workhouse master. It was felt that the formula was biased too much in favour of the Labour-controlled high-spending authorities, and the RSG became a political weapon to curb their excesses.

The hand of the centre The Local Government Planning and Land Act (1980) abolished the needs and resources elements of the RSG, replacing them with a new Block Grant more complicated than ever. However, in principle it was the essence of simplicity, merely replacing decisions made by negotiation and calculation with political *dictat*. After a short time an even tougher regime was set up by superimposing a system of centrally determined 'targets' backed up with 'holdback' penalties for 'overspending' which were made increasingly severe. The grant system had been changed from a means of assisting authorities to a means of harrying them. With the abolition of the rates, the grant was renamed the Revenue Support Grant and was made inflexible, so that any marginal changes in local spending would fall entirely on the community charge. Thus a 1 per cent rise in spending would mean a community charge increase of some 4 per cent.

Borrowing

Like individuals and organizations, local authorities have the right to borrow, and they do so for the same kinds of reasons: to purchase things they could not otherwise afford. If we cannot afford a holiday in Disneyland we do not go, but when we purchase a car or a house, we borrow because there is a tangible asset to act as collateral. Thus, local authorities generally only borrow for *capital expenditure* (schools, houses, machines, and so on). This has the additional advantage of spreading costs over the successive generations which will also use the asset.

The hand of the centre However, once again authorities do not have freedom. Before 1981 they were obliged to gain central approval through a loan sanction process. The original purpose of this was to ensure local prudence, but in the post-war era it became an instrument of demand management. When the Thatcher government renounced Keynesianism there was promise that borrowing controls would be relaxed, and the Local Government Planning and Land Act (1980) scrapped the old procedure. However, it introduced a general power of the centre to set ceilings on total annual capital expenditure for each authority. With the introduction of the community charge, central government gave itself even more power over capital spending through a system of 'credit approvals'.

The audit

Like other organizations, local authorities must submit their accounts for annual audit. Before 1983 this was undertaken by district auditors who, although operating impartially, were civil servants. Traditionally such a review was meant to ensure good accounting practice, prevent corruption, and identify *ultra vires* expenditure.

The hand of the centre In 1983 the system was toughened up wtih the creation of a new Audit Commission, a centralized watchdog quango with its 15 members appointed by the government. In addition to the old set of auditing functions, the new body was to undertake special 'value-for-money' audits. The auditors would go into an authority to make a critical scrutiny of its practices according to private-sector criteria, even demanding cuts and redundancies.

•   •   •

It is clear that local authorities are bound to the central state with chains of gold. In the following section we address directly this major and controversial issue of local politics: the central–local relationship.

Conclusion: Local Government in a Centralist State

> The fundamental idea of Centralisation is, *distrust*. It puts no Faith in Man; believes not in Hope, nor in the everlastingness of truth; and treats charity as an idle word.
>
> Its synonyms are, irresponsible control; meddling interference; and arbitrary taxation.
>
> J. Toulmin Smith, *Local Self-Government and Centralization* (1851)

The 1980s saw local government projected from the wings of the political stage into the limelight. The New Right policies of the Conservative government were intended to shatter the mould of the post-war consensus. They centred upon public expenditure cuts and rolling back the social-democratic advances of the post-war era, and boded ill for local government as the major arm of the welfare state. Indeed the 1980s were a period of fierce central–local battle, with much of the local dynamic coming from a movement termed the New Urban Left.

The rise of the New Urban Left

As the New Right programme bit deeper into the economy and the welfare state, the local government commitment to maintain social services was increased more than ever because of the social traumas of rising unemployment and inner-city tension. Two broad sets of factors combined to facilitate the rise of the **New Urban Left**: a *new vision of the role of local government* and the *political configuration*.

With the retreat from Keynesianism many left-wing authorities began to act on their local economies, taking a number of policy initiatives in areas

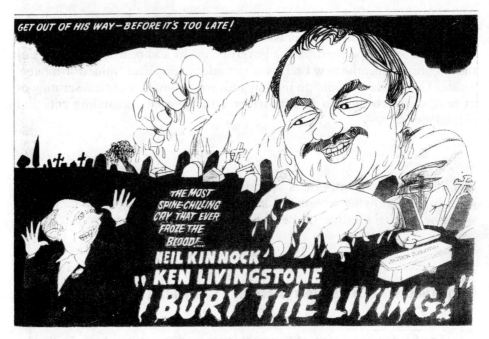

GET OUT OF HIS WAY – BEFORE IT'S TOO LATE!

THE MOST SPINE-CHILLING CRY THAT EVER FROZE THE BLOOD!

NEIL KINNOCK

"KEN LIVINGSTONE

'I BURY THE LIVING!'"

Reproduced by permission of *Punch*

such as industrial incentives and job creation (Chandler and Lawless 1985). When Ken Livingstone became leader of the GLC in 1982, he widened the vision of what an authority with limited powers could do, from public transport subsidies to cycle lanes, arts subsidies and policies in areas of personal morality, including positive orientations towards homosexuals, women and racial minorities, although they earned for their advocates the media title 'loony left'. Two features of the political configuration helped the movement. In the first place, there was the natural swing against the party of government (see table 16.1), which increased the number of Labour-controlled councils. Secondly, Labour's parliamentary defeat began to suggest a long-term loss of central power, giving local government a new strategic position for a last-ditch stand.

In addition, councils became more radical as the left began to displace the right within the party associations and the possibility of fighting for socialism from the town halls produced an infusion of fresh blood. Movements of the far left, churches, community organizations, women's movements, radical sections of the public-sector workforce, black rights groups,

> Local government can be a tool for achieving socialist change. This has been submerged in parliamentary, centralist views of progress.
>
> David Blunkett (leader of Sheffield City Council), interviewed in M. Boddy and C. Fudge (eds), *Local Socialism: the Way Ahead* (1984)

the CND and environmentalists began to forge the kind of alliance which scholars such as Eric Hobsbawm had long advocated as a panacea for the British left.

Central government recognized a major threat, and policy during the 1980s was often designed as much to attack local government as to pursue official objectives. Power to legislate was the centre's key weapon. In addition to the financial legislation (which was resisted through various forms of 'creative accounting'), a battery of laws were passed to weaken local government. A *coup de grace* came in the abolition of the GLC and the metropolitan counties, zapped from the political screen like space invaders. The intergovernmental relationship was even dragged into the courts as, for example, when Lord Denning ruled against the GLC's 'Fares Fair' policy. The councillors of Liverpool (who refused to set a rate) incurred, not only bankrupting surcharges at the hands of the auditors, but crippling court costs after their case failed in the House of Lords.

The end of the story? Central consternation at what was seen as the unconstitutional 'politicization' of local government led to the establishment of the Widdicombe Committee on the Conduct of Local Authority Business, which reported in 1986. It argued that the fact that a local authority is elected

> may lend political authority to its actions within the law, ... but does not provide a mandate to act outside or above the law. Its continued existence ... depends on the contribution it can make to good government.
>
> (Widdicombe 1986a: ch. 3, para. 49)

What this seemingly reasonable statement does not explain is that the 'law' is anything the central government wishes to drive through Parliament, and 'good government' is no more than whatever the Cabinet or Prime Minister approve of.

For many authorities the object of the enervating struggle had been to hang on until a white knight, in the form of a Labour Secretary of State for the Environment, could secure their rescue. Hence the Conservatives' 1987 election victory marked a significant turning point, signalling a sombre mood of 'new realism' at all levels of the party. For a number of reasons the New Urban Left cannot be considered a philosophical or practical counterpoise to the New Right. It lacked homogeneity, it lacked the clear intellectual articulation of the New Right, and was essentially a protest movement rather than a promise of lasting political power. David Blunkett, as leader of Sheffield Council, declared: 'We may lose, but we will lose honourably and lose in the traditions of the Labour movement that fought and struggled and didn't keep its head down' (1984: 247).

Conceptualizing central–local intergovernmental relations

The decline in the autonomy of local government since the nineteenth century has taken place without any formal change in the constitution. In this concluding section we examine a variety of models advanced to explain the **central–local relationship**, including agency, partnership, stewardship, power-dependence, Marxist, and the dual state thesis.

The agency model The idea that local government should be an agency of the centre, with little will of its own, is essentially the Benthamite position. It is justified on grounds of efficiency. In the 1960s, W. A. Robson (an academic and local councillor) began a loud lament for what he saw as the death of local autonomy (Robson 1966), arguing that local initiative was being sacrificed on the altar of centralism. However, there were few to mourn the passing of the golden age, as the Labour Party (and its Fabian mentors) lost interest in 'gas-and-water socialism' once the idea of a hand on the levers of central power left the realms of pipe-dreams.

The partnership model In the late 1960s, orthodox opinion seemed to suggest that Robson had been scare-mongering and, although local actors *felt* a sense of oppression, with the loss of functions and some highly centralist legislation such as the 1944 Education Act, the agency model was systematically discredited. Scholars argued that differentials in levels of per capita spending on particular services (education, housing, social services) demonstrated local autonomy (Boaden 1971; Davies 1972). It was argued that central and local government existed together in a largely harmonious partnership.

The stewardship model It can be argued that the idea of stewardship, in which a local employee manages the estate in the absence of the landlord, is a better analogy for the central–local relationship. The steward has discretion for the simple reason that he is on the spot and has greater understanding of local problems than the landlord; he may at times even persuade the landlord to adopt a certain policy. However, there is no suggestion that this implies any degree of power to resist the employer. The steward is expected to defer, otherwise he may be removed (Chandler 1988: 185–6).

The power-dependence model The benign partnership model was period-bound, providing a comfortable orthodoxy for the years of long-boom plenty in the 1950s and 1960s. Rhodes (1981) offered a more realistic version of partnership in the power-dependence model. This stressed that local authorities, like other organizations, were actors engaged in a bargaining process, and as such they had a number of resources (expertise, organization, information, and a crucial role in policy implementation). This view brings in the concept of a local government policy community (see

p. 420) which also takes us beyond a mere central–local institutional relationship to a more complex network of interacting interests set in the wider political system (Rhodes 1988). There is no reason to believe that the wishes of the centre will always prevail. This was underlined throughout the 1980s as the centre was repeatedly forced to legislate following successive failures to control local authorities.

The orthodox Marxist model A Marxist view of central–local relations can be seen as a variant of the agency model in as much as the local authorities are portrayed as the mandatories of a greater power. However, this is not central government but the forces of wealth and capital which lie behind the facade (Cockburn 1977). The history of local government can indeed be read as a series of responses to the needs of the capitalist economy.

The dual state model This neo-Marxist idea (see p. 480), depicting central government as a closed system of corporate decision-making (concerned mainly with investment policies to ensure profitability of private enterprise) and local government as a relatively open system permitting the involvement of non-capitalist interests (concerned mainly with collective consumption services), provides a sophisticated framework for an analysis of the relationship between the two levels (Saunders 1984: 24). It can predict central–local conflict in four arenas: the *organizational* (bargaining between officials), the *functional* (investment versus consumption policy), the *political* (corporatism versus open participation), and the *ideological* (market allocation of resources versus collectivist provision). Of course in a capitalist society the logic is in each case in favour of central domination, because the interests of capitalism must come first.

●　●　●

In the light of events it is difficult to accept the bargaining models and explain central–local relations in terms of power dependence, when the resources of the combatants are so grossly maldistributed. In the 1980s, central government has been a matador in some surrealistic bullring, with the ability to alter the length of the pike, file the bull's horns, ask judges for support, and change the rules. The declining trends in the scale of British local government are shown in figure 16.9.

Justifying local democracy

> It is but a small proportion of the public business of a country which can be well done, or safely attempted, by the central authorities; ... the legislative portion at least of the governing body busies itself far too much with local affairs.
>
> John Stuart Mill (1806–73; utilitarian philosopher), *On Representative Government* (1861)

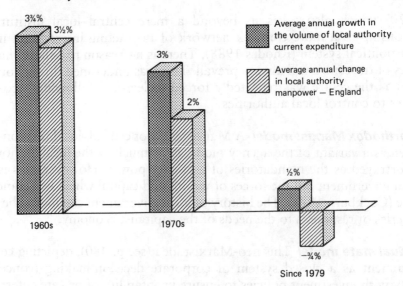

Figure 16.9 Declining trends in local government expenditure and manpower

Source: HMSO (1986: 4)

In conclusion, we may ask whether in fact local government is, like all other institutions of the constitution, subservient to the doctrine of the supremacy of Parliament, left shorn of all claims to autonomy. Has it any constitutional defence against central government?

The answer to this is very clearly 'Yes', providing we go beyond the lawyer's wig and gown and address the question in moral terms. It must be remembered that the British constitution is unwritten and largely based upon convention. Throughout the history of local government there has been a localist strain, evincing a spontaneous desire by communities to provide services collectively, and predating central legislation. The idea that local government is nothing more than a creation of the central state is a myth established by nineteenth-century legislation and perpetuated by centralist politicians of all political shades. There is nothing morally superior about central government; historically the development of the parish was more vital to people than that of the county, the latter being little more than a

> When you have provided the proper constitution of local authority you must provide that the local authority must have sufficient powers; and that it gets these powers by diminishing the excessive and exaggerated powers that have been heaped on the central authorities in London.
>
> Lord Salisbury (Conservative Prime Minister) speaking on his government's creation of the LCC (1888), quoted in K. Young and P. L. Garside, *Metropolitan London* (1982)

mechanism for the king to gain funds and fighting-men. Thus localism can be said to be deeply embedded in the evolution of the British constitution. As in many other aspects of its policy, the Thatcher government's assault on local democracy was by no means characteristic of the party which venerates the evolutionary principles and age-old constitutional convention.

Moreover, local democracy, by permitting ordinary people to participate in politics, enriches life. Aristotle declared that one who lives without politics is either a god or a beast. When local authorities like the GLC are wiped off the map because we do not like what they say, perhaps we take a step back towards the jungle.

Key points

- Britain has a long history of local government, arising from localism (the desire of local communities to regulate themselves) and centralism (the desire of the central authority to control through local agents).
- The reality of local government lies in what services it is able to provide. Without a portfolio of important functions the idea of local democracy is a hollow myth.
- Generally local government has provided consumption, as opposed to investment, functions. Hence it is a major arm of the welfare state.
- The industrial revolution marked a traumatic break with the past. The new bourgeoisie claimed that the old institutions were outdated and the reforms they introduced secured their hold over the municipal institutions.
- Within each territory local government is essentially political and cannot be understood without reference to political parties and interest groups.
- A key to understanding local government and politics lies in finance. Much of the effective power of the centre is derived from its control of financial sources.
- In studying local government it is impossible to ignore the presence of the central government. No atom of the system is untouched by the hand of the Westminster–Whitehall leviathan.
- At the end of the day, in spite of the legislative supremacy of Westminster, local government retains a moral justification derived from the ancient traditions and conventions of communal life.

Questions for discussion

1 Identify and classify the functions of local authorities. Is there any rationale underlying the distribution of functions between central and local government?
2 'It is impossible to understand the internal working of local government without reference to the role of political parties and interest groups.' Discuss.
3 'The low turnout at local elections demonstrates that the British people have attached little importance to local democracy.' Discuss.
4 'The professional expertise of senior local government officers means that they must inevitably dominate councillors.' Discuss.

5   What were the implications of the industrial revolution for the development of English local government?
6   Examine the criticism levelled at the local government system in the decades prior to the Redcliffe-Maud Report.
7   'Central government dominates local government, not because of the constitutional supremacy of Parliament, but because it stands for the interests of capital while local government stands only for the community.' Discuss.

Assignment

Study the extract from the *Independent* and answer the following questions.

Scottish councillors burn payment books in poll tax protest

By Mark Douglas Home
Scottish Correspondent

FOUR LABOUR councillors yesterday burned their poll tax payment books outside the Scottish Office in Edinburgh in protest at the introduction of the tax in Scotland today.

Three members of Lothian Regional Council and one of Edinburgh District Council joined two dozen protesters who dropped poll tax books and bills into a dustbin of burning paper. Further protests are expected in the city today.

Anne Aylett, a Lothian councillor, said: "The poll tax is a completely unacceptable method of financing local government. It puts the main burden on those who can least afford it."

The protest, organised by the Federation of Edinburgh Anti-Poll Tax Groups, followed a demonstration by 13 Labour MPs and two Labour Euro MPs. They stood outside the Scottish Office behind anti-poll tax banners, but drifted away before the burning of the books.

Labour has set itself against joining or leading a non-payment campaign. But Donald Dewar, the party's Scottish spokesman, said yesterday that its campaign against the tax had scored "very considerable success" against the

Government. "The Government is sounding very defensive. They are going to pay a very real political price where it hurts most — when the General Election votes are counted."

The introduction of the tax, or "community charge", to replace domestic rates in Scotland is the biggest revolution in local authority finance for at least a century. Although the first bills will be paid this month, the change-over is still causing regional councils considerable problems. Neil Lindsay, one of the Labour councillors who burnt his payment book, said 1,400 callers an hour were ringing Lothian region yesterday with poll tax queries.

But the rebate scheme is the biggest remaining administrative worry. Malcolm Rifkind, Secretary of State for Scotland, said last year that 1.2 million people in Scotland would be eligible for rebates of up to 80 per cent. But it has emerged this week that tens of thousands of people have either not applied for rebates or have applied too late for them to be deducted from the first batch

of poll tax bills. Councils are now warning that people risk losing part of their rebate if they do not apply within 56 days.

John Mullin, chairman of Strathclyde region's finance committee, said he was "very concerned" about the low uptake of rebates. His council expected that 580,000 adults out of the 1.8 million on the Strathclyde poll tax register would be eligible for rebates. But only about 60 per cent had applied so far.

The poll tax, a flat-rate charge on most adults, spreads the burden of paying for local services to 3.9 million Scots, 1.8 million more than paid rates. The bills this year range from just over £114 in Shetland to £392 in Edinburgh. The average tax is £301, compared with average rates of £495.

Thousands of demonstrators are expected to march through Edinburgh today in a protest organised by the cross-party All Scotland Anti-Poll Tax Steering Committee. The Government dismisses such demonstrations as futile. But it will watch the workings of the poll tax in Scotland with interest as it will indicate problems likely to be encountered when the tax is introduced in England and Wales next spring.

Independent, 1 April 1989

% mark

1 Why is it claimed that the poll tax 'puts the main burden on those who can least afford it'? 10

2 Why do you think the 13 Labour MPs and two Euro-MPs 'drifted away before the burning of the books'? 10

3 Why do you think the government dismisses demonstrations of thousands of people as 'futile'? 10

4 Assess the likely effects on local government policy-making of the introduction of the poll tax. 20

5 'The poll tax ... spreads the burden of paying for local services to 3.9 million Scots, 1.8 million more than paid rates'. Is it not fair that the burden should be spread more widely? 25

6 Compare the poll tax with the rates as a system of local taxation. What other alternatives are there? 25

Review your understanding of the following terms and concepts

local government	metropolitan county
local authority	council
ultra vires	local political party
body corporate	local corporatism
investment function	local pluralism
collective consumption	local bureaucracy
local politics	corporate management
local state	city manager
centralism	deregulation
county	rates
localist tradition	rate capping
parish	community charge (poll tax)
borough	specific grant
county borough	block grant
city region	equalization
single-tier system	New Urban Left
shire county	central–local relations

Topics for debate

This house believes that the idea of local democracy is a legitimating myth of the capitalist state.

or

This house believes that a local authority should be free to spend as much as its citizens are prepared to pay in local taxes.

Further reading

Local libraries contain many accounts of local government in the area. These can furnish good material for local projects.

Boddy, M. and Fudge, C. (eds) (1984) *Local Socialism.*
A lively book of readings with essays by those involved (including charismatic figures such as David Blunkett) as well as by academics.

Chandler, J. A. (1988) *Public Policy-making for Local Government.*
An up-to-date view of the central–local relationship with a particular stress on the role and influence of the Whitehall mandarins.

Checkland, S. G. and E. O. A. (eds) (1974) *The Poor Law Report of 1834.*
With a lengthy introduction by the editors, this book offers a unique insight into the utilitarian and moralistic outlook, with its anti-collectivist fixation and obsession with personal blame for poverty, which was central to industrialization.

Dearlove, J. (1973) *The Politics of Policy in Local Government.*
This classic study of the inner political metabolism of a London borough came as a breath of fresh air into the cobwebbed world of local government study.

Dunleavy, P. J. (1980) *Urban Political Analysis.*
Very lively and provocative, though introducing some highly sophisticated analysis. Not for beginners.

Fraser, D. (1976) *Urban Politics in Victorian England.*
A scholarly and lively work which fully recognizes the intensely political nature of Victorian local government.

Henney, A. (1984) *Inside Local Government: a Case for Radical Reform.*
A view from the far right by a local government officer, predictably betraying little affection for local democracy.

Rhodes, R. (1988) *Beyond Westminster and Whitehall: the Sub-central Government of Britain.*
Up-to-date version of the power-dependence analysis.

For light relief

Winifred Holtby, *South Riding.*
Not many novels take county government as their background, but here by-laws, drainage schemes and council resolutions are entwined with the passions of ordinary people.

17

Political Justice

> In this chapter we examine the institutions applying the laws by which society operates. We examine the **courts**, the **legal profession**, the **judges**, and certain special institutions (**tribunals**, **enquiries** and the **ombudsman**) established to safeguard the citizen from the power of the state. The law is supposed to be above politics, and the judges are its high priests, set outside party, class and faction, dispensing justice to rich and poor alike without fear or favour. However, an important thesis of the chapter is that the judicial process is by no means outside the realm of the political, and the questions we address are political, not legal.

Of all the institutions of the constitution, none is as august and dignified as those associated with the administration of justice. Judges deck themselves in the ornate regalia of another age as necessarily as plumbers wear boiler suits, and the leading and most venerable members of the judiciary sit like bishops in the House of Lords. In court judges expect impeccable courtesy and reverent deference (indeed, failure to display this can be punished as *contempt*). This pageantry and splendour is there for a purpose: it is intended to bestow upon the machinery an aura elevating it above the mundane into a superior realm of honesty, equity and integrity. The judiciary will protect the weak from the abuse of power by the mighty, and will protect the citizen from the state itself. It is through the stewardship of these legal custodians that the concept of the rule of law is made manifest.

This is the orthodox view, but in this chapter we find cause to question it.

Hogarth's 'The Bench'
Source: Mary Evans Picture Library

> Judgement must always be passed with complete solemnity –
> because it's such rot. Suppose a judge throws a woman into clink
> for having stolen a corncake for her child. And he isn't wearing his
> robes. Or he's scratching himself while passing sentence . . . then
> the sentence he passes is a disgrace and the law is violated. It
> would be easier for a judge's robe and a judge's hat to pass
> sentence than for a man without all that paraphernalia.
>
> Azdak, in Bertolt Brecht's play *The Caucasian Chalk Circle* (1948)

The courts

Figure 17.1 illustrates the structure of the court system in England and
Wales, which is organized hierarchically, superior courts checking the

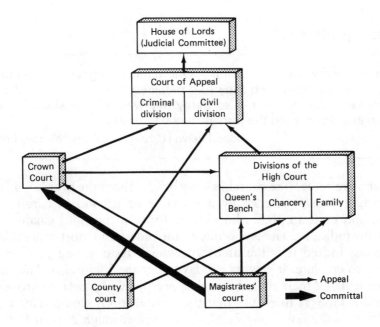

Figure 17.1 The courts in England and Wales

actions of those below through a process of appeal. The organization reflects a fundamental dichotomy between **civil jurisdiction** (one citizen versus another – tort, contract, and so on) and **criminal jurisdiction** (the state versus an offender – burglary, murder, and so on).

Civil jurisdiction Minor cases begin in the county courts, presided over by itinerant circuit judges, while more important ones are heard in the High Court. Appeals from there go to a special Court of Appeal (civil division) and thence, if a further appeal is made, to the House of Lords, the highest court in the land.

Criminal jurisdiction Minor criminal cases are tried summarily (without a jury) in a magistrate's court. These are usually presided over by unpaid magistrates (advised by clerks who are qualified lawyers) appointed from the local community, though in large cities there are also stipendary (professionally qualified and paid) magistrates. For serious criminal cases the magistrate's court conducts committal proceedings, which decide, not the question of innocence or guilt, but whether there is a case to answer. If there is, it will go to the Crown Court (to one of its hundred or so centres around the country) to be tried before a jury and presided over by a High Court judge or circuit judge. Appeals from the Crown Court may be taken to the High Court (on a point of law) or the Court of Appeal (Criminal Division), and thence to the House of Lords.

The legal profession

> I dined at my Lord Chancellor's, where three Sergeants at law told their stories, how long they had detained their clients in tedious processes by tricks, as if so many highway thieves should have met and discovered the purses they had taken.
>
> John Evelyn (1620–1706), *Diary* (26 Nov. 1686)

The courts are rather like churches – nothing without the people inside them. Control is jealously guarded by a veritable priesthood of curates, vicars, bishops, and even an archbishop in the form of the Lord Chancellor, the head of the judiciary. The law is one of the oldest and most venerable of the professions; indeed it is the archetype which most young professions try enviously to emulate. It saw its heyday under the Victorians. The capitalist bourgeoisie based their claim to wealth, prestige and power on property and they needed lawyers to ensure that their acquisitions would remain secure. The reform of the law along Benthamite lines, through Acts of Parliament, was the basis for establishing the new order, and the huge increase in private and public legislation in the early part of the century made Parliament an earthly paradise for the great Victorian lawyers. They were the natural partners of the capitalists, with whom they coexisted in warm symbiosis in the courts and in Parliament. Like the bourgeoisie they were hard working, generally became immensely wealthy, and registered this with a profound sense of their own dignity and importance. The hallowed respect for the law became, in practice, a veneration for lawyers which endures to this day.

> The Law is the true embodiment
> Of everything that's excellent.
> It has no kind of fault or flaw,
> And I, my lords, embody the law.
>
> Sung by the Lord Chancellor in
> Gilbert and Sullivan's *Iolanthe*

In the administration of justice lawyers fall into three categories: **solicitors**, **barristers** and the **judiciary** (judges). Although the three branches are bound together with dense legal bindweed, they have long practised a strict division of labour. Though not entirely unique to Britain, the system is relatively unusual, and not much admired by lawyers from other countries.

Solicitors Solicitors can be employed in various contexts (see table 17.1). They mainly practise privately, usually in partnerships, dealing directly with the public. They are collectively represented by their 'trade union', the Law Society, which has enjoyed considerable influence as an 'insider' pressure

> The Lawyer is exclusively occupied with the details of predatory fraud either in achieving or in checking chicanery, and success in the profession is therefore accepted as marking a large endowment of that barbarian astuteness which has always commanded men's respect and fear.
>
> Thorstein Veblen, *The Theory of the Leisure Class* (1899)

group *par excellence*. Although they may work very closely with clients, and perhaps understand every nuance of their cases, they have been by convention prohibited from appearing in a superior court, having to instruct a barrister, their superior in the legal pecking order, to do this.

Table 17.1   Number of solicitors, England and Wales 1988

	Men	Women
Partners	21,009	2,047
Sole practitioners	3,389	525
Consultants/retired	1,722	113
Assistants/associates	6,913	4,722
Local and national government	2,467	791
Commerce/other	2,202	690
Not known	2,573	1,174
Total	40,275	10,062

Source: Bar Council (1989: 41)

Barristers   Known collectively as 'the Bar', barristers are far less numerous than solicitors and, despite their superior status, dependent on the latter for business. As a group they remain socially insulated, over half operating in the hothouse of London (see table 17.2) in one of the four great Inns of Court, marked by much tradition, ritual and snobbery. The Inns of Court, which control the profession through the General Council of the Bar and a Bar Secretariat, have an ancient lineage, being regarded as well established in the fifteenth century. They were originally concerned with training barristers through lectures and 'arguments', and successful students would duly be 'called to the Bar'. This function gradually declined until, by the early nineteenth century, the call was a formality, the student being merely required to pay an appropriate fee and symbolize attendance for 12 terms by consuming a prescribed number of dinners at the Inns of Court. Today the

Table 17.2   Number of barristers, 1988

	Men	Women
London	3,260	937
Outside London	1,438	309
Queen's Council	576	25

Source: Bar Council (1989: 42)

organization continues to reflect that of the ancient Oxbridge colleges (Jackson 1960: 217), although nineteenth-century reforms added to wealth and gastronomic capacity a requirement to pass examinations. Barristers, like solicitors, form a group which mirrors the upper-middle-class establishment; they are predominantly masculine (see tables 17.1 and 17.2) and white (see table 17.3).

Barristers may advance to a higher grade by 'taking silk', meaning that they are formally appointed a Queen's Counsel (QC) by the Lord Chancellor. At the very top of the heap stand two political appointees: the *Attorney General* (the government's attorney) and the *Solicitor General* (the government's solicitor).

Table 17.3   Proportion of barristers from ethnic minorities

	QCs	Juniors	Pupils
Percentage from ethnic minority	1	6	12

Source: Bar Council (1989: 267)

The judiciary For historical reasons it is mainly from the Bar that judges have been chosen. This has an important implication for the legal system because judicial office is seen as legal business rather than as an aspect of public service. It helps to legitimate the law by reinforcing the impression of independence. Yet paradoxically these appointments are in effect political ones (though not subject to parliamentary approval), being made by the Crown on the advice of the Prime Minister and the Lord Chancellor (who is also a member of the government of the day).

The judiciary may be regarded as the top of the legal profession in the sense that appointment is seen by barristers as promotion (although it is promotion that the richest barristers will spurn). Like other sections of the profession, judges form a hierarchy (see figure 17.2), from the Lord Chancellor and the Law Lords down to the unpaid magistrates sitting in the local courts. The 30 or so senior members of this hierarchy constitute the most politically significant part of the judiciary; it is they who move in the circles of power and make the sensitive judgements which can actually shape the constitution.

Magistrates At the very opposite end of the judicial pecking order come the **Justices of the Peace** (JPs) sitting in the magistrates' courts. Most are laymen and not really members of the legal profession at all. For a long time JPs were key figures in local government, but the industrial revolution swept them from the centre stage. They did however retain a role in the law, and their work was increased with responsibility for juvenile cases after 1908. However, the system remained elitist, with strong attachments to the local landowning classes. The Attlee government declined the opportunity to reform the system of local justice, preferring only to inject some working-class blood through the trade unions and local Labour parties.

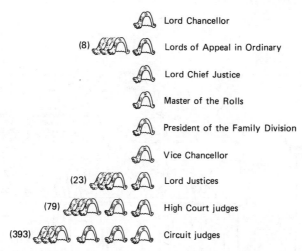

Figure 17.2   The judicial hierarchy, 1987

Source: Data from *Judicial Statistics* (1987)

Today JPs are formally appointed by the Lord Chancellor, although he acts on the advice of local committees. The system is potentially democratic, for technically anyone can become a magistrate, but the process of making recommendations to the Lord Chancellor is controlled by secretive middle-class oligarchies consisting of the great and the good from the Freemasons, political parties, and chambers of commerce in the locality.

The jury system

Although we have introduced the highest and most mighty we have not encompassed the British judicial system until we consider the 12 ordinary people who form the juries in many trials. Juries are made up of people selected randomly from the population, although there are certain disqual-ifications (including those who have received prison sentences of over five years). This is without doubt the most democratic aspect of the legal system; perhaps the most democratic aspect of the whole political system. In the eighteenth century Lord Camden said that 'trial by jury is indeed the foundation of our free constitution; take that away and the whole fabric will soon moulder into dust' (quoted in Jackson 1960). Through the jury system it is possible for ordinary citizens (however they may be directed by the judge) to speak so authoritatively that the most lofty in the land must heed their words. It was a jury which acquitted Clive Ponting of charges of treason (against the direction of the judge) for acting according to his conscience and against the interests of his political masters in the *Belgrano* affair.

However, unlike other elements of the judicial system, juries are under threat. The police in particular find them tiresome, conducting an unceasing campaign for their abolition or limitation. In 1965 Robert Mark (as Chief Constable of Leicester) made a speech calling for the introduction of majority verdicts (rather than unanimity) and in the Criminal Justice Act

"The jury will ignore that last remark..."

Reproduced by permission of *Punch*

(1967) the Labour government duly obliged (Kettle 1980: 17). This by no means satisfied Sir Robert who, in his Dimbleby Lecture, carped how 'illogical it is to confer it [the right to decide] upon any one of twelve random jurymen, least fitted by deafness, stupidity, prejudice or one of a hundred other reasons so to do' (Mark 1978: 281). In July 1989, Metropolitan Police Commissioner Sir Peter Imbert argued in a lecture to the Police Foundation that Britain could usefully move away from its adversarial method of trying cases, with barristers arguing with each other before a jury, to a French-style inquisitorial system, where an examining magistrate with powers of arrest takes charge of the investigation at an early stage, and where it is the judge who questions the witnesses in court, leaving juries less leeway to form judgements on the basis of conflicting arguments.

By the 1980s the system was in a state of crisis and causing alarm in middle-class circles. The tendency of professional people to be excused service on the grounds of their work was leading to a preponderance of working-class jurors, manual workers and the unemployed. Horror stories were recounted in the media of jurors celebrating 'over a pint' with the defendants after finding them not guilty (Gibb 1988).

The system has declined over the years and today juries are only employed in a minority of cases; they are no longer used in magistrates' courts, or in Crown Courts where the accused pleads guilty – which most do. Yet the demise of the system would constitute a grave threat to democracy. In Northern Ireland juries were dispensed with for certain cases of alleged terrorism in 1973, following the recommendations of Lord Diplock. In these 'Diplock courts' convictions have often been made on the basis of confessions obtained during long hours of police interrogation, where allegations of beatings and other forms of ill treatment were subsequently proved. Such developments may be contrasted with the US Grand Jury system (the equivalent of British magistrates' courts in committal proceedings), where juries award compensation in civil claims (sometimes resulting in huge payments against corporate interests).

A 'Big Bang' for lawyers: the Mackay proposals

> A client is fain to hire a lawyer to keep from the injury of other lawyers – as Christians that travel in Turkey are forced to hire Janissaries, to protect them from the insolencies of other Turks.
>
> Samuel Butler (1835–1902; British writer), *Prose Observations*

In January 1989 the new Lord Chancellor, Lord Mackay of Clashfern, unveiled three green papers proposing a reform of the legal profession. This placed a very lively cat among the legal pigeons by attacking some cherished principles of restrictive practice. The far-reaching shake-up designed to introduce free-market, Thatcherite principles into the cloistered world of wig and gown included: breaking the barristers' monopoly, with advocacy rights in all courts for any qualified lawyer; ending solicitors' conveyancing monopoly; and allowing lawyers to take on cases on a US-style 'no-win, no-fee' basis, to advertise and to publish fees. Barristers were to be allowed to take instruction directly from members of the public and there was also to be a lay-dominated Lord Chancellor's advisory committee on legal education and conduct.

The proposals threw the legal profession into turmoil, even arousing the opposition of Lord Hailsham, the recently retired Lord Chancellor and once staunch member of the Thatcher Cabinet. On 19 July, after much lobbying, a white paper, *Legal Services: a Framework for the Future*, duly appeared in which the original green paper proposals were modified in certain important respects. The Lord Chancellor bravely summarized the purpose of his proposed legislation in the House of Lords as 'designed to further the interests of the administration of justice, to increase access to justice, and to extend the range of those possessing rights of audience before the courts'. However, critics saw the white paper as a triumph for one of the most powerful interests in the country, describing the amendments as a climb-down. Both the Law Society and the Bar seemed much mollified and there was every expectation that the bill planned for Autumn 1989 would have a smooth passage. The barristers could expect to maintain their hegemony in the high terrains of the upper courts and the smaller solicitors had been protected against the competition threatened by the formation of multidisciplinary practices and the banking juggernauts in the lucrative area of conveyancing.

Access to the law

> In England, Justice is open to all, like the Ritz hotel.
> Attributed to James Matthew (1830–1908; British judge)

The nature of the legal profession is not merely a matter of sociological curiosity, it has important implications for the nature of democracy. A prerequisite of a just legal system is that all sections of the community have equal access, but this is by no means the case. Many of the characteristics of the profession serve to restrict access, lawyers' clientele remaining predominantly middle class (Zander 1969). There are various reasons for this.

- *Cost.* Lawyers' fees, which are protected by the monopolistic practices of the Law Society, mean that the law is not cheap. For many it is better to suffer a wrong than risk an expensive lawsuit.
- *Legal expertise.* It is in the nature of the legal profession to take a greater interest in the problems of the wealthy than the poor. The intricacies of business and commerce and the transfer of real property tend to preoccupy the legal mind, to the exclusion of problems with landlords, local authorities and social security agencies.
- *The nature of the law.* The law places its greatest emphasis on the management and protection of property. Indeed, it can be argued with credibility that the law is the real culprit in the problem of access (Harris 1988: 371), though of course the law is itself fashioned by lawyers.
- *Class.* The upper-middle-class image of the profession is itself a deterrent. In accent, dress, job and education a yawning gulf exists between working-class people and the typical smooth-talking, self-confident lawyer. Fear of embarrassment, of appearing foolish, tends to keep the ordinary person away from the intimidating solicitor's consulting room.

However, attempts have been made to improve access. First, there is a system of *legal aid*, whereby the state gives financial assistance to litigants. This was introduced in the Legal Aid and Advice Act (1949) and represents a significant development, both for the law and for British democracy in the wider sense. Generally aid in either civil or criminal cases depends upon income and the merits of the case. The Thatcher era saw a great rise in the number of claimants for legal aid as problems resulting from unemployment meant that more people were in debt and experiencing mortgage difficulties. Attempts were made to curtail the system: in 1986 a cut in the dependants' allowance in the means test effected a reduction in the number of claimants and the Legal Aid Bill (1987) removed the administration of the system from the Law Society, placing it in the hands of a new government quango, the Legal Aid Board. By the end of the 1980s the Law Society adjudged the system to be in a state of crisis (Harris 1988: 366).

In 1971 a group of radical lawyers set up a Legal Action Group, to direct legal attention away from the preoccupation with business and property matters to concerns affecting ordinary people, such as welfare legislation, consumer affairs and employment problems. In large cities Law Centres have been established to provide advice and representation, financed by charities and local authorities. Citizens' Advice Bureaux are another source of legal advice, although their workers are generally not lawyers and may not recognize where legal action is possible.

Judges and Politics

The twin constitutional principles of the separation of powers and the rule of law embody the notion that the function of judges is to discover and apply the law rather than make it, and to favour neither the rich nor the poor in so doing. This picture is essential to the legitimation of liberal-democratic government. The famous statue above the Central Criminal Court (the Old Bailey) shows Justice blindfolded in order not to know who sits on the balance she holds.

Judges shaping law

The constitutional subordination of the judiciary to Parliament is shown by the absence of a system of **judicial review**. In many countries (such as the US and France) judges are responsible for reviewing legislation to decide whether it accords with the constitution and basic civil rights. Since Britain's entry into the EC, courts do now have a limited capacity to review legislation to ensure its harmony with the Treaty of Rome, but the concept of judicial law-making is said to be abhorrent to the British constitution. However, this view is fictitious, for judges play an exceedingly important role in shaping the law and are by no means independent of the politically motivating forces of class and state.

The evolving nature of the common law   Much British law is no more than a body of past judgements, a great coral reef of wisdom from successive ages. When a particular case is tried the lawyers will delve into the records to find how similar disputes were settled in the past, and early decisions are treated as *precedents* to guide current decisions. Moreover, this body of **case law** is ever-changing. Where two or more cases appear to have been resolved differently, or where social conditions have changed so as to reduce the relevance of the earlier judgement, then the contemporary judge will exercise discretion and so create a further precedent. This continuing accretion forms the **common law**, which has the great moral virtue of developing with society in an organic manner, rather than being state imposed.

Statute law However, the new capitalists of the nineteenth century were impatient with the idea of a slowly evolving law, which could be seen as a recipe for the maintenance of the status quo. Bentham argued from his utility principle that each generation should fashion its own laws in accordance with the needs of the age. The result was a vast increase in the amount of **statute law**, made by politicians in the reformed Parliament, which was given precedence over the common law.

This change of emphasis might seem to rule out the creative powers of the judiciary, but this is by no means so. No Act of Parliament can possibly take into account all the circumstances of any particular case and invariably some interpretation, or *statutory construction*, is required. This can considerably alter the legislators' original intentions. For example, the Law Lords decided that the Race Relations Act (1971), seemingly intended to outlaw racial discrimination generally, did not apply to private clubs. Much legislation invokes the concept of 'reasonableness' in determining standards of acceptable behaviour, which in practice means what the *judge* regards as reasonable.

> The Common Law of England has been laboriously built about a mythical figure – the figure of the 'reasonable man'.
>
> A. P. Herbert (1890–1971; British writer and politician),
> *Uncommon Law* (1935)

The Law Commission This is a quango composed entirely of lawyers, with responsibility for revising the law. Its role is defined formally as a technical, non-political one, concerned with clarifying obscure language, repealing obsolete statutes, and consolidating and codifying masses of complicated statute or common law. However, the commission can make major recommendations with more than a cosmetic impact. For example, the important 1986 Public Order Act (replacing that of 1936 and consolidating various pieces of relevant law in the area), incorporated most of the recommendations of a report made by the commission three years earlier.

Involvement in policy debates In the great public debates of the day judges are by no means shrinking violets. Even when delivering judgements their exegesis will often pass comment on various matters of social concern, such as the role of the family, discipline in schools, moral standards, and so on. Moreover, where important public questions are being addressed it is usual to appoint a member of the judiciary to head an official investigation. Figures like Lord Scarman and Lord Denning appear as leading actors in the political drama, more famous than many ministers.

Suction into politics Governments can even create laws designed to suck judges into the political realm. Such an attempt was made by Edward Heath in 1971 with the establishment of the Industrial Relations Court. Legislation during the 1980s made dramatic efforts to bring judges into a bitter political struggle with the working class, obliging them to sequestrate union funds and surcharge socialist councillors. In the GLC 'Fares Fair' case (1981), Lord Denning took it upon himself to tell us that party manifestos do not matter, that they were issued to get votes and not to be taken as the Gospel'.

Questioning judicial impartiality

The impartiality of judges reflects a fundamental principle of natural justice – no one should be the judge in their own cause. This does not only mean that they will be expected to be impartial between all litigants, it also means that they will intervene between citizen and state to prevent the rise of oppressive government. Judges must appear to stand above the confused mêlée in which classes, parties and interests vie with each other for control or influence over the state. But do they? We can begin to answer this question by considering their background.

The background of the judiciary The British judiciary has for long been tied by silken threads of class to the establishment. Indeed it is very much part of that comfortable elite which exercises eternal vigilance in maintaining its privileges and advantages over the mass, monopolizing the key positions in the state, the professions and the economy, sending its sons to the very cream of the public schools, and thence along a comfortable inside track to Oxbridge. Most importantly, it is the class which self-confidently nurses a deep conviction of its divine right to rule.

As successful barristers they will have learned to move smoothly in the world of country houses and London clubs. A number of them become MPs, their allegiance falling (not surprisingly) predominantly to the party of property and privilege. Here they will blossom until plucked for the judiciary by the hand of the Lord Chancellor, acting largely on the advice of senior members of the profession. The career path ensures that they will be relatively old, predominantly male, and the likelihood that their faces will be white is as certain as that their wigs will be so. This system cannot produce men of a radical turn of mind. When those from less propitious backgrounds receive the call – and there is evidence of a widening entry to the Inns of Court School of Law (Bar Council 1989: 51), they are unlikely to make any impression on the impassive face of the legal establishment. In the first place, they are likely to be motivated by individualistic social aspiration, with little desire to challenge the status quo, and, secondly, they will have been subject to a battery of socializing pressures in attitudes and behaviour. Most important of all, the golden patronage will not be bestowed on any suspect characters: at each stage selection is by their seniors, who fashion the clay into their own image before administering the breath of life.

As a group, they manifest nothing of the heterogeneity of the society they presume to judge. They have no experience of being unemployed, unqualified, discriminated against, dispossessed and demoralized by society. They are the high and the mighty and, if the Sermon on the Mount is to be believed, such worries which they may have concern the next world rather than this. All this means that when judges have decided what is in the *public interest*, as they are constantly asked to do, it is a public interest as seen from a very narrow perspective. They have consistently exercised a conservative bias, being led ineluctably to the view that 'stability above all is necessary for the health of the people and is the supreme law' (Griffith 1981: 235).

Judicial bias

In seeking evidence of judicial bias we can isolate sentencing, moral issues, police powers, national security, property rights versus civil rights, cases involving trade unions and relations between central and local government.

Sentencing Generally judges are more lenient towards members of the professions (such as accountants or architects) than they are towards the working class or the unemployed (Box 1971). Prudent solicitors recognize this when advising working-class clients to wear a conventional middle-class uniform in court.

Moral issues Members of sexual minorities, holders of unorthodox views, squatters, student protesters, and so on can all expect rough justice in the British courts. In 1976, for example, the House of Lords opined, in dispensing with his right to refuse the adoption of his child, that a homosexual had nothing to offer his son. In the area of race relations, judges have proceeded 'on the basis that legislation is primarily an interference with the rights of individuals to discriminate and that the public interest is best served by restricting the impact of that legislation as far as possible' (Griffith 1981: 225).

Police powers The judiciary has generally supported the police in areas such as questioning, seizure, obtaining 'confessions', conduct of identification parades, and telephone tapping, where legal powers have been exceeded. It is generally recognized by the Director of Public Prosecutions, in deciding whether or not to proceed against the police, that it is exceedingly difficult to secure a conviction.

National security In matters of national security the judiciary is willing to set most other considerations aside in siding with the state. In the *Hosenball* case (1977), an American journalist was ordered to be deported by Merlyn Rees, the Labour Home Secretary, for obtaining for publication material said to be harmful to UK security. Lord Denning, in dismissing an appeal, said 'when the state is in danger ... even the rules of natural justice had to take second place' (*The Times*, 30 March 1977). In the case of Sarah Tisdall (see p. 363), a sentence of extreme severity was imposed for leaking a memo,

FUN.—October 13, 1866.

NUPKINS'S JUSTICE.

Learned Magistrate :—" HEAR THE EVIDENCE FOR THE DEFENCE? NONSENSE! I WON'T HEAR A WORD OF IT!
WHAT'S THE USE?——I COULD NOT THINK OF DOUBTING A POLICEMAN'S WORD."

Source: Mary Evans Picture Library

while in the Ponting case (see p. 363) the judge explicitly equated the interests of the state with those of the government, directing the jury to convict (a recommendation they actually chose to ignore).

Property rights versus civil rights The rise of the bourgeoisie was dependent upon their ability to secure property. Property rights are legally vested in individuals through contracts and leases, their protection being one of the primary purposes of the law. In the absence of a Bill of Rights or a written constitution, human rights are not vested, so when judges consider such matters they are asked not to *protect* a right but to *assert* it, often against a powerful private institutional interest. This is alien to their principal function, which is 'not the enlargement of liberty, but the preservation of legally vested [property] rights' (Griffith 1981: 222).

Where it is the state which threatens individual property rights the judiciary is placed on the horns of a dilemma, its natural propensities leading it to support both parties. However, here it appears more willing to take its function of protecting the individual from the state more seriously. In the *Amisminic* case (1969) a company was aggrieved by the refusal of the Foreign Compensation Commission to recompense it for the forced sale of its Egyptian property to the Egyptian government at a loss. Although there was no right of appeal to the courts, the House of Lords insisted on hearing the case and found in favour of the company. In another case, in 1976–7, a minister instructed the Civil Aviation Authority to refuse a permit for entrepreneurial Freddie Laker to offer cut-price fares over the Atlantic. The courts supported Laker. Interestingly, in both cases the government was Labour.

Cases involving trade unions Trade unions are seen by capitalists as a threat to profit and since their inception have been consistently opposed by judges. In the nineteenth century, a series of Combination Acts sought to restrict their growth, an intention assisted by the judiciary in statutory interpretation and in additions to common law.

Indeed, towards the end of the century, when Parliament began to doubt the value of legal penalties in this area, it was actually necessary to curb judicial anti-unionist fervour with legislation. Most important was the Conspiracy and Protection of Property Act (1875), which effectively legalized strikes. The notorious Taff Vale Judgement of 1900 held that trade unions could be sued by employers for losses sustained as a result of strikes, and had to be reversed by the 1906 Liberal government in its Trade Disputes Act. Another blow came in the Osborne Judgement of 1910, preventing the use of union funds for procuring parliamentary representation, thereby undermining the base of the fledgling Labour Party. Again Parliament had to curb the excess of judicial zeal with the Trade Union Act (1913). More recently Parliament was obliged to nullify a vicious House of Lords judgement in *Rookes* v. *Barnard* (1964), which came at a time when the unions were being blamed for industrial decline. It was seen as a direct attack on the right to strike.

In 1971 the Heath government passed an Act to regulate industrial relations, establishing a special National Industrial Relations Court (NIRC), presided over by former High Court judge Sir John Donaldson. In July 1972, five dockers who refused to comply with a ruling of the court were actually imprisoned for contempt, resulting in a furore with widespread threats of industrial disruption, and even a general strike. In some extremely Machiavellian manoeuvring the House of Lords delivered an unprecedentedly speedy judgement on an unconnected case, holding that a union was responsible for its shop stewards. This decision allowed the NIRC off the hook by presenting an excuse for the dockers' hasty release, thereby foiling their willing martyrdom. The case remains an extraordinary example of naked political action by the judiciary.

Conservative policy during the 1980s was to enact a whole new corpus of law designed to push more industrial relations issues into the courts. They were not laggard in responding, ordering the large-scale sequestration of funds from the miners', printers' and seamens' unions. In the dispute between right-wing press baron Rupert Murdoch and the print union SOGAT 82, the courts, in finding members guilty of secondary picketing, refused to take account of the fact that Murdoch had forced this upon them by cunningly splitting his newspaper holding into separate companies.

Central–local relations The relationship between central and local government is a political minefield and again the courts have frequently been extremely friendly to the forces of the right, as a number of *causes célèbres* show.

In the *Tameside* case in 1976 a newly elected Conservative council cancelled a plan for comprehensive education prepared by its Labour predecessor under the requirements of the Labour government's policy. The Labour Secretary of State intervened under powers in the 1944 Education Act, on the grounds that the council was acting 'unreasonably'. However, the House of Lords supported the council.

In 1979, the Conservative government's strategy of shifting political disputes into the courts was used in its bitter struggle with the Labour-controlled local authorities and again received judicial support. The *Norwich* case of 1981–2 saw the Court of Appeal upholding the government in its insistence that the city council sell its council houses; it was told by Lord Denning to 'get a move on'. In the GLC 'Fares Fair' case the High Court upheld the council's right to reduce the fares charged by London Transport, but the Appeal Court, and subsequently the Law Lords, ruled that the statutory duty of the GLC to provide 'economic' transport facilities ruled out the policy. No consideration was made of the wider economic and environmental benefits involved. Few public transport systems in the world break even, and the decision appeared highly political. In other cases the courts have upheld crippling surcharges on Labour councillors.

Judges and party politics

Prima facie the evidence suggests a natural bias of the judiciary towards the interests of property and the Conservative Party. If this is not precisely true, it certainly appears that Labour governments are more likely 'to act in ways which offend the judicial sense of rightness, the judicial sense of where the public interest lies' (Griffith 1981: 236–7). Either way, it amounts to the same thing in practice.

Administrative Justice

The threat of the state

Throughout the present century ordinary citizens have come increasingly into contact with the state. This has arisen as a result of the growth of the welfare state, intensified activity by coercive forces such as the police and immigration control, and increased regulation in social life, as in rent control, race relations and gender equality. All this increases the possibility that a citizen may need to seek **redress of grievance**, not from a fellow citizen, but from the state itself.

Some countries meet this contingency with separate systems of administrative courts and a special body of **administrative law** such as the *droit administratif* of France. However, in Britain most of the relevant law is in the form of general public statutes concerned with setting up, or modifying, some particular service, supplemented with a haphazard collection of common-law decisions.

Dissatisfaction with this state of affairs reached a climax in a major *cause célèbre*: the Crichel Down case of 1953–4, where improper behaviour by civil servants seriously embarrassed the government, which sought the time-honoured escape route by setting up a committee of enquiry, the Franks Committee. The British section of the international association of jurists, Justice, also conducted an enquiry, resulting in the Whyatt Report (1961). Both reports were highly critical, making recommendations leading to changes in the system of administrative tribunals and public enquiries, and the establishment of the office of ombudsman.

The Crichel Down affair

The question of the relationship between a minister and his civil servants was brought to the fore in 1954 in the Crichel Down Affair. This case concerned the restoring to agricultural use of a piece of land previously requisitioned by the government for military purposes. Despite the fact that the former owners wished to regain possession, officials at the Ministry of Agriculture thwarted them with underhand, though not illegal, tactics. The owners, members of the upper middle class and well connected, were able to battle on for their rights, and after a public inquiry the civil servants were severely censured and the Minister, Sir Thomas Dugdale, resigned.

Administrative tribunals

Although taking multifarious forms, **administrative tribunals** are essentially committees appointed by ministers to adjudicate in certain categories of cases where a citizen feels aggrieved by some action of a government official. Most are standing bodies, concerned with areas such as rents, rates, social security, pensions, supplementary benefits, immigration, housing and health, though others are set up on an *ad hoc* basis to consider some particular matter. They hardly constitute a system, more a rather motley counterpane sewn loosely together over time. They defy precise enumeration because some are so closely woven into the bureaucratic fabric that it is difficult to discover whether they are formal tribunals or just committees. However, the network is extensive, with over 70 different systems (Pliatzky 1980: 2) and hundreds of tribunals receiving over 150,000 cases each year. The Franks Report (1957) contained a number of indictments of the system.

- The minister whose department was subject to the complaint appointed the tribunal, which could, as a consequence, function as judge in its own cause.
- Members were not legally qualified, and in many cases legal representation was denied.
- The methods of hearing evidence were not strictly controlled.
- Decisions were often given without reasons.
- Whether or not justice was done, it was not *seen* to be done; hearings were often conducted like masonic rituals.
- There was no appeals machinery.

Franks wanted to see the tribunal chairpersons appointed like judges by the Lord Chancellor, and the establishment of a special independent body to appoint tribunals and keep them under constant review. He also argued for greater openness, legal representation, reasoned decisions, and a right of appeal to the courts for unsatisfied complainants. The fact that such fundamental, self-evident recommendations had actually to be asserted is in itself a severe indictment of the ethos of British administrative justice.

Following Franks some grudging and limited changes have been made in the system: proceedings are usually public, there is limited scope for appeals (both to special appelate tribunals and to the courts), and some legal representation is permitted. It is often claimed that the most important reform was the establishment in 1958 of a Council on Tribunals, a watchdog quango of around 10–15 members appointed by the Lord Chancellor, to whom it is responsible. This is a less powerful body than that envisaged by Franks: it does not appoint tribunals and cannot award compensation, hear appeals, or overturn decisions. Its pleas for more powers have been unheeded and it remains little more than a legitimating sop to the spirit of Franks, demonstrating the ability of the bureaucracy to cocoon itself against the winds of natural justice.

Although some of the tribunal chairpersons are now legally qualified,

Table 17.4   Caseload of various administrative tribunals, 1986–1987

Tribunal	Cases received	Cases heard
Income tax commissioners	–	565,995
Lands Tribunal	1,283	672
Local valuation panels	179,752	37,668
Mental Health Review	4,812	2,829
Misuse of Drugs	10	3
Pensions Appeals	1,994	2,761
Performing Rights	1	0
Police Appeals	27	46
Rent assessment panels	19,808	18,650
Vaccine Damage	42	26
VAT	1,317	547

Source: Data from *Social Trends* (1988: table 11.5)

appointment still remains within the patronage of the minister, selecting from a list approved by the Lord Chancellor. Tribunal members continue to be appointed by ministers, which means in practice they are largely made by officials of the interested department.

Much is made by apologists for the friendly informality of tribunals. However, developments in the post-Franks era have tended to take them more in the direction of formality, and the experience of appearing before one is, for ordinary people, daunting and intimidatory. The virtue of expertise is also questionable; in practice this can mean the opportunity for technocrats to obfuscate the issues with esoteric fog which a skilled judge would insist on disentangling into terms that all can understand. To citizens, administrative tribunals can appear as Kafkaesque castles of the establishment, peopled by upper-middle-class bureaucrats generally more anxious to protect themselves than pursue justice. Yet the demand for this rather rough form of justice continues unabated (see table 17.4).

Public inquiries

Government and its officials have a further alternative to the courts in the **public inquiry**, which may be employed in cases where the aggrieved party is not an individual but a section of the population. Such mass grievance can easily be generated by the state in areas like economic or land use planning, state acquisition of land, the construction of motorways, and so on.

In order to settle or pre-empt a dispute a minister may set up a public inquiry, entailing the appointment of an inspector to conduct hearings in which those with an interest may appear like witnesses to put their arguments. The Franks Report led to more stringency in the handling of inquiries, so that the reports are now published, and reasons given for recommendations. However, they remain heavily dominated by officials; the inspector is usually a civil servant, socialized into the ways and habits of technocracy, secrecy and self-confidence. Ministers tend to follow the advice tendered, which is not surprising, because the inspectors are from the heavenly list of the great and the good, who can be relied upon to favour an orthodox establishment line.

As with tribunals, bureaucrats like to pretend that these exercises are merely administrative operations (Wraith and Lamb 1971: 13). However, the siting of airports, nuclear power stations and motorways can incite the most intense political feeling involving the organized actions of pressure groups, local authorities and private companies. Large-scale public hearings, such as that considering the siting of the nuclear reactor at Sizewell, arrest considerable media attention. However, the general feeling of those who attend is one of impotence before a bland wall of intensely polite bureaucratic intransigence. Where protestors give vent to their feelings in some un-English display of emotion, they are likely to be removed by the inspector's ever-present henchmen in blue.

The ombudsmen

A further defect of the tribunal network was that not all areas of administration were covered. Some departments, such as the DSS, are heavily tribunalized, while others, such as the DES, deal with complaints on an informal basis. Moreover, tribunals are set up to deal only with certain categories of complaint and cannot cover the full scope of administrative discretion. It was not only Hamlet who was troubled by delay and the insolence of office, there exists an infinite variety of ways in which officials can annoy, inconvenience and cause suffering for individuals, while acting quite legally and giving no cause for complaint to a tribunal.

The 1961 Justice report (Whyatt 1961) recommended the introduction of an **ombudsman system** based on the Scandinavian model of a citizens' trouble-shooter with a remit to investigate complaints against bureaucrats. The idea was received frostily by officials, who argued that it would undermine the quintessential genius of the British constitution, with its supremacy of Parliament and ministerial responsibility. Initially the Conservative government rejected the idea but Labour took a more sympathetic view in 1967. However, the British variant of the office was so locked into the existing institutions and conventions that it was but a pale shadow of the Nordic prototype; even the friendly term 'ombudsman' was translated through Whitehallspeak into the crusty and inelegant 'Parliamentary Commissioner for Administration' (PCA).

The PCA was to be seen as a servant of Parliament rather than the people, and there was also to be a special select committee to monitor his work, investigate his reports, and observe the extent to which bureaucrats attempted to right their wrongs. Following the initial decision to usher an ombudsman onto the stage, the principle was guardedly extended in 1969 to Northern Ireland, to the NHS in 1973, and to local government in 1974.

Restrictions on the PCA

In 1977 Justice published another report (the Widdicombe Report) assessing the impact of the new institution. Its title, *Our Fettered Ombudsman*, encapsulated its conclusion (Widdicombe 1977). The PCA is shackled by heavy chains forged by the unharmonious blacksmiths of Whitehall. There are restrictions on access and on defining maladministration, limited jurisdiction, absence of autonomy and problems of enforcement.

Access Unlike their Scandinavian cousins, the British people cannot address their ombudsman directly; they must go through their MP. This is entirely against the ombudsman spirit as a 'friend of the people'. One of the arguments put forward for this arrangement was to prevent the PCA being swamped – a curious alternative to providing a larger staff. Another reason for the MP 'filter' is said to have been a desire to protect the traditional role of Parliament in the redress of grievances. However, beneath all constitutional cant is the bureaucracy, ever alert in protecting itself from the prying eyes of outsiders. A number of authorities, including the Widdicombe Committee and the PCA itself, have argued for direct access. However, the select committee and the civil service continue obdurately to resist formal change.

The concept of maladministration A further difficulty lies in the meaning of **maladministration**. The term has proved both confusing and restrictive, defying precise definition. Richard Crossman, when introducing the bill in Parliament, provided a lurid catalogue of bureaucratic natural shocks to add to Hamlet's soliloquy, including 'bias, neglect, inattention, delay, incompetence, ineptitude, perversity, turpitude, arbitrariness, and so on'. Generally the stress on maladministration means that the PCA is permitted to consider only the *procedure* of decision-making, not the nature of the decisions, yet it is often the latter which causes the suffering. The 1977 Justice report recommended lifting this restriction so that 'unreasonable, unjust, or oppressive decisions' could be investigated, as in other countries. However, uneasy bureaucrats have managed to ensure that this alarming suggestion gathers dust in the vaults of Whitehall.

Limited jurisdiction A serious problem lies in the ombudsman's limited jurisdiction. All complaints which may be pursued through the courts or tribunals are excluded, as are sensitive parts of the public sector like the armed forces, police, and government contracting with the private sector. This restriction accounts for a large proportion of the rejected cases.

Limited autonomy Although formally free of the executive, the ombudsman's real autonomy is questionable. The executive cannot sack him, but it makes the appointment in the first place. It also appoints his staff, the size of which is controlled by the almighty Treasury. Where legal advice is required it is taken mainly from the Treasury Solicitor rather than from the courts (although since Widdicombe sources of advice have slightly broadened). Astonishingly, until the appointment of Cecil Clothier in 1979 (a judge), the first three incumbents were ex-civil servants. This was justified on the grounds that, as ex-poachers, they alone would be able to stalk their prey along the burrows of Whitehall. However, they have not been inclined to become particularly ferocious gamekeepers; rather they have acted like civil servants, sidling shyly out of the limelight, denying any political role, shunning the media, and delivering pious apologias for their role. Sir Edmund Compton, in evidence to the select committee, gushingly eulogized on the excellent standards of administration achieved by the mandarins, stressing with pride how few of his investigations had found in favour of the complainant.

Enforcement of judgements Finally there are great weaknesses over the enforcement of the PCA's recommendations. Upon completing an investigation he will submit a report, not to the citizen, but to the MP and department concerned. Although this may contain recommendations, the PCA, unlike a court or tribunal, has no power to enforce them. He must rely on the willingness of departments to accept his suggestions in order to avoid fuss, bad publicity, and further scrutiny by the select committee.

Ombudsmouse or ombudseunuch?

This was a designer ombudsman system for one of the most deferential and secretive polities in the world. It remains on the sidelines of political life; few know of its existence, and even fewer use it.

This does not mean that the British ombudsmen are not politically significant, but their value lies, not in their capacity to provide redress of citizens' grievances, but in their role in legitimating state bureaucracy. The low level of complaints made, and the low proportion of these to be upheld (around a quarter) are explained complacently by the high standards of British public life. Of course, those who suffer are not the wealthy and powerful, but the poor and humble, those not street-wise to the ways of the state.

Towards an administrative court

In 1971 Justice suggested the creation of a special division of the High Court to provide an avenue to appeal from tribunals on points of law. This would resemble the powerful and prestigious *Conseil d'Etat* in France, which is a supreme administrative tribunal through which ordinary citizens can, at small cost, obtain a wide range of remedies against officialdom. The suggestion met with bureaucratic opposition on the grounds that the court would lack expertise; a weak objection given that cases requiring expert knowledge are not unusual in the ordinary courts and may be dealt with by the use of expert witnesses. However, increasingly use has been made of the Queen's Bench Division for judicial review of tribunal *procedure*, where some 12 judges specialize in administrative law. With this growing expertise the demands that the British government drop its objection to a formal system of administrative courts become more compelling.

Conclusion: the Law and the Neutrality Myth

> If the law suppose that . . . the law is a ass.
> Mr Bumble in Charles Dickens's novel *Oliver Twist* (1837–8)

The British constitution makes much of the notion of the rule of law, which avows that no person or group, including the government, is above it. This implies that in some mysterious way the law is God-given, beyond the meddling hand of mankind. Yet this idea is clearly fictitious; laws are made by people, the people who make the laws are the economically powerful, and the laws they make are designed to keep them that way. The law 'says what shall be property and what shall be crime – and it mediates class relations with a set of appropriate rules and sanctions, all of which, ultimately, confirm and consolidate class power' (Thompson 1975: 259). This does not mean that gains cannot be made by the unpowerful, but these tend to be modest and seemingly necessary for a minimum level of civilization (extension of the franchise, health and safety at work, trade union rights, welfare services, and so on), and are only secured against stout resistance.

The myth of neutrality may be buttressed by the argument that the law protects the 'public interest'. This concept is crucial to the legitimating process and it is worth pondering its meaning. When British judges (or the pseudo judges of the bureaucracy) consider what is in the public interest, the public they have in mind is not the great mass; it is the public in public school rather than in public convenience. This is the 'public' which existed in the days of parsimonious franchise, when certain people were seen to matter, and others were equally seen not to matter. It is a world which still remains deeply engrained within the heart of the deferential British political culture; a museum world of which the judiciary are the faithful curators. Thus, when the agencies of coercion and force claim to be enforcing a neutral law in the public interest, they are walking a perilous psychological tightrope. That they are able to defy political gravity with such conspicuous success is testimony to the forces of socialization which must necessarily underlie popular belief in the neutral law.

Key points

- Within the British constitution the legal institutions are the most august and venerated; the law is formally held to be above politics and impartial between classes, parties and factions.
- The legal profession assumed great importance during the eighteenth and nineteenth centuries as the rising industrial bourgeoisie sought a means of safeguarding the property and wealth it was rapidly accumulating.
- The legal profession comprises solicitors, barristers and judges. The latter are appointed from the ranks of the barristers. This means that judging is seen as a job for lawyers rather than public representatives.
- The jury system is the only democratic chink in the legal system though it is under fire on a number of fronts.
- Although the role of judges is formally seen as interpreting and applying the law, they are in reality more powerful than this, able to shape the law in a number of ways.
- Lawyers are generally from the upper middle classes. The record shows that they tend to favour the interests of capital against those of working people.
- Britain does not have a special set of laws and courts to deal with cases involving the citizen and the state. To fill this vacuum a system of administrative tribunals has grown up, where justice is dispensed by the state officials themselves. There is also a system of ombudsmen, which is but a pale shadow of the Scandinavian prototype.
- In reality, law and the legal system cannot be regarded as above the game like a football referee.

Review your understanding of the following terms and concepts

civil jurisdiction	common law
criminal jurisdiction	statute law
solicitor	judicial impartiality
barrister	redress of grievance
judiciary	administrative law
Justices of the Peace	administrative tribunal
jury system	public inquiry
judicial review	ombudsman
case law	maladministration

Assignment

Study figure 17.3 and answer the following questions.

% mark

1 What are the principal reasons for the rejection of cases by the ombudsman? 20

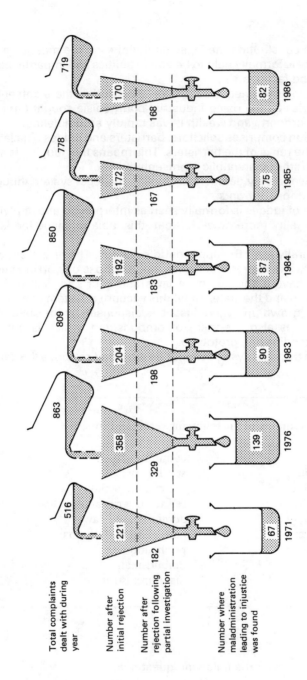

Figure 17.3 Complaints to the Parliamentary Commissioner: the filtering process

Source: Data from annual reports of the Parliamentary Commissioner for Administration

2 Do the figures suggest that the public are becoming more familiar with 40
   the system?
3 What filtering takes place before cases reach the ombudsman? Is this a 40
   benefit or hindrance to administrative justice?

Questions for discussion

1 Why did the nineteenth century see great developments in the legal profession?
2 Evaluate the principle of trial by jury. Why do you think bodies such as the
   police are unhappy with it?
3 'The absence of a formal system of judicial review of legislation means that
   British judges play no part in shaping the law.' Discuss.
4 'The manner in which judges are appointed means that they must nurse
   conservative leanings and have little understanding of, or sympathy with, the
   aims of working people or left-wing movements.' Discuss.
5 'The British ombudsmen do little more than legitimate bureaucratic power.'
   Discuss.
6 'The British legal profession has existed in warm symbiosis with the interests
   of capital.' Discuss.
7 Is Britain's system of administrative tribunals an adequate substitute for a
   full-scale system of administrative law such as the French *droit administratif*?

Topic for debate

This house believes that our system of law places property rights above civil
rights.
   or
This house believes that the office of British Parliamentary Commissioner for
Administration operates to protect the state from the citizen.

Further reading

Bar Council (1989) *Quality of Justice: the Bar's Response.*
The Bar Council's response to the Lord Chancellor's proposed reforms of the
judiciary. Not surprisingly, it attempts to defend the status quo, but is highly
informative.

Franks, O. (1957) *Report of the Committee on Administrative Tribunals and
Inquiries.*
The influential report on Britain's system of administrative justice.

Griffith, J. A. G. (1981) *The Politics of the Judiciary.*
A lively and forceful critique of the judiciary and its alleged political neutrality which
caused a stir within the establishment when published.

Harris, P. (1988) *An Introduction to the Law.*
An original kind of introductory legal text, ideal for the student of politics in that it

portrays the law and the legal system as living institutions within society and politics.

Kairys, P. (ed.) (1982) *The Politics of Law: a Progressive Critique*.
Readings on law in society.

Thompson, E. P. (1975) *Whigs and Hunters*.
Explores the relationship between the law and economic power.

Whyatt, J. (1961) *The Citizen and the Administration*.
The celebrated Justice report leading to the creation of the office of PCA.

Widdicombe, D. (1977) *Our Fettered Ombudsman*.
Report by Justice which cast a withering eye at the British ombudsman experiment.

Zander, M. (1976) 'Independence of the legal profession: what does it mean?', *Law Society's Gazette* (22 Sept.).
Discussion by a leading scholar.

For light relief

Charles Dickens, *Bleak House*.
A vigorous satire on the Court of Chancery, with its delays and costs which brought ruin to so many of its suitors. Tells of *Jarndyce and Jarndyce*, a case which continues interminably, for the profit of the lawyers concerned, only ending when the legal costs have absorbed the entire estate in dispute.

B. M. Gill, *The Twelfth Juror*.
A judicial thriller.

Franz Kafka, *The Trial*.
A nightmare vision of a judicial system. Begins menacingly: 'Someone must have slandered Joseph K., because one morning, without his having done anything wrong, he was arrested'.

Twelve Angry Men.
Gripping classic film starring Henry Fonda which takes place in a jury room.

18

The Coercive State

One of the defining characteristics of the state is the legitimate right to the use of physical force. Although a necessary power, it is one fraught with danger, with implications for the 'police state', where force is used to support oppressive rule. The world is full of such examples. This chapter is in three main sections. We begin by examining the **evolution of the police service**, its **organization**, the **political nature** of its role, and the **culture** which determines the way it operates in its twin functions of **fighting crime** and **maintaining public order**. The second section considers trends in modern policing. Finally attention goes beyond the police force to consider the role of other vital agencies – the **military** and the **secret services**. We conclude by asking whether the coercive policing of modern times can ever revert to the consensus policing of a (partly mythological) past.

The Political Role of the Police

There are grounds for believing that policing in the UK is a model for the world. Certainly many men and women in all ranks serve with dedication, tact and often great bravery. Yet the position they are in is necessarily one of acute political sensitivity. Policing can only enjoy legitimacy in a society which constantly debates its role and evaluates its operation. It is a measure of the success of British policing that a number of associated issues feature openly in modern political debate.

Evolution

The history of British policing may be traced back before the Norman

Conquest, lying in the principle that a community accepted a joint responsibility for maintaining the peace, with ordinary citizens appointed for limited terms and known by various titles: in Anglo-Saxon times they were hundredmen or reeves, to the Normans they were constables and sheriffs, and by the eighteenth century they were watchmen and constables.

Although considered a civic duty, service as a constable was open to corruption (Keith Lucas 1980: 84–5). From the eighteenth century the system became organized under the Justices of the Peace (JPs) who, in addition to their judicial duties, appointed the constables. Since the JPs were largely in the pockets of the landowning gentry, they operated largely in their interests. However, with servants to guard 'their plate and their wives' (Hay 1975: 59) they had little need of anything resembling a modern police force and the system remained rudimentary.

However, like most of the apparatus of the modern state, the police force evolved not from these medieval roots but was a nineteenth-century creation, part of the grand strategy of the rising bourgeoisie to create a society fit for industrial capitalism. In the dense, unhealthy, urban communities created by industrialization, lawlessness could thrive and there was an ever-present threat of civil unrest, made more terrifying to the newly propertied classes by the example of the French revolution and its terrible aftermath. An early move to strengthen the forces of law and order was made in the eighteenth century by Henry Fielding (author of the classic *Tom Jones*), a justice at London's Bow Street Court, who gathered together a group of upper-class vigilantes to work as a team of detectives: the celebrated Bow Street Runners (Stead 1985).

Radical agitation in the period 1815–19 culminated in the appalling Peterloo Massacre in Manchester in August 1819, where the magistrates brought in the cavalry to break up a large but peaceful working-class demonstration. This created a scandal and was clearly not a method which could secure the legitimacy of the political order, a fact well recognized by Sir Robert Peel who, as Home Secretary, secured a number of important penal reforms. He introduced the concept of the modern police force in the Metropolitan Police Act (1829). It was Peel's Metropolitan Force – a paid, uniformed, full-time, disciplined and specially trained corps, formed by amalgamating a number of parishes – which became the model for other municipalities, and developments were consolidated under the County and Borough Police Act of 1856.

The traditional character which the British police service has inherited from its evolution is that it is decentralized, non-militaristic and apolitical. This remains the official picture today but, like so much of the constitution, the formal principles often mask the reality. Before examining this issue, we look first at the structure and culture of the police service.

Structure, accountability and control of today's force

Today the police service is formally a local government function lying largely with the counties and, since the abolition of the metropolitan counties, joint bodies formed from the metropolitan districts. The administrative framework resembles that of other local government services, but the image of the police service as just another local government function is exceedingly misleading; the **police authority** is unique in its autonomy. The **police committee**, one-third of which must be non-elected JPs, has virtually no control over the policing of its area; the chief constable is in sole command (figure 18.1).

The original version of the Bains Report on management in local government had regarded the **chief constable** as one of the local authority team of officers, subject to the constraints of corporate management. However, when the report came out it alarmed the Assistant to the Chief Inspector of Constabulary, James Anderton, who immediately complained to the Home Office, with the result that it was withdrawn and redrafted to read: 'The Chief Constable is not an officer of the local authority but an independent officer of the crown' (Oliver 1987: 51–2).

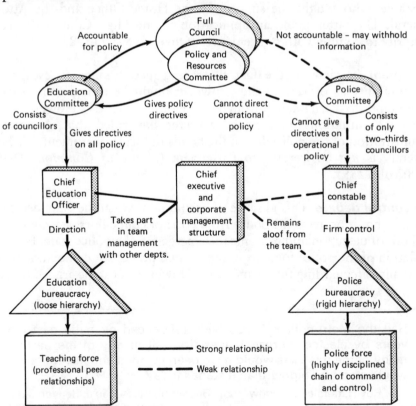

Figure 18.1 Comparison between local government as a police authority and as an authority for any other service (such as education)

> Not only can the chief constable do what he likes, but he can spend all our money doing it.
>
> Gabrielle Cox (chairperson of the Manchester Police Committee), quoted in the *Guardian* (11 Aug. 1984)

The Home Secretary The Home Secretary is in a sense the minister for the police but, although having considerable formal powers, incumbents have been exceedingly timid where the police are concerned. In the 1980s Douglas Hurd was admired for the way he was able to cultivate 'an appearance of almost deliberate powerlessness when it comes to police operation' (Evans 1986a). When the Home Secretary does use his authority it is to coerce the police authorities rather than the chief constable. In South Yorkshire during the 1984 miners' strike, the council, alarmed by the tactics of their force in policing the troubles at the Orgreave coking plant, requested the chief constable to stop the passage of coke (the objective of the strikers) as a logical means of averting disorder. They also tried to withhold the supply of funds for policing the strike. In all this they were opposed by the chief constable, who sought the support of the Home Office and the Attorney General. The latter made an application to the High Court to force the authority to comply with police desires (Oliver 1987: 215–21).

Parliament In view of the fact that the police manage to escape local accountability as officers of the Crown, it might be thought that they are accountable to Parliament through the Home Secretary. However here a 'catch 22' situation obtains: the Speaker has ruled that, because the administration of the police lies in the hands of local government, the Home Secretary is *not* answerable to Parliament (*House of Commons Debates* 1958: col. 1259).

The control debate This absence of **accountability** can be defended on the grounds that it protects the police from corrupt councillors, safeguards their methods of detection and prevents the emergence of a **police state**. Hence the insulation of the police force from the normal process of democratic politics is actually safeguarding that democracy. However, it can be argued that evils

> Had the Metropolitan Police been influenced over the past ten years by elected representatives from all or any of the parties, many of the mistakes would have been avoided and its reputation would stand far higher than it stands today.
>
> Roy Hattersley (Shadow Home Secretary), quoted in J. Benyon (ed.), *Scarman and After* (1984: 108)

are more likely to occur in the absence of democratic accountability and control. At best it can lead to rule by technocrats, and at worst to *de facto* political control by covert means. Police autonomy from elected representatives is actually a new idea. In the nineteenth century watch committees were 'able to exercise considerable control over policing policies and, backed up by powers to dismiss officers, they could, and often did, call for weekly reports' (Baldwin and Kinsey 1982: 106).

Police culture

The police have two broad functions – fighting crime and maintaining public order, both involving them in the exercise of considerable discretion and allowing them to shape society. They have an essentially political role and, because they dwell in a part of the state which democracy cannot reach, it becomes important to study the ideas and attitudes which inform their actions – the **police culture**.

> Reading isn't an occupation we encourage among police officers. We try to keep the paperwork down to a minimum.
>
> Joe Orton (1933–67; British dramatist), *Loot* (1965)

Racism A traditional reluctance to employ blacks, and a disinclination of blacks to apply, reinforces white culture in the police force. This has attracted increasing attention since the 1970s and is without doubt one of the major problems of British policing today. Research by the Policy Studies Institute in the 1980s found the casual manner in which racist language was used its most telling feature. West Indians were regularly referred to as 'nigger', 'sootie', 'coon', 'spade', 'monkey' and 'spook', while Asians were invariably 'Pakis', regardless of their real origins. The norms led officers who did not think of themselves as racists to use such language (Smith and Gray 1985: 390–3).

> I freely admit that I hate, loath and despise niggers . . . I don't let it affect my job though.
>
> Police officer quoted in D. J. Smith and J. Gray, *Police and People in London* (1985: 403)

Attitudes like this have helped to precipitate race riots, such as those in Bristol, Liverpool and Birmingham. The 1986 Broadwater Farm riots illustrated the intensity of feeling when a policeman was horribly murdered. Subsequent research revealed that 75 per cent of young blacks perceived the police as acting unjustly towards them, and as many as 67 per cent of young

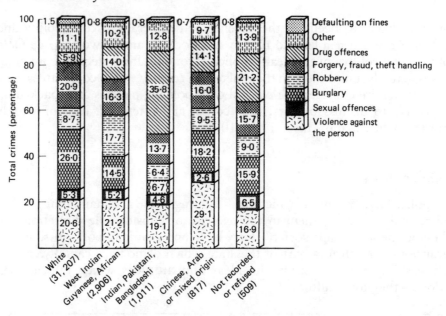

Figure 18.2 Sentenced prison population by offence and ethnic group, June 1986 (total numbers in brackets)

Source: Data from *Social Trends* (1988: table 12.15)

whites agreed with this (Lea et al. 1986). The popular view that blacks are more prone to violent crime is entirely unjustified (see figure 18.2).

Sexism The dominant values and ethos of the police are overtly masculine, similar to those found in other predominantly male preserves like the army or rugger clubs (the police field formidable teams, often including internationals).

One result of this is that women police officers experience great difficulty in fitting in and developing a career, and they continue to constitute only a small proportion of the force (see figure 18.3). The conversation and jokes portray women colleagues ('plonks') as inferior. Smith and Gray, choosing a deliberately mild example, report an older constable enthusing over the practice whereby WPCs arriving for the first time at the station were always 'stamped on the bare bum' with the official rubber stamp (1985: 373). The absence of women is a question not merely of unequal opportunity (though this is important), it has deep political implications. The non-consensual pattern of policing which can actually incite violence is a product of the macho culture.

Attitudes towards women in general are similarly sexist A particular problem arises with rape, the crime to which women are uniquely vulnerable. In the first place, victims are loath to report it (only about one in four do so), and when they do are subject to humiliating doubt and scepticism from the time they contact the police until the trial (Benn et al. 1983).

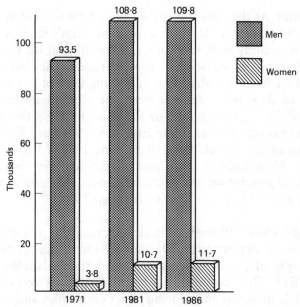

Figure 18.3   Size of the police force in England and Wales, 1971–1986

Source: Data from *Social Trends* (1988: table 12.27)

The Greenham Common demonstrations, where women stepped outside the traditional structures of protest to express a particularly female view of the arms race, created a new awareness of the problem. The policing of the encampments saw a huge number of arrests for trivial offences, intimidating dawn raids, many injuries, sexual harassment, strip searching, and photographing. Similarly, wives who became involved in the miners' strikes experienced humiliation and abuse: mocked for their poverty, locked in vans for up to two hours and 'refused access to a toilet . . . offered a milk bottle instead' (Benn 1985: 132).

Class The police stand in a curious position socially. They are approved of by the middle classes, whom they generally admire and whose privileges they work to protect. In the Metropolitan force ('the Met'), officers divided the citizenry broadly into two categories – 'slag' or 'rubbish' on the one hand and 'respectable people' on the other – and these groups were 'defined partly, but not entirely, in terms of social class' (Smith and Gray 1985: 434). Traditionally the service has recruited from the working class (Reiner 1982). This is not surprising, because the job can be variously onerous, boring, and dangerous: between 1981 and 1987, 111 police officers in England and Wales were killed on duty (Lambert 1988a). Recruits from a higher class are under social pressure to conform and may even affect a lower-class accent (Smith and Gray 1985: 435). With their rigid discipline, deeply ingrained sense of hierarchy and demanding machismo norms to live up to, the police are among the most oppressed of the working class, resulting in an alarming rise in the incidence of stress-related illnesses (Evans 1986a).

Leisure patterns   At the same time, the police tend to drift away from their working-class moorings, to be left in a social no-man's land. As a result, they tend to socialize mainly with each other, becoming cut off from society and reinforcing their racist, sexist and class attitudes. They seem particularly drawn to the Freemasons, a shadowy right-wing kind of boy scout organization. In spite of denials by Peter Imbert, the Commissioner, freemasonry appears rife in the upper echelons of the Met. In 1988 the *Sunday Times* acquired a list of no fewer than a hundred senior Scotland Yard officers who were active members. In addition, there were believed to be some 5,000 masons in the Metropolitan force and allegations were made that membership enhanced promotion prospects, influenced the cases to which officers were assigned and led to cover-ups (Chittenden 1988).

Political complexion   Although officially neutral, the police service is very clearly a right-wing organization. One survey found that as many as 80 per cent of a sample of police officers described themselves as Conservative (Kettle 1980: 31). The National Front has, despite its venomous message, experienced little difficulty in seducing 'chief constables and even the Home Office into providing the movement with the necessary facilities for its public campaigns' (Walvin 1984: 142).

Socialization and conformity   The police culture exerts a constant socializing effect. As recruits work their way up the pressure is to conform, to become more macho, more right wing and more racist. The successful officer will not be one who stands out against prevailing norms, and those in positions of authority will tend to promote in their own image.

Exercising discretion: fighting crime

One misapprehension on the part of the public is that the police indulge in detective work and as a result catch criminals without fear or favour. This model belongs to the world of cops and robbers fantasy and is evidenced in only a minority of real cases (Lambourne 1984). The result of the police culture is to favour the white, the wealthy and the owners of property. Offences relating to property dominate crime statistics.

The weight of police suspicion bears most heavily on the lower sections of the working class (unskilled workers, the unemployed and the young), who are more likely to be treated with contempt and abuse. Researchers listened to an officer, not considered unusual, addressing a boy in the absence of his parents: 'You're a fucking little cunt aren't you? You've been at it again haven't you, you little bastard? . . . I'm going to nail your fucking hide to the wall' (Smith and Gray 1985: 420). It is unlikely that a stockbroker would be addressed in such terms.

The evidence is that blacks, particularly West Indians, are far more likely than others to be stopped, the capricious use of the infamous 'sus' laws seeing the arrest of innocent blacks purely on the grounds of intuition.

Various areas have caused concern, including brutality, false confessions, and the decision to prosecute.

Police brutality The macho image of the police has resulted in a harrowing catalogue of atrocities. For example, in 1971 in Leeds, David Oluwale, a Nigerian, was singled out for 'special treatment', in which he was subject to deep humiliation, urinated on, beaten severely, and abandoned dead in the countryside; in an ensuing cover-up notebooks were doctored. In 1976, Liddle Towers was set upon by police outside a Gateshead club, subsequently dying from injuries received; though his doctor described his body as 'pulped', a Labour Home Secretary refused to set up an official enquiry. In June 1979, Jimmy Kelly was set upon by police as he walked home from a pub in Huyton, Liverpool, subsequently dying in police custody; the police pathologist's report suggested heart failure, but independent examination established that he had been savagely beaten. Further journalistic investigations into this particular force disclosed a long trail of beatings and sadism.

False confessions Formal protection for the arrested was traditionally scanty, based on the famous, though ill-understood **Judges' Rules**, permitting prisoners the right to silence and access to a solicitor or friend while in custody. These did not carry statutory force, were applied capriciously and were subject to abuse. In addition, 'confessions' extracted by police officers appeared to owe more to the talents of Agatha Christie than Sherlock Holmes. A major *cause célèbre* was the *Confait* case, where three boys were convicted of murder and arson on the basis of false confessions after a male homosexual had been found dead in his blazing home in April 1972. This case led in 1977 to a Royal Commission on Criminal Procedure set up against police wishes. Sir David McNee, Metropolitan Police Commissioner, prepared evidence for the commission arguing, not that the police should be circumscribed, but that the things they did were necessary and should therefore be legalized (Koffman 1985: 15). The resultant Police and Criminal Evidence Act (1984) actually increased the powers of the police to stop and search, and to detain for questioning.

A dramatic example of conviction on the basis of false confessions involved the 'Guildford Four', released in January 1990 from serving life sentences for the Guildford pub bombings of 5 October 1974. In 1989, the West Midlands serious crime squad was suspended pending an inquiry into its activities after a series of trials collapsed amidst allegations of fabricated evidence. Officers from the squad had been involved in the controversial conviction of the 'Birmingham Six', imprisoned for the pub bombings of 21 November 1974.

The decision to prosecute The fact that an arrest has been made does not in itself mean that a criminal prosecution will follow. Traditionally the police enjoyed great discretion over which categories of crime, and which types of offender, to prosecute, and when to employ a caution. This unsatisfactory state of affairs eventually led in 1986 to the establishment in England and Wales of a body of lawyers to make these decisions – the Crown Prosecution Service – under the Director of Public Prosecutions.

Exercising discretion: public order

In spite of the increase in powers under the 1984 Act, the police record in crime-fighting is not at all good. The prolonged failure to catch the Yorkshire Ripper in the 1980s provided bizarre evidence of ineptitude. However, in the second of their functions they can appear more effective. The maintenance of **public order** is more overtly political than fighting crime and has become more visible since the 1980s, with the police increasingly cast as instruments of government policy. In this role, the police often act as if they are protecting, not public order, but the state itself, working through the Special Branch and in liaison with the secret service.

A show of force against Liverpool strikers, 1911
Source: Mary Evans Picture Library

At the beginning of the 1980s the powers of the police in this area rested mainly on the Public Order Act (1936). This was replaced by a designer Public Order Act (1986) intended to legitimize many of the powers which the police had been assuming without authorization. In making public order decisions police culture leaves officers with little empathy with the sort of people who march in support of causes such as anti-fascism, gay lib, CND, troops out of Ireland, Greenpeace, and so on. They see such marches as unpatriotic and undermining the state, rather than as attacking inequalities of wealth and power, expressing views such as: 'It's the scum of the earth. Why should we protect that?' (Smith and Gray 1985: 436).

Trends in Modern Policing

In recent decades the British police force has seen three highly significant developments greatly altering its traditional character: centralization, militarization and politicization.

Centralization: a national police force?

The principle of local policing, and the notion of a plurality of forces, was part of the evolution of the service, justified in the same way as for any other local government service in terms of fostering local democracy and ensuring responsiveness to local conditions. However, with the police the case for localism is even stronger: the absence of a single national force is a crucial protection against the growth of a monolithic police state. The police themselves have consistently resisted the creation of a single force under the Home Secretary and responsible to Parliament. However, throughout the century an insidious **centralization** has taken place beneath a pluralistic facade, so that the potential for repression is actually greater, being insulated from parliamentary scrutiny. This has been facilitated in various ways, including amalgamation of forces into larger units, the emergence of centralized staff organizations, advances in communications technology, the creation of specialist squads, and the strategy of the central government.

Amalgamations From the outset, central government was concerned to make police areas larger than communities. In 1882 an Act forbade new boroughs with populations less than 20,000 to establish their own forces, and the 1888 Local Government Act insisted that boroughs with populations below 10,000 merge their forces with those of the parent county under joint committees. Amalgamation was further advanced during the second world war.

A royal commission reviewing the constitutional position of the police in 1962 recognized that a single force would be more efficient, and would offer a clear line of accountability through the Home Secretary. However, it stopped short of radical centralization, recommending tripartite control between Home Secretary, chief constables and the local authority. The 1964 Police Act gave the Home Secretary increased power to effect amalgamations and strengthen the system of central inspection.

Both Conservative and Labour governments pursued the policy of amalgamations; a pattern of small and diverse police authorities reflecting local conditions was gradually eroded. The Local Government Act (1972), which made the top-tier counties the police authorities, completed the process. The result is a relatively small number (52 in the UK as a whole) of large forces. In 1989 the Home Affairs Select Committee recommended the regionalization of the service. Although the case for large supra-communal forces is mainly couched in terms of efficiency, the effect is to weaken the capacity for diversity and local control.

Centralized staff associations A *de facto* centralization of the police service has largely been effected by the police themselves through the development of national associations. Important among these is the Police Federation, a kind of trade union representing all officers up to the rank of chief inspector (officially the police are not allowed to join a trade union). The federation speaks for its members in negotiations with government, and through public pronouncements, as if for a single force.

Of even greater moment is the Association of Chief Police Officers (ACPO) representing senior officers, including chief constables. ACPO does more than speak for its members, it organizes policing on a national basis, particularly through the National Reporting Centre (NRC), which is in effect an operational centre, coordinating the work of police throughout the country and liaising with the Home Office and MI5 (Boateng 1985: 240). It was established at Scotland Yard in response, not to the rise in crime, but to fears for public order in the early 1970s. ACPO also operates the Mutual Aid Coordination Centre set up by the 1964 Police Act, whereby police may be deployed anywhere in the country like a national force. The system was particularly visible during the miners' strike, when convoys of blue minibuses became a familiar sight on the M1.

Advanced communications technology Each force now operates a sophisticated computer and electronic communications system and assists in the collection and collation of vast quantities of data for national records, facilitating systems of 'precise and rapid central control' (Campbell 1980: 65). In 1959 a department was set up by the Home Office, the Metropolitan Police and the Prison Commission known as the Joint Automatic Data Processing Unit, which has continued to extend the use of central and regional computers. This led in 1969 to the establishment of the Police National Computer Unit as a department of the Home Office, housed at Hendon in North London to control and supervise a complex communications network of almost a thousand terminals located throughout the country.

Specialist squads Further centralization has been promoted by the development of specialist CID squads working on a national or regional basis, including regional crime squads, the National Drugs Intelligence Unit, the National Identification Bureau and the Serious Fraud Office; even the Crown Prosecution Service can be seen as part of the centralizing tendency. In addition, there are the specialist squads of the Metropolitan force such as the Special Branch, concerned with national security and working with MI5, and the Royalty and Diplomatic Protection Service.

Central government strategy Finally, there is the role of central government. Whitehall's ability to influence policing from the centre is by no means a new phenomenon; it has been part of the hidden police constitution since the beginning of the century, particularly in class dispute (Morgan 1987). The policing of the miners' strike gave a number of important insights into how government can control from the centre. Strategy was coordinated by a high-powered cabinet committee (Misc 101) chaired by Mrs Thatcher, which included leading ministers and a representative of the armed forces and received regular reports from the NRC. The Cabinet Office also played a part, although this was done by word of mouth in order to mask any link between Coal Board and police (Boateng 1985: 239).

Towards a British 'FBI' In July 1989, Metropolitan Police Commissioner Peter Imbert called, in a lecture to the Police Foundation, for an even tighter degree of central control with the creation of a single, national detective force along the lines of the US Federal Bureau of Investigation (FBI). This would consist of police, customs officers, lawyers, accountants, computer experts and immigration officers. The new body would be centrally funded, responsible to Parliament through the Home Secretary, and would have access to a national computerized intelligence system. Local forces would exist alongside the central body but be required to yield some of their sovereignty.

Official arguments against the formal creation of a national force are couched in terms of democracy. However, this is questionable. Democracy in Britain has never depended upon such a principle; it is based only on the rule of law and the sovereignty of Parliament. Hence it is difficult to resist the conclusion that the fragmentation of the police force serves as a convenient fiction to evade inconvenient accountability to Parliament.

Militarization

The economic problems of the 1970s saw waves of unrest in Britain with much of the 'goodwill' between police and people breaking down. The policing of demonstrations and industrial disputes began to display a **militaristic** style, with marching in troops, charges, the use of various weapons, visors, and intimidation such as the rhythmic beating of riot shields as in primitive war rituals. In the urban anti-police riots CS gas was used and most forces now have gruesome arsenals of rubber bullets, riot shields, water cannons and armoured vehicles. New recruits receive training in the use of these weapons as well as conventional firearms training, and forces have special crack firearms squads. In the period 1970–2 police were issued with guns on 5,244 occasions; by the end of the decade, during 1975–8, this happened 14,574 times (Rollo 1980: 166–7). In 1983, an innocent man, Stephen Waldorf, had the appalling experience of being shot in his car by the police, who mistook him for someone else.

Policing of the industrial dispute between the print unions and Rupert Murdoch's News International at Wapping led to some 440 complaints from the public, many concerning the action of mounted police who charged demonstrators like the cavalry of old (*Independent*, 10 Dec. 1988), while the miners' strike introduced television viewers and strikers to alarming visions of a specialized paramilitary force.

A third force? In some countries there exists within the coercive apparatus of the state a third force, poised between the police and the military. This avoids the drastic step of using the military to quell civil disturbance, while protecting police relationships with citizens. However, the hallmark of such forces is the savagery which they bring to the task. In France, for example, the *Compagnie Republicaine de Securité* is dreaded: in the Paris riots of 1968 it injured 1,500 in a single night. Britain has traditionally eschewed such a force, but today special groups have developed with much of the appearance of **paramilitary units**.

In the early 1970s, establishment fears of working-class movements led to the setting up of a National Security Committee with representatives of the military, intelligence services, Home Office, Department of Trade and police, to prepare for nothing less than an internal attack on the state (Bunyan 1977: 293). It recommended better training in riot control, the use of firearms, and regular joint police–military exercises. Additionally, a Special Patrol Group (SPG), established in London by the Labour government some years earlier to concentrate on crime and vandalism, was given a paramilitary function while remaining formally within the police force. A key figure in this move was Sir Robert Mark, Chief Commissioner of the Metropolitan Police, who had made detailed studies of the methods used by the Royal Ulster Constabulary (RUC) and the B-Specials in Northern Ireland. The new elite corps was to have an independent command structure based on Scotland Yard. Members, distinguished by the letters CO on their shoulders, serve for two-year terms and are selected from young volunteers from the London police divisions.

The SPG's existence remained largely unknown until the India House incident in 1973, when two Pakistanis from Bradford invaded the Indian High Commission with toy guns in a religious protest. Within four minutes, and without being asked to drop the guns, they were shot dead by the SPG officers guarding the embassy, who became overnight heroes. Another celebrated operation was the Grunwick industrial dispute of 1977, where an employer sought to deprive his employees (Asian women) of trade union rights. When mass picketing took place Metropolitan Commissioner Sir David McNee sent in the SPG and their brutality astonished prominent figures present. Despite Labour being in power, TUC demands for a Home Office enquiry were not met and the Home Secretary himself, Merlyn Rees, loyally supported the SPG.

The Blair Peach affair in April 1979 brought home the extent to which the

SPG operated in a realm above the law. Peach, one of the objectors to a National Front demonstration (held with extreme provocation in the largely black area of Southall), was struck on the head with a rubber cosh filled with lead (an unauthorised weapon) by a member of the SPG. Before long he was dead. The events following this outrage had all the characteristics of a cover-up and no officer was ever prosecuted (Rollo 1980: 165).

> His tongue was stuck to his upper jaw, and the upper part of his head was all red as if he was bleeding inside.
>
> Local resident who attempted to administer aid to Blair Peach, quoted in J. Rollo, 'The Special Patrol Group', in P. Hain (ed.), *Policing the Police*
> (1980: 158)

The paramilitary model quickly spread: today most forces have some kind of SPG clone, composed of members from the uniformed branches, under an independent chain of command. Known variously (Mobile Support Unit, Special Operations Unit, Tactical Aid Group), they share the paramilitary characteristics of the prototype. Some have themselves been involved in *causes célèbres* such as the James McGeown case (1978) in Strathclyde (a man with hands tied behind his back was kicked to death by members of the Strathclyde Support Unit).

Politicization

Much of the formal case put forward by the police for remaining beyond parliamentary accountability rests on the argument that policing is outside politics, existing only to serve the state by impartially upholding the law. However, it has already been shown that the exercise of discretion in policing has deep and lasting political consequences. Where there is inequality, the police must constantly seek to restrain the 'have nots' from threatening the 'haves'. Hence, it is a logical necessity that the police will feel a certain affinity with the political right. However, police involvement in politics goes beyond this to an overt presence as a political pressure group.

Publicity campaigning Although the Police Federation and ACPO are statutorily restricted in what they can do politically, they have broken out of this straitjacket to become mouthpieces of collective police views. Unlike the civil service, the police do not subscribe to the Trappist Monk school of public relations, giving opinions on many issues. They have argued against the right of suspects to remain silent, for tougher penalties for the convicted, against juries, against community policing, and they make strong moral judgements about schools, parents, the church, industrial relations, homosexuality, and so on.

The **politicizing** of the police was never better illustrated than when the

Police Federation actually launched a Law and Order Campaign in 1975. The movement arose over frustration that 'soft' minority groups were exercising too liberalizing an effect on the law, policing and penal policy. Their campaign copied the methods of other pressure groups with members taking public speaking engagements, feeding the media and lobbying Parliament. After some confrontation with the Labour government, the federation announced in February 1978 its intention to make 'law and order' an issue in the forthcoming general election, even sponsoring large newspaper advertisements. The Conservative Party became an enthusiastic part of the movement, pledging its 'unstinting backing' for the police. On the Conservative victory, the federation broke with its formal non-party stance by appointing as its parliamentary spokesman, not a member of the opposition as had been the tradition, but Eldon Griffiths, a Conservative who had demonstrated a fervent commitment to their cause.

Police superstars In addition to expressing collective views, leading personalities within the service have sought to project themselves as national celebrities, as visible as elected figures like trade unionists and ministers. In particular, Metropolitan Police Commissioners have found in their positions a unique platform for self-publicity and influence. Notable was Sir Robert Mark, brought in by the libertarian Home Secretary, Roy Jenkins, in 1967 to clear up the deep-seated corruption which had, through the pornography trade, gnawed to the very core of the force. However, Mark's opposition to pornography proved to be but one facet of a strongly anti-libertarian stance on life in general (Kettle 1980: 13).

A major event in his life occurred in 1973 when he was invited to deliver the BBC Dimbleby Lecture, which offered him the largest audience he, or any other policeman, had ever had. Here he astonished with the extremity of his views, arguing, *inter alia*, for law reforms to strengthen the police and for an easier road for the prosecution in criminal trials, castigating 'crooked lawyers' with the temerity to defend those the police wished to prosecute. The lecture has been seen as the coming of age of politically assertive policing in Britain.

Following this example a number of senior officers have become celebrities. James Anderton, Chief Constable of Greater Manchester, was particularly prominent during the 1980s, proclaiming that AIDS sufferers and drug addicts dwelt in 'a cess-pit of their own making'. He charmed the establishment, appearing on TV and radio current affairs programmes and chat shows.

A climate of corporatism Senior officers do not only seek to influence the political culture, they enjoy direct links with Whitehall, the Home Office in particular. We have already noted how Anderton was able to have the Bains Report changed. A more telling example occurred when Michael Foot put forward proposals to amend the law on picketing. Sir Robert Mark recounts that he told 'Jimmy Waddell [Sir James Waddell, a high-ranking Home

Office civil servant] in no uncertain terms' that, if there was ever any possibility of these becoming law he would conduct a vigorous public campaign against them. 'Happily they were abandoned and no harm was done' (Mark 1978: 151–2).

Today the police force may be seen unequivocally as a pressure group within the political system, enjoying the power of publicity as well as close insider-group status. Whenever there is a proposal for a change of law relating to criminal or judicial procedure, or whenever there is a *cause célèbre* involving the police, a well-lubricated lobby rolls smoothly into action.

Quis Custodiet Ipsos Custodes: Who Guards the Guards?

It is clear that the modern police force is powerful in society, with many attendant dangers. The absence of democratic control throws into prominence the question of the redress of citizens' grievances.

The case for a complaints procedure

If in a democratic society a particular group is given weapons and authority denied other citizens, it becomes crucially important that these will be exercised only in accordance with public interest. Yet we have seen that there is little redress available to the public through normal democratic channels.

The 1962 royal commission considered the question and the subsequent Police Act (1964) placed a statutory obligation on chief constables to investigate all complaints by the public, bringing in officers from other forces if they so wished. If the chief constable formed the impression that a criminal offence might have occurred, a report was sent to the Director of Public Prosecutions (DPP), who decided whether to prosecute.

The system left many unhappy. In the 1970s, some alarming cases of deaths in police custody occurred and investigations into allegations of police brutality were felt by victims' families to be unsatisfactory. Police response to such criticism tended to allege irresponsible agitation by left-wing extremists but, despite this opposition, the Police Act (1976) was passed. This ended chief constables' exclusive right in the area by establishing a quango, the Police Complaints Board (PCB), a body of laymen with the power, not to receive complaints or investigate the police, but to play a limited supervisory role in cases where no disciplinary action was taken by the chief constable, or where the issue was contested. The system had many weaknesses, the greatest being that the conduct of the investigation remained in police hands, justified on the grounds that, as experts in crime detection, they were the only ones to do the job, a suspect claim given the large number of private police and investigative agencies in existence.

Intense debate continued, with recommendations for independent investigation from many quarters, including the NCCL, Justice, the Law Society, the Runnymede Trust, the local ombudsman and the Labour Party. In 1980, the PCB itself recommended that an independent team of seconded police officers should investigate serious complaints.

After Scarman

When the Scarman Report on the Brixton riots surfaced in November 1981 it cited the absence of an independent **complaints procedure** as one of five crucial factors contributing to the breakdown of police–community relations (Scarman 1981: para. 4.2). Public cynicism was such that people with genuine grievances did not even bother to make complaints. The Police and Criminal Evidence Act (1984) established a three-tiered approach, adding to the existing system a conciliation mechanism for non-serious complaints and provision for independent supervision of police investigation into serious ones. This supervision was to come from a Police Complaints Authority (PCA), which would replace the PCB. Although the first chairman, Sir Cecil Clothier, had functioned for six years as the ombudsman, the reform fell very short of truly independent investigation.

Today a complainant may approach the chief constable (or police authority if it concerns a senior officer), who decides whether the matter can be solved by informal conciliation. If not, he must appoint an officer to conduct an enquiry and prepare a report in the traditional manner. Where appropriate, the PCA (serious cases) is informed, and it decides whether or not to supervise the investigation.

The PCA's 1987 annual report revealed that in 1986 it received 15,865 complaints and supervised 681 investigations. Criminal proceedings were brought against only 48 officers (40 for assault). In the vast majority of cases (12,505) no disciplinary charges were made owing to insufficient or conflicting evidence. The Metropolitan force (accounting for a quarter of all complaints) was heavily criticized for its operation of the procedure and Sir Cecil Clothier claimed it had proved uniquely difficult to achieve 'a dialogue at senior level'.

In November 1988 the Commons Home Affairs Committee recommended that the procedure be subject to regular parliamentary scrutiny, as suggested to the committee by Sir Cecil Clothier himself. It also advocated strengthening the PCA's ability to acquire evidence (Home Affairs Committee 1988). The response of the Police Federation in its 1989 annual conference was to

---

> If one of the boys working for me got himself into trouble, I would get all of us together and I would literally script him out of it. I would write all the parts out and if we followed them closely we couldn't be defeated.
>
> Metropolitan Police sergeant interviewed by D. J. Smith and J. Gray,
> *Police and People in London* (1985: 355)

pass a vote of no confidence in the PCA, which they believed to be siding with the complainants.

However, in principle it is still the police who investigate the police, clearly violating the fundamental principle of natural justice that no person should be judge in their own cause. The police have a tradition of sticking together when under attack; this prevented the identification of Blair Peach's killer.

Beyond the Blue Horizon

The military

Ostensibly states have a military arm to defend themselves from external invasion and to attack and subjugate other states. During the days of the empire the British military pursued the second of these goals, becoming a feared power in Europe and around the world. In two hellish world wars the military became even more central to the state, but subsequently, with the dismantling of the empire, it was anticipated that the men on horseback would return quietly to their barracks. However, they were to seek a role rather nearer home, as another arm with which the state could fight the 'enemy within'.

Policy-making for the military   Control of the military is vested formally in government ministers responsible to Parliament, which grants its annual supply of funds. The modern history of the political control of the military may be dated from the establishment of the Committee of Imperial Defence in 1902 as a result of the experience of the Boer War. With the outbreak of the second world war this was replaced by the War Cabinet, and in 1947 a formal Ministry of Defence was set up. In 1964 the three service departments were amalgamated under the Secretary of State for Defence and a Defence Council.

The service chiefs are, like civil servants, heavily involved in decision-making. Often among the more arrogant of the British upper class, they take it extremely hard if elected politicians try to resist their 'advice'. Here is another instance of a corporatist area in British politics where a select inner circle influence the destiny of the nation away from the prying eyes of democracy. Few outsider groups are as 'outside' as the CND. Parliament and the full Cabinet has very little hold on the reins; thus defence spending reaches astronomical heights (see figure 18.4) and the arms industry grows fat.

Class and the military   Although the vast majority of those who marched to venues like the Somme as cannon fodder were from the working class, the people who matter in the military, the top brass, follow very much in the traditions of British elitism. Before the rise of the industrial bourgeoisie, commissions in the army and navy were reserved for the sons of the

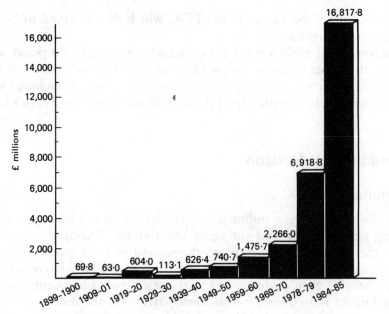

Figure 18.4   Total defence expenditure, 1899–1985

Source: Data from Butler and Butler (1986: 473)

aristocracy, and great wealth was needed both to purchase them and to achieve subsequent promotion. However, the worldwide policing necessary to protect free trade made the new bourgeoisie more than a little concerned with its efficiency, and they sought to gain control, which has thus remained squarely in the hands of the British elite. The high social prestige of military rank is such that, unlike privates or sergeants, retired officers continue to wear their titles like honours, even having them engraved on their tomb-stones to proclaim their greatness long after the worms have digested their entrails.

The military on the home front   The military in any state contains the most fearsome potential for violence. Most *coups d'état* are military backed if not military led, and it is not unusual for a state to direct such power on its own citizens. In Britain, the 1714 Riot Act enabled magistrates to call in the military to quell disturbances, while today governments can make 'reason-able' use of troops in riotous situations. Indeed, the Crown prerogative, which is effectively held by the Prime Minister, means that in a state of emergency troops can be used in any way at all.

Compelling military theatricals in civil situations have been mounted in recent times. An army–police anti-terrorist operation at Heathrow airport in 1974 greatly alarmed Prime Minister Wilson, who realized how easily troops could be turned against the government (James 1987). It was chillingly explained afterwards that the purpose of the exercise was 'to accustom the public to the reality of troops deploying through the high street' (*Guardian*, 8 Jan. 1974).

Such overt military involvement in civil affairs has been conducted by a specially trained elite corps – the Special Air Service (SAS) – which first caught the public imagination when it daringly ended the siege of the Iranian Embassy in 1980, under the very eyes of television cameras. However, the most telling use of the army in civil situations has been in Northern Ireland since 1969. In 1976 the Prime Minister announced that the SAS would be joining the army to operate under cover. In the province, codes permit extra military freedoms, buttressed by special emergency powers granted by Parliament. Although codes and conventions restrict the extent to which the authorities might use troops in mainland Britain, there is nothing to prevent these being changed.

The security services: the 'cloak and dagger' of the state

Textbooks on British government ignore the **security services**, not because such matters are not to be discussed in front of the young but because they are things which nobody at all is supposed to talk about. Here we meet agencies operating below the level of public accountability and consciousness. People have some vague notion that they exist from the novels of John Le Carré and Ian Fleming, but these are chauvinistic fantasies about impossible figures like George Smiley and James Bond.

The services are not new. The Home Office has had an historic responsibility for ensuring the safety of the state, maintaining an *ad hoc* network of spies and informers which was created as a partner to industrial capitalism in the eighteenth century (Bunyan 1977: 153). They comprise a number of agencies.

- The *Special Branch* of the Metropolitan Police Force was set up in 1883 to be concerned mainly with criminal offences against the security of the state and with terrorist or subversive organizations. It has always been heavily involved with the affairs of Ireland. The emphasis is on intelligence gathering and 'watching'; that is, with 'political policing' (Bunyan 1977: ch. 3).
- *MI5* was established in 1909 to root out subversive activity at home. Today it works closely with the Special Branch, calling on police powers (of arrest and so on) when required.
- *MI6*, the *Secret Intelligence Service*, is concerned with organizing espionage overseas. For example, in 1919 'MI6 poured in agents and several million pounds in a vain effort to subvert the [Russian] revolution' (Bunyan 1977: 155).
- The *Government Communications Headquarters* (GCHQ) at Cheltenham is concerned with worldwide electronic surveillance.
- The *Defence Intelligence Staff* of the Ministry of Defence, oversees the work of the intelligence staffs of each of the armed services.
- The ordinary *police service* (liberally interpreting its public order function) is increasingly concerned with matters of security.

Though separate organizations, all work closely together at various levels,

"None of you knows each other, I trust."

Reproduced by permission of *Punch*

with major coordination at Scotland Yard (Campbell 1980: 116).

The paranoid secrecy surrounding all the institutions of the state is never more tight lipped than here, serving not merely to safeguard Britain's secrets from potential enemies, but to protect the fact that the agencies sail extremely close to the legal wind. When joining MI5, Peter Wright was told that the organization could not be part of the Whitehall machinery because its work 'very often involved transgressing propriety or the law' (Wright 1987: 31).

The British government long fostered the idea that the security services did not exist. For example, the Head of MI6 in 1956 (and former head of MI5), Sir Dick Goldsmith White, was officially listed as Deputy Under Secretary at the Foreign Office and Superintending Under Secretary of the Library and Records Department (Bunyan 1977: 189–90).

The class factor Unlike the predominantly working-class police service, the security services remain very much a bastion of the lordly amateur male establishment world of John Buchan, even to the extent, according to Peter Wright (1987: 36), of closing down MI5 once a year for the Lord's test match, where they have an unofficially reserved patch in the Lord's Tavern. The girls managing the files are debutantes recruited from the aristocracy, believed to be the best vetting of all. Recruitment to the security services is conducted on an informal basis, and most members (including the spies) come from the public school–Oxbridge hothouse.

What do they do? The security services have the broad function of protecting the system of government from those who would destroy it, safeguarding the state from subversion and espionage. Clearly the definition of **subversion** must have a considerable bearing on whom the security services may fix their attentions on. The standard modern definition, given by Lord Denning in his report on the Profumo case in 1963, described subversives as those contemplating 'the overthrow of the government by unlawful means'. This obviously includes potential foreign enemies, and conceivably includes political extremists of left or right. However, in 1978, Labour Home Secretary Merlyn Rees redefined subversion to cover those who 'threaten the safety or well being of the state, and are intended to undermine or overthrow parliamentary democracy by political, industrial, or violent means'. The removal of 'unlawful' gave the green light to the security services (Kettle 1980: 52–3). They have been able to turn inward on the body politic like an invading virus, investigating left-wing politicians, trade unionists and anyone daring to express an unorthodox political opinion.

The tragedy of the Police State is that it always regards all opposition as a crime, and there are no degrees.

Lord Vansittart, House of Lords speech (June 1947)

The activities of the security services are potentially infinite in their variety. In the years following the first world war, working-class reformers were portrayed as subversives and subjected to severe harassment and even imprisonment. The National Unemployed Worker's Movement was kept under constant surveillance by the Special Branch, its leaders eventually arrested, its officers sacked and its documents confiscated. The most notorious act of MI5 and MI6 concerned the Zinoviev letter scandal. In spite of its fury about this, the Labour Party when in government did not, and has never, conducted the scourge of the security services which it promised. Indeed, such is the power of mind politics in Britain that ordinary working-class people would see such an act as profoundly unpatriotic.

The Zinoviev letter

This forged letter was reputedly uncovered during the 1924 general election campaign. Apparently sent by Gregory Zinoviev, president of the Communist International, to a prominent member of the British Communist Party, it urged armed revolution. The resulting paranoia effectively ruined Labour's election chances. The letter's authenticity was never proved and it appears to have been the product of a dirty tricks operation involving 'members of MI6 and MI5, the top personnel at the Foreign Office, and the Tory party' (Bunyan 1977: 159). In addition, a middle man named Thurn was involved who received £7,500 from the Conservative Party, touted the letter around and ensured its publication in the *Daily Mail*.

However, it is in the post-war era that the surveillance of British subjects innocent of any crime has come into its own. The security services are even suspected of working against an elected Labour government. In the soft-focus days of the 1960s, when the Beatles, Mary Quant and student uprisings seemed to symbolize a new classless era, and Harold Wilson appeared to be making Labour a natural party of government, members of the establishment talked long into the nights of *coups* to prevent the drift into left-wing anarchy as the allegedly sick nation came under the grip of the working class. In 1965, the Lord Chancellor was reduced to driving around Green Park when he wanted to discuss something with the Attorney General, believing it 'more likely than not that MI5 were bugging the telephones in my office'. In this Orwellian scenario he could hardly complain to the Prime Minister, because Wilson believed that he too was under MI5 surveillance (Knightly 1986). In 1990, Colin Wallace claimed, astonishingly, that as an army public relations officer in the 1970s, he had been involved in MI5 operations ('Clockwork Orange') to smear the characters of British politicians including David Owen, Jeremy Thorpe, Edward Heath, Denis Healey, Merlyn Rees and the Prime Minister, Harold Wilson (*Observer*, 4 Feb. 1990).

When Labour returned to office in 1974 the establishment again began to tremble. MI5 built up an unprecedented bank of computer data focusing on leaders of groups like CND, Greenpeace, the trade unions, schools and universities, hospitals, the theatre and the media. In the media world, for example, MI5 tried to have newsreader Anna Ford sacked on the grounds that a former boyfriend had once been a communist. BBC management was shown by the *Observer* newspaper to have had long-standing links with MI5 in order to blacklist left-wing journalists (Leigh and Lashmar 1987). Phones are tapped, people are photographed, and mail is opened by the Post Office or by MI5. During the 1984 miners' strike, a complex operation involved informers, spies and *agents provocateurs*. The advance of technology lifts the capability of the security services to gather, collect and collate information to truly Kafkaesque levels of nightmare.

Who watches the watchers? The secretive agencies operate beyond the realm of parliamentary scrutiny. We can have no idea what they cost, because money for them is surreptitiously granted under misleading heads, and even less idea what they are actually doing at any particular time. Of the elected politicians, only the Prime Minister formally knows what is going on, but even this is doubtful. The British tradition of the neutral civil service which shelters civil servants from public scrutiny has created a situation in which 'Ministers, and Prime Ministers, increasingly become putty, on questions of "security", in their senior adviser's hands' (Thompson 1980: 157).

The Blunt case in particular called into question the relationship of the security services to their putative elected masters. In 1964 this aristocratic self-confessed Russian spy, a former member of MI5, struck a curious deal with the security agencies: he was granted immunity from prosecution (and allowed to retain his prestigious position as the Surveyor of the Queen's Pictures, a royal appointment) in exchange for information on other spies. All took place in the darkest secrecy.

Dissatisfaction with the state of the security services led in November 1988 to a Security Service Bill which for the first time gave official recognition to the existence of MI5, though not of MI6. This recommended a tribunal to hear complaints from those who felt aggrieved, and a commissioner (a Law Lord) to oversee warrants for bugging and entering, who would make an annual report to Parliament, though this could be edited by the Prime Minister. Critics such as the Campaign for Freedom of Information regarded this as rather little rather late, and stopping well short of full parliamentary oversight.

If you ask me to strike a balance in my own life, I'd say that the right I've done is greater than the wrong I've done.
Kim Philby (Russian spy), 1988 interview in Moscow in the *Sunday Times*
(27 March 1988)

The spies Although the security services have an impressive record of probing and harassing the political left, they have enjoyed rather less success in catching real spies. The result has been some embarrassing post-war scandals, including those of Blake, Burgess, Maclean, Philby, Vassall and Blunt. Generally the spies were from upper-class backgrounds (not surprisingly, given the social make-up of the security network) and it is quite clear why the establishment cannot tolerate such behaviour from within its ranks: they are not merely traitors, they are class traitors. Kim Philby enjoyed the institutional warmth of the inside track his background had given him, but could not help wondering 'what about the millions outside the establishment, those millions whom the establishment manipulates with such off-handed ease?' (Knightly 1988). Consequently, in popular demonology they are made the very quintessence of evil, and the enemy, not of privilege but of the ordinary people of Britain.

Conclusion: the Coercive State and the Community

> I never saw any of them again – except the cops. No way has yet been invented to say goodbye to them.
>
> Philip Marlowe in Raymond Chandler's novel *The Long Goodbye* (1954)

It would of course be absurd to expect policing and other forms of state coercion to operate without force and violence; it is to employ such means that they are created in the first place. If there were no conflict within society there would be no need for legitimate **state violence**. Capitalism, with its tendency to create classes based on wealth, has a particular need for policing, and the emergence of the modern police force in Britain was unequivocally tied to the industrial revolution and the rise of the capital-owning bourgeoisie. Yet the modern police force managed to develop an ethos of community spirit which was linked with the gradual and by no means perfect assimilation of the working class into the capitalist system, reaching a peak in the post-war corporatist decades of the mixed economy. Dixon of Dock Green, a friendly and caring 'bobby' featuring in a long-running television series, did not seem grossly at variance with reality.

Yet the hard right was never entirely happy with the idea of **consensus policing** or of a consensus society. The possibility that the Labour Party might become entrenched as the natural party of government was seen as a deep threat, occasioning some shadowy cloak-and-dagger manoeuvres, and from the late 1970s consensus building was explicitly rejected as a goal of government as the New Right viewed the trade unions as the 'enemy within'. The government recognized the key role they would place on the police in their law-and-order rhetoric, Mrs Thatcher promising in the 1979 Conservative manifesto to 'spend more on fighting crime even while we economize elsewhere'. The bitter events of the miners' strike in 1984–5 starkly revealed the position: while criticism of police tactics reached a crescendo, the government refused to encourage a negotiated settlement. All the time, society continued to be darkened by the spectre of violence (figure 18.5).

The Scarman Report and a 'new' approach

Against the trend came the Scarman Report on the 1981 Brixton riots,

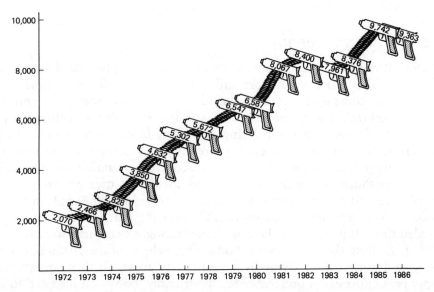

Figure 18.5 A more violent society? Number of notifiable offences reported by the police where firearms were reported to have been used, 1972–1986

Source: Data from *Social Trends* (1988: table 12.4)

expressing the belief that crime, riots and public disorder are largely explicable in terms of the social environment (Scarman 1981: para. 2.38). It aroused considerable public and official interest and made various recommendations favouring the community approach:

- new recruitment procedures to screen out racists, encourage black entrants, and more women in the force;
- outlawing of discriminatory practices;
- increased consultation with the community;
- reduction in police discretionary powers;
- increased accountability by means of lay visitors to police stations.

The law-and-order lobby have consistently opposed genuine **community policing.** Responses to Scarman often involved cosmetic reforms such as the employment of one or two per cent of the force in a communal policing capacity. These officers were isolated, often ridiculed, and given nicknames like 'Sambo'.

One of the most prominent advocates of genuine community policing has been the ex-Chief Constable of Devon and Cornwall, John Alderson (a former barrister), who sought to change the very culture of the force so that *every* officer was concerned with community relations. However, the New Right political atmosphere produces an ecology in which advocates of a return to a softer approach to policing, as seen in the decades of consensus politics, cannot flourish. Alderson was consistently opposed by the Police Federation, which sent deputations to argue over his use of resources. He finally left to take up an academic post.

Coercion at arm's length

Whether Britain could ever 'return' to a community approach must remain debatable. The Scarman Report did not recognize all the problems. It ignored the contradictions between the community approach and the increased centralization, militarization and incorporation of other arms of the security forces into the policing role, and failed to recognize greater democratic control through elected representatives as the way to secure the accountability it advocated. Without such control, a number of community policing methods are seen by critics as insidious attempts to conduct surveillance and control over the community (Gordon 1984: 56). In March 1990, a report commissioned by ACPO from the Harris Research Centre revealed that 70 per cent of the population thought that there were too few police patrolling their neighbourhoods. The feelings of dissatisfaction were strongest amongst those living in the inner-city areas. Of those questioned, 74 per cent expressed a preference for the friendly 'bobby on the beat' to the 'Sweeny' image of fast cars and tough policing (*Guardian*, 9 March 1990). Yet today the administration of the coercive forces of the state is very much at 'arm's length' – indeed it is the proverbial 'long arm of the law'.

PC Attilla Rees, ox broad, barge booted, stamping out of Handcuff House in a heavy beef-red huff, blackbrowed under his damp helmet . . . limbering down to the strand to see that the sea is still there.

Dylan Thomas (1914–53; Welsh poet), *Under Milk Wood* (1954)

Key points

- Every state requires a right to use physical force and coercion to impose its will. The liberal-democratic state is no exception; indeed the freedom for free-market forces tends to require particularly strong coercive forces to maintain inequalities in wealth and property.
- Hence the modern police force in Britain was a creature of the industrial revolution which imposed the new capitalist order. Before this time policing was relatively unorganized and undertaken on a voluntary basis by local communities.
- Today Britain formally has a number of separate police forces administered by local government. However, local authorities really have very little influence; forces are under the firm control of their chief constables.
- It is sometimes said that the police force must be outside politics, but the twin functions of crime-fighting and maintaining public order are intrinsically political in that they have a profound effect upon the lives of ordinary people and involve the exercise of considerable political discretion on the part of the police.

- Since the 1970s the British police have become increasingly centralized, militarized and politicized.
- Through ACPO the police can enjoy most of the advantages of a national force without the costs of responsibility to Parliament.
- Complaints against the police is an area of heated controversy but it is still the case that the police themselves conduct any inquiries into alleged police misconduct.
- The police are not the only source of force and coercion on the home front. The military and security services play a part, although they do so covertly and with less accountability than the police themselves.
- The services remain deeply suspicious of those on the left, including the supposed 'enemy within' in the trade unions and even Labour governments.

Review your understanding of the following terms and concepts

police authority	militarization
police committee	paramilitary unit
chief constable	politicization
accountability	police complaints procedure
police state	security services
police culture	subversion
Judges' Rules	community policing
public order	consensus policing
centralization	violence, state

Assignment

Study the extract from the *Guardian* on p. 570 and answer the following questions.

% mark

1 From the summary of the recommendations in the Gifford riot report, what would you take to be its opinion on the causes of the Broadwater Farm estate race riots?   10

2 What conclusions would you draw from the fact that the Gifford report is held by Lord Scarman to be 'saying much the same as [his] Brixton report five years ago'?   30

3 Explain what Lord Scarman means when he says: 'They are confusing a very complicated constitutional issue with a very necessary political measure'.   40

4 Critically examine the concept of the consultative committee for bringing together police and community interests.   20

Questions for discussion

1 Why did the industrial revolution lead to a breakdown in traditional methods of policing local communities?

2 'Policing is no job for a woman.' Discuss.

Scarman backs Gifford riot report

By Martin Wainwright

Lord Scarman yesterday endorsed the main points of Lord Gifford's report on the Broadwater Farm riots in north London last October when a policeman was murdered, guns were fired, and petrol bombs were thrown.

"Stripped of some of its rhetoric, it is saying very much the same as the Brixton report five years ago," he said.

Lord Gifford's report calls for greater consultation between police and the community, more economic aid for inner cities, and changes in housing and education policies to combat racism. It was commissioned by Haringey council after the Government had refused a formal inquiry into the riot on October 6.

Lord Scarman also made a strong attack on Labour councils like Lambeth, and the Labour opposition at Westminster, which have boycotted policy consultative committees. He accused them of prejudice, intellectual confusion, and damaging one of the most important means of improving inner city communities.

"It is a tragedy that extreme political views have prevailed in Lambeth town hall, views which are now supported, to some extent, by one of the major political parties in this country," he said.

"One gets the feeling that until they get local authority control of the police they will have no truck with consultation. They are confusing a very complicated constitutional issue with a very necessary practical measure."

Lord Scarman said that support for consultative committees, which were given a statutory basis after his report, were one of the main recommendations of the Brixton inquiry.

Guardian, 6 July 1986

---

3 'Allegations of police brutality and the obtaining of false confessions only undermine the morale of police officers and reduce their effectiveness.' Discuss.

4 'The security services are not part of the political system, they are apolitical.' Discuss.

5 Is there any truth in the allegation that Britain has a national police force in all but name?

6 Identify the weaknesses in the police complaints procedures. How could it be improved?

7 What is meant by 'community policing'? What factors inhibit its development in Britain today?

Topic for debate

This house believes that the police forces of Britain should be made into a single national force responsible to Parliament.

   or

This house believes that the British police force is a model for the world.

Further reading

Baxter, J. and Koffman, L. (eds) (1985) *Police, the Constitution and the Community.*
Book of readings. See especially Benn, M. 'Policing women', for a discussion on a little-studied subject, and Boateng, P. 'Crisis in accountability'.

Benn, M. et al. (1983) *The Rape Controversy.*
Looks at the area where the macho police culture is at its most destructive.

Bunyan, A. (1977) *The History and Practice of the Political Police in Britain.*
A controversial and lively study which presaged some of the problems to surface in the next decade.

Hain, P. et al. (eds) (1980) *Policing the Police.*
Critical book of readings. See especially Kettle, M. 'The politics of policing and the policing of politics' and Campbell, D. 'Society under surveillance', written by crusading journalist Duncan Campbell, the 'C' of the notorious 'ABC' *cause célèbre*.

Home Affairs Committee (1988) *Parliamentary Accountability of the Police Complaints Authority.*
Parliament's view of a fundamental issue.

Knightly, P. (1986) *The Second Oldest Profession: the Spy as Bureaucrat, Fantasist and Whore.*
Specialist journalist's account of a field too boggy for most academics to venture into.

Mark, R. (1978) *In the Office of Constable.*
The world through the eyes of Sir Robert Mark.

Scarman, Lord (1981) *The Brixton Disorders, 10–12 April 1981.*
The celebrated Scarman Report which gave the police establishment pause for thought.

Smith, D. J. and Gray, J. (1985) *Police and People in London.*
A powerful study of the Metropolitan Police Force at work. Captures much of the tension (and the boredom) by following the police through their daily routines, listening to their conversations, and observing them with the public.

For light relief

Most of the accounts in the extensive genre of cops and spies are too fantastical to be of much serious value.

S. Knight, *The Brotherhood.*
An exposé of freemasonry in Britain in the higher reaches of the establishment, including the church, the judiciary and the police.

G. F. Newman, *Law and Order.*
A powerful and realistic novel inspired by police corruption and exploring the relationship between the police and the forces of the establishment.

PART VI

Conclusion

In this final section the aim is not to present any essentially new material for study, but to consider how we may review the substance of the previous chapters in overall terms.

19

Getting it Together: Thinking Holistically

> The objective of this chapter is to stress the importance of seeing the various aspects of politics studied throughout the book as part of a single whole. Only in this way can we find the order beneath the bewildering complexity. We begin by considering the basic idea of a **holistic perspective**, and then go on to consider various approaches to this, including organic theories of the state and systems theory, an intellectual idea of inestimable importance for the development of the social sciences. The Further Reading section directs your attention to the future, which is uncharted, and about which the novelist may have more to tell us than the academic. It is in your hands.

Thinking Holistically

An important theme of this book has been the interrelatedness of the subject matter. Government is seen as deeply enmeshed in a dense biomass of political life, and politics as a process involving, not merely the institutions of state, but of the economy and civil society, and subject to a range of influences emanating from the global context of the state. Political energy has been shown to issue from multifarious sources, including differences in wealth, education, employment status, class, gender, race, geographical location, and so on. Moreover, the process embraces institutions well beyond the formal Westminster–Whitehall terrain, encompassing the judiciary, the police, the military, the secret services, trade unions, private firms, thousands of pressure groups espousing an infinity of causes, and giant peak organizations like the TUC and CBI. Yet despite this seamless cohesion the previous chapters have been characterized by distinct focuses. There are two principal reasons for this.

- *Verisimilitude.* The world of government and politics really is to some extent formally compartmentalized through the organizational structures of the state. Thus, for example, the judiciary is distinct from the civil service, Parliament is distinct from local government, and so on. We saw in chapter 2 that this division is actually part of the constitution: the division of authority is seen as a protection from overpowerful government.
- *Intellectual necessity.* It is a natural characteristic of the human intellect to split up, compartmentalize and classify any subject of matter under study; it is only by doing this that we can make sense of the complexity of the world which surrounds us. This is partly what we mean by 'analysis'. Thus, for example, actors will split up a play into its scenes, acts and dialogues in the process of mastering it.

However, ultimately the actors will want to rebuild the play in its entirety to reveal its dramatic intent. Otherwise the real purpose and meaning of the parts will not make sense: an exciting and well-played scene which adds nothing to the overall development of the plot becomes a waste of time when the play is viewed as a totality. When we take a **holistic perspective** we view our subject as a whole **system**, rather than in terms of its parts, and it may be argued that it is only from such a perspective that the political drama can be fully understood. To take another analogy, a football team is something qualitatively different from the eleven individuals who compose it. To assess its likely success we need to understand how these individuals relate together. The potential energy of the team as a goal-scoring machine may be greater than the sum of that of each individual; this increase gained from working together is termed **synergy**.

There are various ways of conceiving politics in holistic terms. We shall introduce two which are closely related and which underly much political study and debate – the organic and the systemic.

Organic theories of the state

> States, like men, have their growth, their manhood, their decrepitude, their decay.
> Walter Savage Landor (1775–1864; English writer), *Imaginary Conversations* (1824–9)

A long-prevailing view of the state has pictured it as a living organism (usually the human body) with its various organs fulfilling particular functions but bound together in mutual dependence. This goes back to the Ancient Greeks, but a particular version flourished in the nineteenth century amongst a school of biological political theorists. Here the notion of the organism was not merely metaphor; the state was believed to be a life form, capable of birth, life, disease and death. They also spoke of the state's adaptation to its environment through a slow process of evolution, in which some organs became more important and others (like the human appendix) became unwanted and withered away.

This **organic thinking** was exemplified *par excellence* by the German philosopher Friedrich Hegel, one of the most significant of modern thinkers, his influence spreading in widely divergent directions. He argued that the meaning of individual lives could only be understood, and ethically evaluated, in terms of their relationship to the state, which was essentially not a gathering of individuals, but a single, tightly knit collectivity. He exalted the state as the ultimate end of human existence.

Hegel's view lay at the very extremes of collectivism and was modified for English consumption by T. H. Green, who leavened it with an English spirit of radical individualism, believing that the life of the state has no real existence except in the individual existences of its members. For Green, the state was not all-consuming; its interest could not be seen as an end in itself, yet he believed its purpose to be the promotion of the 'common good', arguing that man was most free when he identified himself with this (that is, when seeking to promote the good of the collectivity).

Functionalism   The organic view was to underlie an approach to the study of society and the state termed **functionalism**. This argued that state structures and institutions must, like the organs of the body, perform certain necessary functions (respiration, reproduction, digestion, and so on) for it to survive. This approach was applied by influential anthropologists like Radcliffe-Brown (1881–1955) and Malinowski (1884–1942) to explain and compare primitive societies where formal institutions did not exist. Thus while a society might not have a Parliament in the sense understood by western culture, it would necessarily require the function of making rules.

A function only has meaning in terms of the *whole* and, by the same reasoning, if an institution acts in a manner harmful to the whole then it is, like a disease in an organism, **dysfunctional**. The sociologists Talcott Parsons and Robert Merton adapted the anthropologists' ideas more specifically to industrialized societies, revealing that even here it is possible to ask questions based on functional analysis. Thus we may enquire whether an institution really fulfils the function it is supposed to (does Parliament really make laws?), or whether it is fulfilled elsewhere (the civil service, the Cabinet, and so on). It can be seen that these are similar questions to those discussed in the introductory chapter, which seek to look behind the institutional facade of government.

Ideology and the organic view   However, the organic view is not without ideological implications. It leads to a Burkean form of conservatism that institutions should be allowed to grow naturally and not be tampered with –

a veneration of the status quo. Not surprisingly, this has been favoured by those with the most to gain from opposing radical reform and keeping things as they are: the wealthy and privileged. The organic perspective does not exclude change but it generally stresses slow (Darwinian-style) evolution to fit into the environment. It may seem contradictory in that Marx (by no means a conservative) was greatly influenced by Hegel. However, the organic view can also entail the idea of *death* followed by *rebirth* – in other words, *revolution*.

Systems theory and the political system

The organic view demanded a degree of metaphysical faith and fell out of favour with the development of science and technology. However, it was replaced with the idea of the **political system**. Although the term is often used loosely to denote little more than 'the place where politics takes place', the concept is essentially holistic. It is part of a wider intellectual thrust termed **general systems theory**, an interdisciplinary movement to unify the sciences by identifying concepts which could enable the disciplines to speak to each other and promote intellectual cross-fertilization. (Thus, for example, a biologist might have something to say about the nutritional system in plants which could have relevance to a mechanical engineer studying transport systems.) The approach was pioneered by the biologist Ludwig von Bertal-lanfy who stressed, not only the universality of the application of the concept, but its holistic quality.

> Each part depends not only on conditions within itself, but also ... on conditions within the *whole* of which it is part.
>
> (von Bertallanfy 1952: xix)

The concept was introduced into political science by the American scholar David Easton, who entitled a seminal work *The Political System*, on the holistic premise that 'the phenomena of politics tend to cohere and to be mutually related' (Easton 1953: 97).

Organic and mechanical systems The systems approach advanced thinking by adding to the long-standing (and out of favour) organic view a mechanical one. The two may be distinguished as follows.

- **The organic system.** Here the main goal of the system is self-preservation or survival; processes and structures are functional to the extent that they aid this. This supports the classic conservative position and is a reincarnation of the organic view of the state. The state is seen as something which man cannot change for his own purposes.
- **The mechanistic system.** This system differs fundamentally from the organic in that it does not evolve under some internal dynamic of its own; it is conceived as a machine *designed* by man to fulfil his purpose. Thus a car is

designed to transport us; it will never seek to place its own interest before its rider as might a horse (an organic system). Perceived in this way the state becomes something that can be *changed* by man on the basis of *reason*; we can alter the design of the car, but the horse we must accept in all its equine perversity.

The mechanical approach has been extended by some political scientists into the new field of cybernetics, the study associated with the science of information technology, which looks at the internal control mechanisms within systems through communication networks. Karl Deutsch, for example, in *The Nerves of Government* (1964), characterized government in terms of a complex network of internal informational channels binding all parts together like the printed circuits of a computer. For Deutsch, communication, rather than power, is the key to understanding the process of government.

That the essential difference between the mechanical and organic systems is fundamental will come as no surprise. It mirrors the philosophical dichotomy between the conservative and radical traditions of political thought and also closely parallels that between *Gemeinschaft* and *Gesellschaft* (see p. 11). While the conservatism of Burke urged that the constitution be conceived as something above human contrivance, Bentham and the Philosophical Radicals saw the state as a constitutional Meccano set to be constructed at will. We have seen throughout this book how the rise of the bourgeoisie in the industrial revolution made prolific use of the idea of man-made change, to the extent of sculpting the modern British liberal-democratic state.

There is no doubt at all that much present-day political analysis makes use of the concepts of systems theory (though not always knowingly) and the associated terms (inputs, outputs, feedback, boundaries, homeostasis, and so on) are very much part of the popular vocabulary.

A holistic study strategy

If politics is perceived holistically, one is drawn to conceptualize the parts of the political system in terms of their relationship to the whole and to each other (figure 19.1). This can open the doors to a level of understanding far deeper than that gained from compartmentalized knowledge. We realize that the behaviour of some element (say a pressure group) cannot be fully explained without understanding its relationship with other elements (other pressure groups, the mass media, Parliament, public opinion, the civil service, international organizations, its own rank and file, society at large, and so on).

There is no limit to the level at which the holistic perspective may be focused. Systems may be conceived as consisting of *subsystems* (for example, the committee system may be seen as a subsystem of the House of Commons and the latter as a subsystem of Parliament, and so on) and may themselves

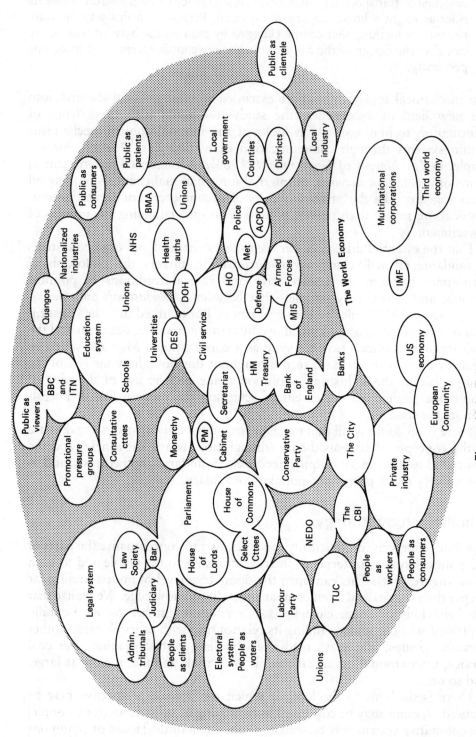

Figure 19.1 Politics as a system

be seen as part of larger systems (for example, the political system itself can be seen as a subsystem of the British social system, or of the national economy, or of the world economy, and so on).

Some lessons on holistic thinking come from science in general and particularly from meteorology, where it is crucially necessary to take a global perspective. The range of influences which shape our weather are so complex that, even with computers capable of performing 600 million calculations a second (the present state of the art), it will always be impossible to include every causal factor; hence we will never be able to predict weather with complete accuracy. Scientists speak of the '**butterfly effect**' wherein a butterfly flapping its wings may set in motion a chain of events which will alter the course of a tornado on the other side of the globe. Politics is full of such causal chains. To think in a consciously holistic way is constantly to pose a battery of relevant questions about any particular part of the political system. When you think about any question on politics try to conceptualize the overall system in the way depicted in figure 19.1 and try to think how the particular part of the system you are concerned with relates to all other aspects. Never imagine that you can fully understand one part without appreciating its place in the whole system.

Key points

- Politics and government can only be fully understood if viewed in holistic terms; each element must be seen as fitting into a larger whole, which defines its function.
- A holistic perspective on politics is offered by the organic view of the state, which depicts it as a kind of living organism, with many of the same characteristics (growth, survival, disease, even death).
- In modern political analysis the concept of the system, derived from the natural sciences, provides a more advanced conceptual framework for the holistic perspective.
- Systems may be dichotomized as organic or mechanistic. The former are held to grow naturally and have an end in their own existence, their main goal being survival. The latter are designed by man and have no purpose or end other than that intended.
- This distinction has important implications for the study and practice of politics; it is further reflected in the sociological concepts of *Gemeinschaft* and *Gesellschaft*.

Review your understanding of the following terms and concepts

holism	political system
system	general systems theory
synergy	organic system
organic theory	mechanistic system
functionalism	butterfly effect
dysfunction	

Further reading

Anthony Burgess, *Clockwork Orange*.
An alarming vision of a future dominated by technology, violence and authoritarian government. Made into a film by Stanley Kubrick in 1971.

Aldous Huxley, *Brave New World*.
A fable set in the seventh century AF (after Ford). Here life is subjugated by science, all under World Controller Mustapha Mond. In *Brave New World Revisited*, Huxley believes his prophecies are already (1958) coming frighteningly true.

William Morris, *News from Nowhere*.
A utopian socialist fantasy.

George Orwell, *Nineteen Eighty-Four*.
A nightmare of totalitarianism with 'newspeak', 'doublethink', where war is peace, freedom is slavery and ignorance is strength.

Chronology of Events

427BC	Birth of Plato, father of western political thought.
384BC	Birth of Aristotle; his *Politics* informs much modern debate.
AD1066	Norman Conquest.
1086	Domesday Book compiled.
1154	First Plantagenet king of England.
1170	Murder of Thomas Becket.
1215	Magna Charta.
1258	Simon de Montfort forces reforms on Henry III.
1265	De Montfort's Parliament; defeat and death of de Montfort.
1284	Completion of English conquest of Wales under Edward I.
1290	Edward I begins conquest of Scotland.
1295	'Model Parliament' of Edward I.
1314	Robert the Bruce secures Scottish independence.
1327	Deposition and murder of Edward II.
1338	Beginning of Hundred Years War between England and France.
1362	English becomes official language in Parliament and courts.
1381	Peasants' Revolt under Wat Tyler.
1399	Richard II deposed by Henry IV.
1400	Welsh revolt under Owen Glendower.
1415	Battle of Agincourt.
1431	Martyrdom of Joan of Arc.
1450	Jack Cade's rebellion against Henry VI.
1453	Final English defeat and end of Hundred Years War.
1455	Beginning of Wars of the Roses.
1476	Caxton sets up printing press.
1485	Battle of Bosworth Field; Tudor dynasty begins.
1493	Vasco da Gama finds sea route to India.

1515   Thomas Wolsey becomes Lord Chancellor and Cardinal.

1517   Martin Luther begins Reformation by nailing up Ninety-five Theses at Wittenberg.

1534   Act of Supremacy; Henry VIII takes control of Church in England.

1535   Thomas More executed.

1536   Ann Boleyn executed.

1588   Elizabeth I becomes Queen.

1577   Drake begins circumnavigation.

1588   Spanish Armada defeated.

1600   English East India Company founded.

1601   Elizabethan Poor Law; introduces rates.

1603   Irish revolts suppressed. Death of Elizabeth I. Accession of James VI of Scotland as James I of England.

1605   Gunpowder plot.

1611   English and Scottish Protestants settle in Ulster.

1620   Pilgrim Fathers settle in New England.

1628   Petition of Right to Charles I by Commons.

1629   Charles I tries to rule without Parliament.

1635   John Hampden refuses to pay ship money.

1642   Charles I attempts to arrest five members of Parliament. Outbreak of civil war.

1644   Battle of Marston Moor; decisive in English civil war. North lost to Charles I. Royalist campaign in Scotland.

1645   Formation of New Model Army. Royalist army crushed at Naseby.

1646   Charles I surrenders to Scots.

1647   Charles I handed over to Parliament, seized by army, flees to Carisbrooke Castle.

1648   Second civil war; New Model Army defeats Scots and Royalists.

1649   Charles I executed; England governed as republic under Cromwell. England suppresses Ireland.

1651   Cromwell becomes supreme in all Britain after the Battle of Worcester. First English Navigation Acts. Thomas Hobbes publishes *Leviathan*.

1655   English take Jamaica.

1658   Cromwell dissolves Rump Parliament, becomes Lord Protector.

1660   Restoration of monarchy; Charles II returns from exile.

1665   Great Plague of London.

1666   Great Fire of London.

1681   Charles II tries to rule without Parliament; establishes Oxford Parliament.

1685   Monmouth's rebellion crushed by James II at Sedgemoor.

1688   William of Orange lands with army in England; flight of James II. The 'Glorious Revolution'. Bill of Rights limits monarchy.

1690   Locke's *Two Treatises on Government*. Battle of the Boyne; William crushes Irish.

1693   National Debt begun.

1694	Bank of England founded.
1701	Act of Settlement establishes Hanoverian succession.
1707	Act of Union of English and Scottish Parliaments.
1714	Death of Queen Anne; accession of Elector of Hanover as George I. Riot Act enables magistrates to call in military to quell civil disorder.
1715	Septennial Act; Parliament prolongs its life from three to seven years.
1720	'South Sea' bubble.
1721	Robert Walpole seen as first Prime Minister.
1733	John Kay invents flying shuttle. Jethro Tull advocates new agricultural technology.
1742	Walpole falls.
1748	Montesquieu publishes *L'Esprit des Lois*.
1760	Beginning of 100-year period termed industrial revolution.
1757	Pitt as Secretary of State is main force in British government. Clive conquers Bengal.
1759	Beginning of canal age.
1763	First British Empire at its height.
1764	John Wilkes expelled from Commons.
1769	Richard Arkwright invents water frame for spinning.
1770	James Cook discovers New South Wales.
1774	Warren Hastings appointed first Governor General of India.
1776	American Declaration of Independence (4 July). Adam Smith's *Wealth of Nations*.
1783	Treaty of Versailles; American independence recognized. Pitt the Younger becomes PM.
1784	Last appearance of monarch in Cabinet.
1785	Cartwright invents power loom.
1787	American Constitution drafted. Consolidated Fund established. Creation of Royal Ulster Constabulary.
1789	Washington first US President. French Revolution begins with storming of the Bastille (14 July). Bentham's *Introduction to the Principles of Morals and Legislation*.
1792	Denmark first country to prohibit slave trade. France becomes republic.
1798	Battle of Vinegar Hill.
1800	Parliamentary union of Great Britain and Ireland.
1804	Napoleon Bonaparte becomes French Emperor.
1805	Battle of Trafalgar; victory and death of Nelson.
1807	Slave trade abolished in British Empire. Napoleon in control of all Europe. Britain blockaded by continent.
1811	Luddite riots against new machinery.
1812	Napoleon's retreat from Moscow; destruction of his Grand Army.
1813	French defeated by Wellington at Vitoria.
1814	Napoleon abdicates; Louis XVIII King of France.
1815	Napoleon escapes from Elba. Battle of Waterloo. Corn law in Britain

protects agricultural interests against imports at expense of commerce.

1819   'Peterloo Massacre'.

1823   'Monroe Doctrine' announced by US.

1824   Repeal of Combination Acts which had outlawed trade unions.

1829   Formation of Metropolitan Police Force.

1832   First Reform Bill.

1833   First British Factory Act. First government grant for education.

1834   Poor Law Amendment Act. 'Tolpuddle Martyrs' transported to discourage working-class association.

1835   Municipal Corporations Act. Peel's 'Tamworth Manifesto'.

1836   Chartist movement formed.

1837   Queen Victoria's accession.

1839   Formation of Anti-Corn Law League.

1842   Chartists present second Charter. Great Irish potato famine.

1846   Corn Laws repealed; Peel resigns; Conservatives split; Disraeli becomes leader.

1848   Revolutionary movement throughout Europe. French Republic proclaimed. Marx and Engels produce *Communist Manifesto*.

1851   Great Exhibition.

1850   *Communist Manifesto* published in English.

1854   Crimean War; France and England declare war against Russia. Much British bureaucratic incompetence exposed; Northcote–Trevelyan Report.

1855   End of Crimean War with fall of Sevastopol.

1856   Bessemer invents process for large-scale steel production.

1858   British Crown assumes government of India.

1859   Darwin's *Origin of the Species*. J. S. Mill's *On Liberty*.

1861   Beginning of American civil war. J. S. Mill's *Considerations on Representative Government*. Public Accounts Committee established.

1864   First Socialist International.

1865   General Lee surrenders to Grant; end of American civil war.

1866   Office of Comptroller and Auditor General established.

1867   Second Great Reform Bill. Bagehot's *The English Constitution*. Volume I of Marx's *Capital*.

1868   Disraeli succeeds Lord Derby as PM, but later defeated by Gladstone in general election.

1870   Forster's Education Act sets up school boards throughout country.

1872   Secret ballot introduced.

1874   General election; Disraeli succeeds Gladstone as PM.

1880   Gladstone returned as PM.

1883   Introduction of national insurance system in Germany. Establishment of Special Branch of the Met.

1884   Third Parliamentary Reform Bill. Fabian Society founded.

1885   Dicey's *Law and the Constitution*.

1886	First Irish Home Rule Bill defeated in Commons. Unionist defectors from Liberal Party join Conservatives.
1888	County Councils Act.
1889	Second Socialist International. Great strike at London Docks. First Official Secrets Act.
1890	Ruination of Parnell by divorce case.
1893	Second Irish Home Rule Bill rejected in Lords. Independent Labour Party formed.
1894	Manchester Ship Canal opened. Gladstone resigns.
1899	Boer War starts.
1900	Labour Party formed. 'Khaki Election'.
1901	Death of Queen Victoria. Taff Vale judgement.
1902	Boer War ends. Committee of Imperial Defence established.
1903	First flight of heavier-than-air flying machine at Kitty Hawk, US. Emmeline Pankhurst forms Women's Social and Political Union, main instrument of suffragettes.
1905	Liberal general election landslide; first Labour MPs appear.
1906	Suffragettes become active. Trades Disputes Act reverses Taff Vale judgement.
1908	Asquith becomes PM.
1909	Old age state pension scheme introduced. Lloyd George's 'People's Budget' rejected by Lords; constitutional crisis. Henry Ford begins to manufacture cheap motor cars. MI5 established.
1910	Edward VII's death; accession of George V. Labour exchanges established. Liberals battle with House of Lords, win two general elections, but become dependent upon Irish MPs. Anti-union Osborne Judgement.
1911	Parliament Act reduces Lords' power. MPs to be paid a salary. National Insurance introduced. Second Official Secrets Act passed with notorious section 2.
1912	Third Irish Home Rule Bill. *Titanic* disaster.
1913	'Cat and Mouse Act'.
1914	Archduke Francis Ferdinand assassinated at Sarajevo; war in Europe. Britain declares war on Germany. Coalition government formed. Irish Bill passed but put in cold storage.
1916	Lloyd George becomes PM. New coalition reduces role of Liberals. Easter uprising in Ireland. Battle of the Somme; 420,000 British soldiers killed owing to inept British strategy.
1917	US declares war on Germany. Russia proclaimed a republic; Bolshevic revolution. Balfour Declaration recognizes Palestine as Jewish 'national home'.
1918	Armistice signed by Germans. Women given vote. 'Coupon Election' preserves wartime coalition under Lloyd George. Sinn Fein MPs win majority of Irish seats but set up own Parliament (Dail). IRA formed under Michael Collins. New Labour Party constitution drawn up with wider commitment to socialism.

1919   Paris peace conference. Peace treaty signed with Germans at Versailles; League of Nations established (Germany excluded).

1920   British send Black and Tans into Ireland.

1921   Irish settlement; Irish Free State set up; Ulster to remain in UK.

1922   Conservatives meet to end coalition; 1922 Committee formed. Conservatives win general election.

1923   Baldwin dissolves Parliament over tariff reform. General election makes Labour second largest party; they rule for 10 months with Liberal support.

1924   First Labour government, under MacDonald (lasts 9 months). Liberals withdraw support over Campbell case. Zinoviev letter affair. Conservatives return triumphantly to office.

1925   Chancellor Winston Churchill puts Britain back on gold standard. Drastic cuts in wages and industrial unrest.

1926   General strike.

1928   Equal Franchise Act; voting age for women lowered to 21.

1929   In general election Labour largest single party for the first time. Second Labour government under MacDonald. Liberal decline becomes inevitable. Wall Street crash. BBC comes into existence.

1931   Economic depression; Cabinet split over public expenditure cuts. MacDonald resigns. Surprise formation of coalition under MacDonald who is denounced by his own party. Coalition overwhelmingly endorsed by electorate. Henderson becomes Labour leader.

1932   Lansbury becomes Labour leader.

1933   Hitler appointed Chancellor by Hindenburg and begins to gain iron control in Germany.

1934   Hitler becomes dictator. Foundation of NCCL.

1935   Baldwin succeeds MacDonald as PM. Attlee becomes Labour leader. General election returns Conservatives.

1936   Spanish civil war breaks out. Public Order Act passed. Keynes publishes *General Theory of Employment, Interest and Money*. BBC TV begins.

1937   Chamberlain forms coalition.

1938   Germany annexes Austria. British navy mobilized. Chamberlain signs Munich Agreement with Hitler.

1939   Britain recognizes Franco government in Spain; civil war ends. Conscription introduced. Poland invaded by Germany. War declared (11 a.m. 3 September). Third Official Secrets Act passed.

1940   Labour agrees to join coalition; Churchill forms National Government. British army evacuated from Dunkirk. Italy declares war on Britain and France. Germans capture Paris. Battle of Britain (1 July–6 Sept). Attlee recognized as deputy PM.

1941   Japanese attack Pearl Harbour.

1942   Beveridge Report.

1943   Mussolini overthrown. Italian Fascist Party dissolved.

1944   D-Day invasion of Europe. Paris liberated. Bretton Woods Agreement; IMF and World Bank established. Great Education Act.

1945   Mussolini and mistress shot by Italian partisans. Suicide of Hitler and mistress. End of second world war against Germany (2 May). UN Charter signed. Landslide Labour election victory. Attlee becomes PM. Britain begins to create modern welfare state; accepts Keynesian principles. Atomic bomb used against Japan. Russia declares war against Japan. Japan surrenders. Lend–Lease terminated. Nuremberg Trials of major war criminals. UN formed. Attlee takes decision that Britain shall manufacture atomic bombs.

1946   After much doubt and argument US House of Representatives approves loan to Britain.

1947   Nationalization begins (coal). 'Marshall Aid' plan begins. India and Pakistan become dominions. Marriage of Princess Elizabeth.

1948   End of British mandate for Palestine; partition into Jewish and Arab states. NHS established. Electricity nationalized. Republic of Ireland Bill signed. Approximate beginning of the 'long boom'.

1949   Parliament Act reduces Lords' power to delay legislation. NATO formed after Russians blockade Berlin. Gas nationalized.

1950   Rebuilt House of Commons opened. Labour secures narrow election victory, but lacks confidence to govern.

1951   Resignation of Bevan over introduction of NHS prescription charges. Attlee dissolves Parliament. Labour wins most votes in election but defeated in terms of seats; Churchill becomes PM.

1952   George VI's death (6 Feb.).

1953   Elizabeth II's coronation (2 June); much ceremony; televised. Steel denationalized.

1954   Crichel Down case. Food rationing ended.

1955   Churchill resigns as PM; succeeded by Eden. Conservative election victory. Independent TV begins. Attlee retires as Labour leader; succeeded by Gaitskell.

1956   Britain's first atomic power station starts working at Calder Hall. Nasser elected President of Egypt; announces nationalization of British- and French-owned Suez Canal; crisis ensues. UN calls for removal of British, French and Israeli troops from Egypt. Anthony Crosland publishes *The Future of Socialism*.

1957   Eden resigns as PM; replaced by Macmillan. Report of Franks Committee on tribunals and inquiries.

1958   European Economic Community treaty comes into force; Britain stays out. CND launched under Bertrand Russell; makes first London–Aldermaston protest march. Life Peerage Act. First women peers introduced in House of Lords.

1959   Conservatives' third successive election victory.

1960   Macmillan's 'wind of change' speech in South African Parliament; Monday Club formed in Conservative Party. Plowden Report on public expenditure; PESC system begins. Kennedy elected US President. Herbert Report on Greater London. Momentous Labour conference; Gaitskell vows to 'fight, fight, and fight again'.

1961   Justice Report, *The Citizen and the Administration*. Neddy established.

1962   Cuban missile crisis. Beeching takes over British Rail; drastic programme of cuts ensues. Macmillan's 'Night of the Long Knives' (13 July). First post-war Immigration Act passed, limiting entry to those with jobs. Vassall spy scandal. Report of royal commission on the police.

1963   British application to join EEC rejected. Gaitskell's unexpected death; Harold Wilson becomes Labour leader. Profumo scandal. Peerage Act enables peers to renounce hereditary titles. Macmillan resigns as PM; succeeded by Sir Alec Douglas-Home. President Kennedy assassinated (22 Nov.).

1964   First elections for New GLC; Labour victory. Nelson Mandela sentenced to life imprisonment at Pretoria. Labour gains narrow majority in general election; Wilson becomes PM. DEA created. Import surcharge and export tax introduced to improve balance of payments. Government, TUC and employers agree policy on productivity, prices and income. Police Act limits local control of police forces.

1965   Douglas-Home resigns as Conservative leader; new electoral process makes Heath leader. BP strike North Sea oil. Death penalty abolished. Prices and Incomes Board created.

1966   Labour increases majority in election to almost 100. Long seamen's strike (16 May–1 July). Frank Cousins resigns from government over incomes policy. Industrial Reorganization Corporation created. Six-month freeze imposed on prices and incomes. Post Office made public corporation. Sir Edmund Compton becomes first Ombudsman.

1967   Jo Grimond resigns as Liberal leader; replaced by Jeremy Thorpe. Britain makes another application to join Common Market. Criminal Justice Act allows majority verdicts from juries. *Rookes* v. *Barnard* attacks right to strike.

1968   George Brown resigns as Foreign Secretary. NHS prescription charges re-introduced. France vetos British entry into EEC. Northern Ireland disturbances begin. Racial unrest felt; Enoch Powell's 'Rivers of Blood' speech. Fulton Report on the civil service.

1969   British army units to be deployed in Northern Ireland. Voting age lowered to 18. Government seeks TUC's voluntary agreement to curb unofficial strikes. Report of the Redcliffe-Maud Commission on local government structure outside Greater London.

1970   Heath gains surprise general election victory. Third application to join EEC. Army uses rubber bullets in Northern Ireland. Heath's economic policy a 'dash for growth'.

1971   Currency decimalized. Immigration Act reduces status of Commonwealth immigrants to that of aliens. Both Houses of Parliament vote to join EEC. Compton Report on interrogation of IRA suspects finds evidence of ill treatment. US balance of trade slides into deficit with consequences for world capitalism. National Industrial Relations Court established (a failure, laid to rest in 1974).

1972   'Bloody Sunday' in Londonderry; 13 civilians killed. Power crisis; state of emergency declared; power cuts. Increased IRA bombing. Direct rule from

Westminster over Northern Ireland introduced. Decision taken to float pound. Local Government Act to reorganize system.

1973   Britain (and Ireland and Denmark) join EEC. Heath U-turns on economic policy; nationalization of lame ducks. Northern Ireland referendum shows strong support for retaining link with Britain. VAT introduced. First sitting of new Ulster Assembly collapses in chaos. Diplock Courts introduced in terrorist cases.

     Arab–Israeli war. Arab oil suppliers announce cut in supplies until Israelis withdraw from occupied territories; oil prices quadruple. Fuel conservation measures announced, including three-day week. Collapse of long boom becomes apparent. 'Snake in the Tunnel' agreement in Europe. India House incident brings existence of Special Patrol Group to public attention. Sir Robert Mark delivers BBC Dimbleby Lecture.

1974   End of direct rule in Northern Ireland. Parliament recalled for two-day debate on energy crisis. Miners' strike. Reorganized local government and NHS systems come into operation. Heath calls general election to decide 'who governs'; no clear result; Heath unsuccessfully flirts with Liberals; Labour becomes minority government. Miners return to work. Ulster assembly collapses; direct rule resumed. Red Lion Square disorders.

     End of statutory incomes policy. Guildford pub bombings kill five. Second general election in October returns Labour (majority of three). Birmingham pub bombings (21 killed). Anti-terrorist bill rushed through Parliament proscribes IRA. IRA bombs in London (Selfridges, Harrods, Heath's home).

1975   Heath forced by 1922 Committee to resubmit to election; defeated by Margaret Thatcher. Referendum on remaining in EEC; 2 to 1 majority 'Yes'. First live broadcast of Commons. Unemployment rises to over 1 million. Balcombe Street siege; two Londoners held in flat by IRA. National Enterprise Board established. Anti-sex discrimination and equal pay legislation comes into force. Ombudsman stystem extended to NHS.

1976   Wilson's unexpected resignation; Callaghan becomes PM. Britain begins exporting N. Sea oil. David Steel elected Liberal leader. Christopher Ewart-Biggs, British Ambassador to the Irish Republic, assassinated. Britain found guilty by European Commission on Human Rights of torturing detainees in Ulster.

     Lord Hailsham expounds 'elective dictatorship' thesis in BBC Dimbleby Lecture. Blunt spy scandal. Police Complaints Board established; Sir Robert Mark resigns in disgust. PM announces death of Keynesianism: 'we cannot . . . spend our way out of a recession'.

1977   Government loses absolute majority; Lib–Lab pact. Grunwick dispute. Violent racist clashes in Lewisham. Firemen's strike; army brought in to deal with fires. *Hosenball* case.

1978   Special Liberal Assembly votes to continue Lib–Lab pact until July. Regular broadcasting of parliamentary proceedings begins. Publication of *The Times* suspended (Nov.) in dispute over new technology (until Nov. 1979). Outbreak of IRA bombing in British cities. IMF Articles redrawn to mark end of Bretton Woods Agreement; currencies no longer tied to gold. Public sector strikes bring 'Winter of Discontent'.

1979   Referendums in Scotland and Wales reject devolution proposals. Government defeated on no-confidence motion; PM announces general election. Blair Peach dies in clash with police in black area of Southall. Thatcher becomes first woman PM in general election. Conservatives also dominate in European elections.

   Earl Mountbatten and others killed by bomb on boat in Sligo. Lancaster House talks to settle Rhodesia's (Zimbabwe's) future. All foreign exchange controls removed. BSC axe over 50,000 jobs; 13-week steel strike. New system of Commons select committees introduced.

1980   Bristol race riots. Zimbabwe becomes independent with Robert Mugabe as PM. National Front and Anti-Nazi League clashes at Lewisham. Iranian Embassy seized; later stormed by SAS. Wave of bombings and violence in Ulster marks ten years of internment.

   Callaghan retires as Labour leader; replaced by Foot. Reagan becomes US President. Alan Walters, right-wing economist, appointed PM's personal economic adviser. Local Government Planning and Land Act reforms block grant system to give more central control.

1981   Special Labour conference at Wembley changes leadership election method to give unions and constituencies a say. 'Gang of Four' establish Council for Social Democracy; SDP formed. Rupert Murdoch buys *The Times*. Engagement of Prince Charles and Lady Diana Spencer. Weekend of racial anti-police violence at Brixton. Death of Bobby Sands after 66-day fast; deaths of other IRA hunger strikers.

   Blanks fired at the Queen during Trooping of the Colour. SDP alliance with Liberals. Public expenditure cuts across a wide front including UGC and BBC. Riots at Toxteth and other cities; savage confrontations with police. Lonhro take over the *Observer*. Wedding of Lady Diana and Prince Charles. Benn's unsuccessful challenge to Healey for Labour deputy leadership. Government announce privatization of state North Sea oil assets. OPEC unify oil price structure.

   Anglo-Irish summit agrees on Intergovernmental Council; uproar in Commons; Ian Paisley promises to make province ungovernable. Benn elected off Shadow Cabinet. Scarman Report on Brixton riots. Arthur Scargill elected NUM leader. Labour NEC investigates Militant Tendency. Law Lords rule against GLC's 'Fares Fair' policy. British Nationality Act closes the door to non-whites.

1982   Unemployment reaches 3 million; Thatcher's popularity at all-time nadir. Group of Argentinians in South Georgia to dismantle a whaling station raise their country's flag, followed by 'invasion'. Emergency cabinet meeting; Foreign Secretary forced to resign; British naval blockade of Falklands; Falklands war breaks out. Ceasefire agreed 14 June. Thatcher's popularity reaches new heights.

   Roy Jenkins becomes SDP leader. IRA bombs in Hyde Park and Regent's Park; 11 killed. Greenham Common missile base ringed by 30,000 women in anti-nuclear, feminist protest.

1983   Labour NEC votes to expel five members of Militant. Ian MacGregor appointed Chairman of NCB. General election ('Falklands election'); Conservative majority of 144. Bernard Weatherill elected Speaker against Thatcher's wishes. Jenkins resigns as SDP leader; succeeded by Owen. New

Chancellor Lawson announces public expenditure cuts of £500 million.

38 IRA prisoners escape from Maze prison; Governor resigns. Kinnock elected Labour leader; Hattersley deputy. Parkinson resigns due to scandal. First US Cruise missiles arrive at Greenham Common. Massive bomb outside Harrods. US invades Grenada. Audit Commission established to toughen up central control of local government.

1984   Government announces ban on trade union membership at GCHQ. NCB announces loss of 20,000 jobs and closure of 21 pits. Miners' strike begins (12 March); NCB gets High Court injunction to prevent flying pickets. Sarah Tisdall jailed for 6 months for leaking documents about Cruise missiles. Greenham Common women evicted by bailiffs. Michael Bettaney jailed for 23 years for espionage. Labour gains in European Parliament elections; Conservatives retain majority.

Immigration rules further toughened. Government defeat in Lords over 'paving bill' for GLC abolition. Mirror Group Newspapers bought by Robert Maxwell. High Court rules ban on union membership at GCHQ illegal. 18 councils rate-capped. TUC votes to rejoin Neddy. Clive Ponting charged under Official Secrets Act. Police and Criminal Evidence Act increases police powers to stop and search; also replaces Police Complaints Board with more powerful Police Complaints Authority.

NUM fined by High Court for contempt. IRA bomb in Brighton hotel housing Conservative leaders for party conference. High Court orders sequestration of NUM assets. Talks between NUM and NCB repeatedly break down. Law Lords support ban on unions at GCHQ. High Court appoints receiver to control NUM funds. British Telecom privatized; massive profits made on first day's trading.

1985   House of Lords televised live. Oxford University refuses Thatcher honorary degree. Clive Ponting aquitted by jury of breaching the Official Secrets Act. Miners drift back to work after repeated failures of talks; end strike without agreement (3 March). Launch of Conservative Centre Forward, ginger group led by Pym to oppose Thatcherite policies. Government defeated for fourth time in Lords over GLC abolition.

European Court of Human Rights holds that Britain discriminates against women in immigration rules. Violent rioting in Brixton after police accidentally shoot Mrs Cherry Groce. Policeman killed during Broadwater Farm riots (Tottenham). Miners in Notts and South Derbyshire leave NUM and join Union of Democratic Mineworkers. Anglo-Irish agreement signed by Thatcher and Dr Garret Fitzgerald gives republic right to participate in Ulster's affairs; mass resignation of Ulster Unionist MPs. Control of *Daily Telegraph* passes to Canadian, Conrad Black. Westland affair begins. Church of England *Faith in the City* report published.

1986   Heseltine resigns criticizing Thatcher. Tory MPs vote against Rate Support Grant Settlement in Commons. Leon Brittan resigns over part in leak of Solicitor General's letter in Westland affair. Murdoch prints *Sunday Times* and *News of the World* at Wapping despite opposition from print unions; violent demonstrations. GLC and metropolitan counties abolished. Labour NEC begins disciplinary action against 16 militants at Liverpool.

John Stalker suspended and taken off Northern Ireland inquiry into RUC 'Shoot to Kill' policy. Derek Hatton (Liverpool militant leader) expelled from Labour Party. Gifford Report on Broadwater Farm riots. Appeal Court imposes ban on *Spycatcher* by former MI5 officer, Peter Wright. Stalker reinstated by Greater Manchester police force. Eric Heffer fails to secure election to Labour NEC. Marmaduke Hussey appointed by Thatcher as BBC Chairman. Launch of new quality national daily, the *Independent* (7 Oct.).

Sale of TSB shares on open market. Pound hits record low. 'Big Bang' in the City as computers are introduced and practices change on the stock exchange. *Spycatcher* case begins in Australian court; British government seeks to prevent publication of Peter Wright's memoirs. British Gas privatized. US air attack on Libya from British bases. Crown Prosecution Service comes into operation. New Public Order Act increases police powers.

1987   Privatization of BA. Large-scale redundancies on Tyneside. Home Secretary refers case of 'Birmingham Six' (pub bombing) to Court of Appeal after much campaigning; they will not be acquitted. SAS shoot eight IRA men and a civilian in County Tyrone. European Court of Human Rights dismisses case of GCHQ workers. Government obtains injunction to prevent showing on BBC of Zircon spy satellite.

Relaunch of formal Liberal–SDP Alliance. Enforced resignation of BBC Director General Alasdair Milne. Police raid on BBC offices in Glasgow to remove film *Secret Society*. Mgr Bruce Kent, leading CND activist, retires as active Catholic priest. Sir Kenneth Newman retires as head of Metropolitan Police; replaced by Peter Imbert. President Reagan admits 'arms for hostages' deal with Iran ('Irangate' scandal).

Three men convicted of murder of PC Blakelock in Broadwater Farm Estate. Moscow talks between Thatcher and Gorbachev. Thawing of cold war; Gorbachev offers to abolish short-range missiles in Europe. Labour Party rejects black activist, Sharon Atkin, chosen by local association at Nottingham East. Third successive general election triumph for Thatcher but great vote of no-confidence in Conservatives from Scotland, Wales and north.

1988   On 3 January Thatcher becomes longest-serving PM of century. Budget creates uproar in Commons; top rate tax reduced to 40 per cent (lowest in Europe); £2,000 million of tax cuts go to wealthiest.

Imports begin to rise faster than exports. Home spending fuelled by consumer credit boom. Ibbs Report on slimming the civil service. SAS gun down three IRA members in Gibraltar. Free vote in Commons decides to admit television cameras. DHSS split into two. Differences between PM and Chancellor; Thatcher announces return in 1989 of economic adviser Sir Alan Walters.

July trade figures reveal record deficit of £2,150 million. Inflation begins to rise. Local Government Finance Bill to introduce poll tax receives royal assent after stormy passage. Hostility aroused by far-ranging changes to social security system. Church continues to attack Thatcherite policies.

SDP and Liberals form new party; Paddy Ashdown emerges as leader of Social and Liberal Democratic Party. Benn and Heffer challenge Kinnock/ Hattersley leadership but easily defeated. Fall in NUM membership means that Arthur Scargill no longer entitled to automatic place on TUC's General Council; fails to get elected.

TUC becomes more favourably disposed towards EC as a result of speech by M. Jacques Delors, President of European Commission, that 1992 means not merely a single market but workers' rights and social reform. Same sentiments evoke opposite reaction in Thatcher, who resists French and German proposals that Britain joins EMS; in Bruges speech she utters dark warnings on EC socialism.

Last act of *Spycatcher* drama; High Court rules newspapers free to comment on and publish extracts. Legislation to replace section 2 of Official Secrets Act; critics say no improvement. Broadcasting Standards Authority set up under Sir William Rees Mogg ostensibly to regulate portrayal of sex and violence on TV, but gives grounds for fear of other forms of censorship.

British Steel privatized. Police Federation passes vote of no confidence in Police Complaints Authority. Government imposes ban on media interviews with members of Sinn Fein. Formation of Charter 88. Health Minister Edwina Currie offends NFU with remarks on salmonella in egg production; forced to resign.

1989   White paper on NHS outlines fundamental reforms; threatens doctors' autonomy. White paper from Lord Chancellor on reforms to legal system. Ayatollah Khomeni passes 'death sentence' on Salman Rushdie; some British Muslims demonstrate against the author; calls for extension of ancient blasphemy laws. European election results deeply alarming to Conservatives. Anomalies in electoral system exposed when Greens gain 15 per cent of votes but no seats. Summer recess preceded by cabinet reshuffle which succeeds in ruffling the feathers of three senior ministers. Televising of Commons begins. Chief Constable of West Midlands disbands Serious Crime Squad after allegations of falsified confessions; largest investigation into police corruption for ten years begins. Water privatized. Thatcher forces dramatic resignation of Lawson by refusing to sack Alan Walters; replaced by John Major.

1990   Nelson Mandela released by South African government. Thatcher's calls for ending of sanctions resisted by rest of world. Release of 'Guildford Four'; doubt about their 'confessions'. Ending of cold war and dramatic changes in Eastern Europe make future shape and role of NATO and the EC problematic. Massive anti-poll tax demonstrations in cities. Labour's popularity over the Conservatives higher than ever before (24 per cent). New crisis in Gulf as Iraq invades Kuwait. Heavy build-up of US troops in the region. UN condemns Iraq. Thatcher takes tough line; British troops sent.

Interest rates rise in an attempt to control inflation; many council house buyers suffer. Conservatives lose safe seats of Mid-Staffs to Labour and Eastbourne to the SLD in by-elections. Local elections debacle for Conservatives though they hold New Right Wandsworth and Westminster. Cabinet splits over Thatcher's vision of Europe; Hurd and Major fight to hold things together. Dramatic and bitter resignation by Geoffrey Howe, with ferocious attack on Thatcher in resignation speech. This signals election fight for Conservative leadership. In November Heseltine humiliates Thatcher by forcing a second ballot; she resigns. After a second ballot John Major emerges as party leader and Prime Minister.

Glossary

Words in **bold** type within entries refer to terms or concepts found elsewhere in the glossary.

Absolute majority A majority greater than the combined votes of all other candidates.

Abstention Non-voting at elections.

Accountability Answerability to a higher authority (the people, in a **democracy**).

Accumulation Amassing capital for investment.

Act of Parliament Package of laws on some matter.

Adjournment debate Debate (usually proposed by a backbencher) at end of parliamentary day.

Administrative law Justice concerned with cases between the citizen and the state.

Administrative tribunal Deals with cases of citizens' grievances against the state.

Advanced capitalism Modern, hi-tech, multinational **capitalist** economy. Distinguished from late capitalism (capitalism in crisis and decay). Technology makes workers less important, increasing opportunities for the few to amass wealth.

Adversary politics Description of British **two-party system**, seeing it based on argument rather than compromise between parties.

Advisory body Set up by government to conduct an inquiry and come up with recommendations.

Affiliated associations Associations linked to **political parties** (e.g. trade unions and cooperative societies), greatly enlarging membership.

Agency capture Control of a **regulatory agency** by the enterprise it is supposed to be regulating.

Alternative vote system Form of **proportional representation**.

Aristocracy Government by an enlightened elite.

Arm's length philosophy Belief that government should set up quasi-autonomous agencies to run various state services and then keep well away.

Art of the possible Classic aphorism used as a pithy definition of politics, drawing attention to compromising and wheeling and dealing evident in real-world politics.

Authoritative allocation of values Definition of politics. May be contrasted with **market** allocation in that allocation is on the basis of political authority, rather than ability to pay.

Authoritative opinion A constitutional source; the views of eminent jurists expressed after learned deliberation.

Authority Form of **power** distinguished by the fact that it is accepted by those over whom it is held.

Autonomy Self-determination; usually of a state.

Barrister Lawyer with right to plead in higher court.

Behaviouralism Approach to social sciences, including political science, taking only observable phenomena as its data.

Bill of Rights Constitutional document guaranteeing citizens' rights.

Bills Legislation is introduced into Parliament in the form of a Bill (when passed it becomes an **Act**). *Public* bills make laws applying to the whole country; *private* bills have only limited application.

Block grant Grant from central to **local government** not earmarked for any particular service.

Block vote Large number of votes tied together and cast at one go; a controversial feature of the Labour Party conference.

Body corporate Organization with a persona in law (e.g. local authority).

Borough Historic **local government** area based on a town which had gained a royal charter entitling it to certain freedoms.

Bourgeoisie French term for town-dweller appropriated by Marx to denote a capital-owning social class spawned by the industrial revolution; to Marx, the ruling class.

Bretton Woods Agreement Outcome of a meeting of 44 nations at Bretton Woods (in US) aimed at repairing the damage to the world capitalist economy inflicted by second world war. IMF and World Bank at heart of the arrangements.

Broadcasting impartiality Requirement that broadcasting media do not display the open bias projected by newspapers.

Budgetary process Method whereby government determines its annual sources of income.

Bureaucracy Strictly speaking, rule by officials. Weber argued that the growth of **socialism** would result in such rule. Used without pejorative connotations to denote a large hierarchical organization.

Bureaucratic power Power of permanent officials in politics; often manifest in the way they are able to manipulate elected politicians.

Butterfly effect Term from meteorology noting how a small disturbance within a system can set in motion great chains of repercussion.

Cabinet committees Bodies set up by Cabinet to concentrate on particular policy areas.

Cabinet government Government by a team rather than a single ruler.

Cabinet Secretariat Special **civil service** department responsible for servicing the Cabinet and its committees; can be influential in policy.

Cabinet Secretary Head of **Cabinet Secretariat** (and of civil service).

Capitalism Mode of production in which private individuals, rather than the state, own materials necessary to produce what society needs for its survival.

Case law Law resulting from previous judicial decisions (precedent).

Central–local relations Relationship between central government and its territorially based agencies; most often in connection with **local government**.

Centralism Central government's dominance over **local government**.

Centralization Central government's dominance over other state agencies.

Ceremonial Ostentatious aspects of government usually with little importance for actual decision-making, but often crucial for **legitimation**.

Chartism   Working-class organization founded in 1838 after dissatisfaction with 1832 Reform Bill. 'Charter' demanded universal male suffrage without property qualification.

Chief constable   Head of local police force.

City manager   'Managing director' appointed by local **council** to run its affairs, replacing old-style town clerk. Usually termed 'chief executive'.

City region   **Local authority** area embracing a major city and its surrounding towns and rural hinterland.

City-state   Political unit about which most Ancient Greek political thought was written; very small and not comparable with complex modern **nation-states**.

Civil jurisdiction   Pertaining to that part of the legal system concerned with cases involving one citizen against another.

Civil rights   Rights accruing to individuals as citizens which may not be infringed by other citizens or by the state.

Civil servant   Member of central government **bureaucracy**.

Class in Marxist terms   Dichotomy arising from the position of individuals in the productive process – the **bourgeoisie** own the means of production; the proletariat (working class) have only their labour to sell – an exploitative relationship; the bourgeoisie is effectively a 'ruling class'.

Coercive policing   See **consensus policing**.

Cold war   State of east–west tension which began after the second world war.

Collective responsibility   Constitutional convention reflecting the idea of **cabinet government**; entails various things including the idea that ministers participate in collective **policy-making**.

Collectivism   **Ideology** seeing the collectivity, rather than the individual, as the essential human unit.

Colonialism   Form of domination of one state over another associated with **imperialism**; may be established after military conquest or economic penetration of a weak economy (**neocolonialism**).

Collective consumption   Services consumed collectively by the population (e.g. education).

Common law   Law formed on the basis of precedents set in previous cases; reflects the accumulated wisdom of the past; is not the product of the legislative process.

Community charge (poll tax)   Local tax introduced to replace **rates**.

Communism   Ideology of equality and the common ownership of property.

Community policing   Form of policing in which the force becomes deeply involved in community affairs to establish mutual trust.

Comparative advantage   Economic theory underpinning the philosophy of **free trade** associated with Adam Smith (1723–90), arguing that if each nation produces that which it does most efficienctly, the world will maximize its wealth.

Consensus   Harmony between possibly opposed factions. The era of consensus politics in Britain (late 1940s–mid-1970s) saw Labour and Conservatives in agreement over a wide range of policies.

Consensus policing   Form of policing based on gaining the consent and cooperation of those policed; contrasted with coercive policing which relies on force.

Conservatism   View of politics, society and the constitution which believes in the wisdom of the past and is suspicious of radical change. Has deep intellectual antecedents; associated particularly with Edmund Burke and the ideology of the Conservative Party.

Consolidated Fund   The government's account at the Bank of England.

Constituency Territorial electoral division (e.g. Glasgow Hillhead). Can also denote the nature of a politician's support (e.g. 'small businessmen are the natural constituency of the Conservative Party').

Constituency association Local branch of a national **political party**.

Constitution Set of rules, customs and conventions defining the composition and powers of the institutions of state and regulating their relationships to each other and to private citizens.

Constitutional amendment Formal change to the **constitution**.

Constitutional convention Regularly observed practices regarded as part of the **constitution**.

Constitutional government Government constrained by rules and procedures laid down in the **constitution**; contrasted with arbitrary government.

Constitutional monarchy Political system in which a **monarchy** exists but is so constrained by the **constitution** that it plays no part in decision-making.

Consultative body Set up by government to bring together interested parties for policy discussions.

Consumer voting model Voting behaviour model seeing voters as shoppers in a political market place, choosing parties on the basis of their shop windows (**manifestos**, etc.).

Corporate management Form of management urged upon **local government** which seeks to unify control of its services under a single chief executive.

Corporatism Theory of **pressure group** activity in which the government incorporates certain groups into the **policy-making** process.

Council Body of people elected by the citizens of a local area to control the **local authority**.

County Top-tier **local authority** with ancient lineage.

County borough Type of **local authority** created in 1888 combining the powers and status of a **county** and a **borough**; not part of the general two-tier system.

Criminal jurisdiction Pertaining to the criminal law in which the crimes are against the state rather than against a particular person.

Cross-bencher Member of House of Lords not owing allegiance to any party.

Cross-class voting Phenomenon whereby individuals belonging to one social class vote for a party ostensibly supporting the interests of another.

D-notice system Voluntary code whereby the press restrains itself from publishing material on defence which officials want kept secret.

De facto In actuality.

De jure According to law.

Deference Belief amongst citizens that they should not play much part in government; they are happy to leave things to those whom they believe to be superior.

Delegated legislation Laws made by **bureaucrats** with power delegated by Parliament.

Demand management Keynesian principle whereby government uses its financial influence in the economy to manipulate the level of aggregate demand to maintain full employment.

Democracy Rule by all citizens in a community.

Demos Greek word for the people as a collectivity (hence **democracy**).

Deregulation Removal by the state of controls tending to protect state services from competition (e.g. local authority transport services).

Détente Reduction of tension between states; used particularly of east–west relations during the **cold war**.

Determinism Doctrine that everything that happens does so because of other forces; downgrades human free choice (**voluntarism**) as a factor explaining events.

Dignified and efficient elements   Distinction between those elements of a **constitution** which have no direct impact on **policy-making** and those which do; does *not* mean that the dignified elements are not important.

Direct democracy   Form of **democracy** in which citizens actually take part in making decisions; almost impossible in the real world.

Dual state thesis   View that policies for private business and the welfare state are made differently, the former closed and secretive, the latter more open to citizens' influence.

Dysfunction   Behaviour by an element of a **system** harmful to the whole.

Economic planning   Government intervention in the economy to achieve certain future goals, such as full employment, economic growth, balance of payments; opposed by **monetarists**.

Election campaign   Efforts made by **political parties** in the run-up to an election to win voters' support.

Electoral quota   Number of votes a candidate requires to be elected under certain systems of **proportional representation**.

Electoral stability   Condition where voters tend to vote the same way in successive elections.

Electoral swing   Mathematical calculation measuring the percentage shift of party support across the country; may or may not be uniform.

Electoral volatility   Condition in which the electorate cannot be relied upon to vote regularly for the same party. *Gross volatility* is the actual amount of vote changing between elections; *net volatility* is the overall effect in terms of the final distribution.

Elitism   Body of thought on **power** in society which sees as inevitable the formation of elites which will consolidate their positions, collude with each other and control government in their own interests.

Embourgeoisement   Process whereby members of the working class acquire middle-class habits and characteristics.

Emergency debates   Debates called under various procedures when Parliament suspends its normal business in order to discuss some matter of great importance.

Endogenous explanation   Explaining national political events solely in terms of factors internal to the country.

Entrenched provision   Constitutional provisions which cannot be changed by the normal process of law-making; absent from the British **constitution**.

Equalization   One of the functions of the central government grant to **local authorities**; redistributes money from richer to poorer areas of the country.

Establishment   Term used for a narrow, upper-middle-class elite with much power over society.

Estimates process   Established in the nineteenth century to allow Parliament to consider government expenditure proposals.

Exchange rate   Value of one currency in terms of that of another country.

Executive, political   Generally, the arm of **government** responsible for carrying out policy; more narrowly, the Cabinet.

Executive body   Quango responsible for actually administering some state function (e.g. Arts Council).

Exogenous explanation   Explanation of internal political events based on external factors.

Fabianism   Approach to social and political reform advocated by the Fabian Society, stressing small incremental advances rather than revolution.

Faction Segment within a party; usually considered more hard edged than a **ginger group** or a **tendency**.

False consciousness Errors of perception concerning one's self-interest; may explain why working-class people support the Conservatives.

Fiscal policy Taxation policy; may be used in pursuit of various objectives (e.g. pollution control).

First-past-the-post system System of election returning a single candidate on the basis of a simple majority, even though he or she may have only a small proportion of the votes cast. Rarely used in democracies, except Britain.

Floating voter Member of electorate who easily changes party allegiance.

Free press Doctrine that newspapers should be free to print what they like without government direction or censorship.

Free trade Free flow of goods in international trade, unimpeded by tariff barriers; has fuelled much political controversy.

Freedom of Information Act Legislation giving citizens a legal 'right to know' much of what happens in government; no such act exists in Britain.

Functionalism Body of theory looking primarily at the way institutions and practices contribute to the working of a social or political system; may be contrasted with an institutional approach.

Gemeinschaft* and *Gesellschaft German terms meaning community (based on bonds of affection, kinship, etc.) and association (based on contract), respectively.

General systems theory Body of theory seeing the **system** concept as a basis for interdisciplinary study.

Generalist **Civil servant** with no special or professional skill; often holding a high position within the British service.

Ginger group Small group within a party devoted to promoting a particular idea or principle; often ideologically extreme.

'Golden Age' of Parliament Period approximately between the 1832 and 1867 Reform Acts when Parliament appeared to have the power to bring down governments; ended by the rise of party discipline.

Golden share State-owned share in a privatized company enabling it to have control over certain key decisions.

Government (verb) The process of ruling a community; (noun) an elite group formally recognized as being in control of the community.

Green paper Government document to stimulate public debate; *see also* **white paper**.

Hansard Official record of parliamentary proceedings.

Health authority Local body set up as part of the NHS to administer the local health service as an unelected 'local council'.

Hegemony Rule or domination; used by neo-Marxists of an upper or ruling class holding leading positions in various walks of life.

Hiving off Chopping off pieces of public **bureaucracy** to form semi-autonomous agencies responsible for some clearly defined block of work.

Holism Theory stressing the *whole* of the object of study rather than the parts.

Ideology Political doctrine claiming to give a universally applicable theory of people and society from which may be derived a programme of political action.

Imperialism Extension of the **hegemony** of one country by conquest (military or economic) and imposed rule over others.

Incrementalism Theory of government decision-making holding that radical steps are impossible or undesirable.

Individualism   Ideology seeing the individual as the prime unit in morality and politics; underlies the theories of classical economists in which individuals pursue their own self-interest.

Industrial revolution   Period between 1760 and 1860 (approximately) based on multiple innovations in production methods and technologies; revolutionary in the social transformation it induced.

Inflation   General rise in prices throughout the economy; often measured by the Retail Price Index (RPI).

Inner cabinet   Unofficial Cabinet consisting of the PM and a few chosen members of the government.

Insider group   **Pressure group** with a close, secretive relationship with government.

Institutional racism   Practices reflecting entrenched **racist** attitudes, such as discrimination in job appointments.

Instrumental explanation   An interpretation of politics seeing the state as an instrument of some greater power behind the throne; in **Marxism**, this is the **bourgeoisie**.

Interest aggregation   Bringing interests together to construct a body sufficiently large (party or group) to have political clout.

Interest group   Association of people with some common concern; *see also* **pressure group**.

International associations   Associations of nations such as NATO and the United Nations Organization.

Investment function (of state)   State role in investing in the economy (e.g. road building).

Iron Curtain   Powerful image employed by the west to describe the separation between the communist East European bloc and the capitalist west.

Iron law of oligarchy   Sociological 'law' postulated by Michels stating that in any **political party** a small elite would eventually gain control.

Judge's Rules   Set of rules governing police questioning of suspects; modified by legislation in the 1980s.

Judicial impartiality   Constitutional principle that judges are impartial between the interests within society.

Judicial review   Part of the principle of the **separation of powers**. The **judiciary** is able to review legislation and actions of the **executive** in terms of their constitutionality. No provision for this in Britain.

Judiciary   Body of judges.

Jury system   Part of judicial system; highly democratic in that the jury is selected at random, so does not include power-seekers in the way electoral politics does. Used by the Greeks not only for legal decisions.

Justice of the Peace (JP)   Generally lay judge with limited jurisdiction; formerly a key local administrator.

Keynesianism   Economic theory arguing that the free **market**, left to itself, will not automatically work for the benefit of all in the way the classical economists (nineteenth century) claimed. Consequently the state must intervene in the **capitalist** market to achieve desirable social ends, particularly full employment.

Laissez-faire   Slogan adopted by classical economists that the state should keep out of the private **capitalist** economy.

Legislative process   Series of stages by which a **bill** becomes an **Act**; entails passage through the Commons and the Lords and is finalized by the royal assent.

Legislature   Institution formally charged with making laws – Parliament.

Legitimacy   Quality of being popularly accepted as rightful and just.

Legitimation   Actions and processes designed to secure **legitimacy**; may entail deception.

Lend–Lease   System whereby the US provided Britain with materials to fight the second world war.

Liberal democracy   Form of **democracy** based upon elections and representative institutions which places great stress upon the idea of individual freedom defined in terms of a *limited* role for government and the state; linked with idea of **market** economy.

Liberalism   **Ideology** seeing minimum government and individual freedom as its prime virtues; attractive to **capitalism** by permitting the operation of the free **market**.

Limited government   Government restrained from arbitrary rule; accomplished variously by **rule of law, separation of powers,** or a **constitution.**

Lobbyist   One practised in the art and craft of dealing with MPs on behalf of **pressure groups.**

Local authority   Body responsible for delivering **local government** services; comprises a work force, a **bureaucracy,** and an elected **council.**

Local bureaucracy   Organization of **local government** officials.

Local corporatism   Theory that **local politics** contains certain groups enjoying a close and intimate relationship with the councillors and officers.

Local government   Self-government by the people of some subnational territorial unit within the state on the basis of delegated authority.

Local pluralism   Interplay of local **pressure groups** in **local politics.**

Local political party   Party fighting for places on, and perhaps power over, the local **council.**

Local politics   Politics taking place in a subnational territorial unit of the state.

Local state   Term used by some writers to designate **local government**; not accurate in a legal sense.

Localist tradition   Tradition in **local government** evolution whereby communities have sought to provide collective services for themselves.

Long boom   Period from the end of the second world war to the beginning of the 1970s when the developed **capitalist** countries enjoyed rising standards of living and a great rise in material wealth.

MEP   Member of the European Parliament.

Machinery of government   Institutions through which **government** works; **civil service** departments, **local authorities,** etc.

Maladministration   Bad administration causing inconvenience or suffering to a citizen.

Managerialism   Approach to government in which the public sector tries to ape private-sector methods; tends to reduce elected politicians' authority.

Mandarin   Term used to describe members of the upper echelons of the **civil service.** Originally used of officials in imperial China.

Mandate   Approval for a set of policies gained by a party elected to office on the basis of a **manifesto.**

Manifesto   Set of policy promises made by the parties to entice electors.

Market   Key mechanism (based on price) in classical economic theory; it is said to work as if controlled by a hidden hand to achieve optimum allocation of the resources in society.

Marshall Aid programme   System of US loans to Europe following the second world war.

Marxism   Body of thought with many strands deriving from the ideas of Marx; sees the private ownership of materials needed for production as the key explaining society and politics.

Mass party   **Political party** organized throughout the country with thousands of members.

Mechanistic system   System made by people to serve their purposes; not a naturally occurring thing.

Medical model of health   Definition of health given by the medical profession, reflecting doctors' interests.

Mercantilism   Economic doctrine favoured in the sixteenth and seventeenth centuries. Argued that a country should seek to export as much as possible, while restricting imports. Did not suit the **capitalists** of the **industrial revolution** who favoured **free trade**.

Meritocracy   Literally, rule by the most able; more colloquially, refers to a system (educational or social) where promotion is based on merit, usually measured by examination performance.

Metropolitan county   Top-tier **local government** area created by 1972 Local Government Act, for the large conurbations.

Militarization (of police)   Greater use of defensive and offensive weapons and militaristic tactics (e.g. marches, charges).

Mind politics   Term used in this book to denote an arena of political activity concerned with influencing what people think, rather than allocating values.

Ministerial adviser   Experts from outside the **civil service** to advise ministers on policy; they adopt openly partisan stances and are not welcomed by the **bureaucrats**.

Ministerial responsibility   Doctrine declaring that the minister in a government department is the only one who should be questioned, praised and blamed. In extreme cases may be expected to resign (e.g. Lord Carrington over the Falklands war).

Mixed economy   One in which **capitalism** is modified so that some of the productive capital in society is owned by the people (e.g. Britain before the **privatization** programme).

Mob rule   The down side of **democracy**; term used by opponents of democracy.

Monarchy   Rule by a single person; usually hereditary.

Monetarism   Economic doctrine holding that governments should do little in the economy, being content to control the rate at which the quantity of money in circulation rises. Everything else is then said to take care of itself through the **market**.

Money supply   Quantity of money in the economy, believed to be causally linked with **inflation**.

Monopoly capitalism   Characteristic of **advanced capitalism** when, by a process of predatory takeovers, production becomes concentrated in a few enormous firms.

Multi-member constituency   Electoral district returning more than one candidate; a prerequisite of **proportional representation**.

Multi-party system   Political system in which three or more parties contest elections and gain seats in the assembly. Often associated with coalition government.

Multinational corporation   Giant private firm located throughout the world; often producing a wide range of unrelated products.

Nation-state   The state as understood today; to be contrasted with the **city-states** of Ancient Greece.

Nationalism   Ideological attachment to the nation and its interests.

Nationalization   (Often compulsory) acquisition by the state of private property or a business within its territory.

Natural law System of law deriving from human nature, rather than invented by reason; an idea present in political thought from the time of the Ancient Greeks. The great Roman statesman Cicero (106–43 BC) spoke of 'right reason – which is in accordance with nature, and is unchangeable and eternal' (*Republic*: III, 22).

Natural monopoly An industry where the technical problems of competition are so great that it is better for society if monopoly is permitted (e.g. telecommunications, railways).

Neocolonialism Form of domination characteristic of the post-war era in which **capitalists** from the developed world effectively dominate the less-developed economies through multinational companies.

Neocorporatism Used to distinguish the practice of post-war **corporatism** from pre-war fascism.

New Right Term for a resurgence of anti-socialist thought in the US, France and Britain; in many ways restating the free-market ideas of the nineteenth-century economists.

New Urban Left Local political movement which sought to resist the Thatcher government's policies in the early 1980s.

Non-aligned world Group of nations professing neutrality during the **cold war**.

North–south divide Political gulf between the north and south of Britain emerging from the late 1970s; by 1987 Scotland, Wales and northern England were solidly Labour while the south was overwhelmingly Conservative.

Official secrecy The keeping of state secrets; justified on the grounds of national security.

Oligarchy Oppressive rule by a small group.

Ombudsman Short name for the Parliamentary Commissioner for Administration, who investigates complaints of **maladministration**.

Opposition Days Set number of days when the parliamentary opposition is able to choose the topic for debate.

Order Paper Agenda for the parliamentary day.

Organic system System which has grown naturally rather than having been designed by people.

Organic theory Body of theory seeing society as a living organism.

Outsider group **Pressure group** which government is unwilling to listen to.

Paramilitary unit Police unit able to use militaristic methods and equipment (e.g. Special Patrol Group).

Parish One of the oldest units of **local government**; very small and based on the area around the church.

Parliamentary cadre Party in Parliament consisting of MPs; may or may not have a mass membership outside Parliament.

Parliamentary debate Considered a central function of the modern Parliament; tends to be dominated by the front-benchers.

Parliamentary privilege Set of privileges accorded to MPs; supposed to enable them to perform better as representatives, without fears of, say, libel.

Parliamentary questions (PQs) Questions from MPs to members of the government on a rota system.

Parliamentary sovereignty Belief that Parliament is the supreme source of sovereignty in the **constitution**. Dicey believed this to be the only morally defensible version of sovereignty in a **democracy**.

Partisan dealignment Tendency of voters to break away from stable identification with a **political party**.

Party bureaucracy Paid employees of **political parties** concerned with administration; characteristic of the modern mass party.

Party cohesion   Party's ability to hold together; the Conservatives are particularly good at this.

Party conference   Usually the annual meeting of all elements of the mass party organization.

Party constitution   Rules determining the internal processes within a party.

Party discipline   MPs' obedience in the House of Commons to their party.

Party executive   Leadership of the party.

Party identification   Used by psephologists to describe voters who always vote for the same party regardless.

Party list   Feature in **proportional representation** electoral systems; displays the candidates of a party, sometimes in order of preference.

Party system   Usually defined in terms of the number of parties taking part in the political fray; main categories are **single-party**, **two-party** or multi-party.

Party whip   An office in the parliamentary party. The chief whip and his assistants ensure that members follow the party line.

Patriarchy   Society in which men dominate women.

Patronage   Making appointments on the basis of favour rather than electoral choice or expertise.

Peak organization   Organization formed by the association of a number of **pressure groups** (e.g. the TUC).

Peer   Member of the House of Lords.

PESC (Public Expenditure Survey Committee) process   Whitehall process for planning **public expenditure**.

Pluralism   Theory of politics seeing **pressure groups** as central to the political process; generally holds their effect to be benign and democratic.

Pluralist stagnation   Right-wing explanation for Britain's post-war economic failure claiming that too many **pressure groups** were being permitted to voice their demands.

Police authority   Body formally controlling local police (the police committee).

Police committee   See above.

Police complaints procedure   System for handling complaints against the police.

Police culture   Characteristic set of attitudes held by the police.

Police state   Totalitarian state under police control.

Policy Cabinet   Used to denote a small Cabinet of about five, the members of which are concerned with the whole area of government policy, rather than being responsible for specific departments. Has never really been tried.

Policy implementation   Carrying out government policy; formally the task of the **bureaucracy**.

Policy-making   Essential act of **government** in the modern state. The extent to which government is free to make policy is a matter of debate.

Polis   Ancient Greek term for city.

Political culture   Set of ideas and attitudes held towards the **political system**.

Political party   Group formed for the purpose of gaining political office, usually through winning elections.

Political philosophy   Generalized answers to fundamental questions such as the nature of justice.

Political science   Term which may be used loosely to denote the study of politics generally, or more rigorously to indicate the application of scientific method.

Political socialization   Social process through which individuals develop an awareness of political values, norms and processes; continues throughout life.

Political system A whole consisting of institutions of **government** and the society they serve, a concept stressing the **holistic** nature of politics – no part can be properly understood without reference to its place in the whole.

Political theory Theories about political institutions, law, **constitutions**, democracy, etc.

Political thought Corpus of theories whereby people have sought to explain political behaviour, values, and mechanisms and institutions of **political systems**.

Politicization Process whereby an institution may become actively involved in politics (e.g. the **civil service** and police).

Politics–administration dichotomy Long-standing distinction saying that making policy and carrying it out are distinct activities; underlies **separation of powers** between **executive** and **legislature**.

Polity Political organization of a state.

Poll tax Tax placed on all citizens equally regardless of ability to pay; last imposed in 1381 (Peasants' Revolt) until **community charge** introduced (1989–90).

Polyarchy Robert Dahl's term for a form of **pluralism** seeing in groups a more effective balance of power than in the **constitution**.

Populism Form of **government** supposed to enshrine the will of the people. Some political leaders have an instinctively populist appeal. Presidents, where directly elected, may claim populist mandate.

'Populist monarchism' Term applied to Thatcher approach to **government**.

Positive law Law believed to have been made by applying human reason rather than by some metaphysical power such as God; *see also* **natural law**.

Power Key concept in the study and practice of politics; the ability to achieve some desired effect regardless of opposition. May take many forms.

Power-sharing executive An **executive** formed to reflect both majority and minority interests.

Presidential government System of **government** by one person, usually elected directly by the people.

Press baron **Capitalist** owner of large-circulation newspapers; today empires extend into the media and entertainments industry.

Press partisanship Political bias shown by newspapers in reporting news and in editorial comment; usually supporting the right.

Pressure group Association wishing to influence government policy.

Primary elections Elections held before the real elections to choose candidates who will stand.

Private members' bills **Bills** introduced into Parliament by MPs in their personal capacity rather than by the government; rarely get very far because the government does not make sufficient time available.

Privatization Transfer of state-owned assets into private hands.

Privy Council Originally the monarch's close advisers; now a ceremonial body of ministers and ex-ministers.

Promotional group **Pressure group** concerned with promoting an ideal rather than the self-interest of its members (e.g. RSPCA).

Proportional representation Electoral system intended to create an assembly which accurately reflects the level of support for the parties in the country.

Protestant work ethic Characteristic attributed by Weber to eighteenth and nineteenth-century British **capitalist** class; a nonconformist belief in austerity, thrift and hard work, which made them uniquely wealthy and powerful.

Psephology   Study of elections and electoral behaviour.

Public choice theory   Body of theory seeking to explain and analyse politics on the basis of the **individualist** premises of classical economics.

Public corporation   Body created by government in the image of a private company but owned by the state, rather than private shareholders.

Public expenditure   Expenditure by the state, including **transfer payments**.

Public health   Area of government policy concerned with the general health of the population (sewers, clean water and air, etc.).

Public inquiry   Official inquiry into some matter of public concern.

Public interest   Vague term meaning the collective interest of society. What is, or is not, in the public interest is often a matter of judgement. In the Ponting case, the judge denied the right of a citizen to make up his own mind on the matter, declaring that only the government could decide.

Public order   Well-regulated civic life.

Public sector borrowing requirement (PSBR)   Amount of money government wishes to borrow in any year.

Quango   QUasi-Autonomous National (or Non-) Government Organization.

Queen's Speech   Great day in the ceremonial calendar of British politics, marking the annual opening of Parliament and outlining the government's proposed programme for the year.

Question Time   One-hour period when MPs address questions to ministers.

Racism   Attribution of characteristics of superiority and inferiority to members of particular races.

Rate-capping   System devised in the 1980s to prevent **local authorities** raising their rates.

Rates   **Local government** property tax (abolished 1989–90).

Rational decision-making   Making a decision on the basis of reason rather than self-interest, political advantage or prejudice.

Redress of grievance   Means taken to right a wrong (often inflicted by the state on a citizen).

Regulatory agency   Body set up by government to regulate economic or social activity (e.g. Office of Fair Trading, Equal Opportunities Commission).

Representative government   Form of **government** in which a minority act on behalf of the rest of the population. There are various theories about the relationship between the represented and the representatives.

Royal prerogative   Set of special privileges enjoyed exclusively by the monarch since medieval times; today many of the most important are effectively held by the PM.

Rule of law   Constitutional doctrine that the ultimate source of **authority** in the state is the law; kings and governments are themselves subject to it.

Scrutiny committee   **Select committee** established to look into some aspect of the work of the **executive**.

Sectional group   **Pressure group** composed of members of society from some sectional interest.

Sectoral cleavage   An alternative to class as an explanation of voting behaviour.

Security services   State agencies concerned with espionage (MI5 and MI6).

Select committee   Committee of MPs established to undertake some particular task on behalf of Parliament.

Selection process   Choice of candidates to stand in election.

Selective incentive   Inducement made by a **pressure group** to recruit and retain members.

Separation of powers Constitutional doctrine that the various institutions of the state share the functions of government in order to limit each other and prevent despotism.

Sexism Attitudes falsely ascribing certain attributes to one sex, usually to justify inequality.

Shadow Cabinet Opposition front-bench team.

Shire county Non-metropolitan **county** usually reflecting ancient boundary patterns.

Simple plurality election Election in which the candidate with the most votes (the first past the post) is elected regardless of the actual proportion of the electorate giving support.

Single-tier system **Local government** areal structure without subdivisions.

Single transferable vote One of the best known systems of **proportional representation**; avoids wasting votes by a system of redistribution on the basis of second preferences.

Single-party system **Political system** in which one party dominates; under totalitarian regimes may actually eliminate its rivals by force.

Social class Section of population sharing a common social status; almost invariably associated with socioeconomic factors.

Social democracy Ideology of moderate **socialism**, mixed economy, welfare state, etc.

Socialism Egalitarian **ideology** under which the state actively cares for citizens.

Society A community sharing a common system of political authority, and conscious of their collective identity and distinctiveness from other groups.

Solicitor Legal general practitioner.

Sovereignty Concept of the ultimate source of **power** within the state.

'Special relationship' Britain's view of its relationship with the US.

Specialist–generalist debate A dichotomy based on two fundamental kinds of expertise found in government **bureaucracy**.

Specific grant Grant made to **local government** by central government to be used to provide some particular service.

Spoils system System of **patronage** in which the victors in an election distribute offices to those who have assisted them.

Sponsorship Relationship of MPs to various non-party organizations (e.g. some Labour MPs are sponsored by trade unions).

Standing committees of Parliament Committees of MPs which consider **bills** during their process through Parliament (the committee stage).

Starred questions **Parliamentary questions** where the MP specifically requests a verbal reply.

State In simple terms, a sovereign community, within a defined territory.

State shareholdings State ownership of shares in a private company.

Statute law Laws made by Parliament.

Structural explanation Explanation of political behaviour which sees it as determined by the structure in which it takes place (e.g. the **capitalist** economy).

Subclass Disadvantaged class developing during the 1980s (unemployed, ethnic minorities, etc.).

Subgovernment Community formed by those concerned with policy in a certain area – **insider pressure groups, civil servants**, the specialist press, ministers, etc; sometimes termed a policy community.

Subversion Attempt to overthrow the government by unlawful means.

Suffragette Woman active in the cause of women's voting rights.

Supragovernmental organizations   International authorities standing above national governments.

Supplementary questions   Probing additions to a **parliamentary question**.

Synergy   Energy generated within a **system** as a result of the interplay of its parts, but greater than the sum of their individual energy.

System   Set of elements interacting together to constitute a larger whole.

Tactical voting   Voting behaviour designed to keep out a disliked candidate by supporting the rival most likely to defeat him or her.

Tendency   Used in politics to designate sections within parties (e.g. Militant Tendency).

Transfer payments   State payments to a section of the population financed by taxation (e.g. pensions).

Tripartism   Form of **corporatism** developed in Britain in the immediate post-war decades involving government, employers and unions.

Two-party system   **Political system** in which two equal parties monopolize in terms of votes and seats in the assembly.

Tyranny   Oppressive rule.

Ultra vires   Legal principle restraining public bodies within a framework of powers prescribed by the **sovereign** body.

Universal franchise   Condition of an electoral system in which all adult citizens have the right to vote.

Unwritten constitution   **Constitution** existing in the form of custom and practice, and various laws, rather than a single document.

Utilitarianism   Basis of a moral philosophy preached by Bentham, J. S. Mill and others which sees the maximization of utility (happiness) as the basis for all law, morality, political institutions and right behaviour.

Violence, political   Settlement of disputes by physical force; often seen as the antithesis of politics.

Violence, state   Legitimate use of force against citizens (e.g. police).

Voluntarism   View that humans control their own actions, rather than acting as the system forces them to do.

War Cabinet   Small Cabinet invariably established by PMs during wars, to be responsible for key decisions.

Ward association   Party organization which is a subdivision of the **constituency association**.

Welfare statism   A social democratic kind of ideology.

White paper   Document published by government to outline and explain its policy; *see also* **green paper**.

World economy   The idea that all countries are interlocked through trade.

World policeman   Linked to the idea of the **world economy**; the one nation (or group) which regulates the world economy, stabilizing **exchange rates**, keeping open trade routes, etc.

Xenophobia   Fear (and often hatred) of foreigners.

Zones of the world economy   The **world economy** may be said to consist of three zones: a core, an intermediate zone, and a periphery.

Bibliography

Abrahams, M. (1958) 'Class distinctions in Britain', in *The Future of the Welfare State*, London, Conservative Political Centre.

Almond, G. A. and Powell, G. B. (1966) *Comparative Politics*, Boston, Little Brown.

Almond, G. A. and Verba, S. (1963) *The Civic Culture*, Princeton, NJ, Princeton University Press.

Almond, G. A. and Verba, S. (eds) (1980) *The Civic Culture Revisited*, Boston, Little Brown.

Althusser, L. (1969) *For Marx* (translated by B. Brewster), Harmondsworth, Penguin.

Amery, L. S. (1947) *Thoughts on the Constitution*, London, Oxford University Press.

Anwar, M. (1984) *Votes and Policies: Ethnic Minorities and the General Election of 1979*, London, Commission for Racial Equality.

Armstrong, P., Glyn, A. and Harrison, J. (1984) *Capitalism since World War II*, London, Fontana.

Atkins, R. (1988) 'Line-up for when the pause in privatisation issues ends', *Financial Times* (20 June).

Atkinson, A. B. (1983) *The Economics of Inequality*, Oxford, Oxford University Press.

Atkinson, A. B. and Harrison, A. J. (1978) *The Distribution of Personal Wealth in Britain*, Cambridge, Cambridge University Press.

Aubrey, C. (1981) *Who's Watching You*, Harmondsworth, Penguin.

Bagehot, W. (1963) *The English Constitution*, London, Fontana (first published 1867).

Bains, M. A. (chairman) (1972) *The New Local Authorities: Management and Structure*, London, HMSO.

Baldwin, N. D. J. (1985) 'Behavioural changes: a new professionalism and a more independent House (of Lords)', in Norton, P. (ed.), *Parliament in the 1980s*, Oxford, Blackwell, pp. 96–113.

Baldwin, R. and Kinsey, R. (1982) *Police Powers and Politics*, London, Quartet.

Balogh, T. (1968) 'The apotheosis of the dilettante: the establishment of mandarins', in Thomas, H. (ed.), *Crisis in the Civil Service*, London, Anthony Blond.

Bar Council (1989) *Quality of Justice: the Bar's Response*, London, Bar Council.

Barret, M. (1980) *Woman's Oppression Today*, London, New Left Books.

Barry, B. (1970) *Sociologists, Economists and Democracy*, London, Macmillan.

Batty, K. and George, B. (1985) 'Finance and facilities for MPs', in Norton, P. (ed.), *Parliament in the 1980s*, Oxford, Basil Blackwell, pp. 169–81.

Baxter, J. and Koffman, L. (eds) (1985) *Police, the Constitution and the Community*, Abingdon, Professional Books.

Beer, S. H. (1965) *Modern British Politics*, London, Faber.

Beer, S. H. (1982) *Britain Against Itself*, London, Faber.

Benn, M. (1985) 'Policing women', in Baxter, J. and Koffman, L. (eds), *Police, the Constitution and the Community*, Abingdon, Professional Books.

Benn, M. et al. (1983) *The Rape Controversy*, London, National Council for Civil Liberties.

Benn, T. (1979) *Arguments for Socialism*, Harmondsworth, Penguin.

Benn, T. (1980) 'Manifestos and Mandarins', in *Policy and Practice: the Experience of Government*, London, Royal Institute of Public Administration.

Bentley, A. F. (1967) *The Process of Government*, Cambridge, MA, Harvard University Press (first published 1908).

Bentley, M. (1984) *Politics Without Democracy, 1815–1914*, London, Fontana.

Beveridge, W. (chairman) (1942) *Social Insurance and Allied Services*, Cmd 6404, London, HMSO.

Bevins, A. and Felton, D. (1988) 'Kinnock demands policies for power', *Independent* (5 Oct.).

Bhavnani, K. K. and R. (1985) 'Racism and resistance in Britain', in Coates, D. et al. (eds), *A Socialist Anatomy of Britain*, Cambridge, Polity, pp. 147–59.

Birch, A. H. (1959) *Small Town Politics*, Oxford, Oxford University Press.

Black, D. (chairman) (1980) *Inequalities in Health*, London, DHSS.

Blacksell, M. (1981) *Post-War Europe*, London, Hutchinson.

Blake, R. (1985) *The Conservative Party from Peel to Thatcher*, London, Fontana.

Blunkett, D. (1984) 'Local socialism: the way ahead', in Boddy, M. and Fudge, C. (eds), *Local Socialism*, London, Macmillan, pp. 242–60.

Boaden, N. (1971) *Urban Policy Making*, Cambridge, Cambridge University Press.

Boateng, P. (1985) 'Crisis in accountability', in Baxter, J. and Koffman, L. (eds), *Police, the Constitution and the Community*, Abingdon, Professional Books, pp. 237–45.

Boddy, M. and Fudge, C. (eds) (1984) *Local Socialism: the Way Ahead*, London, Macmillan.

Bottomore, T. (1964) *Elites in Society*, Harmondsworth, Penguin.

Bower, T. (1988) *Maxwell: the Outsider*, London, Aurum Press.

Box, S. (1971) *Deviance, Reality and Society*, London, Holt, Rinehart and Winston.

Briggs, A. (1963) *Victorian Cities*, Harmondsworth, Penguin.

Brittan, S. (1983) 'Privatisation: a new approach', *Financial Times* (17 Nov.).

Bruce-Gardyne, J. (1984) *Mrs Thatcher's First Administration*, London, Macmillan.

Budd, A. (1978) *The Politics of Economic Planning*, London, Fontana.

Bunyan, A. (1977) *The History and Practice of the Political Police in Britain*, London, Quartet.

Burch, M. and Moran, M. (1984) 'Who are the new Tories?' *New Society* (11 Oct.).

Burke, E. (1861) *Reform of Representation in the House of Commons*, in *Works*, vol. VI, London, Bohn (first published 1782).

Burnham, J. (1942) *The Managerial Revolution*, London, Putnam.

Butler, D. (1960) 'The paradox of party difference', *American Behavioural Scientist*, 4(3).

Butler, D. (ed.) (1978) *Coalitions in British Politics*, London, Macmillan.

Butler, D. and Butler, G. (1986) *British Political Facts 1900–1985*, London, Macmillan.

Butler, D. and Kavanagh, D. (1988) *The British General Election of 1987*, London, Macmillan.

Butler, D. and Rose, R. (1960) *The British General Election of 1959*, London, Macmillan.

Butler, D. and Stokes, D. (1969) *Political Change in Britain*, London, Macmillan.

Campbell, D. (1980) 'Society under surveillance', in Hain, P. et al. (eds), *Policing the Police*, London, John Calder, pp. 65–150.

Camps, M. (1964) *Britain and the European Community 1955–1963*, London, Oxford University Press.

Castells, M. (1977) *The Urban Question*, London, Edward Arnold.

Castle, B. (1980) *The Castle Diaries, 1974–6*, London, Weidenfeld and Nicolson.

Cater, D. (1965) *Power in Washington*, London, Collins.

Cawson, A. (1982) *Corporatism and Welfare*, London, Heinemann.

Cawson, A. (1986) *Corporatism and Political Theory*, Oxford, Basil Blackwell.

Chandler, J. A. (1988) *Public Policy-Making for Local Government*, London, Croom Helm.

Chandler, J. A. and Lawless, P. (1985) *Local Authorities and the Creation of Employment*, Aldershot, Gower.

Checkland, S. G. and E. O. A. (eds) (1974) *The Poor Law Report of 1834*, Harmondsworth, Penguin.

Chester, N. (1979) 'Fringe bodies, quangos and all that', *Public Administration*, 57(1), 51–4.

Chester, N. (1981) 'Questions in the House', in Walkland, S. A. and Ryle, M. (eds), *The Commons Today*, London, Fontana, pp. 175–202.

Chittenden, M. (1988) 'Freemasonry "rife" among top police', *Sunday Times* (10 April).

Chrimes, S. B. (1967) *English Constitutional History*, 4th edn, London, Oxford University Press.

Coates, D., Johnston, G. and Bush, R. (1985) *A Socialist Anatomy of Britain*, Cambridge, Polity.

Cockburn, C. (1977) *The Local State*, London, Pluto Press.

Cockerell, M., Hennessy, P. and Walker, P. (1984) *Sources Close to the Prime Minister: Inside the Hidden World of the News Manipulators*, London, Macmillan.

Cornford, F. M. (ed. and translator) (1941) *The Republic of Plato*, Oxford, Clarendon Press.

Cosgrave, P. (1978) *Margaret Thatcher: a Tory and Her Party*, London, Hutchinson.

Cowe, R. (1989) 'Hard grind is better than greed for private business', *Guardian* (19 May).

Cox, A. (1988) 'The old and new testaments of corporatism: is it a political form or a method of policy making?' *Political Studies*, 36(2), 294–308.

Crewe, I. (1986) 'On the death and resurrection of class voting: some comments on *How Britain Votes*', *Political Studies*, 34 (4), 620–38.

Crick, B. (1964) *In Defence of Politics*, Harmondsworth, Penguin.

Crosland, A. (1956) *The Future of Socialism*, London, Jonathan Cape.

Cross, C. (1963) *The Liberals in Power 1905–1914*, London, Pall Mall Press.

Crossman, R. H. S. (1963) 'Introduction', in Bagehot, W., *The English Constitution*, London, Fontana.

Crossman, R. H. S. (1975) *Diaries of a Cabinet Minister, Vol. 1*, London, Jonathan Cape.

Crossman, R. H. S. (1976) *Diaries of a Cabinet Minister, Vol. 2*, London, Jonathan Cape.

Crossman, R. H. S. (1977) *Diaries of a Cabinet Minister, Vol. 3*, London, Jonathan Cape.

Crouch, C. (1979) 'The state, capital and liberal democracy', in Crouch, C., *State and Economy in Contemporary Capitalism*, London, Croom Helm.

Curtice, J. and Steed, M. (1988) 'Analysis', in Butler, D. and Kavanagh, D. (eds), *The British General Election of 1987*, London, Macmillan, pp. 316–62.

Daalder, H. (1964) *Cabinet Reform in Britain, 1914–63*, Stanford, CA, Stanford University Press.

Dahl, R. A. (1956) *A Preface to Democratic Theory*, Chicago, University of Chicago Press.

Dahl, R. A. (1961) *Who Governs?*, New Haven, Yale University Press.

Dangerfield, G. (1936) *The Strange Death of Liberal England*, London, Constable.

Davies, B. (1972) *Variations in Children's Services among British Urban Authorities*, London, Bell.

Day, R. (1963) *The Case for Televising Parliament*, London, Hansard Society.

Deane, P. (1963) *The First Industrial Revolution*, Cambridge, Cambridge University Press.

Dearlove, J. (1973) *The Politics of Policy in Local Government*, London, Cambridge University Press.

de Jonquieres, G. (1983) 'The BT sale: why are the stakes so high?', *Financial Times* (3 May).

Dennis, J., Lindberg, L. and McCrone, D. J. (1971) 'Support for nation and government amongst English schoolchildren', *British Journal of Political Science*, 1(1), 25–48.

Department of the Environment (1983) *Streamlining the Cities*, Cmnd 9063, London, HMSO.

Deutsch, K. W. (1964) *The Nerves of Government*, Glencoe, IL, Free Press.

Diamond, Lord (1975) *Public Expenditure in Practice*, London, George Allen & Unwin.

Dicey, A. V. (1959) *An Introduction to the Study of the Law of the Constitution*, 10th edn, London, Macmillan (first published 1885).

Doig, A. (1984) 'Public service and private gain', *Public Money*, 4(3).

Douglas, I. and Lord, S. (1986) *Local Government Finance: a Practical Guide*, London, Local Government Information Unit.

Downs, A. (1957) *An Economic Theory of Democracy*, New York, Harper and Row.

Drewry, G. and Butcher, T. (1988) *The Civil Service Today*, Oxford, Basil Blackwell.

Drucker, H. (1979) *Multi-Party Britain*, London, Macmillan.

Dunleavy, P. (1980) *Urban Political Analysis*, London, Macmillan.

Dunleavy, P. (1981) *The Politics of Mass Housing in Britain: Corporate Power and*

Professional Influence in the Welfare State, Oxford, Clarendon Press.

Dunleavy, P. (1985) 'Fleet Street: its bite on the ballot', *New Socialist* (Jan), 24–6.

Dunleavy, P. and Husbands, C. T. (1985) *British Democracy at the Crossroads: Voting and Party Competition in the 1980s*, London, George Allen & Unwin.

Easton, D. (1953) *The Political System*, New York, Knopf.

Eckstein, H. (1960) *Pressure Group Politics*, London, George Allen & Unwin.

Englefield, D. (ed.) (1984) *Commons Select Committees: Catalysts for Progress?*, London, Longman.

Evans, P. (1986a) 'Police are all too often a target of those frustrated by society', *The Times* (10 Nov.).

Evans, P. (1986b) 'The low profile policy', *The Times* (11 Nov.).

Expenditure Committee (1977) *The Civil Service: Eleventh Report and Volumes of Evidence, 1976/7, Vols. I–III*, HC 535, London, HMSO.

Eysenck, H. J. (1951) 'Primary social attitudes', *British Journal of Sociology*, 2, 198–209.

Fay, S. and Young, H. (1976) 'The fall of Heath: part III', *Sunday Times* (7 March).

Finer, S. E. (1968) *Anonymous Empire*, London, Pall Mall.

Finer, S. E. (ed.) (1975) *Adversarial Politics and Electoral Reform*, London, Anthony Wigram.

Fletcher, P. (1969) 'An explanation of variations in turnout in local elections', *Political Studies*, 17(4), 495–502.

Fox, J. (1975) 'The brains behind the throne', in Herman, V. and Alt, J. E. (eds), *Cabinet Studies*, London, Macmillan, pp. 277–92.

Franks, O. (1957) *Report of the Committee on Administrative Tribunals and Inquiries*, Cmnd 218, London, HMSO.

Franks, Lord O. (1972) *Departmental Committee on Section 2 of the Official Secrets Act 1911*, Cmnd 5104, London, HMSO.

Fraser, D. (1976) *Urban Politics in Victorian England*, Leicester, Leicester University Press.

Friedman, M. and R. (1985) *The Tyranny of the Status Quo*, Harmondsworth, Penguin.

Fry, G. K. (1985) *The Changing Civil Service*, London, George Allen & Unwin.

Fry, G. K. (1986) 'Inside Whitehall', in Drucker, H. et al. (eds), *Developments in British Politics*, London, Macmillan.

Fulton, Lord (1968) *The Civil Service, Vol. 1: Report of the Committee*, Cmnd 3638, London, HMSO.

Gallup (1976) 'Voting behaviour in Britain, 1945–1974', in Rose, R. (ed.), *Studies in British Politics*, 3rd edn, London, Macmillan.

Gamble, A. (1979) 'The Conservative Party', in Drucker, H. (ed.), *Multi-Party Britain*, London, Macmillan.

Gamble, A. (1985) *Britain in Decline*, London, Macmillan.

Gardener, R. N. (1956) *Sterling–Dollar Diplomacy*, London, Oxford University Press.

Garnsey, E. (1982) 'Women's work and theories of class stratification', in Held, D. and Giddings, A. (eds), *Classes, Power and Conflict*, London, Macmillan.

Gibb, F. (1988), 'Justice by lottery?', *The Times* (25 Oct.).

Giddens, A. (1979) *The Class Structure of the Advanced Societies*, London, Hutchinson (2nd edn 1980).

Giddens, A. (1986) *Sociology: a Brief but Critical Introduction*, London, Macmillan.

Giddens, A. (1989) *Sociology*, Cambridge, Polity.

Gilmour, I. (1969) *The Body Politic*, London, Hutchinson.

Gladden, E. N. (1967) *Civil Services of the United Kingdom*, London, Frank Cass.

Glasgow University Media Group (1976) *Bad News*, (1980) *More Bad News*, (1982) *Really Bad News*, London, Routledge and Kegan Paul.

Goodin, R. E. (1986) 'The principle of voluntary agreement', *Public Administration*, 64(4), 435–44.

Gordon, P. (1984) 'Community policing: towards the local police state', *Critical Social Policy*, 4(1), 39–58.

Gough, I. (1979) *The Political Economy of the Welfare State*, London, Macmillan.

Gould, B. (1978) 'The MP and constituency cases', in Mackintosh, J. P. (ed.), *People and Parliament*, Farnborough, Saxon House, pp. 84–94.

Gramsci, A. (1971) *Selections from Prison Notebooks*, London, Lawrence and Wishart.

Grant, W. (1984) 'The role and power of pressure groups', in Borthwick, R. L. and Spence, J. E. (1984) *British Politics in Perspective*, Leicester, Leicester University Press, pp. 123–44.

Grant, W. and Marsh, D. (1977), *The CBI*, London, Hodder and Stoughton.

Gray, A. and Jenkins, W. I. (1985) *Administrative Politics in British Government*, Brighton, Harvester.

Greenwood, J. and Wilson, D. (1989) *Public Administration in Britain Today*, London, Unwin Hyman.

Greer, G. (1970) *The Female Eunuch*, London, MacGibbon & Kee.

Griffith, J. A. G. (1980) 'Unequal before the law', *Spectator* (2 Feb.).

Griffith, J. A. G. (1981) *The Politics of the Judiciary*, London, Fontana.

Griffiths, R. (1988) *Community Care: Agenda for Action*, London, HMSO.

Gunn, S. (1988) 'Reining in the peers', *Marxism Today*, 32 (June), 3.

Guttsman, W. S. (1963) *The British Political Elite*, London, MacGibbon & Kee.

Gyford, J. (1976) *Local Politics in Britain*, London, Croom Helm.

HMSO (1985) *The Health Service in England: Annual Report*, London, HMSO.

HMSO (1986) *Paying for Local Government*, London, HMSO.

HMSO (1988) *Reform of Section 2 of the Official Secrets Act 1911*, Cm 408, London, HMSO.

HMSO (1989) *Britain: an Official Handbook*, London, HMSO.

Hailsham, Lord (1978) *The Dilemma of Democracy*, London, Collins.

Hain, P. et al. (eds) (1980) *Policing the Police*, London, Calder.

Hampton, W. (1970) *Democracy and Community*, London, Oxford University Press.

Hanson, A. H. (1963) *Nationalisation*, London, George Allen & Unwin.

Harden, I. and Lewis, N. (1986) *The Noble Lie*, London, Hutchinson.

Hargreaves, I. and Lawson, D. (1985) 'Challenges in the pipeline to the sell-off of British Gas', *Financial Times* (2 July).

Harris, L. (1985) 'British capital: manufacturing, finance and multinational corporations', in Coates, D. et al. (eds), *A Socialist Anatomy of Britain*, Cambridge, Polity, pp. 7–28.

Harris, P. (1988) *An Introduction to the Law*, 3rd edn, London, Weidenfeld and Nicolson.

Harrison, M. (1988) 'Broadcasting', in Butler, D. and Kavanagh, D. (eds), *The British General Election of 1987*, London, Macmillan, pp. 139–62.

Hartmann, H. (1982) 'Capitalism, patriarchy and job segregation by sex', in Held, D. and Giddings, A. (eds), *Classes, Power and Conflict*, London, Macmillan.

Hay, D. (1975) 'Property, authority and the criminal law', in Hay, D. (ed.), *Albion's Fatal Tree*, Harmondsworth, Penguin.

Heady, B. (1975) 'Cabinet ministers and senior civil servants: mutual requirements and expectations', in Herman, V. and Alt, J. E. (eds), *Cabinet Studies*, London, Macmillan.

Heath, A., Jowell, R. and Curtice, J. (1985) *How Britain Votes*, Oxford, Pergamon Press.

Heath, A., Jowell, R. and Curtice, J. (1987) 'Trendless fluctuation: a reply to Crewe', *Political Studies*, 35(2), 256–77.

Heath, E. (1972) *My Style of Government*, London, Evening Standard Publications.

Heclo, H. and Wildavsky, A. (1974) *The Private Government of Public Money*, London, Macmillan.

Heffer, S. (1988) 'Labour brings the House down on its own head', *Daily Telegraph* (8 April).

Henke, D. (1989) 'The grip of a ruling passion', *Guardian* (1 March).

Hennessy, P. (1985) 'The megaphone theory of "Yes Minister"', *Listener* (19 and 26 Dec.).

Hennessy, P. (1986) *Cabinet*, Oxford, Basil Blackwell.

Hennessy, P. (1988) *Whitehall*, London, Fontana.

Hennessy, P., Cockerell, M. and Walker, D. (1984) *Sources Close to the Prime Minister: Inside the Hidden World of the News Manipulators*, London, Macmillan.

Henney, A. (1984) *Inside Local Government: a Case for Radical Reform*, London, Sinclair Browne.

Heseltine, M. (1986) 'Deliberate attempt made to avoid discussion of issues', *The Times* (10 Jan.).

Hewart, Lord (1929) *The New Despotism*, London, Ernest Benn.

Higgins, J. (1988) 'The private market in health care', *Social Sciences: News from the ESRC* (June).

Hill, D. (1974) *Democratic Theory and Local Government*, London, George Allen & Unwin.

Hills, J. (1981) 'Britain', in Lovenduski, J. and Hills, J. (eds), *The Politics of the Second Electorate: Women and Public Participation*, London, Routledge and Kegan Paul, pp. 8–32.

Himmelweit, H., Humphreys, P. and Jaeger, M. (1985) *How Voters Decide*, Milton Keynes, Open University Press.

Hodgson, G. (1984) *The Democratic Economy*, Harmondsworth, Penguin.

Hoggart, R. (1958) *The Uses of Literacy*, Harmondsworth, Penguin.

Holland, P. (1981) *The Governance of Quangos*, London, Adam Smith Institute.

Hollingsworth, M. (1986) *The Press and Discontent: a Question of Censorship*, London, Pluto Press.

Holme, R. and Elliot, M. (eds) (1988) *1688–1988: Time for a New Constitution*, London, Macmillan.

Home, Lord (1976) *The Way the Wind Blows*, London, Collins.

Home Affairs Committee (1988) *Parliamentary Accountability of the Police Complaints Authority, Fourth Report*, Session 1987–88, London HMSO.

Hood, C. (1979) 'Keeping the centre small: explanations of agency type', *Political Studies*, 26(1), 30–46.

Hood Phillips, O. (1987) *Constitutional and Administrative Law*, 7th edn, London, Sweet and Maxwell.

Hoskyns, Sir J. (1984) 'Conservatism is not enough', *Political Quarterly*, 55(1), 3–16.

Hoskyns, Sir J. (1985) *An Agenda for Change*, London, Institute of Directors.

Hughes, C. (1988) 'Whitehall to employ more women in top jobs', *Independent* (22 Oct.).

Hume, D. (1882) 'That politics may be reduced to a science', reprinted in Dahl, R. and Neubauer, D. E. (1968) *Readings in Modern Political Analysis*, Englewood Cliffs, Prentice Hall.

Hunter, F. (1953) *Community Power Structure*, Chapel Hill, NC, University of North Carolina Press.

Hutton, W. (1986) *The Revolution that Never Was*, London, Longman.

Ingle, S. (1987) *The British Party System*, Oxford, Basil Blackwell.

Jackson, R. M. (1960) *The Machinery of Justice in England*, Cambridge, Cambridge University Press.

James, B. (1987) 'The coup that never was . . .', *The Times* (7 Aug.).

Jenkins, S. (1986) *The Market for Glory: Fleet Street Ownership in the Twentieth Century*, London, Faber.

Johnson, R. W. (1985) *The Politics of Recession*, London, Macmillan.

Johnston, R. J., Pattie, C. J. and Allsopp, J. G. (1988) *A Nation Dividing? The Electoral Map of Great Britain 1979–87*, London, Longman.

Jones, G. W. (1969) *Borough Politics: a Study of the Wolverhampton Borough Council 1888–1964*, London, Macmillan.

Jones, G. W. (1983) 'Prime ministers' departments really do create problems: a rejoinder to Patrick Weller', *Public Administration*, 61(1), 79–84.

Judge, D. (ed.) (1983) *The Politics of Parliamentary Reform*, London, Heinemann.

Jennings, I. (1966) *The British Constitution*, 5th edn, Cambridge, Cambridge University Press.

Kairys, P. (ed.) (1982) *The Politics of Law: a Progressive Critique*, London, Pantheon.

Kavanagh, D. (1980) 'Political culture in Britain: the decline of the civic culture', in Almond, G. A. and Verba, S. (eds) (1981) *The Civic Culture Revisited*, Boston, Little Brown.

Kavanagh, D. (ed.) (1982) *The Politics of the Labour Party*, London, George Allen & Unwin.

Keegan, W. (1984) *Mrs Thatcher's Economic Experiment*, Harmondsworth, Penguin.

Keith-Lucas, B. (1980) *The Unreformed Local Government System*, London, Croom Helm.

Kellner, P. and Crowther-Hunt, Lord (1980) *The Civil Servants: an Enquiry into Britain's Ruling Class*, London, Macdonald.

Kettle, M. (1980) 'The politics of policing and the policing of politics', in Hain, P. et al. (eds), *Policing the Police*, London, Calder, pp. 9–64.

King, A. (ed.) (1976) *Why is Britain Becoming Harder to Govern?*, London, BBC Publications.

Kingdom, J. E. (ed.) (1989) *The Civil Service in Liberal Democracies*, London, Routledge.

Klein, R. (1983) *The Politics of the National Health Service*, London, Longman.

Knightly, P. (1986) *The Second Oldest Profession: the Spy as Bureaucrat, Fantasist and Whore*, London, André Deutsch.

Knightly, P. (1988) 'Philby: no regrets', *Observer* (10 April).

Koffman, L. (1985) 'Safeguarding the rights of the citizen', in Baxter, J. and

Koffman, L. (eds), *Police, the Constitution and the Community*, Abingdon, Professional Books, pp. 11–37.

Lambert, A. (1988a) 'Who should police the police?', *Independent* (10 Sept.).

Lambert, A. (1988b) 'Ulster: civil war or law and order?', *Independent* (17 Sept.).

Lambourne, G. (1984) *The Fingerprint Story*, London, Harrap.

Laski, H. J. (1938) *Parliamentary Government in England*, London, George Allen & Unwin.

Lasswell, H. D. (1936) *Politics: Who Gets What, When, How?*, New York, McGraw Hill (reprinted 1958).

Lasswell, H. D. and Kaplan, A. (1950) *Power and Society*, New Haven, Yale University Press.

Lawrence, D. H. (1950) 'Nottingham and the mining country', in *Selected Essays*, Harmondsworth, Penguin.

Layton Henry, Z. (ed.) (1980) *Conservative Party Politics*, London, Macmillan.

Lea, J. et al. (1986) 'The fear and loathing at Broadwater Farm', *Guardian* (4 June).

Lehmbruch, G. and Schmitter, P. (eds) (1982) *Patterns of Corporatist Policy-Making*, London, Sage.

Leigh, D. and Lashmar, P. (1987) 'MI5 wanted ITN man as media spy', *Observer* (4 Oct.).

Lindblom, C. E. (1959) 'The science of muddling through', *Public Administration Review*, 19, 79–88.

Lively, J. (1978) 'Pluralism and consensus', in Birnbaum, P., Lively, J. and Parry, G. (eds), *Democracy, Consensus and Social Contract*, London, Sage.

MacDonald, M. (1986) *Children of Wrath: Political Violence in Northern Ireland*, Cambridge, Polity.

McIntosh, R. (chairman) (1976) *A Study of the UK Nationalised Industries*, NEDO Report, London, HMSO.

McKenzie, R. (1967) *British Political Parties*, 2nd rev. edn, London, Heinemann.

McKenzie, R. and Silver, A. (1968) *Angels in Marble*, London, Heinemann.

Mackenzie, W. J. M. (1969) *Politics and Social Science*, Harmondsworth, Penguin.

McKeown, T. (1979) *The Role of Medicine: Dream or Mirage*, Oxford, Basil Blackwell.

Mackintosh, J. P. (1977) *The British Cabinet*, London, Stevens.

Mackintosh, J. P. (ed.) (1978) *People and Parliament*, Farnborough, Saxon House.

Magnus, P. (1963) *Gladstone*, London, Murray.

Mallalieu, J. P. W. (1941) *Passed to You Please*, London, Victor Gollancz.

Mair, L. (1970) *Primitive Government*, Harmondsworth, Penguin.

Mandel, E. (1975) *Late Capitalism*, London, New Left Books.

Mandel, E. (1983) 'Economics', in McLellan, D., *Marx: The First Hundred Years*, London, Fontana, pp. 189–238.

Manser, W. A. P. (1982) 'Nationalization or privatization: the case for each', *Banker*, 132 (Dec.).

Mark, R. (1978) *In the Office of Constable*, London, Collins.

Marsh, A. (1978) *Protest and Political Consciousness*, London, Sage.

Marsh, D. and Locksley, G. (1983) 'Labour: the dominant force in British politics?', in Marsh, D. (ed.), *Pressure Politics*, London, Junction Books.

Marsh, D. and Locksley, G. (1987) 'The influence of business', in *British Politics: a Reader*, Manchester, Manchester University Press, pp. 215–26.

Marsh, D. and Read, M. (1988) *Private Members' Bills*, Cambridge, Cambridge University Press.

Marsh, J. W. (1985) 'Representational changes: the constituency MP', in Norton, P.

(ed.), *Parliament in the 1980s*, Oxford, Basil Blackwell, pp. 69–93.

Marwick, A. (1982) *British Society Since 1945*, Harmondsworth, Penguin.

Marx, K. (1969) 'Towards a critique of Hegel's Philosophy of Right', in Feuer, L. S. (ed.), *Marx and Engels: Basic Writings on Politics and Philosophy*, London, Fontana, pp. 303–8.

Maud, Sir J. (chairman) (1967) *Management of Local Government*, London, HMSO.

Mellors, C. (1978) *The British MP*, Farnborough, Saxon House.

Michael, J. (1982) *The Politics of Secrecy*, Harmondsworth, Penguin.

Michels, R. (1962) *Political Parties*, New York, Collier (first published 1920).

Middlemass, K. (1979) *Politics in Industrial Society*, London, André Deutsch.

Miliband, R. (1961) *Parliamentary Socialism*, London, Merlin.

Miliband, R. (1984) *Capitalist Democracy in Britain*, Oxford, Oxford University Press.

Miller, J. B. D. (1962) *The Nature of Politics*, Harmondsworth, Penguin.

Milne, A. (1988) *DG: Memoirs of a British Broadcaster*, London, Hodder and Stoughton.

Mills, C. W. (1959) *The Power Elite*, New York, Oxford University Press.

Mitchell, A. (1982) *Westminster Man*, London, Methuen.

Mitchell, D. (1982) 'Intervention, control and accountability: the National Enterprise Board', *Public Administration Bulletin*, 38, 40–65.

Mitchell, J. (1971) *Womans' Estate*, Harmondsworth, Penguin.

Moore, J. (1985) Treasury press release, 17 July.

Morgan, J. (1987) *Conflict and Order: the Police and Labour Disputes in England and Wales 1900–1939*, Oxford, Clarendon Press.

Morley, J. (1903) *Life of William Ewart Gladstone, Vol. I*, London, Macmillan.

Morrison, H. (1933) *Socialism and Transport*, London, Constable.

Muller, W. D. (1977) *The Kept Men*, Hassocks, Harvester.

Navarro, V. (1974) *Medicine under Capitalism*, London, Croom Helm.

Newton, K. (1986) 'Mass media', in Drucker, H. et al. (eds), *Developments in British Politics 2*, London, Macmillan, pp. 313–28.

Newton, K. (1976) *Second City Politics*, Oxford, Clarendon Press.

Nicolson, N. (1958) *People and Parliament*, London, Weidenfeld and Nicolson.

Niskanen, W. A. (1973) *Bureaucracy: Servant or Master?*, London, Institute of Economic Affairs.

Norton, P. (1981) *The Commons in Perspective*, Oxford, Martin Robertson.

Norton, P. and Aughey, A. (1981) *Conservatives and Conservatism*, London, Temple Smith.

O'Connor, J. (1973) *The Fiscal Crisis of the State*, New York, St Martin's Press.

Oliver, F. R. and Stanyer, J. (1969) 'Some aspects of the financial behaviour of County Boroughs', *Public Administration*, 47, 169–84.

Oliver, I. (1987) *Police Government and Accountability*, London, Macmillan.

Olson, M. (1968) *The Logic of Collective Action*, New York, Schocken.

Olson, M. (1982) *The Rise and Decline of Nations*, New Haven, Yale University Press.

Ostrogorski, M. (1902) *Democracy and the Organisation of Political Parties*, London, Macmillan.

Paley, W. (1842) *Works*, London, Bohn (first published 1785).

Peele, G. (1986) 'The state and civil liberties', in Drucker, H. et al. (eds), *Developments in British Politics 2*, London, Macmillan, pp. 144–74.

Pelling, H. (1968) *A Short History of the Labour Party*, 3rd edn, London, Macmillan.

Perrigo, S. (1985) 'The women's movement: patterns of oppression and resistance', in Coates, D. et al. (eds), *A Socialist Anatomy of Britain*, Cambridge, Polity, pp. 124–45.

Pienaar, J. (1987) 'Contemptible smear by Livingstone', *Independent* (10 July).

Pienaar, J. (1988) 'A cabinet exile reflects on the cravings of power', *Independent* (15 Sept.).

Pillay, V. (1981) 'The international economic crisis', in Currie, D. and Smith, R. (eds), *Socialist Economic Review*, London, Merlin.

Pinto-Duschinsky, M. (1972) 'Central Office and power in the Conservative Party', *Political Studies*, 20(1), 1–16.

Piven, F. and Cloward, R. (1972) *Regulating the Poor*, London, Tavistock.

Pliatzky, L. (1980) *Report on Non-Departmental Public Bodies*, Cmnd 7797, London, HMSO.

Plowden, Lord (chairman) (1961) *The Control of Public Expenditure*, Cmnd 1432, London, HMSO.

Ponting, C. (1986) *Whitehall: Tragedy and Farce*, London, Hamish Hamilton.

Popper, K. (1957) *The Poverty of Historicism*, London, Routledge and Kegan Paul.

Poulanzas, N. (1973) *Political Power and Social Classes*, London, New Left Books.

Pryke, R. (1981) *The Nationalized Industries*, Oxford, Martin Robertson.

Punnett, R. M. (1975) 'Her Majesty's shadow government', in Herman, V. and Alt, J. E. (eds), *Cabinet Studies*, London, Macmillan, pp. 140–56.

RIPA (1980) *Party Politics in Local Government: Officers and Members*, London, Royal Institute of Public Administration/Policy Studies Institute.

Ramphal, S. (1988) 'Reflections on "Vancouver"', *Round Table*, no. 305, 10–20.

Raphael, A. and Wansell, G. (1979) 'The selling of Maggie', *Observer* (22 April).

Redcliffe-Maud, Lord (chairman) (1969) *Royal Commission on Local Government in England 1966–69, Vol. I*, Cmnd 4040, London, HMSO.

Redlich, J. and Hirst, F. W. (1970) *Local Government in England, Vol. II* (edited by Keith-Lucas, B.), London, Macmillan (first published in 1903).

Rees, M. (1987) 'The parameters of politics', in Chapman, R. A. and Hunt, M. (eds), *Open Government*, Beckenham, Croom Helm, pp. 31–8.

Reiner, R. (1982) 'Who are the police?', *Political Quarterly*, 53(2).

Rhodes, R. A. W. (1981) *Control and Power in Central–Local Government Relations*, Farnborough, Gower.

Rhodes, R. A. W. (1988) *Beyond Westminster and Whitehall: the Sub-central Government of Britain*, London, George Allen & Unwin.

Richards, P. G. (1970) *Parliament and Conscience*, London, George Allen & Unwin.

Richards, P. G. (1981) 'Private members' legislation', in Walkland, S. A. and Ryle, M. (eds), *The Commons Today*, London, Fontana, pp. 137–53.

Richardson, J. J. and Jordan, A. G. (1979) *Government under Pressure*, Oxford, Martin Robertson.

Riddell, P. (1985) *The Thatcher Government*, Oxford, Basil Blackwell.

Ridley, F. F. (1966) 'The importance of constitutions', *Parliamentary Affairs*, 19, 312–23.

Robson, W. A. (1966) *Local Government in Crisis*, London, George Allen & Unwin.

Rollo, J. (1980) 'The Special Patrol Group', in Hain, P. (ed.), *Policing the Police*, London, John Calder, pp. 153–208.

Rose, R. (1962) 'The political ideas of English party activists', *American Political Science Review*, 56(2), 360–71.

Rose, R. (1964) 'Parties, factions and tendencies in British politics', *Political Studies*, 12(1), 33–46.

Rose, R. (1980) *Do Parties Make a Difference?*, London, Macmillan.

Rose, R. and McAllister, I. (1986) *Voters Begin to Choose: From Closed Class to Open Elections*, Beverly Hills, Sage.

Roth, A. (1981) *The Business Backgrounds of MPs*, London, Parliamentary Profiles.

Rowbotham, S. (1973) *Woman's Consciousness, Man's World*, Harmondsworth, Penguin.

Royal Commission on the Distribution of Income and Wealth (1976) *Report No. 3: Higher Incomes from Employment*, London, HMSO.

Salisbury, R. H. (1969) 'An exchange theory of interest groups', *Midwest Journal of Political Science*, 13, 1–32.

Sarlvik, B. and Crewe, I. (1983) *Decade of Dealignment: the Conservative Victory of 1979 and Electoral Trends in the 1970s*, Cambridge, Cambridge University Press.

Sartori, G. (1976) *Parties and Party Systems: a Framework for Analysis*, Cambridge, Cambridge University Press.

Saunders, P. (1980) *Urban Politics: a Sociological Interpretation*, Harmondsworth, Penguin.

Saunders, P. (1984) 'Rethinking local politics', in Boddy, M. and Fudge, C. (eds), *Local Socialism*, London, Macmillan, pp. 22–48.

Scarman, Lord (1974) *English Law: the New Dimension*, London, Stevens.

Scarman, Lord (1981) *The Brixton Disorders, 10–12 April 1981: Report of an Inquiry*, Cmnd 8427, London, HMSO (reprinted by Penguin Books, 1982).

Scattschneider, E. E. (1960) *The Semi-Sovereign People*, New York, Holt, Rinehart and Winston.

Schmitter, P. (1974) 'Still the century of corporatism', *Review of Politics*, 36, 85–131.

Scott, J. (1985) 'The British upper class', in Coates, D. et al. (eds), *A Socialist Anatomy of Britain*, Cambridge, Polity, pp. 29–54.

Seaton, J. and Pimlot, B. (eds) (1987) *The Media in British Politics*, Aldershot, Avebury.

Sedgemore, B. (1980) *The Secret Constitution*, London, Hodder and Stoughton.

Segal, A. (1970) 'The case for not televising Parliament', in Crick, B. (ed.), *The Reform of Parliament*, London, Weidenfeld and Nicolson, pp. 300–10.

Select Committee on Defence (1982) *The Handling of Press and Public Information During the Falklands Conflict: First Report*, HC 17–1, London, HMSO.

Self, P. and Storing, H. (1962) *The State and the Farmer*, London, George Allen & Unwin.

Seltman, C. (1956) *Women in Antiquity*, London, Pan.

Simon, H. A. (1947) *Administrative Behaviour*, 1st edn, London, Macmillan.

Sivanandan, V. (1981) 'From resistance to rebellion', *Race and Class*, 23 (Autumn).

Smith, B. C. (1976) *Policy Making in British Government*, Oxford, Martin Robertson.

Smith, D. J. and Gray, J. (1985) *Police and People in London*, Aldershot, Gower.

Stead, J. (1985) *The Police of Britain*, London, Collier Macmillan.

Steel, D. (1984) 'Managing health authorities: one member's view', *Public Money*, 4(1), 37–40.

Stenton, F. M. (1941) *Anglo Saxon England*, Oxford, Clarendon Press.

Stuart, C. (ed.) (1975) *The Reith Diaries*, London, Collins.

Studlar, D. T. (1983) 'The ethnic vote 1983: problems of analysis and interpretation', *New Community*, 9(1–2), 92–100.

Taylor, A. J. P. (1965) *English History 1914–1945*, London, Oxford University Press.

Thomas, H. (ed.) (1959) *The Establishment*, London, Anthony Blond.

Thomas, R. (1987) 'The experience of other countries', in Chapman, R. A. and Hunt, M. (eds), *Open Government*, Beckenham, Croom Helm, pp. 235–71.

Thompson, E. P. (1975) *Whigs and Hunters*, London, Allen Lane.

Thompson, E. P. (1980) 'The logic of exterminism', *New Left Review*, 121 (May–June), 3–32.

Thompson, E. P. (1982) 'The heavy dancers of the air', *New Society* (11 Nov.), 244.

Todd, J. and Butcher, B. (1982) *Electoral Registration in 1981*, London, Office of Population Census and Surveys.

Treasury (1988a) Press release, 27 July.

Treasury (1988b) *Civil Service Statistics*, London, Government Statistical Service.

Treasury (1989) 'The Public Expenditure Survey', in *Economic Progress Report*, London, HMSO.

Tunstall, J. (1970) *The Westminster Lobby Correspondents*, London, Routledge and Kegan Paul.

Turner, D. R. (1969) *The Shadow Cabinet in British Politics*, London, Routledge and Kegan Paul.

Urry, J. (1985) 'The class structure', in Coates, D. et al. (eds), *A Socialist Anatomy of Britain*, Cambridge, Polity.

Von Bertallanfy, L. (1952) *General Systems Theory*, New York, Harper.

Wainwright, W. (1978) 'Women and the division of labour', in Abrahams, P. (ed.), *Work, Urbanism and Inequality*, London, Weidenfeld and Nicolson.

Walker, P. G. (1972) *The Cabinet*, London, Fontana.

Walkland, S. A. and Ryle, M. (eds) (1981) *The Commons Today*, London, Fontana.

Wallerstein, I. (1979) *The Capitalist World Economy*, Cambridge, Cambridge University Press.

Walvin, J. (1984) *Passage to Britain*, Harmondsworth, Penguin.

Wass, Sir D. (1984) *Government and the Governed* (BBC Reith Lectures), London, Routledge and Kegan Paul.

Wass, Sir D. (1986) 'Foreword', in Harden, I. and Lewis, N. *The Noble Lie*, London, Hutchinson, pp. ix–xiii.

Weber, M. (1978) *Economy and Society, Vol. II*, Berkeley, University of California Press (first published 1922).

Weller, P. (1983) 'Do prime ministers' departments really create problems?', *Public Administration*, 61(1), 59–78.

Whiteley, P. and Winyard, S. (1984) 'The origins of the "New Poverty Lobby"', *Political Studies*, 32(1), 32–54.

Whyatt, J. (1961) *The Citizen and the Administration*, London, Justice.

Widdicombe, D. (1977) *Our Fettered Ombudsman*, London, Justice.

Widdicombe, D. (1986a) *The Conduct of Local Authority Business*, Cmnd 9797, London, HMSO.

Widdicombe, D. (1986b) *Research Volume 1: The Political Organisation of Local Authorities*, Cmnd 9798, London, HMSO.

Wilkinson, M. (1985) 'Regulation: vital but difficult to get right', *Financial Times* (29 Nov.).

Williams, F. (1969) 'A prime minister remembers: the war and post-war memories of the Rt. Hon. Earl Attlee', in King, A. (ed.), *The British Prime Minister*, London, Macmillan.

Wilson, H. (1974) *The Labour Government 1964–70*, Harmondsworth, Penguin.

Wilson, H. H. (1961) *Pressure Group: the Campaign for Commercial Television*, Harmondsworth, Penguin.

Wilson, J. Q. (ed.) (1980) *The Politics of Regulation*, New York, Basic Books.

Wilson, T. (1966) *The Downfall of the Liberal Party 1914–1935*, London, Collins.

Witherow, J. (1986) 'Defence report: MPs on warpath over Westland', *Sunday Times* (13 July).

Wraith, R. E. and Lamb, G. B. (1971) *Public Inquiries as Instruments of Government*, London, George Allen & Unwin.

Wright, P. (1987) *Spycatcher*, New York, Viking.

Wyatt, W. (1973) 'Parliament the waste land', *Sunday Times* (4 Nov.).

Young, H. (1989) *One of Us*, London, Macmillan.

Zander, M. (1969) 'Who goes to solicitors?', *Law Society's Gazette*, 66.

Zander, M. (1976) 'Independence of the legal profession: what does it mean?', *Law Society's Gazette* (22 Sept.).

Index